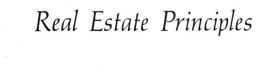

Real Estate Principles

BRUCE HARWOOD

Real Estate Principles

RESTON PUBLISHING COMPANY, INC.

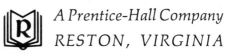

A Prentice-Hall Company
RESTON, VIRGINIA

Library of Congress Cataloging in Publication Data

Harwood, Bruce M
    Real estate principles.

    Bibliography:
    Includes index.
    1.   Real estate business—United States.   I.   Title.
HD1375.H38
333.3'3
76–53781
ISBN 0–87909–719–1

© 1977 by Reston Publishing Company, Inc.
A Prentice-Hall Company
RESTON, VIRGINIA

10 9 8 7 6

*This book is dedicated
to the reader's success in the field of real estate.*

A SPECIAL NOTE TO READERS

The author anticipates that as many women will read this book as men. However, it would make the sentences in this book harder to read if "he and she" and "his and her" were used on every possible occasion. Therefore, when you read, "he," "his," or "him" in this book, please note they are being used in their grammatical sense and refer to women as well as men.

*   *   *

The forms in this text are for information only and are not intended for use as legal documents. In such matters, an attorney should be consulted.

CONTENTS

Real estate is an exciting business. But it is also a demanding one since it requires that one know the ethical and business principles fundamental to the successful selling and buying of houses and land. There are some who say that the only way to learn these principles is by experience. That can be extremely time-consuming and costly, no matter how good a teacher experience is. A more logical approach is to learn a substantial portion of this complicated body of knowledge from experts already at work in the field. Then personal experience can be acquired. With that in mind, this book has been written to provide you with an understanding of the basic principles and business fundamentals of real estate. Emphasis is placed on an easily readable presentation that combines explanations of "how" things are done in real estate with "why" they are done.

Sketches and diagrams are used wherever they help to explain and sort out the complex rights and interests that are involved in real property. The essentials of real estate forms and documents are also dealt with carefully. Wherever possible, simplified versions are used so that their key elements can be easily identified and are not lost in a maze of legal language. Warranty deeds, quit-claim deeds, trust deeds, grant deeds, title insurance policies, promissory notes, and mortgages are among the real estate "apparatus" so treated.

At the beginning of each chapter there is a list of the new "key" terms that will be learned, along with brief definitions. And at the end of each chapter, there are review questions and problems based on the material just studied. Persons who intend to make a career in real estate may want to consider additional questions, problems and situations that will test and improve their grasp of the subject. The accompanying workbook by John T. Ellis and Bruce M. Harwood is designed to fill that need. It is available from bookstores and the publisher of this book and is called the *Real Estate Principles Resource Book.*

No author can cover every topic that a reader might conceivably be interested in learning. That holds true for this book. Nevertheless, its topics were not randomly selected. Instead, the choice of topics was the result of extensive market research conducted at privately organized real estate schools, at community colleges and at four-year colleges that offer real estate courses to non-business majors. The topics include those often covered in such courses, as well as those listed in the outline of real estate principles published by the National Association of Real Estate License Law Officials.

Criticisms of and suggestions for improving this book and its workbook are welcome of course. They should be sent to the publisher for the author.

ACKNOWLEDGMENTS   *Special thanks to the following people for their assistance in preparing this book: Stewart Angus, Larry Baldwin, Donald Bell, Wayne Brunkan, Beverly Dordick, Joe Eagle and Associates, John Ellis, Carroll Gentry, Robert Goforth, Rosanna Hanna, Richard Hobert, Jack Hunter, Patrice LaLiberté, Robert Martin, Dallas Patterson, Weldon Rackley, Mary Phillips Rainey, Donald Tallman, David Ungerer, Sidney Uyetake, Olive Ziegler.*

B.H.

Introduction to Real Estate

This book has been written for the reader who has not studied the principles of real estate before. Therefore, emphasis is placed on an orderly and interesting presentation of the subject in a simple and readable style. The two main objectives are (1) to help the reader better understand the whys and wherefores of real estate as they apply to his or her own real estate transactions, and (2) to educate those who plan to offer competent and professional services in the real estate business. This latter group includes prospective real estate salesmen and brokers, real estate appraisers, property managers, land surveyors, real estate tax experts and advisors, escrow and title closing agents, abstracters and title searchers, and real property insurance agents.

In Chapter 2 we will consider what is and what is not real estate, how land is described, and what makes it physically and economically different from other commodities. We then discuss the right of an individual to own land and the right of government to control land uses (Chapter 3), joint ownership of property (Chapter 4), the process by which real estate ownership is conveyed from one person to another (Chapter 5), and how ownership is determined (Chapter 6). In Chapters 7 and 8, we turn to contract law and its application to offers, acceptances, and other real estate agreements.

Chapters 9-12 are devoted to real estate finance. In Chapter 9, mortgages and the laws regarding their use are explained. Chapter 10 covers trust deeds and is intended for readers in those states where trust deeds are used in place of mortgages. Amortized loans, points, FHA and VA programs, and mortgage insurance are discussed in Chapter 11. Mortgage lenders, loan approval and interest rates, as well as financing alternatives to banks and savings institutions, are covered in Chapter 12.

In Chapter 13, we show how property taxes and assessments are calculated, and in Chapter 14 explain title closing and escrow processes. Chapters 15-17 are devoted to real estate value. Why real property has a value is discussed in Chapter 15, and in Chapters 16 and 17 we appraise (estimate) real estate value through the market, cost, and income approaches. In Chapter 18, we examine the relationship between real estate agents and buyers and sellers, and in Chapter 19 discuss the procedure by which a person can become licensed as a real estate salesman or broker. Next, in special recognition of their growing popularity, Chapter 20 covers condominiums, townhouses and cooperatives. Property insurance, property management, and land planning and zoning are discussed in Chapters 21, 22, and 23, respectively. The book concludes with a chapter on real estate investing for individuals and a combined Glossary-Index.

Thus, the study of this book will provide an excellent exposure to both the principles and practices of modern-day real estate.

LICENSING PROCEDURES   If you are studying real estate to obtain a real estate license, you should write to your real estate regulatory agency to obtain specific instructions regarding the license application procedure. To obtain the address, check your telephone directory or call your local Board of Realtors.

Those seeking real estate licenses should also read that portion of Chapter 19 dealing with license laws. Briefly, the usual procedure for obtaining a license is that, at your request, your state's regulatory agency will send you a license application form and an application to take a real estate examination. Fill out the forms and return them with a license application fee and an exam fee. You will then receive a notice telling you when and where to report for the exam. Four to six weeks after the examination, you will be notified of the results. If you passed, you mail in the required license fee and shortly thereafter receive your license. If you did not pass, you may take the next available examination by paying a new exam fee. Because a large number of states offer real estate exams only four times a year, it is advisable to write for your application materials now before you finish this book.

The requirement that real estate salesmen and brokers should take real estate education courses, in addition to passing a license examination, is gaining widespread support among state legislatures. This recognizes the fact that, for most persons, purchases and sales of real property are the largest transactions in their lives. Therefore, a person who seeks the aid of a real estate broker and his sales staff should have knowledgeable and competent help. Moreover, real estate industry groups, such as the National Association of Realtors, support the concept of more education as a means of acquiring professional status for the real estate industry. Another reason for education requirements is that legislatures and law courts are demanding that **licensees** (persons holding licenses) offer the public professional-quality service. A licensee can be held responsible for money damages if he does not. The law is beginning to side more with the public, and courts are finding fewer instances where the licensee can successfully plead ignorance. The philosophy of "Let the buyer beware" is also losing its traditional support. In its place we are beginning to see a growing number of malpractice lawsuits against real estate licensees.

Lastly, the better educated can compete more successfully in the real estate field. The future is not bright for a person who can do no more than hold open house on Saturday or Sunday and wait for someone to drop by, look around once, and say, "I'll buy it." The person who can value property, identify a prospect's needs, draft a legally sound offer and acceptance, find financing, understand the title transfer and closing process, and the like, will be more successful.

EDUCATIONAL REQUIREMENTS

Thirty-six states require salesmen and thirty-eight states require brokers to take real estate education courses. In most of these states, required courses must be completed before a license will be issued. In a few states, a license can be obtained before meeting the education requirement, but the required courses must be taken to renew the license. In a small, but increasing number of states, courses are required to obtain as well as renew real estate licenses. Thus, there is a growing interest in obliging licensees to expand their proficiency in the field through continued education.

STATE REQUIREMENTS

Table 1:1   **REAL ESTATE EDUCATION AND EXPERIENCE REQUIREMENTS**

STATE	SALESMAN		BROKER		
	Education Requirement	Mandatory Continued Education	Additional Education Required	Experience Requirement	Mandatory Continued Education
Alabama	High school & 45 hours	No	No	2 years	No
Alaska	None	No	No	2 years	No
Arizona	45 hours	Yes	90 hours	3 years	Yes
Arkansas	30 hours	No	60 hours *or*	2 years	No
California	None	Yes	270 hours	2 years	Yes
Colorado	48 hours	Yes	48 hours	2 years	Yes
Connecticut	30 hours	No	2 courses	2 years	No
Delaware	75 hours	No	45 hours	5 years and 30 sales	No
District of Columbia	None	No	No	None	No
Florida	48 hours	Yes	51 hours	1 year	Yes
Georgia	24 hours	No	60 hours	3 years	No
Hawaii	30 hours	No	40 hours	2 years	No
Idaho	30 hours	No	60 hours	2 years	No
Illinois	High school & 30 hours	No	60 hours	1 year	No
Indiana	High school & 40 hours	No	No	2 years	No
Iowa	30 hours	Yes	No	1 year	Yes
Kansas	High school	No	No	2 years	No
Kentucky	48 hours	Yes	48 hours	2 years	Yes
Louisiana	30 hours	No	60 hours	1 year	No
Maine	High school	No	90 hours	1 year	No
Maryland	45 hours	No	90 hours	3 years	No
Massachusetts	None	No	No	None	No
Michigan	30 hours if fails exam	No	90 hours if fails exam	3 years	No
Minnesota	90 hours	Yes	90 hours	2 years	Yes

Key: Hours are clock-hours in the classroom; experience requirement is experience as a licensed real estate salesman.

Table 1:1 summarizes real estate education and experience requirements in the United States now in effect. In this table you can see your state requirements and compare them with others. The education requirement column shows the number of hours that a license applicant must spend in a classroom. Broker education requirements are in addition to

Table 1:1 *continued*

STATE	SALESMAN		BROKER		
	Education Requirement	Mandatory Continued Education	Additional Education Required	Experience Requirement	Mandatory Continued Education
Mississippi	45 hours	No	90 hours	1 year	No
Missouri	32 hours	No	No	1 year	No
Montana	Tenth grade	No	High school	2 years	No
Nebraska	High school & 60 hours	Yes	60 hours	2 years	No
Nevada	90 hours	Yes	270 hours	2 years	Yes
New Hampshire	None	No	None	1 year	No
New Jersey	45 hours	No	90 hours	2 years	No
New Mexico	60 hours	No	30 hours	2 years	No
New York	45 hours	No	45 hours *or*	2 years	Yes
North Carolina	30 hours	No	30 hours	1 year	No
North Dakota	30 hours	No	30 hours	1 year	No
Ohio	60 hours	No	60 hours	2 years & 30 sales	No
Oklahoma	30 hours	No	30 hours	1 year	No
Oregon	90 hours	Yes	60 hours	3 years	Yes
Pennsylvania	60 hours	No	180 hours	3 years	No
Rhode Island	None	No	90 hours *or*	1 year	No
South Carolina	30 hours	No	60 hours *or*	2 years	No
South Dakota	30 hours	No	60 hours	2 years	No
Tennessee	45 hours	No	45 hours	2 years	No
Texas	90 hours	Yes	90 hours	2 years	No
Utah	High school & 60 hours	No	120 hours	3 years	No
Vermont	High school	No	None	1 year	No
Virginia	60 hours	No	90 hours	3 years	No
Washington	30 hours	No	60 hours	2 years	No
West Virginia	None	No	None	2 years	No
Wisconsin	30 hours	Yes	30 hours	None	
Wyoming	None	Yes	None	2 years	

Source: National Association of Real Estate License Law Officials. Check with your state for any changes that may have occurred since this book was printed.

those required to obtain a salesman's license. The mandatory continued education columns give the hours the licensee must spend in the classroom in order to renew his license.

The hours of education required and the types of courses that a person must take to be licensed are set by an act of each state's legislature. However, the individual topics covered in each course and the amount of time spent on each is usually left to the discretion of the state's real estate department or commission. The courses themselves are offered in public schools and colleges, by state Realtor associations, and by private real estate schools. To make certain that students receive education of approximately equal quality, no matter where they attend, state-approved course guidelines are established and instructors are required to be knowledgeable in the courses that they teach.

In most states real estate salesman applicants complete a course in real estate principles. This typically lasts from 30 to 48 hours and includes the topics in this text. Later, when the salesman wants to obtain a broker's license, he takes additional courses, such as real estate law, finance, appraisal, economics, property management, office administration, and closings (escrows). Generally, states without education requirements are adding them, and states with requirements are increasing them.

In 47 states, the broker license applicant is required to have one to five years experience as a real estate salesman (see Table 1:1). Some states will reduce the experience requirement if the broker applicant has taken certain real estate courses or has a college degree. Such arrangements are too lengthy for treatment here; one should inquire for details from his state real estate regulatory agency if he plans to substitute education for experience.

QUESTIONS *To help answer these, obtain a copy of your state's real estate license laws.*

1. What are the current education requirements for the salesman and broker licenses in your state?
2. What is the application fee for a real estate salesman's license? For the examination? For the license itself?
3. How much real estate sales experience is required of a broker's license applicant?

4. Are broker's license applicants permitted to substitute education for experience?
5. Under what conditions is a person exempt from holding a real estate license? (See also Chapter 19.)

There are several real estate principles texts that will give you valuable additional information. Read them whenever you wish to investigate further those matters that each treats particularly.

Chief among them is the fifty-five year old classic by Alfred Ring. It is now in its eighth edition.

*   *   *

ADDITIONAL READINGS

Real Estate Principles and Practices, by Alfred A. Ring and Jerome Dasso, is best known for its thorough treatment, including chapters on home ownership, real estate marketing and advertising, subdividing and development, housing legislation, and mobile homes. (8th ed. Prentice-Hall, 1977, 715 pages.)

Real Estate Principles and Practices, by Maurice A. Unger, is relatively easy to read and gives special emphasis to the legal side of real estate. (5th ed. South-Western, 1974, 760 pages.)

Real Estate, by Arthur M. Weimer, Homer Hoyt, and George F. Bloom, emphasizes a decision-oriented approach. (6th ed. The Ronald Press, 1972, 831 pages.)

Modern Real Estate Practice, by F. W. Galaty, W. J. Allaway, and R. C. Kyle, is aimed primarily at introducing candidates for license exams to real estate principles. (7th ed. Real Estate Education Corp., 1975, 320 pages.)

Real Estate and Urban Development, by H. C. Smith, C. J. Tschappat, and R. L. Racster, is a college-level text that includes much of the material traditionally taught in principles courses and focuses on the application of theory and research to real estate problems and decision making. (Richard D. Irwin, 1973, 481 pages.)

Real Estate: Principles and Practices, by Karl G. Pearson, includes many traditional real estate principles subjects, and, in addition, treats mobile homes, computerized real estate, farms, shopping centers, resort and retirement property, transportation and real estate values, and urban renewal. (Grid, Inc., 1973, 456 pages.)

Fundamentals of Real Estate, by Jerome Dasso, Alfred A. Ring, and Douglas McFall, covers topics suggested in a thirty-hour course outline prepared by the National Association of Real Estate License Law Officials (Prentice-Hall, 1977, 730 pages).

*   *   *

The suggested readings at the end of each chapter in this book are annotated so that you can refer to their special treatment of the topics you have just studied.

2

Nature and Description of Real Estate

Base line: an imaginary latitude line selected as a reference in the rectangular survey system; there are 36 base lines in the United States

Fixture: an object that has been attached to the land

Improvements: any form of land development, such as buildings, roads, fences, pipe lines, etc.

Meridians: imaginary lines running north and south, used as references in mapping land

Metes and bounds: a method of mapping land using distance (metes) and compass direction (bounds)

Monument: an iron pipe, stone, tree or other fixed object used in surveying the boundaries of a parcel of land

Personal property: a right or interest in things of a temporary or movable nature; anything not classed as real property

Real estate: land and improvements in a physical sense as well as the rights to own or use them

Recorded plat: a subdivision map filed in the county recorder's office that shows the location and boundaries of individual parcels of land

Riparian right: the right of a landowner whose land borders a river or stream to use and enjoy that water

What is real estate? Real estate is land and improvements made to land, and the rights to use them. Let us begin by looking more closely at what is meant by land and improvements. Then in Chapter 3 we shall focus our attention on the rights one may possess in land and improvements.

Often we think of land as only the surface of the earth. But, it is substantially more than that. As Figure 2:1 illustrates, land starts at the center of the earth, passes through the earth's surface, and continues on into space. An under-

LAND

standing of this concept is important because, given a particular parcel of land, it is possible for one person to own the rights to use its surface (**surface rights**), another to own the rights to drill or dig below its surface (**subsurface rights**), and still another to own the rights to use the airspace above it (**air rights**).

Figure 2:1

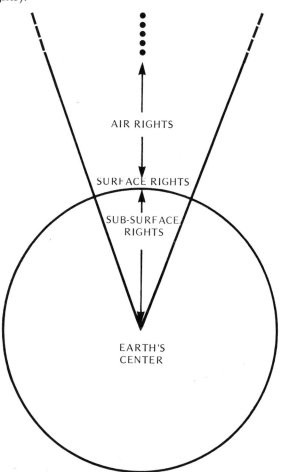

Land includes the surface of the earth and the sky above and everything below to the center of the earth.

IMPROVEMENTS   Anything affixed to land with the intent of being permanent is considered to be part of the land and therefore real estate. Thus houses, schools, factories, barns, fences, roads, pipelines and landscaping are real estate. As a group, these are referred to as **improvements** because they improve or develop land.

Being able to identify what is real estate and what is not, is important. For example, in conveying ownership to a house, only the lot is described in the deed. It is not necessary to describe the dwelling unit itself, or the landscaping, driveways, sidewalks, wiring or plumbing. Items that are not a part of the land, such as tables, chairs, beds, desks, automobiles, farm machinery, and the like, are classified as **personal property**; if the right to use them is to be transferred to the buyer, there must be a separate **bill of sale** in addition to the deed.

When an object is attached to the land by virtue of its being imbedded in the land or affixed to the land by means of cement, nails, bolts, etc., it is called a **fixture**. Ordinarily, a fixture is the property of the landowner and when the land is conveyed to a new owner, it is automatically included with the land. *FIXTURES*

In determining whether or not an object is considered to be part of the land, we apply what are called the five tests of a fixture. They are (1) the manner of attachment, (2) the adaptation of the object, (3) the intent of the person affixing the object, (4) the relationship of the parties involved, and (5) the existence of an agreement.

The first test, **manner of attachment,** refers to how the object is attached to the land. To illustrate, when asphalt and concrete for driveways and sidewalks are still on the delivery truck, they are movable and therefore personal property. But once they are poured into place, the asphalt and concrete become part of the land. Similarly, lumber, nails, wiring, pipes, doors, toilets, sinks, water heaters, furnaces and other construction materials change from personal property to real estate when they become part of a building. Items brought into the house that do not become permanently affixed to the land, for example, furniture, clothing, cooking utensils, radios and television sets, remain personal property. *Attachment*

Adaptation

Historically, the manner of attachment was the only method of classifying an object as personal property or real estate, but as time progressed, this test alone was no longer adequate. For example, how would you classify storm windows, which for a few months of the year are temporarily clipped or hung in position? For the answer, we must apply a second test: **How is the article adapted** to the building? If the storm windows were custom cut for the windows in the building, they are automatically included in the purchase or rental of the building. Storm windows of a general design and suitable for use on other buildings are personal property and are not automatically included with the building. Note the difference: in the first case, the storm windows were specifically adapted to the building; in the second case, they were not.

Intent and Relationship

It is sometimes necessary to consider the **intent and relationship of the parties involved** in order to classify an object as real or personal. This is particularly true for a landlord-tenant relationship. Normally, when a tenant makes permanent additions to the property that he is renting, the additions belong to the landlord when the lease or rental agreement expires. However, this can work a particular hardship on tenants operating a trade or business. For example, a supermarket moves into a rented building and bolts to the floor its display shelves, meat and dairy coolers, frozen-food counters and checkout stands. When the supermarket later moves out, do these items, by virtue of their attachment, become the property of the building owner? Modern courts rule that they do not; the tests of intent and relationship of the parties involved indicate that **trade fixtures** are not intended to become the property of the landlord. However, for the tenant to keep the trade fixtures, they must be removed before the expiration of the lease and without seriously damaging the building.

When applied to different situations, the tests of intent and relationship can bring different results. For example, consider a refrigerator and a window air conditioner, neither of which is permanently attached. If a tenant rents a house or apartment and installs these items, the tenant may remove them upon departing because they are not permanently attached and therefore are personal property. But, if they belong to the apartment owner and he is selling his building, they are considered a part of the building because their purpose is to produce rental income, which is the reason why someone would buy the building.

The final test is the **existence of an agreement** between the parties involved. For example, a seller can clarify in advance and in writing to his real estate broker what he considers personal property and thus will take when he leaves, and what he does not consider personal property and thus will leave for the buyer. Likewise, a tenant may obtain an agreement from his landlord that items installed by the tenant will not be considered fixtures by the landlord. When it is not readily clear if an item is real or personal property, the use of an agreement can avoid later argument or a court case.

Agreement

Trees, cultivated perennial plants, and uncultivated vegetation of any sort are classed as **fructus naturales** and are considered part of the land. Annual cultivated crops are called **emblements** and most courts of law regard them as personal property even though they are attached to the soil.

Ownership of Plants, Trees and Crops

The ownership of land that borders on a river or stream carries with it the right to use that water in common with the other landowners whose land borders the same watercourse. This is known as a **riparian right.** The landowner does not have absolute ownership of the water that flows past his land, but he may use it in a reasonable manner. In some states, riparian rights have been modified by the **doctrine of prior appropriation:** the first owner to divert water for his own use may continue to do so, even though it is not equitable to the other landowners along the watercourse. Where land borders on a lake or sea, it is said to carry **littoral rights** rather than riparian rights. Littoral rights allow a landowner to use and enjoy the water touching his land provided he does not alter the water's position by artificial means.

WATER RIGHTS

Ownership of land normally includes the right to drill for and remove water found below the surface. Where water is not confined to a defined underground waterway, it is known as **percolating water.** In some states a landowner has the right, in conjunction with neighboring owners, to draw his share of percolating water. Other states subscribe to the doctrine of prior appropriation. When speaking of underground water, the term **water table** refers to the level of percolating water below the earth's surface. This may be only a few feet below the surface or hundreds of feet down.

REALTY, REAL PROPERTY AND PERSONALTY

Realty refers to land and buildings and other improvements from a physical standpoint; **real property** refers to the right to own land and improvements; and **real estate** refers to land and improvements and the rights to own or use them. As a practical matter, however, these three terms are used interchangeably in everyday usage. A similar situation also exists with regard to the terms personal property and personalty. Technically, **personal property** refers to ownership rights to items of a temporary or movable nature, whereas **personalty** refers to the physical object itself. Again, everyday usage is to refer to both the object and the right to own it as "property." In this book, we shall follow everyday usage because it is used in the real estate industry and because most people are already familiar with it.

LAND DESCRIPTIONS

There are five commonly used methods of describing the location of land: (1) informal reference, (2) metes and bounds, (3) rectangular survey system, (4) recorded plat, and (5) reference to documents other than maps. We shall look at each in detail.

INFORMAL REFERENCES

Street numbers and place names are informal references: the house located at 7216 Maple Street; the apartment identified as Apartment 101, 875 First Street; the office identified as Suite 222, 3570 Oakview Boulevard; or the ranch known as the Rocking K Ranch—in each case followed by the city (or county) and state where it is located—are informal references. The advantage of an informal reference is that it is easily understood. The disadvantage from a real estate standpoint is that it is not a precise method of land description: a street number or place name does not provide the boundaries of the land at that location, and these numbers and names change over the years. Consequently, in real estate the use of informal references is limited to situations in which convenience is more important than precision. Thus, in a rental contract, Apartment 101, 875 First Street, city and state, is sufficient for a tenant to find his apartment unit. His apartment need not be described by one of the following formal land descriptions.

Early land descriptions in America depended on convenient natural or man-made objects. A stream might serve as one side of a parcel, an old oak tree as a corner, a road as a side, a pile of rocks as a corner, a fence as a side, and so forth. This method was handy, but it had two major drawbacks: there might not be a convenient corner or boundary marker where one was needed, and over time, oak trees died, stone heaps were moved, streams and rivers changed, stumps rotted, fences were removed, and unused roads became overgrown with vegetation. The following description in the Hartford, Connecticut, probate court records for 1812 illustrates what is sometimes encountered:

METES AND BOUNDS

> Commencing at a heap of stone about a stone's throw from a certain small clump of alders, near a brook running down off from a rather high part of said ridge; thence, by a straight line to a certain marked white birch tree, about two or three times as far from a jog in a fence going around a ledge nearby; thence by another straight line in a different direction, around said ledge and the Great Swamp, so called; thence, in line of said lot in part and in part by another piece of fence which joins on to said line, and by an extension of the general run of said fence to a heap of stone near a surface rock; thence, as aforesaid, to the "Horn," so called, and passing around the same as aforesaid, as far as the "Great Bend," so called, and from thence to a squarish sort of a jog in another fence, and so on to a marked black oak tree with stones piled around it; thence, by another straight line in about a contrary direction and somewhere about parallel with the line around by the ledge and the Great Swamp, to a stake and stone bounds not far off from the old Indian trail; thence, by another straight line on a course diagonally parallel, or nearly so, with "Fox Hollow Run," so called, to a certain marked red cedar tree out on a sandy sort of a plain; thence, by another straight line, in a different direction,

to a certain marked yellow oak tree on the off side of a knoll with a flat stone laid against it; thence, after turning around in another direction, and by a sloping straight line to a certain heap of stone which is, by pacing, just 18 rods and about one half a rod more from the stump of the big hemlock tree where Philo Blake killed the bear; thence, to the corner begun at by two straight lines of about equal length, which are to be run by some skilled and competent surveyor, so as to include the area and acreage as herein before set forth.*

Permanent Monuments   The drawbacks of this method of land description are resolved by setting a permanent man-made **monument** at one corner of the parcel, and then describing the parcel in terms of distance (**metes**) and direction (**bounds**) from that point. Distances are measured in feet, usually to the nearest tenth or one-hundredth of a foot. Direction is shown in degrees, minutes and seconds. There are 360 degrees (°) in a circle, 60 minutes (') in each degree and 60 seconds ('') in each minute. The abbreviation 29°14'52'' would be read as 29 degrees, 14 minutes, and 52 seconds. Figure 2:2 illustrates a parcel of land mapped in metes and bounds.

At the corner where the survey begins, a monument in the form of an iron pipe or bar 1 to 2 inches in diameter is driven into the ground. Alternatively, concrete or stone monuments are sometimes used. To guard against the possibility that the monument might later be destroyed or removed, it is referenced by means of a **connection line** to a nearby **permanent reference mark** established by a government survey agency. The corner where the parcel survey begins is called the **point of beginning** or **point of commencement.** From this point in Figure 2:2, we travel clockwise along the parcel's perimeter, reaching the next corner by going in the direction 80 degrees east of south for a distance of 180 feet. We then travel in a direction 15 degrees west of south for 160 feet, thence 85 degrees west of south for 151 feet, and thence 4 degrees, 11 minutes and 18 seconds east of north for 199.5 feet back to the point of beginning. In mapping shorthand,

---

* Harry Borchard, *Surveying* (Scranton, Pa.: International Textbook Company, 1947), pp. 435–36. By permission.

this parcel would be described by first identifying the monument, then the county and state within which it lies, and "thence S80°0'0"E, 180.0'; thence S15°0'0"W, 160.0'; thence S85°0'0"W, 151.0'; thence N4°11'18"E, 199.5' back to the p.o.b."

DESCRIBING LAND BY METES AND BOUNDS   **Figure 2:2**

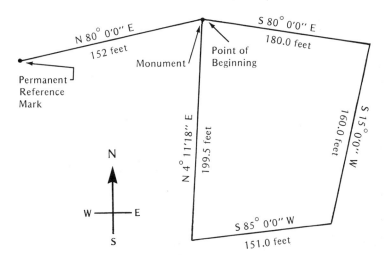

The compass illustrated in Figure 2:3A shows how the direction of travel along each side of the parcel in Figure 2:2 is determined. Note that the same line can be labeled two ways depending on which direction you are traveling. To illustrate, look at the line from *P* to *Q*. If you are traveling toward *P* on the line, you are going N45°W. But, if you are traveling toward point *Q* on the line, you are going S45°E.   *Compass Directions*

Curved boundary lines are produced by using arcs of a circle. The length of the arc is labeled *L* or *A*; the radius of the circle producing the arc is labeled *R*. The symbol ∆ (delta) indicates the angle used to produce the arc (see Figure 2:3B). Where an arc connects to a straight boundary or another arc the connection is indicated by the symbol ——●—— or the symbol ——○——.

Bench marks are commonly used as permanent reference markers. They are round bronze disks, 3¼ inches across, set in vertical steel pipes or in concrete at ground level by government agencies, such as the United States Geological

Survey (USGS) and the United States Coast and Geodetic Survey (USCGS). These marks are referenced to each other by distance and direction. The advantages of this type of reference point, compared to trees, rocks, and the like, are permanence and accuracy to within a fraction of an inch.

Figure 2:3   METES AND BOUNDS MAPPING

(A) NAMING DIRECTIONS FOR
A METES & BOUNDS SURVEY

(B) MAPPING A CURVE

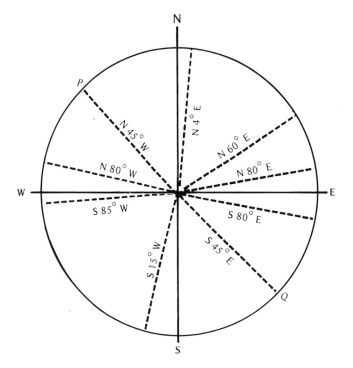

A = Length of the arc. (Some maps use the letter 'L")
R = Radius of the circle necessary to make the required arc (shown here by the broken lines)
△ = Angle necessary to make the arc, i.e., the angle between the broken lines

Moving in a clockwise direction from the point of beginning, set the center of a circle compass (like the one shown above) on each corner of the parcel to find the direction of travel to the next corner. (*Note:* Minutes and seconds have been omitted above for clarity)

Additionally, even though it is possible to destroy a reference point or monument, it can be replaced in its exact former position because each is related to other reference points.

It is also possible to describe a parcel using metes and bounds when there is no physical monument set in the ground. This is done by identifying a corner of a parcel of land by using the rectangular survey system or a recorded plat map, and then using that corner as a reference point to begin a metes and bounds description. As long as the starting place for a metes and bounds description can be accurately located by future surveyors, it will serve the purpose.

The rectangular survey system was established by Congress in May 1785. It was designed to provide a faster and simpler method than metes and bounds for describing land in newly annexed territories and states. Rather than using physical monuments, the rectangular survey system, also known as the **government survey** or **public lands survey,** is based on imaginary lines. These lines are the east-west **latitude** lines and the north-south **longitude** lines that encircle the globe, as illustrated in Figure 2:4.

Certain longitude lines were selected to act as **principal** or **prime meridians.** For each of these an intercepting latitude line was selected as a **base line.** Every 24 miles east and west of a principal meridian, **guide meridians** were established, and every 24 miles north and south of a base line, **correction lines** or **parallels** were established. These are needed because the earth is not a flat surface; as one travels north in the United States, longitude (meridian) lines come closer together. Figure 2:4 shows how guide meridians and correction lines adjust for this problem. Each 24 by 24-mile area created by the guide meridians and correction lines is called a **check.**

There are 36 principal meridians and accompanying base lines. Figure 2:5 shows the states in which the rectangular survey system is used and the land area for which each principal meridian and base line act as a reference. For example, the Sixth Principal Meridian is the reference point for land surveys in Kansas, Nebraska, and portions of Colorado, Wyoming, and South Dakota. In addition to the U.S. rectangular survey system, a portion of western Kentucky was surveyed into townships by a special state survey. Also, the state of Ohio contains eight public lands surveys that are rectangular in design, but which use state boundaries and major rivers rather than latitude and longitude as reference lines.

Figure 2:6 shows how land is referenced to a principal

RECTANGULAR SURVEY SYSTEM

meridian and base line. Every 6 miles east and west of each principal meridian, parallel imaginary lines are drawn. The resulting 6-mile-wide columns are called **ranges** and are numbered east and west of the principal meridian. For example, the first range west is called Range 1 West and abbreviated R1W. The next range west is R2W, and so forth. The fourth range east is R4E.

Figure 2:4

LATITUDE AND LONGITUDE LINES PROVIDE BASE LINES AND MERIDIANS

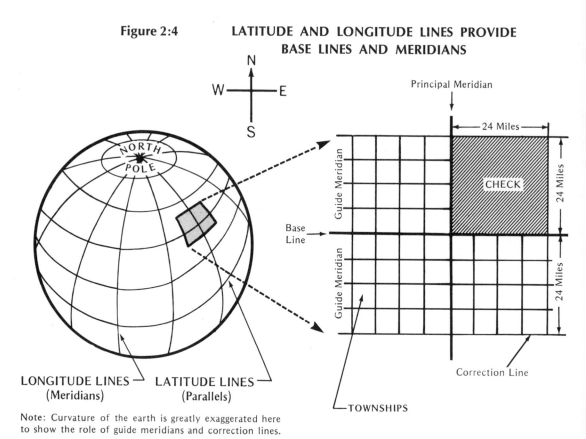

LONGITUDE LINES
(Meridians)

LATITUDE LINES
(Parallels)

TOWNSHIPS

Note: Curvature of the earth is greatly exaggerated here to show the role of guide meridians and correction lines.

Every six miles north and south of a base line, township lines are drawn. They intersect with the range lines and produce 6 by 6-mile imaginary squares called **townships** (not to be confused with the word township as applied to political subdivisions). Each tier or row of townships thus created is numbered with respect to the base line. Townships lying in

Figure 2:5

THE PUBLIC LAND SURVEY SYSTEMS OF THE UNITED STATES

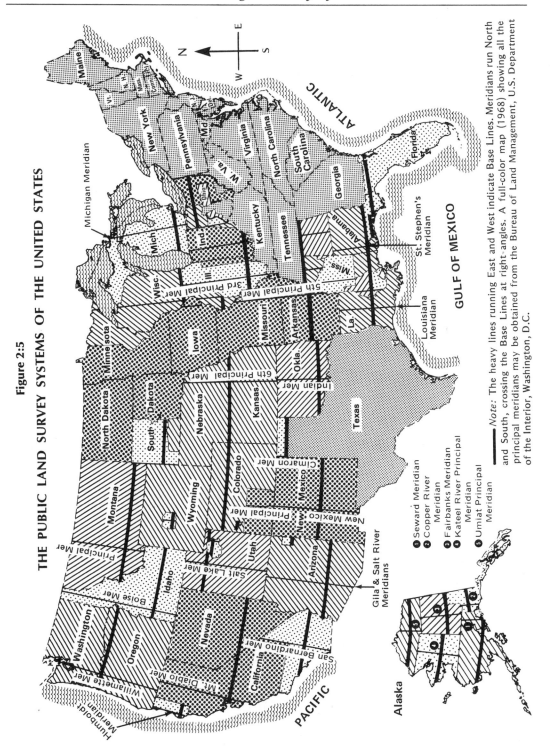

— *Note:* The heavy lines running East and West indicate Base Lines. Meridians run North and South, crossing the Base Lines at right-angles. A full-color map (1968) showing all the principal meridians may be obtained from the Bureau of Land Management, U.S. Department of the Interior, Washington, D.C.

❶ Seward Meridian
❷ Copper River Meridian
❸ Fairbanks Meridian
❹ Kateel River Principal Meridian
❺ Umiat Principal Meridian

the first tier north of a base line all carry the designation Township 1 North, abbreviated T1N. Townships lying in the first tier south of the base line are all designated T1S, and in the second tier south, T2S. By adding a range reference, an individual township can be identified. Thus, T2S, R2W would identify the township lying in the second tier south of the base line and the second range west of the prime meridian. T14N, R52W would be a township 14 tiers north of the base line and 52 ranges west of the principal meridian.

Each 36 square-mile township is divided into 36 one-square-mile units called **sections.** When one flies over farming areas, particularly in the Midwest, the checkerboard pattern of farms and roads that follow section boundaries can be seen. Sections are numbered 1 through 36, starting in the upper-right corner of the township. This numbering system is illustrated in Figure 2:6 where the shaded section is described as Section 32, T2N, R3E, 6th Principal Meridian.

Figure 2:6   **IDENTIFYING TOWNSHIPS AND SECTIONS**

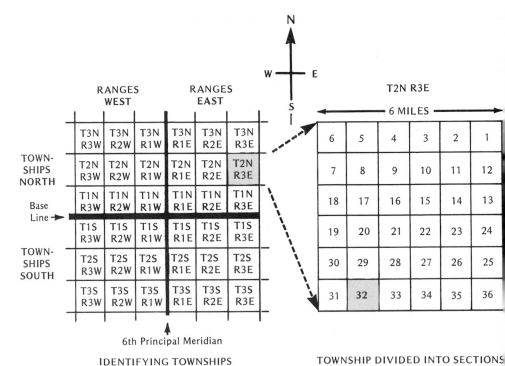

IDENTIFYING TOWNSHIPS   TOWNSHIP DIVIDED INTO SECTIONS

Each square-mile section contains 640 acres, and each **acre** contains 43,560 square feet. If a parcel of land is smaller than a full 640-acre section, it is identified by its position in the section. This is done by dividing the section into quarters and halves and other fractions, as shown in Figure 2:7. For example, the shaded parcel shown at (A) is described by dividing the section into quarters and then dividing the southwest

SUBDIVIDING A SECTION   Figure 2:7

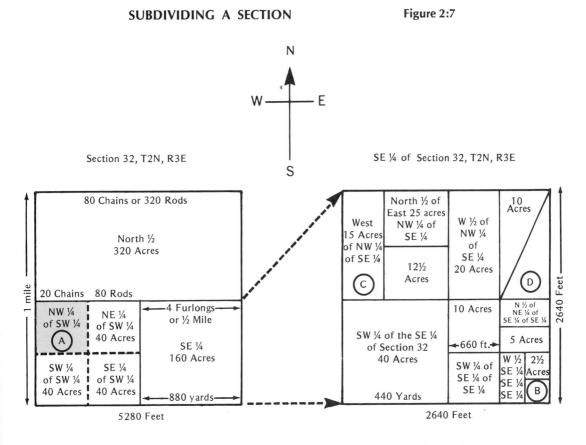

ONE SECTION (640 Acres) SUBDIVIDED   SE ¼ (160 Acres) SUBDIVIDED FURTHER

quarter into quarters. Parcel (A) is described as the NW¼ of the SW¼ of Section 32, T2N, R3E, 6th P.M. Additionally, it is customary to name the county and state in which the land lies. How much land does the NW¼ of the SW¼ of a section contain? A section contains 640 acres; therefore, a quarter-section contains 160 acres. Dividing a quarter-section again into quarters results in four 40-acre parcels. Thus, the northwest quarter of the southwest quarter contains 40 acres.

The rectangular survey system is not limited to parcels of 40 or more acres. To demonstrate this point, the 160 acres in the SE¼ of section 32 are expanded in the right half of Figure 2:7. Parcel (B) is described as the SE¼ of the SE¼ of the SE¼ of the SE¼ of section 32 and contains 2½ acres. Parcel (C) is described as the west 15 acres of the NW¼ of the SE¼ of section 32. Parcel (D) would be described in metes and bounds using the northeast corner of the SE¼ of section 32 as the starting point.

In terms of surface area, more land in the United States is described by the rectangular survey system than by any other survey method. But in terms of number of properties, the recorded plat is the most important survey method.

RECORDED PLAT   When a tract of land is ready for subdividing into lots for homes and businesses, reference by recorded plat provides the simplest and most convenient method of land description. Also known as the **lot-block-tract system, recorded map,** or **recorded survey,** it is based on the filing of a surveyor's plat map in the public recorder's office of the county where the land is located. Figure 2:8 illustrates a plat map. Notice that a metes and bounds survey has been made and a map prepared to show in detail the boundaries of each parcel of land. Each parcel is then assigned a lot number. Each block in the tract is given a block number, and the tract itself is given a name or number. The maps showing all the blocks in the tract are delivered to the county recorder's office, where they are placed in **map books** or **survey books,** along with maps of other subdivisions in the county.

Each plat map is given a book and page reference number, and all map books are available for public inspection. From that point on, it is no longer necessary to reference a monument and then give a lengthy metes and bounds description to describe one of the parcels. Instead, one need only refer to the lot and block number, tract name, map book

LAND DESCRIPTION BY RECORDED PLAT MAP   **Figure 2:8**

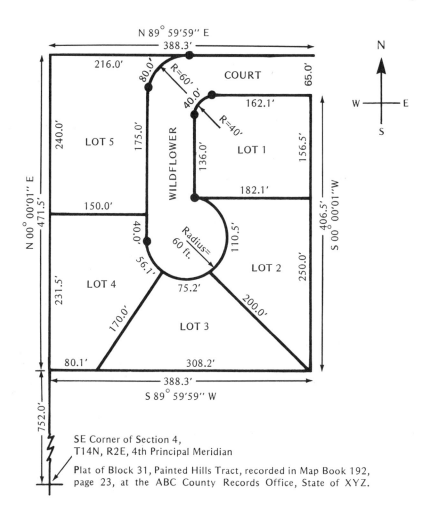

SE Corner of Section 4,
T14N, R2E, 4th Principal Meridian

Plat of Block 31, Painted Hills Tract, recorded in Map Book 192, page 23, at the ABC County Records Office, State of XYZ.

reference, county, and state. To find the location and dimensions of a recorded lot, one need only refer to the map book at the county recorder's office.

Note that the plat map in Figure 2:8 combines all the land descriptions discussed thus far. The boundaries of the numbered lots are in metes and bounds, and these in turn are referenced to a section corner in the rectangular survey system.

REFERENCE TO
DOCUMENTS OTHER
THAN MAPS

Land can also be described by referring to another publicly recorded document, such as a deed or a mortgage, that
contains a full legal description of the parcel in question. For
example, suppose that several years ago Baker received a deed
from Adams which contained a long and complicated metes
and bounds description. Baker recorded the deed in the public records office, where a photocopy was placed in Book 1089,
page 456. If Baker later wants to deed the same land to
Cooper, Baker can describe the parcel in his deed to Cooper
by saying, "all the land described in the deed from Adams to
Baker recorded in Book 1089, page 456, county of ABC, state
of XYZ, at the public recorder's office for said county and
state." As these books are open to the public, Cooper (or anyone else) could go to Book 1089, page 456 and find a detailed
description of the parcel's boundaries.

The key test of a land description is: "Can another
person, reading what I have written or drawn, understand my
description and go out and locate the boundaries of the
parcel?"

VERTICAL LAND
DESCRIPTION

In addition to surface land descriptions, land may also be
described in terms of vertical measurements. This type of
measurement is necessary when air rights or subsurface rights
need to be described.

The point, line, or surface from which a vertical height or
depth is measured is called a **datum.** The most commonly used
datum in the United States is mean sea level, although a number of cities have established other data surfaces for use in
local surveys. From the datum point, **bench marks** are set by
government survey teams; thus, a surveyor need not travel
to the datum point to determine an elevation. These same
bench marks are used as metes and bounds reference points.

In selling or leasing subsurface drilling or mineral rights,
the chosen datum is often the surface of the parcel. For example, an oil lease may permit the extraction of oil and gas
from a depth greater than 500 feet beneath the surface of a
parcel of land.

An **air lot** (a space over a given parcel of land) is described by identifying both the parcel of land beneath the air

lot and the elevation of the air lot above the parcel (see Figure 2:9A).

Contour maps (topographic maps) indicate elevations. On these maps, **contour lines** connect all points having the same elevation. The purpose is to show hills and valleys, slopes, and water runoff. If the land is to be developed, the map shows where soil will have to be moved to provide building lots. Figure 2:9B illustrates how vertical distances are shown using contour lines.

AIR LOT AND CONTOUR LINES   Figure 2:9

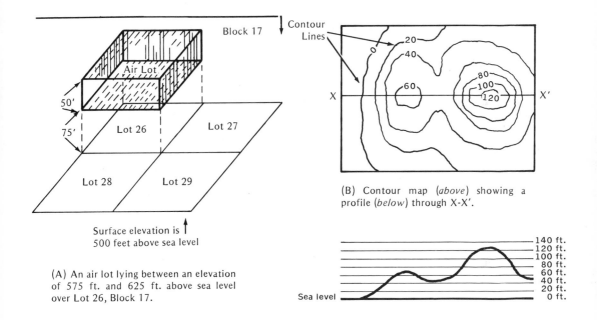

(A) An air lot lying between an elevation of 575 ft. and 625 ft. above sea level over Lot 26, Block 17.

(B) Contour map (*above*) showing a profile (*below*) through X-X'.

The physical characteristics of land are immobility, indestructibility, and nonhomogeneity. This combination of characteristics makes land different from other commodities and directly and indirectly influences man's use of it.

PHYSICAL CHARACTERISTICS OF LAND

A parcel of land cannot be moved. It is true that soil, sand, gravel, and minerals can be moved by the action of

Immobility

nature (erosion) or man (digging); however, the parcel itself still retains its same geographical position on the globe. Because land is **immobile,** a person must go to the land; it cannot be brought to him. When land is sold, the seller cannot physically deliver his land to the buyer. Instead, the seller gives the buyer a document called a deed that transfers to the buyer the right to go onto that land and use it. Because land is immobile, real estate offices nearly always limit their sales activities to nearby properties; even then a great deal of a salesperson's effort is used in traveling to show properties to clients. Immobility also creates a need for property-management firms, because, unless an owner of rental property lives on the property or nearby, neither land nor buildings can be efficiently managed.

Indestructibility   Land is **indestructible,** that is, durable. For example, today one can travel to the Middle East and walk on the same land that was walked on in Biblical days, and most of the land that we use in the United States today is the same land used by the American Indians a thousand years ago.

The characteristic of physical durability has encouraged many people to buy land as an investment because they feel paper money, stocks and bonds, and other commodities may come and go, but land will always be there. Although this is true in a physical sense, whether a given parcel has economic value depends on one's ability to protect his ownership coupled with the demand for that land by other persons. In other words, physical durability must not be confused with economic durability.

Nonhomogeneity   The fact that no two parcels of land are exactly alike because no two parcels can occupy the same position on the globe is known as **nonhomogeneity** (heterogeneity). Courts of law recognize this characteristic of land and consequently treat land as a **nonfungible** (pronounced non·fun'je'ble) commodity (i.e., nonsubstitutable). Thus, in a contract involving the sale or rental of land (and any improvements on that land), the courts can be called upon to enforce specific performance of the contract. For example, in a contract to sell a home, if the buyer carries out his obligations and the seller fails to convey ownership to the buyer, a court of law will force the seller to convey ownership of *that* specific home to the buyer. The court will not require the buyer to accept a substitute home. This is different than a homogeneous or **fungible** commodity which is freely substitutable in carrying out a contract. For example, one bushel of No. 1 grade winter wheat can be freely replaced by another bushel of the same grade, and one share of United States Steel common stock can be substituted for another as all are identical.

Although land is nonhomogeneous, there can still be a high degree of physical and economic similarity. For example, in a city block containing 20 house lots of identical size and shape, there will be a high degree of similarity even though the lots are still nonhomogeneous. Finding similar properties is, in fact, the basis for the market-comparison approach to appraising real estate. However, the lack of exact similarity means that an appraisal is only an estimate.

The dividing line between the physical and economic characteristics of land is sometimes difficult to define, because the physical aspects of land greatly influence man's economic behavior toward land. However, four economic characteristics are generally recognized: scarcity, modification, permanence of investment (fixity), and area preference (situs, pronounced sī'tus).

ECONOMIC CHARACTERISTICS OF LAND

*scarcity,
situs
fixity
modification*

The shortage of land in a given geographical area where there is great demand for land is referred to as **scarcity.** It is a man-made characteristic. For example, land is scarce in Miami Beach, Florida, because a relatively large number of people want to use a relatively small area of land. Another well-known example is 2-mile-wide, 13-mile-long Manhattan Island in New York City, where more than 1,000,000 people live and twice that number work. Yet one need only travel 25 miles west of Miami Beach or into central New York State to find plenty of uncrowded land available for purchase at very reasonable prices. The sheer quantity of undeveloped land in the United States as seen from an airplane on a cross-country flight is staggering.

Land scarcity is also influenced by man's ability to use

Scarcity

land more efficiently. To illustrate, in agricultural areas, production per acre of land has more than doubled for many crops since 1940. This is not due to any change in the land, but is the result of fertilizers, irrigation systems, better seeds and modern crop management. In urban areas, an acre of land that once provided space for five houses can be converted to high-rise apartments to provide homes for 100 or more families.

Thus, although there is a limited physical amount of land on the earth's surface, scarcity is chiefly a function of demand for land in a given geographical area and the ability of man to make land more productive. The persistent notion that all land is scarce has led to periodic land sale booms in undeveloped areas, which are often followed by a collapse in land prices when it becomes apparent that that particular land is not economically scarce.

Modification   Land use and value are greatly influenced by **modification,** that is, improvements made by man to surrounding parcels of land. For example, the construction of an airport will increase the usefulness and value of land parallel to runways but have a negative effect on the use and value of land at the ends of runways because of noise from landings and takeoffs. Similarly, land subject to flooding will become more useful and valuable if government-sponsored flood control dams are built upriver.

One of the most widely publicized cases of land modification occurred near Orlando, Florida, when Disney World was constructed. Nearby land previously used for agricultural purposes suddenly became useful as motel, gas station, restaurant, house, and apartment sites and increased rapidly in value.

Fixity   The fact that land and buildings and other improvements to land require long periods of time to pay for themselves is referred to as **fixity** or **investment permanence.** For example, it may take 20 or 30 years for the income generated by an apartment or office building to repay the cost of the land and building plus interest on the money borrowed to make the purchase. Consequently, real estate investment and land use decisions must consider not only how the land will be used next month or next year, but also the usefulness of the improvements 20 years from now. There is no economic logic in spending money to purchase land and improvements that will require 20 to 30 years to pay for themselves, if their usefulness is expected to last only 5 years.

Fixity also reflects the fact that land cannot be moved from its present location to another location where it will be more valuable. With very few exceptions, improvements to land are also fixed. Even with a house, the cost of moving it, plus building a foundation at the new site, can easily exceed the value of the house after the move. Thus, when an investment is made in real estate, it is regarded as a **fixed** or **sunk cost.**

Location preference or **situs** refers to location from an economic rather than a geographic standpoint. It has often been said that the single most important word in real estate is "location." What this means is the preference of people for a given area. For a residential area, these preferences are the result of *natural* factors, such as weather, air pollution, scenic views, and closeness to natural recreation areas, and *man-made* factors, such as employment availability, transportation facilities, shopping, and schools. For an industrial area, situs depends on such things as an available labor market, adequate supplies of water and electricity, nearby rail lines, and highway access. In farming areas, situs includes soil and weather conditions, water and labor availability, and transportation facilities.

Situs location !!!!

Situs is the reason that house lots on street corners sell for more than identical-sized lots not on corners. This reflects a preference for open space. The same is true in apartments; corner units usually rent for more than similar-sized non-corner units. In a high-rise apartment building, units on the top floors, if they offer a view, command higher prices than identical units on lower floors. On a street lined with stores, the side of the street that is shaded in the afternoon will attract more shoppers than the unshaded side. Consequently, buildings on the shade side will generate more sales and as a result be worth more.

It is important to realize that, since situs is a function of people's preferences and preferences can change with time, situs can also change. For example, the freeway and expressway construction boom, that started up in the 1950s, and accelerated during the 1960s, increased the preference for suburban areas. This resulted in declining property values in inner city areas and increasing land values in the suburbs. Today, with gasoline prices and transportation costs rapidly increasing, people are starting to show a preference for living closer to the centers of cities.

VOCABULARY REVIEW

Match terms a–r with statements 1–18.

a. Acre
b. Base line
c. Contour lines
d. Datum
e. Emblements
f. Fixity
g. Fixture
h. Government survey
i. Lot–block–tract

j. Meridian
k. Metes and bounds
l. Monument
m. Quarter-section
n. Riparian right
o. Section
p. Subsurface rights
q. Township
r. Water table

1. An object that has been attached to the land.
2. Contains 36 sections of land.
3. The depth below the surface at which water-saturated soil can be found.
4. A survey line running east and west from which townships are established.
5. Contains 640 acres of land.
6. The right of a landowner to use water flowing across his land.
7. An iron pipe or other object set in the ground to establish land boundaries.
8. A survey line that runs north and south in the rectangular survey system.
9. Annual crops produced by man.
10. A horizontal plane from which height and depth are measured.
11. Refers to the permanence of real estate investments.
12. A system of land description based on compass bearings and measured distances.
13. A land survey system based on imaginary latitude and longitude lines.
14. Includes the right to mine minerals and drill for oil.

15. Lines on a map that connect points having the same elevation.
16. Land description by reference to a recorded map.
17. 43,560 square feet.
18. Contains 160 acres of land.

1. Is the land upon which you make your residence described by metes and bounds, lot–block–tract, or the rectangular survey system?
2. On a sheet of paper sketch the following parcels of land in Section 6, T1N, R3E: (a) the N½; (b) the SW¼ of the SW¼; (c) the W½ of the SE¼; (d) the N17 acres of the E½ of the NE¼; (e) the SE¼ of the SE¼ of the SE¼ of the NW¼.
3. How many acres are there in each parcel described in number 2?
4. Describe the parcels labeled A, B, C, D, and E in the section shown at the right. How many acres does each contain?
5. Using an ordinary compass and ruler, sketch the following parcel of land. Beginning at monument M, thence due east for 40 feet, thence south 45° east for 14.1 feet, thence due south for 40 feet, thence north 45° west for 70.7 feet back to the point of beginning.
6. If a landowner owns from the center of the earth to the limits of the sky, are aircraft that pass overhead trespassers?
7. Would you classify the key to the door of a building as personal property or real property?
8. With regard to your own residence, itemize what you consider to be real property and what you consider to be personal property.
9. With regard to riparian rights, does your state follow the doctrine of prior appropriation or the right to a reasonable share?
10. What effects do you think changes in the location of the magnetic north pole would have on surveys over a long period of time? How would earthquakes affect bench marks?

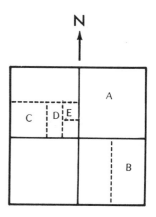

Brown, Curtis M., and **Eldridge, Winfield H.** *Evidence and Procedures for Boundary Location.* New York: John Wiley, 1962, 484 pages. Procedures for correctly locating a parcel of land in accordance with a property description are discussed.

Dunscombe, Carroll. *Riparian and Littoral Rights.* New York: The William-Frederick Press, 1970, 84 pages. A survey of legal problems involved in residential and commercial land use along the water's edge.

Herubin, Charles A. *Principles of Surveying*. Reston, Va.: Reston Publishing Co., 1974, 288 pages. Covers basic surveying theory and techniques, including horizontal and vertical distance measurement, angle measurement, and mapping.

Moss, Frank E. *The Water Crisis*. New York: Praeger, 1967, 305 pages. Water supplies in the United States are limited but demand is increasing. Water research, water conservation, and the impact of water availability on land values are covered.

Semenow, Robert W. *Selected Cases in Real Estate*. Englewood Cliffs, N.J.: Prentice-Hall, 1973, 638 pages. See pages 365–384 for court decisions as to what are considered fixtures and what are not.

Smith, Chester H., and **Boyer, Ralph E.** *Survey of the Law of Property*, 2nd ed. St. Paul, Minn.: West Publishing Co., 1971, 510 pages. Chapters 7–14 in Part II deal with the legal aspects of air, surface, and subsurface rights, water rights, fixtures, and emblements.

3

Rights and Interests in Land

Chattels: things deemed by law to be personal property; includes movable items (personal chattels) and less than freehold estates in land (real chattels)

Curtesy: the legal right of a widower to a portion of his deceased wife's real property

Dower: the legal right of a widow to a portion of her deceased husband's real property

Easement: the right or privilege one party has to use land belonging to another for a special purpose not inconsistent with the owner's use of the land

Eminent domain: the right of government to take privately held land, provided fair compensation is paid

Encroachment: the trespass of a building or other improvement onto another person's land

Fee simple: the largest, most complete, bundle of rights one can hold in land; land ownership

Lien: a hold or claim which one person has on the property of another to secure payment of a debt or other obligation

Title: a person's evidence of ownership; for example, a deed or a bill of sale

Early man was nomadic and had no concept of real estate. Roaming bands followed game and the seasons, and did not claim the exclusive right to use a given area. When man began to cultivate crops and domesticate animals, the concept of an exclusive right to the use of land became important. This right was claimed for the tribe as a whole, and each family in the tribe was given the right to the exclusive use of a portion of the tribe's land. In turn, each family was obligated to aid in defending the tribe's claim against other tribes.

As time passed, individual tribes allied with each other for mutual protection; eventually these alliances resulted in political states. In the process, land ownership went to the head of the state, usually a king. The king, in turn, gave the right (called a feud) to use large tracts of land to select individuals, called lords. The lords did not receive ownership. They were tenants of the king, and were required to serve and pay duties to the king and to help fight the king's wars. It was customary for the lords to remain tenants for life, subject, of course, to the defeat of their king by another king. This system, wherein all land ownership rested in the name of the king, became known as the **feudal system.**

The lords gave their subjects the right to use small tracts of land. For this, the subjects owed their lord a share of their crops and their allegiance in time of war. The subjects (vassals) were, in effect, tenants of the lord and subtenants of the king. Like the lord, the vassal could not sell his rights nor pass them to his heirs.

Allodial System

The first major change in the feudal system occurred in 1285 when King Edward I of England gave his lords the right to pass their tenancy rights to their heirs. Subsequently, tenant vassals were permitted to convey their tenancy rights to others. By the year 1650, the feudal system had come to an end in England; in France it ended with the French Revolution in 1789. In its place arose the **allodial system** of land ownership under which individuals were given the right to own land. Initially, lords became owners rather than tenants of the king, and peasants remained tenants of the lord. As time passed, the peasants became landowners either by purchase or by gift from the lord.

When the first European explorers reached North American shores, they claimed the land in the name of the king or queen whom they represented. When the first settlers later came to America from England, they claimed the land in the name of their mother country. However, since the feudal system had been abolished in the meantime, the king of England granted the settlers private ownership of the land upon which they settled, while retaining the claim of ownership to the unsettled lands.

Claims by the king of England to land in the 13 colonies were ended with the American Revolution. Subsequently, the U.S. government acquired the ownership right to additional lands by treaty, wars, and purchase, resulting in the borders of the United States as we know them today. The United States adopted the allodial system of ownership, and not only permits but encourages its citizens to own land within its borders.

Under the feudal system, the king was responsible for organizing defense against invaders, making decisions on land use, providing services such as roads and bridges, and the general administration of the land and his subjects. An important aspect of the transition from feudal to allodial ownership was that the need for these services did not end. Consequently, even though ownership could now be held by private citizens, it became necessary for the government to withhold the rights of taxation, eminent domain, police power, and escheat. Let us look at each of these more closely.

GOVERNMENT RIGHTS IN LAND

Government restricts rights

Under the feudal system, governments financed themselves by requiring lords and vassals to share a portion of the benefits they received from the use of the king's lands. With the change to private ownership, the need to finance governments did not end. Thus, the government retained the right to collect **property taxes** from landowners. Before the advent of income taxes, taxes levied against land were the main source of government revenues. Taxing land was a logical method of raising revenue for two reasons: (1) until the Industrial Revolution, which started in the mid-eighteenth century, land and agriculture were the primary sources of income; the more land one owned, the wealthier one was considered to be and therefore the better able to pay taxes to support the government; (2) land is impossible to hide, making it easily identifiable for taxation. This is not true of other valuables such as gold or money.

Property Taxes

The real property tax has endured over the centuries, and today it is still a major source of government revenue. The major change in real estate taxation is that initially it was used to support all levels of government, including defense. Today, defense is supported by the income tax, and real estate taxes are sources of city, county, and, in some places, state revenues. At state and local government levels, the real property tax provides money for such things as schools, fire and police protection, parks, and libraries. To encourage property owners to pay their taxes in full and on time, the right of taxation also gives the government the right to seize ownership of real estate upon which taxes are delinquent and to sell the property to recover the unpaid taxes.

Eminent Domain   The right of government to acquire ownership of privately held real estate regardless of the owner's wishes is called **eminent domain.** Land for schools, freeways, streets, parks, urban renewal, public housing, public parking, and other social and public purposes is obtained this way. Quasi-public organizations, such as utility companies and railroads, are also permitted to obtain land needed for utility lines, pipes, and tracks by state law. The legal proceeding involved in eminent domain is a **condemnation proceeding,** and the property owner must be paid the fair market value of the property taken from him. The actual condemnation is usually preceded by negotiations between the property owner and an agent of the public body wanting to acquire ownership. If the agent and the property owner can arrive at a mutually acceptable price, the property is purchased outright. If an agreement cannot be reached, a formal proceeding in eminent domain is filed against the property owner in a court of law. The court hears expert opinions from appraisers brought by both parties, and sets the price the property owner must accept in return for the loss of ownership.

When only a portion of a parcel of land is being taken, **severance damages** may be awarded in addition to payment for land actually being taken. For example, if a new highway requires a 40-acre strip of land through a 160-acre farm, the farm owner will not only be paid for the 40 acres; he will also receive severance damages to compensate for the fact that his farm will be more difficult to work because it is no longer in one piece.

An **inverse condemnation** is a proceeding brought about by a property owner demanding that his land be purchased from him. In a number of cities, homeowners at the end of airport runways have forced airport authorities to buy their homes because of the deafening noise of jet aircraft during takeoffs. Damage awards may also be made when land itself is not taken but its usefulness is reduced because of a nearby condemnation. These are **consequential damages,** and might be awarded, for instance, when land is taken for a sewage treatment plant, and privately owned land downwind from the plant suffers a loss in value owing to foul odors.

The right of government to enact laws and enforce them   *Police Power*
for the order, safety, health, morals, and general welfare of the public is called **police power.** Examples of police power applied to real estate are zoning laws, planning laws, building, health and fire codes, and rent control. A key difference between police power and eminent domain is that, although police power restricts how real estate may be used, there is no legally recognized "taking" of property. Consequently, there is no payment to an owner who suffers a loss of value through the exercise of police power. A government may not utilize police power in an offhand or capricious manner; any law that restricts how an owner may use his real estate must be deemed in the public interest and evenly applied to be valid. The breaking of a law based upon the right of police power results in a civil or criminal penalty rather than the seizing of real estate, as in the case of unpaid property taxes.

The right of government to take ownership when a per-   *Escheat*
son dies and leaves no heirs and no instructions as to how to dispose of his real and personal property is known as **escheat.** Escheat solves the problem of property becoming ownerless for lack of an heir.

It cannot be overemphasized that, to have real estate,   *PROTECTING*
there must be a system or means of protecting rightful claims   *OWNERSHIP*
to the use of land and the improvements thereon. In the United States, the federal government is given the task of organizing a defense system to prevent confiscation of those rights by a foreign power. The federal government, in combination with state and local governments, also establishes laws and courts within the country to protect the ownership rights of one citizen in relation to another citizen. Whereas armed forces protect against a foreign takeover, within a country, deeds, public records, contracts, and other documents have

replaced the need for brute force to prove and protect ownership of real estate.

BUNDLE OF RIGHTS IDEA   The concept of real estate ownership can be more easily understood when viewed as a bundle of rights. Under the allodial system, the rights of taxation, eminent domain, police power, and escheat are retained by the government. The remaining bundle of rights, called **fee simple**, is available for private ownership (see Figure 3:1).

Figure 3:1   **THE FEE SIMPLE BUNDLE OF RIGHTS**

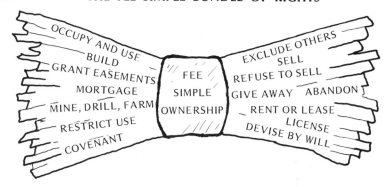

OCCUPY AND USE
BUILD
GRANT EASEMENTS
MORTGAGE
MINE, DRILL, FARM
RESTRICT USE
COVENANT

FEE SIMPLE OWNERSHIP

EXCLUDE OTHERS
SELL
REFUSE TO SELL
GIVE AWAY   ABANDON
RENT OR LEASE
LICENSE
DEVISE BY WILL

Real estate ownership is, in actuality, the ownership of rights to land. The largest bundle available for private ownership is called "fee simple."

The fee simple bundle of rights can be held by a person and his heirs forever, or until his government can no longer protect those rights. The term **estate** is synonymous with bundle of rights; thus, fee simple is the largest estate one can hold in land. Most real estate sales are for the fee simple estate; when a person says he or she "owns" or has "title" to real estate, it is usually the fee simple estate that is being discussed. **Title** refers to a person's evidence of property ownership.

Real estate is concerned with the sticks in the bundle: how many there are, how useful they are, and who possesses the sticks not in the bundle. With that in mind, let us pull sticks out of the bundle and describe the results.

The stick most commonly removed from the bundle is the right to offer the property as collateral for a loan. This stick is removed when the owner signs a mortgage agreement (in some states a trust deed) whereby the lender is given the right to force the sale of the mortgaged property if the borrower does not repay his loan. The bundle that remains is a fee simple estate subject to a mortgage or trust deed. Once the loan is repaid, the stick held by the lender is returned to the main bundle.

Another stick in the bundle that is often removed for varying lengths of time is the right to lease to another the possession and use of one's property. To illustrate, the fee owner of a house rents it to a tenant. As long as the tenant has a valid lease, abides by it, and pays the rent on time, the owner, even though he owns the house, cannot move in and use it until the lease has expired. During the lease period, the fee owner is said to hold a **reversionary interest.** His bundle is called a fee simple estate subject to a lease. Figure 3:2 illustrates the fee simple bundle with the mortgage and lease sticks removed. The deed restrictions and easement sticks, which are discussed next, are also taken out.

Deed Restrictions and Covenants

Private agreements that govern the use of land are known as **deed restrictions** and **covenants.** For example, a land subdivider can require that persons who purchase lots from him build only single-family homes containing 1,200 square feet or more. The purpose would be to protect those who have already built houses from an erosion in property value due to the construction of nearby buildings not compatible with the neighborhood. Where scenic views are important, deed restrictions may limit the height of buildings and trees to 15 feet. A buyer would still obtain fee simple ownership, but at the same time would voluntarily give up some of his rights to do as he pleases. As a buyer, he is said to receive a fee simple title subject to deed restrictions. The right to enforce the restrictions is usually given by the developer to the subdivision's homeowner's association.

Easements

An **easement** is a right or privilege one party has to the use of land of another for a special purpose consistent with the general use of the land. The landowner is not dispossessed

Figure 3:2   REMOVING STICKS FROM THE FEE SIMPLE BUNDLE

OCCUPY AND USE
BUILD
GRANT EASEMENTS
MORTGAGE
MINE, DRILL, FARM
RESTRICT USE
COVENANT

FEE SIMPLE OWNERSHIP

EXCLUDE OTHERS
SELL
REFUSE TO SELL
GIVE AWAY   ABANDON
RENT OR LEASE
LICENSE
DEVISE BY WILL

MINUS THE FOLLOWING:

RIGHT TO FORECLOSE

RIGHT TO LEASE

EASEMENT RIGHTS

DEED RESTRICTIONS

LEAVES AS A BALANCE

1. A MORTGAGE

FEE SIMPLE SUBJECT TO

3. AN EASEMENT AND

2. A LEASE

4. DEED RESTRICTIONS

Note that the fee simple bundle shrinks as an owner voluntarily removes rights from it.

from his land, but rather coexists side by side with the holder of the easement. Examples of easements are those given to telephone and electric companies to erect poles and run lines over private property, easements given to people to drive or walk across someone else's land, and easements given to gas and water companies to run pipelines to serve their customers. Figure 3:3 illustrates several examples of easements.

COMMONLY FOUND EASEMENTS   Figure 3:3

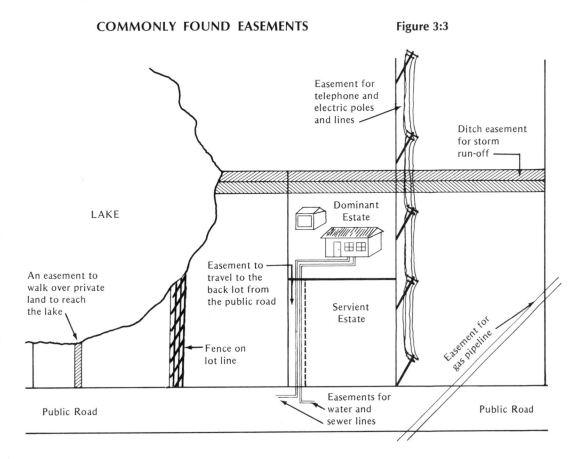

The usual procedure in creating an easement is for the landowner to use a written document to specifically grant an easement to someone else or to reserve an easement to himself in the deed when he sells the property. A land developer may reserve easements for utility lines and then grant them to the utility companies that will service the lots.

It is also possible for an easement to arise without a written document. For example, a parcel of land fronts on a road and the owner sells the back half of the parcel. If the only access to the back half is by crossing over the front half, even if the seller did not expressly grant an easement, the law will generally protect the buyer's right to travel over the front half to get to his land. The buyer cannot be landlocked by the seller. This is known as an **easement by necessity.** Another method of acquiring an easement without a written document is by constant use, or **easement by prescription:** if a person acts as though he owns an easement long enough, he will have a legally recognized easement. Persons using a private road without permission for a long enough period of time can acquire a legally recognized easement by this method.

Easement Appurtenant

An **easement appurtenant** is one that attaches itself to a parcel of land. When a person sells the back half of his lot, the easement to travel over the front to reach the back attaches to the land in the back and is said to "run with the land." Whenever the back half is sold, the easement to travel over the front automatically goes to the new owner. The back half of the lot is the **dominant estate** (or dominant tenement) because it acquires the easement; the front half is the **servient estate** (or servient tenement) because it gives up the easement.

An **easement in gross** is given to a person or business, and a subsequent sale of the land does not usually affect ownership of the easement. Telephone, electricity, and gas line easements are examples of easements in gross. The holder of a commercial easement usually has the right to sell, assign, or devise it. However, easements in gross for personal use are not transferable and terminate with the death of the person holding the easement. An example of a personal easement in gross would be a landowner giving a friend an easement to travel over his land to reach a choice fishing area.

Party Wall Easement

Party wall easements exist when a single wall straddles the lot line that separates two parcels of land. The wall may be either a fence or the wall of a building. In either case, each lot owner owns that portion of the wall on his land, plus an easement in the other half of the wall for physical support. Party walls are common where stores and office buildings are built right up to the lot line. Such a wall can present an interesting problem when the owner of one lot wants to demolish his building. Since the wall provides support for the building next door, it is usually his responsibility to either leave the wall or provide special supports for the adjacent building during demolition and until another building is constructed on the lot.

Easements may be terminated when the purpose for the easement no longer exists (a public road is built adjacent to the back half of the lot in the example earlier), when the dominant and servient estates are combined with the intent of extinguishing the easement, by release from the owner of the dominant estate to the servient estate, or by lack of use.

The **life estate** conveys a fee simple estate for the duration of someone's life. It is often used when a person wishes to look after another's financial well-being through a grant of real estate, but does not wish to give that person the right of passing it on to his heirs or devisees. (A devisee is a person named in a will to receive real estate. Heirs are those designated by law to receive the deceased's property when there is no will.) Suppose that you have an aunt who needs financial assistance. One possibility would be to grant her, for the duration of her life, a house to live in or perhaps an income-producing investment property. Your aunt becomes a **life tenant**; when she dies, the estate you granted her will revert back to you. The right to regain the property is called a **reversionary interest.** If you die before her, your reversionary interest goes to your heirs or devisees.

LIFE ESTATES

An alternative arrangement is to tie the length of time a life tenant has an estate to the life of another person. Suppose that you know that your rich uncle is naming your aunt to receive a substantial portion of his wealth upon his death. If this would adequately take care of her financial needs, you could grant your aunt a life estate until your uncle dies. Furthermore, when her life estate terminates, the real property in it need not return to you. It can automatically go to a third party, say, your brother or a charity. Sometimes the life estate is used to avoid the time and expense of probating a will and to reduce inheritance taxes. For example, an aging father could deed his real estate to his children but hold back a life estate for himself.

Since a life estate arrangement is temporary, the life tenant must not commit **waste** by destroying or harming the property. Furthermore, the life tenant is required to keep the property in reasonable repair and to pay any property taxes, assessments, and interest on debt secured by the property. During his or her tenancy, the life tenant is entitled to the profits and income generated by the property, and may sell, lease, rent, or mortgage his interest.

LEGAL LIFE ESTATES

"Legal" life estates are created by state law. They include **dower,** which gives a wife rights in her husband's real property, **curtesy,** which gives a husband rights in his wife's real property, and **homestead,** which is designed to protect the family's home from certain debts and, upon the death of one spouse, provides the other with a home for life. Table 3:1 shows the states that have these laws.

Dower

Historically **dower** came from old English common law, in which the marriage ceremony was viewed as merging the wife's legal existence into that of her husband's. From this viewpoint, property bought during marriage belongs to the husband, with both husband and wife sharing the use of it. As a counterbalance, the dower right recognizes the wife's efforts in marriage and grants her legal ownership to one-third (in some states one-half) of the family's real property for the rest of her life. This prevents the husband from conveying ownership of the family's real estate without the wife's permission and protects her from being left out of her husband's will.

Because the wife's dower right does not ripen into actual ownership until her husband's death, her right is described as being **inchoate** until then. Once she obtains her life estate, she can sell, give, rent, or mortgage it, as described in the previous section.

In real estate sales, the effect of dower laws is that, when a husband and wife sell their property, the wife must relinquish her dower rights. This is usually accomplished by the wife signing the deed with her husband or by signing a separate quit claim deed. If she does not relinquish her dower rights, the buyer (or even a future buyer) may find that, upon the husband's death, the wife may return to legally claim a life estate in one third of the property. This is an important

DOWER, CURTESY, AND HOMESTEAD PROTECTION BY STATE   Table 3:1

	Dower Right for Wife	Curtesy or Dower Right for Husband	Homestead Protection		Dower Right for Wife	Curtesy or Dower Right for Husband	Homestead Protection
Alabama	X		X	Missouri			X
Alaska			X	Montana			X
Arizona			X	Nebraska			X
Arkansas	X	X	X	Nevada			X
California			X	New Hampshire			X
Colorado			X	New Jersey	X	X	
Connecticut				New Mexico			X
Delaware	X	X		New York			X
District of Columbia	X	X		North Carolina			X
				North Dakota			X
Florida			X	Ohio	X	X	X
Georgia			X	Oklahoma			X
Hawaii	X	X		Oregon			X
Idaho			X	Pennsylvania			
Illinois			X	Rhode Island	X	X	
Indiana			X	South Carolina	X		X
Iowa			X	South Dakota			X
Kansas			X	Tennessee	X	X	X
Kentucky	X	X	X	Texas			X
Louisiana			X	Utah			X
Maine			X	Vermont	X	X	X
Maryland				Virginia	X	X	X
Massachusetts	X	X	X	Washington			X
Michigan	X		X	West Virginia	X	X	X
Minnesota			X	Wisconsin	X	X	X
Mississippi			X	Wyoming			X

reason why, if you are buying real estate, you should have the property's ownership researched by a competent abstracter and have the title you receive insured by a title insurance company. Because the wife's dower right is inchoate while her husband is alive, she cannot sell it or otherwise part with it except when they mutually sell family real estate.

Curtesy   Roughly the opposite of dower, **curtesy** gives the husband benefits in his deceased wife's property as long as he lives. However, unlike dower, the wife can defeat those rights in her will. Furthermore, state law may require the couple to have had a child in order for the husband to qualify for curtesy. In some states, husbands are given dower rights rather than curtesy.

If dower and curtesy rights seem confusing, they are. Dower and curtesy came to the United States from English common law when the original 13 colonies were settled. Each state has so modified them that no two states are exactly alike in their administration of these rights. Because the premise of male dominance in marriage and family property ownership is at odds with equal rights for men and women, we shall undoubtedly witness the gradual abandonment of dower and curtesy in favor of more equitable systems of husband–wife ownership, such as community property. Meanwhile, it is intersting to note that England abandoned dower and curtesy over 50 years ago.

Homestead Protection   Nearly all states (see Table 3:1) have passed **homestead protection laws,** usually with two purposes in mind: (1) to provide some legal protection for the husband and wife from debts and judgments against them that might result in the forced sale and loss of the family home, and (2) to provide a home for a widow, and sometimes a widower, for life. Homestead laws also restrict one spouse from acting without the other when conveying the homestead or using it as collateral for a loan. Although dower and curtesy are automatic in those states that have them, the homestead right may require that a written declaration be recorded in the public records. (Homestead as referred to here is not the acquiring of title to state or federally owned lands by filing and establishing a residence.)

FREEHOLD ESTATES   For purposes of classification, legal life estates, conventional life estates, and fee simple estates (plus qualified fee estates and fee tail estates, which are not described here because they are so rarely found) are categorized in law as **freehold estates.** There are two key distinguishing features of freehold estates: (1) there must be actual ownership of the land, and (2) the estate must be of unpredictable duration. If the date of termination is known in advance, the estate cannot be a freehold. It is called a **less than freehold estate** or more commonly, a **leasehold estate.** The lease is the smallest estate that one can hold in land.

LEASEHOLD ESTATES

The most important aspect of a leasehold estate is that the land user is not the land owner.* The user is the **lessee** or **tenant,** and the person from whom he leases is the **lessor** or **landlord.** At the end of the tenant's stay, the landlord recovers possession of his property. Thus, the landlord holds a reversionary interest while the leasehold estate is in effect. There are four categories of leasehold estates.

Estate for Years

Also called a tenancy for years, the **estate for years** is somewhat misleadingly named as it implies that a lease for a number of years has been created. Actually, the key criterion is that the lease have a specific starting time and a specific ending time. It can be for any length of time, ranging from less than a day to many years. An estate for years does not automatically renew itself, and neither the landlord nor the tenant must act to terminate it, as the lease agreement itself specifies a termination date.

Usually the lessor is the freehold estate owner. However, the lessor could be a lessee himself. To illustrate, a fee owner leases his property to a lessee, who in turn leases his right to still another person. By doing this, the first lessee has become a **sublessor** and is said to hold a **sandwich lease.** The person who leases from him is a **sublessee.** It is important to realize that in no case can a sublessee acquire from the lessee any more rights than the lessee has under his lease. Thus, if a lessee has a 5-year lease with 3 years remaining, he can assign to a sublessee only the remaining 3 years or a portion of that.

---

* This chapter examines leases primarily from the standpoint of estates in realty. Leases as financing tools are discussed in Chapter 12, and leases from the landlord–tenant viewpoint are covered in Chapter 22.

Periodic Estate

Also called an estate from period to period or a periodic tenancy, a **periodic estate** has an original lease period with fixed length; when it runs out, unless the tenant or his landlord acts to terminate it, renewal is automatic for another like period of time. A month-to-month apartment rental is an example of this arrangement. To avoid last minute confusion, rental agreements usually require that advance notice be given if either the landlord or the tenant wishes to terminate the tenancy.

Estate at Will

Also called a tenancy at will, an **estate at will** is a landlord–tenant relationship with all the normal rights and duties of a lessor–lessee relationship, except that the estate may be terminated by either the lessor or the lessee at anytime. However, most states recognize the inconvenience a literal interpretation of "anytime" can cause and require that reasonable advance notice be given.

Estate at Sufferance

Also called a tenancy at sufferance, an **estate at sufferance** occurs when a tenant stays beyond his legal tenancy without the consent of the landlord. In other words, the tenant wrongfully holds the property against the owner's wishes. In a tenancy at sufferance, the tenant is commonly called a **holdover tenant,** although once beyond his legal tenancy he is not actually a tenant in the normal landlord–tenant sense. The landlord is entitled to evict him and recover possession of his property, provided he does so in a timely manner. If this is not done, most courts will hold that the tenant's continued occupancy terminates the tenancy at sufferance and creates a periodic estate.

LICENSE

A **license** is not an estate in land, but a personal privilege given to someone to use land. It is nonassignable and can be canceled by the person who issues it. A license to park is typically what an automobile parking lot operator provides for persons parking in his lot. The contract creating the license is usually written on the stub that the lot attendant gives the driver, or it is posted on a sign on the lot. Tickets to theaters and sporting events also fall into this category.

The trespass of a building or other improvement onto another person's land is called an **encroachment.** A tree that overhangs into a neighbor's yard, or a building or eave of a roof that crosses a property line are examples of encroachments. The owner of the property being encroached upon has the right to force the removal of the encroachment. Failure to do so may eventually injure his title and make his land more difficult to sell. Ultimately, inaction may result in the encroaching neighbor claiming a legal right to continue his use. Figure 3:4 illustrates several commonly found encroachments.

ENCROACHMENTS

COMMONLY FOUND ENCROACHMENTS

Figure 3:4

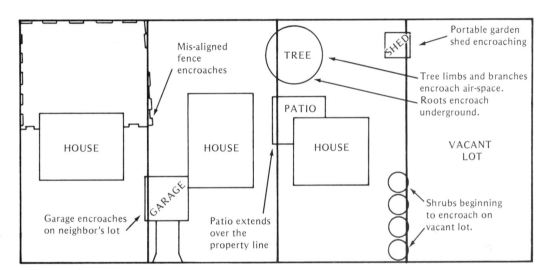

Most commonly found encroachments are not intentional but are due to poor or nonexistent planning. For example, a weekend garden shed, fence, or patio project is built without surveying to find the lot line, or a tree or bush grows so large it encroaches upon a neighbor's land.

A hold or claim that one person has on the property of another to secure payment of a debt or other obligation is called a **lien.** Common examples are property tax liens, mechanic's liens, and judgment liens. **Property tax liens** are a result of the right of government to collect taxes from property owners. At the beginning of each tax year, a tax lien is placed

LIENS

on taxable property. It is removed if the property taxes are paid. If they are not paid, the lien gives the state the right to sell the property and collect the unpaid taxes out of the sale proceeds. **Mechanic's lien** laws give anyone who has furnished labor or materials for the improvement of land the right to place a lien against that land if payment has not been received. A sale of the property can then be forced to recover the money owed. **Judgment liens** arise from lawsuits for which money damages are awarded. The law permits a hold to be placed against the property of the loser until the judgment is paid. Similarly, federal and state income and inheritance tax authorities can place liens on the property of delinquent taxpayers. In some states, mortgages are considered to be liens.

CHATTELS

Chattels are things deemed by law to be personal property. They are divided into two categories: chattels personal and chattels real. **Chattels personal** are movable objects (i.e., personalty). **Chattels real** are interests in real estate that do not qualify as freehold estate in land, for example, a leasehold estate for years. The term "chattels" is broader than "goods" as it includes both movable and intangible property. The significance of this classification system is that property laws in the United States are divided into two categories, those that pertain to real property and those that pertain to personal property. Chattels are governed by personal property laws; freehold estates are governed by real property laws.

A PICTORIAL
SUMMARY

Let us conclude this chapter by combining what has been discussed in Chapter 2 regarding the physical nature of land with what has been covered in this chapter regarding estates and rights in land. The results, diagrammed in Figures 3:5 and 3:6, show why real estate is both complicated and exciting at the same time. A single parcel of land can be divided into subsurface, surface, and air-space components, and each of these carries its own fee simple bundle of rights, which can be divided into the various estates and rights discussed in this chapter.

To more clearly convey this idea, let us turn our attention to Figure 3:5. In parcel A, the fee landowner has leased the

CROSS SECTION OF ESTATES AND RIGHTS IN LAND   **Figure 3:5**

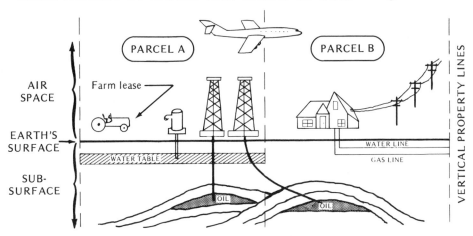

bulk of his surface and air rights, plus the right to draw water from his wells, to a farmer for the production of crops and livestock. This leaves the fee owner with the right to lease or sell subterranean rights for mineral, oil, and gas extraction. With a single parcel of land, the fee owner has created two estates, one for farming and another for oil and gas production. With the minor exception of the placement of the well platforms, pumps, and pipes, neither use interferes with the other and both bring income to the landowner. The farmer, in turn, can personally utilize the leasehold estate he possesses or he can sublease it to another farmer. The oil company, if it has leased its rights, can sublease them; if it has purchased them, it can sell or lease them. A variation would be for an oil company to buy the land in fee, conduct its drilling operations, and lease the remainder to a farmer. In the public interest, the government has claimed the right to allow aircraft to fly over the land. Although technically a landowner owns from the center of the earth out to the heavens, the right given aircraft to fly overhead creates a practical limit on that ownership.

In parcel B, the fee simple landowner has sold the right to extract oil and gas from beneath his land. However, no surface right for the purpose of entering and drilling has been leased or sold. Thus, the oil company must slant drill from a

Surface Right of Entry

nearby property where they do have a **surface right of entry.**
The remaining rights amount to a full fee estate in the surface
and air space. However, use of those rights is subject to
zoning laws and building codes that restrict what can be built.
Deed restrictions may include additional limitations on the
type of structure that can be built. Also, the government
claims air-space rights for passing aircraft, as it does over all
land within its borders. Just above and beneath the surface,
easement rights have been granted to utility companies for
electric, telephone, water, and gas lines.

Despite the fact that this homeowner's bundle of rights is
not complete, what he does have is quite suitable for a home
site. Recognizing this, lenders will accept the owner's offer to
pledge this house and lot as collateral for a loan. This might
not be the case if the oil company had a surface right of entry.
The noise, odor, and fire hazard of a working oil well next to
a house would considerably reduce its value as a residence.

Land Lease   In parcel C shown in Figure 3:6, the fee owner has created
an estate for years by a long-term lease of his land to an
investor, who has subsequently constructed an apartment
building on the land. This estate gives the building owner the
right to occupy and use the land for a fixed period of time,
most often between 55 and 99 years. The rights to any mineral, oil, or gas deposits can either be included in the lease or
reserved by the landowner. At the end of the lease period, the
reversionary interest held by the owner of the fee estate
entitles him to retake possession of his land, including the
buildings and other improvements thereon.

Condominium Lots   In parcel D, fee simple air lots have been sold to individual apartment owners in a condominium apartment build-
ing. The owner of each air lot has a fee simple bundle of
rights with respect to his air lot and is free to dispense the
bundle as he pleases. For example, he can mortgage his apartment, taking the foreclosure stick out of his bundle of rights
and giving it to a lender in exchange for a loan. Also, he can
lease his unit to a tenant, thereby creating a leasehold estate
and a reversionary right.

CROSS SECTION OF ESTATES AND RIGHTS IN LAND Figure 3:6
(continued)

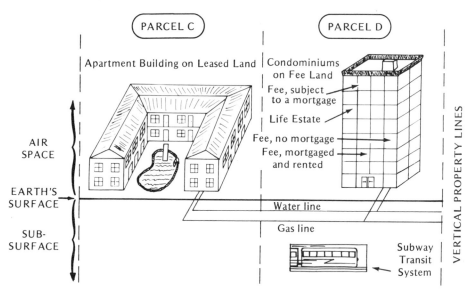

Condominium owners as a group usually own the surface of the land upon which the building rests, the air space not split into air lots, and the subsurface. In parcel D, the owners have either sold, leased, or granted to a transit authority the right to build a subway line under this parcel. Underground rights of this type are very important in cities with subsurface transportation networks and will continue to be so as more cities open underground mass transit systems, such as Washington, D.C. did in 1976.

An alternative to fee owners granting a subsurface right for underground transportation lines is for the line owner to own the fee interest in the entire parcel, use the subsurface portion for its tracks, and sell or lease the use of the surface and air space above. In Chicago and New York City, for instance, railroads have sold or leased surface and air rights above their downtown tracks for the purpose of constructing office buildings and convention halls. Passenger trains run just below the surface, while new buildings occupy the space above.

VOCABULARY REVIEW   *Match terms a–t with statements 1–20.*

a. *Allodial*   k. *Estate for years*
b. *Bundle of rights*   l. *Holdover tenant*
   concept   m. *Inverse condemnation*
c. *Chattel*   n. *Lessee*
d. *Curtesy*   o. *Lessor*
e. *Dower*   p. *Lien*
f. *Easement*   q. *Periodic tenancy*
g. *Eminent domain*   r. *Police power*
h. *Encroachment*   s. *Reversionary interest*
i. *Escheat*   t. *Waste*
j. *Estate*

1. A lease with a specific starting and ending date and no automatic renewal provision.

2. A charge or hold against property to use it as security for a debt.

3. A leasehold estate that automatically renews itself unless cancelled.

4. Movable items and any form of property not classed as a freehold estate in land.

5. The trespass of a building or other improvement upon the land of another.

6. A tenant who wrongfully remains in possession of leased property after his lease expires.

7. The right of government to forcefully acquire property from private owners, who in turn must be compensated.

8. A real property ownership system that allows land to be owned by individuals.

9. The right of government to enact laws and enforce them for the order, safety, health, morals, and general welfare of the public.

10. A lawsuit by a property owner demanding that a public agency purchase his property.

11. The abuse or destructive use of property.

12. Real estate onwership viewed as a collection of many rights.

13. The reversion of property to the state when the owner dies without leaving a will or heirs.

14. The extent of interest which a person has in real property. Also used to describe all the real and personal property owned by a person.

15. One who holds title and leases out his property; the landlord.

16. One who holds the right to use property but does not own it; the tenant.

17. The right that a wife has in her husband's estate at his death.
18. The right that a husband has in his wife's estate at her death.
19. A right or privilege one party has in the use of land belonging to another.
20. The right to the future enjoyment of property presently in the possession of another.

QUESTIONS AND PROBLEMS

1. Distinguish between freehold and less than freehold estates in land.
2. Under what conditions is it possible for an easement to be created without there being specific mention of it in writing?
3. What steps are currently being taken by your state legislature to recognize the legal equality of married women in real estate ownership?
4. Why are dower, curtesy, and homestead protection referred to as "legal" life estates?
5. From the standpoint of possession, what is the key difference between an easement and a lease?
6. What is the legal difference between an heir and a devisee?
7. In your community, name specific examples of the application of police power to the rights of landowners.
8. If your state has a homestead protection law, how much protection does it offer and what must a person do to qualify?
9. Technically speaking, a 99-year lease on a parcel of land is personal property. However, from a practical standpoint, the exclusive right to use a parcel of land for such a long period of time seems more like real property. Do the laws of your state treat a 99-year lease as real or personal property?

ADDITIONAL READINGS

Guitar, Mary Anne. *Property Power*. Garden City, N.Y.: Doubleday & Company, 1972, 322 pages. Discusses rights of the public versus the rights of the private landowner, with particular emphasis on the environmental question.

Kusnet, Jack. "Air Rights: The Third Dimension," *Real Estate Today*, Aug. 1974, pages 12–15. Explains the concept of air space rights and discusses how these rights can be used for real estate development in crowded downtown areas.

"Land in the New World," *Real Estate Today*, Jan. 1976, pages 6ff. Provides an interesting historical perspective on land ownership in the United States. Based on the books *The Great American Land Bubble*, by **A. M. Sakolaski,** and *The Urban Wilderness*, by **Sam Bass Warner, Jr.**

Lawrence, Glenn. *Condemnation—Your Rights When Government Acquires Your Property.* Dobbs Ferry, N.Y.: Oceana Publications, 1967, 123 pages. A short nontechnical book about the legal rights of a property owner whose property is being taken in an eminent domain action.

Semenow, Robert W. *Selected Cases in Real Estate.* Englewood Cliffs, N.J.: Prentice-Hall, 1973, 638 pages. Discusses actual legal cases involving eminent domain (pages 351–364) and liens (pages 504–536).

Smith, Chester H., and **Ralph E. Boyer.** *Survey of the Law of Property,* 2nd ed. St. Paul, Minn.: West Publishing Co., 1971, 510 pages. Part I, Chapter 4 discusses freehold estates, concurrent estates, less than freehold estates, dower, curtesy, and future interests.

Forms of Ownership

KEY TERMS

Community property: a form of property co-ownership for married persons wherein husband and wife are treated as equal partners with each owning a one-half interest

Estate in severalty: owned by one person; sole ownership

Financial liability: the amount of money one can lose; risk exposure

Joint tenancy: a form of property co-ownership that in most states carries the right of survivorship

Joint venture: an association of two or more persons or firms in order to carry out a single business project

Right of survivorship: the remaining co-owners of a property who automatically acquire a deceased co-owner's interest

Tenancy by the entirety: a form of joint ownership reserved for married persons; right of survivorship exists and neither spouse has a disposable interest during the lifetime of the other

Tenants in common: shared ownership of a single property among two or more persons; interests need not be equal and no right of survivorship exists

Undivided interest: ownership by two or more persons that gives each the right to use the entire property

In Chapter 3 we explored the various rights and interests that can be held in land. In this chapter, we shall look at the methods by which a right or interest in land can be held by one or more individuals.

SOLE OWNERSHIP

When title to property is held by one person, it is called an **estate in severalty** or **sole ownership.** Although the word "severalty" seems to imply that several persons own a single property, the correct meaning can be easily remembered by thinking of "severed" ownership. Sole ownership is available to single and married persons. However, in the case of married persons, most states require one spouse to waive community property, dower, or curtesy rights in writing. It is from the estate in severalty that all other tenancies are carved.

The major advantage of sole ownership is flexibility. A sole owner can make all the decisions regarding the property without having to get the agreement of any co-owners. He can decide what property or properties to buy, when to buy, and how much to offer. He can decide whether to pay all cash or to seek a loan by using the property as collateral. Once bought, he controls (within the bounds of the law) how the property will be used, how much will be charged if it is rented, and how it will be managed. If he decides to sell, he alone decides when to offer the property for sale and at what price and terms.

But freedom and responsibility go together. If one purchases a rental property, for instance, one must determine the prevailing rents, find tenants, prepare contracts, collect the rent, and keep the property in repair; or one must hire and pay someone else to manage the property. Another deterrent to sole ownership is the high entry cost. This form of real estate ownership is not possible for someone with only a few hundred dollars to spend.

TENANTS IN COMMON

When two or more persons wish to share the ownership of a single property, they may do so as **tenants in common.** As tenants in common, each owns an **undivided interest** in the whole property. This means that each owner has a right to possession of the entire property. None can exclude the others nor claim any specific portion for himself. In a tenancy in common, these interests need not be the same size, and each owner can independently sell, mortgage, give away, or devise his individual interest. This independence is possible because each tenant in common has a separate legal title to his undivided interest.

Suppose that you invest $20,000 along with two of your friends, who invest $30,000 and $50,000, respectively; together you buy 100 acres of land as tenants in common. Presuming that everyone's ownership interest is proportional to his or her cash investment, you will hold a 20% interest in the entire 100 acres and your two friends will hold 30% and

50%. You cannot pick out 20 acres and exclude the other co-owners from them, nor can you pick out 20 acres and say, "These are mine and I'm going to sell them"; nor can they do that to you. You do, however, have the legal right to sell or otherwise dispose of your 20% interest (or a portion of it) without the permission of your two friends. Your friends have the same right. If one of you sells, the purchaser becomes a new tenant in common with the remaining co-owners.

Wording of Conveyance

As a rule, a tenancy in common is created by naming the co-owners in the conveyance and adding the words "as tenants in common." For example, a deed might read, "Samuel Smith, John Jones, and Robert Miller, as tenants in common." If nothing is said regarding the size of each co-owner's interest in the property, the law presumes that all interests are equal. Therefore, if the co-owners intend their interests to be unequal, the size of each co-owner's undivided interest must be stated as a percent or a fraction (e.g., 60% and 40% or one-third and two-thirds). In nearly all states, if a conveyance document such as a deed names two or more persons as owners, and there is no specific indication as to how they are taking title, they are presumed to be tenants in common. Thus, with regard to a deed made out to "Dennis Adams and Bruce Kelly," the law would consider them to be tenants in common, each holding an undivided one-half interest in the property. An important exception to this presumption is when the co-owners are married to each other. In this case, they may be automatically considered to be taking ownership as joint tenants, tenants by the entirety, or community property depending on state law.

When a tenancy in common exists, if a co-owner dies his interest passes to his heirs or devisees, who then become tenants in common with the remaining co-owners. There is no **right of survivorship;** that is, the remaining co-owners do not acquire the deceased's interest unless they are named in the deceased's last will and testament to do so. When a creditor has a claim on a co-owner's interest and forces its sale to satisfy the debt, the new buyer becomes a tenant in common with the remaining co-owners. If one co-owner wants to sell (or give away) only a portion of his undivided interest, he may; the new owner becomes a tenant in common with the other co-owners.

Any income generated by the property belongs to the tenants in common in proportion to the size of their interests. Similarly, each co-owner is responsible for paying his proportionate share of property taxes, repairs, upkeep, and so on, plus interest and debt repayment, if any. If any co-owner fails to contribute his proportionate share, the other co-owners can pay on his behalf and then sue him for that amount. If co-owners find that they cannot agree as to how the property is to be run and cannot agree on a plan for dividing or selling it, it is possible to request a court-ordered partition. A **partition** divides the property into distinct portions so that each person can hold his proportionate interest in severalty. If this is physically impossible, such as when three co-owners each have a one-third interest in a house, the court will order the property sold and the proceeds divided between the co-owners.

JOINT TENANCY   Another form of multiple-person ownership is **joint tenancy.** Its two key characteristics are that (1) the co-owners are considered to be joint and equal owners of the same undivided interest, and (2) a right of survivorship exists. Let us explore these characteristics in more detail.

Joint and Equal   For a joint tenancy to exist, **four unities** must be present.
Owners   They are the unities of time, title, interest, and possession. **Unity of time** means that each joint tenant must acquire his or her ownership interest simultaneously. Once a joint tenancy is formed, it is not possible to add new joint tenants later unless an entirely new joint tenancy is formed among the existing co-owners and the new co-owner. To illustrate, suppose that B, C, and D own a parcel of land as joint tenants. If B sells his interest to E, then C, D, and E must sign documents to create a new joint tenancy among them. If this is not done, E automatically becomes a tenant in common with C and D who, between themselves, remain joint tenants.

Unity of title means that there is only one title and each co-owner has a share in it. In contrast, each co-owner has a

Table 4:1   CONCURRENT OWNERSHIP BY STATES

	Tenancy in Common	Joint Tenancy	Tenancy by the Entirety	Community Property		Tenancy in Common	Joint Tenancy	Tenancy by the Entirety	Community Property
Alabama	X	X			Missouri	X	X	X	
Alaska	X		X		Montana	X	X		
Arizona	X	X		X	Nebraska	X	X		
Arkansas	X	X	X		Nevada	X	X		X
California	X	X		X	New Hampshire	X	X		
Colorado	X	X			New Jersey	X	X	X	
Connecticut	X	X			New Mexico	X	X		X
Delaware	X	X	X		New York	X	X	X	
District of					North Carolina	X	X	X	
Columbia	X	X	X		North Dakota	X	X		
Florida	X	X	X		Ohio	X		X	
					Oklahoma	X	X	X	
Georgia	X				Oregon	X		X	
Hawaii	X	X	X		Pennsylvania	X	X	X	
Idaho	X	X		X	Rhode Island	X	X	X	
Illinois	X	X			South Carolina	X	X		
Indiana	X	X	X		South Dakota	X	X		
Iowa	X	X			Tennessee	X	X	X	
Kansas	X	X			Texas	X	X		X
Kentucky	X	X	X		Utah	X	X	X	
Louisiana				X	Vermont	X	X	X	
Maine	X	X			Virginia	X	X	X	
Maryland	X	X	X		Washington	X	X		X
Massachusetts	X	X	X		West Virginia	X	X	X	
Michigan	X	X	X		Wisconsin	X	X		
Minnesota	X	X			Wyoming	X	X	X	
Mississippi	X	X	X						

separate legal title to his undivided interest in a tenancy in common. **Unity of interest** means that no single joint tenant will be recognized as having a larger interest in the property than any other joint tenant. No matter how much each has contributed, if there are two joint tenants, each is regarded as having a one-half interest. Three joint tenants each have a one-third interest. If the co-owners attempt to overcome this by listing disproportionate interests, the law will consider them to be tenants in common. Unity of interest also means that, if one joint tenant holds a fee simple interest in the property, the others cannot hold anything but a fee simple interest.

Unity of possession means that the joint tenants must enjoy the same undivided possession of the whole property. All joint tenants have the use of the entire property, and no individual owns a particular portion of it.

Right of Survivorship

The feature of joint tenancy ownership that is most widely recognized is its **right of survivorship.** Upon the death of a joint tenant, his interest in the property is extinguished. In a two-person joint tenancy, when one person dies, the other immediately becomes the sole owner. With more than two persons as joint tenants, when one dies the remaining joint tenants are automatically left as owners. Ultimately, the last survivor becomes the sole owner. For the public record, a copy of the death certificate and an affidavit of death of the joint tenant is recorded in the county where the property is located; and the property must also be released from any estate tax liens.

It is the right of survivorship that has made joint tenancy a popular form of ownership among married couples. Married couples often want the surviving spouse to have sole ownership of the marital property. Any property held in joint tenancy goes to the surviving spouse without the delay of probate and usually with less legal expense. Moreover, in joint tenancy the remaining joint tenant(s) acquires the property free and clear of any liens against the deceased. To illustrate, a judgment lien on the property as the result of a lawsuit against the husband is extinguished by his death, and his wife succeeds as sole owner free of that lien.

"Poor Man's Will"

Because of the survivorship feature, joint tenancy has loosely been labeled a "poor man's will." However, it cannot replace a properly drawn will as it affects only that property held in joint tenancy. Moreover, a will can be changed if the persons named therein are no longer in one's favor. But once a joint tenancy is formed, title is permanently conveyed and there is no further opportunity for changes. One should also be aware of the possibility that ownership in joint tenancy may result in additional estate taxes.

Another important aspect of joint tenancy ownership is that it can be used to defeat dower or curtesy rights. If a married man forms a joint tenancy with someone other than his wife (such as a business partner) and then dies, his wife has no dower rights in that joint tenancy. As a result, courts have begun to look with disfavor upon the right of survivorship. Alaska, Georgia, Louisiana, Ohio, and Oregon either do not recognize joint tenancy or have abolished it.* Of the remaining states that recognize joint tenancy ownership (see Table 4:1), 12 have abolished the automatic presumption of survivorship. In these states, if the right of survivorship is desired in a joint tenancy, it must be clearly stated in the conveyance. For example, a deed might read, "Karen Carson and Judith Johnson, as joint tenants with the right of survivorship and not as tenants in common." Even in those states not requiring it, this wording is often used to ensure that the right of survivorship is intended. In community property states, one spouse cannot take community funds and establish a valid joint tenancy with a third party.

Tenancy by the entirety (also called tenancy by the entireties) is a form of ownership specifically designed for married persons. It is based on the legal premise that a husband and wife are an indivisible legal unit. Two key characteristics of this form of property ownership are (1) the surviving spouse becomes the sole owner of the property upon the death of the other, and (2) neither spouse has a disposable interest in the property during the lifetime of the other. Thus, while both are alive and married to each other, both signatures are necessary to convey title to the property. With respect to the first characteristic, tenancy by the entirety is

TENANCY BY THE
ENTIRETY

---

* In Georgia, Ohio, and Oregon, other means are available to achieve rights of survivorship between nonmarried persons. When two or more persons own property together in Louisiana, it is termed an "ownership in indivision" or a "joint ownership." Louisiana law is based on French civil law.

similar to joint tenancy because both feature the right of survivorship. They are quite different, however, with respect to
the second characteristic. A joint tenancy can be terminated
by one tenant's conveyance of his or her interest, but a
tenancy by the entirety can be terminated only by joint action
of husband and wife. States that recognize tenancy by the
entirety are listed in Table 4:1. Some of these states automatically assume that a tenancy by the entirety is created
when married persons buy real estate. However, it is best to
use a phrase such as "John and Mary Smith, husband and
wife as tenants by the entirety with the right of survivorship"
on deeds and other conveyances. This avoids later questions
as to whether their intention might have been to create a joint
tenancy or a tenancy in common.

Advantages and   There are several important advantages to tenancy by the
Disadvantages   entirety ownership: (1) it protects against one spouse conveying or mortgaging the couple's property without the consent
of the other, (2) it provides in many states some protection
from the forced sale of jointly held property to satisfy a debt
judgment against one of the spouses, and (3) it features
automatic survivorship. Disadvantages are that (1) tenancy
by the entirety provides for no one except the surviving
spouse, (2) it may create inheritance tax problems, and (3) it
does not replace the need for a will to direct how the couple's
personal property shall be disposed.

Effect of   In the event of divorce, the parting spouses become
Divorce   tenants in common. This change is automatic, as tenancy by
the entirety can exist only when the co-owners are husband
and wife. If the ex-spouses do not wish to continue co-
ownership, they can, acting independently, sell their individual interests. If a buyer cannot be found for a partial
interest nor an amicable agreement reached for selling the in-
interests of both ex-spouses simultaneously, either may seek
a court action to partition the property. Note that severalty,
tenancy in common, joint tenancy, and tenancy by the
entirety are called English common law estates because of
their English origin.

Spanish law, inherited from Mexico when vast areas of the western United States were under Mexican control, was the basis for the development of the **community property** form of ownership for married persons. Table 4:1 identifies community property states. The laws of each community property state vary slightly, but the underlying concept is that the husband and wife contribute jointly and equally to their marriage and thus should share equally in any property purchased during marriage. Whereas English law is based on the merging of husband and wife upon marriage, community property law treats husband and wife as equal partners, with each owning a one-half interest and the husband acting as property manager.

COMMUNITY PROPERTY

Property owned before marriage, and property acquired after marriage by gift, inheritance, or purchase with separate funds, can be exempted from the couple's community property. Such property is called **separate property** and can be conveyed or mortgaged without the signature of the owner's spouse. All other property acquired by the husband or wife during marriage is considered community property and requires the signature of both spouses before it can be conveyed or mortgaged. Under community property ownership, each spouse can devise his or her one-half interest as he or she pleases. It does not have to go to the surviving spouse. If death occurs without a will, in five states (California, Idaho, Nevada, New Mexico, and Washington) the deceased spouse's interest goes to the surviving spouse. In Arizona, Louisiana, and Texas, the descendents of the deceased spouse are the prime recipients. Neither dower nor curtesy exist in community property states.

Separate Property

The major advantage of the community property system is found in its philosophy: it treats the spouses as equal partners in property acquired through their mutual efforts during marriage. Even if the wife elects to be a full-time homemaker and all the money brought into the household is the result of her husband's job (or vice versa), the law treats them as equal co-owners in any property bought with that money. This is true even if only one spouse is named as the owner.

In the event of divorce, if the parting couple cannot amicably decide how to divide their community property, the courts will usually do so. If the courts do not, the ex-spouses will become tenants in common with each other. If it later becomes necessary, either can file suit for partition.

TENANCY IN PARTNERSHIP

A **tenancy in partnership** exists when two or more persons, as partners, unite their property, labor, and skill as a business to share the profits created by it. The agreement between the partners may be oral or written. The partners may hold the partnership property either in their own names or in the name of the partnership. If a partnership name is used, the name and a list of the partners must be published in the public records of each county and state where the partnership owns property. From then on, business may be transacted in the name of the partnership. For convenience, especially in a large partnership, the partners may designate two or three of their group to make contracts and sign documents on behalf of the entire partnership. There are two types of partnerships: general partnerships made up entirely of general partners and limited partnerships composed of general and limited partners.

General Partnership

The **general partnership** is an outgrowth of common law. However, to introduce clarity and uniformity into general partnership laws across the United States, 47 states and the District of Columbia have adopted the **Uniform Partnership Act** either in total or with local modifications. (The three exceptions are Georgia, Louisiana, and Mississippi.) Briefly, the highlights of a general partnership are that (1) each partner has, in effect, an undivided interest in the partnership's property and equal right of possession, (2) the partners may own different-sized shares of the partnership, (3) all partners have a voice in the management of the partnership, (4) the partnership can be terminated by agreement and is automatically ended by the death, withdrawal, or bankruptcy of one of the partners, (5) the partnership is not a taxable entity, and (6) all partners have unlimited liability for the debts of the partnership.

As a form of property ownership, the partnership is a method of combining the capital and expertise of two or more persons. Equally important is that, although the partnership files a tax return, it is only for informational purposes. The profits and losses of the partnership are taxable directly to each individual partner in proportion to his or her interest in the partnership. The partnership itself does not pay taxes. Negative aspects of this form of ownership center around continuity, liability, and illiquidity. **Continuity** refers to the fact that, when one partner withdraws, dies, or goes bankrupt, by law the partnership dissolves and must be reorganized in order to continue. **Financial liability** means each partner is personally responsible for all the debts of the partnership. Thus, each general partner can lose not only what he has invested in the partnership, but more, up to the full extent of his personal financial worth. If one partner makes a commitment on behalf of the partnership, all partners are responsible for making good on that commitment. If the partnership is sued, each partner is fully responsible. **Illiquidity** refers to the possibility that it may be very difficult to sell one's partnership interest on short notice.

Because of the negative points just discussed, especially unlimited financial liability, an alternative partnership form, the **limited partnership,** has developed. Forty-nine states, plus the District of Columbia, have adopted the **Uniform Limited Partnership Act.** (The exception is Louisiana, which has its own general and limited partnership laws.) This act recognizes the legality of limited partnerships and requires that a limited partnership be formed by a written document.

Limited Partnership

A limited partnership is composed of general and limited partners. The general partners organize and operate the partnership, contribute capital, and agree to accept the full financial liability of the partnership. The **limited partners** provide the bulk of the investment capital, have little say in the day-to-day management of the partnership, share in the profits and losses, and contract with their general partners to limit the financial liability of each limited partner to the amount he or she invests. Additionally, a well-written partnership agreement will allow for the continuity of the partnership in the event of the death of a general or limited partner.

The advantages of limited liability, minimum management responsibility, and direct pass-through of profits and losses for taxation purposes have made this form of ownership popular. However, being free of management responsibility is only advantageous to the investors if the general partners are capable and honest. If they are not, the only control open to the limited partners is to vote to replace the general partners.

The limited partner must keep in mind that the market for resale of limited partnership interests is practically non-existent. This is partly by design: if they were freely and actively transferable, the partnership would begin to resemble a corporation in the eyes of state and federal taxing authorities and would risk being taxed as such. Because of this illiquidity, partnership organizers should tell prospective investors what type of property the partnership is buying, how it will be financed and operated, and how long it will be held before an attempt is made to sell. Thus, one can better judge if a partnership is suitable for his personal objectives before investing. One should also investigate the past record of the general partners, for this is usually a good indication of how the new partnership will be managed. The investigation should include their previous investments, talking to past investors, and checking court records for any legal complaints brought against them.

JOINT VENTURE   A **joint venture** is an association of two or more persons or firms to carry out a single business project. The association can take the form of a general partnership, limited partnership, or corporation. In any case, the distinguishing feature of the joint venture is that those forming it do not intend to enter into a permanent relationship. Examples of joint ventures in real estate are the purchase of land by two or more persons with the intent of grading it and selling it as lots, the association of a landowner and builder to build and sell, and the association of a lender and builder to purchase land and develop buildings on it to sell to investors. Each member of the joint venture makes a contribution in the form of capital or talent, and all have a strong incentive to make the joint venture succeed.

A **syndicate** (or **syndication**) is not a form of ownership; rather, it refers to individuals or firms combining to pursue an enterprise too large for any of them to undertake individually. The form of ownership might be a tenancy in common, joint tenancy, general or limited partnership, or a corporation. Applied to real estate investing, the term "syndicate" usually refers to a limited partnership in which the limited partners provide the investment capital and the general partners provide the organizational talent and ongoing management services. The general partners receive compensation for purchasing, managing, and reselling the properties. The limited partners receive a return on and a return of their investment if the syndicate is successful. Most states require that real estate syndicates be registered with the state before they can be sold to investors. Federal registration may also be necessary.

SYNDICATES

Each state has passed laws to permit groups of people to create **corporations** that can buy, sell, own, and operate in the name of the corporation. The corporation, in turn, is owned by stockholders, who possess shares of stock as evidence of their ownership.

CORPORATIONS

Because the corporation is an entity (or legal being) in the eyes of the law, the corporation must pay income taxes on its profits. What remains can be used to pay dividends to the stockholders, who in turn pay personal income taxes on their dividend income. This double taxation of profits is the most important negative factor in the corporate form of ownership. On the positive side, the entity aspect shields the investor from unlimited liability. Even if the corporation falls on the hardest of financial times and owes more than it owns, the worse that can happen to the stockholder is that the value of his stock will drop to zero. Another advantage is that shares of stock are much more liquid than any previously discussed form of real estate ownership, even sole ownership. Stockbrokers and stock exchanges specialize in the purchase and sale of corporate stock, usually completing a sale in a week or less. Furthermore, shares of stock in most corporations sell for less than $100, thus enabling an investor to operate with small amounts of capital. In a corporation, the stockholders elect a board of directors, who in turn hire the management needed to run the day-to-day operations of the company. As a practical matter, however, unless a person is a major shareholder in a corporation, he will have little control over management. His alternative is to buy stock in firms where he likes the management and sell where he does not.

Under a special set of Internal Revenue Service (IRS) rules, a corporation with 10 or fewer shareholders may avoid double taxation. Upon qualification, the IRS will allow the shareholders to elect to be taxed only on their proportional interest in the corporation's profits. Because the limited liability aspect remains in effect, this **tax-option corporation** (also called a "Sub-chapter S" corporation) has much to recommend it as a means of sharing real estate ownership. However, with only 10 shareholders allowed, the market for selling one's shares at a later time is small.

REAL ESTATE INVESTMENT TRUSTS

The idea of creating a trust that in turn carries out the investment objectives of its investors is not new. State laws have long provided for the trust form of ownership wherein one person holds property for the benefit of another. What is relatively new is that in 1961 Congress passed a law allowing trusts that specialize in real estate investments to avoid double taxation by following strict rules. These real estate investment trusts **(REITs)** pool the money of many investors for the purchase of real estate, much like mutual funds do with stocks and bonds. Investors in a REIT are called **beneficiaries** and they purchase **beneficial interests** somewhat similar to shares of corporate stock. The trust officers, with the aid of paid advisors, buy, sell, mortgage, and operate real estate investments on behalf of the beneficiaries. If a REIT follows a strict set of IRS rules designed to ensure that it confines its activities to real estate investments, and if the REIT has at least 100 beneficiaries and distributes at least 90% of its net income every year, then the IRS will collect tax on the distributed income only once—at the beneficiaries' level. Failure to follow the rules results in double taxation.

The REIT is an attempt to combine the advantages of the corporate form of ownership with single taxation status. Like stock, the beneficial interests are freely transferable and usually sell for $100 each or less, a distinct advantage for the investor with a small amount of money to invest in real estate. Beneficial interests in the larger REITs are sold on a national basis, thus enabling a REIT to have thousands of beneficiaries and millions of dollars of capital for real estate purchases.

Equity Trusts

Because the individual beneficiary has little influence on how the REIT is managed, management usually announces its investment policy, and a prospective investor can decide if that policy is suitable for him before investing. REIT investment policies tend to fall into three major categories: equity trusts, mortgage trusts, and hybrid trusts. **Equity trusts** specialize in buying and owning land and buildings, often using the investors' money as a down payment and borrowing the balance. **Mortgage trusts** specialize in lending money on real estate. **Hybrid trusts** own as well as lend.

The REITs offer several important advantages. They are capable of assembling large amounts of capital from numerous investors, the investor is free of day-to-day property management problems, and the investor's financial liability appears to be limited to the value of his investment, although some argue that this feature has not been thoroughly tested in court.

Unfortunately, between 1973 and 1976 a great number of REITs did not do as well as anticipated. A substantial number of mortgage trusts paid more interest for loan money than they were earning, and in more than a few cases large loans were made that later went into default. This is not the fault of the REIT form of ownership itself. Syndications, joint ventures, etc., are just as susceptible. The problem lies with the selection and operation of the investment properties.

CONDOMINIUMS

Condominium ownership is designed to provide exclusive use and ownership of a portion of a larger property, plus shared use and ownership of common areas. The most popular application is in the apartment-type homes and townhouses currently being offered for sale across the country. Under the condominium arrangement, the individual owner buys the exclusive right to occupy the space where his unit is located. If his unit is located in a multistory building with other units above or below him, his exclusive right is to the air space his unit occupies. The apartment owner also receives an undivided interest in the land and common areas, such as the lobby, hallways, elevators, structure of the building, and, as a rule, the recreation facilities. The common areas are administered by a board of directors elected by the unit owners. The board also sets house rules by which all unit owners are expected to abide.

The major advantages of condominium ownership are that, despite living in the same building, each individual owner can buy, sell, or mortgage his unit like a single-family house. The use of common walls, floors, and ceilings and the ability to place more dwelling units on a given parcel of land have helped to reduce dwelling unit costs. The disadvantages of condominium living center on people getting along with each other at close range; community living requires the sacrifice of some individual rights for the benefit of the group. For those accustomed to the freedom of a single-family residence, a set of house rules may be distasteful.

The condominium form of ownership is not limited to residences. It is also used for medical, office, and industrial buildings, although less frequently than for dwelling units.

COOPERATIVES

Under the **cooperative** form of ownership, a nonprofit corporation is formed to purchase a building in severalty. Stock in the corporation is then sold to pay for the building. When a person buys stock in a cooperative apartment building, the stock gives him the right to occupy a specific apartment in the building. The better apartment units in the building require the purchase of more shares of stock than do smaller or poorly located apartments. If money was borrowed by the corporation to buy the building, it is a debt of the corporation; each shareholder must contribute to the payments in proportion to the number of shares he holds. When an owner sells, he does not sell his apartment unit, but rather his shares of stock, which in turn carry the privilege of occupying the unit.

The key negative aspect of cooperative ownership is that only the corporation can mortgage the building. The individual cannot mortgage, refinance, or pay off the loan as he can in a condominium. For many cooperative owners, this disadvantage is offset by the fact that the board of directors has the right to approve or disapprove a new shareholder, thus preserving a certain amount of ingroup exclusiveness.

CAVEAT

The purpose of this chapter has been to acquaint you with the fundamental aspects of the most commonly used forms of real estate ownership in the United States. You undoubtedly saw instances where you could apply these. Unfortunately, it is not possible in a real estate principles book to discuss each detail of each state's law (many of which change frequently), nor to take into consideration the specific characteristics of a particular transaction. In applying the principles in this book to a particular transaction, you should add competent legal advice regarding your state's legal interpretation of these principles.

VOCABULARY REVIEW

Match terms a–q with statements 1–17.

a. *Community property*
b. *Estate in severalty*
c. *Financial liability*
d. *General partnership*
e. *Joint tenancy*
f. *Joint venture*
g. *Limited partner*
h. *Partition*
i. *Real estate investment trust*
j. *Right of survivorship*
k. *Syndicate*
l. *Tax-option corporation*
m. *Tenancy by the entirety*
n. *Tenants in common*
o. *Undivided interest*
p. *Unity of interest*
q. *Unity of time*

1. Owned by one person only. Sole ownership.
2. Each owner has a right to use the entire property.
3. Undivided ownership by two or more persons without right of survivorship; interests need not be equal.
4. The remaining co-owners automatically acquire the deceased's undivided interest.

5. A form of co-ownership in which the most widely recognized feature is the right of survivorship.
6. All co-owners have an equal interest in the property. A requirement for joint tenancy.
7. All co-owners acquired their ownership interests at the same time. A requirement for joint tenancy.
8. Spouses are treated as equal partners with each owning a one-half interest. Spanish law origin.
9. An English law form of ownership reserved for married persons. Right of survivorship exists and neither spouse has a disposable interest during the lifetime of the other.
10. Each partner is fully liable for all the debts and obligations of the partnership.
11. A member of a limited partnership whose financial liability is limited to the amount invested.
12. Two or more persons joining together on a single project as partners.
13. A general term that refers to a group of persons who organize to carry out a project requiring a large amount of capital.
14. A type of mutual fund for real estate investment and ownership wherein a trustee holds property for the benefit of the beneficiaries.
15. Combines the corporate form of ownership with income taxation similar to that of a partnership.
16. Refers to the amount of money a person can lose.
17. To divide jointly held property so that each owner can hold a sole ownership.

QUESTIONS AND PROBLEMS

1. What is the key advantage of sole ownership? What is the major disadvantage?
2. Explain what is meant by the term "undivided interest" as it applies to joint ownership of real estate.
3. Name the four unities of a joint tenancy. What does each mean to the property owner?
4. What does the term "right of survivorship" mean in real estate ownership?
5. Suppose that a deed was made out to "John and Mary Smith, husband and wife" with no mention as to how they were taking title. Which would your state assume: joint tenancy, tenancy in common, tenancy by the entirety, or community property?
6. Does your state permit the right of survivorship among persons who are not married?

7. If a deed is made out to three women as follows, "Susan Miller, Rhoda Wells, and Angela Lincoln," with no mention as to the form of ownership or the interest held by each, what can we presume regarding the form of ownership and the size of each woman's ownership interest?

8. In a community property state, if a deed names only the husband (or the wife) as the owner, can we assume that only that person's signature is necessary to convey title? Why or why not?

9. List two ways in which a general partnership differs from a limited partnership.

10. What advantages does a real estate investment trust offer a person who wants to invest in real estate?

ADDITIONAL READINGS

Grange, William J., and **Woodbury, Thomas C.** *Manual of Real Estate Law and Procedures,* 2nd ed. New York: Ronald Press, 1968, 470 pages. A nontechnical guide to current practice in real estate transactions. Chapter 4 covers various forms of co-ownership.

Powell, Richard R. *The Law of Property.* New York: Matthew Bender, 1975. Chapter 4 in volume 1 reviews the history of American property law and includes a short discussion of how the property laws of each state developed. Chapters 49–53 in volume 4A cover in detail the legal aspects of tenancy in common, joint tenancy, tenancy by the entirety, community property, and partnerships.

Reader's Digest. *You and the Law,* rev. ed. Pleasantville, N.Y.: Reader's Digest Association, 1973, 863 pages. Presents in nontechnical language one's legal rights and obligations under the law. Contains sections on contract law, landlord–tenant law, home purchase, mortgages, real estate taxes, and rights and interests of spouses. Charts show how laws vary from state to state.

Ross, Martin J. *Handbook of Everyday Law,* 3rd ed. New York: Harper & Row, 1975, 361 pages. Written for the layman; describes his legal rights and shows how to protect them. Includes sections on purchasing real estate, contracts, agency, joint ownership, and taxes. With glossary.

5

Transferring Title

KEY TERMS

Adverse possession: acquisition of real property through prolonged occupation

Bargain and sale deed: a deed that contains no covenants, but does imply the grantor owns the property being conveyed by the deed

Cloud on the title: a lien or encumbrance or other condition that affects the fee owner's title

Color of title: some plausible, but not completely clear-cut indication of ownership rights

Consideration: anything of value given to produce a contract

Covenants: binding agreements

Grantee: the person named in a deed who acquires ownership

Grantor: the person named in a deed who conveys ownership

Quitclaim deed: conveys whatever title the grantor has; it contains no covenants, warranties, nor implication of the grantor's ownership

Warranties: assurances or guarantees

The previous three chapters emphasized how real estate is described, the rights and interests available for ownership, and the forms that ownership can take. In this chapter we shall discuss how ownership of real estate is conveyed from one owner to another. We begin with the voluntary conveyance of real estate by deed, and then continue with conveyance after death, and conveyance by occupancy, accession, public grant, dedication, and forfeiture.

DEEDS

A **deed** is written legal evidence that ownership of real property has been conveyed from one party to another. Written deeds were not always used to transfer real estate. In early England, when land was sold its title was conveyed by inviting the purchaser onto the land. In the presence of witnesses, the seller picked up a clod of earth and handed it to the purchaser. Simultaneously, the seller stated that he was delivering ownership of the land to the purchaser. In times when land sales were rare, because ownership usually passed from generation to generation, and when witnesses seldom moved from the towns or farms where they were born, this method worked. However, as transactions became more common and people more mobile, this method of title transfer became less reliable. Furthermore, it was susceptible to fraud if enough persons could be bribed or forced to make false statements. As a result, in 1677, England passed a law known as the **Statute of Frauds.** This law, subsequently adopted in the United States, required that transfers of real estate ownership be in writing in order to be enforceable. Thus, the need for a deed was created.

Essential Elements of a Deed

What makes a written document a deed? What special phrases and statements are necessary to convey the ownership rights one has in land and buildings? First, a deed must identify the **grantor,** who is the person giving up ownership, and the **grantee,** the person who is acquiring that ownership. The actual act of conveying ownership is known as a **grant.** To be legally enforceable, the grantor must be of legal age (18 years in most states) and of sound mind. Second, the deed must state that **consideration** was given by the grantee to the grantor. Except in the state of Nebraska, where the actual amount of consideration paid must be shown, it is common to use the phrase, "For ten dollars ($10.00) and other good and valuable consideration," or the phrase, "For valuable consideration." These meet the legal requirement that consideration be shown, but retain privacy regarding the exact amount paid. If the conveyance is a gift, the phrase, "For natural love and affection," may be used, provided the gift is not for the purpose of defrauding the grantor's creditors. Third, the deed must contain **words of conveyance.** With these words the grantor clearly states that he is making a grant of real property to the grantee, and identifies the quantity of the estate being granted. Usually, this is the fee simple estate, but it may also be a lesser estate, such as a life estate or an easement. When written, these words accomplish the same objective as the oral statement that accompanied the passing of the clod of earth prior to written deeds.

A land **description** that cannot possibly be misunderstood is the fourth requirement. Acceptable legal descriptions are made by the metes and bounds method, the government survey system, recorded plat map, or reference to another recorded document that in turn uses one of these three description methods. Street names and numbers are not used as they do not identify the exact boundaries of the land and because street names and numbers can and do change over time. If the deed conveys only an easement or air right, the deed would state that fact along with the legal description of the land. The key point is that a deed must clearly outline what the grantor is granting to the grantee.

Delivery and Acceptance

Fifth, the grantor must **sign** his name on the deed. Eight states also require that the grantor's signature be witnessed and that the witnesses sign the deed. If the grantor is unable to write his name, he may make a mark, usually an ✗, in the presence of witnesses. They in turn print his name next to the ✗ and sign as witnesses. If the grantor is a corporation, the corporation's seal is affixed to the deed and an officer of the corporation with the proper authority signs. The sixth and final step is **delivery and acceptance.** Although a deed may be completed and signed, it does not transfer title to the grantee until the grantor voluntarily delivers it to the grantee and the grantee accepts it. At that moment title passes. The following example illustrates the essential elements combined to form a deed.

Witnesseth, _____John Stanley_____ *, grantor, for valuable consideration given by* _____Robert Brenner_____ *, grantee, does hereby grant and release unto the grantee, his heirs and assigns to have and to hold forever, the following described land: [insert legal description here].*

_____
Grantor's signature

Notice that the example includes an identification of the grantor and grantee, fulfills the requirement for consideration, has words of conveyance, a legal description of the land involved, and the grantor's signature. The words of conveyance are "grant and release" and the phrase, "to have and to hold forever," says that the grantor is conveying all future benefits, not just a life estate or a tenancy for years. Ordinarily, the grantee does not sign the deed.

Covenants and Warranties

Although legally adequate, a deed meeting the preceding requirements can still leave a very important question unanswered in the grantee's mind: "Does the grantor possess all the rights, title, and interest he is purporting to convey by this deed?" As a protective measure, the grantee can ask the grantor for **covenants** (binding agreements) and **warranties** (assurances or guarantees). Five have evolved over the centuries for use in deeds, and a deed may contain none, some, or all of them, in addition to the essential elements already discussed. They are seizin, quiet enjoyment, encumbrances, further assurance, and warranty forever.

Under the **covenant of seizin** (sometimes spelled seisin), the grantor warrants that he is the owner and possessor of the property being conveyed and that he has the right to convey it. Under the **covenant of quiet enjoyment**, the grantor warrants to the grantee that the grantee will not be disturbed, after he takes possession, by someone else claiming an interest in the property.

In the **covenant against encumbrances**, the grantor guarantees to the grantee that the title is not encumbered with easements, restrictions, or any unpaid property taxes, assessments, mortgages, judgments, or the like, except as stated in the deed. If the grantee later discovers an undisclosed encumbrance, he can sue the grantor for the cost of removing it. The **covenant of further assurance** requires the grantor to procure and deliver to the grantee any subsequent documents that might be necessary to make good the grantee's title. **Warranty forever** is the absolute guarantee by the grantor to the grantee that the title and rights to possession of the property are as stated in the deed. If at any time in the future someone else can prove that he is the rightful owner, the grantee can sue the grantor for damages up to the value of the property at the time of the sale.

Although it is customary to show on the deed the **date** it was executed by the grantor, it is not essential to the deed's validity. Remember that title passes upon **delivery** of the deed to the grantee, and that this may not necessarily be the date it was signed.

It is standard practice to have the grantor appear before a notary public or other public officer and formally declare that he signed the deed as a voluntary act. This is known as an **acknowledgment.** Most states consider a deed to be valid even though it is not witnessed or acknowledged, but very few states will allow such a deed to be recorded in the public records. Acknowledgments and the importance of recording deeds will be covered in more detail in Chapter 6. Meanwhile, let us turn our attention to examples of the most commonly used deeds in the United States.

The **full covenant and warranty deed,** also known as the general warranty deed or warranty deed, contains all five covenants and warranties. It is thus considered to be the best deed a grantee can receive, and is used extensively in most states.

The circled numbers in Figure 5:1 identify the various parts of a warranty deed. Beginning at ①, it is customary to identify at the top of the document that it is a warranty deed. At ② the wording begins with "This deed. . . ." These words are introductory in purpose. The fact that this is a deed depends on what it contains, not what it is labeled. A commonly found variation starts with "This indenture" (meaning this agreement or contract) and is equally acceptable. The place the deed was made ③ and the date it was signed ④ are customarily included, but are not necessary to make the deed valid.

At numbers ⑤ and ⑥ the grantor is identified by name and, to avoid confusion with other persons having the same name, by address. Marital status is also stated: husband and wife, bachelor, spinster, widow, widower, divorced and not remarried. To avoid the inconvenience of repeating the

Figure 5:1

WARRANTY DEED ①

② THIS DEED, made in the city of ____③____ , state of _____ , on the ④ day of_____ , 19___, between _____⑤_____ , residing at _____⑥_____ , herein called the GRANTOR⑦ and _____⑧_____ residing at _____⑨_____ , herein called the GRANTEE:⑩

WITNESSETH that in consideration⑪ of ten dollars ($10.00) and other valuable consideration, paid by the Grantee to the Grantor, the Grantor does hereby grant⑫ and convey unto the Grantee, the Grantee's⑬ heirs and assigns forever, the following described parcel of land:

[legal description of land] ⑭

together with the buildings⑮ and improvements thereon and all the estate⑯ and rights pertaining thereto,

⑰ TO HAVE AND TO HOLD the premises herein granted unto the Grantee, the Grantee's heirs⑱ and assigns forever.

The premises are free from encumbrances except as stated herein: ⑲

[note exceptions here]

The Grantee shall not: ⑳

[list restrictions imposed by Grantor on the Grantee]

The Grantor is lawfully seized㉑ of a good, absolute, and indefeasible estate in fee simple and has good right, full power, and lawful authority to convey the same by this deed.

The Grantee, the Grantee's heirs and assigns, shall peaceably㉒ and quietly have, hold, use, occupy, possess, and enjoy the said premises.

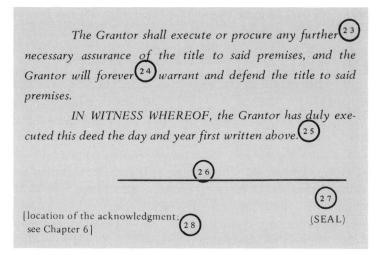

The Grantor shall execute or procure any further (23) *necessary assurance of the title to said premises, and the Grantor will forever* (24) *warrant and defend the title to said premises.*

IN WITNESS WHEREOF, the Grantor has duly executed this deed the day and year first written above. (25)

_____ (26)

(27)

[location of the acknowledgment; (28)   (SEAL)
see Chapter 6]

grantor's name each time it is needed, the wording at ⑦ states that in the balance of the deed the word "Grantor" (plural, "Grantors") will be used instead. A common variation of this is to call the first party named "the party of the first part." Next appears the name and marital status of the "Grantee" ⑧ (plural, "Grantees") and the method by which title is being taken (severalty, tenants in common, joint tenants, etc.). The grantee's address appears at ⑨, and the wording at ⑩ states that the word "Grantee" will now be used instead of the grantee's name. The alternative method is to call him "the party of the second part."

The legal requirement that consideration be shown is fulfilled at ⑪. Next we come to the granting clause at ⑫. Here the grantor states that the intent of this document is to pass ownership to the grantee, and at ⑬ the grantor describes the extent of the estate being granted. The phrase, "The grantee's heirs and assigns forever," indicates a fee simple estate. The word **assigns** refers to anyone the grantee may later deed the property to, such as by sale or gift. The legal description of the land involved is then shown at ⑭. When a grantor is unable or does not wish to convey certain rights of ownership, he can list the exceptions here. For example, a grantor either not having or wishing to hold back oil and gas rights for himself may grant to the grantee the land described, "except for the right to explore and recover oil and gas at a depth below 500 feet beneath the surface." The separate mention at numbers ⑮ and ⑯ of buildings, estate, and rights is not an essential requirement as the definition of land already includes these items.

The **habendum clause,** sometimes called the "To have and to hold clause," begins at ⑰ and continues through ⑱. This clause, together with the statements at ⑫ and ⑬, forms the deed's words of conveyance. For this reason, the words at ⑱ must match those at ⑬. Number ⑲ identifies the covenant against encumbrances. The grantee warrants that there are no encumbrances on the property except as listed here. The most common exceptions are property taxes, mortgages, and assessment (improvement district) bonds. For instance, a deed may recite, "Subject to an existing mortgage . . . ," and name the mortgage holder and the original amount of the loan, or "Subject to a city sewer improvement district bond in the amount of $1,500." At ⑳ the grantor may impose restrictions as to how the grantee may use the property. For example, "The grantee shall not build upon this land a home with less than 1,500 square feet of living space."

Special Wording   The covenants of seizin and quiet enjoyment are located at ㉑ and ㉒, respectively. Number ㉓ identifies the covenant of further assurance, and at ㉔ the grantor agrees to warrant and defend forever the title he is granting. The order of grouping of the five covenants is not critical, and in some states there are laws that permit the use of two or three special words to imply the presence of all five covenants. For example, in Alaska, Illinois, Kansas, Michigan, Minnesota, and Wisconsin, if the grantor uses the words "convey and warrant" he implies the five covenants even though he does not list them in the deed. The words "warrant generally" accomplish the same purpose in Pennsylvania, Vermont, Virginia, and West Virginia, as do "grant, bargain, and sell" in the states of Arkansas, Florida, Idaho, Missouri, and Nevada.

At ㉕ the grantor states that he signed this deed on the date noted at ④. This is the **testimony clause;** although customarily included in deeds, it is redundant and could be left out as long as the grantor signs the deed at ㉖. Historically, a seal made with hot wax was essential to the validity of a deed. Today, those few states that require a seal ㉗ accept a hot wax seal, a glued paper seal, the word "seal," or the letters "L.S." "L.S." is an abbreviation for the Latin words "locus sigilli" (place of the seal). The acknowledgment is placed at ㉘, the full wording of which is given in Chapter 6. If an acknowledgment is not used, this space is used for the signatures of witnesses to the grantor's signature. Their names would be preceded by the words, "In the presence of, ..."

Style

The exact style or form of a deed is not critical as long as it contains all the essentials clearly stated and in conformity with state law. For example, one commonly used warranty deed format begins with the words "Know all men by these presents," is written in the first person, and has the date at the end. The writing of deeds should be left to experts in the field. In fact, some states permit only attorneys to write deeds. Even the preparation of preprinted deeds from stationery stores and title companies should be left to knowledgeable persons. Preprinted deeds contain several pitfalls for the unwary. First, the form may have been prepared and printed in another state and, as a result, may not meet the laws of your state. Second, if the blanks are incorrectly filled in, the deed will not be legally recognized. This is a particularly difficult problem when neither the grantor nor grantee realizes it until several years after the deed's delivery. Third, the use of a form deed presumes that the grantor's situation can be fitted to the form and that the grantor will be knowledgeable enough to select the correct form.

GRANT DEEDS

Some states, notably California, Idaho, and North Dakota, use a grant deed instead of a warranty deed. In a **grant deed** the grantor covenants and warrants that (1) he has not previously conveyed the estate being granted to another party, (2) he has not encumbered the property except as noted in the deed, and (3) he will convey to the grantee any title to the property he may later acquire. These covenants are fewer in number and narrower in coverage than those found in a warranty deed, particularly the covenant regarding encumbrances. In the warranty deed, the grantor makes himself responsible for the encumbrances of prior owners as well as his

Figure 5:2

GRANT DEED ①

For a valuable ② *consideration, receipt of which is hereby*
acknowledged, _____ ③ _____ *hereby*
(name of the grantor)
GRANT(S, ④ *to* _____ ⑤ _____ *the*
(name of the grantee)
following described real property in the _____ ⑥ _____ ,
(city, town, etc.)
County of _____ *, State of California:*
[legal description of land here] ⑦

Subject to:

[note exceptions and restrictions here] ⑧

Dated ⑨ _____   _____ ⑩ _____
(Grantor's signature)

⑪ [location of the acknowledgment]

own. The grant deed limits the grantor's responsibility to the period of time he possessed the property. Figure 5:2 summarizes the key elements of a California grant deed.

Referring to the circled numbers in Figure 5:2, ① labels the document, ② fulfills the requirement that consideration be shown, and ③ is for the name and marital status of the grantor. By California statutory law, the single word GRANT(S) at ④ is the granting clause *and* habendum, *and* implies the covenants and warranties of possession, prior encumbrances, and further title. Thus, they need not be individually listed.

Number ⑤ is for the name and marital status of the grantee and the method by which title is being taken. Numbers ⑥ and ⑦ identify the property being conveyed. Easements, property taxes, conditions, reservations, restrictions, and the like, are noted at ⑧. The deed is dated at ⑨, signed at ⑩, and acknowledged at ⑪.

Why have grantees, in states with more than one-tenth of the total U.S. population, been willing to accept a deed with fewer covenants than a warranty deed? The primary reason is the early development and extensive use of title insurance in these states, whereby the grantor and grantee acquire an insurance policy to protect themselves if a flaw in ownership is later discovered. Title insurance is now available in nearly all parts of the country and is explained in Chapter 6.

The **special warranty deed** contains only one covenant, wherein the grantor covenants and warrants he has not encumbered the property except as stated in the deed under the exceptions and restrictions section. Except for containing just one covenant instead of all five, it is identical to the deed shown in Figure 5:1. The special warranty deed is also known in some states as a bargain and sale deed with a covenant against the grantor's acts.

SPECIAL WARRANTY DEED

The basic **bargain and sale** deed contains no covenants, and only the minimum essentials of a deed (see Figure 5:3). It has a date, identifies the grantor and grantee, recites consideration, describes the property, contains words of conveyance, and has the grantor's signature. But lacking covenants, what assurance does the grantee have that he is acquiring title to anything? Actually, none. In this deed the grantor only *implies* that he owns the property described in the deed, and that he is granting it to the grantee. Logically, then, a grantee will much prefer a warranty deed over a bargain and sale deed, or require title insurance.

BARGAIN AND SALE DEED

A quitclaim deed has no covenants or warranties (see Figure 5:4). Moreover, the grantor makes no statement, nor does he even imply that he owns the property he is quitclaiming to the grantee. Whatever rights the grantor possesses at the time the deed is delivered are conveyed to the grantee. If the grantor has no interest, right, or title to the property described in the deed, none is conveyed to the grantee. However, if the grantor possesses fee simple title, fee simple title will be conveyed to the grantee.

QUITCLAIM DEEDS

The critical wording in a quitclaim deed is the grantor's statement that he "does hereby remise, release, and quitclaim

Figure 5:3

BARGAIN AND SALE DEED

THIS DEED made _____, between _____
(date)

residing at _____, herein

called the Grantor, and _____

residing at _____,

herein called the Grantee.

WITNESSETH, that the Grantor, in consideration of

_____, does hereby grant and

release unto the Grantee, the Grantee's heirs, successors, and

assigns forever, all that parcel of land described as

[land description here]

TOGETHER WITH the appurtenances and all the

estate and rights of the Grantor in and to said property.

TO HAVE AND TO HOLD the premises herein

granted together with the appurtenances unto the Grantee

IN WITNESS WHEREOF, the Grantor sets his hand

and seal the day and year first written above.

_____ L.S.
(Grantor)

[location of the acknowledgment]

forever." The word "quitclaim" means to renounce all possession, right, or interest. "Remise" means to give up one's
claim, as does the word "release" in this usage. If the grantor
subsequently acquires any right or interest in the property, he
is not obligated to convey it to the grantee.

At first glance it may seem strange that such a deed
should even exist, but it does serve a very useful purpose.
Situations often arise in real estate transactions when a person claims to have a partial or incomplete right or interest in
a parcel of land. Such a right or interest, known as a **cloud on**

QUITCLAIM DEED

Figure 5:4

THIS DEED, made the _____ day of _____ , 19_ ,
BETWEEN _____ of_____ ,
party of the first part, and _____
of _____ , party of the second part,

WITNESSETH, that the party of the first part, in consideration of ten dollars ($10.00) and other valuable consideration, paid by the party of the second part, does hereby remise, release, and quitclaim unto the party of the second part, the heirs, successors and assigns of the party of the second part forever,

ALL that certain parcel of land, with the buildings and improvements thereon, described as follows,

[insert legal description here]

TOGETHER WITH the appurtenances and all the estate and rights of the Grantor in and to said property.

TO HAVE AND TO HOLD the premises herein granted unto the party of the second part, the heirs or successors and assigns of the party of the second part, forever.

IN WITNESS WHEREOF, the party of the first part has duly executed this deed the day and year first above written.

_____
(Grantor)

[location of the acknowledgment]

the title, may have been due to an inheritance, a dower, curtesy, or community property right, or to a mortgage or right of redemption due to a court-ordered foreclosure sale. By releasing that claim to the fee simple owner through the use of a quitclaim deed, the cloud on the fee owner's title is removed.

OTHER TYPES
OF DEEDS

A **gift deed** is created by simply replacing the recitation of money and other valuable consideration with the statement, "in consideration of his [her, their] natural love and affection." This phrase may be used in a warranty, special warranty, or grant deed. However, it is most often used in quitclaim or bargain and sale deeds as these permit the grantor to avoid committing himself to any warranties regarding the property.

A **guardian's deed** is used to convey a minor's interest in real property. It contains only one covenant, that the guardian and minor have not encumbered the property. The deed must state the legal authority (usually a court order) that permits the guardian to convey the minor's property.

Life estate deeds fall into two categories. A deed for the life of the grantor contains the wording, "for and during the term of the remainder of the natural life of the grantor," in the granting clause and the habendum. A deed for the life of the grantee contains the wording, "for and during the term of the remainder of the natural life of the grantee," in the granting clause and habendum. In both deeds, the remaining wording usually follows either the quitclaim or bargain and sale deed format.

Sheriff's deeds and **referee's deeds in foreclosure** are issued to the new buyer when a person's real estate is sold as the result of a mortgage or other court-ordered foreclosure sale. The deed should state the source of the sheriff's or referee's authority and the amount of consideration paid. Such a deed conveys only the foreclosed party's title, and, at the most, carries only one covenant: that the sheriff or referee has not damaged the property's title.

A **correction deed,** also called a deed of confirmation, is used to correct an error in a previously executed and delivered deed. For example, a name may have been misspelled or an error found in the property description. A quitclaim deed containing a statement regarding the error is used for this purpose. A **cession deed** is a form of a quitclaim deed wherein a property owner conveys street rights to a county or municipality. A **deed of trust** is used to pledge real property as security for a loan. It is discussed in Chapter 10.

If a person dies without leaving a last will and testament (or leaves one that is subsequently ruled void by the courts because it was improperly prepared), he is said to have died **intestate,** which means without a testament. When this happens, state law directs how the deceased's assets shall be distributed. This is known as **title by descent** or **intestate succession.** The surviving spouse and children are the dominant recipients of the deceased's assets. The deceased's grandchildren receive the next largest share, followed by the deceased's parents, brothers and sisters, and their children. These are known as the deceased's **heirs** or, in some states, **distributees.** The amount each heir receives, if anything, depends on individual state law and on how many persons with superior positions in the succession are alive. If no heirs can be found, the deceased's property escheats to the state.

CONVEYANCE AFTER DEATH

A person who dies and leaves a valid will is said to have died **testate,** which means that he died leaving behind a testament telling how his property shall be distributed. The person who made the will, now deceased, is known as the **testator.** In the will, the testator names the persons or organizations who are to receive his real and personal property after he dies. Real property that is willed is known as a **devise** and the recipient, a **devisee.** Personal property that is willed is known as a **bequest** or **legacy,** and the recipient, a **legatee.** The will usually names an **executor** to carry out its instructions. If one is not named, the court will appoint an **administrator.**

Testate, Intestate

Notice an important difference between the transfer of real estate ownership by deed and by will: once a deed is made and delivered, the ownership transfer is permanent, the grantor cannot change his mind and take back the property. With respect to a will, the devisees, although named, have no rights to the testator's property until he dies. Until that time the testator can change his mind and his will.

Upon death, the deceased's will must be filed with a court having power to admit wills, usually called a **probate** or **surrogate court.** This court determines if the will meets all the requirements of law: in particular, that it is genuine, properly

Probate Court

signed and witnessed, and the testator was of sound mind when he made it. At this time anyone may step forward and contest the validity of the will. If the court finds the will to be valid, the executor is permitted to carry out its terms. If the testator owned real property, its ownership is conveyed using an **executor's deed** prepared and signed by the executor. The executor's deed is used both to transfer title to a devisee and to sell real property to raise cash. It contains only one covenant, a covenant by the executor that he has not encumbered the property.

Protection for the Deceased   Because the deceased is not present to protect his assets, state laws attempt to ensure that fair market value is received for the deceased's real estate by requiring court approval of proposed sales, and in some cases by sponsoring open bidding in the courtroom. To protect his interests, a purchaser should ascertain that the executor has the authority to convey title.

For a will to be valid, and subsequently bind the executor to carry out the instructions, it must meet specific legal requirements. All states recognize the **formal** or **witnessed** will, a written document prepared, in most cases, by an attorney. The testator must declare it to be his will and sign it in the presence of two to four witnesses (depending on the state), who, at the testator's request and in his presence, sign the will as witnesses. A formal will prepared by an attorney is the preferred method, as the will then conforms to the law. This greatly reduces the likelihood of its being contested after the testator's death. Additionally, an attorney may offer valuable advice on how to word the will to reduce inheritance taxes.

Holographic Wills   **Holographic wills** are wills that are entirely handwritten, dated, and signed by the testator; but there are no witnesses. Nineteen states recognize holographic wills as legally binding. Persons selecting this form of will generally do so because it saves the time and expense of seeking professional legal aid, and because it is entirely private. Besides the fact that holographic wills are considered to have no effect in 31 states, they often result in much legal argument in states that do accept them. This can occur when the testator is not fully aware of the law as it pertains to the making of wills. Many otherwise happy families, relatives, and friends have been torn by dissension when a relative dies and the will is opened, only to find that there is a question as to whether or not it was properly prepared and hence valid. Unfortunately, what follows is not what the deceased intended; those who would receive more from intestate succession will contest that the will be declared void and of no effect. Those with more to gain if the will stands as written will muster legal forces to argue for its acceptance by the probate court.

An **oral will,** more properly known as a **noncupative will,** *Oral Will*
is a will spoken by a person who is very near death. The witness must promptly put what he has heard in writing and submit it to probate. An oral will can only be used to dispose of personal property. Any real estate belonging to the deceased would be disposed of by intestate succession.

A **codicil** is a supplement or amendment made to a previously existing will. It is used to change some aspect of the will or to add a new instruction, without the work of rewriting the entire will. The codicil must be dated, signed, and witnessed in the same manner as the original will. The only way to change a will is with a codicil or by writing a complete new will. The law will not recognize crossouts, notations, or other alterations made on the will itself.

By occupying another person's land for a long enough *ADVERSE*
period of time, it is possible under certain conditions to *POSSESSION*
acquire ownership through title by **adverse possession.** The historical roots of adverse possession go back many centuries to a time before written deeds were used as evidence of ownership. At that time, in the absence of any claims to the contrary, a person who occupied a parcel of land was presumed to be its owner. Today, adverse possession is, in effect, a statute of limitations that bars a legal owner from claiming title to land when he has done nothing to oust an adverse occupant during the statutory period. From the adverse occupant's standpoint, adverse possession is a method of acquiring title by possessing land for a specified period of time under certain conditions.

Courts of law are quite demanding before they will issue

Table 5:1   ADVERSE POSSESSION: NUMBER OF YEARS OF OCCUPANCY REQUIRED TO CLAIM TITLE*

	Adverse Occupant Lacks Color of Title & Does Not Pay the Property Taxes	Adverse Occupant Has Color of Title &/or Pays the Property Taxes		Adverse Occupant Lacks Color of Title & Does Not Pay the Property Taxes	Adverse Occupant Has Color of Title &/or Pays the Property Taxes
Alabama	20	3–10	Missouri	10	10
Alaska	10	7	Montana		5
Arizona	10	3	Nebraska	10	10
Arkansas	15	2–7	Nevada		5
California		5	New Hampshire	20	20
Colorado	18	7	New Jersey	30–60	20–30
Connecticut	15	15	New Mexico	10	10
Delaware	20	20	New York	10	10
District of Columbia	15	15	North Carolina	20–30	7–21
Florida		7	North Dakota	20	10
Georgia	20	7	Ohio	21	21
Hawaii	20	20	Oklahoma	15	15
Idaho	5	5	Oregon	10	10
Illinois	20	7	Pennsylvania	21	21
Indiana		10	Rhode Island	10	10
Iowa	10	10	South Carolina	10–20	10
Kansas	15	15	South Dakota	20	10
Kentucky	15	7	Tennessee	20	7
Louisiana	30	10	Texas	10–25	3–5
Maine	20	20	Utah		7
Maryland	20	20	Vermont	15	15
Massachusetts	20	20	Virginia	15	15
Michigan	15	5–10	Washington	10	7
Minnesota	15	15	West Virginia	10	10
Mississippi	10	10	Wisconsin	20	10
			Wyoming	10	10

*As may be seen, in a substantial number of states, the waiting period for title by adverse possession is shortened if the adverse occupant has color of title and/or pays the property taxes. In California, Florida, Indiana, Montana, Nevada, and Utah, the property taxes must be paid to obtain title. Generally speaking, adverse possession does not work against minors and other legal incompetents. However, upon obtaining competency, the adverse possession must be broken within the time limit set by each state's law (the range is one to 10 years). In the states of Louisiana, Oklahoma, and Tennessee, adverse possession is referred to as title by prescription.

a new deed to a person claiming title by virtue of adverse possession. The claimant must have maintained actual, visible, continuous, hostile, exclusive, and notorious possession, and be claiming ownership to the property. These requirements mean that the claimant's use must have been visible and obvious to the legal owner, continuous and not just occasional, and exclusive enough to give notice of the claimant's individual claim. Furthermore, the use must have been without permission and the claimant must have acted as though he were the owner, even in the presence of the actual owner. Finally, the adverse claimant must be able to prove that he has met these requirements for a period ranging from 3 to 30 years, as shown in Table 5:1.

The required occupancy period is shortened and the claimant's chances of obtaining legal ownership are enhanced in many states if he has been paying the property taxes and the possession has been under "color of title." **Color of title** suggests some plausible appearance of ownership interest, such as an improperly prepared deed that purports to transfer title to the claimant or a claim of ownership by inheritance. In accumulating the required number of years, an adverse claimant may **tack on** his period of possession to that of a prior adverse occupant. This could be done through the purchase of that right. The current adverse occupant could in turn sell his claim to a still later adverse occupant until enough years were accumulated to present a claim in court.

Color of Title

Although the concept of adverse possession often creates the mental picture of a trespasser moving onto someone else's land and living there long enough to acquire title in fee, this is not the usual application. More often, adverse possession is used to extinguish weak or questionable claims to title. For example, if a person buys property at a tax sale, takes possession, and pays the property taxes each year afterward, adverse possession laws act to cut off claims to title by the previous owner. Another source of successful adverse possession claims arises from encroachments. If a building extends over a property line and nothing is said about it for a long enough period of time, the building will be permitted to stay.

EASEMENT BY
PRESCRIPTION

An easement can also be acquired by prolonged adverse use. This is known as acquiring an **easement by prescription.** Like adverse possession, the laws are strict: the usage must be openly visible, continuous and exclusive, as well as hostile and adverse to the owner. Additionally the use must have occurred over a period of 5 to 20 years, depending on the state. All these facts must be proved in a court of law before the court will issue the claimant a document legally recognizing his ownership of the easement. As an easement is a right to use land for a specific purpose, and not ownership of the land itself, courts rarely require the payment of property taxes to acquire a prescriptive easement.

As may be seen from the foregoing discussion, a landowner must be given obvious notification *at the location* of his land that someone is attempting to claim ownership or an easement. Since an adverse claim must be continuous and hostile, an owner can break it by ejecting the trespassers, preventing them from trespassing, or giving them permission to be there. Any of these actions would demonstrate the landowner's superior title. Stores and office buildings that have privately owned sidewalks or streets upon which the public is allowed to pass take action to break any possible claims to a public easement by either periodically barricading the sidewalk or street or by posting signs giving permission to pass. These signs are often seen in the form of brass plaques embedded in the sidewalk or street. In certain states, a landowner may record with the public records office a **notice of consent.** This is evidence that subsequent uses of his land for the purposes stated in the notice are permissive and not adverse. The notice may be later revoked by recording a **notice of revocation.** Federal, state, and local governments protect themselves against adverse claims to their lands by passing laws making themselves immune.

OWNERSHIP BY
ACCESSION

The extent of one's ownership of land can be altered by **accession.** This can result from natural or man-made causes. With regard to natural causes, the owner of land fronting on a lake, river, or ocean may acquire additional land due to the gradual accumulation of rock, sand, and soil. This process is called **accretion** and the results are referred to as alluvion and reliction. **Alluvion** is the increase of land that results when waterborne soil is gradually deposited to produce firm dry ground. **Reliction** (or dereliction) results when a lake, sea or river permanently recedes, exposing dry land. When land is rapidly washed away by the action of water, it is known as **avulsion.** Man-made accession occurs when man attaches personal property to land. For example, when lumber, nails, and cement are used to build a house, they alter the extent of one's land ownership.

A transfer of land by a government body to a private individual is called a **public grant.** The grants of land made by the governments of England, France, Spain, and Mexico to their citizens when those countries claimed large landholdings in North America are examples. The granting by the U.S. government of federally owned land to railroads for laying track is a form of public grant. Individuals can obtain a public grant of 160 acres of land from the U.S. government. The Homestead Act of 1862 permits persons wishing to settle on otherwise unappropriated federal land to acquire fee simple ownership by paying a small filing charge and occupying and cultivating the land for 5 years. Similarly, for only a few dollars, a person may file a mining claim to federal land for the purpose of extracting whatever valuable minerals he can find. To retain the claim, a certain amount of work must be performed on the land each year. Otherwise, the government will consider the claim abandoned and another person may claim it. If the claim is worked long enough, a public grant can be sought and fee simple title obtained. In the case of both the homestead settler and the mining claim, the conveyance document that passes fee title from the government to the grantee is known as a **land patent.**

PUBLIC GRANT

When an owner makes a voluntary gift of his land to the public, it is known as **dedication.** To illustrate, a land developer buys a large parcel of vacant land and develops it into streets and lots. The lots are sold to private buyers, but what

DEDICATION

about the streets? In all probability they will be dedicated to the town, city, or county. By doing this, the developer, and later the lot buyers, will not have to pay taxes on the streets, and the public will be responsible for maintaining them. The fastest way to accomplish the transfer is by either statutory dedication or dedication by deed. In **statutory dedication,** the developer prepares a map showing the streets, has the map approved by local government officials, and then records it as a public document. In **dedication by deed** the developer prepares a deed that identifies the streets and grants them to the city.

Common law dedication takes place when a landowner, by his acts or words, shows that he intends part of his land to be dedicated even though he has never officially made a written dedication. For example, a landowner may encourage the public to travel on his roads in an attempt to convince a local road department to take over maintenance.

FORFEITURE

Forfeiture can occur when a deed contains a condition or limitation. For example, a grantor states in his deed that the land conveyed may be used for residential purposes only. If the grantee constructs commercial buildings, the grantor can reacquire title on the grounds that the grantee forfeited his interest by not using the land for the required purpose. Similarly, a deed may prohibit certain uses of land. If the land is used for a prohibited purpose, the grantor can claim forfeiture has occurred.

FORMS OF ALIENATION

A change in ownership of any kind is known as an **alienation.** In addition to the forms of alienation discussed in this chapter, alienation can result from court action in connection with escheat, eminent domain, partition, foreclosure, execution sales, and quiet title suits. Marriage can also result in property alienation. These are discussed in other chapters.

Match terms a–t with statements 1–20.

a. *Adverse possession*
b. *Alluvion*
c. *Bargain and sale deed*
d. *Cloud on the title*
e. *Codicil*
f. *Color of title*
g. *Consideration*
h. *Covenants and warranties*
i. *Dedication*
j. *Deed*

k. *Easement by prescription*
l. *Grantee*
m. *Grantor*
n. *Holographic will*
o. *Intestate*
p. *Land patent*
q. *Probate*
r. *Quitclaim deed*
s. *Statute of Frauds*
t. *Warranty deed*

1. A written document that, when properly executed and delivered, conveys title to land.
2. Requires that transfers of real estate be in writing to be enforceable.
3. Person named in a deed who conveys ownership.
4. Person named in a deed who acquires ownership.
5. Anything of value given to produce a contract. It may be personal or real property, or love and affection.
6. Agreements and guarantees found in a deed.
7. A lien or encumbrance or other condition that affects the fee owner's title.
8. A deed that contains the covenants of seizin, quiet enjoyment, encumbrances, further assurance, and warranty forever.
9. A deed that contains no covenants; it only implies that the grantor owns the property described in the deed.
10. A deed with no covenants and no implication that the grantor owns the property he is deeding to the grantee.
11. To die without a last will and testament.
12. A will written entirely in one's own handwriting and signed but not witnessed.
13. The process of verifying the legality of a will and carrying out its instructions.
14. A supplement or amendment to a previous will.
15. Acquisition of real property through prolonged occupation.
16. Some plausible, but not completely clear-cut, indication of ownership rights.
17. Acquisition of an easement by prolonged use.
18. Waterborne soil deposited to produce firm, dry ground.
19. A document for conveying government land in fee to settlers and miners.
20. Private land voluntarily conveyed to the government.

QUESTIONS AND
PROBLEMS

1. Is it possible for a document to convey fee title to land even though it does not contain the word "deed"? Why?
2. In the process of conveying real property from one person to another, at what instant in time does title actually pass from the grantor to the grantee?
3. What legal protections does a full covenant and warranty deed offer a grantee?
4. As a real estate purchaser, which deed would you prefer to receive: warranty, special warranty, bargain and sale? Why?
5. Does your state require a seal on deeds?
6. What are the hazards of preparing your own deeds?
7. Name five examples of title clouds.
8. What is meant by the term "intestate succession"?
9. With regard to probate, what is the key difference between an executor and an administrator?
10. Does your state consider holographic wills to be legal? How many witnesses are required by your state on a formal will?
11. Can a person who has rented the same building for 30 years claim ownership by virtue of adverse possession? Why or why not?
12. Cite examples from your own community or state where land ownership has been altered by alluvion, reliction, or avulsion.

ADDITIONAL READINGS

Kling, Samuel G. *Your Will and What to Do About It.* Chicago: Follett, 1971, 149 pages. Defines key terms used in wills, discusses the importance of wills, and answers the questions of whether or not to write your own will. Contains sample forms and information for all states.

Quinlan, Elsie M. "Adverse Possession," *Real Estate Review,* Winter 1974, pages 128–130. This article recounts three adverse possession cases that reached the courts in 1973: 13 acres of oceanfront land in Delaware, a logging road in Vermont, and a sewer line in Colorado.

Richards, Ralph. *You Can't Take It With You.* New York: Crown, 1970, 96 pages. Written for laymen. Talks about what should be in a will, how an estate is administered, and what the death taxes and other costs will be.

Semenow, Robert W. *Questions and Answers on Real Estate.* Englewood Cliffs, N.J.: Prentice-Hall, 1972, 672 pages. Chapter 3 contains text and questions on title transfer, parts of a deed, kinds of deeds, and adverse possession.

Semenow, Robert W. *Selected Cases in Real Estate.* Englewood Cliffs, N.J.: Prentice-Hall, 1973, 638 pages. Pages 266–332 deal with actual legal cases regarding deeds. Pages 1–37 discuss adverse possession cases.

6

Recordation, Abstracts, and Title Insurance

KEY TERMS

Abstract: a complete historical summary of everything affecting title to a given parcel of land

Acknowledgment: a formal declaration of authenticity

Actual notice: notice of ownership or claim given by one's physical presence on property

Chain of title: a chronological list that shows the present owner and all previous owners of a given parcel of land

Constructive notice: notice of ownership or claim given by means of a document placed into the public records

Marketable title: title free from reasonable doubt as to who the owner of a given property is

Mechanic's lien: a lien placed against land by unpaid workmen and materials suppliers

Quiet title suit: court ordered hearings held to determine land ownership

Title insurance: an insurance policy against defects in title not listed in the title report or abstract

Torrens system: a state-sponsored method of registering land titles

In this chapter we shall focus on (1) the need for a method of determining real property ownership, (2) the process by which current and past ownership is determined from public records, (3) the availability of insurance against errors made in determining ownership, (4) the Torrens system of land title registration, and (5) the Uniform Marketable Title Act.

Until the enactment of the Statute of Frauds in England in 1677, determining who owned a parcel of land was primarily a matter of observing who was in physical possession. This is known as **actual notice:** a landowner gave notice to the world of his claim to ownership by being in actual possession of his land. After 1677 written deeds were required to show transfers of ownership. The problem then became one

NEED FOR A RECORDING SYSTEM

of finding the person holding the most current deed to the land. This was easy if the deedholder also occupied the land, but was more difficult if he did not. The solution was to create a government-sponsored public recording service where a person could record his deed. These records would then be open free of charge to anyone. In this fashion, an owner could post notice to all that he had an interest in a parcel of land. This is known as **constructive notice** and Figure 6:1 illustrates the concept.

Figure 6:1

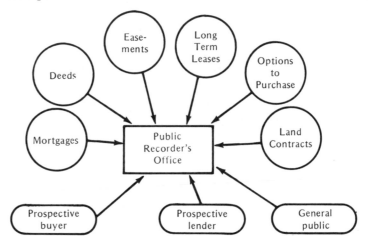

The public recorder's office serves as a central information station for changes in rights, estates, and interests in land.

Recording Acts

All states have passed **recording acts** to provide for the recording of every instrument (i.e., document) by which an estate, interest, or right in land is created, transferred, or encumbered. Within each state, each county has a **public recorder's office**, known variously as the County Recorder's Office, County Registrar's Office, or Bureau of Conveyances. The person in charge is the recorder, registrar or commissioner of deeds. Located at the seat of county government, each public recorder's office records those documents submitted to it that pertain to real property in that county. Thus a deed to property in XYZ County is recorded with the public recorder in XYZ County. Similarly, anyone seeking information regarding ownership of land in XYZ County would go to the recorder's office in XYZ County. Some cities also maintain record rooms where deeds are recorded. The recording process itself involves photocopying the documents and filing them for future reference.

To encourage people to use public recording facilities, laws in each state decree that (1) a deed, mortgage, or other instrument affecting real estate is not effective as far as subsequent purchasers and lenders are concerned if it is not recorded, and (2) prospective purchasers, mortgage lenders, and the public at large are presumed notified when a document is recorded.

To illustrate the effect of constructive and actual notice laws, suppose that Brown offers to sell his land to Carver. Carver then inspects both the land and the public records and finds Brown to be the owner. Satisfied as to Brown's ownership, Carver pays Brown and receives a deed in return. Suppose that Carver does not occupy the land, but he does record his deed with the public recorder's office in the county where the land is located. If Brown now approaches Dawson and attempts to sell the same land, Dawson will find, upon visiting the public records office, that Brown has already conveyed title to Carver. But what if Dawson assumes that Brown is telling the truth and does not trouble himself to inspect the land or the records? Even though Dawson pays for the land and receives a deed from Brown, the law will not regard Dawson as the owner, even if Dawson records his deed. When Dawson discovers that Carver is the true owner, the only recourse open to Dawson is to sue Brown for the return of his money, presuming he can still locate Brown.

Example of Notice Laws

What would the result be if Carver did not record the deed he received and did not occupy the land? If Dawson became interested in buying the land and inspected the public records, he would find Brown still listed as the owner. Upon inspecting the land, Dawson would find no notice of Carver's ownership either. Having satisfied the law and himself regarding the land's ownership, Dawson would pay Brown and receive a deed to the land. If Dawson records his deed before Carver does, the law will consider Dawson to be the new owner. The only recourse open to Carver is to try to get his money back from Brown. Even if

Carver later records his deed and claims that the date on his deed is earlier than the date on Dawson's deed, it is of no avail. Priority is established by the date of recording, not by the date written on the deed. Failure to record does not invalidate the deed itself; it is still binding between the parties who made it. But it is not valid with respect to the rest of the world.

If Carver does not record the deed he receives, but does occupy the land, the law holds Dawson responsible for visiting the land and asking Carver what his rights are. At that point Dawson would learn of Brown's deed to Carver. Any time a person buys property knowing that it has been sold before to another and the deed has not been recorded, the buyer will not receive good title.

Although recording acts permit the recording of any estate, right, or interest in land, many lesser rights are rarely recorded because of the cost and effort involved. Month-to-month rentals and leases for less than a year fall into this category. Consequently, only an on-site inspection would reveal their existence, or the existence of any developing adverse possession or prescriptive easement claim.

With respect to actual and constructive notice, we can draw two important conclusions. First, a prospective purchaser (or lessee or lender) is presumed by law to have inspected both the land itself and the public records to determine the present rights and interests of others. Second, upon receiving a deed, mortgage, or other document relating to an estate, right, or interest in land, one should have it *immediately* recorded in the county in which the land is located.

REQUIREMENTS FOR RECORDING

Nearly all states require that a document be **acknowledged** before it is eligible to be recorded. A few states will permit **proper witnessing** as a substitute. Some states require both. The objective of this requirement is to make certain that the person who signs the document is the same person named in the document. This is done to ensure the accuracy of the public records and to eliminate the possibility of forgery and fraud. To illustrate, suppose that you own 50 acres of vacant land and someone is intent on stealing it from you. Since the physical removal of your land is an impossibility, an attempt would be made to change the public records. A deed would be typed and the forger would sign your name to it. If he were successful in recording the deed, and then attempted to sell the land, the buyer would, upon searching the records, find a deed conveying the land from you to the forger. A visual inspection of the vacant 50 acres would not show you in actual possession. Although innocent of any wrongdoing and buying in good faith, the buyer would be left with only a worthless piece of paper, as there was no intent on your part to convey title to him.

Witnesses

In states that accept witnesses, the person executing the document signs in the presence of at least two witnesses, who in turn sign the document indicating that they were witnesses. To protect themselves, witnesses should not sign unless they know that the person named in the document is the person signing. An example of a witness statement is shown in Figure 6:2.

Figure 6:2

IN WITNESS whereof, the grantor has duly executed this deed in the presence of:

_____   _____
Witness   Grantor

_____
Witness

Acknowledgment

An **acknowledgment** is a formal declaration of authenticity made in the presence of a person legally authorized to take acknowledgments. Like witnessing, its purpose is to prove the genuineness of the signature on the document. Persons authorized to take acknowledgments include notaries public, recording office clerks, commissioners of deeds, judges of courts of record, justices of the peace, and certain others as authorized by state law. Commissioned military officers are authorized to take the acknowledgments of persons in the military; foreign ministers and consular agents can take acknowledgments abroad. If an acknowledgment is taken outside the state where the document will be recorded, either the recording county must already recognize the out-of-state official's authority or the out-of-state official must provide certification that he or she is qualified to take acknowledgments. The official seal or stamp of the notary on the acknowledgment normally fulfills this requirement.

Figure 6:3

ACKNOWLEDGMENT FOR AN INDIVIDUAL

STATE OF _____ }
COUNTY OF_____ } ss

On this_____ day of_____, 19___ , before me, the undersigned, a Notary Public in and for said State, personally appeared_____ [name of person executing document]_____ known to me to be the person whose name is subscribed to the within instrument and acknowledged that he (she) executed the same. Witness my hand and official seal.

space for seal or
stamp of the
notary public | _____
                                           Signature of notary public

[in some states, the   My commission expires _____
words "by his (her)   Date
free act and deed"
are added here]

The acknowledgment illustrated in Figure 6:3 is typical of those used by an individual. Notice that the person signing the document must personally appear before the notary, and that the notary states that he or she knows that person to be the person described in the document. If they are strangers, the notary will require proof of identity. The person executing the document states that he or she acknowledges executing the document by signing it in the presence of the notary. At the completion of the signing, a notation of the event is made in a permanent record book kept by the notary, which is later given to the state government for safekeeping.

Each document brought to a public recorder's office for recordation is photocopied and then returned to its owner. The photocopy is arranged in chronological order with photocopies of other documents and bound into a book. These books (often referred to by the Latin name for book, **liber**) are placed in chronological order on shelves that are open to the public for inspection. When the word liber is used, pages within the book are called **folios.** Otherwise, these are simply called **book and page.**

Filing incoming documents in chronological order makes sense for the recorder's office, but it does not provide an easy means for a person to locate all the documents relevant to a given parcel of land. To illustrate, suppose that you are planning to purchase a parcel of land and want to make certain that the person selling it is the legally recognized owner. Without an index to guide you, you would have to inspect every document in every volume, starting with the most recent book, until you located the current owner's deed. In a heavily populated county, your search might require you to look through hundreds of books, each containing up to 1,000 pages of documents. Consequently, recording offices have developed systems of indexing. The two most commonly used are the grantor and grantee indexes, used by all states, and the tract index, used by nine states. Of the two, the **tract index** is the simplest to use. In it, one page is allocated to either a single parcel of land or to a group of parcels, called a tract. On that page you will find a reference to all the recorded deeds, mortgages, and other documents at the recorder's office that relate to that parcel. Each reference gives the book and page where the original document is recorded.

Grantor and grantee indexes are alphabetical indexes and are usually bound in book form. There are several variations in use in the United States, but the basic principle is the same. For each calendar year, the **grantor index** lists in alphabetical order all grantors named in the documents recorded

*PUBLIC RECORDS
ORGANIZATION*

*Grantor and
Grantee Indexes*

that year. Next to each grantor's name is the name of the grantee named in the document, the book and page where a photocopy of the document can be found, and a few words describing the document. The **grantee index** is arranged by grantee names and gives the name of the grantor and the location and description of the document.

Example of
Title Search

    As an example of the application of the grantor and grantee indexes to a title search, suppose Robert T. Davis states that he is the owner of Lot 2, Block 2, in the Hilldale Tract, in your county and you would like to verify that statement in the public records. You begin by looking in the grantee index for his name, starting with this year's index and working backward in time. The purpose of this first step is to determine if the property was ever granted to Davis. If it was, you will find his name in the grantee index and, next to his name, a book and page reference to a photocopy of his deed to that parcel. The next step is to look through the grantor index for the period of time starting from the moment he received his deed up to the present. If he has granted the property to someone else, Davis's name will be noted in the grantor index with a reference to the book and page where you can see a copy of the deed. (Davis could have reduced your efforts by showing you the actual deed conveying the lot to him. However, you would still have to inspect the grantor index for all dates subsequent to his taking title to see if he had conveyed title to a new grantee. If you do not have the name of the property owner, you would first have to go to the property tax office.)

    Suppose your search shows that on July 1, 1974, in Book 2324, page 335, a warranty deed from John S. Miller to Davis, for Lot 2, Block 2 of the Hilldale Tract was recorded. Furthermore, you find that no subsequent deed showing Davis as grantor of this land has been recorded. Based on this, it would appear that Davis is the fee owner. However, you must inquire further to determine if Miller was the legally recognized owner of the property when he conveyed it to Davis. In other words, on what basis did Miller claim his right of ownership and, subsequently, the right to convey that ownership to Davis? The answer is that Miller based his claim to ownership on the deed he received from the previous owner.

By looking for Miller's name in the 1974 grantee index and then working backward in time through the yearly indexes, you will eventually find his name and a reference to Lot 2, Block 2 in the Hilldale Tract. Next to Miller's name you will find the name of the grantor and a reference to the book and page where the deed was recorded.

By looking for that name in the grantee index, you will locate the next previous deed. By continuing this process you can construct a **chain of title.** This is a chronological list of all the owners of a parcel of land beginning, in most cases, with the original sale or grant of the land from the government to a private citizen. It is used to prove how title came to be **vested** in (i.e., possessed by) the current owner. The figure at the right illustrates the chain-of-title concept.

Sometimes, while tracing a chain of title back through time, an apparent break or dead end will occur. This can happen when the grantor is an administrator, executor, sheriff, or judge, because the owner died or a mortgage against the land was foreclosed. To regain the title sequence, one must search outside the recorder's office by checking probate court records in the case of a death, or civil court actions in the case of a foreclosure.

In addition to constructing the chain of title, known as **running the chain,** a search must be made for any outstanding mortgages, judgments, actions pending, liens, and unpaid taxes that may affect the title. With regard to searching for mortgages, states again differ slightly. Some place mortgages in the general grantor and grantee indexes, listing the borrower (mortgagor) as the grantor and the lender (mortgagee) as the grantee. Other states have separate index books for mortgagors and mortgagees. The process involves looking for the name of the property owner in each annual **mortgagor index** published while he owned the land. If a mortgage is found, a further check will reveal whether or not it has been satisfied and released. If it has been released, the recorder's office will have noted on the margin of the recorded mortgage the book and page where the release is located. Or if one has

CHAIN OF TITLE

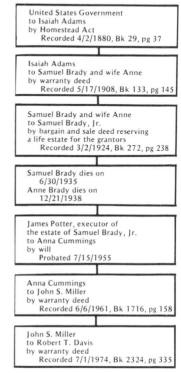

... in some states, when a person sells his land, he presents a chain of title as evidence that he is the owner of the land.

the lender's name, the mortgage location and its subsequent release can also be found by searching the **mortgagee index.**

Public records must also be checked to learn if any lawsuits have resulted in judgments against recent owners, or if any lawsuits are pending that might later affect title. This information is found, respectively, on the **judgment rolls** and in the **lis pendens index** at the office of the county clerk. The term "lis pendens" is Latin for pending lawsuits. A separate search must also be made for **mechanic's liens** against the land that may have been filed by unpaid workmen and material suppliers. This step should also include an on site inspection of the land for any recent construction activity or material deliveries. A visit must also be made to the local tax assessor's office to check the tax rolls for unpaid property taxes. This does not exhaust all possible places that must be visited to do a thorough title search. A title searcher may also find himself researching birth, marriage, divorce, and adoption records, probate records, military files, and federal tax liens in an effort to identify all the parties with an interest or potential interest in a given parcel of land.

ABSTRACT

Although it is useful for the real estate practitioner to be able to find a name or document in the public records, full-scale title searching should be left to professionals. In a sparsely populated county, title searching is usually done on a part-time basis by an attorney. In more heavily populated counties, a full-time **conveyancer** or **abstracter** will search the records. These persons are experts in the field of title search, and for a fee they will prepare an abstract for a parcel of land. An **abstract** is a complete historical summary of everything affecting the title of a property. It includes not only the title chain, but also identifies recorded easements, mortgages, wills, tax liens, judgments, pending lawsuits, marriages, and the like, that affect title. The abstract is then sent to an attorney. Based on his knowledge of law and the abstract he is reading, he renders an **opinion** as to who the fee owner is and names anyone else he feels has a legitimate right or interest in the property. This opinion, when written, signed by the attorney, and attached to the abstract is known in many states as a **certificate of title.** In some parts of the

United States, this certified abstract is so valuable that it is brought up to date each time the property is sold and passed from the seller to the buyer.

TITLE INSURANCE

Despite the diligent efforts of conveyancers, abstracters, and attorneys to give as accurate a picture of land ownership as possible, there is no guarantee that the finished abstract, or its certification, is completely accurate. Persons preparing abstracts and opinions are liable for mistakes due to their own negligence, and they can be sued if that negligence results in a loss to a client. But what if a recorded deed in the title chain is a forgery? Or what if a married person represented himself on a deed as a single person, thus resulting in unextinguished dower rights? Or what if a deed was executed by a minor or an otherwise legally incompetent person? These situations can result in substantial losses to a property owner, yet the fault does not lie with the conveyancer, abstracter, or attorney. The solution has been the organization of private companies to sell insurance against possibilities such as these.

Efforts to insure titles date back to the last century and were primarily organized by and for the benefit of attorneys who wanted protection from errors that they might make in the interpretation of abstracts. As time passed, **title insurance** or **title guarantee** became available to anyone wishing to purchase it. The basic principle of title insurance is similar to any form of insurance: many persons pay a small amount into an insurance pool that is then available if any one of them should suffer a loss.

Title Report

From the property owner's viewpoint, title insurance is a two-step process: first, a title report is prepared, and second, a title insurance company offers to insure the findings in the report. The **title report** is based on an abstract prepared by an independent abstracter or by one employed by the insurance company. A company attorney then reviews these findings and prepares a report that shows the current owner and lists any title defects, liens, or encumbrances. This information is reported to the property owner in a manner similar to that shown in Figure 6:4.

Notice how a title report differs from an abstract. An ab-

Figure 6:4

TITLE INSURANCE POLICY
Title Report Section

LAND DESCRIPTION: Lot 17, Block M, Atwater's Addition, Jefferson County, State of _____ .

DATE AND TIME OF SEARCH: January 15, 1977, at 10:30 a.m.

NAMES OF THE INSURED: Adolf Adams and wife Barbara, Paul B. Baker

AMOUNT OF INSURANCE: ____$40,000____ *PREMIUM:* ____$200.00____ *POLICY NUMBER:* ___A-12345___

VESTING AS OF THE ABOVE DATE: Paul B. Baker, a single man

ESTATE OR INTEREST: Fee

EXCEPTIONS:

PART I: 1. A mortgage in favor of the First National Bank in the amount of $30,000, recorded June 2, 1974, in Book 2975, Page 245 of the Official County Records.

2. An easement in favor of the Southern Telephone Company along the eastern five feet of said land for telephone poles and conduits. Recorded on June 15, 1946, in Book 1210, Page 113 of the Official County Records.

3. An easement in favor of Coastal States Gas and Electric Company along the north ten feet of said land for underground pipes. Recorded on June 16, 1946, in Book 1210, Page 137 of the Official County Records.

stract is a historical summary of recorded events that have affected the title to a given parcel of land; a title report is more like a snapshot that shows the condition of title at a specific moment in time. A title report does not tell who the

PART II: 1. *Taxes or assessments not shown by the records of any taxing authority or by the public records.*

2. *Any facts, rights, interests, or claims that, although not shown by the public records, could be determined by inspection of the land and inquiry of persons in possession.*

3. *Discrepancies or conflicts in boundary lines or area or encroachments that would be shown by a survey, but which are not shown by the public records.*

4. *Easements, liens, or encumbrances not shown by the public records.*

5. *Unpatented mining claims and water rights or claims.*

previous owners were; it only tells who the current owner is. A title report does not list all mortgage loans ever made against the land, but only those that have not been repaid. The title report in Figure 6:4 states that a search of the public records shows Paul B. Baker to be the fee owner of Lot 17, Block M, at the time the search was conducted. In Part I, the report lists all recorded objections that could be found to Baker's fee estate, in this case, a mortgage and two easements. In Part II, the title company lists sources of information not searched in preparing the report.

Policy Exceptions

If title insurance is purchased, the exceptions in Parts I and II become exceptions to the policy. These exceptions say three things to the insured. First, the insurer takes responsibility for having thoroughly searched the publicly available records as they pertain to the land involved and insures the accuracy of its findings. Second, the insurer does not take responsibility for information pertinent to this land that is not found in the public records. Third, the insurer has not made a visual inspection of the land for signs of actual notice. It is presumed that the insured knows the location of his land

and can make his own inspection. If the insured is not certain of the land's boundaries, a surveyor should be hired.

Although an owner may purchase a title insurance policy on his property at any time, it is most often purchased when land is sold. In some parts of the United States it is customary for the seller to pay the cost of both the title search and the insurance. In other parts, the seller pays for the search and the buyer for the insurance. In a relatively few instances, the buyer pays for both. Customarily, when a property is sold, it is insured for an amount equal to the purchase price. This insurance protects the buyer not only while the buyer owns the property, but at any time in the future that an insured defect is discovered. The insurance premium consists of a single payment. On the average-priced home, the combined charge for a title report and title insurance amounts to about 1/2 of 1% of the amount of insurance purchased. Some companies offer reduced **reissue rates** if the previous owner's policy is available for updating, because the time period that must be searched is shorter.

Owner's and Mortgagee's Policies

The policy carrying the obligations and exceptions illustrated in Figure 6:4 is an **owner's policy.** However, title insurance companies also sell a **mortgagee's policy.** This protects a lender who has taken real estate as collateral for a loan. There are two significant differences between an owner's and a mortgagee's policy. The owner's policy is good for the face amount at any time in the future, whereas the mortgagee's policy protects only for the amount owed on the mortgage loan. Thus, the coverage on a mortgagee's policy declines and finally terminates when the loan is fully repaid. The other major difference is that the mortgagee's policy does not make exceptions for claims to ownership that could have been determined by physically inspecting the property.

The cost of a mortgagee's policy (also known as a lender's policy or loan policy) is similar to an owner's policy. Although the insurance company takes added risks by eliminating some exceptions found in the owner's policy, this is balanced by the fact that the liability decreases as the loan is repaid. When an owner's and a mortgagee's policy are purchased at the same time, as in the case of a sale with new financing, the combined cost is only a few dollars more than the cost of the owner's policy alone.

The last item in a title policy is a statement as to how the company will handle claims. Although this "Conditions and Stipulations Section" is too lengthy to reproduce here, its key aspects can be summarized as follows. When an insured defect arises, the title insurance company reserves the right to either pay the loss or fight the claim in court. If it elects to fight, any legal costs the company incurs are in addition to the amount of coverage named in the policy. If a loss is paid, the amount of coverage is reduced by that amount and any unused coverage is still in effect. If the company pays a loss, it acquires the right to collect from the party who caused the loss.

Claims for Losses

In comparing title insurance to other forms of insurance (e.g., life, fire, automobile), note that title insurance insures against something that has already happened but has not been discovered. A forged deed may result in a disagreement over ownership: the forgery is a fact of history, the insurance is in the event of its discovery. But in some cases the problem will never be discovered. For example, a married couple may be totally unaware of dower and curtesy rights and fail to extinguish them when they sell their property. If neither later claims them, when they die, the rights extinguish themselves, and the intervening property owners will have been unaffected.

Only a small part of the premiums collected by title insurance companies are used to pay claims, largely because they take great pains to maintain on their own premises complete photographic copies of the public records for each county in which they do business. These are called **title plants;** in many cases they are actually more complete and better organized than those available at the public recorder's office. The philosophy is that the better the quality of the title search, the fewer claims that must be paid.

The title insurance business has mushroomed due to four important reasons. First, in a warranty deed, the grantor makes several strongly worded covenants. As you will recall, the grantor covenants that he is the owner, that the grantee will

The Growth of Title Insurance

not be disturbed in his possession, that there are no encumbrances except as stated in the deed, that the grantor will procure any necessary further assurance of title for the grantee, and that the grantor warrants forever the grantee's title and possession. Thus, signing a warranty deed places a great obligation on the grantor. By purchasing title insurance, the grantor can transfer that obligation to an insurance company.

Second, a grantee is also motivated to have title insurance. Even with a warranty deed, there is always the lingering question of whether or not the seller would be financially capable of making good on his covenants and warranties. They are useless if one cannot enforce them. Additionally, title insurance typically provides a grantee broader assurance than a warranty deed. For example, an outsider's claim must produce physical dispossession of the grantee before the covenant of quiet enjoyment is considered broken. Yet the same claim would be covered by title insurance before dispossession took place.

Third, the broad use of title insurance has made mortgage lending more attractive, and borrowing a little easier and cheaper for real property owners, because title insurance has removed the risk of loss due to defective titles. Eliminating this loss means that lenders can charge a lower rate of interest.

Marketable Title   Fourth, title insurance has made titles to land much more marketable. In nearly all real estate transactions the seller agrees to deliver **marketable title** to the buyer. Marketable title is a title that is free from reasonable doubt as to who the owner is. Even when the seller makes no mention of the quality of the title, courts ordinarily require that marketable title be conveyed. To illustrate, a seller orders an abstract prepared, and it is read by an attorney who certifies it as showing marketable title. The buyer's attorney feels that certain technical defects in the title chain contradict certification as marketable. He advises the buyer to refuse to complete the sale. The line between what is and what is not marketable title can be exceedingly thin, and differences of legal opinion are quite possible. One means of breaking the stalemate is to locate a title insurance company that will insure the title as being marketable. If the defect is not serious, the insurance company will accept the risk. If it is a serious risk, the company may either accept the risk and increase the insurance fee or recommend a quiet title suit.

When a title defect (or **title cloud**) must be removed, it is logical to remove it by using the path of least resistance. For example, if an abstract or title report shows unpaid property taxes, the buyer may require the seller to pay them in full before the deal is completed. A cloud on the title due to pending foreclosure proceedings can be halted by either bringing the loan payments up to date or negotiating with the lender for a new loan repayment schedule. A distant relative with ownership rights might be willing, upon negotiation, to quitclaim them for a price.

Sometimes a stronger means is necessary to remove title defects. For example, the distant relative may refuse to negotiate, or the lender may refuse to remove a mortgage lien despite pleas from the borrower that it has been paid. The solution is a **quiet title suit** (also called a suit to quiet title). Forty-seven states have enacted legislation that permits a property owner to ask the courts to hold hearings on the ownership of his land. At these hearings anyone who feels that he has an interest or right to the land in question may present verbal or written evidence of that claim. A judge, acting on the evidence presented and the laws of his state, rules on the validity of each claim. The result is to legally recognize those with a genuine right or interest and to "quiet" those without.

Over a century ago, Sir Robert Torrens, a British gentleman, devised an improved system of identifying land ownership. He was impressed by the relative simplicity of the British system of sailing-ship registration. The government maintained an official ships' registry that listed on a single page a ship's name, its owner, and any liens or encumbrances against it. Torrens felt land titles might be registered in a similar manner. The system he designed, known as the **Torrens system** of land title registration, starts with a landowner's application for registration and the preparation of an

.abstract. This is followed by a quiet title suit at which all parties named in the abstract and anyone else claiming a right or interest to the land in question may attend and be heard.

Certificate of Title

Based on the outcome of the suit, a government-appointed **registrar of titles** prepares a **certificate of title.** This certificate displays the legally recognized fee owner and lists any legally recognized exceptions to that ownership, such as mortgages, easements, long-term leases, or life estates. The registrar keeps the certificate and issues a duplicate to the fee owner. (Although they use the same name, a Torrens certificate of title is not the same as an attorney's certificate of title. The former shows ownership and claims against that ownership as established by a court of law. The latter is strictly an opinion of the condition of title.)

Once a title is registered, any subsequent liens or encumbrances against it must be entered on the registrar's copy of the certificate of title in order to give constructive notice. When a lien or encumbrance is removed, its notation on the certificate is canceled. In this manner, the entire concept of constructive notice for a given parcel of land is reduced to a single-page document open to public view at the registrar's office. This, Torrens argued, would make the whole process of title transfer much simpler and cheaper.

When registered land is conveyed, the grantor gives the grantee a deed. The grantee takes the deed to the registrar of titles, who transfers the title by canceling the grantor's certificate and issuing a new certificate in the name of the grantee. Any liens or other encumbrances not removed at the same time are carried over from the old to the new certificate. The deed and certificate are kept by the registrar; the grantee receives a duplicate of the certificate. If the conveyance is accompanied by a new mortgage, it is noted on the new certificate, and a copy of the mortgage is retained by the registrar.

Except for the quiet title suit aspect, the concept of land title registration is quite similar to that used in the United States for registering ownership of motor vehicles. A department or division of motor vehicles at the state government level maintains a record of the owner and lienholder (lender), if any, for each motor vehicle registered in the state. The state also provides the owner with a certificate of title that lists the owner's name and any lienholders. When the car is sold, the owner signs the reverse of the certificate, indicating that the vehicle has been sold, and requests that a new certificate be issued to the buyer. The state, upon receiving the certificate, cancels it, issues a new one with the new owner's name on it, and records the change of ownership in its files.

Adoption

The Torrens land title registration system was first adopted in 1857 by South Australia. Adoption elsewhere was slow, and 40 years passed before the remaining Australian territories and England enacted similar acts. In the United States, the first state to have a land registration act was Illinois in 1895. Other states slowly followed, but often their laws were vague and cumbersome to the point of being useless. At one point, 20 states had land title registration acts, but since then 9 states have repealed their acts and only 11 remain. Of these 11, only the states of Hawaii, Illinois, Massachusetts, Minnesota, and New York have witnessed its active use. And of these 5 states, only Hawaii has experienced statewide acceptance of land title registration. In Illinois, use has been concentrated in Cook County (Chicago area); in Minnesota, in the Minneapolis area; in Massachusetts, in the Boston area; and in New York, in Suffolk County (eastern Long Island). In the remaining 6 states, Colorado, Georgia, North Carolina, Ohio, Virginia, and Washington, the public has made relatively little use of land title registration.

Why the lukewarm acceptance? One area of controversy has been the need for an assurance or recovery fund. The quiet title suit and the certificate of title are considered to be conclusive evidence of ownership. But what if a legitimate claimant was not aware of the suit, or a mortgage holder is erroneously left off the certificate? What recourse for recovery do they have? The usual solution is to charge every parcel of land a small fee the first time it is registered. Cook County, Illinois, for example, charges 1/10 of 1% of the market value. This is placed in a recovery fund. However, opponents of Torrens registration argue that this may not be enough in the event of substantial claims. To counteract this, Hawaii has moved to reinforce its recovery fund, if the need arises, with state general funds. Cook County has found in its 75-year history of title registration that recovery fees collected have exceeded claims by a ratio of 30 to 1.

A much more devastating blow to the broad acceptance of title registration can be traced to its time and cost and to the widespread availability of title insurance. A routine registration takes about three months, most of it consumed by waiting periods stemming from the quiet title suit process. By comparison, a title insurance policy can be obtained in about a week. Another serious drawback is the cost of registration. In Hawaii, for example, a typical homeowner faces the prospect of costs in the range of $500 to $1,000 to register a title. Most of this covers necessary services, such as a licensed surveyor, an abstracter, and an attorney, rather than the actual registration fee itself. For $200 to $300 the same homeowner can purchase an owner's title insurance policy, which provides equally acceptable assurance of marketable title. Although over the long run the cumulative cost of title insurance policies each time the property changes hands will be higher than the one-time registration cost, the homeowner is more concerned with his cost now, not someone else's cost in the future.

That Hawaii is a leader in the use of title registration is not the result of the small landowner. Rather, it is due to the state's large private landowners, the 50 largest of whom own 85% of the privately held land in the state. These owners have used the Torrens system to remove title defects and to reinforce recognition of their ownership. Also, the cost of registration does not increase proportionately with the area of land. For example, an entire 100-home subdivision might cost only $5,000 to register before the homes are sold. On a per home basis, this is only $50 each.

MARKETABLE TITLE ACTS   At least 10 states have a **Marketable Title Act.** This is *not* a system of title registration. Rather, it is legislation aimed at making abstracts easier to prepare and less prone to error. This is done by cutting off claims to rights or interests in land that have been inactive for longer than the act's statutory period. In Connecticut, Michigan, Utah, Vermont, and Wisconsin, this is 40 years. Thus, in these states, a person who has an unbroken chain of title with no defects for at least 40 years is regarded by the law as having marketable title.* Any defects more than 40 years old are outlawed. The result is to concentrate the title search process on the immediate past 40 years. Thus, abstracts can be produced with less effort and expense, and the chance for an error either by the abstracter or in the documents themselves is greatly reduced. This is particularly true in view of the fact that record-keeping procedures in the past were not as sophisticated as they are today.

The philosophy of a marketable title act is that a person has 40 years to come forward and make his claim known; if he does not, then he apparently does not consider it worth pursuing. As protection for a person actively pursuing a claim that is about to become more than 40 years old, the claim can be renewed for another 40 years by again recording notice of the claim in the public records. In certain situations, a title must be searched back more than 40 years (e.g., when there is a lease of more than 40-year duration or when no document affecting ownership has been recorded in over 40 years). Marketable title acts do not eliminate the need for actual notice nor do they eliminate the role of adverse possession.

Match terms a–q with statements 1–17. VOCABULARY REVIEW

a. *Abstract*
b. *Acknowledgment*
c. *Actual notice*
d. *Chain of title*
e. *Constructive notice*
f. *Grantor index*
g. *Lis pendens index*
h. *Marketable title*
i. *Marketable title acts*

j. *Mechanics lien*
k. *Mortgagee's title policy*
l. *Notary public*
m. *Owner's title policy*
n. *Public recorder's office*
o. *Quiet title suit*
p. *Title report*
q. *Torrens system*

1. Notice given by one's physical presence on the property.
2. Notice given by means of a document placed into the public records.

---

* In Nebraska the statutory period is 22 years; in Florida, North Carolina, and Oklahoma it is 30 years; in Indiana, 50 years.

3. A formal declaration, made in the presence of a notary public or other authorized individual, by a person affirming that he or she signed a document.
4. A person authorized to take acknowledgments.
5. A place where a person can inform the world as to his land ownership by recording his deed.
6. A book at the public recorder's office that lists grantors alphabetically by name.
7. A chronological list that shows the present owner and all previous owners of a given parcel of land.
8. A publicly available index whereby a person can learn of any pending lawsuits that may affect title.
9. A lien placed against land by unpaid workmen and material suppliers.
10. A complete historical summary of everything affecting title to a given parcel of land.
11. Insurance to protect a property owner against monetary loss if his title is found to be imperfect.
12. A report made by a title insurance company showing current title condition.
13. A title policy written to protect a real estate lender.
14. Title that is free from reasonable doubt as to who the owner is.
15. Court-ordered hearings held to determine land ownership.
16. Laws that automatically cut off inactive claims to rights or interests in land.
17. A method of registering land titles that is similar to that of automobile ownership registration.

QUESTIONS AND PROBLEMS

1. Explain in your own words the concepts of actual and constructive notice and the role that they play in real estate ownership.
2. Where is the public recorder's office for your community located?
3. How much does your public recorder's office charge to record a deed? A mortgage? What requirements must a document meet before it will be accepted for recording?
4. What is the purpose of grantor and grantee indexes?
5. Why is it important that a title search be carried out in more places than just the county recorder's office?
6. What is the difference between a certificate of title issued by an attorney and one that results from a Torrens land registration proceeding?
7. How does a title report differ from an abstract?
8. What is the purpose of title insurance?

9. Thorsen sells his house to Williams. Williams moves in but for some reason does not record his deed. Thorsen discovers this and sells the house to an out-of-state investor who orders a title search, purchases an owner's title policy, and records his deed. Thorsen then disappears with the money he received from both sales. Who is the loser when this scheme is discovered: Williams, the out-of-state investor, or the title company? Why?
10. If you are located near the public recorder's office for your county, take a parcel of land (such as your home) and trace its ownership back through three owners.

ADDITIONAL READINGS

Flick, Clinton P. *Abstract and Title Practice*, 2nd ed. St. Paul, Minn.: West Publishing Co., 1958. (Updated with inserts.) A three-volume series that deals with law and practice concerning abstracts, title insurance, Torrens title registration, title defects, tax titles, etc.

Kratovil, Robert. *Real Estate Law*, 6th ed. Englewood Cliffs, N.J.: Prentice-Hall, 1974, 479 pages. Chapter 9 deals with the legal aspects of recording and constructive notice.

Perspective: America's Land Title Industry. Washington, D.C.: American Land Title Association, n.d., 32 pages. A group of six articles that first appeared in the *National Capital Area Realtor*. Included are articles about title plants, abstracting, title lawyers, title insurance, and title losses.

Thau, William A. "Protecting the Real Estate Buyer's Title," *Real Estate Review*, Winter 1974, pages 71–83. A discussion of the role of title insurance in protecting the real estate buyer's title. Explains the standardized American Land Title Association insurance forms, title policy exceptions, title company liability, claim recovery, and policy cost.

Title Insurance. Los Angeles: Title Insurance and Trust Company, 1975, 24 pages. This pamphlet, which is available free from Ticor Title offices across the United States, provides a brief explanation of how title insurance works.

7

Contract Law

Breach of contract: failure without legal excuse to perform as required by a contract

Competent parties: persons considered legally capable of entering into a binding contract

Contract: a legally enforceable agreement to do (or not to do) a particular thing

Duress: the application of force to obtain an agreement

Fraud: an act intended to deceive for the purpose of inducing another to part with something of value

Liquidated damages: an amount of money set forth in a contract that is to be paid in the event the contract is not completed

Minor, Infant: a person under the age of legal competence; in most states, under 18 years

Specific performance: contract performance according to the precise terms agreed upon

Void contract: a contract that has no legal effect on the parties who made it

Voidable contract: a contract that binds one party but gives the other the right to withdraw

A contract is a legally enforceable agreement to do (or not to do) a specific thing. In this chapter we shall see how a contract is created and what makes it legally binding. Topics covered include offer and acceptance, fraud, mistake, lawful object, consideration, performance, and breach of contract. In Chapter 8 we shall turn our attention to the binder, purchase contract, trade agreement, and installment contract as they relate to the buying and selling of real estate.

HOW A CONTRACT IS CREATED

Contracts may be either expressed or implied. An **expressed contract** occurs when the parties to the contract declare their intentions either orally or in writing. (The word "party" [plural, parties] is a legal term that refers to a person or group involved in a legal proceeding.) A lease or rental agreement, for example, is an expressed contract. The lessor (landlord) expresses his intent to permit the lessee (tenant) to use the premises, and the lessee agrees to pay the rent. An **implied contract** occurs when the actions of the parties indicate that they intend to create a contract. For example, when you step into a taxicab, you imply that you will pay the fare. The cab driver, by allowing you in the cab, implies that he will take you where you want to go. The same thing occurs at a restaurant. The presence of tables, silverware, menus, and waitresses implies that you will be served food. When you order, you imply that you are going to pay when the bill is presented.

Bilateral Contract

Contracts are classed as either bilateral or unilateral. A **bilateral contract** occurs when a promise is exchanged for a promise. For example, a seller lists his property with a real estate broker, promising to pay him a commission if he finds a buyer. The broker, in turn, promises to diligently search for a buyer. In the typical real estate sale, the buyer promises to pay the agreed price, and the seller promises to deliver title to the buyer.

Unilateral Contract

A **unilateral contract** is created when one party makes a promise or begins performance without first receiving any promise of performance from the other. For instance, during a campaign to get more listings, a real estate office manager announces to the firm's sales staff that an extra $100 bonus will be paid for each saleable new listing. No promises or agreements are necessary from the salespersons. However, each time a salesperson brings in a saleable listing, he or she is entitled to the promised $100 bonus. An offer to purchase is a unilateral contract until it is accepted by the property owner, at which time it becomes a bilateral contract.

Forbear

Most contract agreements are based on promises by the parties involved to act in some manner (e.g., pay money, find a buyer, or deliver title). However, a contract can contain an agreement to **forbear** (not to act) by one or more of its parties. For example, a lender may agree not to foreclose on a delinquent mortgage loan if the borrower agrees to a new payment schedule.

A **valid contract** is one that meets all the requirements of law. It is binding upon its parties and legally enforceable in a court of law. A **void contract** has no legal effect and, in fact, is not a contract at all. Even though the parties may have gone through the motions of attempting to make a contract, no legal rights are created and any party thereto may ignore it at his pleasure. A **voidable contract** binds one party but not the other. Let us now turn our attention to the requirements of a valid contract.

Valid, Void, Voidable

For a contract to be **legally valid**, and hence binding and enforceable, the following five requirements must be met:

ESSENTIALS OF A VALID CONTRACT

1. Legally competent parties.
2. Mutual agreement.
3. Lawful objective.
4. Sufficient consideration or cause.
5. Contract in writing when required by law.

If these conditions are met, any party to the contract may, if the need arises, call upon a court of law to either enforce the contract as written or award money damages for nonperformance. In reality, a properly written contract seldom ends in court because each party knows it will be enforced as written. It is the poorly written contract or the contract that borders between enforceable and unenforceable that ends in court. A judge must then decide if a contract actually exists and the obligations of each party. Using the courts, however, is an expensive and time-consuming method of interpreting an agreement. It is much better if the contract is correctly prepared in the first place. Let us look more closely at the five requirements of an enforceable contract.

To be legally enforceable, all parties entering into a contract must be legally competent. In deciding competency, the law provides a mixture of objective and subjective standards. The most objective standard is that of age. A person must reach the age of **majority** to be legally capable of entering into a contract. **Minors** do not have contractual capability. Until the voting age in national elections was reduced from 21 to 18 years by Congress, persons were considered to be minors by

Competent Parties

most states until they reached the age of 21. Since then most state legislatures have lowered the age for entering into legally binding contracts to 18 years. The purpose of majority laws is to protect minors (also known as "'infants" in legal terminology) from entering into contracts that they may not be old enough to understand. Depending on the circumstances, a contract entered into by a minor may be void or voidable. For example, the adult might be bound but the minor could withdraw. If a contract with a minor is required, it is still possible to obtain a binding contract by working through the minor's legal guardian.

Persons of unsound mind who have been declared incompetent by a judge may not make a valid contract, and any attempt to do so results in a void contract. The solution is to contract through the person appointed to act on behalf of the incompetent. If a person is not judicially incompetent but nonetheless appears incapable of understanding the transaction in question, he has no legal power to contract. In some states persons convicted of felonies may not enter into valid contracts without the prior approval of the parole board.

Regarding intoxicated persons, if there was a deliberate attempt to intoxicate a person for the purpose of approving a contract, the intoxicated person, upon sobering up, can call upon the courts to void the contract. If the contracting party was voluntarily drunk to the point of incompetence, when he is sober he may ratify or deny the contract if he does so promptly. However, some courts look at the matter strictly from the standpoint of whether the intoxicated person had the capability of formulating the intent to enter into a contract. Obviously, there are some fine and subjective distinctions among these three categories, and a judge may interpret them differently than the parties to the contract.

Power of Attorney   Corporations are considered legally competent parties. However, the individual contracting on behalf of the corporation must have authority from the board of directors. Some states also require that the corporate seal be affixed to contracts. A partnership can contract either in the name of the partnership or in the name of any of its general partners. An individual given the power by another person to act on his behalf has a **power of attorney** and is legally competent to the extent of the powers granted as long as the person granting the power remains legally competent. Finally, executors and administrators can legally contract on behalf of trusts and estates.

The requirement of **mutual agreement** (also called **mutual consent)** means that all parties to a contract must fully understand the contract and be in complete agreement as to its terms and conditions. Specifically, this means that (1) there must be an offer and acceptance, (2) there must be no fraud, misrepresentation, or mistake, and (3) the agreement must be genuine and freely given.

Mutual Agreement

Offer and acceptance: requires that one party (the **offeror)** make an offer to another party (the **offeree)**. The offeree must then communicate to the offeror that he accepts. The means of communication may be verbal, in writing, or by an act that implies acceptance. To illustrate, suppose that you own an apartment and want to rent it. You tell a prospective tenant that he can rent it for $250 per month beginning today, and inform him of the house rules, when the rent is due, how much the deposit is, and under what conditions it will be returned. This is the offer, and you, the offeror, have just communicated it to the offeree. One requirement of a valid contract is that the offer be specific in its terms. Mutual agreement cannot exist if the terms of the offer are vague or undisclosed and/or the offer does not clearly state the obligations of each party involved. If you were to say to a prospective tenant, "Do you want to rent this apartment?" without stating the price, and the prospective tenant said "Yes," the law would not consider this to be a contract.

Upon receiving an offer, the offeree has three options: to agree to it, reject it, or make a counteroffer. If he agrees, he must agree to every item in the offer. An offer is considered by law to be rejected if the offeree either rejects it outright or makes a change in the terms. If he makes any changes, it is a **counteroffer** and, although it would appear the offeree is only amending the offer before he will accept it, in reality the offeree has rejected it and is making an offer of his own. This

Counteroffer

now makes him the offeror. To illustrate, suppose that the prospective tenant for your apartment states that he would like to rent the apartment on the terms you offered, but instead of paying $250 per month, he wants to pay $230 per month. This is a rejection of your offer and the making of a counteroffer. You now have the right to accept or reject his offer. If you counter at $240 per month, this rejects his offer and you are again the offeror. If $240 is agreeable with the offeree, he must communicate his acceptance to you. In this case, a verbal "Yes, I'll take it" would be legally adequate.

If the offeree does not wish to accept the offer nor make a counteroffer, how is the offer terminated? Certainly he can simply say "No." However, if he says nothing, the passage of time can also terminate the offer. This can happen in two ways. The offeror can state how long the offer is to remain open, for example, "You have until 8:00 P.M. tonight to decide if you want the apartment." If nothing is heard by 8:00 P.M., the offer terminates. When nothing is said as to how long the offer is to remain open, the courts will permit a reasonable amount of time, depending on the situation. To illustrate, it is reasonable to presume that if the prospective tenant left without accepting your offer or arranging for time to think about it, your offer terminates with his departure. This frees you to look for another tenant and make another offer without still being committed to the first offeree. When the offer is for the purchase of real estate and no termination date is given, law courts have ruled that a reasonable period of time might be several days or a week.

The best policy is to state the length of time an offer is open to avoid the problem of receiving two acceptances. Selecting a time period depends on the amount of time the offeror feels the offeree needs to decide and the length of time the offeror is willing to tie up his property.

Fraud

Mutual agreement requires that there be no fraud, misrepresentation, or mistake in the contract if it is to be valid. A **fraud** is an act intended to deceive for the purpose of inducing another to part with something of value. It can be as blatant as knowingly telling a lie or making a promise with no intention of performance. For example, you are showing your apartment and a prospective tenant asks if there is frequent bus service nearby. There isn't, but you say, "Yes," as you sense this is important and want to rent the apartment. The prospective tenant rents the apartment, relying on this information from you, and moves in. The next day he calls and says that there is no public transportation and he wants to break the rental agreement immediately. Because mutual agreement was lacking, the tenant can **rescind** (cancel) the contract and get his money back.

Fraud can also result from failing to disclose important information, thereby inducing someone to accept an offer. For example, the day you show your apartment to a prospective tenant the weather is dry. But you know that during a heavy rainstorm the tenant's automobile parking stall becomes a lake of water 6 inches deep. This would qualify as a fraud if the prospective tenant was not made aware of it before agreeing to the rental contract. Once again, the law will permit the aggrieved party to rescind the contract. However, the tenant does not have to rescind the contract. If he likes the other features of the apartment enough, he can elect to live with the flooded parking stall.

If a real estate agent commits a fraud to make a sale and the deceived party later rescinds the sales contract, not only is the commission lost, but explanations will be necessary to the other parties of the contract and perhaps to state license law officials.

Innocent misrepresentation differs from fraud (intentional misrepresentation) in that the party providing the wrong information is not doing so to deceive another for the purpose of reaching an agreement. To illustrate, suppose that over the past year you have observed that city buses stop near your apartment building. If you tell a prospective tenant that there is bus service, only to learn the day after the tenant moves in that service stopped last week, this is innocent misrepresentation. Although there was no dishonesty involved, the tenant still has the right to rescind the contract. If performance has not begun on the contract (in this case the tenant has not moved in), the injured party may give notice that he **disaffirms** (revokes) the contract. However, if the tenant wants to break

Innocent
Misrepresentation

the contract, he must do so in a timely manner; otherwise the law will presume that the situation is satisfactory to the tenant.

Mistake

Mistake as applied to contract law has a very narrow meaning. It does not include innocent misrepresentation nor does it include ignorance, inability, or poor judgment. If a person enters into a contract that he later regrets because he did not investigate it thoroughly enough, or because it did not turn out to be beneficial, the law will not grant relief to him on the grounds of mistake, even though he may now consider it was a "mistake" to have made the contract in the first place. Mistake as used in contract law arises from ambiguity in negotiations and mistake of material fact. For example, you offer to sell your mountain cabin to an acquaintance. He has never seen your cabin, and you give him instructions on how to get there to look at it. He returns and accepts your offer. However, he made a wrong turn and the cabin he looked at was not your cabin. A week later he discovers his error. The law considers this ambiguity in negotiations. In this case the buyer, in his mind, was purchasing a different cabin than the seller was selling; therefore, there is no mutual agreement and any contract signed is void.

To illustrate a mistake of fact, suppose that you show your apartment to a prospective tenant and tell him that he must let you know by tomorrow if he wants to rent it. The next day he visits you and together you enter into a rental contract. Although neither of you is aware of it, there has just been a serious fire in the apartment. Since a fire-gutted apartment is not what the two of you had in mind when the rental contract was signed, there is no mutual agreement.

Occasionally, "mistake of law" will be claimed as grounds for relief from a contract. However, mistake as to one's legal rights in a contract is not generally accepted by courts of law unless it is coupled with a mistake of fact. Ignorance of the law is not considered a mistake.

Mutual agreement also requires that the parties express **contractual intent.** This means that their intention is to be bound by the agreement, thus precluding jokes or jests from becoming valid contracts.

The last requirement of mutual agreement is that the offer and acceptance be genuine and freely given. **Duress** (use of force), **menace** (threat of violence), or **undue influence** (unfair advantage) cannot be used to obtain agreement. The law permits a contract made under any of these conditions to be revoked by the aggrieved party.

Lawful Objective

To be enforceable, a contract cannot call for the breaking of laws. The reason is that a court of law cannot be called upon to enforce a contract that requires that a law be broken. Such a contract is void, or if already in operation, it is unenforceable in a court of law. For example, a debt contract requiring interest rates in excess of those allowed by state law would be void. If the borrower had started repaying the debt and then later stopped, the lender would not be able to look to the courts to enforce collection of the balance. Contracts contrary to good morals and general public policy are also unenforceable.

Consideration

For an agreement to be enforceable, contract laws require that the parties to the agreement exchange valuable or good consideration. **Valuable consideration** is money, property, legal rights, services, promises to forbear, or anything worth money. The legal philosophy is that a person cannot promise to do something of value for another without receiving in turn some form of consideration. Stated in another way, each must give up something; i.e., each must suffer a detriment. In most real estate contracts this is the exchange of money for title to property, rights to use property, or services. Examples are a purchase contract, a rental contract, and a listing agreement, respectively.

If a person wishes to give something of value to a friend or loved one, the courts have ruled that, although love and affection is not valuable consideration in the monetary definition, it is nonetheless **good consideration.** As such it fulfills the requirement of consideration. As long as there is consideration, be it valuable or good, the courts will not look into the sufficiency of the consideration unless there is evidence of fraud, duress, threat, or undue influence. For instance, if a man gave away his property or sold it very cheaply to keep it from his creditors, the creditors could ask the courts to set aside those transfers.

Contract in Writing   Certain types of contracts must be in writing in order to be enforceable in a court of law. With regard to real estate transactions, any agreement that has to do with the purchase or sale of title to real property must be in writing to be enforceable. This includes such things as offers, acceptances, binders, land contracts, deeds, escrows, and options to purchase. Commission agreements, mortgages, trust deeds and their accompanying bonds and notes, and the promise to answer for the debt of another must also be in writing. Agreements that will not be executed within 1 year, such as a lease for 1 year or more, must also be in writing to be enforceable in a court of law. With regard to personal property contracts, a written and signed agreement is required if the value to be exchanged is more than a specified amount, such as $500. A contract that is required to be in writing and is not is unenforceable in a court of law.

The most common real estate contract that does not need to be in writing to be enforceable is a month-to-month rental agreement that can be terminated by either landlord or tenant on 1-month notice. Nonetheless, most are in writing, because people tend to forget verbal promises. While the unhappy party can go to court, the judge may have a difficult time determining what verbal promises were made, particularly if there were no witnesses other than the parties to the agreement. Hence, it is advisable to put all important contracts in writing and for each party to recognize the agreement by signing it. It is also customary to date written contracts, although most can be enforced without showing the date the agreement was reached.

A written contract will supersede an oral one. Thus, if two parties verbally promise one thing and then write and sign something else, the written contract will prevail. This fact has been the basis for many complaints against overzealous real estate agents who make verbal promises that do not appear anywhere in the written sales contract.

Under certain circumstances the **parol evidence rule** permits oral evidence to complete an otherwise incomplete or ambiguous written contract. However, the application of this rule is quite narrow. If a contract is complete and clear in its intent, the courts presume that what the parties put into writing is what they agreed upon.

Having made a valid contract, the parties involved are expected to carry out their respective contractual duties. While the contract is in the process of being completed, it is called **executory.** When all contract duties are completed, the contract is said to be **executed.**

PERFORMANCE AND DISCHARGE OF CONTRACTS

Most contracts are discharged by being fully performed by the contracting parties in accordance with the contract terms. However, alternatives are open to the parties of the contract. One is to sell or otherwise **assign** the contract to another party. Unless prohibited by the contract, rights, benefits, and obligations under a contract can be assigned to someone else. The original party to the contract, however, still remains ultimately liable for its performance. Note, too, that an assignment is a contract in itself and must meet all the essential contract requirements to be enforceable. A common example of an assignment occurs when a lessee wants to move out and sells his lease to another party. When a contract creates a personal obligation, such as a listing agreement with a broker, an assignment may not be made.

A contract can also be performed by **novation.** Novation occurs when a new contract and/or a new party are substituted for an existing one, as when a buyer assumes a seller's loan, and the lender releases the seller from the loan contract. This differs from assignment in that the departing party is released from the obligation to complete the contract.

When a contract is only partially performed and it appears that there will be no further performance, two alternatives are open. The first is to accept **partial performance** as satisfactory discharge of the contract. To illustrate, a painting contractor agrees with a homeowner to paint his house for $800. The house is painted, but before the $800 is paid the homeowner complains that the painters damaged $100 worth of landscaping with their ladders. The contractor agrees to settle the issue by accepting $700 as full payment for the job.

The second alternative is to agree to **money damages** for the unfulfilled part of the contract. For example, a retail store plans to offer a large selection of Christmas decorations and contracts in advance with a nearby warehouse to keep the decorations as they arrive from the manufacturers. If later the warehouse owner substitutes a warehouse that is farther away, the retail owner may accept the new location plus a monetary adjustment to cover the trouble and expense of the extra hauling involved.

If the objective of the contract becomes legally impossible to accomplish, the law will consider the contract discharged. For example, a new legislative statute may forbid what the contract originally intended. If the parties mutually agree to cancel their contract before it is executed, this too is a form of discharge. For instance, you sign a 5-year lease to pay $500 per month for an office. Three years later you find a better location and want to move. Meanwhile, rents for similar offices in your building have increased to $575 per month. Under these conditions the landlord might be happy to agree to cancel your lease.

If one of the contracting parties dies, the contract is considered discharged if it called for some specific act that only the dead person could have performed. For example, if you hired a free-lance gardener to tend your landscaping and he died, the contract would be discharged. However, if your contract was with a firm that employed other gardeners who could do the job, the contract would still be valid. Damage to the premises may also discharge the agreement. As a case in point, it is common in real estate sales contracts to provide that the contract is deemed canceled if the property is destroyed or substantially damaged before title passes. However, if the damage is minor and promptly repaired by the seller, the contract would still be valid.

BREACH OF When one party fails to perform as required by a con-
CONTRACT tract and the law does not recognize the reason for failure to be a valid excuse, there is a **breach of contract.** The wronged

or innocent party has four alternatives: (1) accept the breach and consider the contract ended, (2) rescind the contract unilaterally, (3) sue for specific performance, or (4) sue for money damages. Let us consider each of these.

The innocent party may decide to accept the breach because there may not be a great deal at stake or because the innocent party feels that the time and effort to sue would not be worth the rewards. Suppose that you contracted with a roofing repairman to fix your roof for $400. When he was finished you paid him. But a week later you discover a spot that he had agreed to fix, but missed. After many futile phone calls, you accept the breach and consider the contract discharged, because it is easier to fix the spot yourself than to keep pursuing the repairman.

Under certain circumstances, the innocent party can **unilaterally rescind** a contract. That is, the innocent party can take the position that if the other party is not going to perform his obligations, then the innocent party will not either. An example would be a rent strike in retaliation to a landlord who fails to keep the premises habitable. Unilateral rescission should be resorted to only after consulting an attorney.

Specific Performance

The innocent party may sue in a court of equity to force the breaching party to carry out the remainder of the contract. For example, you make an offer to purchase a parcel of land and the seller accepts. A written contract is prepared and signed by both of you. If you carry out all your obligations under the contract, but the seller changes his mind and refuses to deliver title to you, you may bring a lawsuit against the seller for **specific performance.** If you win your lawsuit, the court will force the seller to deliver title to you as specified in the contract. In reviewing your suit, the court will determine if the contract is valid and legal, if you have carried out your duties to the contract, and if the contract is just and reasonable.

Money Damages

If the damages to the innocent party can be reasonably expressed in terms of money, the innocent party can sue for

money damages. For example, you rent an apartment to a tenant. As part of the rental contract you furnish the refrigerator and freezer unit. While the tenant is on vacation, the unit breaks down and $200 worth of frozen meat and other perishables spoil. Since your obligation under the contract is to provide the tenant with a working refrigerator–freezer, the tenant can sue you for $200 in money damages. He can also recover interest on the money awarded to him from the day of the loss to the day you reimburse him.

Comparison   Note the difference between suing for money damages and suing for specific performance. When money can be used to restore one's position (such as the tenant who can buy $200 worth of fresh food), a suit for money damages is appropriate. In situations where money cannot provide an adequate remedy, and this is often the case in real estate because no two properties are exactly alike, specific performance is appropriate. Notice, too, that the mere existence of the legal rights of the wronged party is often enough to gain cooperation. In the case of the tenant, you would give him the value of the lost food before spending time and money in court to hear a judge tell you to do the same thing. A threat of a lawsuit will often bring the desired results if the defendent knows that the law will side with the wronged party. The cases that do go to court are usually those in which the identity of the wronged party and/or the extent of the damages is not clear.

Liquidated Damages   The parties to a contract may decide in advance the amount of damages to be paid in the event either party breaches the contract. An example is an offer to purchase real estate that includes a statement to the effect that, once the seller accepts the offer, if the buyer fails to complete the purchase, the seller may keep the buyer's deposit (earnest money) as **liquidated damages.** If a broker is involved, the seller and broker usually agree to divide the damages, thus compensating the broker for his time and effort. Another case of liquidated damage occurs when a builder promises to finish a building by a certain date or pay the party that hired him a certain number of dollars per day until it is completed. This impresses upon the builder the need for prompt completion and compensates the property owner for losses due to the delay.

The **statute of limitations** limits by law the amount of time a wronged party has to seek the aid of a court in obtaining justice. The aggrieved party must start legal proceedings within a certain period of time or the courts will not help him. The amount of time varies from state to state and by type of legal action involved. However, time limits of 3 to 7 years are typical for breach of contract.

STATUTE OF LIMITATIONS

As was pointed out at the beginning of this chapter, one can incur contractual obligations by implication as well as by oral or written contracts. Home builders and real estate agents provide two timely examples. For many years, if a homeowner discovered poor design or workmanship after he had bought a new home, it was the buyer's problem. The philosophy was **caveat emptor,** let the buyer beware before he buys. Today, courts of law find that in building a home and offering it for sale, the builder simultaneously implies that it is fit for living. Thus, if a builder installs a toilet in a bathroom, the implication is that it will work.

IMPLIED OBLIGATIONS

Similarly, real estate agent trade organizations, such as the National Association of Realtors and state and local Realtor associations, are constantly working to elevate the status of real estate brokers and salesmen to that of a competent professional in the public's mind. But as professional status is gained, there is an implied obligation to dispense professional-quality service. Thus, an individual agent will find himself not only responsible for acting in accordance with written laws, but will also be held responsible for being competent and knowledgeable in his field. Once recognized as a professional by the public, the real estate agent will not be able to plead ignorance.

In view of the present trend towards consumer protection, it appears that the concept of "Let the buyer beware" is being replaced with "Let the seller (and his agent) beware."

VOCABULARY REVIEW   *Match terms a–q with statements 1–17.*

a. *Assign*
b. *Breach*
c. *Competent party*
d. *Contract*
e. *Counteroffer*
f. *Duress*
g. *Executory*
h. *Forbear*
i. *Liquidated damages*

j. *Minor*
k. *Money damages*
l. *Offeror*
m. *Rescind*
n. *Specific performance*
o. *Statute of limitations*
p. *Unilateral contract*
q. *Void contract*

1. A legally enforceable agreement to do (or not to do) something.
2. A contract in which one party makes a promise or begins performance without first receiving any promise to perform from the other.
3. Not to act.
4. A person who is considered legally capable of entering into a contract.
5. A person who is not old enough to enter into legally binding contracts.
6. A contract that is not legally binding on any of the parties that made it.
7. The party who makes an offer.
8. An offer made in response to an offer.
9. To cancel a contract and restore the parties involved to their respective positions before the contract was made.
10. Use of force to obtain contract agreement.
11. A contract that is in the process of being carried out.
12. To transfer one's rights in a contract to another person.
13. Damages that can be measured in and compensated by money.
14. Failure, without legal excuse, to perform any promise called for in a contract.
15. Contract performance according to the precise terms agreed upon.
16. A sum of money called for in a contract that is to be paid if the contract is breached.
17. Laws that set forth the period of time within which a lawsuit must be filed.

QUESTIONS AND   1. What is the difference between an expressed contract and
PROBLEMS   an implied contract? Give an example of each.
2. Name the five requirements of a legally valid contract.

3. What is the difference between a void contract and a void-able contract?
4. Give four examples of persons not considered legally competent to enter into contracts.
5. How can an offer be terminated prior to its acceptance?
6. What does the word "mistake" mean when applied to contract law?
7. Why must consideration be present for a legally binding contract to exist? Give examples of three types of consideration.
8. If a contract is legally unenforceable, are the parties to the contract stopped from performing it? Why or why not?
9. If a breach of contract occurs, what alternatives are open to the parties to the contract?
10. Assume that a breach of contract has occurred and the wronged party intends to file a lawsuit over the matter. What factors would he consider in deciding whether to sue for money damages or for specific performance?

ADDITIONAL READINGS

Deming, Richard. *Man Against Man*. New York: Hawthorn Books, 1972, 210 pages. Written to explain in as clear and interesting terms as possible how civil law works in the United States. Includes the role of civil courts, steps in litigation, and procedures to enforce judgments.

Farmer, Robert A., and Associates. *What You Should Know About Contracts*. New York: Arco, 1969, 173 pages. A guide to contract law written for the layman. Outlines requirements for a valid contract, how to interpret a contract, remedies for contract breach, and contract dissolution.

Hogue, Arthur R. *Origins of the Common Law*. Bloomington, Ind.: Indiana University Press, 1966, 276 pages. Provides a fascinating historical review of the origins of common law in England and how it became transplanted to the United States to serve as the basis for so many U.S. laws.

Loeb, Robert H., Jr. *Your Legal Rights as a Minor*. New York: Franklin Watts, 1974, 154 pages. Discusses special legal restrictions and privileges that pertain to minors including their rights in commercial transactions and the ownership of real and personal property.

Semenow, Robert W. *Selected Cases in Real Estate*. Englewood Cliffs, N.J.: Prentice-Hall, 1973, 638 pages. Discussion and actual legal cases pertaining to contract rescission are found on pages 537–585.

8

Real Estate Sales Contracts

"As is": said of property offered for sale in its present condition with no guaranty nor warranty of quality provided by the seller

Binder: a short purchase contract used in certain states to hold a real estate transaction together until a more formal contract can be signed

Closing: the day on which title is conveyed; also refers to the process and paperwork between signing the purchase contract and conveying title

Default: failure to perform a legal duty; such as failure to carry out the terms of a contract

Deposit receipt: a receipt given for a deposit that accompanies an offer to purchase; also refers to a purchase contract that includes a deposit receipt

Earnest money deposit: money that accompanies an offer to purchase as evidence of good faith

Escrow company: a firm that specializes in handling the details of a transaction once a contract has been made

Installment contract: a method of selling and financing property whereby the buyer obtains possession but the seller retains the title

Pro-rate: to apportion ongoing income and expense items when a property is sold

"Time is of the essence": means that the time limits of a contract must be faithfully observed

Contracts are essential to nearly every aspect of real estate. Real estate mortgages (discussed in Chapter 9) are contracts between borrowers and lenders. Listing agreements (discussed in Chapter 18) are contracts that create an agency relationship between a real estate broker and a property owner. Leases and rental agreements (discussed in Chapter 22) are contracts between lessors and lessees.

The present chapter will focus on contracts used to initiate the sale or exchange of real estate. Specifically, we shall look at the binder, then at the purchase contract, and at the exchange agreement, and finally at the installment contract.

PURPOSE OF SALES
CONTRACTS

What is the purpose of a real estate sales contract? If a buyer and a seller agree on a price, why can't the buyer hand the seller the necessary money and the seller simultaneously hand the buyer a deed? The main reason is that the buyer needs time to ascertain that the seller is, in fact, legally capable of conveying title. To protect himself, the buyer will enter into a written and signed contract with the seller, stating that the purchase price will be paid only after title has been searched and found to be in satisfactory condition. The seller in turn agrees to deliver a deed to the buyer when the buyer has paid his money. A contract also gives the buyer time to arrange financing and to specify how such matters as taxes, mortgage debts, existing leases, and fire insurance on the property will be discharged.

A properly prepared contract commits each party to its terms. Once a sales contract is in writing and signed, the seller cannot suddenly change his mind and sell his property to another person. He is obligated to convey title to the buyer when the buyer has performed everything required of him by the contract. Likewise, the buyer must carry out his promises, including paying for the property, provided the seller has done everything required by the contract.

CONTRACT
PREPARATION

In some areas of the United States, notably the northeastern states, real estate sales contracts are prepared almost exclusively by attorneys. In other states, real estate agents prepare a wide variety of sales contracts for their clients by using preprinted forms available from banks, title companies, real estate associations, escrow companies, and stationery stores. The agent fills in the purchase price, down payment, and other terms of the transaction. Why are there two different approaches? All states prohibit the practice of law by anyone except attorneys. Courts and bar associations in some states interpret this to include the filling in of blank spaces on preprinted contract forms by real estate agents for their clients. The reasoning is that an attorney, being a specialist in law, is the best-qualified person to prepare a contract. Courts and bar associations in states that permit the broad use of preprinted contract forms reason that the printed form was prepared by an attorney and the real estate agent is adding only a few specific facts as they apply to a particular transaction.

The difference in who prepares the sales contract is very important. Where real estate agents are given wide latitude in the use of preprinted contract forms, a valuable psychological advantage is gained. The moment a buyer and seller agree to a sale, the agent can prepare a formal binding contract and have it signed before either party changes his mind. The major negative aspect of preprinted forms is that the blank spaces still leave considerable room for error.

THE BINDER

In localities where real estate agents do not prepare the formal purchase contract, once a buyer and seller have agreed upon the terms of the sale, it is customary to arrange a meeting at the office of the seller's attorney. In attendance are the seller and his attorney, the buyer and his attorney, and the agents responsible for bringing about the sale. Together they prepare a written contract, which the buyer and seller sign. As it may take several days to arrange this meeting, a psychological disadvantage occurs: the buyer or seller may have second thoughts about the transaction and refuse to attend the contract meeting. The need to "get something on paper" to hold a deal together until the formal contract meeting has resulted in the binder. In the **binder** the buyer and seller agree in writing on price and terms and to meet at a later date to draw up a more formal contract. The binder is prepared by the real estate agent, who asks the buyer and seller to sign it as soon as an agreement is reached. A sample binder is illustrated in Figure 8:1.

While it is easy to play down the binder because it is to be replaced by "a more formal contract," it does, nonetheless, meet all the requirements of a legally binding contract. In the absence of a more formal contract, it can be used to enforce completion of a sale by a buyer or seller. Referring to Figure 8:1, notice that the binder starts out as a unilateral contract in which the purchaser offers to buy the seller's property. The

Figure 8:1

BINDER

THIS AGREEMENT *made and entered into between*
①_____ *, as Seller,*
and the undersigned as Purchaser. Purchaser agrees to purchase
_____②_____
at the price of $ _____③_____ *, with a deposit of*
$ ___④_____ *, receipt of which is hereby acknowledged,*
and $ _____⑤_____ *when a more formal contract, such*
as is used by Title Companies, is signed by Seller and Pur-
chaser, which is to be signed on or about _____⑥_____ *,*
19__ , at _____ *. The*
*Purchaser agrees to pay $*_____⑦_____ *, cash at closing, and*
$ ____⑧____ *by assuming and agreeing to pay mortgage*
for that amount now on subject property. The balance of
$ ___⑨___ *is to be paid by Purchaser as follows:* _____
_____⑩_____
_____
_____
_____ *. In the event the Seller is*
not willing to accept the above price and terms, the deposit
is to be promptly returned. In the event the Seller accepts
and the Purchaser does not comply, the deposit shall be
*forfeited.*⑪
_____
_____⑫_____
_____
This agreement is approved and accepted by the Seller, who
agrees to pay _____⑬_____ *,*
licensed real estate broker, _____⑭_____ *%*
of the purchase price as commission.

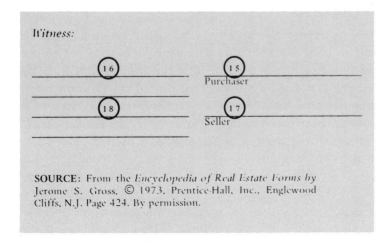

Witness:

_____ (16)

_____ (15)
Purchaser

_____ (18)

_____ (17)
Seller

_____

SOURCE: From the *Encyclopedia of Real Estate Forms* by Jerome S. Gross. © 1973. Prentice-Hall, Inc., Englewood Cliffs, N.J. Page 424. By permission.

blank space at ① is for the name of the seller, and at ② the legal description of the property is given. Number ③ states the price the purchaser is willing to pay for the property.

It is customary for the purchaser to make a deposit ④ in the form of cash or a check. Sometimes a promissory note in favor of the seller is used. The purpose of the deposit is twofold: it shows the serious intent of the purchaser's offer, and it gives the seller something for his time and trouble if he accepts and the buyer fails to complete his part of the agreement. This forfeiture provision is located at ⑪.

Provision for A Formal Contract

At ⑤, the purchaser agrees to increase his deposit if the offer is accepted and to meet with the seller at an agreed time and place ⑥ to sign a more formal contract. This allows time for an attorney to prepare a more detailed contract for the buyer and seller to sign. If the seller's attorney writes the formal contract the contract will favor the seller at every possible opportunity. This is only logical. The seller's attorney is expected to protect the seller's best interests at all times. The purchaser, to protect his interests, should not rely on the seller's attorney at the contract meeting, but should bring his own attorney.

Lines ⑦ to ⑩ deal with how the purchaser proposes to pay the remaining difference between the deposit already made and the purchase price being offered. More specifically, at ⑦ the purchaser states how much additional down payment he will make, and at ⑧ he shows how much existing debt against the property he will assume from the seller. If additional financing is needed, the amount is inserted at ⑨ and the buyer proposes how he will obtain it at ⑩. The blank lines at ⑫ provide space for anything not covered by the printed part of the binder. For example, if the purchaser wanted the seller to include his furniture in the sales price, a statement to that effect would be inserted at ⑫.

At ⑮, the purchaser signs the binder. In some localities it is customary to have the purchaser's signature witnessed at ⑯. Once signed, the binder is delivered to the seller. If the seller agrees to the offer, lines ⑬ and ⑭ dealing with the brokerage commission that the seller will pay are completed, and the seller signs at ⑰. Where witnesses are required, they sign at ⑱.

If the seller refuses the offer, he has the choice of making a written counteroffer or refusing and waiting for another offer. To keep negotiations alive, the real estate agent will usually recommend that a counteroffer be made. For example, a seller lists his property with a broker at a price of $70,000. A buyer offers $66,000. The seller refuses, but counters by offering to take $68,000. The buyer can either accept, refuse, or counter again, say for $67,000. This continues until the buyer and seller either refuse to negotiate further or are in agreement on the price and all other aspects of the binder.

Additional Negotiation

The binder's major weakness, and one to be well aware of, is in what the binder *does not say*. In its apparent simplicity, the binder leaves open much room for future argument. To illustrate, consider the problem of termites. The binder shown makes no mention of a termite inspection, nor does it say who is to pay for repairs and extermination if termites are present. Unless an agreement on this matter is written in at ⑫ on the binder, the question must be resolved later at the formal contract meeting. If at the meeting the buyer's attorney, wishing to protect his client's interests, asks for inspection, extermination, and repairs at the expense of the seller, and the seller agrees, there is no problem. But if the seller does not want to incur the expense of the inspection and/or is fearful of finding termites and termite damage, he may take the position that, since the purchaser did not mention termites in the binder, the property is to be sold "as is."

The binder makes no mention of the type of deed that the seller will deliver to the buyer. The buyer may ask for a warranty deed at the formal contract meeting. However, the seller may be planning to convey title using a bargain and sale deed. In some states a seller is not obligated to deliver a warranty deed unless he so agreed.

Although the preprinted part of the binder calls for a closing, it does not state when the closing will be or when the buyer may take possession, nor does it address the problem of closing delays. The buyer may be anxious to close and take possession as quickly as possible, while the seller may want more time. Unless these points and others can be resolved at the formal contract meeting, a dilemma results.

The binder is a binding contract wherein the buyer agrees to buy and the seller agrees to sell. Yet if a more formal and detailed contract cannot be agreed upon, how is the sale to be completed? Certainly, the buyer will wonder if his refusal to meet all the seller's demands at the contract meeting will result in the loss of his deposit money. If a stalemate develops, the courts may be asked to decide the termite question, deed type, closing date, and any other unresolved points. However, because this is costly and time consuming for all involved, there is give-and-take negotiation at the contract meeting. If a completely unnegotiable impasse is reached, as a practical matter the binder is usually rescinded by the buyer and seller and the buyer's deposit returned.

THE PURCHASE CONTRACT

The alternative to the two-step process of a binder followed by a more formal contract is to eliminate the binder and prepare a formal contract at the outset. Variously known as a purchase contract, deposit receipt, offer and acceptance, purchase offer, or purchase and sales agreement, these preprinted forms contain four key parts: (1) provision for the buyer's earnest money deposit, (2) the buyer's offer to pur-

Figure 8:2

REAL ESTATE PURCHASE CONTRACT

(1)

City of _____Riverdale_____ , State of _____ ,

October 10, 19— (2)

(3) Samson Byers _____ *(herein called the Buyer) agrees*

to purchase and (4) William and Sarah Ohner _____ *(herein*

called the Seller) agree to sell the following described real

property located in the City of (5) Riverdale _____ , *County*

of _____Lakeside_____ , *State of* _____ .

a single-family dwelling commonly known as 1704 Main

Street , *and legally described as* Lot 21, Block C of Madi-

son's Subdivision as per map in Survey Book 10, page 51, in

the Office of the County Recorder of said County .

(6) *The total purchase price is* forty-five thousand

Dollars ($45,000.00) , *payable as follows.* One thousand

dollars ($1,000.00) is given today as an earnest money

deposit, receipt of which is hereby acknowledged. An addi-

tional $7,000.00 is to be placed into escrow by the Buyer

before the closing date. The remaining $37,000.00 is to be by

way of a new mortgage on said property .

(7) *Seller will deliver to the Buyer a* warranty *deed to*

said property. Seller will furnish to the Buyer at the Seller's

expense a standard American Land Title Association title

insurance policy issued by First Security Title *Company*

showing title vested in the Buyer and that the Seller is con-

veying title free of liens, encumbrances, easements, rights and

conditions except as follows: People's Gas and Electric Com-

pany utility easement along eastern five feet of lot .

(8) *The escrow agent shall be* First Security Title Com-

pany *and escrow instructions shall be signed by the Buyer*

and Seller and delivered to escrow within five days upon

Figure 8:2 *continued*

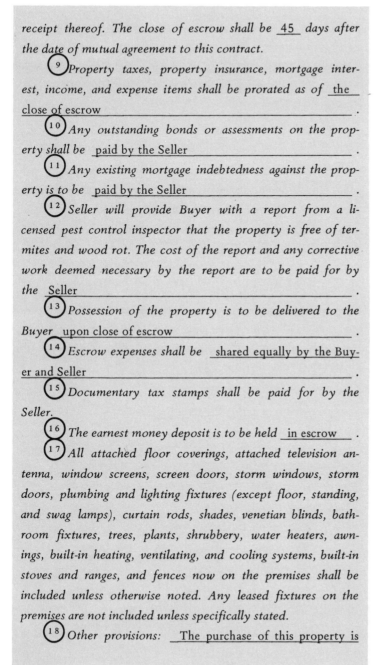

receipt thereof. The close of escrow shall be __45__ days after the date of mutual agreement to this contract.

(9) Property taxes, property insurance, mortgage interest, income, and expense items shall be prorated as of _the close of escrow_ .

(10) Any outstanding bonds or assessments on the property shall be _paid by the Seller_ .

(11) Any existing mortgage indebtedness against the property is to be _paid by the Seller_ .

(12) Seller will provide Buyer with a report from a licensed pest control inspector that the property is free of termites and wood rot. The cost of the report and any corrective work deemed necessary by the report are to be paid for by the _Seller_ .

(13) Possession of the property is to be delivered to the Buyer _upon close of escrow_ .

(14) Escrow expenses shall be _shared equally by the Buyer and Seller_ .

(15) Documentary tax stamps shall be paid for by the Seller.

(16) The earnest money deposit is to be held _in escrow_ .

(17) All attached floor coverings, attached television antenna, window screens, screen doors, storm windows, storm doors, plumbing and lighting fixtures (except floor, standing, and swag lamps), curtain rods, shades, venetian blinds, bathroom fixtures, trees, plants, shrubbery, water heaters, awnings, built-in heating, ventilating, and cooling systems, built-in stoves and ranges, and fences now on the premises shall be included unless otherwise noted. Any leased fixtures on the premises are not included unless specifically stated.

(18) Other provisions: _The purchase of this property is_

Figure 8:2 *continued*

subject to the Buyer obtaining a mortgage loan on this property in the amount of $37,000 or more, with a maturity date of at least 25 years, at an interest rate no higher than 9½% per year and loan fees not to exceed two points. Purchase price to include the refrigerator currently on the premises. Purchase is subject to buyer's approval of a qualified building inspector's report. Report to be obtained within 7 days at Buyer's expense.

(19) *If the improvements on the property are destroyed or materially damaged prior to the close of escrow, or if the Buyer is unable to obtain financing as stated herein, or if the Seller is unable to deliver title as promised, then the Buyer, at his option, may terminate this agreement and the deposit made by him shall be returned to him in full. If the Seller fails to fulfill any of the other agreements made herein, the Buyer may terminate this agreement with full refund of deposit, accept lesser performance, or sue for specific performance.*

(20) *If this purchase is not completed by reason of the Buyer's default, the seller is released from his obligation to sell to the Buyer and shall retain the deposit money as his sole right to damages.*

(21) *Upon the signature of the Buyer, this document becomes an offer to the Seller to purchase the property described herein. The Seller has until* 11:00 p.m., October 13, 19 ____ *to indicate acceptance of this offer by signing and delivering it to the Buyer. If acceptance is not received by that time, this offer shall be deemed revoked and the deposit shall be returned in full to the Buyer.*

(22) *Time is of the essence in this contract.*

Real Estate Broker Riverdale Realty Company

By **Ima D. Salesman**

Address 1234 Riverdale Blvd. (23) *Telephone* 333-1234

(24) *The undersigned offers and agrees to buy the above described property on the terms and conditions stated herein and acknowledges receipt of a copy hereof.*

Buyer ___**Samson Byers**___

Address ___2323 Cedar Ave., Riverdale___

Telephone ___666-2468___

Acceptance

(25) *The undersigned accepts the foregoing offer and agrees to sell the property described above on the terms and conditions set forth.*

(26) *The undersigned has employed* ___Lakeside Realty Company___ *as Broker and for Broker's services agrees to pay said Broker as commission the sum of* ___twenty-seven hundred___ -------------------- *dollars* ($2,700.00) *payable upon recordation of the deed or if completion of this sale is prevented by the Seller. If completion of this contract is prevented by the Buyer, Broker shall share equally in any damages collected by the Seller, not to exceed the above stated commission.*

(27) *The undersigned acknowledges receipt of a copy hereof.*

Seller ___**Sarah Ohner**___

Seller ___**William Ohner**___

Address ___1704 Tenth St., Riverdale___

Telephone ___333-3579___ Date ___10/10/——___

Notification of Acceptance

(28) *Receipt of a copy of the foregoing agreement is hereby acknowledged.*

Buyer ___**Samson Byers**___ Date ___10/11/___

chase, (3) the acceptance of the offer by the seller, and (4) provisions for the payment of a brokerage commission. Taken together, these form a binding purchase contract that is meant to include all the details found in a more formal contract.

Figure 8:2 illustrates in simplified language the highlights of a real estate purchase contract.* The purchase contract begins at ① and ② by identifying the location and date of the deposit and offer. At ③, the name of the buyer is written, and at ④, the name of the property owner (seller). At ⑤, the property for which the buyer is making his offer is described. Although the street address and type of property (in this case a house) are not necessary to the validity of the contract, this information is often included for convenience in locating the property. The legal description that follows is crucial. Care must be taken to make certain that it is correct.

Deposit Money

The price that the buyer is willing to pay, along with the manner in which he proposes to pay it, is inserted at ⑥. Of particular importance in this paragraph is the **earnest money deposit** that the buyer submits with his offer. With the exception of court-ordered sales, no laws govern the size of the deposit or even the need for one. Generally speaking though, the seller and his agent will want a reasonably substantial deposit to show the buyer's earnest intentions and to have something for their trouble if the seller accepts and the buyer fails to follow through. The buyer will prefer to make as small a deposit as possible, as a deposit ties up his capital and there is the possibility of losing it. However, the buyer also recognizes that the seller may refuse to even consider the offer unless accompanied by a reasonable deposit. In most parts of the country, a deposit of $500 to $2,000 on a $45,000 offer would be considered acceptable. In court-ordered sales, the required deposit is usually 10% of the offering price.

---

*This illustration has been prepared for discussion purposes only and not as a form to copy and use in a real estate sale. For that purpose, the reader should obtain a contract specifically prepared for his state.

At ⑦, the buyer asks the seller to convey title by means of a warranty deed and to provide and pay for a policy of title insurance showing the condition of title to be as described here. Before the offer is made, the broker and seller will tell the buyer about the condition of title. However, the buyer has no way of verifying that information until the title is actually searched. To protect himself, the buyer states at ⑦ the condition of title that he is willing to accept. If title to the property is not presently in this condition, the seller is required by the contract to take whatever steps are necessary to place title in this condition before the close of escrow. If, for example, there is an existing mortgage or judgment lien against the property, the seller must have it removed. If there are other owners, their interests must be extinguished. If anyone has a right to use the property (such as a tenant under a lease), or controls the use of the property (such as a deed restriction), or has an easement, other than what is specifically mentioned, the seller must remove these before conveying title to the buyer.

Deed and Title Condition

In a growing number of states, escrow agents (described in more detail in Chapter 14) handle the details of a sale once the buyer and seller have signed a purchase agreement. Number ⑧ names the escrow agent, states that the escrow instructions must be signed promptly, and sets the closing date for the transaction. It is on that date that the seller will receive his money and the buyer, his deed. The selection of a closing date is based on the estimated length of time necessary to carry out the conditions of the purchase contract. Normally, the most time consuming item is finding a lender to make the necessary mortgage loan. Typically, this takes from 30 to 60 days, depending on the lender and the availability of loan money. The other conditions of the contract, such as the title search and arrangements to pay off any existing liens, take less time and can be done while arranging for a new mortgage loan. Once a satisfactory loan source is found, the lender makes a commitment to the buyer that the needed loan money will be placed into escrow on the closing date. In regions of

Closing Agent

the United States where the custom is to use a closing meeting rather than an escrow, this section of the contract would name the attorney, broker, or other person responsible for carrying out the paperwork and details of the purchase agreement. A date would also be set for the closing meeting at which the buyer and seller and their attorneys, the lender, and the title company representative would be present to conclude the transaction.

Prorating   Number ⑨ deals with the question of how ongoing property expenses, such as property taxes, insurance, and mortgage interest, will be divided between the buyer and the seller. For example, if the seller pays $160 in advance for a 1-year fire insurance policy and then sells his house halfway through the policy year, what happens to the remaining 6 months of coverage that the seller paid for but will not use? One solution is to "sell" the remaining six months of coverage to the buyer for $80. Income items are also prorated. Suppose that the seller has been renting the basement of his house to a college student for $60 per month. The student pays the $60 rent in advance on the first of each month. If the property is sold partway through the month, the buyer is entitled to the portion of the month's rent that is earned while he owns the property. This process of dividing ongoing expenses and income items is known as **prorating.** More information and examples regarding the prorating process are included in Chapter 14.

At ⑩, the buyer states that, if there are any unpaid assessment bonds currently against the property, the seller shall pay them as a condition of the sale. Alternatively, the buyer could agree to assume responsibility for paying them off. At ⑪, the buyer wants the property free of mortgages so that he can arrange for his own loan, and, therefore, asks the seller to remove any existing indebtedness. On the closing date, part of the money received from the buyer is used to clear the seller's debts against the property. Alternatively, the buyer could agree to assume responsibility for paying off the existing debt against the property as part of the purchase price.

At ⑫, the buyer asks that the property be inspected at the seller's expense for signs of termites and rotted wood (dry rot), and that the seller pay for extermination and repairs. The seller's decision of whether or not to accept an offer with this stipulation depends on his knowledge of the existence of these problems, how easily he thinks the property will sell, and whether or not at the price offered he could reasonably be expected to accept this condition. If the property is offered for sale as being in sound condition, a termite and wood rot clause is reasonable. If the property is being offered for sale on an "as is" basis with a price to match, the clause is not reasonable. If the seller is quite sure that there are no termites or wood rot, this condition would not be a major negotiating point, as the cost of an inspection without corrective work is a minor cost in a real estate transaction.

Termite Inspection

The date that actual physical possession of the property will be turned over to the buyer is inserted at ⑬. As a rule, this is the same day as the close of escrow. If the buyer needs possession sooner or the seller wants possession after the close of escrow, the usual procedure is to arrange for a separate rental agreement between the buyer and seller. Such an agreement produces fewer problems if the closing date is later changed or if the transaction falls through and the closing never occurs.

Possession

closing

At ⑭, the purchase contract calls for the buyer and seller to share escrow expenses equally. The buyer and seller could divide them differently if they mutually agreed. At ⑮, the seller is to pay for the documentary tax stamps placed on the deed that he delivers to the buyer. At ⑯, the buyer and seller agree as to where the buyer's deposit money is to be held pending the close of the transaction. It could be held by the escrow agent, the broker, the seller, or an attorney.

The paragraph at ⑰ is not absolutely essential to a valid real estate purchase contract, since what is considered real estate (and is therefore included in the price) and what is personal property (and is not included in the price) is a matter of law. However, because the buyer and seller may not be familiar with the legal definitions of real versus personal property, this information is often included to avoid misunderstandings. Moreover, such a paragraph can clarify whether or not an item like a storm window, which may or may not be real property depending on its design, is included in the purchase price. If it is not the intention of the buyer and seller that an item mentioned here be included, it is crossed out and initialed by them.

Loan Conditions   At ⑱, space is left for conditions and agreements not provided for elsewhere in the preprinted contract. To complete his purchase of this property the buyer must obtain a $37,000 loan. However, what if he agrees to the purchase but cannot get a loan? Rather than risk losing his deposit money, the buyer makes his offer subject to obtaining a $37,000 loan on the property. To further protect himself against having to accept a loan "at any price," he states the terms on which he must be able to borrow. The seller, of course, takes certain risks in accepting an offer subject to obtaining financing. If the buyer is unable to obtain financing on these terms, the seller will have to return the buyer's deposit and begin searching for another buyer. Meanwhile, the seller may have lost anywhere from a few days to a few weeks of selling time. But without such a condition buyers will hesitate to make an offer at all. The solution is for the seller to accept only those loan conditions that are reasonable in the light of current loan availability. For example, if loans on similar-type properties are available at 9% interest, the seller would not want to accept an offer subject to the buyer obtaining a $7\frac{1}{2}\%$ interest loan. The possibility is too remote. If the buyer's offer was subject to obtaining a loan at $9\frac{1}{2}\%$ interest or less, the probability of the transaction collapsing on this condition is greatly reduced. The same principle applies to the amount of loan needed, the number of years to maturity, and loan fees.

Additional Conditions   In the paragraph at ⑱, we also find that the buyer is asking the seller to include an item of personal property in the selling price. While technically a bill of sale is used for the sale of personal property, if the list of items is not long, it is often included in the real estate purchase contract. If the refrigerator was real property rather than personal, no mention would be required, as all real property falling within the descriptions at ⑤ and ⑰ is automatically included in the price. The third item in the paragraph at ⑱ gives the buyer an opportunity to have the property inspected by a professional building inspector. Most home buyers do not know what to look for in the way of structural defects that may soon require expensive repairs. Consequently, in the past several years property inspection clauses in purchase contracts have become more common. The cost of the inspection is borne by the buyer. The inspector's report should be completed as soon as possible so that the property can be returned to the market if the buyer does not approve the findings.

Property Damage

The paragraph at ⑲ sets forth conditions under which the buyer can free himself of his obligations under this contract and recover his deposit in full. It begins by addressing the question of property destruction between the contract signing and the closing date. Fire, wind, rain, earthquake, or other damage doe: occasionally occur during that period of time. Whose responsibility would it be to repair the damage, and could the buyer point to the damage as a legitimate reason for breaking the contract? It is reasonable for the buyer to expect that the property will be delivered to him in as good a condition as when he offered to buy it. Consequently, if there is major damage or destruction, the wording here gives the buyer the option of rescinding the contract and recovering his deposit in full. Note, however, that this clause does not prevent the buyer from accepting the damaged property or the seller from negotiating with the buyer to repair any damage in order to preserve the transaction.

Paragraph ⑲ also states that, if the buyer is unable to obtain financing as outlined at ⑱ or the seller is unable to convey title as stated at ⑦, the buyer can rescind the contract and have his deposit refunded. However, if the buyer is ready to close the transaction and the seller decides he does not want to sell, perhaps because the value of the property has increased between the signing of the contract and the closing date, the buyer can force the seller to convey title through use of a lawsuit for specific performance.

Buyer Default   Once the contract is signed by all parties involved, if the buyer fails to carry out his obligations, the standard choices for the seller are to (1) release the buyer and return his deposit in full, (2) sue the buyer for specific performance, or (3) sue the buyer for damages suffered. Returning the deposit does not compensate for the time and effort the seller and his broker spent with the buyer, nor for the possibility that, while the seller was committed to the buyer, the real estate market turned sour. Yet the time, effort, and cost of suing for specific performance or damages may be uneconomical. Consequently, it has become common practice in many parts of the country to insert a clause in the purchase contract whereby the buyer agrees in advance to forfeit his deposit if he defaults on the contract, and the seller agrees to accept the deposit as his sole right to damages. Thus, the seller gives up the right to sue the buyer and accepts instead the buyer's deposit. The buyer knows in advance how much it will cost if he defaults, and the cost of default is limited to that amount. This is the purpose of the paragraph at [20].

Time Limits   At [21], the buyer clearly states that he is making an offer to buy and gives the seller a certain amount of time to accept. If the seller does not accept the offer within the time allotted, the offer is void. This feature is automatic: the buyer does not have to contact the seller to tell him that the offer is no longer open. The offer must be open long enough for the seller to physically receive it, make a decision, sign it, and return it to the buyer. If the seller lives nearby, the transaction is not complicated, and the offer can be delivered in person, 3 days is reasonable. If the offer must be mailed to an out-of-town seller, 7 to 10 days is appropriate.

If the buyer has another property that he wants to make an offer on if the first offer is not accepted, he may make his offer valid for only a day, or even a few hours. A short offer life also limits the amount of time the seller has to hold out for a better offer. If a property is highly marketable, a buyer will want his offer accepted before someone else makes a better offer. Some experienced real estate buyers argue that a purposely short offer life has a psychological value. It motivates the seller to accept before the offer expires. Note that a buyer can withdraw and cancel his offer at any time before the seller has accepted and the buyer is aware of that acceptance.

"Time is of the essence" at ㉒ means that the time limits set by the contract must be faithfully observed or the contract is void. The major objective is to draw attention to the time limit at ㉑ and the closing date at ⑧. Neither buyer nor seller should expect extensions of time to complete their obligations. This clause does not prohibit the buyer or seller from voluntarily giving the other an extension. Rather, extensions cannot be received upon demand.

Signatures

The real estate agency and salesperson responsible for producing this offer to buy are identified at ㉓. At ㉔, the buyer clearly states that this is an offer to purchase. If the buyer has any doubts or questions regarding the legal effect of the offer, he should take it to an attorney for counsel before signing it. After he signs, the buyer retains one copy and the rest are delivered to the seller for his consideration. By retaining one copy, the buyer has a written record to remind him of his obligations under the offer. Equally important, the seller cannot forge a change on the offer, as he does not have all the copies. Regarding delivery, the standard procedure is for the salesperson who obtained the offer to make an appointment with the agent who obtained the listing, and together they call upon the seller and present the offer.

Acceptance

For an offer to become binding, the seller must accept everything in it. The rejection of even the smallest portion of the offer is a rejection of the entire offer. If the seller wishes to reject the offer but keep negotiations alive, he can make a counteroffer. This would be a written offer to sell to the buyer at a specific price and specific terms that are closer to the buyer's offer than the seller's original asking price and terms. Suppose, for example, that the seller is willing to accept $46,000 for the property, will allow the buyer to make his offer subject to obtaining a $38,000 loan, and will not include the refrigerator. The agent prepares the counteroffer by either filling out a fresh purchase contract identical in all ways to the buyer's offer except for these changes, or by writing on the back of the offer (or on another sheet of paper) that the seller offers to sell at the terms the buyer had offered except for the three stated changes. The counteroffer is then dated and signed by the seller, and a time limit is given to the buyer to accept. The seller keeps a copy, and the counteroffer is delivered to the buyer for his decision. If the counteroffer is acceptable to the buyer, he signs and dates it, and the contract is complete. Another commonly used, but undesirable, practice is to take the buyer's offer, cross out each item unacceptable to the seller, and write above or below it what the seller will accept. Each change is then initialed by the seller and buyer.

Returning to Figure 8:2, suppose that the seller accepts the offer as presented to him. At ㉕, he indicates his acceptance; at ㉖, he states that he employed the Lakeside Realty Company and agrees on a commission of $2,700 for their services, to be paid upon closing and recordation of the deed. Provisions are also included as to the amount of the commission if the sale is not completed. At ㉗, the sellers sign and date the contract and acknowledge receipt of a copy. The last step is to notify the buyer that his offer has been accepted, give him a copy of the completed agreement, and at ㉘ have him acknowledge receipt of it.

Negotiation   One of the most important principles of purchase contracts (and real estate contracts in general) is that nearly everything is negotiable and nearly everything has a price. In preparing or analyzing any contract, consider what the advantages and disadvantages of each condition are to each party to the contract. A solid contract results when the buyer and seller each feel that they have gained more than they have given up. The prime example is the sales price of the property itself. The seller prefers the money over the property, while the buyer prefers the property over the money. Each small negotiable item in the purchase contract has its price too. For example, the seller may agree to include the refrigerator for $200 more. Equally important in negotiating is the relative bargaining power of the buyer and seller. If the seller is confident he will have plenty of buyers at his asking price, he can elect to refuse offers for less money, and reject those with numerous conditions or insufficient earnest money. However, if the owner is anxious to sell and has received only one offer in several months, he may be quite willing to accept a lower price and numerous conditions.

EXCHANGE AGREEMENTS

Most real estate transactions involve the exchange of real estate for monetary consideration. However, among sophisticated real estate investors, exchanging real property for real property has become popular for two important reasons. First, real estate trades can be accomplished without large amounts of cash by trading a property you presently own for one you want. This sidesteps the intermediate step of converting real estate to cash and then converting cash back to real estate. Second, by using an exchange, you can dispose of one property and acquire another without paying income taxes on the profit in the first property at the time of the transaction. As a result, the phrase "tax-free exchange" is often used when talking about trading. To illustrate, suppose that an investor owns an apartment building with a value on his accounting books of $150,000. Due to rising property values, it is worth $200,000 today. If the investor sells for cash, he will have to pay income taxes on the difference between the value of the property on his accounting books and the amount he receives for it. If instead of selling for cash, he finds another building that he wants and can arrange a trade, then for income tax purposes the new building acquires the accounting book value of the old and no income taxes are due at the time of the trade. Taxes will, however, be due if and when the investor finally sells rather than trades. Owner-occupied dwellings are treated differently. The Internal Revenue Service permits the homeowner to sell his home for cash and still postpone paying taxes on the gain if he purchases and occupies another home of equal or greater value within 18 months; 24 month if he builds.

Figure 8:3   **POSSIBLE TRADING COMBINATIONS**

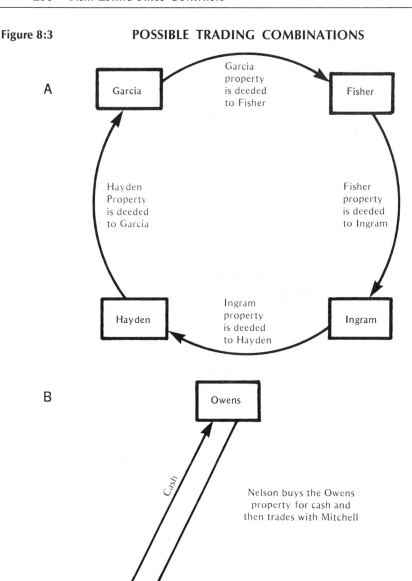

Trading Up   Real estate exchanges need not involve properties of equal value. For example, if you own a small office building worth $100,000 that is free of debt, you could trade it for a building worth $500,000 that has $400,000 of mortgage debt against it.

Alternatively, if the building you wanted was priced at $600,000 with $400,000 in debt against it, you could offer your building plus $100,000 in cash.

When a simple two-way trade does not leave each party satisfied, exchanges involving several parties can be arranged. In the four-way trade in Figure 8:3A, Fisher would like to own Garcia's property but cannot arrange a trade because Garcia does not want Fisher's property. Fisher then looks for a property Garcia would like to own. He finds one that belongs to Hayden. However, Hayden does not want Fisher's property, and the search must continue to find someone who will take Fisher's property and who has something acceptable to Hayden. Ingram fills this gap, and the four-way trade is possible. Fisher gets Garcia's property, who in turn gets Hayden's property, who in turn acquires Ingram's property, who in turn takes Fisher's property.*

In Figure 8:3B, a combination trade and cash sale is shown. Nelson wants Mitchell's property and is willing to pay cash for it. Mitchell refuses to sell for cash because of the income taxes he would have to pay; he will only trade. Owens has a property for sale that Mitchell would like to have. To make the deal, Nelson buys it and gives it to Mitchell, receiving Mitchell's property in return.

Although trading is a complicated business, it is also very lucrative for real estate agents. Whereas an ordinary sale results in one brokerage commission, a two-party exchange results in two commissions, and a four-party exchange, in four commissions.

Space does not permit a detailed review of a trade contract. However, very briefly, a typical trade contract identifies the traders involved and their respective properties; names the type of deed and quality of title that will be conveyed; names the real estate brokers involved and how much they are to be

Typical
Trade Contract

---

* Although recent tax developments indicate a "wheel" type exchange can be carried out tax-free exactly as shown in Figure 8.3A, a few tax experts feel they are on safer ground by working the trade as a series of two-party exchanges.

paid; discusses prorations, personal property, rights of tenants, and damage to the property; provides a receipt for the deposit that each trader makes; requires each trader to provide an abstract of title; and sets forth the consequences of defaulting on the contract. If the same broker represents more than one trader, he must disclose this to each trader that he represents.

INSTALLMENT CONTRACTS

An **installment contract**, also known as a land contract, conditional sales contract, contract for deed, or agreement of sale, is used to sell property in situations where the seller does not wish to convey title until all, or at least a substantial portion, of the purchase price is paid by the buyer. This is different from the purchase contract shown in Figure 8:2, wherein the buyer receives possession and a deed at the closing. With an installment contract, the buyer is given the right to use the property upon closing, but he does not acquire title. Instead, he receives a contract promising that a deed will be delivered at a later date.

The widest use of the installment contract occurs when the buyer does not have the full purchase price in cash or he cannot borrow it from a lender. Under these conditions, the seller must be willing to accept a down payment plus monthly payments until the property is paid for. The seller can either deliver a deed to the buyer at closing and simultaneously have the buyer pledge the property as collateral for the balance owed or the seller can agree to deliver title only after the buyer has completed his payments.

Delivering title after payment is advantageous to the seller because if the buyer fails to make his payments, the title to the property is still in the name of the seller. This avoids the time and costs consumed by foreclosure, a requirement if title has already been conveyed to the buyer.

Sample Contract

Figure 8:4 is a simplified illustration of an installment contract. In section ① the buyer and seller are identified, the purchase price is given, and the amount and terms of the balance due are stated. In section ②, the seller promises to deliver a deed to the buyer when the buyer has made all the

Figure 8:4

INSTALLMENT CONTRACT

①*RECEIVED this* 15th *day of* October, 19 ,
from Cliff Fisher and wife Sandy *(hereafter called the
"buyer") of* 7778 Spinner Street, Bridgetown, Anystate
the sum of $ 200.00 *as down payment toward the sales price
of $* 10,000.00 *. The balance of $* 9,800.00 *is to be
paid in equal monthly installments of $* 98.00 *until paid in
full. The monthly payment includes principal and interest
of* 8 *% per annum on the unpaid balance. Payments are to
be made on the first of each month to the Sunrise Lakes Land
Company (hereafter called the "seller").*

②*BE IT AGREED: if the buyer makes the payments
and performs the agreements stated in this contract, the seller
agrees to convey to the buyer in fee simple, clear of all encumbrances whatsoever, by special warranty deed, Lot #* 17 *,
Block* B-1 *, Sunrise Lakes Tract, situated and recorded in
the County of Sunrise, State of Anywhere.*

③*IF THE BUYER fails to make any of the payments
herein designated or fails to perform any of the other agreements made herein, this contract shall be terminated and the
buyer shall forfeit all payments made on this contract. Such
payments will be retained by the seller as accumulated rent on
the property described above, and the seller shall have the
right to reenter and take possession of the premises.*

④*THE BUYER AGREES to pay all property taxes subsequent to the year* 19-- *.*

⑤*CONSTRUCTION shall be limited to residences built
with new materials. Structures must be located at least twenty
feet from the front lot line and five feet from the other lot
lines. Shacks or unsightly structures are not permitted.*

⑥ *THE BUYER AND SELLER agree that this contract, or any assignment thereof, is not to be recorded without the permission of the seller. To do so shall result in any existing balance on this contract becoming due and payable immediately.*

⑦ *THE BUYER AND SELLER agree that prompt payment is an essential part of this contract and that this contract is binding upon their assigns, heirs, executors, and administrators.*

⑧ *THE BUYER HAS the right to examine the master abstract.*

BUYER   ⑨   SELLER   *Salem Bigland*

Cliff Fisher

Sandy Fisher   Salem Bigland
                        President, Sunrise Lakes Land Company

payments stated in section ①. Section ② also describes the property. Section ③ deals with the possibility that the buyer may fail to make the required payments or fail to abide by the other contract terms. The strong wording in this section is typical of the installment contract, particularly when it is utilized to sell vacant land. If you read section ③ carefully, you will see that, in the event of the buyer's default, the seller can retain all payments made *and* retake possession of the property. This is the feature that makes the installment contract popular with sellers. Section ④ deals with property taxes. In this example, the buyer agrees to pay them. Sometimes the seller will agree to pay the property taxes until a deed is delivered to the buyer. This is not an act of kindness but protection for the seller. The seller does not want to risk the possibility of the buyer's failure to pay the taxes, thus giving the county tax collector the right to take the property.

Repossession   In section ⑤, the seller sets construction restrictions. The object is to prevent unsightly structures from being built that would have a negative impact on surrounding property values. This enhances the buyer's resale value; for the seller, it means that the property is more valuable if the buyer defaults. In agreement with the provisions in section ③, section ⑥ provides the seller with a means of smooth recovery of possession and ownership in the event of default by the buyer. If the buyer records his contract with the public recorder, he serves notice that he has an interest in the property. This creates a cloud on the seller's title. If the buyer were to default, the effort necessary to remove this cloud would be inconsistent with the seller's objective of easy recovery. Also, such a cloud makes it more difficult for the seller to borrow against the property. However, a nonrecording provision is definitely not to the advantage of the buyer, as anyone inspecting the public records would not find a record of the buyer's interest. The seller would still be shown as the owner. In view of this, some states outlaw these clauses.

Section ⑦ reemphasizes that payments must be made promptly and adds that the terms of the contract are binding on anyone to whom the buyer may sell or assign the contract. In the illustrated contract, the buyer does not receive a title report or title insurance for his individual lot when he signs the contract. However, at ⑧, he is invited to see the abstract; presumably it shows the seller as the owner of the land. The balance of the contract, ⑨, is for the signatures of the buyer and seller and, when required, witnesses or an acknowledgment.

The installment contract has received much consumer criticism because its wording so strongly favors the seller. In numerous instances, buyers, although they have paid a portion of the purchase price, have lost the property and their money due to one or two late payments. Strictly interpreted, that is what the contract says; if the buyer signs it, presumably he agrees. However, the courts and legislatures in several states have found this too harsh. Iowa and Minnesota give the buyer a statutory grace period in which to cure his default. Florida and Maryland require an installment sales contract to be foreclosed like a regular mortgage. Georgia, Montana,

Consumer Criticism

South Dakota, Wisconsin, Utah, and California allow a buyer whose contract has been forfeited to recover the amount paid less a reasonable allowance for rent for the time the buyer had the right to use the land. In this age of consumerism, more states will undoubtedly side with the buyer in the future.

Another key weakpoint in the installment sale concept is that the seller does not deed ownership to the buyer until some later date. Thus, a buyer might make payments for several years only to find that the seller cannot deliver title as promised. At that point, unless the seller is willing to give the buyer a refund, the buyer's only recourse is to sue the seller for specific performance or money damages. However, a lawsuit works only if the buyer has the time and money to pursue the matter, if the suit is successful, and if the seller has the money to pay the judgment.

If an installment contract is used for the purchase of real estate, it should be done with the help of legal counsel to make certain that it provides adequate safeguards for the buyer as well as the seller.

VOCABULARY REVIEW

Match terms a–j with statements 1–10.

a. *"As is"*
b. *Bill of sale*
c. *Binder*
d. *Closing date*
e. *Deposit*

f. *Dry rot*
g. *Installment sale contract*
h. *Nonrecording provision*
i. *Purchase contract*
j. *Time is of the essence*

1. A written and signed agreement specifying the terms at which a buyer will purchase and an owner will sell.
2. A short-form purchase contract used in certain states to hold a real estate transaction together until a more formal contract can be prepared and signed.
3. Money that accompanies an offer to purchase as evidence of good faith. Also called earnest money.
4. Property offered for sale in its present condition with no guarantee or warranty of quality provided by the seller.
5. Rotted wood; usually the result of alternate soaking and drying over a long period of time.
6. The day on which the buyer pays his money and the seller delivers title.
7. Written evidence of the sale of personal property.

8. A phrase meaning that all parties to a contract are expected to perform on time as a condition of the contract.

9. Also known as a conditional sales contract, land contract, contract for deed, or agreement of sale.

10. A clause in a land contract that requires immediate payment of the entire balance still owing if the contract is recorded.

QUESTIONS AND PROBLEMS

1. Why is it necessary to include the extra step of preparing and signing a purchase contract when it would seem much easier if the buyer simply paid the seller the purchase price and the seller handed the buyer a deed?

2. How does a binder differ from a more formal purchase contract?

3. What are the advantages and disadvantages of using pre-printed real estate purchase contract forms?

4. Is it legal for a seller to accept an offer that is not accompanied by a deposit? Why or why not?

5. In this chapter, the statement was made that what a contract does not say is as important as what it does say. Explain what this means.

6. If a purchase contract for real property describes the land, is it also necessary to mention the fixtures? Why or why not?

7. How will the relative bargaining strengths and weaknesses of the buyer and seller affect the contract negotiation process?

8. What are the advantages of trading real estate rather than selling it? What would you consider the disadvantages to be?

9. Under an installment contract, what is the advantage to the seller if he does not have to deliver title to the buyer until all required payments are made?

10. What position does your state take toward payment forfeiture and nonrecording clauses in land contracts?

ADDITIONAL READINGS

Gross, Jerome S. *Encyclopedia of Real Estate Forms.* Englewood Cliffs, N.J.: Prentice-Hall, 1973, 458 pages. Contains examples of binders, sales contracts, and exchange agreements.

Klarreich, Harold L. "Land Contracts: An Aid to Selling Homes," *Real Estate Today,* Oct. 1970, pages 16ff. Explains the application of land contracts to selling houses and discusses seller default.

Kling, Samuel G. *The Complete Guide to Everyday Law,* 3rd ed. Chicago: Follett, 1973, 709 pages. A law book written for the nonlawyer. Includes explanations of legal words and phrases and has chapters on real estate law. Contains sample legal forms and a glossary.

Kratovil, Robert. *Real Estate Law,* 6th ed. Englewood Cliffs, N.J.: Prentice-Hall, 1974, 479 pages. Chapter 11 discusses sales contracts, deposits, installment contracts, possession, rescission, and fraud. Contains suggestions on how to draft real estate sales contracts.

Menchor, Melvin. *The Fannie Mae Guide to Buying, Financing and Selling Your Home.* Garden City, N.Y.: Doubleday, 1973, 315 pages. Written especially to guide the consumer through the home-buying and home-selling transaction.

Ringsdorf, R. Royce. *The Basic Steps in Real Estate Exchanging.* n.p. Published by the author, 1974, 129 pages. Explains step by step the process of exchanging real estate. Discusses exchange counseling, negotiations, offer, acceptance, and escrow.

9

Mortgage Theory and Law

KEY TERMS

Acceleration clause: allows the lender to speed up the remaining payments

Deficiency judgment: the amount the borrower must pay the lender if the sale of the pledged property at foreclosure does not bring in enough to pay the balance still owed

Foreclose: to terminate, shut off, or bar

Hypothecate: to pledge property to secure a debt but without giving up possession of it

Junior mortgage: any mortgage on a property that is below the first mortgage in priority

Mortgage: a pledge of property to secure a debt

Mortgagee: the party receiving the mortgage; the lender

Mortgagor: the person who gives a mortgage pledging his property; the borrower

Power of sale: allows a mortgagee to conduct a foreclosure sale without first going to court

Subordination: to voluntarily accept a lower mortgage priority in a financial agreement

A mortgage is a pledge of property to secure a debt. If the debt is not repaid as agreed between the lender and borrower, the lender can force the sale of the pledged property and apply the proceeds to repayment of the debt. To better understand present-day mortgage laws, it is helpful to first look at their history.

EARLY MORTGAGES

The concept of pledging property as collateral for a loan is not new. According to historians, the mortgage was in use when the pharaohs ruled Egypt and during the time of the Roman Empire. According to Roman laws, loans could be secured by mortgages on either personal or real property. In the early years of the Empire, nonpayment of a mortgage loan entitled the lender to make the borrower his slave. In the year 326 B.C. Roman law was modified to allow the debtor his freedom while working off his debt. Later, Roman law was again changed, this time to permit an unpaid debt to be satisfied by the sale of the mortgaged property.

Hypothecation

Mortgages were also an important part of English law and, as a result of the English colonization of America, ultimately were incorporated into the laws of each state. In England, the concept of pledging real estate by temporarily conveying its title to a lender as security for a debt was in regular use by the eleventh century. However, the Christian church at that time did not allow its members to charge interest. Because of this, the Christian lender took possession of the mortgaged property and collected the rents it produced instead of charging interest. In contrast, Jewish lenders in England charged interest and left the borrower in possession. It was not until the fourteenth century that charging interest, rather than taking possession, became universal. Leaving the borrower in possession of the pledged property is known as **hypothecation.** The borrower conveyed his title to the lender, but he still had the use of the property.

Defeasance

Most importantly though, the conveyance of title in the mortgage agreement was conditional. The mortgage stated that, if the debt it secured was paid on time, the mortgage was defeated and title returned to the borrower. This was and still is known as a **defeasance clause.** If the borrower did not repay the debt on time, the opportunity to defeat it was lost forever. The lender became the absolute owner and the borrower was forced from the land. Furthermore, losing the property did not cancel the debt; it was still owed. Happy to be able to borrow at all, for a long time borrowers never questioned the harsh system.

EQUITABLE REDEMPTION

In time, borrowers began to receive more equitable and reasonable treatment. By the time of Columbus's discovery of America, borrowers who had lost their property were beginning to petition the king for help. These petitions contained the borrower's offer to pay the lender the debt and all interest due, plus a request that the king compel the lender to return the lost property to the borrower. The king studied the circumstances that caused the borrower to default on his debt; if he felt the borrower deserving of another chance, he granted the petition. Thus the king superimposed what he felt was equitable upon the mortgage contract. The idea of petitioning for more equitable treatment spread rapidly, and soon the king was forced to appoint a chancellor to handle the petitions. The number of petitions continued to increase, and by the early seventeenth century, instead of hearing each petition individually, a set of rules and instructions regarding property redemption was published. By following these, a borrower, upon repayment of his defaulted loan plus interest, could force a lender to return his property. What was previously granted by special request was now an automatic right of the borrower. This was and still is known as the **equitable right of redemption** or **equity of redemption.**

However, redemption rights under these laws became so generous to the borrower that mortgage agreements no longer provided reasonable and adequate security for lenders. As a result, some lenders stopped making mortgage loans and channeled their money elsewhere. Those lenders who continued to make loans began including a **waiver of right of redemption** clause in their mortgage contracts. By signing a mortgage with this clause, the borrower waived (surrendered) his equitable right of redemption. The courts of law found this arrangement to be unreasonable for the borrower, and refused to enforce these clauses even though borrowers had agreed to them.

Foreclosure Suit

Having failed with the waiver clause, lenders took a new approach. When a default occurred on a loan, the lender would go to court and ask that a limit be placed on the time the borrower had to redeem his property. This became and still is known as a **foreclosure suit.** If the property was not redeemed by the date set, the right to redeem the property ended. By this time in history, the English concept of mortgages was being introduced into America through the establishment of the 13 original colonies.

LIEN THEORY VERSUS TITLE THEORY

Although the United States inherited the whole of English mortgage law, it began to be modified following independence. In 1791 in South Carolina, lawmakers asked the question,

"Should a mortgage actually convey title to the lender subject only to the borrower's default? Or does the mortgage, despite its wording, simply create a lien with a right to acquire title only after proper foreclosure?" Their decision was that a mortgage was a lien rather than a conveyance, and South Carolina became the first "lien" theory state in regard to mortgages. Today, 32 states have adopted this viewpoint.* Fourteen jurisdictions adhere to the older idea that a mortgage is a conveyance of title subject to defeat when the debt it secures is paid. They are classified as "title" theory states† Five states are classified as "intermediate" theory states because they take a position midway between the lien and title theories.‡ In the intermediate states, title does not pass to the lender with the mortgage, but only upon default. In real estate practice, as long as default does not occur the differences among the three theories are more technical than real.

FURTHER MODIFICATIONS IN MORTGAGES

As the mortgage concept originally developed in England, the borrower conveyed title to the lender, but the borrower could defeat the conveyance by paying his debt on time. However, once foreclosed, the borrower could no longer defeat the conveyance, and it became a fee simple title for the lender. This was termed **strict foreclosure.** If the value of the property being foreclosed exceeded the debt owed, the lender benefited at the expense of the borrower. To equalize the situation, one by one the American states began requiring that the foreclosed property be sold to the highest bidder at public auction. The price received was then to be applied to the debt owed. If the property sold for more than the debt it secured, the bor-

---

* Alaska, Arizona, California, Colorado, Delaware, Florida, Georgia, Hawaii, Idaho, Indiana, Iowa, Kansas, Kentucky, Louisiana, Michigan, Minnesota, Missouri, Montana, Nebraska, Nevada, New Mexico, New York, North Dakota, Oklahoma, Oregon, South Carolina, South Dakota, Texas, Utah, Washington, Wisconsin, and Wyoming.

† Alabama, Arkansas, Connecticut, Maine, Maryland, Massachusetts, New Hampshire, Pennsylvania, Rhode Island, Tennessee, Vermont, Virginia, West Virginia, and the District of Columbia.

‡ Illinois, Mississippi, New Jersey, North Carolina, and Ohio.

rower received the surplus. This method, known as **fore-closure by sale,** is the standard foreclosure procedure in 47 states. Only in the states of Vermont, Connecticut, and Illinois is strict foreclosure practiced to any extent, and then only under conditions that prevent the lender from taking unfair advantage.

Another modification to mortgage law has been the introduction of **statutory redemption.** A number of state legislatures have passed laws that permit foreclosed-property owners to redeem even after the foreclosure sale. The first step in this direction was taken in 1820 by the state of New York. The idea spread to other states as a result of a collapse in land values in 1836, and still later to more states. Today, 25 states offer foreclosed owners from as little as 5 months (Arizona, Colorado, Utah, and Wyoming) to as long as 18 months (Kansas) and 2 years (Alabama) after the foreclosure sale to step forward, pay the debt owed, and reclaim title.

Statutory Redemption

A person can pledge his real estate as collateral for a loan by using any of four methods: the regular mortgage, the equitable mortgage, the deed as security, and the trust deed. The **standard or regular mortgage** is the mortgage handed down from England and the one commonly found and used in the United States today. In it, the borrower conveys his title to the lender as security for his debt. The mortgage also contains a statement that it will become void if the debt it secures is paid in full and on time. In title theory states, the conveyance feature of the mortgage stands. In lien theory states, such a mortgage is considered to be only a lien against the borrower's property despite its wording.

PLEDGE METHODS

An **equitable mortgage** is a written agreement that, although it does not follow the form of a regular mortgage, is considered by the courts to be one. For example, Black sells his land to Green, with Green paying part of the price now in cash and promising to pay the balance later. Normally, Black would ask Green to execute a regular mortgage as security for the balance due. However, instead of doing this, Black makes a note of the balance due him on the deed before handing it to Green. The laws of most states would regard this notation as an equitable mortgage. For all intents and purposes, it is a mortgage, although not specifically called one. Another example of an equitable mortgage can arise from the money deposit accompanying an offer to purchase property. If the seller refuses the offer and refuses to return the deposit, the courts will hold that the purchaser has an equitable mortgage in the amount of the deposit against the seller's property.

Occasionally, a borrower will give a bargain and sale or warranty deed as security for a loan. On the face of it, the lender (grantee) would appear to be able to do whatever he pleases since he has the title. However, if the borrower can prove that the deed was, in fact, security for a loan, the lender must foreclose like a regular mortgage if the borrower fails to repay. If the loan is repaid in full and on time, the borrower can force the lender to convey the land back to him. Like the equitable mortgage, a deed used as security is treated according to its intent, not its label.

Deed of Trust   In some states, debts are often secured by trust deeds. Whereas a mortgage is a two-party arrangement with a borrower and a lender, the **trust deed**, also known as a **deed of trust,** is a three-party arrangement consisting of the borrower (the trustor), the lender (the beneficiary), and a neutral third party (a trustee). The key aspect of this system is that the borrower executes a deed to the trustee rather than to the lender. If the borrower pays the debt in full and on time, the trustee reconveys title back to the borrower. If the borrower defaults on the loan, the lender asks the trustee to sell the property to pay off the debt. Trust deeds are covered in more detail in Chapter 10.

Chattel Mortgage   Mortgages can also be used to pledge personal property as security for a debt. These are **chattel mortgages.** The word chattel is a legal term for personal property and originated from the Old English word for cattle. As with real property mortgages, chattel mortgages permit the borrower to use the mortgaged personal property as long as the loan payments are made. If the borrower defaults, the lender is permitted to take possession and sell the mortgaged goods. In a number of states, chattel mortgages are being replaced by security agreements under the Uniform Commercial Code.

Two documents are involved in a standard mortgage loan, a promissory note and the mortgage itself; both are contracts. The **promissory note** establishes who the borrower and lender are, the amount of the debt, the terms of repayment, and the interest rate. A sample promissory note, usually referred to simply as a note, is shown in Figure 9:1. Some states use a **bond** to accomplish the same purpose as the promissory note. What is said here regarding promissory notes also applies to bonds.

PROMISSORY NOTE

To be valid as evidence of debt, a note must (1) be in writing, (2) be between a borrower and lender who both have contractual capacity, (3) state the borrower's promise to pay a certain sum of money, (4) show the terms of payment, (5) be signed by the borrower, and (6) be voluntarily delivered by the borrower and accepted by the lender. If the note is secured by a mortgage or trust deed, it must say so. Otherwise, it is solely a personal obligation of the borrower. Although interest is not required to make the note valid, most loans do carry an interest charge; when they do, the rate of interest must be stated in the note. Finally, in some states it is necessary for the borrower's signature on the note to be acknowledged and/or witnessed.

Referring to Figure 9:1, number ① identifies the document as a promissory note and ② gives the location and date of the note's execution (signing). At ③, the borrower states that he has received something of value and in turn promises to pay the debt described in the note. Typically, the "value received" is a loan of money in the amount described in the note; it could, however, be services or goods or anything else of value.

Obligor-Obligee

The section of the note at ④ identifies to whom the obligation is owed, sometimes referred to as the **obligee**, and where the payments are to be sent. The words "or order" at ⑤ mean that the lender can direct the borrower (the **obligor**) to make his payments to someone else, if the lender sells the right to collect the note.

Figure 9:1

PROMISSORY NOTE SECURED BY MORTGAGE ①

_____City, State② _____   _____March 31, 1977_____

③*For value received, I promise to pay to* ④_Penney-wise Mortgage Company_ , ⑤*or order at* _2242 National Blvd., [City, State]_ , *the sum of* ⑥_Thirty thousand and no/100_ - - - - - - - - - - - - - - - *Dollars, with interest from* _March 31, 1977_ , *on unpaid principal at the rate of* _nine_ ⑦*percent per annum; principal and interest payable in installments of* ⑧_two hundred fifty-one and 80/100_ - - - - - - - - - - - - - - - - - - - *Dollars on the* first *day of each month beginning* ⑨_May 1, 1977_ , *and continuing until said principal and interest have been paid.*

⑩*This note may be prepaid in whole or in part at any time without penalty.*

⑪*There shall be a ten-day grace period for each monthly payment. A late fee of $12.50 will be added to each payment made after its grace period.*

⑫*Each payment shall be credited first on interest then due and the remainder on principal. Unpaid interest shall bear interest like the principal.*

⑬*Should default be made in payment of any installment when due, the entire principal plus accrued interest shall immediately become due at the option of the holder of the note.*

⑭*If legal action is necessary to collect this note, I promise to pay such sum as the court may fix.*

⑮*This note is secured by a mortgage bearing the same date as this note and made in favor of* _Pennywise Mortgage Company_ _____ .

⑰   ⑯   *Hap P. Toborrow*

[this space for witnesses &/or acknowledgment as required by state law   Borrower

The **principal** or amount of the obligation, $30,000, is shown at ⑥. Number ⑦ gives the rate of interest on the debt and the date from which it will be charged. The amount of the periodic payment at ⑧ is calculated from the loan tables discussed in Chapter 12. In this case, $251.80 each month for 25 years will return the lender's $30,000 plus interest at the rate of 9% per year on the unpaid portion of the principal. Number ⑨ outlines when payments will begin and when subsequent payments will be due. In this example, they are due on the first day of each month until the full $30,000 and interest have been paid. The clause at ⑩ is a **prepayment privilege** for the borrower. It allows the borrower to pay more than the required $251.80 per month and to pay the loan off early. Without this very important privilege, the note requires the borrower to pay $251.80 per month, no more and no less, until the $30,000 plus interest has been paid.

At ⑪, the lender gives the borrower a 10-day grace period to accommodate late payments. For payments made after that, the borrower agrees to pay a late charge of $12.50. The clause at ⑫ states that, whenever a payment is made, any interest due on the loan is first deducted, and then the remainder is applied to reducing the loan balance. Also, if interest is not paid, it too will earn interest at the same rate as the principal, in this example 9% per year. The provision at ⑬ allows the lender to demand immediate payment of the entire balance remaining on the note if the borrower misses any of the individual payments. This is called an **acceleration clause**, as it "speeds up" the remaining payments due on the note. Without this clause, the lender can only foreclose on the payments that have come due and not been paid. In this example, that could take as long as 25 years. This clause also has a certain psychological value: knowing that the lender has the option of calling the entire loan balance due upon default makes the borrower think twice about being late with his payments.

At ⑭, the borrower agrees to pay any collection costs incurred by the lender if the borrower falls behind in his payments. At ⑮, the promissory note is tied to the mortgage that secures it, making it a mortgage loan. Without this reference, it would be a personal loan. At ⑯, the borrower signs the note. A person who signs a note is sometimes referred to as a **maker** of the note. If two or more persons sign the note, it is common to include a statement in the note that the borrowers are "jointly and severally liable" for all provisions in the note. Thus, the terms of the note and the obligations it creates are enforceable upon the makers as a group and upon each maker individually. If the borrower is married, lenders generally require both husband and wife to sign. Finally, if state law requires an acknowledgment or witnesses, they would appear at ⑰. Usually, they are not required, as it is the mortgage rather than the note that is recorded in the public records.

THE MORTGAGE INSTRUMENT

The mortgage is a separate agreement from the promissory note. Whereas the note is evidence of a debt and a promise to pay, the mortgage pledges collateral that the lender can sell if the note is not paid. The sample mortgage in Figure 9:2 illustrates in simplified language the key provisions most commonly found in mortgages used in the United States. Let us look at these provisions.

The mortgage begins at ① with the date of its making and the names of the parties involved. In mortgage agreements, the person or party who pledges his property and gives the mortgage is the **mortgagor.** The person or party who receives the mortgage (the lender) is the **mortgagee.** For the reader's convenience, we shall refer to the mortgagor as the borrower and the mortgagee as the lender.

At ②, the debt for which this mortgage acts as security is identified. This mortgage does not act as security for any other debts of the borrower. The key wording in the mortgage occurs at ③, where the borrower conveys to the lender the property described at ④. The pledged property is most often the property that the borrower purchased with the loan money, but this is not a requirement. The mortgaged property need only be something of sufficient value in the eyes of the lender; it could just as easily be some other property the borrower owns. At ⑤, the borrower states that the pledged property is his and that he will defend its ownership. The lender will, of course, verify this with a title search before making the loan.

Figure 9:2

MORTGAGE

(1) *THIS MORTGAGE is made this* __31st__ *day of* __March__ *, 19 77 , between* __Hap P. Toborrow__ *hereinafter called the Mortgagor, and* __Penneywise Mortgage Company__ *hereinafter called the Mortgagee.*

(2) *WHEREAS, the Mortgagor is indebted to the Mortgagee in the principal sum of* __Thirty thousand and no/100 - - - - -__ *Dollars, payable* __$251.80, including 9% interest per annum,__ __on the first day of each month starting May 1, 1977, and con-__ __tinuing until paid__ *, as evidenced by the Mortgagor's note of the same date as this mortgage, hereinafter called the Note.*

(3) *TO SECURE the Mortgagee the repayment of the indebtedness evidenced by said Note, with interest thereon, the Mortgagor does hereby mortgage, grant, and convey to the Mortgagee the following described property in the County of* __Evans__ *, State of* _____ *.*

(4) *Lot 39, Block 17, Harrison's Subdivision, as shown on Page 19 of Map Book 25, filed with the County Recorder of said County and State.*

(5) *FURTHERMORE, the Mortgagor fully warrants the title to said land and will defend the same against the lawful claims of all persons.*

(6) *IF THE MORTGAGOR, his heirs, legal representatives, or assigns pay unto the Mortgagee, his legal representatives or assigns, all sums due by said Note, then this mortgage and the estate created hereby SHALL CEASE AND BE NULL AND VOID.*

(7) *UNTIL SAID NOTE is fully paid:*
(8) *A. The Mortgagor agrees to pay all taxes on said land.*

(9) B. *The Mortgagor agrees not to remove or demolish buildings or other improvements on the mortgaged land without the approval of the lender.*

(10) C. *The Mortgagor agrees to carry adequate insurance to protect the lender in the event of damage or destruction of the mortgaged property.*

(11) D. *The Mortgagor agrees to keep the mortgaged property in good repair and not permit waste or deterioration.*

IT IS FURTHER AGREED THAT:

(12) E. *The Mortgagee shall have the right to inspect the mortgaged property as may be necessary for the security of the Note.*

(13) F. *If the Mortgagor does not abide by this mortgage or the accompanying Note, the Mortgagee may declare the entire unpaid balance on the Note immediately due and payable.*

(14) G. *If the Mortgagor sells or otherwise conveys title to the mortgaged property, the Mortgagee may declare the entire unpaid balance on the Note immediately due and payable.*

(15) H. *If all or part of the mortgaged property is taken by action of eminent domain, any sums of money received shall be applied to the Note.*

(16) *IN WITNESS WHEREOF, the Mortgagor has executed this mortgage.*

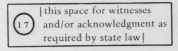

(17) | this space for witnesses and/or acknowledgment as required by state law |

Hap P. Toborrow (SEAL)
Mortgagor

As you may have already noticed, the wording of the sections ③, ④, and ⑤ is strikingly similar to that found in a warranty deed. In states taking the title theory position toward mortgages, this wording is interpreted to mean that theory states, this wording gives only a lien right to the lender, and the borrower (mortgagor) retains title. In either case, the borrower is allowed to remain in physical possession of the mortgaged property as long as he abides by the terms of the note and mortgage.

Provisions for the defeat of the mortgage are given at ⑥. The key words here state that the "mortgage and the estate created hereby shall cease and be null and void" when the note is paid in full. This is the defeasance clause.

At ⑦, there is a list of covenants (promises) that the bor-   *Covenants*
rower makes to the lender. They are the covenants of taxes, removal, insurance and repair. These covenants protect the security for the loan.

In the **covenant to pay taxes** at ⑧, the borrower agrees to pay the taxes on the mortgaged property even though the title may be technically with the lender. This is important to the lender, because if the taxes are not paid on time they become a lien on the property that is superior to the lender's.

In the **covenant against removal** ⑨, the borrower promises not to remove or demolish any buildings or improvements. To do so may reduce the value of the property as security for the lender.

The **covenant of insurance** at ⑩ requires the borrower to carry adequate insurance against damage or destruction of the mortgaged property. This protects the value of the collateral for the loan, for without insurance, if buildings or other improvements on the mortgaged property are damaged or destroyed, the value of the property might fall below the amount owed on the debt. With insurance, the buildings can be repaired or replaced, thus restoring the value of the collateral.

The **covenant of good repair** at ⑪, also referred to as the covenant of preservation and maintenance, requires the borrower to keep the mortgaged property in good condition. The clause at ⑫ gives the lender specific permisison to inspect the property to make sure that it is being kept in good repair and has not been damaged or demolished.

If the borrower breaks any of the mortgage covenants or note agreements, the lender wants the right to terminate the loan. Thus, an acceleration clause at ⑬ is included to permit the lender to demand the balance be paid in full immediately. If the borrower cannot pay, foreclosure takes place and the property is sold.

Alienation Clause   When used in a mortgage, an **alienation clause** (also called a **due-on-sale clause**) gives the lender the right to call the entire loan balance due if the mortgaged property is sold or otherwise conveyed (alienated) by the borrower. An example is shown at ⑭. The purpose of an alienation clause is two-fold. If the property is for sale and the buyer proposes to assume the existing loan, the lender can refuse to accept the buyer as a substitute borrower if the buyer's credit is not good. But, most importantly, it gives the lender an opportunity to eliminate old loans with low rates of interest. All mortgages do not contain alienation clauses, although the trend today is to include them.

Condemnation Clause   Number ⑮ is a **condemnation clause.** If all or part of the property is taken by action of eminent domain, any money so received used to reduce the balance owing on the note.

At ⑯, the mortgagor states that he made this mortgage. Actually, the execution statement is more a formality than a requirement; his signature alone indicates his execution of the mortgage and agreement to its provisions. At ⑰, the mortgage is acknowledged and/or witnessed as required by state law for placement in the public records. Like deeds, mortgages must be recorded if they are to be effective against the world at large. The reason the mortgage is recorded, but not the promissory note, is that the mortgage deals with rights and interests in real property, whereas the note represents a personal obligation.

MORTGAGE   By far, most mortgage loans are paid in full either on or
SATISFACTION   ahead of schedule. When the loan is paid, the standard practice is for the lender to cancel the promissory note and to issue to the borrower a document called a **satisfaction of mortgage (or a release of mortgage).** These are receipts signed by the lender which state that the promissory note or bond has been paid in full and the accompanying mortgage may be

discharged from the public records. It is extremely important that this document be promptly recorded by the public recorder in the county where the mortgage is recorded. Otherwise, the records will continue to indicate that the property is mortgaged. When a satisfaction or release is recorded, the recording office makes a note of its book and page location on the margin of the recorded mortgage. This is done to assist title searchers and is called a **marginal release.**

Partial Release

Occasionally, the situation arises where the borrower wants the lender to release a portion of the mortgaged property from the mortgage after part of the loan has been repaid. This is known as asking for a **partial release.** For example, a land developer purchases 40 acres of land for a total price of $50,000 and finances his purchase with $10,000 in cash and a $40,000 mortgage loan. In the mortgage agreement he might ask that the lender release free and clear of the mortgage encumbrance 10 acres for each $10,000 paid against the loan.

"SUBJECT TO" VERSUS "ASSUMPTION"

Often, when mortgaged real estate is sold, the existing mortgage debt against the property is not paid off as part of the transaction. In this case, the buyer can either purchase the property "subject to" the existing loan or he can "assume" the loan. When the buyer purchases **subject to the existing loan,** he states that he is aware of the existence of the loan and the mortgage that secures it, but takes no personal liability for it. Although the buyer pays the remaining loan payments as they come due, the seller continues to be personally liable to the lender for the loan. As long as the buyer faithfully continues to make the loan payments, which he would normally do as long as the property is worth more than the debts against it, this arrangement presents no problem to the seller. However, if the buyer stops making payments before the loan is fully paid, even though it may be years later, in most states the lender can require the seller to pay the balance due plus interest. This is true even though the seller thought he was free of the loan because he sold the property.

The seller is on safer ground if he requires the buyer to **assume the loan.** Under this arrangement, the buyer promises in writing to the seller that he will pay the loan, thus personally obligating himself. In the event of default on the loan or a breach of the mortgage agreement, the lender will first expect the buyer to remedy the problem. If the buyer does not pay, the lender will look to the seller, because the seller's name is still on the original promissory note. The safest arrangement for the seller is to ask the lender to substitute the buyer's liability for his. This releases the seller from the personal obligation created by his promissory note, and the lender can now require only the buyer to repay the loan. The seller is also on safe ground if the mortgage agreement or state law prohibits deficiency judgments, a topic that will be explained momentarily.

When a buyer is to continue making payments on an existing loan, he will want to know exactly how much is still owing. A **certificate of reduction** is prepared by the lender to show how much of the loan remains to be paid. If a recorded mortgage states that it secures a loan for $35,000, but the borrower has paid the loan down to $25,000, the certificate of reduction will show that $25,000 remains to be paid. Somewhat related to a certificate of reduction is the **estoppel certificate.** This is used when the holder of a mortgage loan sells it to another investor. In it, the borrower is asked to verify the amount still owed and the rate of interest.

DEBT PRIORITIES

Unless the mortgage prohibits it, the same property can be pledged as collateral for additional mortgages. This presents no problems to the lenders involved as long as the borrower makes the required payments on each note secured by the property. The difficulty arises when a default occurs on one or more of the loans, and the price the property brings at its foreclosure sale does not cover all the loans against it. As a result, a priority system is necessary. The debt with the highest priority is satisfied first from the foreclosure sale proceeds, and then the next highest priority debt is satisfied, then the next, until either the foreclosure sale proceeds are exhausted or all debts secured by the property are satisfied.

First Mortgage

In the vast majority of foreclosures, the sale proceeds are not sufficient to pay all the outstanding debt against the property; thus, it becomes extremely important that a lender know his priority position before making a loan. Unless there is a compelling reason otherwise, a lender will want to be in the highest position possible. This is normally accomplished by being the first lender to record a mortgage against a property that is otherwise free and clear of mortgage debt; this lender is said to hold a **first mortgage** on the property. If the same property is later used to secure another note before the first is fully satisfied, the new mortgage is a **second mortgage,** and so on. The first mortgage is also known as the **senior mortgage.** Any mortgage with a lower priority is a **junior mortgage.** As time passes and higher priority mortgages are satisfied, the lower priority mortgages move up in priority. Thus, if a property is secured by a first and a second mortgage and the first is paid off, the second becomes a first mortgage.

Subordination

Sometimes a lender will voluntarily take a lower priority position than he would otherwise be entitled to by virtue of his recording date. This is known as **subordination** and it allows a junior loan to move up in priority. For example, the holder of a first mortgage can volunteer to become a second mortgagee and allow the second mortgage to move into the first position. Although it seems irrational that a lender would actually volunteer to lower his priority position, it is sometimes done by landowners to encourage developers to buy their property.

THE FORECLOSURE PROCESS

Although only about one in 175 real estate loans is foreclosed in the United States in a given year, it is important to have a basic understanding of what happens when foreclosure takes place. First, knowledge of what causes foreclosure can help in avoiding it, and, second, if foreclosure does occur, one should know the rights of the parties involved.

Although noncompliance with any part of the mortgage agreement by the borrower can result in the lender calling the entire balance immediately due, in most cases foreclosure occurs because the note is not being repaid on time. When a borrower is behind in his payments, the loan is said to be **delinquent** or **nonconforming.** At this stage, rather than presume foreclosure is automatically the next step, the borrower and lender meet and attempt to work out an alternative payment program. Contrary to early motion picture plots in which lenders seemed anxious to foreclose their mortgages, today's lender considers foreclosure to be the last resort. This is because the foreclosure process is time consuming, expensive, and unprofitable. The lender would much rather have the borrower make regular payments. Consequently, if a borrower is behind in his loan payments, the lender prefers to arrange a new, stretched-out, payment schedule rather than immediately to declare the acceleration clause in effect and move toward foreclosing the borrower's rights to the property.

If the borrower realizes that stretching out payments is not going to solve his financial problem, instead of presuming foreclosure to be inevitable, he can seek a buyer for the property who will make the payments. More than any other reason, this is why relatively few real estate mortgages are foreclosed. The borrower, realizing he is in, or is about to be in, financial trouble, sells his property. It is only when the borrower cannot find a buyer and when the lender sees no further sense in stretching the payments that the acceleration clause is invoked and the path toward foreclosure taken. Let us look at a summary of the foreclosure process for a standard mortgage. (See Chapter 10 for Trust deed foreclosures.)

The Lawsuit   The mortgage foreclosure process begins with a title search. Next, the lender files a lawsuit naming as defendants the borrower and anyone who acquired a right or interest in the property after the lender recorded his mortgage. In the lawsuit the lender identifies the debt and the mortgage securing it, and states that it is in default. The lender then asks the court for a judgment directing that (1) the defendants' interests in the property be cut off in order to return the condition of title to what it was when the loan was made, (2) the property be sold at a public auction, and (3) the lender's claim be paid from the sale proceeds.

Surplus Money   A copy of the complaint along with a summons is de-
Action   livered to the defendants. This officially notifies them of the pending legal action against their interests. A junior mortgage holder who has been named as a defendant has

basically two choices; he will choose the one that he feels will leave him less worse off. One choice is to allow the foreclosure to proceed and file his own **surplus money action.** By doing this, he hopes that the property will sell at the foreclosure sale for enough money to pay all claims senior to him as well as his own claim against the borrower. The other choice is to halt the foreclosure process by making up the delinquent payments on behalf of the borrower and adding them to the amount the borrower owes him. To do this, the junior mortgage holder must take cash out of his own pocket and decide whether this is a case of "good money chasing bad." It is true that he can add these sums to the amount owed him, but he must also consider whether he will have any better luck being paid than did the holder of the senior mortgage.

At the same time that the lawsuit to foreclose is filed with the court, a **notice of lis pendens** is filed with the county recorder's office where the property is located. This informs the world that a legal action is pending against the property. If the borrower attempts to sell the property at this time, the prospective buyer, upon making his title search, would learn of the pending litigation. He can still proceed to purchase the property if he wants, but he has been informed that he is buying under the cloud of an unsettled lawsuit.

Notice of Lis Pendens

The borrower, or any other defendant named in the lawsuit, may now reply to the suit by presenting his side of the issue to the court judge. If no reply is made, or the issues raised by the reply are found in favor of the lender, the judge will order that the interests of the borrower and other defendants in the property be foreclosed and the property sold. The sale is usually a **public auction.** The objective is to obtain the best possible price for the property by inviting competitive bidding and conducting the sale in full view of the public. To announce the sale, the judge orders a notice to be posted on the courthouse door and advertised in local newspapers.

Public Auction

The sale is conducted by the **county sheriff** or by a **referee** or **master** appointed by the judge. At the sale, which is held at either the property or the courthouse, the lender and all parties interested in purchasing the property are present. If the borrower should suddenly locate sufficient funds to pay the judgment against him, he can, up to the minute the property goes on sale, step forward and redeem his property. This privilege to redeem property anytime between the first sign of delinquency and the moment of foreclosure sale is the borrower's **equity of redemption.** If no redemption is made, the bidding begins. Anyone with adequate funds can bid. Typically, a cash deposit of 10 percent of the successful bid must be made at the sale, with the balance of the bid price due upon closing, usually 30 days later.

While the lender and borrower hope that someone at the auction will bid more than the amount owed on the defaulted loan, the probability is not high. If the borrower was unable to find a buyer at a price equal to or higher than the loan balance, the best cash bid will probably be less than the balance owed. If this happens, the lender usually enters a bid of his own. The lender is in a unique position as he can "bid his loan." That is, he can bid up to the amount owed him without having to pay cash. All other bidders must pay cash, as the purpose of the sale is to obtain cash to pay the defaulted loan. In the event the borrower bids at the sale and is successful in buying back his property, the junior liens against the property are not eliminated.

Deficiency Judgment   If the property sells for more than the claims against it, including any junior mortgage holders, the borrower receives the excess. For example, if a property with $25,000 in claims against it sells for $27,000, the borrower will receive the $2,000 difference, less expenses of the sale. However, if the highest bid is only $20,000, how is the $5,000 deficiency treated? The laws of the various states differ on this question. Most allow the lender to request a **deficiency judgment** for the $5,000, with which the lender can proceed against the borrower's other unsecured assets. In other words, the borrower is still personally obligated to the lender for $5,000 and the lender is entitled to collect it. This may require the borrower to sell other assets.

Several states have outlawed deficiency judgments in most

foreclosure situations so that a lender cannot reach beyond the mortgaged property for debt satisfaction. In these states the lender would stand the $5,000 deficiency loss. These states are California, Montana, North Dakota, and North Carolina. In a large number of states, if the property sells for an obviously depressed price at its foreclosure sale, a deficiency judgment will be allowed only for the difference between the court's estimate of the property's fair market value and the amount of the mortgage judgment against it. Quite naturally, borrowers prefer to sign mortgages without deficiency clauses. Even in states that do allow them, if the borrower is in a strong enough bargaining position, he can negotiate for a mortgage contract that prohibits the lender from seeking a deficiency judgment.

In states that do not give a foreclosed borrower a statutory redemption period, the purchaser at the foreclosure sale receives either a **referee's deed in foreclosure** or a **sheriff's deed**. These are usually special warranty deeds that convey the title the borrower had at the time the foreclosed mortgage was originally made. The purchaser may take immediate possession and the court will assist him in removing anyone in possion who was cut off in the foreclosure proceedings.

In those states with statutory redemption laws, the foreclosed borrower has, depending on the state, from 2 months to 2 years after the foreclosure sale to pay in full the judgment against him and retake title. This leaves the high bidder at the foreclosure auction in a dilemma: he does not know for certain whether he will get the property he bid on until the statutory redemption period has run out. Meanwhile, he receives a **certificate of sale** entitling him to a referee's or sheriff's deed if no redemption is made. Depending on the state, the purchaser may or may not get possession until then. If he does not, the foreclosed borrower may allow the property to deteriorate and lose value. Knowing this, prospective purchasers bid less than what the property would be worth if title and possession could be delivered immediately after the foreclosure sale. In this respect, statutory redemption works against the borrower.

Statutory Redemption

POWER OF SALE   Forty-two states permit the use of **power of sale**, also known as **sale by advertisement**, as a means of simplifying and shortening the foreclosure proceeding itself. If it is necessary to foreclose, this clause in the mortgage gives the lender the power to conduct the foreclosure and sell the mortgaged property without taking the issue to court. States that permit the use of the power of sale require a waiting period between default and the sale. This is the borrower's equity of redemption. The property is then advertised and sold at an auction held by the lender and open to the public. The precise procedures the lender must follow are set by state statutes. After the auction, the borrower can still redeem the property if his state offers statutory redemption. The deed the purchaser receives is prepared and signed by the lender. A major weak point with power of sale is that in many states junior claimants need not be personally notified of a pending sale. Thus, conceivably, a junior claimant could have his rights cut off without being aware of it.

DEED IN LIEU OF   To avoid the hassle of foreclosure proceedings, a bor-
FORECLOSURE   rower may voluntarily deed his property to the lender. In turn, the borrower should demand cancellation of the unpaid debt and a letter to that effect from the lender. This method relieves the lender of foreclosing and waiting out any required redemption periods, but it presents the lender with a sensitive situation. With the borrower in financial distress and about to be foreclosed, it is quite easy for the lender to take advantage of the borrower. As a result, courts of law will usually side with the borrower if he complains of any unfair dealings. Thus, the lender must be prepared to prove conclusively that the borrower received a fair deal by deeding his property voluntarily to the lender in return for cancellation of his debt. If the property is worth more than the balance due on the debt, the lender must pay the borrower the difference in cash. A deed in lieu of foreclosure is a voluntary act by both borrower and lender; if either feels he will fare better in regular foreclosure proceedings, he need not agree to it. Note also that a deed in lieu of foreclosure will not cut off the rights of junior mortgage holders.

Match terms a–t with statements 1–20.

VOCABULARY REVIEW

a. *Alienation clause*
b. *Assumption*
c. *Chattel mortgage*
d. *Covenant of insurance*
e. *Defeasance clause*
f. *Deficiency judgment*
g. *Equitable mortgage*
h. *Equity of redemption*
i. *Foreclosure suit*
j. *Junior mortgage*

k. *Mortgage*
l. *Mortgagor*
m. *Nonconforming*
n. *Partial release*
o. *Power of sale*
p. *Promissory note*
q. *Satisfaction*
r. *Statutory redemption*
s. *Subject to*
t. *Subordination*

1. A pledge of property to secure a debt.
2. A clause in a mortgage stating that the mortgage is defeated if the borrower repays the accompanying note on time.
3. The borrower's right, prior to the day of foreclosure, to repay the balance due on a delinquent loan.
4. A lawsuit filed by a lender that asks a court to set a time limit on how long a borrower has to redeem his property.
5. An agreement that is considered to be a mortgage in its intent even though it may not follow the usual mortgage wording.
6. A pledge of personal property to secure a promissory note.
7. The evidence of debt; contains amount owed, interest rate, repayment schedule, and a promise to repay.
8. The person who gives a mortgage pledging his property; the borrower.
9. A clause in a mortgage that permits the lender to demand full payment of the loan if the property changes ownership. Also called a due-on-sale clause.
10. A clause in a mortgage whereby the mortgagor agrees to keep mortgaged property adequately insured against destruction.
11. Discharge of a mortgage upon payment of the debt owed.
12. Release of a portion of a property from a mortgage.
13. The buyer personally obligates himself to repay an existing mortgage loan as a condition of the sale.
14. The buyer of an already mortgaged property makes the payments but does not take personal responsibility for the loan.
15. Any mortgage lower than a first mortgage in priority.
16. A loan on which the borrower is behind in his payments.
17. A clause in a mortgage that gives the mortgagee the right to conduct a foreclosure sale without first going to court.
18. The amount the borrower must pay the lender if the sale of the pledged property at foreclosure does not bring in enough to pay the balance still owing.

19. The right of a borrower, after a foreclosure sale, to reclaim his property by repaying his defaulted loan.
20. To voluntarily accept a lower mortgage priority position than one would otherwise be entitled to based on the date of recording.

QUESTIONS AND PROBLEMS

1. Is a prepayment privilege to the advantage of the borrower or the lender?
2. What are the legal differences between lien theory and title theory?
3. How does strict foreclosure differ from foreclosure by sale? Which system does your state use?
4. A large apartment complex serves as security for a first, a second, and a third mortgage. Which of these are considered junior mortgage(s)? Senior mortgage(s)?
5. Describe the procedure in your county that is used in foreclosing delinquent real estate loans.
6. What do the laws of your state allow real estate borrowers in the way of equitable and statutory redemption?
7. Do the laws of your state allow a delinquent borrower adequate opportunity to recover his mortgaged real estate? Do you advocate more or less borrower protection than is presently available?
8. In a promissory note, who is the obligor? Who is the obligee?
9. Why does a mortgage lender insist on including covenants pertaining to insurance, property taxes and removal, in the mortgage?
10. What roles do a certificate of reduction and an estoppel certificate play in mortgage lending?

ADDITIONAL READINGS

Gross, Jerome S. *Encyclopedia of Real Estate Forms.* Englewood Cliffs, N.J.: Prentice-Hall, 1973, 458 pages. Contains numerous examples of real estate mortgages, promissory notes, and other mortgage-related documents.

Hoagland, Henry E. and **Leo D. Stone.** *Real Estate Finance,* 5th ed. Homewood, Ill.: Richard D. Irwin, 1973, 603 pages. Chapters 2–6 deal with the legal nature of mortgages, kinds of mortgages, default, foreclosure, alternatives to default, and junior liens.

Kratovil, Robert. *Modern Mortgage Law and Practice.* Englewood Cliffs, N.J.: Prentice-Hall, 1972, 350 pages. Includes the history of mortgage, law, types of mortgages, contents of a mortgage, subordination, foreclosure, redemption, and other mortgage topics.

10

Trust Deeds

KEY TERMS

Assignment of rents clause: the right to collect the rents generated from a property in the event the borrower does not repay the note

Beneficiary: one for whose benefit a trust is created; the lender under a trust deed arrangement

Naked title: title in a strictly legal sense but lacking the rights and privileges usually associated with ownership

Reconveyance: the return to the borrower of legal title to his property upon repayment of the debt against it

Release deed: a document used to reconvey title back from the trustee to the property owner once the debt has been paid

Trust deed: a document that conveys legal title to a neutral third party as security for a loan

Trustee: one who holds property in trust for another

Trustor: one who creates a trust; the borrower under a trust deed arrangement

The basic purpose of a **trust deed,** also referred to as a deed of trust or deed in trust, is the same as a mortgage. Real property is used as security for a debt; if the debt is not repaid, the property is sold and the proceeds are applied to the balance owed. In a few states (Georgia, for example), a security deed that is similar to a trust deed is used for this purpose. The main legal difference between a trust deed and a mortgage is diagrammed in Figure 10:1.

PARTIES TO A TRUST DEED

Figure 10:1A shows that when a debt is secured by a mortgage the borrower delivers his promissory note and mortgage to the lender, who keeps them until the debt is paid. But when a note is secured by a trust deed, three parties are involved: the borrower (the **trustor**), the lender (the **beneficiary**), and a neutral third party (the **trustee**). The lender makes a loan to the borrower, and the borrower gives the lender a promissory

Figure 10:1   **COMPARING A MORTGAGE WITH TRUST DEED**

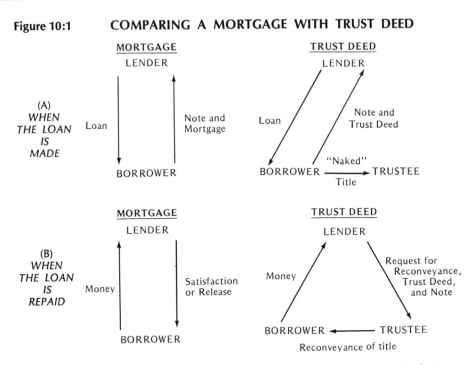

note (like the one shown in Chapter 9) and a trust deed. In the trust deed document, the borrower conveys title to the trustee, to be held in trust until the note is paid in full. The trust deed is recorded in the county where the property is located and then is usually given to the lender for safekeeping. A variation used in some areas of the country is to deliver the recorded trust deed to the trustee to be held in a long-term escrow until the note is paid in full. Anyone searching the title records on the borrower's property would find the trust deed conveying title to the trustee. This would alert the title searcher to the existence of a debt against the property.

The title that the borrower grants to the trustee is sometimes referred to as a "naked" title, because the borrower still retains the usual rights of an owner such as the right to occupy and use the property, and the right to sell it. The title held by the trustee is limited only to what is necessary to carry out the terms of the trust. In fact, as long as the note is not in default, the trustee's title lies dormant. The lender does not receive title, but only a right that allows him to request the trustee to act.

Referring to Figure 10:1B, when the note is repaid in full under a regular mortgage, the lender cancels the note and issues the borrower a mortgage satisfaction or release. Upon recordation, this document informs the world at large that the mortgage is nullified and no longer encumbers the property. Under the trust deed arrangement, the lender sends to the trustee the note, the trust deed, and a **request for reconveyance.** The trustee cancels the note and issues to the borrower a **reconveyance deed,** or a **release deed,** which reconveys title back to the borrower. The borrower records this document to inform the world that the trustee no longer has title. At the recorder's office, a marginal note is made on the record copy of the original trust deed to show it has been discharged.

Reconveyance

If a borrower defaults under a trust deed, the lender delivers the trust deed to the trustee and instructs him to sell the property and pay the balance due on the note. The trustee can do this because of two important features found in the trust deed. First, by virtue of signing the trust deed, the borrower has already conveyed title to the trustee. Second, the power of sale clause found in trust deeds gives the trustee the authority to sell the pledged property without having to go through a court-ordered foreclosure proceeding.

In nearly all states, private trustees, such as a title, trust, or escrow company or the trust department of a bank, may act as trustee. An individual can be named as a trustee in most jurisdictions. However, this can present a problem if the person dies before reconveyance is made. Therefore, a corporate trustee is preferred because its life span is not limited by the human life span. In a few jurisdictions, Colorado for example, the role of trustee is performed by a government official known as a public trustee. Whether public or private, the trustee is expected to be neutral and fair to both the borrower and lender. To accomplish this, the trustee carefully abides by the agreements found in the trust deed.

Figure 10:2 is a simplified example of a trust deed that shows the agreements between the borrower and lender and states the responsibilities of the trustee. Beginning at ①, the document is identified as a deed of trust. This is followed by the date of its execution and the names of the trustor, bene-

THE TRUST DEED

Figure 10:2

DEED OF TRUST WITH POWER OF SALE

(1) *This Deed of Trust, made this* 15th *day of* April *,*
19——— *, between* Fred and Mary Olsen, Husband and Wife *,*
herein called the Trustor, and Blue Sky Mortgage Company
herein called the Beneficiary, and Safety Title and Trust Co.,
Inc. *herein called the Trustee.*

(2) *WITNESSETH: To secure the repayment of one*
promissory note in the principal sum of $ 70,000 *executed*
by the Trustor in favor of the Beneficiary and bearing the
same date as this Deed, and to secure the agreements shown
below, the Trustor irrevocably grants (3) *and conveys to the*
Trustee, in trust, with power (4) *of sale, the following described*
real property in the County of San Juan *, State of_____ .*

Lot 21, Block "A," of (5) *Tract 2468, as shown*
in Map Book 29, Page 17, filed in the Public
Records Office of the above County and State.

(6) *FURTHERMORE: The trustor warrants the title to*
said property and will defend the same against all claims.

(7) *UPON WRITTEN REQUEST by the Beneficiary to*
the Trustee stating that all sums secured hereby have been
paid, and upon surrender of this Deed and said Note to the
Trustee for cancellation, the Trustee shall reconvey the above
described property to the Trustor.

(8) *THIS DEED BINDS all parties hereto, their succes-*
sors, assigns, heirs, devisees, administrators, and executors.

(9) *UNTIL SAID NOTE IS PAID IN FULL:*

A. The Trustor agrees to pay all taxes on said
property.

B. The Trustor agrees not to remove or demolish any
buildings or other improvements on said property without the
approval of the Beneficiary.

C. The Trustor agrees to carry adequate insurance to protect the Beneficiary in the event of damage or destruction of said property.

D. The Trustor agrees to keep the mortgaged property in good repair and not permit waste or deterioration.

E. The Beneficiary shall have the right to inspect said property as may be necessary for the security of the Note.

F. If all or part of said property is taken by eminent domain, any money received shall be applied to the Note.

UPON DEFAULT BY THE TRUSTOR in payment of the debt secured hereby, or the nonperformance of any agreement hereby made, the Beneficiary:

G. May declare all sums secured hereby immediately due and payable.

(10) H. May enter and take possession of said property and collect the rents and profits thereof.

(11) I. May demand the Trustee sell said property in accordance with state law, apply the proceeds to the unpaid portion of the Note, and deliver to the purchaser a Trustee's Deed conveying title to said property.

(12) *THE TRUSTEE ACCEPTS THIS TRUST* when this Deed, properly executed and acknowledged, is made a public record. The Beneficiary may substitute a successor to the Trustee named herein by recording such change in the public records of the county where said property is located.

(13)
Trustor

Fred Olsen
Trustor

(14) |acknowledgment of trustor's signature is placed here|

ficiary, and trustee. For discussion purposes, this chapter will continue to refer to them as the borrower, lender, and trustee, respectively. At ②, the promissory note that accompanies this trust deed is identified, and, it is clearly stated that the purpose of this deed is to provide security for that note. In other words, although this deed grants and conveys title to the trustee at ③, it is understood that the quantity of title the trustee receives is only that which is necessary to protect the note. This permits the borrower to continue to possess and enjoy the use of the property as long as the promissory note is not in default.

Power of Sale   Under the power of sale clause shown at ④, if the borrower defaults, the trustee has the right to foreclose and sell the pledged property and convey ownership to the purchaser. If the borrower does not default, this power lies dormant. Having a power of sale right does not prohibit the trustee from using a court-ordered foreclosure. If the rights of the parties involved, including junior trust deed holders and other claimants, are not clear, the trustee can ask for a court-ordered foreclosure.

At ⑤, the property being conveyed to the trustee is described, and at ⑥ the borrower states that he has title to the property and that he will defend that title against the claims of others. At ⑦, the procedure that must be followed to reconvey the title is described. Note that state laws provide that, when the note is paid, the lender must deliver a request for reconveyance to the trustee. The lender must also deliver the promissory note and trust deed to the trustee. Upon receiving these three items, the trustee reconveys title to the borrower and the trust arrangement is terminated. Figure 10:3 is a sample reconveyance request.

Continuing in Figure 10:2, the sections identified at ⑧ and ⑨ (paragraphs A through G) are similar to those found in a regular mortgage and were discussed in Chapter 9. At ⑩, the lender reserves the right to take physical possession of the pledged property, operate it, and collect any rents or income generated by it. The right to collect rents in the event of default is called an **assignment of rents** clause. The lender

REQUEST FOR FULL RECONVEYANCE

Figure 10:3

To: Safety Title and Trust Company, Inc., *trustee.*

The undersigned is the owner of the debt secured by the above Deed of Trust. This debt has been fully paid and you are requested to reconvey to the parties designated in the Deed of Trust, the estate now held by you under same.

_____
Beneficiary

Date _____

|as a matter of convenience, this form is often printed at the bottom or on the reverse of the trust deed itself|

would only exercise this right if the borrower continued to collect rental income from the property without paying on the note. The right to take physical possession in the event of default is important as it gives the lender the opportunity to preserve the value of the property until the foreclosure sale takes place. Very likely, if the borrower has defaulted on the note, his financial condition is such that he is no longer maintaining the property. If this continues, the property will be worth less by the time the foreclosure sale occurs.

At ⑪, the lender establishes his right to instruct the trustee to sell the pledged property in the event of the borrower's default on the note or nonperformance of the agreements in the trust deed. This section also deals with the ground rules by which the trustee is to conduct the foreclosure sale. Either appropriate state laws are referred to or each step of the process is listed in the deed at this point. Generally, state laws regarding power of sale foreclosure require that (1) the lender demonstrate conclusively to the trustee that there is reason to cut off the borrower's interest in the property, (2) a notice of default be filed with the public recorder, (3) the notice of default be followed by a 90- to 120-day waiting period before

Foreclosure

advertising begins, (4) advertising of the proposed fore-closure sale occur for at least 3 weeks in public places and a local newspaper, (5) the sale itself be a public auction held in the county where the property is located, and (6) the purchaser at the sale be given a trustee's deed conveying all title held by the trustee. This is all the right, title, and interest the borrower had at the time he deeded his property, in trust, to the trustee. Proceeds from the sale are used to pay (1) the expenses of the sale and any unpaid property taxes, (2) the lender, (3) any junior claims, and (4) the borrower, in that order. Once the sale is held, the borrower's equitable right of redemption is ended. In some states, statutory redemption may still exist. Anyone can bid at the sale, including the borrower. However, junior claims that would normally be cut off by the sale are not extinguished if the borrower is the successful bidder.

The wording at ⑫ reflects what is called the **automatic form** of trusteeship. The trustee is named in the deed, but is not personally notified of the appointment. In fact, the trustee is not usually aware of the appointment until called upon to either reconvey or proceed under the power of sale provision. The alternative method is called the **accepted form**: the trustee is notified in advance and either accepts or rejects the appointment. Its primary advantage is that it provides positive acceptance of appointment. The main advantage of the automatic form is that it is faster and easier. In the event the trustee cannot or will not perform when called upon by the lender, the wording at ⑫ permits the lender to name a substitute trustee. This would be necessary if an individual appointed as a trustee had died, or a corporate trustee was dissolved, or an appointed trustee refused to perform. Finally, the borrowers sign at ⑬, their signatures are acknowledged at ⑭, and the trust deed is recorded in the county where the property is located.

WHERE TRUST DEEDS ARE USED   Trust deeds are used almost exclusively in place of regular mortgages in California, the District of Columbia, Mississippi, Missouri, Tennessee, Texas, and West Virginia. They are also used to a certain extent in Alabama, Alaska, Colorado, Delaware, Illinois, Montana, Nevada, New Mexico, North

Carolina, Oregon, Utah, Virginia, Washington, and a few other states. The extent of their use in a state is governed by that state's attitude toward conveyance of title to the trustee, power of sale, and statutory redemption privileges. Many states not listed here allow the use of trust deeds, but consider them to be liens. As such they are treated no differently than a mortgage with a power of sale clause.

A few states recognize some, but not all, of the provisions of a trust deed. For example, a state may allow power of sale clauses in trust deeds but not in regular mortgages. Or it may rule that foreclosed mortgages must have a statutory redemption period while trust deeds do not. In those states that allow all the provisions of the trust deed to function without hindrance, the trust deed has flourished. In California, for example, where it is legally well established that a trust deed does convey title to the trustee, that the trustee has the power of sale, and that there is no statutory redemption on trust deeds, trust deed recordings outnumber regular mortgages by a ratio of more than 500 to 1.

ADVANTAGES OF THE TRUST DEED

The popularity of the trust deed can be traced to the following attributes: (1) if a borrower defaults, the lender can take possession of the pledged property to protect it and collect the rents; (2) the time between default and foreclosure is relatively short, on the order of 90 to 180 days; (3) the foreclosure process under the power of sale provision is far less expensive and complex than a court-ordered foreclosure; (4) title is already in the name of the trustee, thus permitting him to grant title to the purchaser after the foreclosure sale; and (5) once the foreclosure sale takes place, there is usually no statutory redemption. These are primarily advantages to the lender, but such advantages have attracted lenders and made real estate loans easier for borrowers to obtain and less expensive. Some states prohibit deficiency judgments against borrowers when trust deeds are used.

Property can be purchased "subject to" an existing trust deed or it can be "assumed," just as with a regular mortgage. Debt priorities are established as for mortgages: there are first and second, senior and junior trust deeds. Trust deeds can be subordinated and partial releases are possible.

VOCABULARY REVIEW   *Match terms a–f with statements 1–6.*

a. *Beneficiary*   **d.** *Trust deed*
b. *Public trustee*   **e.** *Trustee*
c. *Reconveyance*   **f.** *Trustor*

1. A document that conveys legal title to a neutral third party as security for a loan.
2. One who creates a trust; the borrower under a trust deed arrangement.
3. The lender.
4. One who holds property in trust for another.
5. Transfer of title from the trustee to the trustor.
6. A publicly appointed official who acts as a trustee in some states.

QUESTIONS AND PROBLEMS

1. How does a trust deed differ from a mortgage?
2. Does possession of a trust deed give the trustee any rights of entry or use of the property in question as long as the promissory note is not in default? Explain.
3. What role does a request for reconveyance play?
4. What is the purpose of a power of sale clause in a trust deed?
5. Explain the purpose of an assignment of rents clause.
6. How does the automatic form of trusteeship differ from the accepted form?
7. What is your state's attitude toward trust deeds, power of sale, statutory redemption, and deficiency judgments?

ADDITIONAL READINGS

California Department of Real Estate. *Reference Book.* Sacramento: Department of Real Estate, 1974, 729 pages. Trust deeds are discussed and compared to mortgages on pages 190–199.

Powell, Richard R. *The Law of Property.* New York: Matthew Bender, 1975, 7 volumes. Volume 3, section 439, and Volume 4A, section 574, explain the trust deed and its use and application from a legal point of view.

Thompson, George W. *Commentaries on the Modern Law of Real Property.* Indianapolis: Bobbs-Merrill, 1963 (plus 1975 supplement), 13 volumes. Volume 9, Chapter 59, discusses the use of trust deeds in place of mortgages. Volume 10, Chapters 73 and 74, deal with enforcing trust deeds and mortgages.

11

Mortgage Lending

Amortized loan: a loan requiring periodic payments that include both interest and partial repayment of principal

Balloon loan: a loan in which the final payment is larger than the preceding payments

Conventional loans: real estate loans that are not insured by the FHA or guaranteed by the VA

Equity: The market value of a property less the debt against it

Impound, Escrow, or Reserve account: an account into which the lender places monthly tax and insurance payments

PITI payment: a loan payment that combines principal, interest, taxes and insurance

Point: one percent of the loan amount; one-hundredth of the total amount of the mortgage

Principal: the balance owing on a loan

Purchase money mortgage: a loan used to purchase the real property that serves as its collateral

Take-out loan: a permanent loan arranged to replace a construction loan

The previous two chapters were primarily devoted to the legal aspects of mortgages and trust deeds. In this and the following chapter we shall focus on the financial side of real estate lending. Let us begin by looking at the three basic patterns that mortgage loan repayment can follow: term, amortized, and partially amortized.

TERM LOANS

A loan that requires only interest payments until the last day of its life, at which time the full amount borrowed is due, is called a **term loan** (or straight loan). Because the final payment is larger than the previous payments, term loans are classed as **balloon loans** and the final payment is referred to as a **balloon payment.** Until 1930, the term loan was the standard method of financing real estate in the United States. These loans were typically made for a period of 3 to 5 years. The borrower signed a note or bond agreeing to (1) pay the lender interest on the loan every 6 months and (2) repay the entire amount of the loan upon maturity (i.e., at the end of the life of the loan). As security, the borrower mortgaged his property to the lender.

Loan Renewal   In practice, most real estate term loans were not paid off when they matured. Instead, the borrower asked the lender, typically a bank prior to the 1930s, to renew the loan for another 3 to 5 years. The major flaw in this approach to lending was that the borrower might never own his property free and clear of debt. This left him continuously at the mercy of the lender for renewals. As long as the lender was not pressed for funds, the borrower's renewal request was granted. However, if the lender was short of funds, no renewal was granted and the borrower was expected to pay in full. The borrower might then go to another lender. But there have been periods during America's economic history when loans from any source have been difficult to obtain. If the borrower's loan came due during one of these periods, going to other lenders would not solve the borrower's problem. With the borrower unable to repay, the lender foreclosed and applied the sale proceeds to the amount due on the loan.

The inability to renew a term loan was the cause of hardship to thousands of property owners during the first 155 years of U.S. history, but at no time were the consequences so harsh as during the Great Depression that began in 1930 and lasted most of the decade. Banks were unable to accommodate requests for loan renewals and at the same time satisfy unemployed depositors who needed to withdraw their savings to live. As a result, owners of homes, farms, office buildings, factories, and vacant land lost their property as foreclosures reached into the millions. So glutted was the market with properties being offered for sale to satisfy unpaid mortgage loans that real estate prices fell at a sickening pace.

AMORTIZED LOANS   In 1933, a congressionally legislated Home Owner's Loan Corporation (HOLC) was created to assist financially distressed homeowners by acquiring mortgages that were about to be foreclosed. The HOLC then offered monthly repayment plans tailored to fit the homeowner's budget and aimed at repaying the loan in full by its maturity date without the need for a balloon payment. The HOLC was terminated in 1951 after rescuing over 1 million mortgages in its 18-year life. However, the use of this stretched-out repayment plan, known as an **amortized loan,** took hold, and today it is the accepted method of loan repayment.

REPAYING A 6-YEAR $1,000 AMORTIZED LOAN
Carrying 9% Interest per Year

Figure 11:1

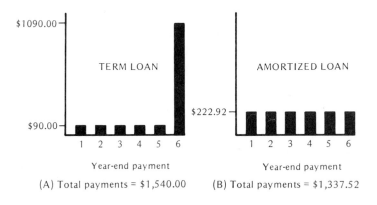

(A) Total payments = $1,540.00   (B) Total payments = $1,337.52

The amortized loan requires regular payments during the life of the loan, in sufficient size and number, to pay all interest due on the loan and reduce the amount owed to zero by the loan's maturity date. Figure 11:1 illustrates the concept of amortization and contrasts it with a term loan. Figure 11:1A shows a 6-year, $1,000 term loan with interest of $90 due each year of its life. At the end of the sixth year the entire principal (the amount owed) is due in one lump sum payment along with the final interest payment. In Figure 11:1B, the same $1,000 loan is fully amortized by making six equal annual payments of $222.92. From the borrower's standpoint, $222.92 once each year is easier to budget than $90 for 5 years and suddenly $1,090 in the sixth year. Furthermore, the amortized loan shown here actually costs the borrower less than the term loan. The total payments made under the term loan are $90 + $90 + $90 + $90 + $90 + $1,090 = $1,540. Amortizing the same loan requires total payments of 6 × $222.92 = $1,337.52. The difference is due to the fact that under the amortized loan the borrower is beginning to pay

back part of the $1,000 principal with his first payment. In the
first year, $90 of the $222.92 payment goes to interest and the
remaining $132.92 reduces the principal owed. Thus, the bor-
rower starts the second year owing only $867.08. At 9% in-
terest per year, the interest on $867.08 is $78.04; therefore,
when the borrower makes his second payment of $222.92,
only $78.04 goes to interest. The remaining $144.88 is applied
to reduce the loan balance, and the borrower starts the third
year owing $722.20.

Figure 11:2   **REPAYING A 6-YEAR $1,000 AMORTIZED LOAN**
Carrying 9% Interest per Year

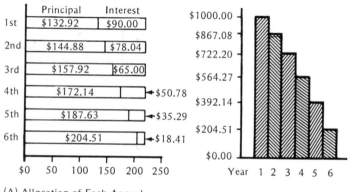

(A) Allocation of Each Annual
Payment to Principal and Interest

(B) Loan (Principal) Balance

Figure 11:2 charts this repayment program. Notice that as
the loan balance is reduced, the interest that must be paid is
reduced, thus allowing a larger and larger portion of each suc-
cessive payment to be used to reduce the loan balance. As a
result, the balance owed drops faster as the loan becomes
older.

Calculating the payments on a term loan is relatively
simple compared to calculating amortized loan payments. As
a result, amortization payment tables are published and used
throughout the real estate industry. Table 11:1 shows the
monthly payments necessary to fully amortize loans carrying
interest rates of 8½% and 9½% for periods ranging from 5
to 40 years. (Amortization tables are also published for quarterly, semiannual, and annual payments.) In using an amorti-

Table 11:1 **AMORTIZATION TABLES FOR MONTHLY LOAN PAYMENTS**

$8^1/2\%$ Interest per Year during Life of Loan

Amount	5 years	10 years	15 years	20 years	25 years	30 years	35 years	40 years
$ 100	$ 2.06	$ 1.24	$ 0.99	$ 0.87	$ 0.81	$ 0.77	$ 0.75	$ 0.74
500	10.26	6.20	4.93	4.34	4.03	3.85	3.74	3.67
1,000	20.52	12.40	9.85	8.68	8.06	7.69	7.47	7.34
5,000	102.59	62.00	49.24	43.40	40.27	38.45	37.35	36.66
10,000	205.17	123.99	98.48	86.79	80.53	76.90	74.69	73.31
15,000	307.75	185.98	147.72	130.18	120.79	115.34	112.03	109.97
20,000	410.34	247.98	196.95	173.57	161.05	153.79	149.38	146.62
25,000	512.92	309.97	246.19	216.96	201.31	192.23	186.72	183.28
30,000	615.50	371.96	295.43	260.35	241.57	230.68	224.06	219.93
35,000	718.08	433.95	344.66	303.74	281.83	269.12	261.41	256.59
40,000	820.67	495.95	393.90	347.13	322.10	307.57	298.75	293.24
45,000	923.25	557.94	443.14	390.53	362.36	346.02	336.09	329.90
50,000	1,025.83	619.93	492.37	433.92	402.62	384.46	373.44	366.55
60,000	1,231.00	743.92	590.85	520.70	483.14	461.35	448.12	439.86
70,000	1,426.16	867.90	689.32	607.48	563.66	538.24	522.81	513.17

$9^1/2\%$ Interest per Year during Life of Loan

Amount	5 years	10 years	15 years	20 years	25 years	30 years	35 years	40 years
$ 100	$ 2.11	$ 1.30	$ 1.05	$ 0.94	$ 0.88	$ 0.85	$ 0.83	$ 0.82
500	10.51	6.47	5.23	4.67	4.37	4.21	4.11	4.06
1,000	21.01	12.94	10.45	9.33	8.74	8.41	8.22	8.11
5,000	105.01	64.70	52.22	46.61	43.69	42.05	41.09	40.51
10,000	210.02	129.40	104.43	93.22	87.37	84.09	82.17	81.01
15,000	315.03	194.10	156.64	139.82	131.06	126.13	123.25	121.51
20,000	420.04	258.80	208.85	186.43	174.74	168.18	164.33	162.02
25,000	525.05	323.50	253.75	233.04	218.43	210.22	205.41	202.52
30,000	630.06	388.20	313.27	279.64	262.11	252.26	246.49	243.02
35,000	735.07	452.90	365.48	326.25	305.80	294.30	287.57	283.53
40,000	840.08	517.60	417.69	372.86	349.48	336.35	328.65	324.03
45,000	945.09	582.29	469.91	419.46	393.17	378.39	369.73	364.53
50,000	1,050.10	646.99	522.12	466.07	436.85	420.43	410.81	405.04
60,000	1,260.12	776.39	626.54	559.28	524.22	504.52	494.97	486.04
70,000	1,470.14	905.79	730.96	652.50	611.59	588.60	575.13	567.05

Source: *Expanded Payment Table for Monthly Mortgage Loans,* publication 193. (Boston: Financial Publishing Company, 1969), pp. 109–117 and 149–157. By permission.

zation table, notice that there are five variables: (1) frequency of payment, (2) interest rate, (3) maturity, (4) amount of the loan, and (5) amount of the periodic payment. If you know any four of these, you can obtain the fifth variable from the tables. For example, suppose that you want to know the monthly payment necessary to amortize a $30,000 loan over 25 years at 8½% interest. The first step is to turn to the monthly payment, 8½% table. Then locate the 25-year column and the $30,000 line. Where they cross you will find the necessary monthly payment: $241.57. Suppose, however, that the loan amount was $30,110 instead of $30,000. Since the table does not have $30,110, an additional step is necessary and is illustrated in Table 11:2.

Table 11:2   **CALCULATING A MONTHLY AMORTIZED LOAN PAYMENT**

Loan Amount	Monthly Payment
$30,000	$241.57
100	0.81
10	0.08
Total $30,110	**Total** $242.46

Note: Alternative methods are to multiply the $10,000 payment of $80.53 by 3.011, or to multiply $80.53 by $0.011 and add it to the $30,000 monthly payment of $241.57. One can also multiply the $1,000 monthly payment of $8.06 by 30.11. However, this is slightly less accurate than using the $10,000 base.

Amortization tables are most often used to find the payments needed to repay a loan. However, they can also be used in a number of other ways. Suppose that a prospective home buyer can afford monthly principal and interest payments of $350 and lenders are making 25-year loans at 9½% interest. How large a loan can this buyer afford? In the 9½% table in Table 11:1, locate the 25-year column. Find the closest figure to $350. That will be $349.48 on the $40,000 line. This means that a $40,000, 25-year, 9½% loan requires monthly payments of $349.48. Therefore, the prospective home buyer can afford a loan of $40,000. By adding his down payment money, you now know what price property he can afford to purchase. Amortization handbooks in common use today are in loan increments of $500. This makes it easier to quickly zero in on a solution. These handbooks also typically include interest rates from 5% to 12% by ¼% increments, and maturities of from 1 to 30 years by 1-year increments, plus 35 and 40 years.

With amortization tables you can find the number of years necessary to repay a loan when you know the interest rate, loan amount, and the periodic payment. For example, an 8½% loan for $25,000 with monthly payments of $192.23 will require 30 years for repayment. The tables can also help you find the interest rate when you know the length of the loan, loan amount, and monthly payments. For example, a 20-year, $50,000 loan with monthly payments of $466.07 would yield the lender 9½% interest per year.

Change in Interest

Several other interesting facets of real estate financing are shown by amortization tables. For example, what happens to the monthly payment when the interest rate is raised from 8½% to 9½% on a 30-year, $35,000 loan? At 8½% the monthly payment is $269.12. At 9½% the same loan requires $294.30, an increase of $25.18 per month. If the borrower could not afford the extra $25.18 per month, he would have to settle for a loan of $32,000.

Change in Maturity

An amortization table also shows the impact on the size of the monthly payment when the life of a loan is extended. For example, a loan of $25,000 for 10 years at 8½% interest requires payments of $309.97 per month. By increasing this loan's life to 20 years, the monthly payment drops dramatically to $216.96, and at 30 years to $192.23. Thus, the longer the life of the loan, the lower the payments, or the larger a loan a borrower can afford, given the same monthly payment. Unfortunately, going beyond 30 years does not reduce the monthly payment significantly. For example, extending the life of the above $25,000 loan from 30 to 40 years reduces the monthly payment by only $8.95 while adding 10 additional years of payments. In terms of loan size, that $8.95 will support only $1,220 of extra principal. Going beyond 40 years produces even smaller decreases in monthly payments. Thus, as a practical matter, amortized real estate loans are seldom made for more than 30 years.

The 30-year practical maximum is also affected by the life span of the property being mortgaged. As a rule of thumb, lenders do not like to lend for longer than three quarters of the remaining useful life of a building. This would permit a

30-year loan on a property with 40 remaining useful years and a 15-year loan on a property with only 20 remaining years.

Budget Mortgages

The **budget mortgage** takes the amortized loan one step further. In addition to collecting the monthly principal and interest payment (often called P + I), the lender collects one twelfth of the estimated cost of the annual property taxes and hazard insurance on the mortgaged property. The money for tax and insurance payments is placed in an **impound account** (also called an escrow or reserve account). When taxes and insurance payments are due, the lender pays them. Thus, the lender makes certain that the value of the pledged property will not be undermined by unpaid property taxes or by uninsured fire or weather damage. This form of mortgage also helps the borrower to budget for property taxes and insurance on a monthly basis. To illustrate, if hazard insurance is $180 per year and property taxes are $1200 per year, the lender will collect an additional $15 and $100 each month along with the regular principal and interest payments. The combined principal, interest, taxes, and insurance payment is often referred to as a **PITI payment.**

PARTIAL AMORTIZATION

When the repayment schedule of a loan calls for a series of amortized payments followed by a balloon payment at maturity, it is called a **partially amortized loan.** For example, a lender might agree to a 15-year amortization schedule with a provision that at the end of the tenth year all the remaining principal be paid in a single balloon payment. The advantage to the borrower is that for 10 years his monthly payments will be smaller than if he completely amortized his loan in 10 years. (You can verify this in Table 11:1.) However, the disadvantage is that the balloon payment due at the end of the tenth year might be his financial downfall. Just how large that balloon payment will be can be determined in advance by using a **loan progress chart.** Presuming an interest rate of 9½% for each $1,000 of the original 15-year loan, at the end of 10 years the loan progress chart in Table 11:3 shows that $497 would still be owed. If the original loan was for $40,000, at the end of 10 years 40 × $497 = $19,880 would be due as one payment. This qualifies it as a balloon loan.

A loan progress chart is not only useful for determining in advance the amount of the final payment in a partially amortized loan, but also for determining what portion of a fully amortized loan remains to be paid at any given moment in time. For example, a $10,000 amortized loan originally made for 30 years at 9½% interest is 6 years old. How much of the loan has been paid off and how much remains to be paid?

Table 11:3   BALANCE OWING ON A $1,000 AMORTIZED LOAN

Age of loan (years)	8½% Annual Interest — Original Life (years)						Age of loan (years)	9½% Annual Interest — Original Life (years)					
	10	15	20	25	30	35		10	15	20	25	30	35
2	$861	$928	$958	$975	$984	$990	2	$868	$925	$963	$978	$987	$992
4	697	843	909	945	966	978	4	708	853	918	952	971	983
6	503	742	851	909	943	964	6	515	756	864	921	953	971
8	273	622	782	867	917	947	8	282	639	799	883	930	957
10		480	700	818	886	928	10		497	720	837	902	940
12		312	603	759	849	904	12		326	625	781	869	920
14		113	488	689	806	876	14		119	510	714	828	896
16			352	606	754	843	16			371	633	780	866
18			191	508	693	805	18			203	535	721	830
20				392	620	758	20				416	650	787
22				255	534	704	22				273	564	735
24				92	432	639	24				100	460	671
26					312	562	26					335	595
28					169	472	28					183	503
30						364	30						391
32						237	32						256
34						86	34						94

Source: *Expanded Payment Table for Monthly Mortgage Loans,* op. cit., pp. 209 and 213.

In Table 11:3, enter the column marked "30" under the heading "original life in years." Then under "age of loan" find the 6-year line. Where these intersect you will find the number $953. This means that for each $1,000 of original loan, $953 remains to be paid. For a $10,000 loan, multiply by 10 and you will find that $9,530 remains to be paid. As you can see, on amortized loans with long maturities, relatively little of the debt is paid off during the initial years of the loan's life. Nearly all the early payments go for interest, and little remains for principal reduction. For example, the loan progress chart shows that when a 30-year, 9½% loan reaches its midpoint,

80½% of the loan is still unpaid. Not until this loan is about 6½ years from maturity will half of it have been repaid.

PACKAGE MORTGAGES

Normally, we think of real estate mortgage loans as being secured solely by real estate. However, it is possible to include items classed as personal property in a real estate mortgage, thus creating a **package mortgage.** In residential loans, such items as the refrigerator, clothes washer and dryer can be pledged along with the house and land in a single mortgage. The purpose is to raise the value of the collateral in order to raise the amount a lender is willing to loan. For the borrower, it offers the opportunity of financing major appliances at the same rate of interest as the real estate itself. This rate is usually lower than if the borrower finances the appliances separately. Once an item of personal property is included in a package mortgage, it is a violation of the mortgage to sell it without the prior consent of the lender.

BLANKET MORTGAGES

A mortgage secured by two or more properties is called a **blanket mortgage.** Suppose you want to buy a house plus the vacant lot next door, financing the purchase with a single mortgage that covers both properties. The cost of preparing one mortgage instead of two would be a savings. Also, by combining the house and lot, the lot can be financed on better terms than if it were financed separately, as lenders more readily loan on a house and land than on land alone. Note, however, if the vacant lot is later sold separately from the house before the mortgage loan is fully repaid, it will be necessary to have it released from the blanket mortgage. This is usually accomplished by including a release clause in the original mortgage agreement that specifies how much of the loan must be repaid before the lot will be released.

OPEN-END MORTGAGES

When a mortgage allows a borrower to obtain further money advances at a later date, it is called an **open-end mortgage.** Suppose that 10 years ago you purchased a home by borrowing $20,000 on an open-end mortgage. Since then you have reduced the balance owed to $14,000. Now you would like to convert the unfinished basement into a recreation room, extra bedroom, and bathroom. The cost will be $5,000, and you want to borrow that amount. Under an open-end mortgage the lender who originally advanced the $20,000 would advance an additional $5,000, returning the loan balance to $19,000. This saves the expense of arranging for a $5,000 second mortgage or obtaining an entirely new first mortgage for $19,000 and paying off the existing first mortgage, perhaps with penalties. Advances under open-end mortgages may also be used for such things as structural repairs, a swimming pool, a porch, a patio, extra rooms, or a bigger garage. The amount of the advance is usually limited to the difference between the original loan amount and the current amount owing. Terms of repayment will depend on prevailing interest rates and the condition and value of the pledged property at the time of the advance.

CONSTRUCTION LOANS

Under a **construction loan,** also called an interim loan, money is advanced as construction takes place. For example, a vacant lot owner arranges to borrow $30,000 to build a house. The lender does not advance all $30,000 at once because the value of the collateral is insufficient to warrant that amount until the house is finished. Instead, the lender will parcel out the loan as the building is being constructed, always holding a portion until the property is ready for occupancy, or in some cases actually occupied. Some lenders specialize only in construction loans and do not want to wait 20 or 30 years to be repaid. If so, it will be necessary to obtain a permanent long-term mortgage from another source for the purpose of repaying the construction loan. This is known as a permanent commitment or a **take-out loan;** since it takes the construction lender out of the financial picture when construction is completed and allows him to recycle his money into new construction projects.

PURCHASE MONEY MORTGAGES

A loan used to purchase the real property that serves as its collateral is called a **purchase money mortgage** or, in trust deed states, a **purchase money trust deed.** Most real estate loans made in connection with a sale fall into this category. For example, an investor buys a $2 million apartment building with a cash down payment of $400,000 and the cash he receives from a $1.6 million mortgage loan for which he pledges the building as security.

A purchase money mortgage or trust deed is also created when a seller agrees to accept part of the purchase price in the form of a promissory note or bond accompanied by a mortgage or trust deed. For instance, suppose that you are interested in buying a $100,000 farm. The seller owns the property free and clear of all debt and offers to deed title to you if you will give him $20,000 in cash and your promissory note for the remaining $80,000, secured by a mortgage against the farm.

LOAN-TO-VALUE RATIO

The relationship between the amount of money a lender is willing to loan and the lender's estimate of the fair market value of the property that will be pledged as security is called the **loan-to-value ratio** (often abbreviated **L/V ratio**). For example, a prospective home buyer wants to purchase a house priced at $60,000. A local lender appraises the house, finds it a has a fair market value of $60,000, and agrees to make an 80% L/V loan. This means that the lender will loan up to 80% of the $60,000 and the buyer must provide at least 20% in cash. In dollars, the lender will loan up to $48,000 and the buyer must make a cash down payment of at least $12,000. If the lender appraises the home for more than $60,000, the loan will still be $48,000. If the appraisal is for $60,000 and the buyer is paying $64,000, the loan will be for $48,000 and the buyer must put down $16,000 in cash. The rule is that price or value, whichever is lower, is applied to the L/V ratio.

EQUITY

The difference between the market value of a property and the debt owed against it is called the owner's **equity.** On a newly purchased $60,000 home with a $12,000 cash down payment, the buyer's equity is $12,000. As the value of the property rises or falls and as the mortgage loan is paid down, equity changes. For example, if the value of the home rises to $70,000 and the loan is paid down to $46,000 the owner's equity will be $24,000. If the owner pays the loan off so that there is no debt against the home, his equity will be equal to the value of the property.

FHA INSURANCE

The Great Depression marked a major turning point in the attitude of the U.S. government toward home mortgage financing. In 1934, one year after the Home Owners Loan

Corporation was established, Congress passed the National Housing Act. The act's most far-reaching provision was to establish the Federal Housing Administration (FHA) for the purpose of encouraging new construction as a means of creating jobs. To accomplish this goal, the FHA offered to insure lenders against losses due to nonrepayment when they made loans on both new and existing homes. In turn, the lender would have to grant up to 20-year amortized loan terms and loan-to-value ratios of up to 80% rather than the 3- to 5-year, 50% to 60% term loans common up to that time. Lenders were at first skeptical regarding the change, but finally reasoned that, if the U.S. government would insure against losses, they would make the loans.

Meanwhile, the FHA did its best to keep from becoming a continuous burden to the American taxpayer. When a prospective borrower approached a lender for a home loan, the FHA stepped in and reviewed the borrower's income, expenses, assets, and debts in the light of the proposed loan. The objective was to determine if there was adequate room in the borrower's budget for the proposed loan payments. The FHA also sent inspectors to the property to make certain that it was of acceptable construction quality and to determine its fair market value. To offset losses that would still inevitably occur, the FHA charged the borrower an annual insurance fee of ½ of 1% of the balance owed on his loan. The FHA was immensely successful in its task. Not only did it create construction jobs, but it raised the level of housing quality in the nation and, in a pleasant surprise to taxpayers, actually returned annual profits to the U.S. Treasury. In response to its success, in 1946 Congress changed its status from temporary to permanent.

Current Coverage

Although the FHA insures only a portion of the home loans in the United States (presently about one home loan in five is FHA insured), it has had a marked influence on lending policies and construction techniques throughout the real estate industry. Foremost among these is the widespread acceptance of the high loan-to-value, amortized loan. In the 1930s, lenders required FHA insurance before making 80% L/V loans. By the 1960s, lenders were readily making 80%

L/V loans without FHA insurance. Meanwhile, the FHA insurance program was working so well that the FHA raised the portion it was willing to insure. By 1976, for a fee of ½ of 1% per year, the FHA offered to insure a lender for 97% of the first $25,000 of appraised value, 90% of the next $10,000 of appraised value, and 80% above that, up to a maximum loan guarantee of $45,000. To illustrate, on a $20,000 home, the FHA would insure a lender against a loss of up to 97% of $20,000, that is, up to $19,400. This allowed a borrower to purchase a $20,000 home with as little as $600 down. On a $34,000 home, the FHA would insure 97% of the first $25,000 and 90% of the remaining $9,000, for a total of $32,350. This required a down payment of only $1,650. The borrower is not permitted to use a second mortgage to raise his down payment money. The FHA requires some down payment; otherwise, it is too easy for the borrower to walk away from his debt obligation and leave the FHA to pay the lender's insurance claim. A strong argument can be made that even if a buyer places 3% cash down he still owes more than he owns the moment he takes title. This is because it would cost about 6% in brokerage fees plus another 1% to 2% in closing costs to resell the home. Inflation in home prices since the 1940s has kept the FHA's insurance losses relatively low.

The FHA led the way in other respects. Once 20-year amortized mortgage loans were shown to be successful investments for lenders, loans without FHA insurance were made for 20 years. Later, when the FHA successfully went to 30 years, non-FHA-insured loans followed. The FHA also established loan application review techniques that have been widely accepted and copied throughout the real estate industry. The biggest step in this direction was to analyze a borrower's loan application in terms of his earning power. Prior to 1933, emphasis had been placed on how large the borrower's assets were, a measurement that tended to exclude all but the already financially well-to-do from home ownership. Since 1933, the emphasis has shifted primarily to the borrower's ability to meet monthly PITI payments. The oft-quoted rule of thumb, that a borrower should have a monthly income four times his monthly payment, is said to have originated with the FHA.

The FHA has also been very influential in construction techniques. When the property for which FHA insurance is requested is of new construction, the FHA will impose on the builder minimum construction requirements regarding the quantity and quality of materials to be used. Lot size, street access, landscaping, and general house design must also fall within the broad guidelines set by the FHA. During construction, an FHA inspector will come to the property several times to check if the work is being done correctly. A home that was not FHA inspected during construction can still qualify for an FHA-insured loan if it has been occupied for 1 year and meets certain FHA requirements.

Construction Requirements

The establishment of construction standards is a two-edged sword. The FHA recognizes that if a building is defective either from a design or construction standpoint, the borrower is more likely to default on his loan and create an insurance claim against the FHA. Furthermore, the same defects will lower the price the property will bring at its foreclosure sale, thus increasing losses to the FHA. An important side effect has been to establish certain national standards of housing construction that have raised the quality of construction in regions where FHA standards are more stringent than local building codes.

Thus far, our discussion of the FHA has centered on insuring home mortgage loans under **Section 203(b)** of Title II of the National Housing Act. This FHA program has insured over 11 million home loans, and is the program for which the FHA is most widely known. However, the FHA administers a number of other real estate programs. Several of the better known programs will be briefly discussed.

Other FHA Programs

Under **Title I** of the National Housing Act, the FHA will insure lenders against losses on loans made to finance repairs, improvements, alterations, or conversions of existing residences. Under **Title II, Section 207** provides for insuring mortgage loans on rental housing projects of eight or more family units and on mobile home parks. **Section 213** provides for insuring mortgages on cooperative housing projects of eight or more family units. **Section 220** insures financing used to rehabilitate salvageable housing and to replace slums with new housing. **Section 221(d)(2)** operates similar to 203(b), but permits 100% insured financing for low- and moderate-income family housing. Under **Section 234,** the FHA will insure individual housing units in a multifamily building of five or more units operated on a condominium basis.

Sections 237 and 238 deal with special credit risks. Under **Section 237,** a low- or moderate-income applicant with a poor credit history must agree to accept budget advice and debt counseling before the FHA will insure his loan. **Section 238** contains a "Special Risk Insurance Fund" to insure mortgages when the real property serving as collateral does not present an otherwise economically sound insurance risk.

The rent-supplement program of **Section 221(d)(3),** the single-family residence interest-subsidy program of **Section 235,** and **Section 236** that subsidized owners of low-rent apartment buildings, were suspended in January 1973. Products of the 1960 decade, these programs were designed to subsidize low- and moderate-income families in their quest for shelter. However, these programs did not meet their projected goals and were too expensive in relation to the benefits received. In their place, the FHA now administers a **Title II, Section 8** housing assistance program. Under this program, low- and moderate-income families, including single, elderly, disabled, or handicapped persons, can obtain FHA certificates that permit them to negotiate for suitable rental dwellings. Aided families then contribute between 15% and 25% of their total family income to the dwelling unit's rent. The difference between that amount and the actual rent is subsidized by the U.S. government through the Department of Housing and Urban Development (HUD).

Under **Title VIII,** also called the Capehart Act, the FHA offers insurance on rental projects on or near military bases for the use of Armed Forces personnel and civilian employees. Under **Title X,** the FHA will insure land purchase financing in approved new town developments.

To show its appreciation to servicemen returning from World War II, in 1944 Congress passed far-reaching legislation to aid veterans in areas of education, hospitalization, employment training, and housing. In the area of housing, the popularly named G.I. Bill of Rights empowered the comptroller general of the United States to guarantee the repayment of a portion of first mortgage real estate loans made to veterans. For this guarantee, no fee would be charged to the veteran. Rather, the government itself would stand the losses. The original 1944 law provided that lenders would be guaranteed against losses up to 50% of the amount of the loan, but in no case more than $2,000.

VETERANS ADMINISTRATION

The objective was to make it possible for a veteran to buy a home with no cash down payment. Thus, on a house offered for sale at $5,000 (houses were much cheaper in 1944) this guarantee enabled a veteran to borrow the entire $5,000. From the lender's standpoint, having the top $2,000 of the loan guaranteed by the U.S. government offered the same asset protection as a $2,000 cash down payment. If the veteran defaulted and the property went into foreclosure, it would have to net less than $3,000 before the lender suffered a loss.

No Down Payment

In 1945, Congress increased the guarantee amount to $4,000 and 60% of the loan, and turned the entire operation over to the Veterans Administration (VA). The VA was quick to honor claims and the program rapidly became popular with lenders. Furthermore, the veterans turned out to be excellent credit risks, bettering, in fact, the good record of FHA-insured home owners. (The FHA recognizes this and gives higher insurance limits to FHA borrowers who have served in the Armed Forces. The limits are 100% of the first $25,000, 90% of the next $10,000, and 85% above that to a maximum of $45,000.) The program blossomed, and to date over 8 million home loans have been guaranteed by the VA, over two thirds of them with no down payment.

To keep up with the increased cost of homes, the guarantee has been increased several times and in mid-1977 was at $17,500. Generally, a $17,500 guarantee means a veteran can purchase up to a $70,000 home with no down payment, provided, of course, that the veteran has enough income to support the monthly PITI payments. Whether or not a lender will make a no down payment VA loan is entirely up to the lender. Some lenders feel the borrower should make at least a token down payment so as to have a sense of ownership. However, the majority of lenders, if they have the funds available, require none.

In the original G.I. Bill of 1944, eligibility was limited to World War II veterans. However, subsequent legislation has broadened eligibility to include any veteran who served for a period of at least 90 days in the armed forces of the United States, or an ally, between September 16, 1940, and July 25, 1947, or between June 27, 1950, and January 31, 1955. Any veteran of the United States who has served 180 days or more since January 31, 1955, to the present is also eligible. The veteran's discharge must be on conditions other than dishonorable and the guarantee entitlement is good until used. Spouses of veterans who died as a result of service can also obtain housing guarantees, if not remarried. Active duty personnel can also qualify.

VA Certificates   To find out what his benefits are, a veteran should make application to the Veterans Administration for a **certificate of eligibility.** This shows if the veteran is qualified and the amount of guarantee available. It is also one of the documents necessary to obtain a VA-guaranteed loan.

The VA works diligently to reduce its exposure to foreclosure losses. When a veteran applies for a VA guarantee, the property is appraised and the VA issues a **certificate of reasonable value.** Often abbreviated **CRV,** it informs the veteran of the appraised value of the property and the maximum VA guaranteed loan a private lender may make. Similarly, the VA establishes income guidelines to make certain that the veteran can comfortably meet the proposed loan payments. It makes no sense, for the veteran or the VA, to approve a loan that the veteran will have trouble repaying.

The VA will guarantee loans for periods of up to 30 years on homes, and there is no prepayment penalty if the borrower wishes to pay sooner. VA loans are also available to obtain farms and farm equipment, farm buildings, and farm capital, to buy or establish a business, or to purchase a mobile home as a residence. A veteran wishing to refinance his existing home or farm can also obtain a VA-guaranteed loan. The VA will also make direct loans to veterans if there are no private lending institutions nearby.

No matter what loan guarantee program is elected, the veteran should know that in the event of default and subsequent foreclosure he is required to eventually make good any losses suffered by the VA on his loan. (This is not the case with FHA-insured loans. There the borrower pays for protection against foreclosure losses that may result from his loan.) Even if the veteran sells his property and the buyer assumes the VA loan, the veteran is still financially responsible if the buyer later defaults. To avoid this, the veteran must arrange with the VA to be released from liability.

In addition to raising the VA guarantee from $12,500 to $17,500, legislation that took effect in 1975 also permits a veteran a full new guarantee entitlement if he has completely repaid a previous VA-guaranteed loan. Even if the veteran has sold his home and let the buyer assume the VA loan, the 1975 law change is still valuable. For example, if a veteran has used $10,000 of his entitlement to date, he still has $7,500 available to him.

As Congress frequently changes eligibility and benefits, a person contemplating a VA or FHA loan should make inquiry to the field offices of these two agencies and to mortgage lenders to ascertain the current status and details of the law, as well as the availability of loan money.* One should also query lenders as to the availability of state veteran benefits. A number of states offer special advantages, including mortgage loan assistance, to residents who have served in the armed forces.

---

* Consult the telephone directory white pages under U.S. government for Veterans Administration and Housing and Urban Development—FHA headings, and the yellow pages for Real Estate Loans.

PRIVATE MORTGAGE
INSURANCE

The financial success of the FHA's Section 203(b) loan insurance program was not lost on private industry. In 1957, the Mortgage Guaranty Insurance Corporation (MGIC) was formed in Milwaukee, Wisconsin, as a privately owned business venture to compete with the FHA in insuring home mortgage loans. Growth was slow but steady for the first 10 years. However, in the late 1960s several things happened that allowed MGIC to enjoy a sudden burst of growth. The first was a red-tape snarl at the FHA that resulted in loan insurance applications taking 4 to 8 weeks to process, much too long a wait for sellers, buyers, brokers, and lenders who were anxious to close. In contrast, MGIC offered 3-day service. Then, too, FHA terms were not keeping up with the times; moderately priced homes required larger down payments with FHA insurance than with private insurance, and the FHA-imposed interest rate ceiling hindered rather than helped many borrowers. Also, private mortgage insurance was priced at one half the FHA fee. Then in 1971 the Federal Home Loan Bank Board, overseer of savings and loan institutions, approved the use of private mortgage insurers. By 1972 private insurers in the United States were regularly insuring more new mortgages than the FHA.

PMI Coverage

Success spawns competition, and today about a dozen firms offer **private mortgage insurance,** or **PMI.** MGIC, however, is still the dominant force in the industry. Like FHA insurance, the object of PMI is to insure lenders against losses due to nonrepayment of low down payment mortgage loans. But unlike the FHA, PMI insures only the top 20% to 25% of a loan, not the whole loan. This allows a lender to make 90% and 95% L/V loans[*] with about the same exposure to

---

[*] The mathematics of this statement are as follows: On 90% L/V loans, the borrower, by placing 10% cash down, takes the top 10% of risk exposure to falling real estate prices. PMI takes 20% of the next 90%, that is, 18%, and the lender takes the bottom 72%. On 95% L/V loans, the borrower takes the top 5% of risk exposure with his 5% down payment. PMI takes 25% of the next 95%, that is, 23.75%, and the lender takes the remaining 71.25%.

foreclosure losses as a 72% L/V loan.* The borrower, meanwhile, can purchase a home with a cash down payment of either 10% or 5%. Under the 10% down payment program, the borrower pays a mortgage insurance fee of ½ of 1% the ✓ first year and of ¼ of 1% thereafter. When the loan is partially repaid (e.g., to a 70% L/V), the premiums and coverage can be terminated at the lender's option. PMI is also available on apartment buildings, offices, stores and warehouses, but at higher rates than on homes.

Private mortgage insurers work to keep their losses to a minimum by first approving the lenders with whom they will do business. Particular emphasis is placed on the lender's operating policy, appraisal procedure, and degree of government regulation. Once approved, a lender simply sends the borrower's loan application, credit report, and property appraisal to the insurer. Based on these documents, the insurer either agrees or refuses to issue a policy. Although the insurer relies on the appraisal prepared by the lender, on a random basis the insurer sends its own appraiser to verify the quality of the information being submitted. When an insured loan goes into default, the insurer has the option of either buying the property from the lender for the balance due or letting the lender foreclose and then paying the lender's losses up to the amount of the insurance. As a rule, insurers take the first option because it is more popular with the lenders and it leaves the lender with immediate cash to relend. The insurer has the task of foreclosing, of course.

POINTS

Probably no single term in real estate finance causes as much confusion and consternation as the word **points.** The word **point** means one percent of the loan amount. Thus, on a $60,000 loan, one point would be $600. On a $40,000 loan, three points would be $1,200. On a $10,000 loan, eight points would be $800.

The use of points in real estate mortgage finance can be split into two categories: (1) loan origination fees expressed in terms of points and (2) the use of points to change the effective yield of a mortgage loan to a lender. Let us look at these two uses in more detail.

Origination Fee   When a borrower asks for a mortgage loan, the lender incurs a number of expenses, including such things as the time its loan officer spends interviewing the borrower, office overhead, the purchase and review of credit reports on the borrower, an on-site appraisal of the property to be pledged, title searches and review, legal and recording fees, and so on. For these, some lenders make an itemized billing, charging so many dollars for the appraisal, credit report, title search, and so on. The total becomes the **loan origination fee,** which the borrower pays to get his loan. Other lenders do not make an itemized bill, but instead simply state the origination fee in terms of a percentage of the loan amount, for example, one point. Thus, a lender quoting a loan origination fee of one point is saying that, for a $45,000 loan, its fee to originate the loan will be $450.

Discount Points   Points charged to raise the lender's monetary return on a loan are known as **discount points.** A simplified example will illustrate their use and effect. If you are a lender and agree to make a term loan of $100 to a borrower for 1 year at 8% interest, you would normally expect to give the borrower $100 now (disregard loan origination fees for a moment), and 1 year later the borrower would give you $108. In percentage terms, the effective yield on your loan is 8% per annum (year) because you received $8 for your 1-year, $100 loan. Now suppose that, instead of handing the borrower $100, you handed him $99 but still required him to repay $100 plus $8 in interest at the end of the year. This is a charge of one point ($1 in this case), and the borrower paid it out of his loan funds. The effect of this financial maneuver is to raise the effective yield (yield to maturity) to you without raising the interest rate itself. Therefore, if you loan out $99 and receive $108 at the end of the year, you effectively have a return of $9 for a $99 loan. This gives you an effective yield of $9 ÷ $99 or 9.1%, rather than 8%.

Calculating the effective yield on a discounted 20- or 30-year mortgage loan is more difficult because the amount owed drops over the life of the loan, and because the majority are paid in full ahead of schedule due to refinancing. However, a useful rule of thumb states that on the typical home loan each point of discount raises the effective yield by ⅛ of 1%. Thus, four discount points would raise the effective yield by approximately ½ of 1% and eight points would raise it by 1%. Discount points are most often charged during periods of **tight money,** that is, when mortgage money is in short supply. During periods of **loose money,** when lenders have adequate funds to lend and are actively seeking borrowers, discount points disappear.

The use of discount points is an important part of FHA and VA loans, because the FHA and VA set interest-rate ceilings on loans they insure or guarantee. With only two exceptions since 1950, the FHA and VA ceilings have been below the prevailing rates on **conventional loans** (non-FHA or non-VA loans). Thus, if the prevailing open-market interest rate on conventional loans is 9½% and the FHA and VA ceilings are at 9%, a borrower will not be able to obtain an FHA or VA loan without offering the lender enough discount points to raise the effective yield to 9½%. If loans can be made at 9½% interest, it is illogical for the lender to accept 9%. To obtain a 9% loan, the borrower must pay the lender four discount points.

Rate Ceilings

However, the FHA and VA limit the number of points that the borrower is allowed to pay to 1 point for existing homes and 2½ points for homes under construction, and these are usually consumed by loan origination costs. These are called **borrower's points.**

Any discount points must be paid for by the seller. For example, on a $30,000 loan, when the market rate is 9½% and the FHA and VA ceilings are 9%, this would amount to $1,200 in **seller's points.** In other words, out of the proceeds from the sale, the seller would have to pay the lender $1,200 so the buyer could enjoy the privilege of obtaining a loan with an interest rate ½% below the market.

By placing yourself in the seller's position, you can see the situation this creates. A buyer making an offer under the above conditions is in effect asking you to take a $1,200 cut in price. If you were planning on reducing your price $1,200 anyway, you would accept the offer. However, if you felt you could readily sell at your price to a buyer not requiring seller's points, you would refuse the offer. The alternative is to price the property high enough to allow for anticipated points. However, this is an effective solution only if your price does not exceed the FHA appraisal or VA certificate of reasonable value. If it does, the FHA or VA buyer is either prohibited from buying or must make a larger cash down payment. One reason for the success of private mortgage insurers is that they impose no restrictions on either interest rates or discount points.

REGULATION Z   Popularly known as the **Truth-in-Lending Law,** Regulation Z of the Federal Consumer Credit Protection Act went into effect on July 1, 1969. Its basic purpose is to require that a borrower be clearly shown how much he is paying for credit in both dollar terms and percentage terms before committing himself. The law covers a broad range of consumer lending activity and extends to real estate mortgage loans (with certain exceptions) and to advertising that contains the offering of credit.

Let us briefly review the act's application and basic provisions as they pertain to real estate. The act applies (1) when the credit transaction is for family, household, agricultural, or personal purposes (but not business or commercial), (2) to banks, savings and loan associations, finance companies, loan brokers, and others who regularly arrange consumer credit, and (3) to advertising that contains the mention of credit.

Annual
Percentage Rate   A key provision of the act is that lenders must use a uniform measure of the annual cost of credit, called the **annual percentage rate,** or **APR.** This combines the interest rate, loan fee, and discount points into a single figure that shows the true annual cost of borrowing. The lender must also tell the borrower the total dollar cost of repaying the loan. The goal is to give the borrower a convenient yardstick with which to

compare financing costs. Regarding advertising, the act requires that whenever credit is promoted all credit terms must be disclosed. Statements such as "Only $210 per month" or "Try no down payment" by themselves are prohibited, because they promote credit but do not fully disclose all the credit terms. The following real estate advertisement would be acceptable: "Try $5,000 down payment; 360 monthly payments of $300 per month (including estimated hazard insurance and property taxes) at 9½% annual percentage rate. Cash price: $35,000." General statements, such as "assumable loan" or "financing available" are not construed by the act to promote credit and thus do not require the full treatment shown above.

On the loan agreement itself, the lender is required to state all fees and discounts in connection with the loan, plus the interest rate, the APR, and the total amount of dollars necessary to repay the loan in full. For some types of loans, the act permits the borrower a 3-day "cooling-off" period after signing the loan papers during which he can cancel the loan. The total dollar amount of the finance charge is not required and the borrower does not have a 3-day "cooling-off" period on a purchase money first mortgage or purchase money first trust deed. Anyone regularly arranging for loans or credit should become familiar with Regulation Z through pamphlets available from commercial lenders and through the Federal Reserve Board.

It is important to recognize that Regulation Z is concerned only with the disclosure of lending charges to the borrower. It does not place a limit on how much a lender can charge for a loan.

VOCABULARY REVIEW   *Match terms a–p with statements 1–16.*

a. *APR*
b. *Blanket mortgage*
c. *Conventional loan*
d. *CRV*
e. *Discount points*
f. *Impound account*
g. *Loose money*
h. *L/V ratio*
i. *PITI*

j. *PMI*
k. *Point*
l. *Principal*
m. *Purchase money mortgage*
n. *Take-out*
o. *Term loan*
p. *Tight money*

1. Balance owing on a loan.
2. A loan that requires the borrower to pay interest only until maturity, at which time the full amount of the loan must be repaid.
3. Refers to a monthly loan payment that includes principal, interest, property taxes, and property insurance.
4. An escrow or reserve account into which the lender places monthly tax and insurance payments.
5. A mortgage secured by more than one property.
6. A permanent loan used to repay a construction loan.
7. A mortgage given by the buyer as part or all of the purchase price of a property.
8. The amount a lender will loan on a property divided by the valuation the lender places on the property.
9. A document issued by the Veterans Administration showing the VA's estimate of a property's value for loan purposes.
10. Mortgage guaranty insurance sold by privately owned companies.
11. One hundredth of the total amount; 1 percent.
12. Used by lenders to adjust the effective interest rate on a loan so that it is equal to the prevailing market interest rate.
13. Refers to periods when mortgage loan money is in short supply and loans are hard to get.
14. Lenders have adequate funds to lend and are actively seeking borrowers.
15. A real estate loan made without FHA insurance or a VA guarantee.
16. A uniform measure of the annual cost of credit.

QUESTIONS AND PROBLEMS

1. What is the major risk that the borrower takes when he agrees to a term loan or a balloon loan?
2. Explain how an amortized loan works.

3. Using the amortization tables in Table 11:1, calculate the monthly payment necessary to completely amortize a $65,000, 30-year loan at $9\frac{1}{2}\%$ interest.

4. A prospective home buyer has a $10,000 down payment and can afford $420 per month for principal and interest payments. If 30-year, $9\frac{1}{2}\%$ amortized loans are available, what price home can the buyer afford?

5. Same information as in number 4 except that the interest rate has fallen to $8\frac{1}{2}\%$. What price home can the buyer afford now?

6. If a mortgaged property is sold and the buyer assumes the loan, what happens to the money in the impound account?

7. Using the loan progress chart shown in Table 11:3, calculate the balance still owing on a $90,000, $9\frac{1}{2}\%$ interest, 30-year amortized loan that is 10 years old.

8. Explain the purpose and operation of the FHA 203(b) home mortgage insurance program.

9. What advantage does the Veterans Administration offer veterans who wish to purchase a home?

10. Explain "points" and their application to real estate lending.

11. What is the basic purpose of Regulation Z, the Truth-in-Lending Law?

ADDITIONAL READINGS

Beaton, William R. *Real Estate Finance.* Englewood Cliffs, N.J.: Prentice-Hall, 1975, 248 pages. Provides an introduction to principles and practices of real estate finance. Deals with finance law, construction and permanent financing, residential financing, etc.

Financial Publishing Company. *Expanded Table for Monthly Mortgage Loans.* Boston: Financial Publishing Company, 1969, 224 pages. This and similar publications by the same company contain tables detailing the monthly and annual payments necessary to amortize 1- to 40-year loans. Includes loan progress charts.

Rohan, Patrick J. *Real Estate Financing.* New York: Matthew Bender, 1975. Volume 4, Chapter 3, discusses the use of private mortgage insurance and Chapter 4 discusses Regulation Z.

Runner, Edward J. "Points—Good, Bad or Indifferent?" *Real Estate Today,* July 1971, page 23ff. Written to help the sales person or realtor better understand and explain to the prospective home owner the role of mortgage discount points, particularly as they apply to FHA and VA mortgages.

To the Home-Buying Veteran, VA Pamphlet 26-6, revised. Washington, D.C.: Veterans Administration, 1973, 34 pages. This free booklet discusses such topics as house selection, costs of home ownership, the purchase contract, VA loans, and closing procedures.

Wiedemer, John P. *Real Estate Finance.* Reston, Va.: Reston Publishing Co., 1974, 331 pages. Chapter 1 provides a historical background of real estate lending in the United States. Chapter 8 deals with federal government mortgage loan programs. Chapter 14 discusses loan closing procedures. Contains a glossary of real estate finance terms.

12

Mortgage Lenders and Alternatives

Alienation clause: provides that the loan against a property must be paid in full if the property is sold

Fannie Mae: a real estate industry nickname for the Federal National Mortgage Association

Illiquid assets: assets that require several weeks or months to convert to cash

Liquid assets: cash plus assets that can be converted to cash in a few days

Mortgage banker: a person or firm that makes mortgage loans and then sells them to investors

Participation loans: real estate loans that require interest plus a percentage of the profits from rentals

Redlining: the practice of refusing to make loans in certain neighborhoods

Step-up rental: a lease with built-in rent increases

Usury: the charging of a rate of interest higher than that permitted by law

Variable rate mortgage: a mortgage on which the interest rate rises and falls with changes in prevailing interest rates

Chapters 9–11 dealt with mortgage and trust deed law, amortized loans, and the FHA and VA. In this chapter we will turn our attention to the lenders themselves, the loan application process, secondary mortgage markets, and alternatives to lending institutions.

SAVINGS AND LOAN ASSOCIATIONS

As a group, the nation's 5,500 savings and loan associations are the single most important source of loan money for residential real estate. Historically, their origin can be traced to early building societies in England and Germany. These were cooperative lending associations where members pooled their money to make home loans to each other.

The first American building society, the Oxford Provident Building Association, was started in 1831 in Pennsylvania. In early associations, members agreed to purchase shares of stock in the amount that they wished to later borrow. The shares were paid for by regular and mandatory payments. When enough money was collected to make a loan, the loan would be auctioned off among the association's members. The loan carried a fixed rate of interest, usually 6%, and the member bidding the highest number of discount points got the loan. At some associations, loans were awarded by a drawing or on a first-come, first-served basis. Loan-to-value ratios were high, even by today's standards, and the borrower pledged both his home and his shares as collateral. Meanwhile, each member continued to pay for his shares and, with the interest from the first loan, another was soon made. To keep members from lagging on their share payments, fines were levied against the tardy member's shares. The method of loan repayment was also unique. Each borrowing member continued to purchase the shares for which he originally subscribed. When their value, plus his portion of the association's earnings equaled the amount he borrowed (usually about 10 years later), his loan and shares were canceled and the borrower left the association. This was an early form of the self-amortizing mortgage. As each member received a loan and repaid it, the association shrank, until the last member received a loan that was, in effect, a return of his own savings plus earnings. At that point, the association was terminated.

Savers and Borrowers

The emergence of two distinct groups led to the savings and loan associations of today: those who wanted to save and those who wanted to borrow. As a result, borrowers did not have to be savers, the requirement that specific amounts be deposited at specific times was dropped, and the associations no longer dissolved after the last member received his loan. Associations also began offering savers stated interest rates rather than a return based on the success of the association. Today savers with passbook accounts can make deposits at any time and in any amount, and withdrawals, for all practical purposes, are available on demand. (Technically, passbook savers are required to give 30-day notice before withdrawing. However, this is rarely enforced for fear that savers would take their deposits elsewhere.)

Savings and loan associations (S&Ls) are now found in all 50 states (in Louisiana they are called Homestead Associations and in Massachusetts, Cooperative Banks). As may be seen in Figure 12:1, their importance to mortgage lending is tremendous. In 1976 mortgage loans held by S&Ls numbered 13 million and amounted to $279 billion. Of this vast amount 75% was for loans on single-family homes, 5% for loans on two-to-four family buildings, 9% for apartment buildings and 9% for commercial real estate. Additionally, S&Ls held $5 billion worth of mobile homes, home improvement, and educational loans.

S&L Growth

MAJOR HOME MORTGAGE LENDERS

Figure 12:1

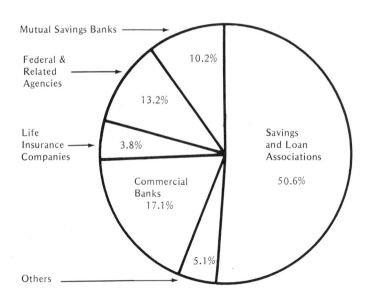

Mutual Savings Banks → 10.2%

Federal & Related Agencies → 13.2%

Life Insurance Companies → 3.8%

Commercial Banks 17.1%

Savings and Loan Associations 50.6%

5.1%

Others

Distribution of One- to Four-Family Nonfarm, Home Mortgage Loans, by Type of Lender, March 31, 1976

Sources: Federal Reserve Board; Federal Home Loan Bank Board

For the most part, S&Ls are locally oriented, collecting the bulk of their deposits and making loans within 100 miles of their offices. It is specialization in limited geographic areas that has been a major factor in their enviable record for making sound loans.

Regulation and
Deposit Insurance

A savings and loan association may be either state or federally chartered. In the latter case, the word "Federal" will appear in its name. A charter is an association's permit to operate. Federal charters are issued by the Federal Home Loan Bank Board (FHLBB). A federally chartered association must be mutually owned (owned by its depositors), be a member of the Federal Home Loan Bank System (FHLBS), and carry Federal Savings and Loan Insurance Corporation (FSLIC) insurance. (The FHLBB is the governing body of the FHLBS.)

An outgrowth of the 1930 depression, the FSLIC is an agency of the U.S. government that insures savers' deposits against the possibility they will not be available whenever the savers wish to withdraw them. For this insurance, the S&L pays an insurance premium to the FSLIC of 1/12 of 1% per year times its savings deposits. The FHLBS was also a product of the Great Depression; it was formed to bring order to chaotic and often weak state banking and savings laws. Today the FHLBS regulates the geographic area a federally chartered S&L can lend in, maximum loan size, maximum loan-to-value ratios, and the ratio of home loans to other types of loans. The FHLBS also provides S&Ls with access to the nation's capital markets, as will be shown later.

State-chartered associations can be mutually owned by depositors or by corporations owned by stockholders. FHLBS membership and FSLIC insurance are optional. Whether federal or state in origin, to be chartered an association must be financially healthy, have a sound lending policy, and maintain adequate amounts of cash and other liquid assets to meet depositors' withdrawal demands. The FHLBB and the FSLIC periodically audit the accounting books of members to assure compliance with regulations and sound lending practices. State-chartered associations are subject to audit by state banking boards.

Interest Ceilings

In 1966, the FHLBB began setting ceilings on the interest rates that could be paid to savers at state and federal associations. The Board also created **savings certificates** (also called **time deposits**), which permit associations to pay savers higher rates when they agree to leave funds on deposit rather than in passbook accounts. At mid-1977, interest ceilings on passbook accounts were 5¼% per annum, 1-year certificates were 6½% and 6- to 10-year certificates were 7¾%. The purpose of encouraging longer-term accounts is to improve the stability of deposits. A built-in problem S&Ls face is that they make 25- and 30-year loans, yet their savers can withdraw on much shorter notice. Thus, although savings certificates cost the S&L more, they do commit the saver to leaving his money on deposit for longer periods of time. By 1977, over one-half of all S&L deposits in the United States were in the form of certificates.

There are two main reasons for setting ceilings on the interest rates paid to savers. First, as ceilings are also imposed on banks by the Federal Reserve Board, "rate wars" are avoided. Second, because the rates S&Ls pay depositors directly affect what they must charge borrowers, savings ceilings keep loan rates down. However, there are no interest ceilings on what the U.S. Treasury and American corporations can pay. As a result, when their interest rates rise above the federally imposed ceilings at S&Ls and banks, money moves out of S&Ls and banks. When Treasury and corporate interest rates fall below the ceilings, money flows back to savings accounts and real estate loans from S&Ls and banks are again readily available. The 12 Federal Home Loan Banks absorb some of this shock by lending money to member S&Ls during savings outflows and then allowing members to repay during inflows.

COMMERCIAL BANKS

The nation's 14,200 commercial banks store far more of the country's money than the S&Ls. However, only one dollar in six goes to real estate lending. As a result, in total number of dollars, commercial banks rank second behind S&Ls in importance in real estate lending. Each bank dollar that does go to real estate lending is distributed as shown in Figure 12:2.

Of the loans held by banks on real estate, the tendency is to emphasize short-term maturities since the bulk of a bank's deposit money comes from demand deposits (checking accounts) and a much smaller portion from savings and time deposits. Consequently, banks are particularly active in making loans to finance real estate construction as these loans have maturities of 6 months to 3 years. They are less inclined to hold long-term real estate loans. When they do, maturities

Figure 12:2

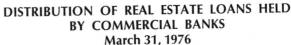

DISTRIBUTION OF REAL ESTATE LOANS HELD
BY COMMERCIAL BANKS
March 31, 1976

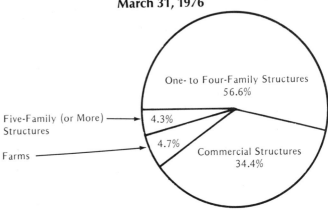

One- to Four-Family Structures
56.6%

Five-Family (or More) ⟶ 4.3%
Structures

4.7%

Farms

Commercial Structures
34.4%

are usually 5 to 15 years rather than 25 to 30 years. There are, however, two exceptions to this. In rural areas where longer-term savings deposits make up a larger portion of a bank's money sources, the town bank is a major source of long-term real estate loans. The other exception is the bank that makes 20- and 30-year loans but sells them rather than keeping them in its own investment portfolio.

Commercial banks operate under state or national charters, the latter being identified by the word "National" in the bank's name. National banks are chartered and supervised by the U.S. Comptroller of the Currency, and are required to be members of the Federal Reserve System (FRS) and the Federal Deposit Insurance Corporation (FDIC). The Federal Reserve System is the "nation's bank," and the FDIC provides insurance to checking and savings depositors. As of mid-1977, the FDIC insured account holders to $40,000, an amount identical to that offered by the FSLIC to S&L depositors. State-chartered banks are controlled by state banking regulatory agencies, usually in a manner similar to the national banks. State banks can voluntarily join the FRS and the FDIC.

MUTUAL SAVINGS　　Important contributors to real estate credit in several
BANKS　　states are the nation's 500 mutual savings banks. Historically, these banks were started in Philadelphia in 1816 and in Boston in 1817 for the purpose of providing a place where a person of

small financial means could save money for any purpose. Today, mutual savings banks are found primarily in the northeastern United States, where they compete aggressively for the savings dollar. The states of Massachusetts, New York, and Connecticut account for 75% of the nation's total.

As the word "mutual" implies, the depositors are the owners, and the "interest" they receive is the result of the bank's success or failure in lending. To protect depositors, laws require mutual savings banks to place deposits in high-quality investments. This includes sound real estate mortgage loans. Loan-to-value ratios can be 70% to 80% (higher for FHA and VA loans), maturities are of 20 to 30 years, and as a rule, loans are made within a 100-mile radius of the bank. Presently, real estate loans account for three out of every four loan dollars at mutual savings banks. Figure 12:3 shows how they are distributed. Mutual savings banks are chartered and controlled by state regulatory agencies. Membership in the FDIC is available and optional.

DISTRIBUTION OF REAL ESTATE LOANS HELD BY MUTUAL SAVINGS BANKS & LIFE INSURANCE COMPANIES
March 31, 1976

Figure 12:3

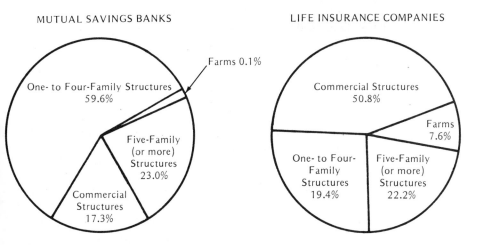

MUTUAL SAVINGS BANKS

Farms 0.1%

One- to Four-Family Structures
59.6%

Five-Family
(or more)
Structures
23.0%

Commercial
Structures
17.3%

LIFE INSURANCE COMPANIES

Commercial Structures
50.8%

Farms
7.6%

One- to Four-
Family
Structures
19.4%

Five-Family
(or more)
Structures
22.2%

As a group, the nation's 1,800 life insurance companies have long been active investors in real estate, both as owners and as long-term lenders. Their source of money is the pre-

LIFE INSURANCE COMPANIES

miums paid by policyholders. These premiums are invested and ultimately returned to the policyholders. Because premiums are collected in regular amounts on regular dates and because policy payoffs can be calculated from actuarial tables, life insurers are in ideal positions to commit money to long-term investments.

Life insurance companies are state chartered and state regulated. Requirements regarding investments vary from state to state, but generally speaking, states allow insurers to place their funds wherever sound investments can be found that will protect policyholder money. Within these guidelines, life insurers channel their funds primarily into government and corporate bonds and real estate. The dollars allocated to real estate are used for purchases of land and buildings, which are leased to users, and to real estate loans on commercial, industrial, and residential property. Generally, life insurers specialize in large-scale projects and mortgage packages such as shopping centers, office and apartment buildings, and million dollar blocks of home mortgage loans (see Figure 12:3).

Participation

Repayment terms on loans for shopping centers, office buildings, and apartment complexes sometimes call for interest and a percentage of any profits from rentals over a certain level. This **participation** feature, or "piece of the action," is intended to provide the insurance company with more inflation protection than a fixed rate of interest.

Few insurers maintain their own loan offices. Most purchase loans originated by commercial banks and mortgage bankers. As a result, the lending activity of life insurers is often not as visible as savings and loan associations, mutual savings banks, or commercial banks.

MORTGAGE BANKERS AND BROKERS

A **mortgage banker** makes a mortgage loan and then sells it to a long-term investor. The process begins by locating borrowers, qualifying them, preparing the necessary loan papers, and making the loans. Once the loan is made, it is sold for cash to a life insurance company, pension or trust fund, savings institution, or government agency. The mortgage banker is usually retained by the mortgage purchaser to **service the loan,** that is, to collect the monthly payments and to handle such matters as insurance and property tax impounds, delinquencies, early payoffs, and mortgage releases.

Mortgage bankers often take the form of **mortgage companies,** that vary in size from one or two persons up to several dozen. As a rule, they are locally oriented, finding and making loans within 25 or 50 miles of their offices. This gives them a feel for their market, greatly aids in identifying sound loans, and makes loan servicing much easier. For their efforts, mortgage bankers typically receive 1% of the amount of the loan when it is originated, and from ¼ to ½ of 1% of the outstanding balance each year thereafter for servicing. On very large loans, such as a major shopping center or office building, the fee drops to 1/10 of 1%.

Mortgage banking is not limited to mortgage companies. Commercial banks, savings and loan associations, and mutual savings banks in active real estate areas often originate more real estate loans than they can hold themselves, and these are sold to other investors. Mortgage bankers are important sources of FHA and VA loans.

Mortgage brokers, in contrast to mortgage bankers, specialize in bringing together borrowers and lenders, just as real estate brokers bring together buyers and sellers. The mortgage broker does not lend his own money, nor does he usually service the loans he has arranged.

Pension funds and trust funds traditionally have channeled their money to high-grade government and corporate bonds and stocks. However, the trend now is to place more money into real estate loans. Since rapid growth in fund size has been projected, pension and trust funds will likely become a major source of real estate financing in the future. At present, pension and trust funds purchase mortgages through mortgage bankers or on the open market. In some localities, pension fund members can tap their own pension funds for home mortgages at very reasonable rates.

Finance companies that specialize in making business and consumer loans also provide limited financing for real estate. As a rule, finance companies seek second mortgages at interest rates 2 to 5 percent higher than the rates prevailing on first mortgages. First mortgages are also taken as collateral; how-

OTHER LENDERS

ever, the lenders already discussed usually charge lower interest rates for these loans and thus are more competitive.

Credit unions normally specialize in consumer loans. However, some of the country's 23,000 credit unions have recently branched out into first and second mortgage loans on real estate.

Individuals are sometimes a source of cash loans on real estate, with the bulk of these loans coming from relatives or friends. Generally, loan maturities are shorter than those obtainable from the institutional lenders already described. In some cities, persons can be found who specialize in making or buying second and third mortgage loans of up to 10-year maturities.

LOAN APPLICATION AND APPROVAL

When a mortgage lender reviews a real estate loan application, the primary concern for both applicant and lender is to approve loan requests that show a high probability of being repaid in full and on time, and to disapprove requests that are likely to result in default and eventual foreclosure. How is this decision made? Figure 12:4 summarizes the key items that a loan officer considers when making a decision regarding a loan request. Let us review these items and observe how they affect the acceptability of a loan to a lender.

In section ①, the lender begins the loan analysis procedure by looking at the property and the proposed financing. Using the property address and legal description, an appraiser is assigned to prepare an appraisal of the property and a title search is ordered. These steps are taken to determine the fair market value of the property and the condition of title. In the event of default, this is the collateral the lender must fall back upon to recover the loan. If the loan request is in connection with a purchase, rather than the refinancing of an existing property, the lender will know the purchase price. As a rule, loans are made on the basis of appraised value or purchase price, whichever is lower. If the appraised value is lower than the purchase price, the usual procedure is to require the buyer to make a larger cash down payment. The lender does not want to overloan simply because the buyer overpaid for the property.

Continuing in section ①, the year the home was built is useful in setting the loan's maturity date. The idea is that the length of the loan should not outlast the remaining economic life of the structure serving as collateral. Note however, chronological age is only part of this decision because age must be considered in light of the upkeep and repair of the structure and its construction quality.

In the past, it was not uncommon for lenders to refuse to make loans in certain neighborhoods regardless of the quality of the structure or the ability of the borrower to repay. This was known as **redlining** and it effectively shut off mortgage loans in many older neighborhoods across the country. Today, under pressure from consumer groups and government agencies, lenders are abandoning this practice.

Redlining

The lender next looks at the amount of down payment the borrower proposes to make, the size of the loan being requested and the amount of other financing the borrower plans to use. This information is then converted into loan-to-value ratios. As a rule, the more money the borrower places into the deal, the safer the loan is for the lender. On an uninsured loan, the ideal loan-to-value (L/V) ratio for a lender on owner-occupied residential property is 70% or less. This means the value of the property would have to fall more than 30% before the debt owed would exceed the property's value, thus encouraging the borrower to stop making loan payments. Because of the nearly constant inflation in housing prices since the 1940's, very few residential properties have fallen 30% or more in value.

Loan-to-Value Ratios

Loan-to-value ratios from 70% through 80% are considered acceptable but do expose the lender to more risk. Lenders sometimes compensate by charging slightly higher interest rates. Loan-to-value ratios above 80% present even more risk of default to the lender, and the lender will either increase the interest rate charged on these loans or require that an outside insurer, such as the FHA or a private mortgage insurer, be supplied by the borrower. When a lender, for example, offers 70% L/V loans for 9% interest, 80% L/V loans

Figure 12:4

RESIDENTIAL MORTGAGE LOAN ANALYSIS

Property address _____

Legal description _____

Appraised value $ _____ Purchase price $ _____ Year Built _____

Down payment $ _____ Total cash required for settlement $ _____

Amount of this mortgage loan $ _____ Other financing $ _____

Loan to value ratio: This mortgage loan _____ % All financing _____ %

Source of settlement funds? _____

Purpose of loan? _____

Attitude of borrower _____

Occupancy of property? _____

② Borrower

Name _____

Age _____

Dependents other than co-borrower _____

Number _____ Ages _____

Employer _____

Years with current employer _____

Years this line of work _____

Position/Title _____

Type of business _____

Self-employed? _____

Previous employer _____

Position _____ Years _____

③ Co-Borrower

Name _____

Age _____

Dependents other than co-borrower _____

Number _____ Ages _____

Employer _____

Years with current employer _____

Years this line of work _____

Position/Title _____

Type of business _____

Self-employed? _____

Previous employer _____

Position _____ Years _____

④ Gross Monthly Income

	Borrower	Co-borrower
Base income	$	$
Overtime		
Bonuses		
Commissions		
Interest/Dividends		
Rental income		
Other		
Other		
Total	$	$

⑤ Monthly Housing Expense

	Previous	Proposed
Rent	$	$
First loan (P+I)		
Other loans (P+I)		
Mortgage insurance		
Hazard insurance		
Real estate taxes		
Assessments		
Owners' Assn.		
Total	$	$

Ratio of monthly housing expense to gross monthly income _____ % ⑥

⑦ Assets

Cash towards purchase	$
Checking and savings	
Stocks and bonds	
Life insurance cash value (Face amount $ _____)	
Sub-total liquid assets	$
Real estate owned	
Retirement fund	
Net worth of business	
Automobiles	
Furniture	
Other assets	
Total Assets	$

Liabilities

⑧

Installment debts	Mo. Pymt/Mos.	Balance
	$ /	$
	/	$
Auto loan		$
Real estate loans	/	$
Other debts	/	$
		$
Alimony/Child support	/	$
Total Mo. Payments	$	
Total Debts		$

Net Worth: ⑩ Total assets minus total debts equals $ _____

Report from credit bureau _____
Any bankruptcies? _____ Any pending lawsuits? _____
Is either applicant a co-maker or endorser on any other loans? _____
Do applicants have health insurance? _____ Disability insurance? _____

⑨

for 9¼% and 90% L/V loans for 9½%, the added ¼% and ½%, respectively, are not interest to the lender but rather compensation for the larger losses the lender will incur on loans made at higher L/V ratios. By comparison, FHA insurance costs the borrower an extra ½ of 1% and private mortgage insurers charge ¼ of 1%.

Settlement Funds   Next in section ①, the lender wants to know if the borrower has adequate funds for settlement. Are these funds presently in a checking or savings account, or are they coming from the sale of the borrower's present property? In the latter case, the lender knows the present loan is contingent on closing that escrow. If the down payment and settlement funds are to be borrowed, then the lender will want to be extra cautious as experience has shown that the less of his own money a borrower puts into a purchase, the higher the probability of default and foreclosure.

Purpose of Loan   The lender is also interested in the proposed use of the property. Lenders feel most comfortable when a loan is for the purchase or improvement of a property the loan applicant will actually occupy. This is because owner-occupants usually have pride-of-ownership in maintaining their property and even during bad economic conditions will continue to make the monthly payments. An owner-occupant also realizes that if he stops paying, he will have to vacate and pay for shelter elsewhere.

If the loan applicant intends to purchase a dwelling to rent out as an investment, the lender will be more cautious. This is because during periods of high vacancy, the property may not generate enough income to meet the loan payments. At that point, a strapped-for-cash borrower is likely to default. Note too, that lenders generally avoid loans secured by purely speculative real estate. If the value of the property drops below the amount owed, the borrower may see no further logic in making the loan payments.

Lastly in this section, the lender assesses the borrower's attitude towards the proposed loan. A casual attitude, such as, "I'm buying because real estate always goes up," or an applicant who does not appear to understand the obligation he is

undertaking would bring a low rating here. Much more welcome is the applicant who shows a mature attitude and understanding of the loan obligation and who exhibits a strong and
logical desire for ownership.

In sections ② and ③ the lender begins an analysis of the
borrower, and if there is one, the co-borrower. At one time,
age, sex and marital status played an important role in the
lender's decision to lend or not to lend. Often the young and
the old had trouble getting loans, as did women and persons
who were single, divorced or widowed. Today, the Federal
Equal Credit Opportunity Act prohibits discrimination based
on age, sex, race and marital status. Lenders are no longer permitted to discount income earned by women even if it is from
part-time jobs or because the woman is of child-bearing age.
Moreover, the money received by a divorced person for alimony or child support must be counted in full. Young adults
and single persons cannot be turned down because the lender
feels they have not "put down roots." Seniors cannot be
turned down as long as life expectancy exceeds the early risk
period of the loan and collateral is adequate. In other words,
the emphasis in borrower analysis is now focused on job stability, income adequacy, net worth and credit rating. Thus in
sections ② and ③ we see questions directed at how long the
applicants have held their present jobs and the stability of
those jobs themselves. The lender recognizes that loan repayment will be a regular monthly requirement and wishes to
make certain the applicants have a regular monthly inflow of
cash in a large enough quantity to meet the loan payment as
well as their other living expenses. Thus, an applicant who
possesses marketable job skills and has been regularly employed with a stable employer is considered the ideal risk.
Persons whose income can rise and fall erratically, such as
commissioned salespersons, present greater risks. Persons
whose skills (or lack of skills) or lack of job seniority result
in frequent unemployment are more likely to have difficulty
repaying a loan. In these sections the lender also inquires as
to the number of dependents the applicant must support out
of his or her income. This information provides some insight
as to how much will be left for monthly house payments.

Borrower Analysis

Monthly Income

In section ④ the lender looks at the amount and sources of the applicants' income. Sheer quantity alone is not enough for loan approval, the income sources must be stable too. Thus a lender will look carefully at overtime, bonus and commission income in order to estimate the levels at which these may reasonably be expected to continue. Interest, dividend and rental income would be considered in light of the stability of their sources also. Under the "other" category, income from alimony, child support, social security, retirement pensions, public assistance, etc. is entered and added to the totals for the applicants.

In section ⑤ the lender compares what the applicants have been paying for housing with what they will be paying if the loan is approved. Included in the proposed housing expense total are principal, interest, taxes and insurance along with any assessments or homeowner association dues (such as in a condominium). Some lenders add the monthly cost of utilities to this list.

At ⑥, proposed monthly housing expense is compared to gross monthly income. Lenders prefer that 25% or less of the applicants' monthly income go to housing expense. As the ratio approaches 35%, the probability of loan approval becomes slimmer and above that it disappears. Lenders recognize that food, health care, clothing, transportation, entertainment and income taxes must also come from the applicants' income.

Assets and Liabilities

In section ⑦ the lender is interested in the applicants' sources of funds for closing and whether, once the loan is granted, the applicants have assets to fall back upon in the event of an income decrease (a job lay-off) or unexpected expenses (hospital bills). Of particular interest, is the portion of those assets that are in cash or readily convertible into cash in a few days. These are called **liquid assets.** If income drops, they are much more useful in meeting living expenses and loan payments than assets that may require months to sell and convert to cash, i.e., assets which are **illiquid.** Note in this section that two values are shown for life insurance. **Cash value** is the amount of money the policyholder would receive if he surrenderd his policy or, alternatively, the amount he could borrow against the policy. **Face amount** is the amount that would be paid in the event of the insured's death. Lenders feel most comfortable if the face amount of the policy equals or exceeds the amount of the proposed loan. Less satisfactory are amounts less than the proposed loan or none at all. Although a borrower may not be expected to die before the loan is repaid, lenders recognize that the probability of default and foreclosure is lessened considerably if the survivors receive life insurance benefits.

In section ⑧, the lender is interested in the applicants' existing debts and liabilities for two reasons. First, these items will compete each month against housing expenses for available monthly income. Thus high monthly payments in this section may reduce the size of the loan the lender feels the applicants will be able to repay. The presence of monthly liabilities is not all negative: it can also show the lender that the applicants are capable of repaying their debts. Second, the applicants' total debts are subtracted from their total assets to obtain their net worth, reported at ⑨. If the result is negative (more owed than owned) the loan request will probably be turned down as too risky. In contrast, a substantial net worth can often offset weaknesses elsewhere in the application, such as too little monthly income in relation to monthly housing expense.

At number ⑩, lenders examine the applicants' past record of debt repayment as an indicator of the future. A credit report that shows no derogatory information is most desirable. Applicants with no previous credit experience will have a harder time proving they intend to repay; those with a history of collections or judgments will have the hardest time of all. Other factors the lender will consider are past bankruptcies on the part of the applicants and any pending lawsuits that might result in judgments against them. Additionally, the applicants may be considered poorer risks if they have guaranteed the repayment of someone else's debt by acting as a co-maker or endorser. Lastly, the lender may take into consideration whether the applicants have adequate insurance protection in the event of major medical expenses or a disability that prevents returning to work.

Past Credit Record

SECONDARY MORTGAGE MARKET

The secondary mortgage market provides a means by which a lender can sell a loan. It also permits investing in real estate loans without the need for loan origination and servicing facilities.

Federal National Mortgage Association

The best known secondary mortgage market operation in the United States is run by the Federal National Mortgage Association (FNMA), fondly known in the real estate business as **"Fannie Mae."** Originally organized by the federal government and later converted to a part public, part private corporation, Fannie Mae buys and sells FHA, VA, and conventional mortgage loans. Purchases are made, usually every 2 weeks, by inviting mortgage holders to offer their loans for sale to the FNMA. Funds for FNMA purchases come from the issue of corporate stock (which is currently traded on the New York Stock Exchange) and the sale of FNMA bonds and notes. Funds are also generated by selling loans it holds to insurance companies, pension funds, savings associations, and other mortgage investors on a competitive basis. Whether FNMA holds a loan or resells it, the actual month-to-month servicing still rests with the loan originator.

Government National Mortgage Association

Known as **"Ginnie Mae,"** the Government National Mortgage Association (GNMA) was split off from FNMA in 1968 and established as a part of the U.S. Department of Housing and Urban Development (HUD). GNMA is currently best known for its special assistance projects and mortgage-backed securities program. Through GNMA special assistance projects, the U.S. government injects subsidy money into the residential loan market. One subsidy program is the **Tandem Plan** wherein GNMA supports the price of mortgage loans that have been issued at less than current market interest rates. The purpose is to reduce interest rates on home loans, for example from 9% to 7½%, to low- and moderate-income home buyers. Upon direction of the president of the United States, GNMA will also make financing available on homes in areas where established financing is not available. Under its **mortgage-backed securities program,** Ginnie Mae insures the payment of principal and interest on blocks of FHA and VA loans sold to investors. GNMA's intention is to attract individuals, pension funds, and trust funds to provide money for mortgages by buying into these blocks.

The Federal Home Loan Mortgage Corporation (FHLMC), known as **"Freddie Mac,"** was established by an act of Congress in 1970 to provide a secondary market facility for the Federal Home Loan Bank System. Freddie Mac has the authority to buy and sell FHA, VA, and conventional loans, enter into mortgage participations, and issue its own mortgage investment certificates. Under its loan purchase program (the **whole loan program**), the FHLMC will buy individual mortgages from savings and loan associations that meet FHLMC requirements as to loan application, appraisal methods, promissory note, and mortgage format. The FHLMC finances its purchases through the sale of stock to the 12 Federal Home Loan Banks and the sale of bonds and notes on the open market. The FHLMC also currently markets a **guaranteed mortgage certificate** nicknamed "The Answer." Designed to attract pension and trust fund money into home mortgages, these certificates are backed by mortgages held by Freddie Mac. Principal and interest are guaranteed by the FHLMC with interest passed through to certificate holders twice a year and principal once a year. The FHLMC also guarantees to buy back each certificate 15 years later, thus avoiding the need for the investor to wait as long as 30 years for the last mortgage to mature.

Federal Home Loan Mortgage Corporation

In 1972, the MGIC Investment Corporation, originators of the Mortgage Guaranty Insurance Corporation, formed a buying and selling unit to provide the first nonfederal secondary market for conventional mortgages. Promptly nicknamed **"Maggie Mae,"** it provides an outlet where a lender can sell MGIC-insured mortgages to other investors. As with FNMA, GNMA, and FHLMC, the purpose is to attract investors who might not otherwise invest in mortgage loans.

MGIC Investment Corporation

Thus far we have been concerned with the money pipelines between lenders and borrowers. Ultimately though, the money a lender has available for loans must have a source. There are two basic sources: (1) savings generated by indi-

AVAILABILITY AND PRICE OF MORTGAGE MONEY

viduals and businesses as a result of spending less than is earned (**real savings**), and (2) government-created money, commonly referred to as **fiat money** or "printing press money." This second source does not represent unconsumed labor and materials; instead it competes for available goods and services alongside the savings of individuals and businesses.

In the arena of money and capital, real estate borrowers must compete with the needs of government, business, and consumers. Governments, particularly the federal government, compete the hardest when they borrow to finance a deficit. Not to borrow would mean bankruptcy and the inability to pay government employees and provide government programs and services. Strong competition also comes from business and consumer credit sectors. Home buyers do not fare as well because they are much less willing or able to pay high interest and are frequently outbid for available loan money.

One "solution" to this problem is for the federal government to create more money, thus making competition for funds easier and interest rates lower. Unfortunately, the net result is often "too much money chasing too few goods" and prices are pulled upward by the demand caused by the newly created money. This is followed by rising interest rates as savers demand higher returns to compensate for losses in purchasing power. Many economists feel that the higher price levels and interest rates of the 1970s are due to applying too much of this "solution" to the economy since 1965.

The alternative solution, from the standpoint of residential loans, is to increase real savings or decrease competing demands for available money. A number of plans and ideas have been put forth by civic, business, and political leaders. They include incentives to increase productive output from available manpower and machines, incentives to increase savings by exempting savings deposit interest from income taxes, and proposals to decrease competition for funds through a credit allocation (rationing) system.

Usury   An old idea that has been tried, but is currently of dubious value in holding down interest rates, is legislation of interest rate ceilings. Known as **usury laws** and found in

nearly all states, these laws were originally enacted to prohibit lenders from overcharging interest on loans to individuals. However, since the end of World War II, the ceilings
in some states have failed to keep in step with rising interest
rates. For example, a state with an 8% ceiling would have presented no problem to a home buyer in 1965, as home loans
then carried interest rates around 6%. However, a decade later,
when home loan rates were 9% and higher, if the ceiling remained unchanged, the home buyer would be denied a loan.
To charge 9%, even if it is the current fair market rate for a
home loan, is usury if the state-set ceiling is less than 9%.
In states where that has happened, lenders have found it
necessary to divert their funds to out-of-state borrowers,
usually through a mortgage banker or the facilities of the
FNMA, GNMA, FHLMC, and MGIC.

Ultimately, the rate of interest one must pay to obtain a   *Price to the Borrower*
loan is dependent on the cost of money to the lender, reserves
for default, loan servicing costs, and available investment
alternatives. For example, in 1976 the cost of money to savings
and loan associations averaged 6.4%. The cost of maintaining cash in the tills, office space, personnel, advertising,
free gifts for depositors, FSLIC insurance, and loan servicing,
plus loan reserves for defaults added another 1.6%, giving a
total of 8%. Therefore, to meet costs an association needed to
earn an average of 8% on all loans held. Since associations still
held loans made at interest rates of less than 8%, it was necessary to charge new borrowers more than 8%. The result was
rates of 8¾ to 9¼% to obtain home loans.

Life insurance companies do not have to "pay" for their
money because it comes from policyholder premiums. Nonetheless, they do want to earn the highest possible yields, with
safety, on the money in their custody in order to meet policy
claims. Thus, if a real estate buyer wants to borrow from a life
insurance company, he must compete successfully with the
other investment opportunities available to the company. For
example, if high-grade corporate bonds with maturities similar to mortgages are yielding 8½% interest, to be competitive,
real estate mortgage loans must offer 8½%. As mortgage

servicing costs of about ⅜ of 1% must be added to that, the borrower must pay 8⅞% to be equally attractive and 9% to be more attractive than corporate bonds. The same holds true when one wants to borrow from pension or trust funds.

ALIENATION AND PREPAYMENT

From a financial standpoint, when a lender makes a loan with a fixed interest rate, the lender recognizes that, during the life of the loan, interest rates may rise or fall. When they rise, the lender remains locked into the lower rate. By including an **alienation clause** (also called a due-on-sale clause or a call clause) the lender can call the balance due and relend the money at the current rate if the borrower sells the mortgaged property. If the buyer wishes to assume the loan, the lender can use this clause to increase the interest to current rates.

If loan rates drop, for instance from 9% to 8%, it becomes worthwhile for a borrower to shop for a new loan and repay the existing one in full. To discourage this, loan contracts sometimes call for a **prepayment penalty** in return for giving the borrower the right to repay his loan early. Typically, a prepayment penalty amounts to the equivalent of 3 to 6 months interest on the amount that is being paid early.

Note, however, that prepayment penalties vary from loan to loan and from state to state. Some loan contracts permit up to 20% of the unpaid balance to be paid in any one year without penalty. Other contracts make the penalty stiffest when the loan is young. In certain states, laws do not permit prepayment penalties on loans more than 5 years old. By federal law, prepayment penalties are not allowed on FHA, VA, and FNMA standardized loans.

VARIABLE-RATE MORTGAGES

As we have already seen, a major problem for savings institutions is that they are locked into long-term loans while being dependent on relatively short term savings deposits. In anticipation of the day when the average interest rate paid by savings institutions and banks increases to 8% or more, lenders have begun changing from fixed-rate loans to mortgage loans that carry a fluctuating interest rate. Called **variable-rate mortgages,** the interest rate on these loans rises and falls during the life of the loan in step with current interest rates.

Variable-rate mortgages add new dimensions to lending because if a lender and borrower agree to let the interest rate on a loan rise and fall during its life, it must be decided in advance (1) when the interest rate will be changed and by how much, and (2) how this change will affect the repayment terms of the loan. The solution to the first question is to tie the loan to some other interest indicator that reflects current market rates on similar types of debt. For example, interest yield rates as set by FNMA mortgage auctions might provide an indicator. Next, it must be decided what amount of change in the indicator would cause a change in the mortgage rate and how often a change could be made. One arrangement currently being used is to limit increases to $\frac{1}{4}$ or $\frac{1}{2}$ of 1% and to a maximum of two per year and a total of $2\frac{1}{2}$% over the life of the loan.

The second question has three possible answers: (1) raise or lower the monthly payment by the amount of the change, (2) keep the monthly payment constant but shorten or lengthen the maturity, and (3) keep the monthly payment and the maturity constant but change the amount owed. When interest rates fall, any of these three approaches will work satisfactorily and cause no hardship on either the lender or borrower. When rates rise, as they have done in two out of every three years since 1950, none of the answers is an ideal solution. Raising the monthly payment would result in a shock to a finely tuned family budget, although presumably the same inflationary factors that caused interest rates to rise would also cause the incomes of most families to increase. Extending maturities is only effective if the increase in interest is a small one. As was discussed in Chapter 11, increasing maturities beyond 25 or 30 years does little to change monthly payments. For example, lengthening a maturity from 25 to 40 years would not accommodate a change in interest from $8\frac{1}{2}$% to $9\frac{1}{2}$% unless there was also an increase in the size of the monthly payments. Furthermore, a lender may not be willing to extend a maturity to 40 years due to the age of the mortgaged structure. Changing the amount owed is the most radical plan of the three, for it can result in the borrower owing more dollars when the loan matures than when he obtained it. Under

Repayment Terms

this plan, monthly payments and maturity are kept constant. If interest rates rise, unless the borrower voluntarily elects to make larger payments, or interest rates later drop, the loan will not be paid off by maturity.

Although much remains to be settled on the issue of variable-rate mortgages, several observations are worthy of mention. First, the effect of variable-rate mortgages will be to take some of the "profit" out of real estate ownership and share it with whoever is providing the loan. Second, if savings associations can pay enough to keep savers from withdrawing their savings to purchase government and corporate debt, money will be more plentiful for real estate borrowers. Third, variable-rate mortgages, when they are written, carry interest rates below fixed-rate loans. This is because a variable-rate lender knows that, if interest rates rise, he will be compensated, whereas a fixed-rate lender charges more at the start to compensate for the possibility that rates will later rise. Fourth, when a variable-rate mortgage is adjusted upward, the borrower is allowed 30 to 60 days to repay without a prepayment penalty. Fifth, if rates do fall, the variable-rate borrower will automatically get the benefit of the new lower rates. Against this the variable-rate borrower must weigh the possibility that interest rates may continue to rise as they have since the end of World War II.

FLEXIBLE RATE
MORTGAGES

Not to be confused with the variable-rate mortgage is the **flexible-rate mortgage,** the objective of which is to help borrowers qualify for loans by basing repayment schedules on salary expectations. Under a flexible-rate mortgage, the interest rate and maturity are fixed and the monthly payment varies. For example, an 8%, $30,000, 30-year loan normally requires monthly payments of $220 for complete amortization. Under the flexible-rate plan, payments could be $200 for the first 5 years and $230 for the next 25 years.

ALTERNATIVES TO
INSTITUTIONAL
LENDERS

When institutional lenders, such as those already described in this chapter, will not loan on a property, one must seek alternative sources of financing. We shall briefly review some of the more commonly available alternatives.

When a seller is willing to accept part of the purchase price owed him in the form of the buyer's promissory note accompanied by a mortgage or trust deed, it is called **purchase money financing.** This allows the buyer to substitute a promissory note for cash; the seller is said to be "taking back paper." This method of financing is popular for land sales (where lenders rarely loan), on property where an existing mortgage is being assumed by the buyer, and on property where the seller prefers to receive his money spread out over a period of time, with interest, instead of lump-sum cash. For example, a retired couple moves out of a large home into a smaller one. The large home is worth $60,000, and they owe $20,000. If they need only $15,000 to make their move, they might be more than happy to let the buyer assume the existing mortgage and accept the remaining $25,000 as $250 per month payments at current interest rates.

Purchase Money Financing

Another financing alternative is **subordination.** For example, a man owns a $20,000 vacant lot suitable for building, and a builder wants to build an $80,000 building on the lot. The builder has only $10,000 cash. The largest construction loan he can find is for $80,000. If he can convince the seller to take $10,000 in cash and $10,000 later, he would have the $100,000 total. Note, however, that the lender making the $80,000 loan will want to be the first mortgagee to protect its position in the event of foreclosure. The lot owner must be willing to take a subordinate position, in this case a second mortgage. If the project is successful, the lot owner will receive his $10,000, plus interest, either in cash after the building is built and sold or as monthly payments. If the project goes into foreclosure, the lot seller can be paid only if the $80,000 first mortgage claim is satisfied in full from the sale proceeds.

Subordination

A financing device called the **installment contract** (land contract) enables the seller to finance a buyer by permitting him to make a down payment followed by monthly payments. However, title remains in the name of the seller. In addition to its wide use in financing land sales, it has also been a very effective financing tool in several states as a means of selling

Installment Contract (Land Contract)

homes during periods of tight money. For example, a home-owner owes $25,000 on his home and wants to sell it for $45,000. A buyer is found but he does not have the $20,000 down payment necessary to assume the existing loan. He does have $7,000, but for one reason or another money is not available from institutional lenders. If the seller is agreeable, the buyer can pay him $7,000 and they can enter into an installment contract for the remaining $38,000. The contract will call for monthly payments to the seller large enough to allow the seller to meet monthly payments on the $25,000 loan as well as to pay the remaining $13,000 owed to the seller, with interest. Unless property taxes and insurance are billed to the buyer, the seller will also collect for these and pay them. When loan money is later available from institutional lenders, the installment contract and existing loan are paid in full and title is conveyed to the buyer.

Option

When viewed as a financing tool, an **option** provides a method by which the need to immediately finance the full price of a property can be postponed. For example, a developer is offered 100 acres of land for a house subdivision, but he is not sure he can sell that many houses. The solution is to buy 25 acres outright and take three 25-acre options at pre-set prices on the remainder. If the houses he builds on the first 25 acres sell promptly, the builder can exercise his options to buy the remaining land. If sales are not good, the builder can let the remaining options expire and avoid being stuck with acreage he does not want or need. A useful variation on the option idea is the lease–option combination. Under it an owner leases his property to a tenant who, in addition to paying rent and using the property, also obtains the right to purchase it at a preset price for 6 months or 1 year.

The option can also provide speculative opportunities on small amounts of capital. If prices do not rise, the optionee loses only the cost of his option; if prices do rise, the optionee finds a buyer and simultaneously exercises his option, thereby realizing a nice profit.

Rentals and Leases

Even though the tenant does not acquire fee ownership, **rentals and leases** are a means of financing. Whether the tenant is a bachelor receiving the use of a $20,000 apartment for which he pays $250 rent per month, or a large corporation leasing a warehouse for 20 years, leasing is an ideal method of financing when the tenant does not want to buy, cannot raise the funds to buy, or prefers to invest available funds elsewhere. Similarly, **farming leases** provide for the use of land without the need to purchase it. Although some farm leases call for fixed rental payments, the more common arrangement is for the farmer to pay the landowner a share, for instance 25%, of the value of the crop produced. Thus, the landowner shares with the farmer the risks of weather, crop output, and prices.

Under a **sale and leaseback** arrangement, an owner–occupant sells his property and then remains as a tenant. Thus, the buyer acquires an investment and the seller frees his capital for other purposes while retaining the use of the property. A variation is for the tenant to order a building constructed, sell it to a prearranged buyer, and lease it back upon completion.

Although **leased land** arrangements are common through-   *Land Leases*
out the United States for both commercial and industrial users and for farmers, anything other than fee ownership of residential land is unthinkable in many areas. Yet in some parts of the United States (e.g., Baltimore, Maryland, Orange County, California, throughout Hawaii, and in parts of Florida) homes with long-term land leases are an accepted practice. Typically, these leases are from 55 to 99 years in length and, barring an agreement to the contrary, the improvements to the land become the property of the fee owner at the end of the lease. Rents may be fixed in advance for the life of the lease, renegotiated at preset points during the life of the lease, or a combination of both.

To hedge against inflation, when fixed rents are used in a long-term lease, it is common practice to use **step-up rentals.** For example, under a 55-year house-lot lease, the rent may be set at $200 per year for the first 15 years, $300 per year for the next 10 years, $400 for the next 10 years, and so forth. An alternative is to renegotiate the rent at various points during the life of a lease so that the effects of land value changes are more closely equalized between the lessor and the lessee. For example, a 60-year lease may contain renegotiation points at the fifteenth, thirtieth, and forty-fifth years. At those points the property would be reappraised and the lease rent adjusted to reflect any changes in the value of the property. Finally, if the lessor is responsible for paying the property taxes on the land, he will include an escalation clause in the lease contract that permits him to raise the lease rent by the amount of any property tax increase. The alternative is for the lessee to assume direct responsibility for paying property taxes.

VOCABULARY REVIEW

Match terms a–l with statements 1–12.

a. *Fannie Mae*
b. *FHLBS*
c. *Flexible rate mortgage*
d. *HUD*
e. *Illiquid assets*
f. *Liquid assets*

g. *Mortgage banker*
h. *Mortgage broker*
i. *Participation*
j. *Savings certificate*
k. *Usury*
l. *Variable-rate mortgage*

1. A federal agency that regulates federally chartered savings and loan associations.
2. A deposit that the saver agrees not to withdraw for a specified period of time; a time deposit.
3. Real estate loans that require interest plus a percentage of the profits from rentals.
4. A person or firm that makes mortgage loans and then sells them to investors.
5. A person or firm that brings borrowers and lenders together much like real estate brokers bring buyers and sellers together.
6. Cash plus assets that can be converted to cash in a matter of a few days.
7. A lending industry name for the Federal National Mortgage Association.
8. Assets that require several weeks or months to convert to cash.
9. Charging a rate of interest higher than that permitted by state law.
10. A mortgage loan on which the rate of interest can rise and fall with changes in prevailing interest rates.
11. A mortgage repayment plan that allows the borrower to make smaller monthly payments at first and larger ones later. Interest rate and maturity are fixed.

12. Commonly used abbreviation for the U.S. Department of Housing and Urban Development.

1. How have the FSLIC and FDIC helped to make mortgage money more readily available to borrowers?
2. Compared to passbook savings accounts, what advantages do time deposits offer savers and savings institutions?
3. What is meant by the term "loan servicing"?
4. Why may we expect pension funds and trust funds to play a more important role in real estate financing in the years to come?
5. Why does a lender feel more comfortable lending on an owner-occupied home than on a property being purchased as a rental investment?
6. Why is the monthly income of a loan applicant more important to a lender than the sheer size of the applicant's assets?
7. By what financing methods do FNMA and GNMA provide money for real estate loans?
8. If a dollar is a dollar no matter where it comes from, what difference does it make if the source of a real estate loan was real savings or fiat money?
9. Regarding variable-rate mortgage loans, what are the advantages and disadvantages to the borrower and lender?
10. Explain why rentals and leases are considered forms of real estate financing.

Hoagland, Henry E., and **Stone, Leo D.** *Real Estate Finance,* 5th ed. Homewood, Ill.: Richard D. Irwin, 1973, 603 pages. Chapters 11–16 deal with real estate financing through savings and loans associations, banks, life insurance companies, mortgage bankers–brokers, and miscellaneous sources. Chapters 23 and 28 are about FHLMC, FNMA and GNMA.

Lindow, Wesley. *Inside the Money Market.* New York: Random House, 1972, 308 pages. Book discusses the roles of the Federal Reserve System, U.S. Treasury, commercial banks, and money supply and demand in general on the availability and cost of mortgage money.

Rohan, Patrick J. *Real Estate Financing.* New York: Matthew Bender, 1975. In Volume 4, Chapter 2A discusses mortgage application preparation; Chapter 3 discusses sources of construction and permanent financing and usury laws; Chapters 6 and 7 discuss leases as financing devices.

Sirota, David. "Carry Back Financing," *Real Estate Today*, May/June 1974, pages 54–57. Author looks at alternative methods of financing residential property when mortgage money is tight and expensive.

Strauss, Jay J., and **Gottlieb, J. R.** "How to Finance Commercial Properties," *Real Estate Today*, Feb. 1975, pages 20ff. Talks about methods of financing commercial properties under tight money conditions.

Wiedemer, John P. *Real Estate Finance*. Reston, Va.: Reston Publishing Co., 1974, 331 pages. Coverage includes such topics as money and interest rates, sources of mortgage money, federal government mortgage programs, loan analysis, and alternative financing methods.

13

Taxes and Assessments

Adjusted sales price: the sales price of a property less commissions, fix-up, and closing costs

Ad valorem taxes: taxes charged according to the value of a property

Assessed value: a value placed on a property for the purpose of taxation

Assessment appeal board: local governmental body which hears and rules on property owner complaints of overassessment

Capital gains tax: income taxes due on the sale of an appreciated asset held more than 12 months

Documentary tax stamps: a tax on deeds and other convey- ances payable at the time of recordation

Mill rate: property tax rate that is expressed in tenths of a cent per dollar of assessed valuation

Tax basis: the price paid for a property plus closing costs and any brokerage fees paid to help find the property; used in calculating income taxes

Tax certificate: a document is- sued at a tax sale that entitles the purchaser to a deed at a later date if the property is not redeemed

Tax lien: a charge or hold that the government has against property to insure the payment of taxes

PROPERTY TAXES

The largest single source of income for local government pro- grams and services is the property tax. Schools (from kinder- garten through two-year colleges), fire and police departments, local welfare programs, public libraries, street maintenance, parks, and public hospital facilities are supported by prop- erty taxes. Some state governments also obtain a portion of their revenues from this source.

Property taxes are **ad valorem** taxes. This means they are levied according to the value of one's property; the more valuable the property, the higher the tax, and vice versa. The

underlying theory of ad valorem taxation is that those owning the more valuable properties are wealthier and hence able
to pay more taxes.

Determining how much tax a property owner will be
charged involves three basic steps: (1) local government
budget determination and appropriation, (2) valuing taxable
property within the taxation district, and (3) allocating
among individual property owners the amount that needs to
be collected.

Appropriation   Each taxing body with the authority to tax property prepares its budget for the coming year. Taxing bodies include
counties, cities, boroughs, towns and villages, and, in some
states, school boards, sanitation districts, and county road
departments. Each budget along with a list of sources from
which the money will be derived is enacted into law. This is
the **appropriation process.** Then sales taxes, state and federal
revenue sharing, business licenses, and city income taxes are
subtracted from the budget. The balance must come from
property taxes.

Assessment   Next, the valuation of the taxable property within each
taxing body's district must be determined. A county or state
assessor's office appraises each taxable parcel of land and the
improvements thereon. Appraisal procedures vary from state
to state. In some, the appraised value is the fair market cash
value of the property. This is the cash price one would expect
a buyer and a seller to agree upon in a normal open market
transaction. Other states start with the fair market value of
the land and add to it the cost of replacing the buildings and
other improvements on it, minus an allowance for depreciation
due to wear and tear and obsolescence.

The appraised value is converted into an assessed value
upon which taxes are based. In some states, the **assessed value**
is set equal to the appraised value; in others, it is a percentage
of the appraised value. Mathematically, the percentage selected
makes no difference as long as each property is treated equally.
Consider two houses with appraised values of $30,000 and
$60,000, respectively. Whether the assessed values are set
equal to appraised values or are set at a percentage of ap-

praised values, the second house will still bear twice the property tax burden of the first.

Certain types of property are exempt from taxation. The assessed values of the remaining taxable properties are then added together in order to calculate the tax rate. To explain this process, suppose that a building lies within the taxation districts of the Westside School District, the city of Rostin, and the county of Pearl River. The school district's budget for the coming year requires $800,000 from property taxes and the assessed value of taxable property within the district is $32,000,000. By dividing $800,000 by $32,000,000 we see that, for every dollar of assessed valuation, the school district must collect a tax of 4 cents. This levy can be expressed three ways: (1) as a mill rate, (2) as dollars per hundred, or (3) as dollars per thousand. All three rating methods are found in the United States.

Tax Rate

As a **mill rate,** this tax rate is expressed as mills per dollar of assessed valuation. Since 1 mill equals one tenth of a cent, a 4-cent tax rate is the same as 40 mills. Expressed as **dollars per hundred,** the same rate would be $4 per hundred of assessed valuation. As **dollars per thousand,** it would be $40 per thousand.

The city of Rostin also calculates its tax rate by dividing its property tax requirements by the assessed value of the property within its boundaries. Suppose that its needs are $300,000 and the city limits enclose property totaling $10,000,000 in assessed valuation. (In this example, the city covers a smaller geographical area than the school district.) Thus the city must collect 3 cents for each dollar of assessed valuation in order to balance its budget.

The county government's budget requires $2,000,000 from property taxes and the county contains $200,000,000 in assessed valuation. This makes the county tax rate 1 cent per dollar of assessed valuation. Table 13:1 shows the school district, city, and county tax rates expressed as mills, dollars per hundred, and dollars per thousand.

The final step is to apply the tax rate to each property. So applying the mill rate to a home with an assessed value of $10,000, is simply a matter of multiplying the 80 mills (the

Table 13:1   **EXPRESSING PROPERTY TAX RATES**

	Mill rate	Dollars per hundred	Dollars per thousand
School district	40 mills	$4.00	$40.00
City	30	3.00	30.00
County	10	1.00	10.00
Total	80 mills	$8.00	$80.00

equivalent of 8 cents) by the assessed valuation to arrive at property taxes of $800 per year. On a dollars per hundred basis, divide the $10,000 assessed valuation by $100 and multiply by $8. The result is $800. To insure collection, a lien for this amount is placed against the property. It is removed when the tax is paid.

To avoid duplicate tax bill mailings, a common practice is for all taxing bodies in a given county to have the county collect for them at the same time that the county collects on its own behalf.

Property tax years generally fall into two categories: January 1 through December 31 and July 1 through the following June 30. Some states require one payment per year; others collect in two installments. A few allow a small discount for early payment, and all charge penalties for late payments.

UNPAID PROPERTY TAXES

If a property owner fails to pay his property taxes, the property is eventually sold at a public tax sale auction and the proceeds used to pay the delinquent taxes. Tax sale methods vary from state to state. In some, title to delinquent property is transferred to the county or state. A 2- to 5-year redemption period follows during which the owner, or any lienholder, can redeem the property by paying back taxes and penalties. If redemption does not occur, the property is sold at a publicly announced auction and the highest bidder receives a **tax deed.** In other states, the sale is held relatively soon after the delinquency occurs, usually within 1 year. When this occurs, a **tax certificate** is issued to the purchaser. This entitles him to a deed to the property provided the delinquent taxpayer, or anyone holding a lien on the property, does not step forward and redeem it during the redemption period that follows. In other words, the successful bidder for a tax certificate is not certain if he will obtain title to the delinquent property because the redemption period occurs after the sale.

The right of government to divorce a property owner from his land for nonpayment of property taxes is well established by law. However, if the sale procedure is not properly followed, the purchaser may find his title open to successful challenge. Thus, it behooves the purchaser to obtain a title search and title insurance and, if necessary, to conduct a quiet title suit or file a suit to foreclose the rights of anyone previously having a right to the property.

ASSESSMENT APPEALS

By law, assessment procedures must be uniformly applied to all properties within a taxing jurisdiction. To this end, the assessed values of all lands and buildings, as determined by the assessors, are made available for public inspection. These are the **assessment rolls.** They permit a property owner to compare the assessed valuation on his property with assessed valuations on similar properties. If an owner feels he is overassessed, he can file an appeal before an **assessment appeal board,** or before a board of review, board of equalization, or tribunal. Some states also provide further appeal channels or permit appeal to a court of law, if the property owner remains unsatisfied with his assessment. Note that the appeal process deals only with the method of assessment and taxation, not the tax rate or the amount of tax.

In some states, the **board of equalization** performs another assessment-related task: that of equalizing assessment procedures between counties. This is particularly important where county-collected property taxes are shared with the state or other counties. Without equalization, it would be to a county's financial advantage to underassess so as to lessen its contribution. At present, two equalization methods are in common usage: one requires that all counties use the same appraisal procedure and assessed valuation ratio, and the other allows each county to choose its own method and then applies a correction as determined by the board. For example, a state may contain counties that assess at 20%, 24% and 30% of fair market value. These could be equalized by multiplying the 20% counties by 1.50, the 24% counties by 1.25, and the 30% counties by 1.00.

PROPERTY TAX
EXEMPTIONS

More than half the land in many cities and counties is exempt from real property taxation. This is because governments and their agencies do not tax themselves or each other. Thus, government-owned offices of all types, public roads and parks, schools, military bases, and government-owned utilities are exempt from property taxes. Also exempted are properties owned by religious and charitable organizations, hospitals, and cemeteries. In rural areas of many states, large tracts of land are owned by federal and state governments, and these too are exempt from taxation.

Property tax exemptions are also used to attract industries and to appease voters. In the first instance, a local government agency buys industrial land and buildings, and leases them to industries at a price lower than would be possible if they were privately owned and hence taxed. Alternatively, outright property tax reductions can be granted for a certain length of time to arriving firms. The rationale is that the cost to the public is outweighed by the economic boost that the newly attracted industry brings to the community. In the second instance, a number of states grant assessment reductions to homeowners. This increases the tax burden for households that rent and for commercial properties.

PROPERTY TAX
VARIATIONS

Property taxes on similarly priced homes within a city or county can vary widely when prices change faster than the assessor's office can reappraise. As a result, a home worth $30,000 in one neighborhood may receive a tax bill of $600 per year, while a $30,000 home in another neighborhood will be billed $800. When the assessor's office conducts a reappraisal, taxes in the first neighborhood will suddenly rise 33% and undoubtedly result in complaints from property owners who were unaware that they were previously underassessed. In times of slow-changing real estate prices, reappraisals were only made once every 10 years. Today, assessors are working toward computerized assessment systems that can make changes annually.

As an aid to keeping current on property value changes, states are enacting laws that require a real estate buyer to advise the assessor's office of the price and terms of his purchase within 90 days after taking title. This information, coupled with building permit records and on-site visits by assessor's office employees, provides the data necessary to constantly update assessments.

The amount of property taxes a property owner may expect to pay varies quite widely across the United States. On a home worth $40,000, for example, property taxes range from less than $400 per year to more than $1,600 per year. Why do differences exist and why are they so great? The answers fall into four basic categories: level of services offered, other sources of revenue, type of property, and government efficiency. Generally, cities with low property taxes offer fewer services to their residents. This may be by choice, such as smaller welfare payments, lower school expenditures per student, no subsidized public transportation, fewer parks and libraries, or because the city does not include the cost of some services in the property tax. For example, sewer fees may be added to the water bill and trash may be hauled by private firms. Lower rates can also be due to location. Wage rates are lower in some regions of the country, and a city not subject to ice and snow will have lower street maintenance expenses. Finally, a city may have other sources of revenue, such as oil royalties from wells on city property.

Supplemental Funding

Property tax levels are also influenced by the ability of local tax districts to obtain federal revenue sharing funds, money from state revenues (especially for schools), and to share in collections from sales taxes, license fees, liquor and tobacco taxes, and fines. For example, in Hawaii, property tax rates are relatively low because schools from kindergarten through the state university are paid for largely through the state income tax. Conversely, in some states property taxes are a major source of state government income.

The amount and type of taxable property in a community greatly affects local tax rates. Taxable property must bear the burden avoided by tax exempt property whereas privately owned vacant land, stores, factories, and high-priced homes generally produce more taxes than they consume in local government services and help to keep rates lower. Finally, one must look at the efficiency of the city. Has it managed its affairs in prior years so that the current budget is not burdened with large interest payments on debts caused by deficits in previous years? Is the city or county itself laid out in a compact and efficient manner, or does its sheer size make administration expensive? How many employees are required to perform a given service?

SPECIAL ASSESSMENTS   Often the need arises to make local municipal improvements that will benefit property owners within a limited area, such as the paving of a street, the installation of street lights, curbs, storm drains, and sanitary sewer lines, or the construction of irrigation and drainage ditches. Such improvements can be provided through special assessments on property.

The theory underlying special assessments is that the improvements must benefit the land against which the cost will be charged, and the value of the benefits must exceed the cost. The area receiving the benefit of an improvement is the **improvement district** or **assessment district,** and the property within the district bears the cost of the improvement. This is different from a **public improvement.** A public improvement, such as reconstruction of the city's sewage plant, benefits the general public and is financed through the general (ad valorem) property tax. A local improvement, such as extending a sewer line into a street of homes presently on septic tanks (cesspools), does not benefit the public at large and should properly be charged only to those that directly benefit. Similarly, when streets are widened, owners of homes lining a 20-foot-wide street in a strictly residential neighborhood would be expected to bear the cost of widening to 30 or 40 feet and to donate the needed land from their frontyards. But a street widening from two lanes to four to accommodate traffic not generated by the homes on the street is a different situation, as the widening benefits the public at large. In this case the widening should be funded from public monies and the homeowners be paid for any land taken from them.

An improvement district can be formed by the action of a group of concerned citizens who want and are willing to pay for an improvement. Property owners desiring the improvement take their proposal to the local board of assessors or similar public body in charge of levying assessments. A public notice showing the proposed improvements, the extent of the improvement district, and the anticipated costs is prepared by the board. This notice is mailed to landowners in the proposed improvement district, posted conspicuously in the district, and published in a local newspaper. The notice also contains the date and place of public hearings on the matter at which property owners within the proposed district are invited to voice their comments and objections.

Hearing and Confirmation

If the hearings result in a decision to proceed, then under the authority granted by state laws regarding special improvements, a local government ordinance is passed that describes the project and its costs and the improvement district boundaries. An assessment roll is also prepared that shows the cost to each parcel in the district. Hearings are held regarding the assessment roll. When everything is in order, the roll is **confirmed** (approved). The contract to construct the improvements is let and work is started.

The proposal to create an improvement district can also come from a city council, board of trustees, or board of supervisors. When this happens, notices are distributed and hearings held to hear objections. Objections are ruled upon by a court of law and if found to have merit, the assessment plans must be revised or dropped. Once approved, assessment rolls are prepared, more hearings held, the roll confirmed, and the contract let.

Bonds

Upon completion of the improvement, each landowner receives a bill for his portion of the cost. If the cost to a landowner is less than $100, the landowner either pays the amount in full to the contractor directly or to a designated public official who, in turn, pays the contractor. If the assessment is larger, the landowner can immediately pay it in full or let it **go to bond.** If he lets it go to bond, local government officials will prepare a bond issue that totals all the unpaid assessments in the improvement district. These bonds are either given to the contractor as payment for his work or sold to the public through a securities dealer with the proceeds used to pay the contractor. The collateral for the bonds is the land in the district upon which assessments have not been paid.

The bonds spread the cost of the improvements over a period of 5 to 10 years and are payable in equal annual (or semiannual) installments plus accumulated interest. Thus, a $2,000 sewer and street-widening assessment on a 10-year bond would be charged to a property owner at the rate of $200 per year (or $100 each 6 months) plus interest. As the bond is gradually retired, the amount of interest added to the regular principal payment declines.

Like property taxes, special assessments are a lien against the property. Consequently, if a property owner fails to pay his assessment, the assessed property can be sold in the same manner as when property taxes are delinquent.

Apportionment

Special assessments are apportioned according to benefits received, rather than by the value of the land and buildings being assessed. In fact, the presence of buildings in an improvement district is not usually considered in preparing the assessment roll; the theory is that the land receives all the benefit of the improvement. Several illustrations can best explain how assessments are apportioned. In a residential neighborhood, the assessment for installation of storm drains, curbs, and gutters is made on a **front-foot basis.** A property owner is charged for each foot of his lot that abuts the street being improved.

In the case of a sanitary sewer line assessment, the charge per lot can either be based on front footage or on a simple count of the lots in the district. In the latter case, if there are 100 lots on the new sewer line, each would pay 1% of the cost. In the case of a park or playground, lots nearest the new facility are deemed to benefit more and thus are assessed more than lots located farther away. This form of allocation is very subjective, and usually results in spirited objections at public hearings from those who do not feel they will use the facility in proportion to the assessment that their lots will bear.

INCOME TAXES ON
THE SALE OF
A RESIDENCE

We now turn to the income taxes one must pay if he sells his home for more than he paid for it. Income taxes are levied by the federal government, 43 states (the exceptions are

Florida, Nevada, New Jersey, South Dakota, Texas, Washington, and Wyoming), and by 48 cities, including New York City, Baltimore, Pittsburgh, Philadelphia, Cincinnati, Cleveland, and Detroit. The discussion here will center on the federal income tax. State and city income tax laws generally follow the pattern of federal tax laws.

The first step in determining the amount of taxable gain upon the sale of an owner-occupied residence is to calculate the home's **basis.** This is the price paid for the home plus fees paid for closing services and legal counsel, and any fee or commission paid to help find the property. If the home was built rather than purchased, the basis is the cost of the land plus the cost of construction, such as the cost of materials and construction labor, architect's fees, building permit fees, planning and zoning commission approval costs, utility connection charges, and legal fees. The value of labor contributed by the homeowner and free labor from friends and relatives cannot be added. If the home was received as compensation, a gift, an inheritance, or in a trade, or if a portion of the home was depreciated for business purposes, special rules apply that will not be covered here and the seller should consult the Internal Revenue Service (IRS).

Basis

Assessments for local improvements and any improvements made by the seller during his occupancy are added to the original cost of the home. An improvement materially adds to the value of a home, prolongs its life, or changes its use. For example, finishing an unfinished basement or upper floor, building a swimming pool, adding a bedroom or bathroom, installing new plumbing or wiring, installing a new roof, erecting a new fence, and paving a new driveway are classed as improvements and are added to the home's basis. Maintenance and repairs are not added as they merely maintain the property in ordinary operating condition. Fixing gutters, mending leaks in plumbing, replacing broken windowpanes, and painting the inside or outside of the home would be considered maintenance and repair items. However, repairs, when done as part of an extensive remodeling or restoration job, may be added to the basis.

Table 13:2   CALCULATING THE GAIN ON A SALE

May 1, 1967	*Buy home for $20,000, closing costs are $300*	Cost basis, $20,300
July 1, 1968	*Add swimming pool for $3,000*	Cost basis, $23,300
Dec. 1, 1969	*Add extra bedroom and bathroom for $3,500*	Cost basis, $26,800
Aug. 1, 1975	*Sell home for $36,500; sales commission & closing costs are $2,500*	Net sales price, $34,000
June 1, 1975	*Paint and fix-up of home in preparation for above sale, $800*	Adjusted sales price, $33,200

Calculation of gain: Adjusted sales price		$33,200
Less cost basis		$26,800
Gain		$ 6,400

Adjusted Sales Price

The next step is to calculate the **adjusted sales price.** This is the sales price reduced by the sales commission, closing costs, and expenses for fix-up and repair work performed on the home to make it more salable. For fix-up and repair work to be deductible from the selling price, the work must be performed during the 90-day period ending on the day the contract to sell is signed, and it must be paid for before another 30 days elapses after that date. Table 13:2 demonstrates the calculation of basis, adjusted sales price, and taxable gain.

Tax Postponement

The seller has three choices if he wants to postpone paying income taxes on the $6,400 gain shown in Table 13:2. He can either buy another residence costing at least $33,200 within 18 months before or after the August 1, 1975, closing date, or he can start construction on a new home costing at least $33,200 within 18 months and finish and occupy it within 24 months. The third alternative is to buy another home for less than $33,200 within the 18 months, and before the 24-month limit has expired add improvements, such as a new bathroom, bedroom or garage, or perform general reconstruction to bring

Table 13:3   **CALCULATING A NEW TAX BASIS**

July 15, 1975	*Buy or build another home for $38,000; closing costs are $300*	Cost of new home,	$38,300
August 1, 1975	*Settlement date on previous home*	Subtract postponed gain	6,400
		Income tax basis for the new home	$31,900

the purchase price plus the improvements to $33,200 or more. If the seller elects any of these postponement methods, the gain of $6,400 becomes a part of the basis of his new home and he is not taxed at this time. Table 13:3 demonstrates this procedure.

If the replacement home costs less than the one sold, some *Taxable Gain* or all of the gain will be recognized and taxed. Suppose that the basis on a home is $30,000, and it sells for an adjusted sales price of $39,000. The seller purchases another home within the time limitations for $35,000. He can transfer his old home's basis to the newly acquired home, but the new home does not cost enough to absorb the entire $9,000 gain. Only $5,000 can be absorbed and avoid being taxed at this time. The remaining $4,000 is recognized now and is subject to taxation. If the new home is $30,000 or less including closing costs, taxes will be due on the full $9,000 gain from the sale of the first residence. If he has owned the property more than 12 months (9 months on sales closed in 1977), the recognized gain is taxed as a **capital gain;** thus he will pay only about half the taxes that would be due if the money had been classed as ordinary income. If the adjusted sales price of the residence just sold is less than the basis, the IRS does not permit the taxpayer to deduct that loss against his other income.

The system of postponing taxes on gains in the value of one's residence works well as long as consistently more expensive homes are purchased. However, when a family's children eventually move away, a smaller and presumably less expensive home is needed. To soften the tax burden that such a move would cause, Congress has enacted a special law that permits persons 65 years of age and over to take a once-in-a-lifetime exclusion from taxable gain of up to $35,000.

To qualify, the owner must be at least 65 years old at the time of the transaction and have owned and occupied the home as his or her principal residence for 5 of the previous 8 years. When married couples own jointly, either upon reaching age 65 will qualify if they file a joint income tax return. This exclusion applies only to the first $35,000 of sales price, thus favoring those in less expensive homes with a low basis. When the sales price, adjusted for selling costs and fix-up expenses, is $35,000 or less, the entire gain is excludable. Above that, the adjusted sales price is divided by $35,000. The answer is divided into the capital gain on the home. The result is the amount that is exempt from taxation.

Installment Sale   Another method of easing the income tax bite upon the sale of a home when a subsequent purchase does not permit postponement of gains is the installment method of reporting income.

Suppose that your home, which is free and clear of debt, is sold for $100,000. The real estate commission and closing costs are $7,500 and your basis is $40,000. As a result, the gain on this sale is $52,500, and you will be required to pay all the income taxes due on that gain in the year of sale, a situation that will undoubtedly force you into a higher tax bracket. A solution is to sell to the buyer on terms rather than sending him to a lender to obtain a loan. If he pays you no more than 30% of the selling price per year (including down payment and principal payments), you may elect to pay income taxes on only that portion of the gain received in any given year. Thus, if the buyer pays you $20,000 down and gives you a promissory note calling for payments of $5,000 and interest this year, and $25,000 plus interest in each of the next 3 years, your gains would be calculated and reported as follows. Of each dollar of sales price received, 52½¢ would be reported gain. Thus, $13,125 would be reported this year and in each of the next 3 years. The interest you earn on the promissory note is reported and taxed separately as interest income.

If there was a $30,000 mortgage on the property that the buyer agreed to assume, the $100,000 sales price would be reduced by $30,000 to $70,000 for tax-calculating purposes. The portion of each dollar paid to you by the buyer that must be reported as gain is $52,500 divided by $70,000, or 75%. If the down payment is $20,000 followed by $10,000 per year for 5 years, you would report 75% of $20,000, or $15,000 this year and $7,500 in each of the next 5 years.

Since the federal income tax began in 1913, owners of single-family residences have been permitted to claim as itemized personal deductions money paid for state and local realty taxes, as well as interest on debt secured by their homes. Subsequently, this deduction was extended to condominium and cooperative apartment owners. The deduction allowed for property taxes does not extend to special assessment taxes for improvement districts. However, if the assessment goes to bond, that portion of each payment attributable to interest is deductible. With regard to mortgages, the IRS also permits the deduction of loan prepayment penalties, and the deduction of points on new loans that are clearly distinguishable as interest and not service fees for making the loan. Loan points paid by a seller to help a buyer obtain an FHA or VA loan are not deductible as interest (it is not the seller's debt), but can be deducted from the home's selling price in computing a gain or loss on the sale.

From an individual taxpayer's standpoint, the ability to deduct property taxes and mortgage interest on a personal residence becomes more valuable as wage gains and inflation push a person into successively higher tax brackets. With $32,000 of taxable income, a single person enters the 50% federal tax bracket, as does a married couple filing jointly with $44,000 in taxable income. At the 50% bracket, every dollar spent for something tax-deductible costs the taxpayer only 50¢ in after-tax money. Or seen from another viewpoint, the taxpayer obtains the full enjoyment of the money he spends on interest and property taxes without having to first pay income taxes on it. Although progressively less dramatic, the same argument applies to persons in the 40%, 30%, and 20% tax brackets. As viewed from a national standpoint, the de-

PROPERTY TAX AND INTEREST DEDUCTIONS

ductibility of interest and property taxes encourages widespread ownership of the country's land and buildings.

INCOME TAXES ON
INVESTMENT
PROPERTY

When one owns real estate for investment purposes, income tax rules vary somewhat from the preceding discussion. Very briefly, the rental income a property produces is fully taxable. However, against this income one can deduct all expenses incurred in earning it, such as property taxes, interest, maintenance, repairs, management, utilities, insurance, and depreciation. Money spent on improvements is not immediately deductible from rental income, but must be added to the basis of the property and depreciated when the property is ultimately sold. Capital gains tax treatment is possible if the property was owned more than 12 months. Also the owner can elect to report his gains by the installment method if he receives no more than 30% of the purchase price in any one year. Tax treatment of investment property is covered in more detail in Chapter 24, where the ability of investment property to "shelter" the owner's other sources of income from taxation is discussed.

Finally, it should be pointed out that if a property owner fails to pay his income taxes, the government may place a lien against his property by issuing a tax warrant. When properly filed, this lien makes the property security for payment of the delinquent taxes.

CONVEYANCE
TAXES

Prior to 1968 the federal government required the purchase and placement of federal documentary tax stamps on deeds. The rate was 55¢ for each $500 or fraction thereof computed on the "new money" in the transaction. Thus, if a person bought a home for $50,000 and either paid cash or arranged for a new mortgage, the tax was based on the full $50,000. If the buyer assumed or took title subject to an existing $30,000 loan, then the tax was based on $20,000. Examples of federal documentary tax stamps, which look much like postage stamps, can still be seen on deeds recorded prior to 1968.

Effective January 1, 1968, the federal deed tax program was ended and many states took the opportunity to step in and begin charging a deed tax of their own. Whereas only a handful of states required a tax on conveyances prior to 1968, today only a handful do not. A large number of states have adopted fee schedules that are substantially the same as the federal government previously charged. Others base their fee on the purchase price without regard to any existing indebtedness left on the property by the seller. The amount of transfer taxes charged by various states (plus some counties and cities) ranges from just a few dollars to as much as $500 or more on the sale of a $50,000 property. These fees are paid to the county recorder prior to recording and are in addition to the charge for recording the document itself. Some states also charge a separate tax on the value of any mortgage debt created by a transaction.

Match terms a–l with statements 1–12.

VOCABULARY REVIEW

a. *Adjusted sales price*
b. *Ad valorem*
c. *Appropriation process*
d. *Assessed valuation*
e. *Assessment roll*
f. *Capital gains tax*
g. *Front-foot basis*
h. *Installment reporting*
i. *Mill rate*
j. *Special assessments*
k. *Tax certificate*
l. *Tax deed*

1. A tax rate expressed in tenths of a cent per dollar of assessed valuation.
2. According to value.
3. A document issued at a tax sale that entitles the purchaser to a deed at a later date if the property is not redeemed.
4. The enactment of a taxing body's budget and sources of money into law.
5. A book that contains the assessed valuation of each property in the county or taxing district.
6. A document conveying title to property purchased at a tax sale.
7. A value placed on a property for the purpose of taxation.
8. Assessments levied to provide publicly built improvements that will primarily benefit property owners within a small geographical area.
9. A charge or levy that varies directly with the measured distance that a parcel of land abuts a street.
10. Sales price of a property less fix-up costs and sales commissions, closing and other selling costs.
11. Refers to income taxes due on the sale of an appreciated asset held more than 12 months.
12. Sale of an appreciated property for less than 30% down in order to spread out the payment of income taxes on the gain.

QUESTIONS AND
PROBLEMS

1. Explain the process for calculating the property tax rate for a taxation district.

2. The Southside School District contains property totalling $120,000,000 in assessed valuation. If the district's budget is $960,000, what will the mill rate be?

3. Continuing number 2, if a home lying in the Southside School District carries an assessed valuation of $40,000, how much will the homeowner be required to pay to support the district this year?

4. The Lakeview Mosquito Abatement District levies an annual tax of $0.05 per $100 of assessed valuation to pay for a mosquito-control program. How much does that amount to for a property in the district with an assessed valuation of $10,000?

5. In your county, if a property owner wishes to appeal an assessment, what procedure must he follow?

6. If the property taxes on your home were to rise 90% in 1 year, where would you go to protest the increase: the assessment appeal board, the city council, or the county government? Explain.

7. How does the amount of tax-exempt real estate in a community affect nonexempt property owners?

8. What methods and techniques are used by your local assessor's office to keep up to date with changing real estate prices?

9. The Smiths bought a house in 1963 for $21,000 including closing costs. Five years later they made improvements costing $2,000 and 5 years after that more improvements that cost $5,000. Today they sell the house; the sales price is $48,000 and commissions and closing costs total $3,000. For income tax purposes, what is their gain?

10. Continuing number 9, a month after selling, the Smiths purchase a two-bedroom condominium for $38,000, including closing costs. What is their taxable gain now? Will it be taxed at ordinary income tax rates or will it receive capital gains treatment? (Assume that the Smiths are less than 65 years of age.)

11. What is the current documentary transfer tax in your community?

ADDITIONAL READINGS

Federal Tax Course. New York: Commerce Clearing House, 1976. Includes detailed information on federal tax laws including their application to real estate. Published annually.

Holland, Daniel M. *The Assessment of Land Value*. Madison: University of Wisconsin Press, 1970, 292 pages. Looks at the role of property taxation in the community. Discussion centers on finding a property tax method that is both equitable and economically neutral.

Internal Revenue Service. "Tax Information for Homeowners," Publication 530. Washington, D.C.: U.S. Government Printing Office, 1976, 8 pages. Discusses income tax aspects of settlement costs, itemized deductions, rental and business use, repairs, improvements, buying, selling, record keeping, casualty losses, etc., for owners of houses, condominiums, and cooperatives. Published annually. Available free from the IRS.

Internal Revenue Service. "Tax Information on Selling Your Home," Publication 523. Washington, D.C.: U.S. Government Printing Office, 1976, 15 pages. Provides instructions on how to report taxable income from the sale of one's residence. Published annually. Available free from the IRS.

Lindholm, Richard W. *Property Taxation U.S.A.* Madison: University of Wisconsin Press, 1967, 315 pages. A collection of articles on property taxes. Topics include taxation history, tax exemptions, tax inducements, the need for property taxes, special tax problems, and a look into the future for property taxes.

Rohan, Patrick J. *Real Estate Financing*. New York: Matthew Bender, 1975. Volume 4, Chapter 8, discusses the requirements for a tax-free exchange of real property.

14

Title Closing and Escrow

Closing statement: an accounting of funds to the buyer and the seller at the completion of a real estate transaction

Escrow: the deposit of documents and funds with a neutral third party along with instuctions as to how to conduct the closing

Escrow agent: the person placed in charge of an escrow

Prorating: the division of ongoing expenses and income items between the buyer and the seller

RESPA, Real Estate Settlement Procedures Act: a federal law that deals with procedures to be followed in a real estate closing

Seller's affidavit of title: a document provided by the seller at the settlement meeting stating that he has done nothing to encumber title since the title search was made

Settlement meeting: a meeting at which the seller delivers his deed to the buyer, the buyer pays for the property, and all other matters pertaining to the sale are concluded

Title closing: the process that begins with the signed purchase contract and ends with the conveyance of title

Title search: a search of publicly available records and documents to determine current ownership and title condition for a property

Numerous details must be dealt with between the time a buyer and a seller sign a real estate sales contract and the day title is conveyed to the buyer. The seller's title must be searched, loans must be arranged, insurance and property taxes must be prorated, and a deed must be prepared. Finally, when everything is in order, the buyer pays for the property and the seller delivers a deed. This is the **title closing** process; depending on where one resides in the United States, it is referred to as a **closing, settlement,** or **escrow.** All accomplish the same basic goal, but the method of reaching that goal can follow one of two paths.

In some parts of the United States, particularly in the East, and to a certain extent the Mountain states, the Midwest, and the South, the title closing process is concluded at a meeting at which each party to the transaction, or a representative, is present. In the western states, and spreading eastward, title closing is conducted by an escrow agent, who is a neutral third party mutually selected by the buyer and seller to carry out the closing. With an escrow, there is no closing meeting; in fact, most of the closing process is conducted by mail. Let us look at the operation of each method.

CLOSING OR SETTLEMENT MEETING

When a meeting is used to close a real estate transaction, the seller (or his representative) meets in person with the buyer and delivers the deed. At the same time, the buyer pays the seller for the property. To ascertain that everything promised in the sales contract has been properly carried out, it is customary for the buyer and seller to each have an attorney present. The real estate agents who brought the buyer and seller together are also present, along with a representative of the firm that conducted the title search. If a new loan is being made or an existing one is being paid off at the closing, a representative of the lender will be present.

Seller's Responsibilities

To assure a smooth closing, each person attending is responsible for bringing certain documents. The seller and his attorney are responsible for preparing and bringing the deed and the most recent property tax bill (and receipt if it has been paid). If required by the sales contract, they also bring the insurance policy for the property, the termite and wood rot inspection report, deeds or documents showing the removal of unacceptable liens and encumbrances, a bill of sale for personal property, a survey map, documentary tax stamps for the deed, and a statement showing the remaining balance on any loan that the buyer will assume. If the property produces income, existing leases, rent schedules, current expenditures, and letters advising the tenants of the new owner must also be furnished.

The buyer's responsibilities include having adequate settle- *Buyer's Responsibilities*
ment funds ready, making certain his attorney is present to
protect his interests, and, if he is borrowing, obtaining his loan
commitment and advising the lender of the meeting's time and
place. The real estate agent is present because it is the custom
in some localities that he be in charge of the closing and prepare the proration calculations. He will also receive his commission check at that time and will want to be certain that all
goes well. If the broker is not in charge of the closing, the
task falls to the buyer's or seller's attorney, a title company
employee, or a closing agent.

If a new loan is involved, the lender will bring a check
for the amount of the loan along with a note and mortgage
for the borrower to sign. If an existing loan is to be paid off
as part of the transaction, the lender will be present to receive a check and release the mortgage held on the property.
If a lender elects not to attend, the check and/or loan papers
are given to the person in charge of the closing, along with instructions for their distribution and signing. A title insurance
representative is also present to provide the latest status of
title and the title insurance policy. If title insurance is not used,
the seller is responsible for bringing an abstract or asking the
abstractor to be present.

When everyone has arrived at the meeting place, the clos- *The Transaction*
ing begins. Those present record each other's names as witnesses to the meeting. The various documents called for by
the sales contract are exchanged for inspection. The buyer
and his attorney inspect the deed the seller is offering, the title
search and/or title policy, the mortgage papers, survey, leases,
removals of encumbrances, and proration calculations. The
lender also inspects the deed, survey, title search, and title
policy. This continues until each party has had a chance to
inspect each document of interest.

As the title search will have been prepared a day or more
before the meeting, the buyer and lender will want protection
against any changes in title condition since then. One solution
is to obtain a **seller's affidavit of title** from the seller. In this
affidavit, the seller states that he is the true owner of the prop-

erty, that there are no judgments, bankruptcy, or divorce proceedings currently against him, and that he has done nothing
to damage the quality of title since the title search. If a defect
caused by the seller later appears, he may be sued for damages. Furthermore, he may be liable for criminal charges if it
can be shown that he was attempting to obtain money under
false pretenses by signing the affidavit. Another solution is to
require the person in charge of the closing to hold the money
being paid to the seller until a final title search is made and
the new deed recorded.

A settlement statement (discussed in detail later) is given
to the buyer and seller to summarize the financial aspects of
their transaction. It is prepared by the person in charge of the
closing either just prior to or at the meeting. It provides a
clear picture of where the buyer's and seller's money is going
at the closing by identifying each party to whom money is
being paid.

If any questions or disagreements arise, it is hoped they
can be resolved at the meeting, possibly with more negotiating.
If an impasse is reached, the parties can agree to adjourn the
closing to a later date. For example, if the seller did not bring
all the documents required by the buyer, or if there is a cloud
on the title unacceptable to the buyer and the seller feels it
can be removed, an adjournment is appropriate. However, if
the impasse is major, such as a cloud on the title that will be
difficult to clear, a lender who will not make the needed loan,
or a title insurance company that refuses to insure, it may be
necessary to cancel the entire transaction.

If everyone involved in the closing has done his or her
homework and has come prepared to the meeting, the closing
will usually go smoothly. If everything is in order, the seller
hands a completed deed to the buyer. The buyer then gives
the seller a check that combines the down payment and net
result of the prorations. The lender has the buyer sign the
mortgage and note, and hands checks to the seller and the
existing lender if one is involved. The seller writes a check to
his real estate broker, attorney, and the abstracter. The buyer
writes a check to his attorney for his services. This continues
until every document is signed and everyone is paid. At the
end, everyone stands, shakes hands, and departs. The deed,

new mortgage, and release of the old mortgage are then recorded, and the transaction is complete.

The use of escrow to close a real estate transaction involves a neutral third party, called an **escrow agent,** escrow holder, or escrowee, who acts as a trusted stakeholder for all the parties to the transaction. Instead of delivering his deed directly to the buyer at a closing meeting, the seller gives the deed to the escrow agent with instructions that it be delivered only after the buyer has completed all his promises in the sales contract. Similarly, the buyer hands the escrow agent the money for the purchase price plus instructions that it be given to the seller only after he has completed all his promises. Let us look closer at this arrangement.

A typical real estate escrow closing starts when a sales contract is signed by the buyer and seller. They select a neutral escrow agent to handle the closing. This may be the escrow department of a bank or savings and loan or other lending agency, an independent escrow company, an attorney or the escrow department of a title insurance company. Sometimes real estate brokers offer escrow services. However, if the broker is earning a sales commission in the transaction, he cannot be classed as neutral and disinterested. Because escrow agents are entrusted with valuable documents and large sums of money, most states have licensing and bonding requirements that escrow agents must meet.

The escrow agent's task begins with placing the buyer's earnest money in a special bank trust account and preparing a set of escrow instructions based on the signed sales contract; these are to be promptly signed by the buyer and seller. The instructions establish an agency relationship between the escrow agent and buyer and seller, respectively. The instructions also detail in writing everything that each party to the sale must do before the deed is finally delivered to the buyer. In a typical transaction, the escrow instructions will tell the escrow agent to order a title search and obtain title insurance. If an existing loan against the property is to be repaid as part of the sale, the escrow agent is asked to contact the lender to request a statement of the amount of money necessary to repay the loan and ask for a mortgage release. The lender will enter into an agreement with the escrow agent wherein the lender will give the completed release papers to the escrow agent, but the agent is not to deliver them to the seller until the agent has remitted the amount demanded by the lender. If the existing loan is to be assumed, the escrow agent will ask the lender for the current balance and any documents that the buyer must sign.

When the title search is completed, the escrow agent forwards it to the buyer or his attorney for approval. The property insurance and tax papers the seller would otherwise bring to the closing meeting are sent to the escrow agent for proration. Leases, service contracts, and notices to tenants are also sent to the escrow agent for proration and delivery to the buyer. The deed conveying title to the buyer is prepared by the seller's attorney (in some states by the escrow agent), signed by the seller, and given to the escrow agent. Once delivered into escrow, if the seller dies, marries, or is legally declared incompetent before the close of escrow, the deed will still pass title to the buyer.

The Closing   As the closing date draws near, if all the instructions have been completed, the escrow agent requests any additional money the buyer and lender must deposit in order to close. The day before closing the escrow agent calls the title company and orders a last minute check on the title. If no changes have occurred since the first (preliminary) title search, the deed, mortgage, mortgage release, and other documents to be recorded as part of the transaction are recorded. Immediately following the recording, the escrow agent hands or mails a check to every party due funds from the escrow (usually the seller, real estate broker, and previous lender), along with any papers or documents to be delivered through escrow (such as the fire insurance policy, copy of the property tax bill, and tenant leases for the buyer). Several days later the buyer, seller, and lender will receive a title insurance policy in the mail from the title company. The public recorder's office also mails the documents it recorded to each party. The deed will be sent to the buyer, the mortgage release to the seller, and the new mortgage to the lender.

In the escrow closing method, the closing, delivery of title, and recordation usually all take place at the same moment. Technically, the seller does not physically hand a deed to the buyer on the closing day. However, once all the conditions of the escrow are performed, the escrow agent becomes an agent of the seller as to the money in the transaction, and an agent of the buyer as to the deed. Thus, a buyer, through an agent, receives the deed, and the law regarding delivery is fulfilled.

It is not necessary for the buyer and seller to meet face-to-face during the escrow period or at the closing. This can eliminate personality conflicts that might be detrimental to an otherwise sound transaction. The escrow agent, having previously accumulated all the documents, approvals, deeds, and monies prior to the closing date, does the closing alone.

In a brokeraged transaction, the real estate agent is usually the only person who actually meets the escrow agent. All communication can be handled through the broker, by mail, or by telephone. If a real estate agent is not involved, the buyer and/or seller can open the escrow, either in person or by mail. The use of an escrow agent does not eliminate the need for an attorney. Although there is no closing meeting for the attorneys to attend, they play a vital role in advising the buyer and seller on each document sent by the escrow agent for approval and signature.

Escrows can be used for purposes other than real estate or sales transactions. For example, a homeowner can arrange to refinance his property by entering into an escrow with the lender. The conditions of the escrow would be that the homeowner deliver a properly executed note and mortgage to the escrow agent and that the lender deposit the loan money. Upon closing, the escrow agent delivers the documents to the lender and the money to the homeowner. Or, in reverse, an escrow could be used to pay off the balance of a loan. The conditions would be the borrower's deposit of the balance due and the lender's deposit of the mortgage release and note. Even the weekly office sports pool is an escrow, with the person holding the pool money being the escrow agent for the participants.

Loan Escrows

PRORATING AT
THE CLOSING

Ongoing expenses and income items must be prorated between the seller and buyer when property ownership changes hands. Items subject to proration include property insurance premiums, property taxes, accrued interest on assumed loans, and rents and operating expenses if the property produces income. If heating is done by oil and the oil tank is partially filled when title transfers, that oil can be prorated, as can utility bills when service is not shut off between owners. The prorating process has long been a source of considerable mystery to real estate newcomers. Several sample prorations common to most closings will help to clarify the process.

Hazard Insurance

Hazard insurance policies for such things as fire, wind, storm, and flood damage are paid for in advance. At the beginning of each year of the policy's life, the premium for that year's coverage must be paid. When real estate is sold, the buyer may ask the seller to transfer the remaining coverage to him. The seller usually agrees if the buyer will reimburse him for the value of the remaining coverage on a prorated basis.

The first step in prorating hazard insurance is to find out how often the premium is paid, how much it is, and what period of time it covers. Suppose that the seller has a 1-year policy costing $120 and starting on January 1, 1977. If the property is sold and the closing date is July 1, 1977, the policy is half used up. Therefore, if the buyer wants the policy transferred to him, he must pay the seller $60 for the remaining 6 months of coverage.

Because closing dates do not always occur on neat, evenly divided portions of the year, nor do most items that are prorated, it is usually necessary to break the year into months and the months into days to make proration calculations. Suppose, in the previous hazard insurance example, that prorations are to be made on June 30 instead of July 1. This would give the buyer 6 months and 1 day of coverage. How much does he owe the seller? The first step is to calculate the monthly and daily rates for the policy: $120 divided by 12 is $10 per month. Dividing the monthly rate of $10 by 30 days gives a daily rate of 33.33¢. The second step is to add 6 months at $10 and 1 day at 33.33¢. Thus, the buyer owes the seller $60.33 for the unused portion of the policy.

When a buyer agrees to assume an existing loan from the seller, an interest proration is necessary. For example, a sales contract calls for the buyer to assume a 9% mortgage loan with a principal balance of $31,111 at the time of closing. Loan payments are due the 10th of each month, and the sales contract calls for a July 3 closing date, with interest on the loan to be prorated through July 2. How much is prorated and to whom? First, we must recognize that interest is normally paid in arrears. On a loan that is payable monthly, the borrower pays interest for the use of the loan at the end of each month he has had the loan. Thus, the July 10 monthly loan payment includes the interest due for the use of $31,111 from June 10 through July 9. However, the seller owned the property through July 2, and from June 10 through July 2 is 23 days. At the closing the seller must give the buyer enough money to pay for 23 days interest on the $31,111. If the annual interest rate is 9%, one month's interest is $31,111 times 9% divided by 12, which is $233.33. Divide this by 30 days to get a daily interest rate of $7.7777. Multiply the daily rate by 23 to obtain the interest for 23 days, $178.89.

In most parts of the country, it is the custom when prorating interest, property taxes, water bills, and insurance to use a 30-day month because it simplifies proration calculations. Naturally, using a 30-day month produces some inaccuracy when dealing with months that do not have 30 days. If this inaccuracy is significant to the buyer and seller, they can agree to prorate either by using the exact number of days in the closing month or by dividing the yearly rate by 365 to find a daily rate. Some states avoid this question altogether by requiring that the exact number of days be used in prorating.

It *is* customary throughout the country to prorate rents on the basis of the actual number of days in the month. Using the July 3 closing date again, if the property is currently rented for $250 per month, paid in advance on the first of each month, what would the proration be? If the seller has already collected the rent for the month of July, he is obligated to hand over to the buyer that portion of the rent earned between July 3 and July 31, inclusive, a period of 29 days. To determine how many dollars this is, divide $250 by the number of days in July. This gives $8.0645, the rent per day. Then multiply the daily rate by 29 days to get $233.87, the portion of the July rent that the seller must hand over to the buyer. If the renter has not paid the July rent by the July 3 closing date, no proration is made. If the buyer later collects the July rent, he must return 2 days rent to the seller.

Property Taxes   Prorated property taxes are common to nearly all real estate transactions. The amount of proration depends on when the property taxes are due, what portion has already been paid, and what period of time they cover. Property taxes are levied on an annual basis, but depending on the locality they may be due at the beginning, middle, or end of the tax year. In most parts of the country, property owners are permitted to pay half their property taxes during the first 6 months of the tax year and the other half during the second 6 months. Suppose that you live in a state where the property tax year runs from July 1 through the following June 30. Property tax bills are sent out in early November; the first half is due by December 10, and the second half by the following April 10. If a transaction calls for property taxes to be prorated to September 5, how is the calculation made?

The problem is complicated by the fact that the new property tax bill will not have been issued by the September 5 closing date. The solution is to use the previous year's tax bill as the best estimate available. Suppose that it was $1,080 for the year. The proration would be from July 1 through September 4, a period of 2 months and 4 days. One month's taxes would be one twelfth of $1,080, or $90. Dividing $90 by 30 gives a daily rate of $3. If you take 2 months at $90 and 4 days at $3, the total is $192. The seller pays the buyer $192.00 because he owned the property through September 4; yet the buyer will later receive a property tax bill for the period starting July 1. If there is a possibility that the November property tax bill will change substantially from the previous year, the buyer and seller can agree to make another adjustment between themselves when the new bill is available.

Let us work one more property tax proration example. Presume that the annual property taxes are $1,350, the tax year runs from July 1 through the following June 30, and the closing and proration date is December 28. First, determine how much of the annual property tax bill has been paid by the seller. If the seller has paid the taxes for July 1 through December 31, the buyer must reimburse the seller for the taxes from December 28 through December 31, a period of 4 days. The amount is calculated by taking one twelfth of $1,350 to find the monthly tax rate of $112.50, and dividing by 30 to get the daily rate of $3.75. Then multiply the daily rate by 4 days to get the amount, $15, that the buyer must give the seller.

Proration Date

Prorations need not be calculated as of the closing date. In the sales contract, the buyer and seller can mutually agree to a different proration date if they wish. If nothing is said, local law and custom will prevail. For example, in the state of New York, it is customary to prorate as of the day before closing, the theory being that the buyer is the new owner beginning on the day the transaction closes. Other states prorate as of the day of closing. If the difference of 1 day is important to the buyer or seller, they should not rely on local custom, but agree in writing on a proration day of their own choosing.

Special assessments for such things as street improvements, water mains, and sewer lines are not usually prorated. As a rule, the selling price of the property reflects the added value of the improvements, and the seller pays any assessments in full before closing. This is not an ironclad rule, however; the buyer and seller in their sales contract can agree to do whatever they want about the assessment.

RESPA

In response to consumer complaints regarding real estate closing procedures, Congress passed the Real Estate Settlement Procedures Act (RESPA) of 1974. This act became effective June 20, 1975 throughout the United States. However, RESPA generated more criticism than compliments from real estate brokers, mortgage lenders and home buyers. Consequently significant changes were made and these went into effect on June 30, 1976. The purpose of RESPA is to regulate and standardize real estate settlement practices when "federally related" first mortgage loans are made on one- to four-family residences, condominiums and cooperatives. Federally related is defined to include FHA or VA or other government-backed or assisted loans, loans from lenders with federally insured deposits, loans that are to be purchased by FNMA, GNMA, FHLMC or other federally controlled secondary mortgage market institutions, and loans made by lenders who make or invest more than $1 million per year in residential loans. As the bulk of all home loans now made fall into one of these categories, the impact of this law is far-reaching.

Restrictions   RESPA prohibits kickbacks and fees for services not performed during the closing process. For example, in some regions of the United States prior to this act, it was common practice for attorneys and closing agents to channel title business to certain title companies in return for a fee. This increased settlement costs without adding services. Now there must be a justifiable service rendered for each closing fee charge. The act prohibits the seller from requiring that the buyer purchase title insurance from a particular title company. The act also contains restrictions on the amount of advance property tax and insurance payments that a lender can collect and place in an impound or reserve account. The amount is limited to the property owner's share of taxes and insurance accrued prior to settlement, plus one-sixth of the estimated amount that will come due for these items in the twelve month period beginning at settlement. This requirement assures that the lender has an adequate but not excessive amount of money impounded when taxes and insurance payments fall due.

Requirements   To the typical homebuyer who is applying for a first mortgage loan the most obvious aspects of RESPA are that (1) he will receive from the lender a special HUD information booklet explaining RESPA, (2) he will receive a good faith estimate of closing costs from the lender, (3) the lender will use the HUD Uniform Settlement Statement, and (4) the borrower has the right to inspect the Uniform Settlement Statement one business day before the day of closing.

The primary purpose of requiring lenders to promptly give loan applicants an estimate of closing costs is to allow the loan applicant an opportunity to compare prices for the various services his transaction will require. Additionally, these estimates help the borrower calculate how much his total closing costs will be. Figure 14:1 illustrates a good faith estimate form. Note that it is primarily concerned with settlement services. RESPA does not require estimates of escrow impounds for property taxes and insurance, although the lender can voluntarily add these items to the form. Note also that RESPA allows lenders to make estimates in terms of ranges. For example, escrow fees may be stated as $110 to $140 to reflect the range of rates being charged by local escrow companies for that service.

HUD SETTLEMENT STATEMENT

The HUD Settlement Statement is used by the person conducting the settlement. It includes a summary of all charges to be paid by the borrower (buyer) and the seller in connection with the settlement. To illustrate how this statement is used, let us observe a typical closing situation. Mr. Homer Leavitt has listed his home for sale with List-Rite Realty for $41,000, and the sales commission is to be 6% of the selling price. A salesperson from Quick-Sale Realty learns about the property through the multiple listing service and produces a buyer willing to pay $41,000 with $11,000 down. The offer is conditioned on the seller paying off the existing $16,000 mortgage loan and the buyer obtaining a new loan for $30,000. Property taxes, hazard insurance, and heating oil in the home's oil tank are to be prorated as of the closing date. The buyer also asks the seller to pay for a termite inspection and repairs if necessary, a title search, an owner's title insurance policy, deed stamps, and one-half of the closing fee. The seller accepts this offer on August 15, and they agree to close on September 15.

The property-tax year for this home runs from July 1 through June 30; taxes for July 1 through December 31 are

Figure 14:1

GOOD FAITH ESTIMATES OF SETTLEMENT CHARGES

Loan amount $ _____

(This form does not cover all items that must be paid in cash at settlement, for example, deposit in escrow for real estate taxes and insurance. You should inquire as to the amounts of such other items.)

Loan Origination Fee $_____

   (included in this amount is document preparation, appraisal fee and credit report fee)

Interest $_____

   (from date of closing to first of next month)

Mortgage Insurance Premium $_____

Hazard Insurance Premium $_____

   (from date of closing to first of next month)

Settlement or Escrow Fee $_____

Notary Fees $_____

Attorney Fees $_____

Title Insurance $_____

Pest Inspection $_____

Recording Fees $_____

Survey $_____

Document Stamps $_____

TOTAL $_____

NOTE: The above good faith estimates of closing costs are made pursuant to the requirements of the Real Estate Settlement Procedures Act (RESPA). These figures are only estimates and the actual charges due at settlement may be different.

Second Federal Savings & Loan
600 S. Commerce Street
City, State 00000

due October 15 and the second half is due on April 15 for the period January 1 through June 30. Mr. Leavitt has paid the taxes for last year, but not for the current year as yet. Newly issued tax bills show that $420 will be due on October 15 for the current 6-month period. The hazard insurance policy that the buyer wishes to assume was purchased by the seller for $120 and covers the period June 15 through the following June 14. The Safety Title Insurance Company will charge the seller $190 for a combined title search, title examination, and owner's title policy package.

The buyer obtains a loan commitment from the Ajax National Bank for $30,000. To make this loan, the bank will charge a $200 loan origination fee, $75 for an appraisal, and $25 for a credit report on the buyer. The bank also requires a lender's title policy in the amount of $30,000 (cost $20), 6 months of property tax reserves, and 4 months of hazard insurance reserves. The loan is to be repaid in equal monthly installments beginning November 1. The termite inspection by Dead-Bug Pest Company costs $39, and recording fees are $3 for deeds and mortgage releases and $5 for mortgages. The bank charges the buyer and the seller $91 each to conduct the closing plus $10 to prepare a deed for the seller and $1 to notarize it. The state levies a transfer tax on deeds of 50 cents per $500 of sales price and the seller is leaving $40 worth of fuel oil for the buyer.

The buyer and seller have each hired an attorney to advise them on legal matters in connection with the sales contract and closing. They are to be paid $110 and $80, respectively, out of the settlement. List-Rite Realty and Quick-Sale Realty have advised the closing agent they are splitting the $2,460 sales commission equally.

Finally, the buyer made a $1,000 earnest money deposit with his offer that is to be credited toward the down payment. Using this information, which is summarized in Table 14:1 for your convenience, let us see exactly how a settlement statement is prepared.

Referring now to the HUD Settlement Statement shown in Figure 14:2, ① through ⑦ deal with the names of the bor-

Settlement Charges

Table 14:1   **TRANSACTION SUMMARY**

	Amount	Comments
Sales Price	$41,000	
Down Payment	$11,000	
Deposit (Earnest Money)	$1,000	Credit to buyer's down payment.
Existing Mortgage	$16,000	Seller to pay off through settlement.
New Mortgage	$30,000	Monthly payments begin Nov. 1. Interest rate is 9.6% per annum.
Loan Origination Fee	$200 ⎫	⎧ Paid by buyer in connection
Appraisal Fee	$75 ⎬	⎨ with obtaining $30,000 loan.
Credit Report	$25 ⎭	⎩
Owner's Title Policy	$190	Seller pays ⎫ ⎧ Safety Title
		⎬ ⎨ Insurance
Lender's Title Policy	$20	Buyer pays ⎭ ⎩ Company.
County Property Taxes	$840/yr	First half, due Oct. 15 for the period July 1 through Dec. 31, is not yet paid.
Hazard Insurance	$120/yr	Existing policy with 9 months to run to be transferred to buyer.
Fuel Oil	$40	Remaining oil in tank.
Pest Inspection	$39	Seller pays Dead-Bug Pest Co.
Property Tax Reserves	$420	6 months at $70 for lender.
Hazard Insurance Reserves	$40	4 months at $10 for lender.
Buyer's Attorney	$110	
Seller's Attorney	$80	
Closing Fee	$182	Charge by Ajax National Bank; buyer & seller each pay $91.
Deed Preparation	$10	Seller pays bank.
Notary	$2	⎰ $1 to seller for deed. ⎱ $1 to buyer for mortgage.
Deed Stamps	$41	Seller pays.
Record Deed	$3	Buyer pays.
Record Mortgage Release	$3	Seller pays.
Record Mortgage	$5	Buyer pays.
Brokerage Commission	$2,460	Seller pays; to be split equally between List-Rite Realty and Quick-Sale Realty.

Settlement and Proration date is September 15. All prorations are to be based on a 30-day banker's month.

rower (buyer), seller, lender and settlement agent plus the place and date of settlement.

We are now ready to observe the actual accounting of the closing. At ⑧, is a column for a financial summary of the borrower's transaction, and at ⑨, a column for a financial summary of the seller's transaction. However, the easiest place to begin is on page 2 of the form at ⑩, "Settlement Charges." The first item listed is the real estate commission. In our example, it is 6% of the $41,000 sales price and it is charged to the seller at ⑪. Thus, the closing agent will take $2,460 from the money the seller receives and pay the real estate commission. Number ⑫ shows to whom the commission checks are to be made payable. (The division of commission money is established by an agreement between the brokers who produced the sale.)

The section at ⑬ pertains to loan charges. Here the lender's $200 loan origination fee, the $75 appraisal fee, and the $25 credit report fee are charged to the borrower.

Loan Fees

The section at ⑭ deals with items the lender requires to be paid in advance. Our closing date is September 15 and the lender requires that interest from the closing date to the first of the following month be paid at closing. At 9.6% annual interest, this comes to $120. (The first monthly payment on this loan will be due on November 1 and will include interest for the month of October.) If the lender requires mortgage insurance for which a fee or premium is due upon closing, the amount is shown in this section. It will be taken from the borrower's funds and remitted to the insurer. If the buyer is not assuming an existing hazard insurance policy, the lender will require that a new policy be purchased. The borrower can either purchase the policy separately from the closing or through the closing. Any time an item is paid separately from the closing, it is entered on the HUD statement with a notation p.o.c. (paid outside of closing), but it is not added to the total charges.

Reserves

The section at ⑮ deals with reserves required by the lender. As discussed in Chapter 9, mortgage lenders prefer to

Figure 14:2

A.		B. TYPE OF LOAN		
U.S. DEPARTMENT OF HOUSING AND URBAN DEVELOPMENT		1. ☐ FHA 2. ☐ FmHA 3. ☐ CONV. UNINS.		
		4. ☐ VA 5. ☐ CONV. INS.		
SETTLEMENT STATEMENT		6. FILE NUMBER:	7. LOAN NUMBER:	
		8. MORTGAGE INSURANCE CASE NUMBER:		

C. *NOTE: This form is furnished to give you a statement of actual settlement costs. Amounts paid to and by the settlement agent are shown. Items marked "(p.o.c.)" were paid outside the closing; they are shown here for informational purposes and are not included in the totals.*

D. NAME OF BORROWER: ①	E. NAME OF SELLER: ②	F. NAME OF LENDER: ③
Neidi d'Moni 2724 East 22nd Street City, State 00000	Homer Leavitt 1654 West 12th Street City, State 00000	Ajax National Bank 1111 West 1st Street City, State 00000

G. PROPERTY LOCATION: ④	H. SETTLEMENT AGENT: ⑤	I. SETTLEMENT DATE:
1654 West 12th Street City, State 00000	Ajax National Bank	Sept. 15, 19xx at 8:00 am ⑦
	PLACE OF SETTLEMENT: Ajax National Bank ⑥	

J. SUMMARY OF BORROWER'S TRANSACTION		K. SUMMARY OF SELLER'S TRANSACTION	
100. GROSS AMOUNT DUE FROM BORROWER: ⑧		*400. GROSS AMOUNT DUE TO SELLER:* ⑨	
101. Contract sales price	$41,000	401. Contract sales price	$41,000
102. Personal property		402. Personal property	
103. Settlement charges to borrower *(line 1400)* ㉑	1,110	403.	
104.		404.	
105.		405.	
Adjustments for items paid by seller in advance ㉒		*Adjustments for items paid by seller in advance* ㉘	
106. City/town taxes to		406. City/town taxes to	
107. County taxes to		407. County taxes to	
108. Assessments to		408. Assessments to	
109. Hazard insurance 9/15 to 6/15	90	409. Hazard insurance 9/15 to 6/15	90
110. Fuel oil	40	410. Fuel oil	40
111.		411.	
112.		412.	
120. GROSS AMOUNT DUE FROM BORROWER ㉓	$42,240	420. GROSS AMOUNT DUE TO SELLER ㉙	$41,130
㉔ *200. AMOUNTS PAID BY OR IN BEHALF OF BORROWER:*		*500. REDUCTIONS IN AMOUNT DUE TO SELLER:*	
201. Deposit or earnest money	1,000	501. Excess deposit *(see instructions)*	
202. Principal amount of new loan(s)	30,000	502. Settlement charges to seller *(line 1400)* ㉚	2,915
203. Existing loan(s) taken subject to		503. Existing loan(s) taken subject to	
204.		504. Payoff of first mortgage loan ㉛	16,000
205.		505. Payoff of second mortgage loan	
206.		506.	
207.		507.	
208.		508.	
209.		509.	
Adjustments for items unpaid by seller ㉕		*Adjustments for items unpaid by seller* ㉜	
210. City/town taxes to		510. City/town taxes to	
211. County taxes 7/1 to 9/15	175	511. County taxes 7/1 to 9/15	175
212. Assessments to		512. Assessments to	
213.		513.	
214.		514.	
215.		515.	
216.		516.	
217.		517.	
218.		518.	
219.		519.	
220. TOTAL PAID BY/FOR BORROWER ㉖	$31,175	520. TOTAL REDUCTION AMOUNT DUE SELLER ㉝	$19,090
300. CASH AT SETTLEMENT FROM/TO BORROWER		*600. CASH AT SETTLEMENT TO/FROM SELLER*	
301. Gross amount due from borrower *(line 120)*	$42,240	601. Gross amount due to seller *(line 420)*	$41,130
302. Less amounts paid by/for borrower *(line 220)*	($31,175)	602. Less reductions in amount due seller *(line 520)*	($19,090)
303. CASH (☒ FROM) (☐ TO) BORROWER ㉗	$11,065	603. CASH (☒ TO) (☐ FROM) SELLER ㉞	$22,040

L. SETTLEMENT CHARGES ⑩

700. TOTAL SALES/BROKER'S COMMISSION based on price $41,000 @ 6 % = $2,460	PAID FROM BORROWER'S FUNDS AT SETTLEMENT	PAID FROM SELLER'S FUNDS AT SETTLEMENT
Division of Commission (line 700) as follows: ⑫		
701. $ 1,230 to List-Rite Realty		
702. $ 1,230 to Quick-Sale Realty		
703. Commission paid at Settlement		
704.		⑪ $2,460

800. ITEMS PAYABLE IN CONNECTION WITH LOAN ⑬		
801. Loan Origination Fee %	$ 200	
802. Loan Discount %		
803. Appraisal Fee to	75	
804. Credit Report to	25	
805. Lender's Inspection Fee		
806. Mortgage Insurance Application Fee to		
807. Assumption Fee		
808.		
809.		
810.		
811.		

900. ITEMS REQUIRED BY LENDER TO BE PAID IN ADVANCE ⑭		
901. Interest from Sept. 15 to Oct. 1 @ $ 8.00 /day	120	
902. Mortgage Insurance Premium for months to		
903. Hazard Insurance Premium for years to		
904. years to		
905.		

1000. RESERVES DEPOSITED WITH LENDER ⑮		
1001. Hazard insurance 4 months @ $ 10 per month	40	
1002. Mortgage insurance months @ $ per month		
1003. City property taxes months @ $ per month		
1004. County property taxes 6 months @ $ 70 per month	420	
1005. Annual assessments months @ $ per month		
1006. months @ $ per month		
1007. months @ $ per month		
1008. months @ $ per month		

1100. TITLE CHARGES ⑯		
1101. Settlement or closing fee to Ajax National Bank	91	91
1102. Abstract or title search to		
1103. Title examination to		
1104. Title insurance binder to		
1105. Document preparation to Ajax National Bank		10
1106. Notary fees to Ajax National Bank	1	1
1107. Attorney's fees to		
(includes above items numbers;		
1108. Title insurance to Safety Title Insurance Company	20	190
(includes above items numbers; 1102 and 1103		
1109. Lender's coverage $ 30,000		
1110. Owner's coverage $ 41,000		
1111. Buyer's attorney	110	
1112. Seller's attorney		80
1113.		

1200. GOVERNMENT RECORDING AND TRANSFER CHARGES ⑰		
1201. Recording fees: Deed $ 3 ; Mortgage $ 5 ; Releases $ 3	8	3
1202. City/county tax/stamps: Deed $; Mortgage $		
1203. State tax/stamps: Deed $ 41 ; Mortgage $		41
1204.		
1205.		

1300. ADDITIONAL SETTLEMENT CHARGES ⑱		
1301. Survey to		
1302. Pest inspection to Dead-Bug Pest Company		39
1303.		
1304.		
1305.		

| 1400. TOTAL SETTLEMENT CHARGES (enter on lines 103, Section J and 502, Section K) | ⑲ $1,110 | ⑳ $2,915 |

HUD-1 Rev. 5/76

pay such items as property taxes, hazard insurance, and property assessment payments on behalf of the borrower. To do this, the lender collects, along with each monthly principal and interest payment, one twelfth of the amount needed each year. In our example, hazard insurance costs $120 per year, and on June 15 of the following year the lender must have that amount available in the borrower's reserve account. However, collecting one twelfth of $120 each month until June 15 will leave the lender $40 short. Therefore, the lender asks that $40 from the borrower's closing funds be placed into a reserve at the closing date. The same concept also applies to the payment of property taxes. In our example, property taxes are currently $840 per year. On a monthly basis, $70 must be added to each monthly loan payment. However, the lender will not have collected any loan payments by the time the first-half taxes fall due on October 15. Consequently, the lender requires that the borrower place $420 into a tax reserve account at settlement. Once past October 15, $70 per month will accumulate enough to pay the second-half taxes of $420 on April 15.

Insufficient
Reserves

What happens if the amount in the reserve account is not sufficient to pay an item when it comes due? For example, suppose that on next June 15 the lender has accumulated $120 for insurance renewal, but the new policy will cost $132 owing to inflation. The lender must temporarily use its own funds to make up the difference. The lender then bills the borrower for $12 or adds $1 per month to the regular monthly payment for the next 12 months. The lender also adds an extra $1 per month so that next time the policy is renewed $132 will be available. Another solution is for the lender to require the borrower to maintain extra funds in the reserve account to meet insurance and property tax increases. If there is a drop in the amounts the lender must pay out then the monthly reserve requirement can be reduced.

Considerable criticism and debate have raged over the topic of reserves. Traditionally, lenders have not paid interest to borrowers on money held as reserves, effectively creating an interest free loan to the lender. This has tempted many lenders to require overly adequate reserves. HUD's RESPA sets a reasonable limit on reserve requirements and some states now require that interest be paid on reserves. Although not required to do so, some lenders now voluntarily pay interest on reserves.

Turning to section ⑯, various title charges payable by the buyer and seller are set forth. While several of the categories in this section appear redundant, the reason is that title services and charges are handled differently in different parts of the United States. In some regions, it is customary for the attorney of the seller or buyer to prepare and conduct the settlement in addition to giving counsel in the preparation of the sales contract. In that case, a separate settlement fee may not be shown, all attorney's services being lumped under "attorney's fees." In other regions, the real estate broker customarily prepares and conducts the settlement as part of services rendered the seller in return for a sales commission. In our example, the lender provides the settlement services, a very common arrangement when a new loan is involved. In other instances, closing services may be provided by a title company, an independent closing agent, or an escrow agent.

Title Charges

Section ⑯ also allows for variations in affirming the seller's title. In some localities, there will be one bill from an independent abstracter for the title search, another from an attorney for examination and certification, and a third from a title insurance company for a title policy. In other regions, a single title company will provide the search, examination, and insurance policy for a single combined charge. Also included in this section are the settlement fee, deed preparation fee, notary fees, and the charges of the buyer's and seller's attorneys. Unless marked p.o.c., these are paid by the closing agent out of the settlement funds.

At ⑰, recording and transfer charges are itemized. In our example, the buyer pays $3 to have his deed recorded and $5 to record the new mortgage. The seller pays $3 to have the release of the existing mortgage recorded and $41 in documentary tax stamps for the deed.

Recording and Transfer Charges

Other Charges   The section at ⑱ deals with settlement costs not included elsewhere. The $39 pest inspection the seller agreed to is entered here. If the inspection discloses damage and the seller orders the work to be done and the cost to be paid out of the settlement funds, it is itemized in this section and the amount entered in the seller's column.

Then, at ⑲ and ⑳, being careful not to include any charges paid outside of closing, the settlement charges are totaled. These totals are carried to page 1 of the form, where the buyer's total is entered at ㉑ and the seller's at ㉚. We are now ready for the concluding steps.

Borrower's Summary   Beginning with the borrower's side at ⑧, the first entry is the $41,000 sales price. If personal property is being sold to the buyer and itemized separately from the real property purchase price, it would be shown on the next line. Section ㉒ covers items already paid for by the seller that will benefit the buyer. In our example, there is no entry for property taxes as the seller has not prepaid them. The seller has, however, prepaid a 1-year hazard insurance policy at a cost of $120 per year, which the buyer wishes to assume. As there are 9 months of coverage remaining, September 15 to June 15, the buyer must pay the seller nine-twelfths of $120, or $90. (If the buyer does not want the seller's policy, he need not accept it. In that case, the seller would cancel his policy and receive a refund for the unused 9 months from the insurance company.) The next entry accounts for $40 worth of heating oil the seller is leaving for the buyer. Then, at ㉓, the gross amount due from the seller is added and entered.

In section ㉔, the buyer is credited with the $1,000 deposit that accompanied his original offer and the new $30,000 loan he has obtained. At ㉕, the buyer is credited with items unpaid by the seller that the buyer will later have to pay. In our example, $420 in property taxes are due on October 15 for the period July 1 through December 31. As the buyer will be the owner on October 15, he will be responsible for paying them. However, the seller has owned the property from July to September 15, a period of 2½ months. At the rate of $70 per month, this means the seller must give the buyer $175 at the closing. Other items left unpaid by the seller can also be entered in this section. The buyer's credits are then totaled and entered at ㉖.

To find the amount of money the buyer must have to close, the $31,175 credit shown at ㉖ is subtracted from the $42,240 amount due at ㉓. The result, $11,065 at ㉗, is the total amount of cash required from the buyer at the closing. (A negative result at ㉗ would indicate that the amount was payable rather than due.)

Seller's Summary

To calculate how much cash the seller will receive from the settlement, we return to the seller's summary at ⑨. Under the heading "Gross Amount Due to Seller," we begin with the $41,000 sales price. The agreed price for any personal property is entered on the next line. At ㉘, the seller receives prorated adjustments for the hazard insurance policy and fuel oil he is passing on to the buyer. These correspond to the entries previously discussed on the buyer's side at ㉒. Finally, the gross amount due the seller is totaled at ㉙.

Against the gross amount due the seller are several reductions. In our example, there are settlement charges of $2,915 at ㉚, an existing $16,000 loan that is being paid off as part of the settlement at ㉛, and $175 of unpaid property taxes at ㉜. The total of these is entered at ㉝. The concluding step is to subtract the reductions from the gross amount due the seller. The result at number ㉞ is the $22,040 in cash due the seller from the settlement. For privacy, the borrower's information and the seller's information may be provided on separate pages.

HUD Information on RESPA Act

More information on the Real Estate Settlement Procedures Act can be obtained in a free HUD booklet available from lenders and titled "Settlement Costs and You," June 1976 revision.

ALTERNATIVE CLOSING FORMS

In transactions not covered by RESPA, any suitable closing format may be used, including the HUD Settlement Statement. Even in transactions covered by RESPA, the closing agent may use his own closing format in addition to the HUD

Settlement Statement. A sample of an alternative closing format is presented in Figures 14:3 & 14:4. The format is based on the same information that was used to prepare the HUD settlement form.

Purchaser's Closing Statement   In the purchaser's closing statement, note that in the debit column each item that the purchaser is expected to pay is entered. This includes the purchase price, loan fees, purchaser's settlement fees, etc. Against this, the purchaser is credited with his $1,000 deposit, the $30,000 he obtained from the new loan, a $175 tax proration, and $11,065 in additional cash paid at closing. At the bottom of the statement, the total of the debit column must equal the total of the credit column.

Figure 14:3

PURCHASER'S CLOSING STATEMENT

	Debits	Credits
Purchase price	$41,000	$
Earnest money deposit		1,000
New mortgage loan		30,000
Appraisal fee for mortgage loan	75	
Credit report fee	25	
Loan origination fee	200	
Interest from Sept. 15 to Oct. 1	120	
Property tax reserves for new loan	420	
Hazard insurance reserves for new loan	40	
Title policy (lender's coverage portion)	20	
Half of escrow fee	91	
Buyer's attorney fee	110	
Notarize mortgage	1	
Record mortgage	5	
Record deed	3	
Hazard insurance proration	90	
Fuel oil left in tank	40	
Property tax proration		175
	42,240	31,175
Money due from purchaser at closing		11,065
	$42,240	$42,240

In the seller's closing statement, the seller is credited *Seller's Closing*
$41,000 for the purchase price, $90 for remaining insurance *Statement*
transferred to the buyer and $40 for the fuel oil left in the
tank. Against this the seller is charged $16,000 to pay off the
existing loan, $2,460 in brokerage fees, a $175 property tax
proration, etc., for a total of $19,090. This leaves the seller
$22,040 in cash.

SELLER'S CLOSING STATEMENT

Figure 14:4

	Debits	Credits
Sales price		$41,000
Mortgage loan payoff	$16,000	
Record mortgage release	3	
Deed preparation	10	
Notarize deed	1	
Deed stamps	41	
Title policy (owner's coverage portion)	190	
Half of escrow fee	91	
Seller's attorney fee	80	
Pest inspection	39	
Sales commission	2,460	
Property tax proration	175	
Hazard insurance proration		90
Fuel oil left in tank		40
	19,090	41,130
Money due seller at closing	22,040	
	$41,130	$41,130

VOCABULARY REVIEW   *Match terms a–g with statements 1–7.*

a. *Closing statement*   e. *Prorate*
b. *Deed delivery*   f. *Seller's affidavit of title*
c. *Documentary transfer tax* g. *RESPA*
d. *Escrow*

1. An accounting of funds to the buyer and seller at the completion of a real estate transaction.
2. Deposit of documents and funds with a neutral third party plus instructions as to how to conduct the closing.
3. A source of state and local revenue derived from taxing conveyance documents.
4. A document provided by the seller at a settlement meeting stating that he has done nothing to encumber title since the title search was made.
5. The moment at which title passes from the seller to the buyer.
6. To divide the ongoing income and expenses of a property between the buyer and seller.
7. A federal law that deals with procedures to be followed in a real estate closing.

QUESTIONS AND
PROBLEMS

1. What are the duties of an escrow agent?
2. As a means of closing a real estate transaction, how does an escrow differ from a settlement meeting?
3. Is an escrow agent the agent of the buyer or the seller? Explain.
4. The buyer agrees to accept the seller's fire insurance policy as part of the purchase agreement. The policy cost $180, covers the period January 16 through the following January 15, and the settlement date is March 12. How much does the buyer owe the seller (closest whole dollar)?
5. A buyer agrees to assume an existing 8% mortgage on which $45,000 is still owed; the last monthly payment was made on March 1 and the next payment is due April 1. Settlement date is March 12. Local custom is to use a 30-day month and charge the buyer interest beginning with the settlement day. Calculate the interest proration. To whom is it credited? To whom is it charged?

6. In real estate closing, does the buyer or seller normally pay for the following items: deed stamps, deed preparation, lender's title policy, loan appraisal fee, mortgage recording, and mortgage release?

ADDITIONAL READINGS

A General Discussion of Escrows. Los Angeles, Calif.: Title Insurance and Trust Company, 1972, 32 pages. Explains the duties and obligations of an escrow officer in a real estate transaction. Available free from the publisher. (Most title companies in the United States have similar booklets available at no charge.)

American Law Institute. *The Practical Lawyer's Real Property Law Manual, No. 1.* Philadelphia: American Bar Association, 1974, 189 pages. Written in straightforward language for non-lawyers as well as lawyers. Coverage includes prorations, real estate settlements, and the role of the attorney in the closing process. Contains sample forms.

Halper, Emmanuel B. "People and Property: Looking out for the Homebuyer," *Real Estate Review,* Summer 1973, pages 9–13. Written in the form of a short story about a couple purchasing a home in New York State, this article follows the settlement procedure from binder, to formal contract signing, to settlement day.

Taylor, Donald G. *Primary Escrow Text and Advanced Handbook for Escrow Personnel.* n.p. Donald G. Taylor, 1976, 178 pages. Basically two books under one cover. Part I gives general information on preparing, administering, and closing an escrow. Part II goes into more detail and is helpful for those who handle escrows as a business.

U.S. Department of Housing and Urban Development. *Settlement Costs and You.* Washington, D.C.: U.S. Government Printing Office, 1976, 31 pages. Explains homebuyer rights under the 1976 RESPA revision. Demonstrates sample closings using the HUD Settlement forms. Available free.

Ventola, William L., Marks, Lynette K., and **Allaway, Wellington J.** *Mastering Real Estate Mathematics.* Chicago: Real Estate Education Co., 1974, 230 pages. A self-instruction text covering the mathematics of real estate. Chapters 14 and 15 deal with prorations and closing statements.

15

Real Estate Economics

Acceleration principle: that an event has a greater impact on demand or prices than can be traced to that event alone

Buyer's market: one with few buyers and many sellers

Cost-push inflation: higher prices due to increased costs of labor and supplies

Demand-pull inflation: higher prices due to buyers bidding against each other

Economic base: the ability of a region to export goods and services to other regions and receive money in return

Filtering: the process by which higher-priced properties become available to lower income buyers on the used market

Real-cost inflation: higher prices due to greater effort needed to produce the same product today versus several years ago

Service industry: an industry that produces goods and services to sell to local residents

Short cycles: economic cycles averaging about four years in length

Thin market: one with few buyers and few sellers

Economic concepts and ideas are interwoven throughout this book, but the objective of this chapter is to discuss several vital aspects of real estate economics not covered elsewhere.

ECONOMIC BASE

Just as one nation must equalize its imports and exports with the rest of the world to maintain a stable balance of trade, regions and cities must export goods and services so that their residents may purchase goods and services not produced locally. To illustrate, Hollywood produces motion pictures for theaters and television stations across the country. The income earned from these films permits residents in Hollywood to send money to Detroit to purchase automobiles. The money Detroit receives is used to buy farm products and other needed goods and services produced outside Detroit. A farming region produces farm products that are sold outside the region to generate income with which to buy farm machinery, gasoline, fertilizer, clothing, vacations, and so forth.

The ability of a city or region to produce a commodity or service that has exchange value outside its area is its **economic base.** Industries that produce goods and services for export are called **base, export,** or **primary industries.** Thus, film making is a base industry for Hollywood, automobile manufacturing is a base industry for Detroit, and agriculture is a base industry in the Midwest. Producers of goods and services that are not exported are **service, filler** or **secondary industries.** This category includes local school systems, supermarkets, doctors, dentists, drugstores, and real estate agents.

Effect on Real Estate   Because realty is immovable, the existence of base industries is absolutely essential to maintaining local real estate values. Unless a region or city exports, it will die economically, and the value of local real estate will fall. An extreme example of this can be found in the abandoned mining towns of yesteryear. Before the discovery of mineral riches, land was often worth but a few dollars an acre for grazing purposes. With the discovery of minerals and subsequent mine development, land that was suitable for townsites zoomed in value. A new and far richer economic base industry than grazing was bringing wealth and people into the area, and land that had been used for strictly agricultural purposes was now in demand for homesites, stores, and offices. Years later, when the mines played out and mineral wealth could no longer be exported from the area, outside money ceased to flow into the town. As a result, miners were laid off and left for other towns where jobs could be found. Without the miners' money, service industries folded and their employees left. The demand for real estate dropped and, in turn, real estate prices fell, often all the way back to their value for grazing purposes.

The extent to which regions and cities are vulnerable to changes in economic base depends on how many different kinds of base industries are present and their ability to consistently export their products. Thus, a city that relies extensively on one base industry for support is much more economically vulnerable than one with a diversified group of base industries. For example, a city or town that has grown up around a military base will suffer extensively if that base is cut back in size or closed down. In Seattle, real estate prices were adversely affected in the early 1970s by slowdowns of production lines at Boeing Aircraft due to a lack of airplane orders. Agriculturally oriented communities often experience ups and downs in farmland prices that correspond with the rise and fall of farm product prices.

Through the application of employment ratios, economic *Employment Ratios* base study can also tell us what effect a change in base industry employment will have on the local population and economy. Generally, for each additional person employed in a base industry, two persons will be employed in service and intermediate industries. Thus, if an electronics firm moves into a community and creates 100 new base industry jobs, opportunities will be created for another 200 persons in jobs such as retail store clerks, restaurant services, gas station operators, gardeners, bankers, doctors, dentists, lawyers, police and firemen, school teaching, and local government, to name a few.

With economic base data, one can also calculate the total impact on local population and the need for land and housing. For example, the 100 base industry jobs created by the electronics firm result in 200 service jobs, for a total of 300 new job opportunities in the community. If every three jobs require two households (more than one person working in some families) and each household averages 2.9 persons, then 300 jobs will provide income from 200 households containing a total of 580 persons. The ultimate effect of the 300 new jobs on local employment and housing demand will depend on what portion of the jobs can be filled from within the community and the extent of vacant housing. If the community is already operating at full employment and has no vacant housing to speak of, the addition of 100 base jobs will result in a demand for land, building materials, and labor necessary to provide 200 new housing units. From the standpoint of local government, 580 more people must be supplied with schools, parks, water, sewage treatment, street maintenance, police and fire protection, and so forth.

HOUSING DEMAND
OVER THE SHORT RUN

Because it takes time to develop raw land into homes, offices, and stores, the supply of developed real estate is not immediately responsive to sudden changes in demand. Furthermore, because of the high entry and holding costs of developed real estate and the possibility of making improvements to land where they may not be needed, considerable risk is involved in developing land in advance of a known demand. As a result, price changes for developed real property can be rapid and dramatic over short periods of time. Let us explore this economic phenomenon more closely with the use of an example.

Increase in Demand

Suppose that in a given community there are presently 5,000 single-family houses, and their average value is $41,000. A new industry moves into the community and increases the demand for houses by 100. Local builders, recognizing the new demand, set to work adding 100 houses to the available housing stock. However, it will take time to acquire land, file subdivision maps, acquire building permits, grade the land, and construct the houses. The entire process typically takes 10 to 18 months. Meanwhile, despite increased demand, the available supply of houses remains fixed. The result will be an increase in house prices as the newly arriving employees bid against each other for a place to live in the existing housing stock. The result is diagrammed in Figure 15:1. Demand Curve 1 represents the demand for houses at various prices before the new industry's employees arrive. More units would be purchased at lower prices and fewer at higher prices. Prior to the arrival of the new industry, supply and demand are in balance at $41,000 per house, as shown at A.

Now the new industry moves in. Adding new employees to the housing market produces **Demand Curve 2**. Prices rise owing to competition for the existing houses. This increase literally rations the existing stock of 5,000 houses among 5,100 households. Prices rise until enough existing owners decide to sell and enough new buyers are priced out of the market. Once again, supply and demand are in balance with 5,000 houses occupied by 5,000 families. This is point B at $43,000.

SHORT-RUN SUPPLY—DEMAND PICTURE

Figure 15:1

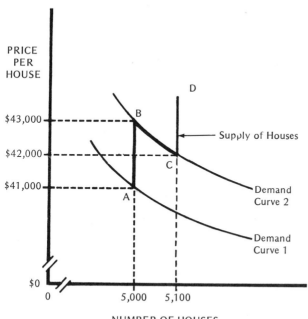

NUMBER OF HOUSES

At last, the 100 new houses that were started in response   *Increase in Supply*
to the new demand are completed and are on the market.
At what price must these be offered in order to sell them
all? It would appear that $43,000 is the answer, as that is what
houses are now selling for. However, the supply–demand relationship in Figure 15:1 shows that only 5,000 houses are
in demand at $43,000, not 5,100 houses. To find out at what
price the additional 100 houses will be absorbed by the market,
we must travel along Demand Curve 2 to 5,100 houses. At
point C, the market will absorb 5,100 houses if they are priced
at $42,000 each. Thus, a temporary glut of homes causes
prices to be reduced slightly. This price softening applies not
only to the builders of the 100 new houses, but also to the
owners of the other 5,000 homes if they wish to sell during
this temporary oversupply situation.

Aware of the oversupply of houses on the market, builders will react by halting building activity until those units are
sold and demand starts pushing prices upward again to D, at

which time the process repeats itself. Over a period of years, the supply pattern for houses takes on a stair-step or rachet-like appearance as temporary shortages and temporary excesses alternate.

Decrease in Demand

Just as a short-run increase in demand can cause a quick run-up in prices, a short-run decrease in demand can have the opposite effect, because supply cannot be decreased as fast as demand falls. This situation is diagrammed in Figure 15:2, with supply and demand in balance at 5,100 houses at $42,000 each. Suppose that there was an overnight cutback of jobs and, as a result, 100 house owners decided to sell and move out of the community. This would cause demand to shift downward from Demand Curve 2 to Demand Curve 1. To sell all 100 houses, it will be necessary for prices to fall from $42,000 at point C to $40,000 at point E. Presuming no increase in the economic base of the community, only a reduction in the supply of existing houses through demolition, disasters, and conversions to other uses will push prices back up along

Figure 15:2   **SHORT-RUN DROP IN DEMAND**

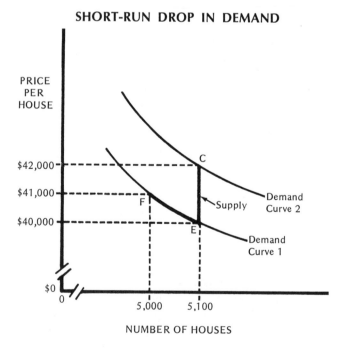

NUMBER OF HOUSES

Demand Curve 1. If supply falls to 5,000 houses, prices will go to $41,000 at point F.

The presence of inflation will cushion the drop in dollar values when demand shifts to Demand Curve 1 in Figure 15:2. Similarly, the drop in prices from B to C in Figure 15:1 will be milder in the presence of moderate inflation. In the presence of high inflation prices may not drop, but actually rise. However, if you strip away the masking effect of inflation, Figures 15:1 and 15:2 accurately portray what actually happens when demand suddenly changes and supply cannot react fast enough. Although we have been talking in terms of houses, the same concept applies to vacant lots, apartment buildings, townhouses, condominiums, office buildings, factories, hotels and motels, store space, and so forth.

Effect of Inflation

Whenever the supply and demand relationship in a market is unbalanced because of an excess supply, a **buyer's market** exists. This means a buyer can negotiate prices and terms more to his liking and a seller, if he wants to sell, must accept them. When the imbalance occurs because demand exceeds supply, it is a **seller's market,** and sellers are able to negotiate prices and terms more to their liking as buyers compete for the available merchandise. Buyer's and seller's markets are usually short term phenomena as buyer's markets tend to attract more buyers and discourage sellers from selling, whereas seller's markets tend to attract more sellers and discourage buyers.

BUYER'S AND SELLER'S MARKETS

A **broad market** means that many buyers and sellers are in the market at the same time. This makes it relatively easy to establish the price of a commodity, and for a seller to find a buyer quickly, and vice versa. In broad markets a sudden, but temporary, surge in sellers or buyers can be accommodated without extreme changes in prices. For instance, if 25 buyers and sellers are active in a residential neighborhood containing 500 homes, it would be a broad market. If, however, only one or two buyers and sellers are active, it would be considered a thin market. **Thin markets** are characterized by relatively

THIN AND BROAD MARKETS

slow turnover, difficulty in obtaining comparable sales so that prices can be established, and a high vulnerability to erratic price changes. The vulnerability is due to the fact that the existing supply and demand balance can easily be upset with the addition of just a few more buyers or sellers.

LONG-RUN DEMAND
FOR HOUSING

Future demand for housing in the United States can be seen by looking at the population in terms of age distribution, and the ability of people to obtain income at various age levels. As shown in Figure 15:3, during the first 10 years of life a person earns no income and is dependent on others, usually parents, for sustenance. During junior high school, high school, and college (if any) a person has part-time jobs but usually is still dependent on others for financial support.

Figure 15:3

LIFETIME INCOME CURVE
Based on Median Dollar Income of all Persons
in the United States

AGE IN YEARS

Upon leaving school and entering the labor market on a full-time basis, a person's income rises quickly, reflecting increased productive capacity in society. As skills increase, income continues to rise rapidly. In another decade the rise stops increasing as rapidly, although it still advances. Then, somewhere between the ages of 40 and 60, depending on a person's skills and the usefulness of those skills in society, health and/or the desire to slow down, the peak earning year occurs.

For those with 4 years of college or the equivalent, this occurs around age 55. For the nation as a whole, it occurs in the mid-forties. The peak earning year is followed at first by mild decreases in income, and then by more rapid decreases as retirement occurs.

With this earning pattern in mind, it can be seen how the progression of housing demand must follow. When a person is young and setting up a household for the first time, income is low and so are accumulated assets. Thus, housing that requires no equity investment at a minimum cost is needed, that is, an inexpensive rental with no frills. During the next decade income increases, enabling the household to increase the quality of its rental unit. Also, savings accumulate, which, coupled with the ability to make mortgage payments, enable the household to meet the down payment and mortgage requirements for a modest housing purchase. As the family grows and income increases, the household can move to larger, more expensive quarters. Typically, this occurs between the ages of 35 and 45. Another upward move in house size and price usually occurs between 45 and 55 when the family reaches its maximum income.

Buying Pattern

As the children move out and income peaks and begins to recede, the household begins to consider a smaller and less expensive dwelling unit. The need for less expensive housing becomes even more compelling upon retirement and a further reduction in income. Retirement income typically is not sufficient to carry mortgage payments on the large home bought during the peak earning years. However, the household has an equity that it can now consolidate into a smaller residence, which is fully or nearly fully paid for.

With this information in mind, let us now turn our attention to Figure 15:4 in which the population of the United States is graphed according to its age distribution. The line labeled 1970 is based on the 1970 U.S. census count; the 1980 and 1990 lines are government-prepared population projections. These are based on the fact that persons on the 1970 line will be 10 and 20 years older, respectively, minus losses due to deaths.

Age Distribution

Figure 15:4

AGE DISTRIBUTION OF THE U.S. POPULATION FOR THE YEARS 1970, 1980 & 1990

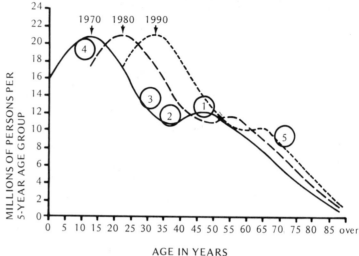

AGE IN YEARS

There are two peaks in the 1970 age distribution line. The smaller of the two, identified as ①, represents persons aged 40 to 50 years in 1970. These persons were born during the decade of the 1920s, a period of economic prosperity in most parts of the United States. Moving to the left, the dip at ② represents children born during the economic depression that spanned the 1930s. By 1970, they were 30 to 40 years old. Moving again to the left, a substantial upward rise is encountered at ③. This is the famed World War II and postwar "baby boom." It started in 1940 and lasted until 1960. In 1960, the number of births per year began to decline and continued to decline in each subsequent year through 1970. This is shown at ④.

Housing Demand

As the two waves in the 1970 line grow older and move to the right across the graph, the impact on housing demand in the United States will be substantial. A wave of demand is being created for more expensive housing accommodations as those who were born between 1920 and 1930 reach their peak income years. In contrast, those born during the 1930s will have many opportunities to move into housing vacated by the

1920 to 1930 group. However, substantial amounts of additional housing will have to be built in order to accommodate the children who were born from 1940 to 1960 as they leave home and establish residences of their own. How does the 1940–1960 "wave" translate into demand? Since the early 1960s, the United States has been experiencing a growing demand for inexpensive rentals by persons under 25 years of age. By 1985, that demand will peak as all children born from 1940 to 1960 will be 25 years or older. Between 1965 and 1975, the number of persons in the United States aged 25 through 34 increased by 9 million and resulted in the formation of 5 million households. Each household required a housing unit suitable to its income characteristics. Between 1975 and 1985, this age group will grow by another 9 million persons and create an additional 5 million households, each of which will require a place to live.

As the population wave caused by the 1940–1960 baby boom continues to move to the right in Figure 15:4, the United States will continue to experience increasing demand by this group for better and more expensive housing. Also, owner–occupants will predominate. Government statistics show that 60% of the households aged 35 through 44 are homeowners, and among those 45 through 54 years old, 75% are owners. (The percentages are even higher if there are children present.) This upgrading process will continue until the year 2015, at which time persons born in 1960 will reach the age of 55. Because personal income patterns decline after that age, a retrenchment into more modest housing will then be observed.

More Homeowners

Although the dominant factor in housing demand in the next several decades will be the maturing members of the 1940–1960 baby boom, we must not overlook the present steady growth in households over the age of 65 years and the dramatic drop in children born since 1960. Households aged 65 and above are growing in numbers and, as may be seen at ⑤, will continue to do so until 1995. At that time there will be a 10-year pause in growth due to persons born during the 1930 decade reaching the age of 65. Following that, this age group will again grow in numbers as those born between 1940 and 1960 reach this age level. As less than 20% of the population over the age of 65 remains in the labor force, the housing demand created by these age groups will primarily be the result of investments, pensions, social security income, public welfare, and assets accumulated earlier in life, including the family home.

When the children born after 1960 reach the age at which they want to have a residence of their own (usually 18 to 25 years of age), they will find large amounts of housing available as the persons born between 1940 and 1960 climb the lifetime income curve and upgrade their housing. Unless some of the housing being abandoned by the 1940–1960 group can be used to accommodate households over the age of 65, this situation will probably cause a slowdown in new housing construction. The United States has already seen a virtual halt in new elementary school construction because of the drop in births after 1960. And this came after a 15-year-long frantic effort to build enough schoolrooms.

It appeared in 1975 that the drop in births that began in 1960 was about to reverse itself as those born between 1940 and 1960 began to have children of their own. If this holds true, we may expect the formation of a third wave in the age distribution of the U.S. population, and, with it, a new surge in housing demand when those children form households.

CITY LAND USE AND
GROWTH PATTERNS

The sites upon which most cities of the world are located today were originally selected on the basis of trade and transportation. On the seacoasts, nearly every major city in the world is located at the site of a natural or man-made harbor. Inland, wagon trails, rivers, road intersections, railway stations, and airports have provided convenient points where persons with excess goods can meet to trade. However, once people begin to congregate in a certain area and a town starts to develop, what process determines how the surrounding land will be used? Is it strictly a haphazard development of homes, offices, shopping facilities, and industrial developments, or are there invisible economic forces at work, which, if identified, would help a city plan for growth and tell real estate investors in advance where demand for land will increase?

One early attempt to explain why land around a city was being put to various uses was made by a German landowner and economist, Johann von Thunen. In *The Isolated State*, published in 1826, he based his explanation of land uses on a hypothetical medieval European city located in the midst of a productive plain and isolated from other cities. He assumed that all goods were transported by ox cart, horseback, or man, and that there was no road network. Under these conditions, von Thunen explained that the city itself would take on a circular shape, and that surrounding land uses would follow the **concentric ring** pattern shown in Figure 15:5. The city would be walled for protection from invaders, and all citizens would live within the walls, leaving only during daylight hours to tend the fields around the city. The concentric ring pattern minimized the travel time to reach a given point outside the city's walls and the effort needed to transport the products produced on the plain to the city for consumption.

Concentric Ring

VON THUNEN'S LAND-USE MODEL   **Figure 15:5**

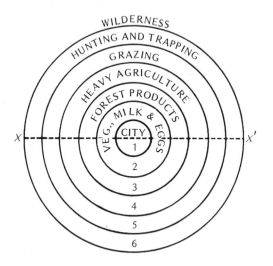

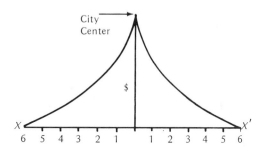

Cross section from X to X' showing land values in the various concentric rings of the model city

In von Thunen's model, ring 1 was the walled city. There shops and homes competed for the available space, often being multistory, since the walls limited outward expansion.

Of all the rings, the land in the center was the most eagerly sought and the most intensely used. Consequently, on a square-foot basis, it commanded a higher price than land in any other ring. The land in ring 2 was the most desirable of all land outside the city walls because of its closeness and hence minimum transportation requirements. Although this land could be used for growing grain or trees or grazing cattle, it was used for vegetable gardens, stall-fed milk cows, and laying chickens, because, of all the agricultural possibilities, these produced the most value of output per square foot of land. Consequently, land value per square foot in ring 2 was the highest of all agricultural rings.

Rings 3 and 4 were used for forest products and bulky crops, respectively. Although it seems strange that forest products would be in ring 3, the need for their closeness to the city was due primarily to transportation considerations: large quantities of wood were used for fuel, the product was bulky and heavy, and ox carts were an inefficient means of transport. Crops such as corn, wheat, hay, and potatoes were grown in ring 4 because they required much land to produce a given amount of food.

Ring 5 was used for the grazing of animals that could travel out of the protective walls of the city during the day and back at night under their own power. Ring 6 was used for hunting and trapping. Beyond that was wilderness.

This arrangement of land uses was not the result of a governmental planning commission, but rather the result of competition for land use based on the value of the product, delivered to the city, that could be produced per square foot of soil. Stated another way, farmers whose products allowed them to pay the highest rents were able to obtain the use of the land closest to the center of the city.

Burgess Model   Recognizing that the industrial revolution had caused startling changes in the use of land around cities, in 1925, an American land economist, Ernest W. Burgess, updated von Thunen's model. Studying the city of Chicago, Burgess found the city center now occupied by shopping facilities, business offices, banks, and government. In ring 2, gardens, cows, and hens had been replaced by manufacturing and wholesale firms. In ring 3, employees of these firms resided in low- and moderate-income homes on modest plots of ground. In ring 4 were found higher-income families who wanted larger lots for their homes and who could afford the commuting costs to jobs in the city. Beyond that were the farms that provided food for the city.

Although Burgess recognized the need for transportation facilities to enable people and goods to move easily between zones, he did not adequately appreciate the effects that transportation routes themselves would have on land use and city

Sector Theory

HOYT'S SECTOR THEORY OF CITY LAND USES   Figure 15:6

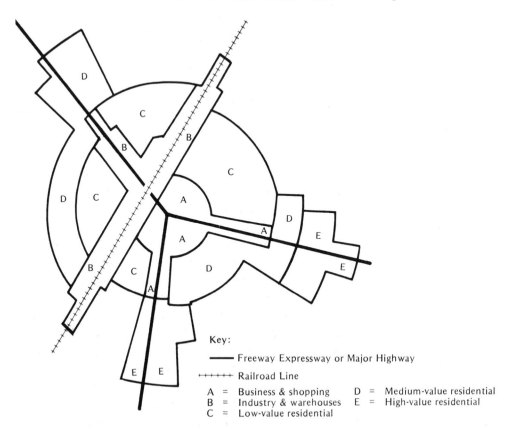

Key:

────── Freeway Expressway or Major Highway

++++++ Railroad Line

A = Business & shopping   D = Medium-value residential
B = Industry & warehouses   E = High-value residential
C = Low-value residential

growth. Consequently, in 1939, real estate economist Homer Hoyt published a study of land uses in 70 American cities.

Sketched in Figure 15:6, Hoyt's approach placed considerable emphasis on land uses that developed in axial patterns along important transportation routes. This has been referred to variously as a **wedge-shaped, pie-shaped,** or **sector theory** of land use and development. By 1939, shopping districts were expanding along major streets due to increased use of the automobile, while wholesale, trade, and factory land uses were expanding along major highways, rail lines, and waterways. Similarly, residential areas extended out along commuter lines. Hoyt also found that low- and modest-cost housing was located near employment opportunities and along transportation arteries, whereas more expensive housing was to be found in suburban areas away from noise, odors, and congestion. Hoyt also pointed out the phenomenon of **filtering** in real estate, wherein higher-priced residential properties are made available to lower paying users as higher-income residents move to new areas. As the land in the direction of the city center has already been developed, the new higher-value areas were carved out of the undeveloped land surrounding the city's outskirts.

Multiple-nuclei City

Economists C. D. Harris and E. L. Ullman felt that the Hoyt model could be improved by emphasizing that in many cities more than one business and shopping district exists. Their concept, published in 1945, was the **multiple-nuclei city.** This concept, diagrammed in Figure 15:7, places the principal business district in the city center and then adds one or more business districts along major streets at some distance from the city center. Each smaller business district in turn becomes the center for a competing set of land uses immediately surrounding it. The creation of these subcenters is the result of several factors, including the absorption of existing outlying towns, growth in automobile ownership, new highway construction, and the availability of parking space at outlying centers. Outward business expansion has also been aided by physical shortages and the high prices of land in central areas, plus concerns about traffic congestion and crime. The telephone has also played a great role in reducing the need for business functions to congregate. From the standpoint of land values, the highest values per square foot were still found in the central city. However, the usual reduction in land prices as one moved away from the city center was interrupted by subcenters.

MULTIPLE-NUCLEI CITY LAND USE PATTERN   Figure 15:7

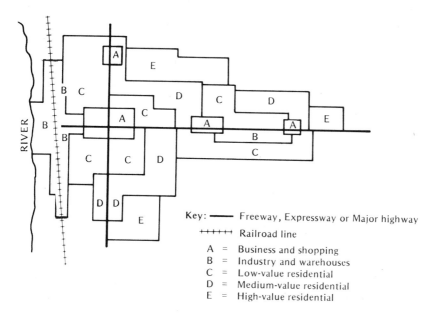

Key: ——— Freeway, Expressway or Major highway

++++++ Railroad line

A = Business and shopping
B = Industry and warehouses
C = Low-value residential
D = Medium-value residential
E = High-value residential

No single pattern describes all cities found in America. *Current Patterns* Land use patterns in a college town will be different from those at a mining site or around a resort area. Moreover, physical barriers such as mountains, rivers, lakes, and oceans play an important role. Nonetheless, several conclusions may be drawn. In rural towns, land use patterns usually extend out along the roads or highways that pass through the town. In medium-sized cities, Hoyt's sector approach appears to be a good description. As a medium-sized city grows to a large city, subcenters spring up, and the sector theory combined with the multiple-nuclei theory provides the best explanation of land uses.

Before leaving this subject, it should be remembered that,

to date, nearly all city growth has been the result of millions of individual decisions made by developers, builders, lenders, and owners of land, homes, stores, offices, and factories, each acting in accordance with self-interest. Today, however, there is a growing trend for deliberate city planning on a scale far more comprehensive than was ever done in the past with local zoning laws. A general plan for an existing city's future growth or a "new town" development designed by a single planner may be different than the result of thousands of individual decisions. Still, even under centralized planning, the basic land use concept recognized by von Thunen and others will hold true: because land is immobile, the single most important factor in land use will continue to be the cost and availability of transportation necessary to get to and from it.

REAL ESTATE CYCLES

When viewed over time, do prices for real estate follow a recurring order or interval, that is, a cyclical pattern? If so, is the pattern predictable in advance with enough accuracy that one can predict when real estate prices will rise and fall in the future? As this section will show, cycles can be found in real estate activity and prices. However, whether the passage of time alone is responsible for these ups and downs is debatable. Let us explore the matter further.

Whether one looks at construction activity, land prices, or deed recordings, over a long enough period of time cyclical patterns appear to repeat themselves every 15 to 20 years. These are called **long cycles.** An excellent example is shown in Figure 15:8. This graph shows how land prices in the United States have alternately risen and fallen since the early 1800s.

Glancing at Figure 15:8, it would appear that a land speculator need only look at a calendar to determine the next upswing. However, although the cycles seem to average 18 years in length, there is no reliability in judging how long the up or down leg of a cycle will last, nor precisely how high prices will go before peaking. For example, the first drop in prices shown took just 1 year: 1818 to 1819. Then it took 17 years to reach the next peak. The next cycle took 7 years to reach bottom and then lasted 11 years on the upswing. If a person had bought in 1837, he would have experienced 6 more

LONG CYCLES IN UNITED STATES LAND PRICES

Figure 15:8

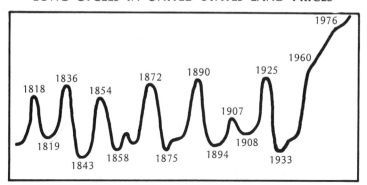

Sources: Graph through 1960 reprinted with permission from ULI—The Urban Land Institute, 1200 8th Street N.W., Washington, D.C. 20036, Technical Bulletin 38, © 1960, From 1961 through 1976, based on FHA statistics.

years of falling prices. If he kept his land in anticipation of prices returning to the 1836 level, he would have waited until 1872. In more recent years, relying on past cycles would have signaled a reverse in land prices sometime in the 1950s, or certainly by 1960. But such a downturn did not occur.

Causes

In looking for the causes of real estate cycles, researchers have found that although cycles sometimes appear to be calendar oriented, in reality they have been caused by events such as the general state of the nation's economy, immigration into the United States, the westward movement, railroad construction, birth-rate changes, the increased use of debt financing to purchase real estate, and government encouragement of home ownership. For example, the low point in real estate prices in 1933 coincided with the depths of the Great Depression. Since then, government programs such as the FHA and VA, general economic prosperity, the 1940–1960 baby boom, and federal fiscal and monetary policies that encouraged inflation have produced a strong upward influence on real estate prices.

Events such as changes in the birth rate, immigration, railway construction and creation of the FHA and VA, are called **secular events.** Secular events often last several decades and are not by themselves cyclical in nature. However, when different types of secular events follow each other, a cyclical pattern can be produced. The fact that a given event can produce a dramatic change in real estate prices is often due to what is called the **acceleration principle.** For example, the completion of railway lines through unsettled areas in the United States resulted in the establishment of thousands of American towns. Many have grown to major cities today, not because everyone works for the railroad, but because the railroad was the catalyst that attracted trade, business, and industry to a given location. The acceleration principle is a well-accepted one, for many land booms have been started on the strength of one railway station. Unfortunately, the psychology of the human mind often tends to exaggerate the effects of acceleration and soon overbidding occurs. When overbidding is finally recognized, prices drop dramatically, and more often than not people become overly pessimistic. This is what tends to give cycles such long, steep sides.

Short Cycles   Superimposed on the long cycles are also real estate **short cycles,** with an average length of about 4 years. These cycles have been particularly apparent since the end of World War II, and it is generally agreed among economists that they result from the ease or difficulty of borrowing money to finance residential real estate. Few home buyers can afford to pay all cash for a place to live; their decision to buy is based on the availability of loan money and the size of the monthly payment. With money available, down payments shrink, and interest rates drop, so that a buyer can afford to buy a more expensive home with the same down payment and monthly payment.

Of the eight housing construction cycles that have occurred since 1945, six have coincided with recessions in the American economy. Called **countercyclical building cycles,** they start when business and consumer loan demand falls owing to a recession. As a result, builders and home buyers who were previously priced out of the loan market now become heavy borrowers. The process comes to a close when the recession ends (an end that is often aided by the upswing in construction activity) and businesses start to compete again for available loan money. Also, if government has been spending more than it has been collecting in taxes in order to stimulate the economy, it, too, is competing with business and home buyers for available loan money. This added competition accelerates interest rate increases and slows down new housing construction. Figure 15:9 illustrates this relationship.

COUNTERCYCLICAL BUILDING CYCLE

Figure 15:9

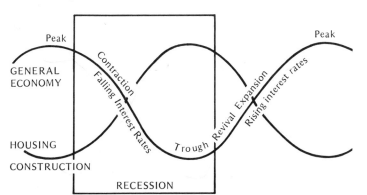

As the general economy contracts, interest rates fall, thus stimulating housing construction. In the expansion stages of the economy, interest rates usually rise causing housing construction to cool.

INFLATION

Each of us is well aware of the upward march in prices of nearly all goods and services offered for sale since the end of World War II. Why has this happened, and why is it likely to continue to happen? The explanations fill volumes. However, for our purposes here, there are four concepts with which you should be familiar: cost-push inflation, demand-pull inflation, monetary inflation, and real-cost inflation.

Cost-push Inflation

The increasing cost of the factors necessary to manu-facture a product or offer a service results in what is called **cost-push inflation.** To illustrate, an automobile manufacturer increases the price of cars because labor and materials cost more. A major reason for increasing new home prices in recent years has been the increase in prices of lumber, bricks, concrete, metal, construction labor, construction loans, and government permits. Moreover, these increases reinforce themselves. If a rental apartment building costs more to build today, higher rents must be charged, in turn causing the tenants to ask for higher wages, which, of course, are built into whatever they are making or doing.

Demand-pull Inflation

When buyers bid against each other to buy something that has been offered for sale **demand-pull inflation** results. For example, three buyers for a single available residence may bid $45,000, $46,000, and $47,000, respectively, in an effort to buy that particular home. Demand-pull inflation usually has little to do with the actual cost of producing the particular goods or services being sought. Thus, from the standpoint of the seller who may have paid $30,000 for the home, the offers of $45,000, $46,000 and $47,000 are more a reflection of what the three buyers feel they would pay elsewhere to obtain similar housing than what the house originally cost the seller.

Monetary Inflation

Demand-pull inflation is basically the result of too much money chasing too few goods. On a local scale, it can result from a certain neighborhood suddenly becoming very popular among buyers. On a national scale, this form of inflation is called **monetary inflation,** as it draws its strength from the creation of excessive amounts of money by government. The classic example of this was in Germany during the first 5 years after World War I. In an effort to provide money to solve all the war-torn country's problems at once, the German government created and spent money on a grand scale. However, there was no parallel increase in goods and services to be purchased with that money. The result was demand-pull inflation as millions of people with pockets, and later wheelbarrows, stuffed with newly printed currency fought to buy everything from bread and vegetables to real estate. Within the space of a few short years, prices rose on the order of 1 million percent before the printing presses were finally shut down.

Much economic arguing over prices in the United States revolves around how much the money supply should be allowed to grow. Allowing the money supply to grow faster than the available supply of goods and services causes a temporary economic stimulus by placing more money in peoples' hands. But the ultimate result is a reduction in the purchasing power of the dollar. The alternative, according to many economists, is for the growth in the money supply to more closely parallel the nation's long-run ability to produce goods and services. Productivity in the United States has grown at the average rate of 3.1% during the current century; presumably, any increase in the money supply over that amount each year would show up as increased prices.

Another factor in higher prices is **real-cost inflation.** This is inflation caused by the increased effort necessary to produce the same quantity of a good or service. The Alaskan pipeline and North Slope oil wells are excellent examples of real-cost inflation. In 1960, all oil produced in the United States came from within the 48 contiguous states and consequently was near the American markets in which it was consumed. Today, at great expense, oil fields are being developed in the frozen North Slope of Alaska. Added to this is a costly transportation network to get the oil to the lower 48 states. Thus, although a gallon of gasoline or fuel oil is chemically the same whether it comes from Oklahoma or Alaska, the one from Alaska involves much more work to get it to the consumer.

Real-cost Inflation

Another good example of real-cost inflation can be found in the iron mining areas of northern Minnesota. For decades, the richest areas of these fields have been tapped to feed America's steel-making industry and provide steel-containing products to American consumers. Today the rich fields have been depleted, and steel companies are forced to mine a lower-grade ore. This ore requires an extra processing step to make it suitable for steel making. The cost of this step must be built into the finished product—an automobile, refrigerator, or the steel frame for a high-rise building.

Real-cost inflation also affects the cost of developing land around cities. Much easy-to-develop land has already been built upon, forcing developers to utilize land that requires more effort to bulldoze into usable lots. To provide water service to new lots, local water districts that once could supply the town's population from a few wells or a nearby lake or river must travel many miles to find water. The additional cost of the water system and pumping charges must be added to the user's water bill. Also, we cannot overlook the nation's efforts to clean up pollution. The generation of electrical power is an excellent example. At one time, our primary concern was the end product—kilowatt hours of electricity produced. Today, we still want electricity, but we also want the smoke emitted by the generating plant to be clean. The cost to do this must be added to the cost of each kilowatt of electricity produced. For many years, improved technology has been able to offset real-cost increases. However, with the beginning of the 1970s, it became apparent that with many products real-cost increases were occurring at rates faster than improved technology could overcome them.

The effect of inflation on existing improved real property since World War II has been dramatic. With land development and construction costs constantly increasing, the prices that prospective buyers are willing to pay for existing buildings are also rising. The result in many cities across the United States is that a house that sold for $20,000 in 1960 will command $40,000 today, despite the fact that it has aged in the meantime. The reason: similar new homes cost $50,000.

VOCABULARY REVIEW

Match terms a–p with statements 1–16.

a. *Acceleration principle*
b. *Base industry*
c. *Buyer's market*
d. *Broad market*
e. *Concentric ring theory*
f. *Cost-push inflation*
g. *Countercyclical building cycle*
h. *Demand-pull inflation*
i. *Long cycles*
j. *Multiple-nuclei theory*
k. *Real-cost inflation*
l. *Secular event*
m. *Seller's market*
n. *Service industry*
o. *Thin market*
p. *Wedge theory*

1. An industry that produces goods or services for export.
2. An industry that produces goods or services to sell to local residents.

3. Many buyers and sellers.
4. Many buyers and few sellers.
5. Few buyers and few sellers.
6. Few buyers and many sellers.
7. Economic patterns that tend to repeat every 15 to 20 years.
8. Long-lasting and noncyclical economic event.
9. A real estate cycle that runs opposite to the general economy.
10. Higher prices due to buyers bidding against each other.
11. Higher prices due to greater effort needed to produce the same product today.
12. Higher prices due to increased costs of labor and supplies.
13. Land use pattern that follows circular rings.
14. Land use pattern that follows a pie-shaped model.
15. City growth pattern with two or more business centers.
16. An event results in a greater impact on demand or prices than can be traced to that event alone.

QUESTIONS AND PROBLEMS

1. List and rank in order of importance the base industries that support your community. How stable are they? Are any new ones coming? Are any existing ones leaving?
2. What would be the effect of a new industry creating 500 new jobs in your community? Is there sufficient vacant housing available? What would be the effect of a loss of 500 jobs?
3. Can you identify buyer's or seller's markets currently existing in your community for specific types of real estate such as vacant land, retail store space, office space, houses, condominiums, and apartment buildings?
4. Does the population age distribution of your community differ from the United States as a whole? How would this affect demand for housing in your area?
5. Obtain a map of your city and show on it present land uses and the direction of city growth. What has caused growth to occur the way it has?
6. Which land use pattern described in this chapter best describes land use patterns in your city?
7. At what point in the building cycle would you say the United States is at this time? On what do you base your answer?
8. What secular events currently appear to be affecting real estate prices in the United States? Do any of these suggest that a drop in real estate prices will occur soon?
9. Identify three specific examples of cost-push inflation that you have personally observed or read about during the past 12 months.

ADDITIONAL READINGS   **Barlowe, Raleigh.** *Land Resource Economics.* Englewood Cliffs, N.J.: Prentice-Hall, 1972, 616 pages. Deals with the economic relationship between man and land, with emphasis on the supply of and demand for land resources, land economics, institutional and social conditions.

Brown, Robert K. *Real Estate Economics.* Boston: Houghton Mifflin, 1965, 388 pages. Emphasis is placed on social and economic influences on real estate.

Case, Fred E. *Real Estate Economics.* Sacramento: California Association of Realtors, 1974, 289 pages. Written especially for the real estate salesman and broker who is seeking a logical and easy to read introduction to real estate economics.

Page, Alfred N., and **Seyfried, Warren R.** *Urban Analysis.* Glenview, Ill.: Scott, Foresman, 1970, 427 pages. An excellent collection of articles on such topics as housing demand, housing location, real estate cycles, property values, racial integration, urban renewal and slums.

16

Appraisal: Market Comparison and Cost Approaches

Comparables: properties similar to the subject property that are used to establish the value of the subject property

Cost approach: property valuation based on land value plus current construction costs less depreciation

Gross rent multiplier (GRM): a number, that when multiplied by a property's gross rents, produces an estimate of the property's worth

Income approach: property valuation based on the monetary returns that a property can be expected to produce

Market approach: a method of valuing a property by looking at prices of recent sales of similar properties

Market value: the cash price that a willing buyer and a willing seller would agree upon, given reasonable exposure of the property to the marketplace, full information as to the potential uses of the property, and no undue compulsion to act

Replacement cost: the cost, at today's prices and using today's methods of construction, of building an improvement having the same usefulness as the one being appraised

Reproduction cost: the cost, at today's prices, of constructing an exact replica of the subject improvements, using the same or similar materials

Subject property: the property that is being appraised

subject

To appraise real estate means to estimate its value. There are three approaches to making this estimate. The first is to compare similar properties that have sold recently, and use them as a guide to estimate the value of the property that you are appraising. This is the **market approach.** The second approach is to add together the cost of the individual components that make up the property being appraised. This is the **cost approach;** it starts with the cost of a similar parcel of vacant land, and adds the cost of the lumber, concrete, plumbing, *341* wiring, and so on, necessary to build a similar building. Depreciation is then subtracted. The third approach is to consider only the amount of net income that the property can reasonably be expected to produce for its owner, plus any anticipated price increase or decrease. This is the **income approach.** For the person who owns or plans to own real estate, knowing how much a property is worth is a crucial part of the buying or selling decision. For the real estate agent, being able to appraise a property is an essential part of taking a listing.

Market Value   In this chapter and the next we shall demonstrate the application of the market, cost, and income approaches as they are used in determining market value. **Market value,** also called **fair market value,** is the highest price in terms of money that a property will bring if (1) the terms are all cash to the seller, (2) the property is exposed on the open market for a reasonable length of time, (3) the buyer and seller are fully informed as to market conditions and the uses to which the property may be put, (4) neither is under abnormal pressure to conclude a transaction, and (5) the seller is capable of conveying marketable title. Market value is at the heart of nearly all real estate transactions.

MARKET
COMPARISON
APPROACH   Let us begin by demonstrating the application of the market comparison approach to a single-family residence. The residence to be appraised is described as follows and is called the **subject property:**

> The subject property is a one-story, wood-frame house of 1,520 square feet containing three bedrooms, two bathrooms, a living room, dining room, kitchen, and utility room. There is a two-car garage with concrete driveway to the street, a 300-square-foot concrete patio in the backyard, and an average amount of landscaping. The house is located on a 10,200-square-foot, level lot that measures 85 by 120 feet. The house is 12 years old, in good repair, and is located in a well-maintained neighborhood of houses of similar construction and age.

Comparables   After becoming familiar with the physical features and amenities of the subject property, the next step in the market approach is to locate houses of similar physical features and

amenities that have sold recently under market value conditions. These are known as **comparables** or "comps." The more
similar they are to the subject property, the fewer and smaller
the adjustments that must be made in the comparison process
and hence the less room for error. As a rule of thumb, it is
best to use comparable sales no more than 6 months old.
During periods of relatively stable prices, this can be extended
to 1 year. However, during periods of rapidly changing prices,
even a sale 6 months old may be out of date.

Sales Records

To apply the market comparison approach, the following
information must be collected for each comparable sale: date
of sale, sales price, financing terms, location of the property,
and a description of its physical characteristics and amenities.
Recorded deeds at public records offices can provide dates and
locations of recent sales. Although a deed seldom states the
purchase price, three-quarters of the states levy a deed transfer tax or conveyance tax, the amount of which is shown on
the recorded deed. This tax can sometimes provide a clue as
to the purchase price.

Records of past sales can often be obtained from title and
abstract companies. In some cities, commercially-operated
financial services publish information on local real estate transactions and sell it on a subscription basis. Property tax assessors keep records on changes in ownership as well as property values. Where these records are kept up to date and are
available to the public, they can provide information on what
has sold recently and for how much. Assessors also keep
detailed records of improvements made to land. This can be
quite helpful in making adjustments between the subject
property and the comparables. For real estate salespeople,
locally operated multiple listing services provide asking prices
and descriptions of properties currently offered for sale by
member brokers, along with descriptions, sales prices, and
dates for properties that have been sold.

Verification

To produce the most accurate appraisal possible, one
should call upon the new owner of each comparable to verify
the purchase price, obtain information on the terms of the
sale, and inspect the premises. One will also need to know the

date the buyer and seller signed their sales contract, for it was on that date, not the date the deed was recorded, that a meeting of minds took place regarding the price and terms of the sale. Failure to verify sales data invites errors. One irony of the market approach is that most people consider their financial dealings to be private information. Yet knowing what someone else paid for a similar property is the very basis of the market comparison approach. Consequently, to obtain cooperation, one must carefully assure owners of comparable properties that information supplied will be kept confidential.

Number of Comparables   As a rule of thumb, from three to five comparables are used. To use only one or two comparables invites too much error. Above five, the additional accuracy must be weighed against the extra effort involved. When the supply of comparable sales is more than adequate, one should choose the sales that require the fewest adjustments.

It is also important that the comparables selected represent current market conditions. Sales between relatives or close friends may result in an advantageous price to the buyer or seller, and sales prices that for some other reason appear to be out of line with the general market should not be used. Listings and offers to buy should not be used in place of actual sales. They do not represent a meeting of minds between a buyer and a seller. Listing prices are, however, useful in establishing the upper limit on prices, whereas offers to buy set lower limits. Thus, if a property is listed for sale at $60,000 and there have been offers as high as $57,000, it is reasonable to presume the market price lies somewhere between $57,000 and $60,000.

Adjustment Process   Let us now work through the example shown in Table 16:1 to demonstrate the application of the market comparison approach to a house. We begin at lines 1 and 2 by entering the address and sales price of each comparable property. For convenience, we shall refer to these as comparables A, B, and C. On lines 3 through 10, adjustments are made to the sale price of each comparable to make it equal to the subject property today. Adjustments are made for changes in prices since each comparable was sold, as well as for differences in

Table 16:1 VALUING A HOUSE BY THE MARKET COMPARISON APPROACH

Line	Item	Comparable Sale A		Comparable Sale B		Comparable Sale C	
1	Address of comparable house	1702 Brookside Ave.		1912 Brookside Ave.		1501 18th St.	
2	Sales price of comparable house		$45,900		$44,000		$44,500
3	Time adjustment	sold 6 mos. ago, add 5%	+2,295	sold 3 mos. ago, add 2½%	+1,100	just sold	0
4	House size	160 sq ft larger at $25 per sq ft	−4,000	20 sq ft smaller at $25/sq ft	+500	same size	0
5	Garage/carport	carport	+2,000	3 car garage	−1,000	two-car garage	0
6	Other	larger patio	−150	no patio	+300	built-in bookcases	−500
7	Age, upkeep, and overall quality of house	superior	−1,000	inferior	+200	equal	0
8	Landscaping	inferior	+500	equal	0	superior	−500
9	Lot size, features, and location	superior	−1,945	inferior	+450	equal	0
10	Terms and conditions of sale	equal	0	special financing	−1,500	equal	0
11	Total adjustments		−2,300		+50		−1,000
12	ADJUSTED MARKET PRICE		$43,600		$44,050		$43,500
13	Correlation process:						
	Comparable A	$43,600 × 20% =	$ 8,720				
	Comparable B	$44,050 × 30% =	$13,215				
	Comparable C	$43,500 × 50% =	$21,750				
14	INDICATED VALUE		$43,685				
	Round to		$43,700				

physical features, amenities, and financial terms. The result indicates the market value of the subject property.

Returning to line 3 in Figure 16:1, assume that house prices in the neighborhood where the subject property and comparables are located have risen 5% during the 6 months that have elapsed since comparable A was sold. If comparable A were for sale today, it would bring 5%, or $2,295,

Time Adjustments

more. Therefore, we must add $2,295 to bring comparable A up to the present. Comparable B was sold 3 months ago, and to bring it up to the present we need to add 2½% or $1,100, to its sales price. Comparable C was just sold and needs no time correction, as its price reflects today's market.

When using the market comparison approach, all adjustments are made to the comparable properties, not to the subject property. This is because we cannot adjust the price of something for which we do not yet have the price. We do, however, have the selling price and date of sale for each comparable and can adjust these prices to make them similar to the subject property in today's market.

House Size   Because house A is 160 square feet larger than the subject house, it is logical to expect the subject property would sell for less money. Hence a deduction is made from the sales price of comparable A on line 4. The amount of the deduction is based on the difference in floor area and the current cost of similar construction, minus an allowance for depreciation. (Methods of calculating construction costs and depreciation are discussed in more detail in the cost approach section found later in this chapter.) If we value the extra 160 square feet at $25 per square foot, we must subtract $4,000. For comparable B, the house is 20 square feet smaller than the subject house. At $25 per square foot, we add $500 to comparable B, as it is reasonable to expect that the subject property would sell for that much more because it is that much larger. Comparable C has the same sized house as the subject property, and no adjustment is needed.

Garage and Patio   Next, the parking facilities (line 5) are adjusted. We first
Adjustments   look at the current cost of garage and carport construction and the condition of these structures. Assume that the value of a carport is $1,000; a one-car garage, $2,000; a two-car garage, $3,000; and a three-car garage, $4,000. Adjustments would be made as follows. The subject property has a two-car garage worth $3,000 and comparable A has a carport worth $1,000. Therefore, based on the difference in garage facilities, we can reasonably expect the subject property to command $2,000

more than comparable A. By adding $2,000 to comparable A, we effectively equalize this difference. Comparable B has a garage worth $1,000 more than the subject property's garage. Therefore, $1,000 must be subtracted from comparable B to equalize it with the subject property. For comparable C, no adjustment is required, as comparable C and the subject property have similar garage facilities.

At line 6, the subject property has a 300-square-foot patio in the backyard worth $300. Comparable A has a patio worth $450; therefore, $150 is deducted from comparable A's selling price. Comparable B has no patio. As it would have sold for $300 more if it had one, a +$300 adjustment is required. The patio at comparable C is the same as the subject property's; however, comparable C has custom built-in bookcases in the living room worth $500 that the subject property does not have. Therefore, $500 is subtracted from comparable C's sales price. Differences between the comparables and the subject property such as swimming pools, fireplaces, carpeting, drapes, roofing materials, and kitchen appliances would be adjusted in a similar manner.

On line 7 we recognize differences in building age, wear and tear, construction quality, and design usefulness. Where the difference between the subject property and a comparable can be measured in terms of material and labor, the adjustment is the cost of that material and labor. For example, the $200 adjustment for comparable B reflects the cost of needed roof repair at the time B was sold. The adjustment of $1,000 for comparable A reflects the fact it has better-quality plumbing and electrical fixtures than the subject property. Differences that cannot be quantified in terms of labor and materials are usually dealt with as lump-sum judgments. Thus, one might allow $500 for each year of age difference between the subject and a comparable, or make a lump-sum adjustment of $1,000 for an inconvenient kitchen design.

Age, Condition, and Quality

Keep in mind that adjustments are made on the basis of what each comparable property was like on the day it was sold. Thus, if an extra bedroom was added or the house was painted after its sale date, these items are not included in the adjustment process.

Landscaping   Line 8 shows the landscaping at comparable A to be inferior to the subject property. A positive correction is necessary here to equalize it with the subject. The landscaping at comparable B is similar and requires no correction; that at comparable C is better and thus requires a negative adjustment. The dollar amount of each adjustment is based on the market value of grass, bushes, trees and the like.

Lot Features   Line 9 deals with any differences in lot size, slope, view, and neighborhood. In this example, all comparables are in the same neighborhood as the subject property, thus eliminating the need to judge, in dollar terms, the relative merit of one neighborhood over another. However, comparable A has a slightly larger lot and a better view than the subject property. Based on recent lot sales in the area, the difference is judged to be $445 for the larger lot and $1,500 for the better view. Comparable B has a slightly smaller lot judged to be worth $450 less, and comparable C is similar in all respects.

Terms and Conditions   Line 10 in Table 16:1 accounts for differences in financing. As a rule, the more accommodating the terms of the sale to the buyer, the higher the sales price, and vice versa. We are looking for the highest cash price the subject property may reasonably be expected to bring, given adequate exposure to the marketplace and a knowledgeable buyer and seller not under undue pressure. If the comparables were sold under these conditions, no corrections would be needed in this category. However, if it can be determined that a comparable was sold under different conditions, an adjustment is necessary. For example, if the going rate of interest on home mortgages is $9\frac{1}{2}\%$ per year and the seller offers to finance the buyer at 8% interest, it is reasonable to expect that the seller can charge a higher selling price. Similarly, the seller can get a higher price if he has a low-interest-rate loan that can be assumed by the buyer. Favorable financing terms offered by the seller of comparable B enabled him to obtain an extra $1,500 in selling price. Therefore, we must subtract $1,500 from comparable B. Another situation that requires an adjustment on line 10 is if a comparable was sold on a rush basis. If a seller is in a hurry to sell, he must usually accept a lower selling price than if he can give his property longer exposure in the marketplace.

Adjustments for each comparable are totaled and either added or subtracted from its sales price. The result is the **adjusted market price** shown at line 12. This is the dollar value of each comparable sale after it has gone through an adjustment process to make it the same as the subject property. If it were possible to precisely evaluate every adjustment, and if the buyers of comparables A, B, and C had paid exactly what their properties were worth at the time they purchased them, the three prices shown on line 12 would be the same. However, buyers are not that precise, particularly in purchasing a home where amenity value influences price and varies considerably from one person to the next.

Adjusted Market Price

While comparing the properties, it will usually become apparent that some comparables are more similar to the subject property than others. The **correlation** step gives the appraiser the opportunity to assign more weight to the more similar comparables and less to the others. At 13, comparable C is given a weight of 50% since it is more similar to the subject and required fewer adjustments. Moreover, this sameness is in areas where adjustments tend to be the hardest to estimate accurately: time, age, quality, location, view, and financial conditions. Of the remaining two comparables, comparable B is weighted slightly higher than comparable A because it is a more recent sale and overall required fewer adjustments.

Correlation Process

In the correlation process, the adjusted market price of each comparable is multiplied by its weighting factor and totaled at line 14. The result is the **indicated value** of the subject property. It is customary to round it off to the nearest $50 or $100 for properties under $10,000, to the nearest $100 or $250 for properties between $10,000 and $100,000, to the nearest $500 for properties between $100,000 and $250,000, and to the nearest $1,000 above that.

The process for estimating the market value of a condominium, townhouse, or cooperative living unit by the market approach is similar to the process for houses except that fewer steps are involved. For example, in a condominium complex with a large number of two-bedroom units of identical floor plan, a sufficient number of comparable sales may be available within the building. This would eliminate adjustments for differences in unit floor plan, neighborhood, lot size and features, age and upkeep of the building, and landscaping. The only corrections needed would be those that make one unit different from another. This would include the location of the individual unit within the building (end units and units with better views sell for more), the upkeep and interior decoration of the unit, a time adjustment, and an adjustment for terms and conditions of the sale.

When there are not enough comparable sales of the same floor plan within the same building and it is necessary to use different sized units, an adjustment must be made for floor area. If the number of comparables is still inadequate and units in different condominium buildings must be used, adjustments will be necessary for neighborhood, lot features, management, upkeep, age, and overall condition of the building.

When using the market approach, the main difference between appraising homes and appraising land is that a home is treated as a single unit. This is possible when the property as a whole is basically similar to its comparables. However, such similarity often does not exist in vacant land. For example, how would one establish a value for 21 acres of vacant land when the only comparables available are 16 acre and 25 acre sales? The usual method is to establish a per acre value from comparables and apply it to the subject land. Thus, if 16- and 25-acre parcels sold for $16,000 and $25,000, respectively, and are similar in all other respects to the 21-acre subject property, it would be reasonable to conclude that land is selling for $1,000 per acre. Therefore, the subject property is worth

Table 16:2   LOT VALUATION BY THE MARKET COMPARISON APPROACH

Line	Item	Comparable Sale D		Comparable Sale E		Comparable Sale F	
1	Address of comparable lot	1250 Neptune Dr.		1820 Mercury St.		1765 Venus Ave.	
2	Sales price of comparable lot	$8,100		$8,800		$10,500	
3	Lot size (front by depth in ft)	90 × 125		80 × 125		120 × 125	
4	Price per front foot		$90.00		$110.00		$87.50
5	Time adjustment	prices up 5%	×1.05	just sold	×1.00	prices up 12%	×1.12
6	After time adjustment		$94.50		$110.00		$98.00
7	Depth adjustment	none req'd.	×1.00	none req'd.	×1.00	none req'd.	×1.00
8	After depth adjustment		$94.50		$110.00		$98.00
9	Neighborhood, lot features and financing	subject is superior	×1.10	subject is inferior	×0.95	subject is equal	×1.00
10	Adjusted value per front foot		$103.95		$104.50		$98.00
11	Correlation process:						
	Comparable D	$103.95 × 40% =	$ 41.58				
	Comparable E	$104.50 × 40% =	$ 41.80				
	Comparable F	$ 98.00 × 20% =	$ 19.60				
	INDICATED VALUE		$102.98 per front foot				
	Round to		$103.00 per front foot				
12	Subject property has 86 front feet and therefore is valued at 86 × $103 = $8,858						
			Round to $8,850				

$21,000. On smaller parcels of land, comparisons are made on a square-foot or front-foot basis.

Lot Adjustments

Table 16:2 shows in more detail how differences in location, usefulness, and time are adjusted between a vacant lot and its comparables. In this example, the subject lot has 86 feet of street frontage and is 125 feet deep. The first step is to locate several recent comparable sales. These comparables must be of similar zoning, since a lot zoned for apartments or commercial purposes must not be compared to a lot zoned for a single-family residence, or vice versa. Furthermore, comparable lots should be similar to the subject lot in terms of size, neighborhood, and usefulness. The closer the similarity, the fewer and smaller the adjustments and, hence, the more accurate the final value for the subject lot.

Time   Lines 1 and 2 in Table 16:2 show both the address and sales price of each comparable sale. Line 3 shows the lot size, and line 4, the price of each lot on a front-foot basis. This is calculated by dividing the sales price by the number of front feet of the lot. The next step is the time adjustment. The factor 1.05 for comparable D means that prices have risen by 5% since it was sold. This factor is multiplied by the front-foot price on line 4 to obtain a front-foot price as if the lot had sold today. This is the $94.50 shown on line 6.

Comparable E was just sold; therefore, the multiplier is 1.00 and the front-foot price after the time adjustment remains at $110. Comparable F is the oldest sale of the three, and the multiplier of 1.12 represents a price increase of 12% since its sale. Thus, at today's prices, F would bring $98 per front foot.

Depth   Next, at line 7, an adjustment can be made for differences between the depths of the comparable lots and the subject lot. The major concern here is that the front-foot method of valuation, by itself, does not consider the depth of a lot. To illustrate, in a residential neighborhood where most houses are located on lots 70 feet wide and 90 feet deep, a lot that is 70 feet wide and 180 feet deep will not bring double the price of 70' × 90' lots as long as it is zoned for one house. It will, though, bring some premium if a buyer can be found who wants a large backyard. Just how much extra can be determined by looking at what buyers have paid in the past for the extra depth or by using **depth rules** or **depth tables.** These are formulas that value a square foot of land near the front of a lot more than a square foot at the back.

With small lots, prices do not decrease in direct proportion to size. For example, a lot 75 feet deep will command 80% to 85% of the front-foot price of a lot 100 feet deep as long as the lot is still usable for building purposes. If a lot is too small for building purposes, its value may be negligible unless it can be combined with an adjacent lot.

When we utilize comparable lots outside the subject lot's neighborhood, an adjustment that reflects differences in neighborhood desirability must be made. The appraiser takes into consideration a neighborhood's general popularity and prestige; street improvements such as paving, curbs, gutters, sidewalks and storm drains; services such as water, electricity, telephone, sanitary sewers, fire and police protection; nearness and adequacy of schools, shopping, and transportation facilities; zoning protection; and the age, upkeep, and quality of surrounding structures. Individual lot features—such as lot shape, existing landscaping, and topography—and differences in financing are also dealt with on line 9. Whereas in the appraisal of a dwelling an amount for these items is stated as a lump-sum dollar figure, in lot valuation this adjustment is expressed as a percentage and then multiplied by the front foot price. An appraiser can often look at this entire list of features and, based on experience, name the percentage correction needed for each comparable. An alternative method is to weight each of the above items separately using tables published by the FHA and then add them to obtain a total correction factor.

Neighborhood, Lot Features, and Financing

In the example in Figure 16:2, the subject property has features that make it 10% more valuable than comparable D, hence the 1.10 multiplier. The correction of 0.95 for comparable E reflects the fact that subject lot features were only 95% as good as comparable E. The 1.00 adjustment for comparable F means that the subject lot had features equal in value to comparable F.

Multiplying the adjustment factor shown on line 9 by line 8 produces the final adjusted value per front foot shown on line 10. On line 11, these are correlated, with more weight given to comparables D and E because they are the most recent sales and are more similar in size to the subject lot. The weighted comparables are added at line 12 to give a corrected value per front foot for the subject property, which is then rounded off to the nearest whole dollar. This is multiplied

Final Steps

by the number of front feet in the subject lot to obtain its appraised value.

GROSS RENT
MULTIPLIERS   A popular market comparison method that is used when a property produces income is the **gross rent multiplier,** or GRM. The GRM is an economic comparison that relates the gross rent a property can produce to its purchase price. For apartment buildings and commercial and industrial properties the GRM is computed by dividing the sales price of the property by its gross annual rent. For example, if an apartment building grosses $10,000 per year in rents and has just sold for $70,000, it is said to have a GRM of 7. The use of a GRM to value houses is questionable since houses are usually sold as owner-occupied residences, not as income properties.

Where comparable properties have been sold at fairly consistent gross rent multiples, the GRM technique presumes the subject property can be valued by multiplying its gross rent by that multiplier. To illustrate, suppose that apartment buildings were recently sold in your community, as shown in Table 16:3. These sales indicate that the market is currently paying seven times gross for apartment buildings. Therefore, to find the value of a similar apartment building that grosses $12,000 per year, $12,000 is multiplied by 7.00 to give an indicated value of $84,000.

Table 16:3   **CALCULATING GROSS RENT MULTIPLIERS**

Building	Sales Price		Gross Annual Rents		Gross Rent Multiplier
No. 1	$122,500	÷	$17,450	=	7.02
No. 2	$ 80,000	÷	$11,494	=	6.96
No. 3	$102,000	÷	$14,676	=	6.95
No. 4	$ 98,000	÷	$13,881	=	7.06
As a Group:	$402,500	÷	$57,501	=	7.00

The GRM method is popular because it is simple to apply. Having once established what multiplier the market is paying, one need only know the gross rents of a building to set a value. However, simplicity is also the weakness of the GRM method, because the GRM looks only at the gross rent that a property produces; gross rent does not allow for variations in vacancies, uncollectable rents, property taxes, maintenance, management, insurance, utilities, or reserves for replacements.

To illustrate the problem, suppose that two apartment buildings each gross $100,000 per year. However, the first has expenses amounting to $40,000 per year and the second, expenses of $50,000 per year. Using the same GRM, the buildings would be valued the same. This is illogical since the first produces $10,000 more in net income for its owner, The GRM also overlooks the expected economic life span of a property. For example, a building with an expected remaining life span of 30 years would be valued the same as one expected to last 20 years, if both currently produce the same rents. One method of partially offsetting these errors is to use different GRMs under different circumstances. Thus, a property with low operating expenses and a long expected economic life span might call for a GRM of 7 whereas a property with high operating expenses or a shorter expected life span would be valued using a GRM of 6 or 5 or even less.

Weakness of GRM

The choice of a GRM of 7 in the example and discussion is not by accident. Experience indicates that there is something special about a GRM of 7, particularly among unsophisticated investors and for modest-sized apartment properties. This is undoubtedly due to the widespread belief that a GRM of 7 will automatically provide a good return on one's investment, plus the fact that the GRM method is easy to use. For the more sophisticated investor, the GRM is a valuable tool for getting a rough estimate of a building's worth. However, an income approach to valuation, such as those shown in Chapters 17 and 24, should be conducted before an offer to buy is made.

In the cost approach to value, land is valued as though vacant and added to the depreciated cost of all improvements. Table 16:4 demonstrates the basic procedure. Step 1 is to estimate the value of the land upon which the building is located. The land is valued as though vacant using the market comparison approach described earlier. In step 2, the cost of constructing a similar building at today's costs is estimated. These costs include the current prices of building materials, construction wages, architect fees, contractor's services,

COST APPROACH TO VALUE

Table 16:4 | COST APPROACH TO VALUE

Step 1:	Estimate land as though vacant		$ 9,000
Step 2:	Estimate new construction cost of similar building	$34,000	
Step 3:	Less depreciation	−6,000	
Step 4:	Indicated value of building		28,000
Step 5:	Appraised property value by the cost approach		$37,000

building permits, utility hookups, and the like, plus the cost of financing during the construction stage and the cost of construction equipment used at the project site. Step 3 is the calculation of the amount of money that represents the subject building's wear and tear, lack of usefulness, and obsolescence when compared to the new building of step 2. In step 4, depreciation is subtracted from today's construction cost to give the current value of the subject building on a used basis. Step 5 is to add this amount to the land value. Let us work through these steps.

Estimating New Construction Costs   To choose a method of estimating construction costs, one must decide whether cost will be approached on a reproduction or on a replacement basis. **Reproduction cost** is the cost at today's prices of constructing an exact replica of the subject improvements using the same or very similar materials. **Replacement cost** is the cost, at today's prices and using today's methods of construction, for an improvement having the same or equivalent usefulness as the subject property. Replacement cost is the more practical choice of the two as it eliminates nonessential or obsolete features and takes full advantage of current construction materials and techniques. It is the approach that will be described here.

Quantity Survey Method   For the appraiser, there are several ways to estimate construction costs. The choice depends on the degree of accuracy desired and the amount of effort one can afford to expend. As a rule, the greater the accuracy needed, the more effort one must be willing to put forth, and vice versa. The most detailed method of estimating construction costs is the quantity survey method, also known as a **take-off.** This method requires a complete set of building plans and involves making an extensive list that shows the quantity and cost of each item of material plus the labor necessary to install it. For example, one item on the list might read: 73 electrical wall outlets, material cost 48¢ each, installation cost 72¢ each, total cost $87.60. To this is added building permit fees, ground preparation, clean up, and financing costs. Because of the vast number of different parts that go into a building before it is finished, this method of estimating cost is undertaken when a contractor is making a bid on a construction job, and then only when one of the faster methods discussed next will not provide a reasonably accurate estimate.

Instead of looking at each individual building component and the cost of installing it, the **unit-in-place method** (also called the **segregated cost method**) groups construction costs by building trade or stage of construction. For example, instead of estimating the cost of a concrete perimeter foundation in terms of cubic yards of concrete needed, plus the cost of concrete forms, steel reinforcing bars and labor, the unit-in-place method looks at the total cost of installing one linear foot of foundation. The cost per foot is then multiplied by the total number of feet of foundation necessary for the building. Thus, if the cost of a linear foot of foundation is $4, a building that requires 200 feet of foundation would cost $800 for this item.

Unit-in-Place Method

The various equipment items in a building are also treated on a unit-in-place basis. Thus, the installed cost of a toilet, including piping costs, might be $270, a bathtub $310, a washbasin $210, and a stall shower $315. A floor furnace may cost $360 plus $50 for each duct leading away from it. The process is continued until costs have been found for site excavation, foundation, floors and floor coverings, walls, ceilings, roof, interior partitions, doors, windows, cabinets, counter tops, plumbing fixtures, electrical outlets, hot water, heat and air conditioning, attic and wall insulation, rain gutters, and so on. The installed cost of each item includes a reasonable allowance for contractor's fees, architectural costs, and incidental expenses, and the total represents the cost of the building. The only item not included is the cost of financing the building during construction.

Construction cost information can be obtained from material suppliers and building contractors. A more convenient method is to subscribe to a building-cost information service. Several well-known services are the *Marshall and Swift Cost Handbooks, The National Construction Estimator,* the *Dow Building Cost Calculator,* and the *Boeckh Appraisal Manual.* These services are published annually with monthly and quarterly updates, and provide costs for single-family and multi-family residential structures, stores, office buildings, warehouses, factories, and farm buildings. Cost information is available on a quantity survey basis, unit-in-place basis, or square-foot basis.

Square-Foot Method

The most widely used approach for estimating construction costs is the **square-foot method.** It provides reasonably accurate estimates that are faster and simpler to prepare than the quantity survey or unit-in-place methods.

The first step in the square-foot method is to find a newly constructed building that is similar to the subject building in terms of size, type of occupancy, design, materials, and construction quality. This becomes the base or standard building. The cost of the base building is converted to cost per square foot by dividing its current construction cost by the number of square feet in the building.

It is possible to go into the field to locate similar buildings that have just been completed and then to inquire as to the construction cost, but many appraisers rely on published cost handbooks as they provide much more detailed information and are far more convenient to use. When this approach is used, the appraiser selects a cost handbook appropriate to the type of building that he is appraising. From photographs of houses included in the handbook along with brief descriptions of the buildings' features, the appraiser finds a house that most nearly fits the description of the subject house. There he will find the current cost per square foot to construct it. If the subject house has a better quality roof, floor covering, heating system, greater or fewer built-in appliances, plumbing

SQUARE-FOOT METHOD OF COST ESTIMATING   Figure 16:1

```
20 ft
┌──────────────────┐
│                  │
│     GARAGE       │        5 ft
20 ft 20' x 20' = 400 sf        ┌──────────────────────────┐
│                  │            │          30 ft           │
└──────────────────┤            │                          │
                   │            │        DWELLING          │
                   │   PATIO    │    50' x 20' = 1,000 sf   │
                25 ft 20' x 25' = 500 sf  20' x 30' =  600 sf 20 ft
                   │            │     Total:    1,600 sf    │
                   │            │                          │
```

Dwelling Value per Square Foot:

Base Price $21.56
add   +.62 for shake shingles   ①
add   +.96 for air conditioning
subtract –.80 no hardwood flooring

Total $22.34 per square foot

DRIVEWAY
45' x 20' = 900 sf

45 ft

20 ft

20 ft

40 ft

50 ft

COST ESTIMATE:

Dwelling	1,600 sf @ $22.34	=	$35,744	②
	add dishwasher		+290
	add fireplace		+1,050
	subtract garbage disposal		–120
	Dwelling total		$36,964
Garage	400 sf @ $8.00	=	3,200
Driveway	900 sf @ $1.50	=	1,350
Patio	500 sf @ $1.50	=	750
Landscaping (see text)		=	1,000
	Subtotal		$43,264	③

Construction financing, real estate
taxes & title policy, add 8%   3,461

GRAND TOTAL $46,725

fixtures, or has a garage, basement, porch, or swimming pool, the handbook provides costs for each of these.

Figure 16:1 illustrates the calculations involved in the square-foot method. The appraiser begins by measuring the improvements and making a sketch. Using this sketch, he calculates the square footage of each improvement. Since the dwelling is L-shaped, it requires a two-step area calculation. An imaginary line is drawn that divides the house into a 20-by 50-foot rectangle containing 1,000 square feet and a 20-by 30-foot rectangle containing 600 square feet for a total dwelling area of 1,600 square feet. The patio, garage and driveway calculations are self-explanatory in the illustration.

Adjusting the
Base Price

The next step is to adjust the base price of the dwelling shown in the handbook to the subject dwelling. There are two types of adjustments, square foot and lump sum, and they are made in that order. At ① in Figure 16:1, the subject house has shake shingles, and as these are more expensive than the shingles included in the base house the handbook one must add 62¢ per square foot to the base price. The house in the cost handbook is described as having forced air heat; the subject house has forced air heat and central air conditioning. This adds, according to the handbook, 96¢ per square foot.

The base house includes a hardwood floor while the subject has a plywood floor that is 80¢ per square foot cheaper to build. Therefore, 80¢ must be subtracted from the base price. If there were differences in heating equipment, ceiling insulation, or carpeting, they would also be treated as square-foot adjustments. When all square-foot adjustments have been identified and made, they are totaled and multiplied by the number of square feet in the dwelling. To this are added or subtracted lump-sum adjustments for items such as plumbing fixtures, ranges, ovens, dishwashers, fireplaces, and so forth. The base house comes equipped with certain items, and adjustments are made only if the subject property is different. At ② in Figure 16:1, the subject house has a built-in dishwasher and a fireplace that the base house does not have. However, the base house has a garbage disposal that the subject house does not have. The handbook tells the appraiser how many dollars to add or subtract for each of these items. In each lump-sum adjustment the dollar amount includes the cost of the item and the cost of installation and hookup. The "dwelling total" is the current cost of constructing the subject house. If the subject house has a basement, it is measured and multiplied by the handbook value for basements and then added to the dwelling total.

Garage, Landscaping, etc.

The next step is to calculate the construction cost of the garage by multiplying the number of square feet in the subject garage by the price per square foot shown in the handbook for a garage of similar size and construction materials. The same is done for the driveway and patio. Landscaping is a lump-sum addition computed by the unit-in-place method and takes into consideration excavating costs, soil preparation, sod, sprinklers, shrubs, and trees. The subtotal shown at ③ reflects the current cost of replacing everything on the lot at today's material and construction costs. To this are added the costs of construction financing and real estate taxes during construction. A prudent developer will also purchase title insurance to cover the higher value of the property as a result of the new construction. In the illustration, 8% of the construction cost is added for these three items. This results in a grand total of $46,725 for the current construction cost of all the improvements on the subject property.

Index Method

The index method of estimating cost starts with the original cost of construction and adjusts for changes in construction prices. Thus, if an apartment building was built in 1974 at a cost of $732,000 and construction costs have risen 35% since that time, its construction cost today would be calculated as follows:

Original Construction Cost		Index Number		Current Construction Cost
$732,000	×	1.35	=	$988,200

Index numbers are computed and published by the building cost service companies. Although tables list index numbers for buildings constructed as far back as 30 years, the most accurate results are obtained on buildings not more than a few years old, because the index method presumes an identical building will be built, using identical materials and construction techniques. The older a building is, the less likely it would be built exactly the same way today. The index method is fast if one knows the original construction date and cost, and it can be quite useful in appraising unusual or unique buildings when time does not permit a detailed unit-in-place or quantity survey approach.

Estimating Depreciation   Having estimated the current cost of constructing the subject improvements, the next step in the cost approach is to estimate the loss in value due to depreciation since they were built. In making this estimate, we look for three kinds of depreciation: physical deterioration, functional obsolescence, and economic obsolescence.

Physical deterioration results from wear and tear through use, such as a wall-to-wall carpet that has been worn thin, or a dishwasher, garbage disposal, or water heater that must be replaced. Physical deterioration also results from the action of nature in the form of sun, rain, heat, cold, and wind, and from damage due to plants and animal life, such as tree roots breaking sidewalks and termites eating wood. Physical deterioration can also result from neglect (an overflowing bathtub) and from vandalism.

Functional obsolescence results from outmoded equipment (old-fashioned plumbing fixtures in the bathrooms and kitchen), faulty or outdated design (a single bathroom in a three- or four-bedroom house or an illogical room layout), inadequate structural facilities (inadequate wiring to handle today's household appliance loads), and overadequate structural facilities (high ceilings in a home). Functional obsolescence can be summarized as loss of value to the improvements because they are inadequate, overly adequate, or improperly designed for today's needs.

Economic obsolescence is the loss of value due to external forces or events. The effect can be on the improvements or the land or both. For example, if a home costing $80,000 is built in a neighborhood of $40,000 homes, the surrounding homes will detract from the value of the more expensive home. The more expensive home is an overimprovement of the neighborhood, and the structure suffers depreciation because of that. Economic obsolescence can also occur if a once-popular neighborhood becomes undesirable because of air or noise pollution, or because surrounding property owners fail to maintain their properties. In these cases the adverse effect is usually picked up in the land valuation.

All existing improved properties, to a greater or lesser degree, have depreciated, and it is the appraiser's task to calculate an amount of money that reflects the loss of usefulness due to these causes. Let us look at two methods of attaching a dollar amount of depreciation.

Estimating the dollar amount of depreciation by the observed method requires that a list be made of all observed physical deterioration, functional obsolescence, and economic obsolescence. Each observed item is then identified as **curable** or **incurable.** If curable, the cost to cure is estimated. For example, in a 10-year-old house the carpets may need replacing at a cost of $1,250, the exterior need painting at $650, and the sidewalk need repairing at $100. For items that do not need replacement at the moment, but which are partway through their useful lives and will need replacement later, a reserve for replacement is calculated. Thus, if shingles on the roof will need replacing in another 10 years at a cost of $1,200, then $600 would be charged against the house for the 10 years the existing shingles have already been used. To this is added an allowance for the amount of useful life that has expired for physical items that are not expected to be replaced during the useful life span of the improvement (e.g., the foundation, walls, floor, and roof beams).

Observed Method

Curable functional obsolescence is reflected through the cost of modernizing the subject property to current standards. This would include costs such as modernizing an outdated kitchen, installing more closets, and adding better insulation. Loss in value due to incurable functional obsolescence, such as a poor floor plan, is measured by market resistance. Thus, all other things being equal, a house with a good floor plan and a house the same size with a poor one may differ in market value by $2,000. Losses due to economic obsolescence can be

Table 16:5   METHOD FOR CALCULATING TYPICAL DEPRECIATION

Average-Quality Wood-frame House			
Age	Depreciation	Condition	Multiplier
5 years	5%	Excellent	0.70
6 years	6%	Very good	0.80
7 years	7%		
8 years	8%	Good	0.90
9 years	9%		
		Average	1.00
10 years	10%		
11 years	12%	Badly worn	1.15
12 years	14%		
		Worn out	1.30
13 years	16%		
14 years	18%		
15 years	20%		

Example 1: For an 8-year old, average-quality wood-frame house in very good condition, depreciation would be 8% × 0.80 = 6.4%.

Example 2: For an 11-year-old, average-quality, wood-frame house in badly worn condition, depreciation would be 12% × 1.15 = 13.8%.

Source: Marshall and Swift Publishing Co., © 1976. By permission.

handled similarly or through a process that looks at the loss in rental value of the subject property. However, care must be taken to ensure that only economic losses to the building, and not those to the land, are deducted from the building.

Depreciation Tables   Utilizing the observed method will produce a very accurate estimate of depreciation. However, when time and effort are more valuable than precise accuracy, depreciation tables are often useful. These are precalculated for different types of buildings and different types of construction materials and quality. Table 16:5 is a depreciation table prepared by the Marshall and Swift Publishing Company that shows typical depreciation for an average-quality wood-frame house. Beginning with the chronological age of the structure, one finds the basic amount of depreciation. This amount is then multiplied by a "condition multiplier" that reflects the general condition and state of repair of the structure being appraised. Two examples are given in Table 16:5.

After calculating the current construction cost of the subject improvements and estimating the amount of depreciation, the next step is to subtract the amount of depreciation from the current construction cost to get the depreciated value of the improvements. This is added to the value of the land upon which the subject improvements rest. The total is the value of the property by the cost approach.

Final Steps in the Cost Approach

VOCABULARY REVIEW

Match terms a–n with statements 1–14.

a. Adjustments
b. Comparables
c. Correlation process
d. Cost approach
e. Depth tables
f. Economic obsolescence
g. Functional obsolescence
h. Index method
i. Market approach
j. Physical deterioration
k. Replacement cost
l. Reproduction cost
m. Subject property
n. Take-off

1. Properties similar to the subject property that are used to establish the value of the subject property.
2. Cost, at today's prices and using today's methods of construction, of building an improvement having the same usefulness as the subject property.
3. Cost at today's prices of constructing an exact replica of the subject improvements using the same or similar materials.
4. To establish the value of a given property by looking at the prices for which similar properties have recently sold.
5. Property valuation based on land value plus current construction costs less depreciation.
6. The property that is being appraised.
7. Used in adjusting for differences in lot depth when valuing on a front-foot basis.
8. Corrections made to comparable properties to account for differences between them and the subject property.
9. A weighting operation whereby an appraiser can give more weight to the comparables that he feels are most similar to the subject property.
10. A cost-estimating procedure in which the cost and quantity of each item shown in the building plans plus the labor for installation are itemized and totaled.
11. A procedure for estimating the current construction cost of an improvement by multiplying its original construction cost by an inflation factor.

12. Depreciation resulting from wear and tear of the improvements.

13. Depreciation resulting from improvements that are inadequate, overly adequate, or improperly designed for today's needs.

14. Loss of value due to external forces or events.

QUESTIONS AND
PROBLEMS

1. What is meant by the phrase "fair market value"?

2. In your county, is the amount of documentary transfer tax shown on a deed a good indicator of the sale price? Why or why not?

3. When making a market comparison appraisal, how many comparable properties should be used?

4. How useful are asking prices and offers to buy when making a market comparison appraisal?

5. When an appraiser speaks of curable depreciation and incurable depreciation, what does he mean?

6. In the market approach, are the adjustments made to the subject property or to the comparables? Why?

7. Why is it important when valuing vacant land that comparable properties be of similar zoning, neighborhood characteristics, size, and usefulness?

8. Explain the use of gross rent multipliers in valuing real properties. What are the strengths and weaknesses of this method?

9. What are the five steps in valuing an improved property by the cost approach?

10. Explain briefly the square-foot method of estimating construction costs.

ADDITIONAL READINGS

American Institute of Real Estate Appraisers. *The Appraisal of Real Estate,* 6th ed. Chicago: American Institute of Real Estate Appraisers, 1973, 596 pages. Covers the fundamental concepts of real estate value and its appraisal by the market, cost, and income approaches.

Boyce, Byrl N., ed. *Real Estate Appraisal Terminology.* Cambridge, Mass.: Ballinger Publishing Co., 1975, 306 pages. Jointly sponsored by the AIREA and the SREA. Provides definitions for words and phrases used in appraisal. Contains sections on depreciation, weights and measure conversions, architecture, and sources of information for appraisers.

17

Appraisal: The Income Approach

Capitalize: to convert future income to current value

Highest and best use: that use of a parcel of land which will produce the greatest return

Illiquidity risk: the chance that an asset will have to be sold at less than market value in order to convert it to cash quickly

Investment recapture: return of investment; purpose is to offset decline in the value of the investment due to depreciation

Net operating income (NOI): gross income less operating expenses, vacancies, and collection losses

Operating expenses: expenditures necessary to maintain the production of income

Pro forma statement: a projected annual operating statement that shows expected income, operating expenses and net operating income

Reversionary value: the expected worth of a property at the end of the projected holding period

Scheduled gross, Projected gross: the estimated rent that a fully-occupied property can be expected to produce on an annual basis

The income approach to real estate appraisal considers the expected monetary returns from a property in light of returns on investment currently being demanded by investors. To illustrate, suppose that an available investment promises to return $900 per year in net income to an investor, and at any time the investor wants to withdraw, the money he originally invested will be returned to him in full. The value of this investment depends on the rate of return that must be paid to attract investors. If an investor is willing to accept a 9% per year return on his invested dollars, he would pay $10,000

$$IV = \frac{900}{9\%} = 10,000$$

for this investment opportunity. The calculation is as follows:

$$\frac{\text{income}}{\text{rate}} = \text{value}, \quad \text{or} \quad \frac{\$900}{0.09} = \$10,000$$

This is called capitalizing the income stream. To **capitalize** means to convert future income to current value. In this example, the capitalized value of $900 per year is $10,000, because for each 9 cents of anticipated annual income, $1 will be invested.

The capitalized value of $900 per year changes as the return per dollar invested changes. If a rate of 10% per year is necessary to attract investors, the present value of $900 per year is worth $9,000. This is because a $900 return per year on a $9,000 investment yields the investor a 10% return per year. On the other hand, if investors are willing to accept 8% per year, we divide the $900 annual income by 8% and obtain $11,250, as the value of this investment.

CALCULATING RATE OF RETURN   In applying the income approach to real property, the appraiser is concerned with three things: (1) how much income the property will provide for its owners, (2) how long the income will last, and (3) the rate of return on investment that must be paid to attract investors. Let us begin with the last question by looking at three well-known methods for determining the return on investment that must be paid to attract investors. They are the summation, direct comparison, and band of investment methods.

Summation Method   In the **summation method**, or **built-up method**, the appraiser determines a rate of return on investment by adding together the safe rate, the business risk rate, the illiquidity rate, and the investment management rate:

	per year (%)
Safe rate	8.0
Business risk	2.0
Illiquidity	0.5
Management	0.4
TOTAL	10.9% (Risk rate)

The safe rate, or pure interest rate, is the rate of interest that an investor can obtain by purchasing U.S. government bonds. It is so named because an investor purchasing these bonds is guaranteed by the U.S. government that he will receive his interest and principal on time and in the full amount due him.

For real estate to attract capital, it must offer investors what the U.S. government is offering *plus* an allowance because real estate is riskier, more illiquid, and takes more management. Consequently, an amount to reflect the risk of any loss of investment in the subject property is added to the safe rate. To this is added compensation for the fact that U.S. bonds can be sold and converted to cash in a week, whereas real estate can take months to convert to cash, perhaps forcing the investor to sell below market value to raise cash quickly. Finally, real estate requires more time to manage and the investor must pay higher sales commissions than on government bonds. The total of these four rates is the **risk rate,** which is the rate of return on investment that investors must be offered to attract capital into real estate.

Direct Comparison

As the name implies, the direct comparison approach to finding an appropriate return on investment (risk rate) requires that the appraiser locate several recent sales of properties similar to the subject property. However, instead of placing primary emphasis on what the comparables sold for, as he would in a market approach to value, the appraiser is more interested in the returns that investors are getting on comparable properties.

Comparables should be as similar as possible. Thus, if one were appraising an apartment building, one would look at other apartment buildings, not office or industrial properties. These apartment buildings should be as similar as possible in number of units, age, rent level, upkeep, operating expenses, and neighborhood characteristics. A quality adjustment is applied for any dissimilarities. Table 17:1 illustrates the direct comparison method.

Band of Investment Method

The band of investment method for calculating a return on investment rate is based on the fact that more than eight

Table 17:1

DIRECT COMPARISON

Line		Compara- ble A	Compara- ble B	Compara- ble C
1	Annual net operating income after depreciation	$31,600	$37,500	$33,810
2	Sale price of property	$310,000	$357,000	$345,000
3	Return on investment (Line 1 divided by line 2)	10.2%	10.5%	9.8%
4	Quality adjustment	1.00	0.95	1.05
5	Adjusted return on investment (Line 3 times line 4)	10.2%	10.0%	10.3%

Correlation:	Comparable A	$10.2\% \times 0.40 = 4.08\%$
	Comparable B	$10.0\% \times 0.20 = 2.00\%$
	Comparable C	$10.3\% \times 0.40 = 4.12\%$

INDICATED RETURN ON INVESTMENT   10.20%

out of ten real estate transactions are financed with debt secured by mortgages or trust deeds. If, for example, mortgage debt at an interest rate of 9% per year is available from lenders for up to 70% of the fair market value on good quality rental apartment buildings, second mortgage financing is available at 11% interest for an additional 10% of value, and on the final 20% of value, which is the cash down payment the investor must make—investors are requiring returns of 15%—the rate would be calculated as in Table 17:2:

Table 17:2

BAND OF INVESTMENT

Financing Source	Loan to Value Ratio		Return		Weighted Interest
First mortgage (least risk)	70%	×	9%	=	6.3%
Second mortgage (more risk)	10%	×	11%	=	1.1%
Equity (most risk) —	20%	×	15%	=	3.0%
			TOTAL		10.4%

Notice that the return in each financing "band" varies with the risk that is being taken. If the value of the property drops, the equity holder (the owner), is in the most vulnerable position. A drop of 10% in the overall value of the property erases one half of his investment; a drop of 20% in overall value wipes him out entirely. Therefore, the equity investor demands the highest return of the three capital providers. The second mortgage holder is in a less risky position than the equity holder as the value of the property would have to drop more than 20% before his collateral would be jeopardized. Thus, the second mortgage holder is willing to accept less return than the equity holder. The first mortgage holder is willing to accept an even smaller return as his financial position is the best insulated against loss.

Once the appraiser knows the rate of return necessary to attract investors, his next step is to prepare a forecast of income and expenses for the subject property.

INCOME AND EXPENSE FORECASTING

The goal of income and expense forecasting is to project the probable net income that may be expected from a property. Not only does the net income provide the underlying basis on which value is determined; it is also a critical process, because each $1 error in annual net income can make a difference of from $5 to $10 in the market value of the property.

The best starting point in projecting gross income and expenses is the actual record of income and expenses for the subject property over the past 3 to 5 years. Although the future will not be an exact repetition of the past, the past record of a property is usually the best guide to future performance. These historical data are blended with the current operating experience of similar buildings and the appraiser's estimates as to what the future will bring. The result is a projected operating statement, such as the one shown in Table 17:3, which begins with the estimated rents that the property can be expected to produce on an annual basis. This is the **projected gross**, or **scheduled gross**, and represents expected rentals from the subject property on a fully occupied basis.

Vacancy and collection loss projections are based partly on the building's past experience and partly on the appraiser's judgment as to what may be expected based on the operating experience of similar buildings. For example, if the subject property has experienced unusually low vacancy rates, the appraiser may be justified in using a higher vacancy factor in his forecast if a higher rate is more typical. This would definitely be the case if the low vacancy rate could be traced to below-market rents or to superior management. This is be-

Table 17:3

PROJECTED ANNUAL OPERATING STATEMENT
(Also called a Pro Forma Statement)

Scheduled gross annual income	$84,000	
Vacancy allowance and collection losses	4,200	
Effective Gross Income		$79,800
Operating Expenses		
Property taxes	9,600	
Hazard and liability insurance	1,240	
Property management	5,040	
Janitorial services	1,500	
Gardener	1,200	
Utilities	3,940	
Trash pickup	600	
Repairs and maintenance	5,000	
Other	1,330	
Reserves		
Furniture & furnishings	1,200	
Stoves & refrigerators	600	
Furnace &/or air-conditioning system	700	
Plumbing & electrical	800	
Roof	750	
Exterior painting	900	
Total Operating Expenses		$34,400
Net Operating Income		$45,400

OPERATING EXPENSE RATIO: $34,400 ÷ $79,800 = 43.1%

cause the appraiser is attempting to forecast under normal conditions, that is, with rents at market levels and with competent, but not necessarily superior, management. Similarly, if the subject property is experiencing higher than normal vacancies, the problem may be curable by lowering rents, changing management, or refurbishing the property. Under these circumstances, the appraiser would base his forecast on these problems being corrected.

Operating Expenses   The next step is to itemize anticipated **operating expenses** for the subject property. These are expenses necessary to maintain the production of income. For an apartment building without recreational facilities or an elevator, the list in Table 17:3 is typical. Again, the appraiser will consider both the property's past operating expenses and what he expects those expenses to be in the future. For example, if the property is currently being managed by the owner and little or no management costs are shown, the appraiser will include a typical fee, say 6% of the gross rents.

Not included as operating expenses are outlays for capital improvements, such as the construction of a new swimming pool, the expansion of parking facilities, and assessments for street improvements. Improvements are not classified as expenses because they increase the usefulness of the property, which increases the rent the property will generate and therefore the property's value.

Reserves for replacement are set up for items that do not *Reserves* require an expenditure of cash each year. To illustrate, lobby furniture (and furniture in apartments rented as "furnished") wears out a little each year, eventually requiring replacement. Suppose that these items cost $7,200 and are expected to last 6 years, at which time they must be replaced. An annual $1,200 reserve for replacement not only reflects a cost for that portion of the furniture that was used up during the year, but also reminds us that, to avoid having to meet the entire furniture and furnishings replacement cost out of one year's income, money should be set aside each year. In a similar manner, reserves are established for other items that must be replaced or repaired more than once during the life of the building, but not yearly. Depreciation of the building itself is not included here; it will be accounted for later.

At this point, the **operating expense ratio** can be calculated. *Operating* It is obtained by dividing the total operating expense number *Expense Ratio* by the effective gross income. The resulting ratio provides a handy yardstick against which similar properties can be compared. If the operating expense ratio is out of step, it signals the need for further investigation.

The operating expense total is then subtracted from the *Net Operating* effective gross income. The balance that remains is the **net** *Income* **operating income.** From the net operating income the property owner receives both a return *on* and a return *of* his investment. The return *on* his investment is the interest he receives for investing his money in the property. The return of investment is to compensate him for the fact that the building is wearing out.

INVESTMENT
RECAPTURE

If the net operating income from a property could be expected to remain constant forever, and if improvements were immune to changes in value due to depreciation, one could simply value the property by the method shown on page 368. However, subject improvements do wear out with use and suffer functional and economic obsolescence as they grow older. Thus, income will not remain constant forever, and, as the improvements progress toward the end of their economic life, they will drop in value. The simplest and least accurate method of handling this problem is to assume that the subject improvements will depreciate on a straight-line basis and that net operating income will fall in tandem with the depreciated value of the improvements. Thus, if the expected economic life span of a building is 50 years, the assumption is that 2% of the original value of the building is lost each year and, as a result, net income declines 2% each year. If investors are currently demanding returns *on* investment of 10.2%, then to also allow an investor a return *of* his investment, an additional 2% must be added for a total capitalization rate of 12.2% per year. The 2% return *of* investment is the **recapture rate**.

on invest
of invest

BUILDING RESIDUAL
TECHNIQUE

Because land is not considered to depreciate like buildings, traditionally it has been separated from the improvements in the income valuation process. One well-known method of doing this is the **building residual technique**. Table 17:4 illustrates the procedure.

The first step in the building residual technique requires the appraiser to know the net operating income of the property, the market value of the land as though vacant, the risk rate, and the estimated economic life of the improvements. The appraiser then calculates the amount of net operating income attributable to the land by multiplying the market value of the land by the return that investors are demanding on their investments (the risk rate). This amount is then subtracted from the net operating income; the remainder is the income from the property attributable to the building.

BUILDING RESIDUAL TECHNIQUE

Table 17:4

Step 1: Subtract required return on land from property's net operating income to get income attributable to the building.

Net operating income	$45,400
Less return to land:	
Market value of land $60,000	
times the risk rate $\times 10.2\%$	
	$-6,120$
Equals net operating income attributable to the building	$39,280

Step 2: Develop the capitalization rate for the building.

Return on investment (risk rate)	10.2%
Return of investment (recapture rate)	+2.0%
Capitalization rate for the building	12.2%

Step 3: Value the building.

$$\frac{\text{Income attributed to the building}}{\text{Building capitalization rate}} = \text{building value}$$

$$\frac{\$39,280}{12.2\%} = \$321,967$$

Step 4: Add back land value to find total value of property.

Building value from Step 3		
Plus market value of the land	=	+60,000
TOTAL VALUE		$381,967
Rounded to		$382,000

As the building must provide not only a return on investment but also a return of investment, in step 2 the risk rate of 10.2% is added to the recapture rate of 2% to obtain a capitalization rate for the building. In step 3, the total is divided into the $39,280 to obtain the building's value. The last step is to add the building's capitalized value to the market value of the land. This method is called the building residual technique because the building is valued on the residual portion of the net operating income that remains after the land has been "paid" in accordance with its market worth.

With the **land residual technique,** the building is valued on its replacement cost, and the return *on* and *of* investment in the building is deducted from the net operating income. The

LAND RESIDUAL TECHNIQUE

remainder (the residual) is attributed to the land and, when divided by the return on investment, gives the value of the land. This is added to the replacement cost of the building to obtain the total value of the property. Table 17:5 summarizes the procedure.

Table 17:5

LAND RESIDUAL TECHNIQUE

Step 1: Calculate the return required by the building.

Replacement cost of the building	$321,967 ·
Times building capitalization rate	×12.2%
Equals return required by building	$ 39,280

Step 2: Subtract the return required by the building from the net operating income produced by the property.

Net operating income of property	$45,400
Less return to the building	−39,280
Equals income attributed to land	$ 6,120

Step 3: Value of land.

$$\frac{\text{Income attributed to the land}}{\text{Risk rate}} = \text{land value}$$

$$\frac{\$6,120}{10.2\%} = \$60,000$$

Step 4: Add land and building value to find total value of the property.

Land value from Step 3	$ 60,000
Plus replacement cost of building =	+321,967
TOTAL VALUE	$381,967
Rounded to	$382,000

A special requirement when using the land residual technique is that, to obtain an accurate value for the land, the subject property must be developed to its greatest income-producing potential, i.e., its **highest and best use.** When this requirement is met, both the land residual and building residual approaches will result in the same value for the property. When the land is not developed to its greatest income-producing potential, the net income will be so low that the land will be undervalued.

INCOME PROPERTY—AS SEEN BY   Figure 17:1

(A) STRAIGHT-LINE CAPITALIZATION   (B) TYPICAL OPERATING EXPERIENCE

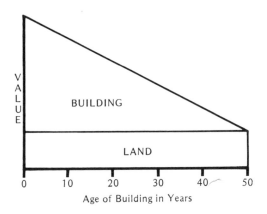

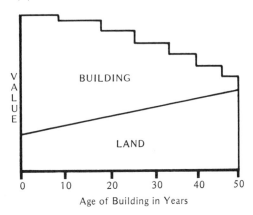

Although the income approach techniques just discussed take into consideration the expected economic life span of the improvements, they have several weaknesses. The two most important are due to the assumption that the value of the property will decline at an even rate throughout its life, and that the income it generates will follow the same pattern. Figure 17:1A illustrates this assumption. However, experience has shown that rents do not drop immediately after a building is constructed. Instead, they stay at the same level for several years, particularly where tenants have fixed-rent leases lasting several years. Then rents drop and stabilize at a new level for several years, dropping and stabilizing several times more until the building is either rebuilt or torn down. This pattern is illustrated in Figure 17:1B. When one adds to this the presence of inflation that may cause rents to rise instead of fall, it can be seen that a better tool is necessary to convert expected net operating income to a single value that will serve as a fair market price for the subject property. This tool is **annuity capitalization.** Not only is this technique capable of handling changes in expected income streams with ease, but it also eliminates the need for a year-by-year forecast of depreciation. Moreover, annuity capitalization eliminates the need to divide

ANNUITY CAPITALIZATION

Table 17:6

COMPOUND INTEREST & PRESENT VALUE TABLES FOR 10% PER YEAR

Year	Column A Compound Interest	Column B Present Value	Column C Accumulated Present Value
1	1.1000	.9091	0.9091
2	1.2100	.8264	1.7355
3	1.3310	.7513	2.4869
4	1.4641	.6830	3.1699
5	1.6105	.6209	3.7908
6	1.7716	.5645	4.3553
7	1.9487	.5132	4.8684
8	2.1436	.4665	5.3349
9	2.3579	.4241	5.7590
10	2.5937	.3855	6.1446
11	2.8531	.3505	6.4951
12	3.1384	.3186	6.8137
13	3.4523	.2897	7.1034
14	3.7975	.2633	7.3667
15	4.1772	.2394	7.6061
16	4.5950	.2176	7.8237
17	5.0545	.1978	8.0216
18	5.5599	.1799	8.2014
19	6.1159	.1635	8.3649
20	6.7275	.1486	8.5136
25	10.8347	.0923	9.0770
30	17.4494	.0573	9.4269
35	28.1024	.0356	9.6442
40	45.2593	.0221	9.7791
45	72.8905	.0137	9.8628
50	117.3909	.0085	9.9148
60	304.4816	.0033	9.9672
70	789.7470	.0013	9.9873
80	2,048.4002	.0005	9.9951
90	5,313.0226	.0002	9.9981
100	13,780.6123	.0001	9.9993
∞	∞	.0000	10.0000

the property's income between the land and the improvements when, in fact, the contributions of the two are inseparable.

The basis of the annuity capitalization method is compound interest and its mathematical inversion, the present value of $1. Although professional appraisers have developed numerous sophisticated tables for converting future income and expenses into current dollars, they all have their basis in

the compound interest and present value tables we shall discuss here. Briefly, compound interest is "interest on interest."
Thus, $1 invested today at 10% per year compound interest
will become $1.10 at the end of 1 year. If this $1.10 is left to
continue growing at 10% per year, at the end of the second
year it will be worth $1.21, at the end of the third year $1.33,
and at the end of the fourth year $1.46. Left to grow at 10%
per year compounded, $1 will reach the values shown in
Column A of Table 17:6.

Present Worth

The figures in Column B show how much money must be
invested at 10% interest per year to have exactly $1 in the
year shown. Whereas compound interest tables start with
exactly $1.00 and tell how much it will grow, a **present value
table,** also called a **present worth table,** tells how much we
must start with in order to finish with $1.00. To illustrate, the
number in Column B opposite year 1, is .9091. This can be
interpreted as $.9091 or as 90.91¢. If this amount is invested
at 10% interest per year for a period of 1 year, it will earn
9.09¢ in interest and together with the original 90.91¢ investment, will be worth $1. As an aid to understanding this pro-
cess, it is sometimes helpful to think of 90.91¢ rounded off to
whole cents, that is, as 91¢. Ninety-one cents invested at 10%
interest will earn 9¢ and together with the original 91¢ investment, will be worth $1.00 a year from now.

The number in the present value column opposite year 2
is .8264, which is $.8264 or 82.64¢. If 82.64¢ is invested for
2 years and earns 10% per year compounded, it will be worth
$1.00 at the end of 2 years. Again using whole cents for ex-
planation purposes, the arithmetic is as follows:

Original investment	83¢
Interest, first year at 10%	+8¢
Accumulation, end of first year	91¢
Interest, second year at 10%	+9¢
Accumulation, end of second year	$1.00

Notice that numbers in the present value column are recip-
rocals of numbers in the compound interest column. In other

words, the number .9091 is the result of dividing 1.1000 into 1. Similarly, .8264 is the result of dividing 1.2100 into 1. This is how the present value table is constructed and why the compound interest table is the source of all income valuation tables.

The numbers in Column C represent an accumulation of the numbers in Column B. Thus, the number 1.7355 at year 2 in Column C is the sum of years 1 and 2 in Column B. At year 3, the accumulated present value figure 2.4869 is the sum of .9091, .8264, and .7513. The purpose of an accumulated table is to reduce the number of mathematical steps necessary when valuing a property that has a stable net income.

Thus far, we have been talking in terms of $1. Once we know what happens to $1.00, by multiplying we can learn what happens to larger amounts of money. For example, if $1 grows to $1.10 in one year, $1,000 would grow to $1,100 in the same length of time. Similarly, if $.7513 will grow to $1.00 in 3 years at 10% compound interest, $75.13 will grow to $100, $7,513 to $10,000, and $751,300 to $1,000,000.

Valuing the Net Operating Income
How are these tables applied to appraising income property? Suppose that you are asked to value an income-producing property. After conducting your investigation you anticipate that rentals will have to be reduced in 1 year upon the expiration of current tenant leases. You estimate rents will remain at the new level for another 4 years, at which time the property will be sold. The dollar figures in your forecast are as follows:

Year	Net Operating Income
1	$8,000
2	$8,000
3	$6,000
4	$6,000
5	$6,000

Estimated value of land and improvements
at the end of the fifth year: $40,000.

In appraising this building, we want to know how many dollars an investor would be justified in paying today in order to receive the above listed amounts of money, assuming that he wants a 10% return on his investment, as well as the return of his investment.

For each dollar of income received 1 year from now, the investor is justified in paying 90.91¢ today. Therefore, the $8,000 in net income he expects to receive in 1 year is worth .9091 × $8,000, or $7,273. (That is, the present value of $8,000 received 1 year from today, discounted at 10% interest, is $7,273.) For $1.00 received 2 years from now, the investor is warranted in paying 82.64¢. Therefore, the $8,000 the subject property is expected to earn in the second year has a present value of .8264 × $8,000 = $6,611.

The present value of $1.00 received 3 years from now is 75.13¢. This makes the $6,000 expected at that time worth $4,508 in today's dollars. The $6,000 received in the fourth year is worth .6830 × $6,000 = $4,098, and the $6,000 received in the fifth year from operations is worth .6209 × $6,000 = $3,725. Five years from today, it is also estimated that the owner can sell the property for $40,000. This is the **reversion** or **reversionary value.** The present value of the reversion is $40,000 × .6209 = $24,836. The present value of the 5 years of income plus the reversion indicates that the value of this property today is $51,051. This is summarized in Table 17:7.

Valuing the Reversion

Table 17:7

Year [a]	Net Operating Income		Present Value Factor		Present Value of Net Operating Income
1	$8,000	×	.9091	=	$7,273
2	$8,000	×	.8264	=	$6,611
3	$6,000	×	.7513	=	$4,508
4	$6,000	×	.6830	=	$4,098
5	$6,000	×	.6209	=	$3,725
Present value of the income stream				=	$26,215
Add the present value of the reversion:					
5	$40,000	×	.6209	=	$24,836
		Total Property Value Today			$51,051
		Round to			$51,000

[a] Amounts are presumed to be received at the end of each year.

Table 17:8

Years	Net Operating Income per year		Present Value Multiplier		Present Value of Net Operating Income
1–2	$8,000	×	1.7355	=	$13,884
3–5	$6,000	×	(3.7908 − 1.7355)	=	$12,332
	Present value of the income stream			=	$26,216
	Add the present value of the reversion:				
5	$40,000	×	.6209	=	$24,836
			Total Property Value Today		$51,052
			Round to		$51,000

Whenever the expected returns from a property remain constant for 2 or more years, it may be possible to cut down the number of steps by using the accumulated present value factors in Column C of Table 17:6. Using the property just discussed, the calculations would be as shown in Table 17:8.

For years 1 and 2, the present value multiplier of 1.7355 represents the value today of $1 received 1 year from now plus $1 received 2 years from now, both discounted at 10% per year. Since the property is expected to produce $8,000 per year in each of its first 2 years, this amounts to $8,000 × 1.7355. For years 3 through 5, take the present value factor for 5 years (3.7908) and subtract the factor for 2 years (1.7355). Then multiply the difference of 2.0553 by $6,000 to get $12,322. To this is added the present value of the reversion.

Instead of having to calculate a rate of depreciation for each year, depreciation (or appreciation if it can be reasonably expected) is built into the estimate of the subject property's reversion value. Thus, if the buyer of this property receives $8,000 per year for 2 years, then $6,000 a year for 3 years, and then sells for $40,000, he will not only recover his $51,051 investment, but will also earn 10% on each dollar for each year it was invested.

Future Increases   Because of inflationary pressures, it may be reasonable to forecast stable or increased rents as a building grows older and, when it is finally torn down, a substantial increase in the value of the land beneath it. To demonstrate, suppose that we want to appraise an apartment building that is currently producing a net operating income of $100,000 per year. Given the location of the building and inflationary expectations, it is expected that, although the building will age, the number of dollars generated in annual net operating income will remain constant until the building is removed. At that time, projected to be 40 years from now, it is estimated the property will be worth $1,000,000. If investors are currently demanding returns of 10% per year on their investments, as well as a return of their investment capital, what is the value of this property in today's market?

In Column C of Table 17:6 we go to year 40 and find that the accumulated present value of $1 per year for 40 years is 9.7791. Thus, the present value of $100,000 per year is 9.7791 × $100,000 = $977,910. To calculate the present value of the $1,000,000 reversion, we go to year 40 in Column B and multiply as follows: .0221 × $1,000,000 = $22,100. Adding together $22,100 and the $977,910, we find that the value of the property is $1,000,010, rounded to $1,000,000.

One apparent problem of this method lies in trying to estimate income and resale value several decades from now. Surprisingly, however, the difference in present value between a life of 40 years and one of 50 years is not that significant. The proof is in Column C, where it can be seen that the present value of $1 a year for 40 years is $9.7791, while for 50 years it is $9.9148. Applied to the property just described, the difference is $991,480 − $977,910 = $13,570, a difference of only 1.4%. Underestimating the land value by $1,000,000 forty years from now also makes a small difference. The present value of $2,000,000 forty years from now is .0221 × $2,000,000 = $44,200. This is only $22,100 (or 2.2%) more than the present value of $1,000,000.

Errors in Forecasting

The point here is that, although the most distant years are the hardest to forecast, the errors made there are the least significant. As Column C shows, even when an asset has an annual income stream expected to last 60 years, given a discount rate of 10% per year, 61% of the property's present worth is accounted for in the first 10 years and 85% by the end of the twentieth year. With higher discount rates, the immediate future is even more important. For example, using a discount rate of 15% per year and an asset with a lifespan of 60 years, 75% of the present worth is generated in the first

10 years and 94% by the end of the twentieth year. Only when the discount rate is relatively low do returns from the distant future take on a significant present worth. For example, at a discount rate of 5%, a 60-year income stream generates 41% of its present worth in 10 years, 66% in 20 years, and 81% in 30 years.

VALUING LEASEHOLDS

Like fee simple title, the right to use real property under a lease arrangement can become quite valuable. Suppose that 10 years ago a parcel of vacant urban land was leased to a parking lot operator for a contract rent of $12,000 per year for 15 years. Today, a similar parcel of land nearby is leased to another parking lot operator for $22,000 a year on a 5-year lease. This transaction indicates that the economic rental value of the first parcel is now $22,000 per year. Yet the operator has a lease contract that allows him to use the land for 5 more years at $12,000 per year. As a result, his lease has become quite valuable, for it entitles him to pay $10,000 per year below comparable rates for the next 5 years.

The value of the lessee's interest (the leasehold estate) is the present worth of the savings that he will enjoy. Presuming a discount rate of 10% per year, Column C in Table 17:6 tells us that $1 per year for 5 years has a present value of $3.7908. Therefore, the present value of saving $10,000 per year is $37,908. This is the value of the lease. It decreases each year and disappears on the day that the lease expires, because the lessee must then negotiate for a new lease at prevailing rates.

The valuation of this parcel of land from the standpoint of the fee simple owner is the present value of the remaining 5 years of lease income at $12,000 per year, plus the present value of the property when the lease expires; i.e., the reversion.

A leasehold interest can also take on a negative value. In the parking lot example, if comparable rents dropped to $7,000 per year and the lot operator was locked into paying $12,000 for 5 more years, not only would his lease have no value, but he would have to pay to be rid of it. How much would he pay? At 10% discount, the amount would be 3.7908 × $5,000 = $18,954.

In periods of rising rents, the lessee is financially better off with a longer lease; during periods of falling rents, a short lease is to his advantage. From the standpoint of the fee owner, the opposite is true.

The most technically advanced income appraisal method is the mortgage equity technique. It combines the sophistication of the present value tables with available mortgage financing. Very briefly, the assumption of this technique is that the buyer of an income-producing property will finance his purchase at terms currently available in the mortgage markets. Therefore, instead of applying the net operating income to the entire purchase price of the property, a deduction is made for mortgage interest. The remainder is the return on the investor's equity, hence the term "mortgage equity." This technique will be covered in Chapter 24.

MORTGAGE EQUITY APPRAISING

In this and the previous chapter, we have described the three approaches to real estate valuation. Whenever possible, all three should be used to provide an indication, as well as a crosscheck, of a property's value. If the marketplace is acting rationally and is not restricted in any way, all three approaches will produce the same value. If one approach is out of line with the others, it may indicate an error in the appraiser's work or a problem in the market itself. It is not unusual to find individual sales that seem out of line with prevailing market prices. Similarly, there are times when buyers will temporarily bid the market price of a property above its replacement cost.

CHOICE OF APPROACHES

For certain types of real property, some approaches are more suitable than others. This is especially true for single-family residences. Here the appraiser must rely almost entirely on the market and cost approaches, as very few houses are sold on their ability to generate cash rent. Unless the appraiser can develop a measure of the "psychic income" in home ownership, relying heavily on rental value will lead to a property value below the market and cost approaches. Applying all three approaches to special-purpose buildings may also prove to be impractical. For example, in valuing a church, bridge, or courthouse, the income and market approaches have limited applicability.

CORRELATING THE THREE APPROACHES

The appraiser's final step is to correlate in dollars the market, cost, and income approaches for the subject property. The appraiser assigns to each approach a weighting factor based on his judgment as to which of the approaches are the most relevant in valuing the property. To demonstrate, he might correlate a single-family house in the following manner:

Market approach	$49,000 × 75% =	$36,750
Cost approach	$48,000 × 20% =	$9,600
Income approach	$45,000 × 5% =	$2,250
FINAL INDICATED VALUE		$48,600

What the appraiser is saying here is that recent sales of comparable properties have the most influence on today's sales prices. He also points out that we must not overlook the fact that the same house can be built for $1,000 less. However, by weighting the cost approach at only 20%, the appraiser is saying that most house buyers want to move in quickly and not wait until a house can be built from scratch. By weighting the income approach by only 5%, the appraiser is recognizing that houses in the area are rarely purchased for rental purposes.

It is important to realize that the appraised value is the appraiser's best *estimate* of the subject property's worth. Thus, no matter how painstakingly it is done, property valuation requires the appraiser to make many subjective judgments as he develops his estimate of a property's worth. Because of this, it is not unusual for three highly qualified appraisers to look at the same property and produce three substantially different appraised values. It is also important to recognize that an appraised value is as of a specific date. For example, if a property was valued at $58,500 on December 18, 1976, the more time that has elapsed since that date, the less accurate that value is as an indication of the property's current worth.

CHARACTERISTICS OF VALUE

Up to this point we have been primarily concerned with value based on evidence found in the marketplace. Before concluding this chapter, let us briefly touch on what creates value, the principles of real property valuation, and appraisal for purposes other than market value.

For a good or service to have value in the marketplace, it must possess four characteristics: demand, utility, scarcity, and transferability. **Demand** is a need or desire coupled with the purchasing power to fill it, whereas **utility** is the ability of a good or service to fill that need. **Scarcity** means there must be a short supply relative to demand. Air, for example, has utility and is in demand, but it is not scarce. Finally, a good or service must be **transferable** to have value to anyone other than the person possessing it.

The **principle of anticipation** reflects the fact that people will pay for a property what they feel they will obtain from it in the future. Thus, the buyer of a home anticipates receiving shelter plus the psychic benefits of home ownership enjoyment.

PRINCIPLES OF VALUE

The **principle of balance** holds that there must be a balance between land uses in a community. In other words, not all the land in a city can be used for high-income-producing purposes such as stores and offices. There must also be land for apartments and houses.

The **principle of substitution** rests on the premise that although real estate is heterogeneous both physically and legally, it is nonetheless quite substitutable from the user's standpoint. In fact, without this neither the market comparison nor the income approach would be possible in real estate appraisal. The principle of substitution also plays an important role in setting an upper limit on prices. If there are two similar houses for sale, or two similar apartments for rent, the lowest priced one will generally be purchased or rented first.

The **principle of highest and best use** reminds us that the present use of a parcel of land may not be the use that makes it the most valuable. Take, for instance, a 30-year-old house located at a busy intersection in a shopping area. To place a value on that property based on its continued use as a residence would be erroneous and misleading, for the house is not

Principle of Highest and Best Use

the highest and best use of the land. Highest and best use changes with the passage of time.

The **principle of competition** recognizes that where substantial profits are being made competition will be encouraged. For example, if apartment rents increase to the point where owners of existing apartment buildings are making substantial profits, builders and investors will be encouraged to build more apartment buildings.

Supply and Demand   Applied to real estate, the **principle of supply and demand** refers to the ability of people to pay for land coupled with the relative scarcity of land. Thus, in evaluating a property's potential worth, attention must be given to such matters on the demand side as population growth, personal income, and the tastes and preferences of people. On the supply side, one must look at the available supply of land and its relative scarcity. When the supply of land is limited and demand is great, the result is rising land prices. Conversely, where land is abundant and there are relatively few buyers, supply and demand will be in balance at only a few cents per square foot.

The **principle of change** serves as a reminder that real property uses are always in a state of change. Although it may be imperceptible on a day-to-day basis, change can easily be seen when longer periods of time are considered. Because the present value of a property is related to its future uses, the more potential changes that can be identified, the more accurate the estimate of its present worth.

The **principle of conformity** is that despite varying construction costs, properties in the same neighborhood will tend to conform in price. This was illustrated on page 362 with the example of the $80,000 house built in the $40,000 neighborhood.

Diminishing Marginal Returns   The principle of **diminishing marginal returns,** also called the principle of contribution, refers to the relationship between added cost and the value it returns. It tells us that we should invest dollars whenever they will return to us more than $1 of value and should stop when each dollar invested returns less than $1 in value.

The **principle of integration and disintegration** refers to the life cycle of all material things. In real estate, the first phase of the cycle is called integration or development, wherein raw land is developed into houses, stores, offices, etc. Once built up, the maturity phase begins. This period is marked by stability in land uses. As time passes, the disintegration phase is reached as wear and tear take their toll. The full cycle typically takes 40 to 60 years and is sometimes followed by redevelopment, in which case the cycle repeats itself.

When we hear the word "value," we tend to think of market value. However, at any given moment in time, a single property can have other values too. This is because value is very much affected by the purpose for which the valuation was performed. The following list gives 20 commonly found types of value.

MULTIPLE MEANINGS OF THE WORD VALUE

1. Assessed value
2. Book value
3. Cash value
4. Capitalized value
5. Condemnation value
6. Estate tax value
7. Exchange value
8. Insurance value
9. Liquidation value
10. Loan value
11. Nuisance value
12. Objective value
13. Plottage value
14. Potential value
15. Rental value
16. Replacement value
17. Reproduction value
18. Salvage value
19. Subjective value
20. Terms value

Assessed value is the value given a property by the county tax assessor for purposes of property taxation. **Book value** is value as seen strictly from an accounting or bookkeeping standpoint. Its primary purpose is in connection with income taxes; as a rule, it is a very poor indicator of market value. **Cash value** refers to what a property is worth on an all-cash-sale basis, and is synonymous with market value. **Capitalized value** is the present value of a property's future net operating income.

Condemnation value is the value placed on a property as a result of an action in eminent domain. By law, it should be equivalent to the market value of the property. **Estate tax value** is the value that federal and state taxation authorities establish for a dead person's property; it is used to calculate the amount of estate taxes that must be paid. **Exchange value** is the value of a property as determined by the marketplace for purposes of exchanging it for something else of value.

Insurance Value   **Insurance value** is concerned with the cost of replacing damaged property. It differs from market value in two major respects: (1) the value of the land is not included, as it is presumed only the structures are destructible, and (2) the amount of coverage is based on the replacement cost of the structures. **Liquidation value** is the price a seller would be forced to take if he were in a hurry to sell. It is lower than market value. **Loan value** is the value set on a property for the purpose of applying a loan-to-value ratio in order to calculate the size of a loan. The **nuisance value** of a property is the price that would probably be paid to be rid of an obnoxious, annoying, or otherwise objectionable condition.

Plottage Value   **Plottage value** results from the combination of two or more parcels of land to form one large parcel that has more usefulness, and hence a greater market value, than the sum of the individual parcels. For example, local zoning laws may permit a six-unit apartment building on a single 10,000-square-foot lot. However, if two of these lots can be combined, zoning laws permit 15 units. This makes the lots more valuable if sold together.

Potential value refers to benefits that are to be received in the future. However, one must estimate the probability that the potential will be achieved and then calculate the present value. **Rental value** is the value of a property expressed in terms of the right to its use for a specific period of time. The fee simple interest in a house may have a market value of $40,000, whereas the market value of 1 month's occupancy might be $300. **Replacement value** is value as measured by the current cost of building a structure of equivalent utility. **Reproduction value** is the current cost of building an exact duplicate.

Salvage Value   **Salvage value** is the price that can be expected for an improvement for purposes of removal and use elsewhere. Because of the high amount of labor necessary to recover salvageable parts, the salvage value of most buildings is usually very low.

Subjective value is the value of a property to a specific individual and is a reflection of the benefits that that individual expects to receive. By comparison, **objective value** reflects prices typical of the market as a whole. From the standpoint of the appraiser, care must be taken that his personal likes and dislikes do not influence the appraisal. **Terms value** is the price a property is expected to bring if offered for sale on financial terms other than cash or prevailing mortgage rates. For example, a vacant site might be equally salable at $16,000 all cash or $18,000 with 20% down.

This list of values is not exhaustive, but it points out that the word value has many meanings. When one hears the word "value," one must ask, "For what purpose?" Thus, the appraiser before starting an appraisal must learn what types of decisions are to be made based on his findings. Is the purpose of the appraisal to buy, sell, lend, insure, or appeal a property tax assessment? Once he knows, he can set forth his assumptions, collect data, and draw conclusions.

PROFESSIONAL APPRAISAL SOCIETIES

During the 1930s, two well-known professional appraisal societies were organized: the American Institute of Real Estate Appraisers (AIREA) and the Society of Real Estate Appraisers. Although a person offering his services as a real estate appraiser need not be associated with either of these groups, there are advantages in official recognition. Both organizations have developed designation systems that are intended to recognize appraisal education, experience, and competence. Within the AIREA, the highest-level designation is the MAI (Member of the Appraisal Institute). To be an MAI requires a 4-year college degree or equivalent education, 16 hours of examinations, a variety of demonstration appraisals, and at least 5 years of appraisal experience, including 3 years in non-single-family real estate. There are about 5,000 MAI's in the United States. Also available is the RM (Residential Member) designation for those with at least a high school education, a passing appraisal examination score, three demonstration appraisal reports, and 3 years of experience in residential real estate.

The highest designations offered by the Society of Real Estate Appraisers are the SREA (Senior Real Estate Analyst) and SRPA (Senior Real Property Appraiser). For members specializing in residential appraisal, the professional designation is SRA (Senior Residential Appraiser). The SRA designation requires completion of basic courses in real estate appraisal, economics and statistics, an examination on appraising and a residential appraisal demonstration report. To this the SRPA designation adds advanced course work in real estate appraisal, plus an income property demonstration appraisal. For the SREA designation further advanced course work and an analytical demonstration appraisal are necessary. For all designations the applicant must have field experience and submit, for review by the Society, actual appraisals he or she has completed.

VOCABULARY REVIEW

Match terms a–p with statements 1–16.

a. *Book value*
b. *Capitalize*
c. *Compound interest*
d. *Net operating income*
e. *Objective value*
f. *Operating expenses*
g. *Plottage value*
h. *Principle of competition*
i. *Principle of conformity*
j. *Principle of substitution*
k. *Reversionary value*
l. *Risk rate*
m. *Safe rate*
n. *Scarcity*
o. *Scheduled gross*
p. *Subjective value*

1. Estimated rent that a fully occupied property can be expected to produce on an annual basis.
2. To convert future income to current value.
3. Income available from a rental property for those who provide the capital.
4. Rate of return on investment demanded by investors before they will invest. Includes the safe rate plus allowances for business risk, illiquidity, and management.
5. Expenses necessary to maintain the production of income.
6. Prevailing rate of interest on U.S. government bonds.

7. Wherever substantial profits are being made, additional suppliers are encouraged to enter the market.
8. Expected worth of a property at the end of the projected holding period.
9. A short supply relative to demand.
10. Interest earning interest.
11. Acts as an upper limit on prices; the lowest priced of two similar properties will usually sell first.
12. States that properties in the same neighborhood will tend to be rather similar in price.
13. Value as seen strictly from an accounting standpoint.
14. Value of a property to a specific individual.
15. Value as seen by the marketplace.
16. Value resulting from the joining of two or more adjacent parcels of land to form a single large parcel.

1. Briefly explain the concept of the income approach to valuing real property.
2. As the rate of return on investment demanded by investors rises, should property values rise or fall?
3. What is a reserve for replacement and what purpose does it serve?
4. What is an operating expense ratio and what role does it play in valuing a property?
5. What is the difference between return *on* investment and return *of* investment?
6. Briefly explain how the land residual technique of appraisal works.
7. What is the present value of $1,000 received in 1 year plus $2,000 received 2 years from now, all discounted at 10% (use Table 17:6)?
8. An investor anticipates that a property currently offered for sale will produce a net operating income of $10,000 per year for 10 years, at which time it can be sold for $90,000. Using a 10% return on investment, what price should the investor offer for the property (see Table 17:6)?
9. What is the purpose of correlating the three approaches to value?
10. Why is transferability necessary before something can have value in the marketplace?
11. What precaution does the principle of diminishing marginal returns suggest to a real estate owner?

QUESTIONS AND PROBLEMS

ADDITIONAL READINGS

American Institute of Real Estate Appraisers. *The Appraisal Journal.* Published quarterly, this periodical deals with current trends and new ideas in real estate appraisal.

Jackson, Peter R. "Contract Rent, Market Rent and Value," *Real Estate Today,* July 1974, pages 34–35. Discusses the appraisal of income properties when the rents currently being charged are different than prevailing rents in the marketplace.

Johnson, Irvin E. *Mini-Math for Appraisers.* Chicago: International Association of Assessing Officers, 1972, 186 pages. Describes how to use compound interest factors for the valuation of real estate. Especially designed for persons who dislike mathematics.

Kinnard, William N., Jr. *A Guide to Appraising Apartments,* 2nd ed. Chicago: Society of Real Estate Appraisers, 1966, 82 pages. Emphasizes the application of appraisal principles and methods to the valuation of apartment properties.

Kinnard, William N., Jr. *Income Property Valuation.* Lexington, Mass.: D.C. Heath—Lexington Books, 1971, 510 pages. Concentrates on the principles and techniques of appraising income-producing real estate.

Wendt, Paul F. *Real Estate Appraisal: Review and Outlook.* Athens, Ga.: The University of Georgia Press, 1974, 268 pages. Reviews the development of appraisal theory and practice and projects its future.

18

The Owner-Broker Relationship

Agent: the person empowered to act by and on behalf of the principal

Commingling: the mixing of clients' funds with an agent's personal funds

Dual agency, Divided agency: one broker representing two or more parties in a transaction

Exclusive right to sell: a listing that gives the broker the right to collect a commission if the property is sold by anyone during the listing period

Middleman: a person who brings two or more parties together but does not conduct negotiations

Principal: a person who authorizes another to act for him; also refers to a property owner

Puffing: nonfactual or extravagant statements a reasonable person would recognize as such

Ready, willing and able buyer: a buyer who is ready to buy now without further coaxing, and who has the financial capability to do so

Third parties: persons who are not parties to a contract but who may be affected by it

AGENCY

When a property owner gives a real estate broker a listing authorizing the broker to find a buyer or a tenant and promising compensation if he does, an **agency relationship** is created. For an agency to exist, there must be a principal and an agent. The **principal** is the person who empowers another to act as his representative; the **agent** is the person who is empowered to act. When someone speaks about the "laws of agency," he refers to those laws that govern the rights and duties of the principal, agent, and the persons (called **third parties**) with whom they deal.

Agencies are divided into three categories: universal, general, and specific. A **universal agency** is very broad in scope, as the principal gives his agent the legal power to transact matters of all types for him. A **general agency** gives the agent the power to transact the principal's affairs in a particular trade or business or at a certain location. For example, a life insurance company appoints a general agent to represent it in a certain city. With a **special agency** the principal empowers his agent to perform only specific acts and no others. Applications of special agency include (1) written power of attorney whereby a principal can empower another person to convey, mortgage, or lease his real property, and (2) real estate listings, the primary topic of this chapter.

LISTING AGREEMENTS

When a property owner signs a listing, all the essential elements of a valid contract, except one, must be present. The owner and broker must be legally capable of contracting, there must be mutual assent, and the agreement must be for a lawful purpose. The exception is mutual consideration: the owner can promise to pay a commission if a buyer is found, but the broker need not promise to find one. In practice, however, many states require that the broker promise that he will actively seek a buyer. A few states simply assume that, when a broker takes a listing, he intends to work on it.

Although some states still do not require that listing agreements be in writing to be valid, the trend is to require that they be written and signed to be enforceable in a court of law.

Figure 18:1 illustrates a simplified listing agreement. Beginning at ①, there is a description of the property plus the price and terms at which the broker is instructed to find a buyer. At ②, the broker promises to make a reasonable effort to find a buyer. This is the broker's part of mutual consideration. The period of time that the listing is to be in effect is shown at ③.

At ④, the owner agrees not to list the property with any other brokers, permit other brokers to have a sign on the property, or advertise it during the listing period. Also, the owner agrees not to revoke the broker's exclusive right to find a buyer as set forth by this contract.

The broker recognizes that the owner may later accept a price and terms that are different from those in the listing. By inserting the words shown at ⑤, the broker assures himself that he will still earn a commission no matter what price and terms the owner ultimately accepts. At ⑥, the amount of compensation the owner agrees to pay the broker is established. The usual arrangement is to express the amount as a percentage of the sale or exchange price, although a stated dollar amount could be used if the owner and broker agreed. No matter how it is computed, the amount of the fee is negotiable between the owner and the broker. The owner knows that if the fee is too high it will pay to sell the property himself. The broker recognizes that if the fee is too low it will not be worthwhile spending time and effort finding a buyer. The typical commission fee in the United States at present is 5% to 7% of the selling price for houses, condominiums, and small apartment buildings, and 6% to 10% on farms, ranches, and vacant land. On multimillion dollar improved properties, commissions usually drop to the 2 to 4% range.

The conditions under which a commission must be paid by the owner to the broker appear next. At ⑦, a commission is deemed to be earned if the owner agrees to a sale or exchange of the property, no matter who finds the buyer. In other words, even if the owner finds his own buyer, or a friend of the owner finds a buyer, the broker is entitled to a full commission fee. Also covered is the possibility that the broker will enlist the aid of other brokers to find a buyer. In this event, called **broker cooperation,** the normal procedure is for the cooperating brokers to enter into an agreement with the broker who took the listing to share the fee paid by the owner. Finally, if the owner disregards his promise at ④ and lists with another broker who then sells the property, the owner will be liable for two full commissions.

Protecting the Broker

The wording at ⑧ is included by the broker to protect against the possibility that the owner may refuse to sell after the broker has expended time and effort to find a buyer at the price and terms of the listing contract. The listing itself is not an offer to sell property. It is strictly a contract whereby the owner employs the broker to find a buyer. Thus, even though a buyer offers to pay the exact price and terms shown in the listing, the buyer does not have a binding sales contract until the offer is accepted in writing by the owner. However, if the owner refuses to sell at the listed price and terms, the broker is still entitled to a commission. If the owner does not pay the broker voluntarily, the broker can file a lawsuit against the owner to collect.

At ⑨, the broker protects himself against the possibility that the listing period will expire while he is working with a prospective purchaser. In fairness to the owner, however, two limitations are placed on the broker. First, a sales contract must be concluded within a reasonable time after the listing expires, and second, the name of the purchaser must have been given to the owner before the listing period expires.

Continuing at ⑩, the owner agrees to let the broker enter the property at reasonable hours to show it. At ⑪, the owner agrees to refer all inquiries regarding the availability of the property to the broker. The purpose is to discourage the owner from thinking that he might be able to save a commission by selling it himself during the listing period, and to increase the broker's chances of generating a sale of the property. Finally, at ⑫, the owner and the broker (or his salesman if the salesman is authorized to do so) sign and date the agreement.

Sample Listing   The sample contract in Figure 18:1 contains the basic requirements of a listing agreement. In practice, however, other promises and information are often included. For example, the listing may remind the owner that the listing price includes built-in furniture, built-in appliances, water heaters, plumbing and electrical fixtures, drapes, curtain rods, and, if attached, television antennas, carpeting and mirrors, plus plants and trees in the ground. Technically, all these are defined as real estate and do not need to be itemized, but their mention in the listing can avoid future disagreements over what the seller can and cannot take when the property is sold. The listing may state that the owner agrees to deliver marketable title and title insurance. It may also include a promise by the owner to post survey stakes so the property boundaries can be easily seen by a prospective buyer, and a provision as to the payment of escrow and closing fees.

When a broker or one of his sales staff shows a listed

Figure 18:1

EXCLUSIVE RIGHT TO SELL
LISTING CONTRACT

(1) *Property Description:* A single-family house at 2424 E.
Main Street, City, State, Legally
described as Block H. Tract 191,
County, State.

Price: $46,500

Terms: Cash

(2) *In consideration of the services of* ABC Realty Company *(herein called the "Broker"), to be rendered to* Roger and Mary Leeving *(herein called the "Owner"), and the promise of said Broker to make reasonable efforts to obtain a purchaser, therefore, the Owner hereby grants to the Broker*

(3) *for the period of time from noon on* April 1, 19—, *to noon on* July 1, 19— *(herein called the "listing period")*

(4) *the exclusive and irrevocable right to advertise and find a purchaser for the above described property at the price and terms shown*

(5) *or for such sum and terms or exchange as the owner later agrees to accept.*

(6) *Owner hereby agrees to pay Broker a cash fee of* 6% *of the selling or exchange price*

(7) *(A) in case of any sale or exchange of the above property within the listing period either by the Broker, the Owner or any person, or*

(8) *(B) upon the Broker finding a purchaser who is ready, willing, and able to complete the purchase as proposed by the owner, or*

⑨ *(C) in the event of a sale or exchange within 60 days of the expiration of the listing period to any party shown the above property during the listing period by the Broker or his representative and where the name was disclosed to the Owner.*

⑩ *The Owner agrees to give the Broker access to the buildings on the property for the purposes of showing them at reasonable hours*

⑪ *and the Owner agrees to refer to Broker all inquiries regarding this property during the listing period.*

⑫ *Accepted:* ABC Realty Company

By: Kurt Kwiklister   *Owner:* Roger Leeving

Owner: Mary Leeving

Date: April 1, 19——

property to prospects, questions about the property will be asked. For example, a home buyer will want to know the number of bedrooms and baths, the number of square feet of living space, lot size, basement size, property taxes, school districts, amount of assumable loan, when possession can be taken, and so forth. Not only must the salesperson have ready answers, but he is also responsible for their accuracy. Thus, it has become a common practice to include in the listing a detailed description of the features of the land and improvements, plus any other pertinent information relating to the property.

EXCLUSIVE RIGHT
TO SELL

The listing illustrated in Figure 18:1 is called an **exclusive right to sell,** or an **exclusive authority to sell,** listing. Its distinguishing characteristic is that no matter who sells the property during the listing period, the listing broker is entitled to a commission. This is the most widely used type of listing in the United States. Once signed by the owner and accepted by the broker, the primary advantage to the broker is that the money and effort he expends on advertising and showing the property will be to his benefit. The advantage to the owner is that the broker will usually put more effort into selling a property on which he holds an exclusive right to sell than on one for which he has only an exclusive agency or an open listing.

The **exclusive agency** listing is similar to the listing shown in Figure 18:1, except that the owner may sell the property himself during the listing period and not owe a commission to the broker. The broker, however, is guaranteed that he is the only broker with the listing during the listing period; hence the term exclusive agency. For an owner, this may seem like the best of two worlds: the owner has a broker looking for a buyer, but if the owner finds a buyer first, he can save a commission fee. The broker is less enthusiastic, as he feels his efforts can too easily be undermined by the owner. Consequently, he may not expend as much effort on advertising and showing the property as with an exclusive right to sell.

EXCLUSIVE AGENCY

Open listings carry no exclusive rights. An owner can give an open listing to any number of brokers at the same time, and the owner can still find a buyer himself and avoid a commission. This gives the owner the greatest freedom of any listing form, but there is little incentive for the broker to expend time and money showing the property as he has little control over who will be compensated if the property is sold. The broker's only protection is that, if he does find a buyer at the listing price and terms, he is entitled to a commission. This reluctance to develop a sales effort usually means few, if any, offers will be received and may result in no sale or a sale below market price. Yet, if a broker does find a buyer, the commission charged may be the same as with an exclusive right to sell.

OPEN LISTINGS

A **net listing** is created when an owner states the price he wants for his property and then agrees to pay the broker anything he can get above that price as his commission. It can be written in the form of an exclusive right to sell, an exclusive agency, or an open listing. If a homeowner asked for a "net $40,000" and the broker sold the home for $50,000, the commission would be $10,000. By using the net listing, many owners feel that they are forcing the broker to look to the

NET LISTINGS

buyer for the commission by marking up the price of the property. In reality though, a buyer will not pay $50,000 for a home that, compared to similar properties for sale, is worth only $40,000 or $45,000. Consequently, we must conclude that the home was actually worth $50,000 and the $10,000 (in effect a 20% commission) came from the seller. If other brokers in the area are charging 5% to 7% of the sales price, a 20% commission invites both public criticism and a lawsuit questioning the broker's loyalty to his seller for accepting such a low listing price. Because of public misunderstanding regarding net listings and because they provide such fertile ground for questionable commission practices, some states prohibit them outright, and most brokers strenuously avoid them even though requested by property owners. There is no law that says a broker must accept a listing; he is free to accept only those listings for which he can perform a valuable service and earn an honest profit.

MULTIPLE LISTING
SERVICE

A "multiple listing" is an exclusive right-to-sell listing taken by a broker who places it into a **multiple listing service** (MLS) organization. Multiple listing organizations enable brokers in a given geographical area to exchange information on listings. The purpose is to inform other brokers and their clients of listings held by each member, thus broadening the market exposure for a given property. Member brokers are permitted to show each others' properties to their clients and, if a sale results, the commission is divided between the broker finding the buyer and the broker obtaining the MLS listing, less a small deduction for the cost of operating the multiple listing service.

A property listed with a broker who is a multiple listing service member receives the advantage of greater sales exposure, which, in turn, means a better price and a quicker sale. For the buyer, it means learning about what is for sale at many offices without having to visit each individually. For the salesman and broker, it means that, if his own office does not have a suitable property for a prospect, the opportunity to make a sale is not lost, because the prospect can be shown the listings of other brokers.

It is to the broker's advantage to make the listing period for as long as possible, as it gives him more time to find a buyer. Sometimes, even an overpriced property will become salable if the listing period is long enough and prices rise fast enough. From a legal standpoint, an owner and a broker can agree to a listing period of several years if they wish. However, most owners are reluctant to be committed for that long and prefer a better balance between their flexibility and the amount of time needed for a broker to conduct a sales campaign. In residential sales, 3 to 4 months is a popular compromise; farm, ranch, commercial, and industrial listings are usually made for 6 months to 1 year.

One problem area is listings that appear on the surface to last for only a few months but, in the fine print, commit the owner to a much longer period. Particularly troublesome is the **automatic renewal clause** that allows a listing to renew itself indefinitely after its expiration date unless canceled in writing by the owner. What often happens is that, after several months pass without a sale of the property, the expiration date arrives and the owner lists with another broker who produces a sale. Then the first broker steps forward to demand "his" commission in addition to the one being paid to the broker who produced the sale. Alternatively, the expiration date arrives without a sale and the owner forgets the matter, only to find the broker on his doorstep a year later with a buyer and a demand for a commission. Because of these problems, many states now outlaw automatic renewals.

Another form of the long-term listing is a 1-year listing period on a residential property that gives the owner the right to cancel after 3 months, provided he gives 30-day advance written notice. If the owner is not satisfied with the broker's efforts or for some other reason wants to terminate the listing at the end of 3 months, he can do so, provided he remembers to write a cancellation letter to the broker by the sixtieth day of the listing period.

When a real estate broker accepts a listing, he takes on a substantial amount of responsibility: he must faithfully perform the agency agreement, be loyal to his principal, exercise reasonable care and account for all funds handled by him in performing the agency. Let us look at these more closely.

Faithful Performance   An agent must obey the instructions given to him by his principal. In the case of a broker, he must perform as promised in the listing contract. A broker who promises to make a "reasonable effort" or apply "diligence" in finding a buyer, and who then does nothing to promote the listing, gives the owner legal grounds for terminating the listing. Faithful performance also means not departing from the principal's instructions. If the agent does so (except in extreme emergencies not foreseen by the principal), it is at his own risk. If the principal thereby suffers a loss, the agent is responsible for that loss. For example, a broker accepts a personal note from a buyer as an earnest money deposit, but fails to tell the seller that the deposit is not in cash. If the seller accepts the offer and the note is later found to be worthless, the broker would be liable for the amount of the note.

Another aspect of faithful performance is that the agent must personally perform the tasks delegated to him. This protects the principal who has selected an agent on the basis of trust and confidence from finding that his agent has delegated that responsibility to another person. However, a major question arises on this point in real estate brokerage, as a large part of the success in finding a buyer for a property results from the cooperative efforts of other brokers and their salesmen. To eliminate the possibility of the owner refusing to pay a commission if a cooperating broker finds a buyer, listing agreements often include a statement that the listing broker is authorized to secure the cooperation of other brokers for the purpose of bringing about a sale.

Loyalty to Principal   Probably no other area of agency is as fertile ground for lawsuits as the requirement that, once an agency is created, the agent must be loyal to his principal. The law is clear in all states that in a listing agreement the broker (and the salespersons working for him) occupy a position of trust, confidence, and responsibility. As such, they are legally bound to keep the property owner fully informed as to all matters that might affect the sale of the listed property and to promote and protect the owner's interests.

Unfortunately, greed and expediency sometimes get in the way. As a result, numerous laws have been enacted for the purpose of protecting the principal and threatening the agent with court action for misplaced loyalty. For example, an out-of-town landowner who is not fully up to date on the value of his land visits a local broker and asks him to list it for $30,000. The broker is much more knowledgeable of local land prices and is aware of a recent city council decision to extend roads and utilities to the area of this property. As a result, he knows that the land is now worth $50,000. The broker remains silent on the matter and the property is listed for sale at $30,000. At this price, the broker can find a buyer before the day is over and have a commission on the sale. However, the opportunity for a quick $20,000 is too tempting to let pass. He buys the property himself or, to hide his identity, in his wife's name or that of a friend and shortly thereafter resells it for $50,000. Whether he sold the property to a client for $30,000 or bought it himself and sold it for $50,000, the broker did not exhibit loyalty to the principal. Laws and penalties for breach of loyalty are stiff: the broker can be sued for recovery of the price difference and the commission paid, his real estate license can be suspended or revoked, and he may be required to pay additional fines and money damages.

Disclosure

If a licensee intends to purchase a property listed for sale by his agency or through a cooperating broker, he is under both a moral and a legal obligation to make certain that the price paid is the fair market value and that the seller knows who the buyer is.

Loyalty to the principal also means that, when seeking a buyer or negotiating a sale, the broker must continue to protect the owner's financial interests. Suppose that an owner lists his home at $62,000 but confides in the broker, "If I cannot get $62,000, anything over $59,000 will be fine." The broker shows the home to a prospect who says, "Sixty-two thousand is too much. What will the owner really take?" or "Will he take fifty-nine thousand?" Loyalty to the principal requires the broker to say that the owner will take $62,000, for that is the price in the listing agreement. If the buyer balks, the broker can suggest that the buyer submit an offer for the seller's consideration. State laws require that all offers be submitted to the owner, no matter what the offering price and terms. This prevents the agent from rejecting an offer that the owner might have accepted if he had known about it. If the seller really intends for the broker to quote $59,000 as an acceptable price, the listing price should be changed; then the broker can say, "The property was previously listed for $62,000, but is now priced at $59,000."

A broker's loyalty to his principal includes keeping him informed of changes in market conditions during the listing period. If, after the listing was taken, an adjacent landowner was successful in rezoning his land to a higher use and the listed property became more valuable, the broker's responsibility is to inform the seller. Similarly, if a buyer is looking at a property priced at $30,000 and tells the broker, "I'll offer $27,000 and come up if need be," it is the duty of the broker to report this to the owner. The owner can then decide if he wants to accept the $27,000 offer or try for more. If the broker does not keep the owner fully informed, he is not properly fulfilling his duties as the owner's agent.

Although the law is clear in requiring the broker to report to the owner all facts that may have a bearing on the property's ultimate sale, it also places the broker in a difficult position if a prospective buyer is not fully aware of this and instead thinks that the broker is *his* agent in the transaction. In this situation, the broker must either make it clear to the buyer that he is the agent of the owner, and therefore loyal to the owner, or the broker becomes a dual agent, in which case the law requires that he make this known to everyone concerned.

Dual Agency   If a broker represents a seller, it is his duty to obtain the highest price and the best terms possible for the seller. If a broker represents a buyer, his duty is to obtain the lowest price and terms for the buyer. When the same broker represents two or more principals in the same transaction, it is a **dual** or **divided agency,** and a conflict of interest results. If he represents both principals in the same transaction, to whom does he owe his loyalty? Does he work equally hard for each principal? This is an unanswerable question; therefore, the law requires that each principal be informed that he cannot expect the agent's full allegiance and thus each is responsible for looking after his own interest personally. If a broker represents more than one principal and does not obtain their consent, he cannot claim a commission and the defrauded principal(s) may be able to rescind the transaction itself. Moreover, his real estate license may be suspended or revoked. This is true even though the broker does his best to be equally fair to each principal.

Dual agency automatically results when one broker represents two or more parties in a real estate exchange. Consequently, the broker must take care to inform his principals of his dual agency in writing before an offer is made.

A dual agency also develops when a buyer agrees to pay a broker a fee for finding a property that suits his needs, and the broker finds one, lists it, and earns a fee from the seller as well as the buyer. Again, both the buyer and seller must be informed of the dual agency in advance of negotiations. If either principal does not approve of the dual agency, he can refuse to participate.

The exception to the dual agency rule is the **middleman.** A middleman is a person who brings two or more parties together who conduct negotiations between themselves without the help of the middleman. If it is clearly understood by all parties involved that the middleman's only purpose was to bring them together, no one expects the middleman's loyalty. If, however, the middleman assists or influences the negotiations, he becomes an agent and is subject to the rules of agency.

Middleman

An agent is expected to exercise reasonable care in carrying out his duties. If a broker is entrusted with a key to an owner's building to show it to prospects, it is the broker's responsibility to see that it is used for only that purpose and that the building is locked when he leaves. Similarly, if a

Reasonable Care

broker receives a check as an earnest money deposit, he must properly deposit it in a bank and not carry it around for several weeks.

Accounting for Funds Received

When a broker obtains an offer on a property, the earnest money that accompanies it belongs to the buyer until the offer is accepted, and upon acceptance, to the seller. The money does not belong to the broker, even though he possesses a check made out to him.

For the purpose of holding clients' money, brokers in the United States (except Alabama, Tennessee, and the District of Columbia) are required to maintain a special trust or escrow account at a bank. This account must be separate from the broker's personal bank account, and the broker is required by law to accurately account for all funds received into and paid out of the trust account. State-conducted surprise audits are made on broker's trust accounts to ensure compliance with the law. One trust account is adequate for all the monies received on behalf of all principals.

Commingling

If a broker places a client's money in his own personal account, it is called **commingling** and, except in the three jurisdictions noted above, is grounds for suspension or revocation of the broker's real estate license. The reason for such severe action is that in the past some brokers have used clients' money for short-term loans to themselves and then have been unable to replace the money. Also, clients' money placed in a personal bank account can be attached by a court of law to pay personal claims against the broker.

If a broker receives a check as an earnest money deposit, along with instructions from the buyer that it remain uncashed, the broker may comply with the buyer's request as long as the seller is informed of this fact when the offer is presented. Similarly, the broker can accept a promissory note, if he informs the seller. The objective is to disclose all material facts to the seller that might influence his decision to accept or reject the offer. The fact that the deposit accompanying the offer is not cash is a material fact. If the broker withholds this information, he violates the laws of agency.

To be legally eligible for compensation, the broker must be able to clearly show that he was employed. Usually, this requirement is fulfilled by using a preprinted listing form approved for use by the local multiple listing service or the state Realtor's association. The broker fills in the blank spaces as they apply to the property he is listing. If listings come in the form of letters or verbal requests from property owners, the broker must make certain that all the essential requirements of a valid listing are present and clearly stated. If they are not, the broker may expend time and money finding a buyer only to be denied a commission because he was not properly employed. To guard against this, the broker should transfer the owner's request to the preprinted listing form that he uses and have the owner sign it.

The broker earns his commission at whatever point in the transaction he and the owner agree upon. In nearly all listing contracts, this point occurs when the broker produces a **"ready, willing, and able buyer"** at the price and terms acceptable to the owner. "Ready and willing" means a buyer who is ready to buy now and needs no further coaxing. "Able" means financially capable of completing the transaction. An alternative arrangement is for the broker and owner to agree to a "no sale, no commission" arrangement whereby the broker is not entitled to a commission until the transaction is closed.

The difference between the two arrangements becomes important when a buyer is found at price and terms acceptable to the owner, but no sale results. The "ready, willing, and able" contract provides more protection for the broker as his commission does not depend on the deal reaching settlement. The "no sale, no commission" approach is to the owner's advantage, for he is not required to pay a commission unless there is a completed sale. However, with the passage of time, court decisions have tended to blur the clear-cut distinction between the two. For example, if the owner has a "no sale, no commission" agreement, it would appear that, if the broker brought a ready, willing, and able buyer at the listing price and terms and the owner refused to sell, the owner would owe no commission, for there was no sale. However, a court of law would find in favor of the broker for the full amount of the commission if the refusal to sell was arbitrary and without reasonable cause or in bad faith. Under a "ready, willing, and able" listing, traditionally, if a broker produced a buyer, it was up to the owner to decide if the buyer was, in fact, financially able to buy. If the owner accepted the buyer's offer and subsequently the buyer did not have the money to complete the deal, the owner still owed the broker a commission. The legal thinking today is that the broker should be responsible, because he is in a much better position to analyze the buyer's financial ability than the owner.

PROCURING CAUSE

A broker who possesses an open listing or an exclusive agency listing is entitled to a commission if he can prove that the resulting sale was primarily due to his efforts. Suppose that a broker shows an open-listed property to a client and, during the listing period or an extension, the client goes directly to the owner and concludes a deal. Even though the owner negotiates his own transaction and prepares his own sales contract, the broker is entitled to a full commission for finding the buyer. This would also be true if the owner and the client used a subterfuge or strawman to purchase the property to avoid paying a commission. State laws protect the broker who in good faith has produced a buyer at the request of an owner.

When an open listing is given to two or more brokers, the first one who produces a buyer is entitled to the commission. For example, Broker 1 shows a property to Client C, but no sale is made. Later C goes to Broker 2 and makes an offer, which is accepted by the owner. Although two brokers have attempted to sell the property, only one has succeeded, and he is the one entitled to a commission. The fact that Broker 1 receives nothing, even though he may have expended considerable effort, is an important reason why brokers dislike open listings.

TERMINATING THE
LISTING CONTRACT

The usual situation in a listing contract is that the broker finds a buyer acceptable to the owner. Thus, in most listing contracts the agency terminates because the objectives of the contract have been completed. In the bulk of the listings for which a buyer is not found, the agency is terminated because the listing period expires. If no listing period is specified, the listing is considered to be effective for a "reasonable" length of time. A court might consider 3 months to be reasonable for a listing on a home and 6 months reasonable for an apartment building or commercial property. Listing contracts without termination dates are revocable by the principal at any time, provided the purpose of the revocation is not to deprive the broker of an earned commission. A major disadvantage of listings without termination dates is that all too often they evolve into expensive and time-consuming legal hassles.

Even when a listing calls for mutual consideration and has a specific termination date, it is still possible to revoke the agency aspect of the listing before the termination date. However, liability for breach of contract still remains, and money damages may result. Thus, an owner who has listed his property may tell the broker not to bring any more offers, but the owner still remains liable to the broker for payment for the effort expended by the broker up to that time. Depending how far advanced the broker is at that point, the amount could be as much as a full commission.

A listing can be terminated by agreement of both the owner and broker without money damages. Because listings are the stock in trade of the brokerage business, brokers do not like to lose listings, but sometimes this is the only logical alternative open, as the time and effort in setting and collecting damages can be very expensive. Suppose, however, that a broker has an exclusive right to sell a listing and suspects that the owner wants to cancel because he has found a buyer and wants to avoid paying a commission. The broker can stop showing the property, but the owner is still obligated to pay a commission if the property is sold before the listing period expires.

Mutual Agreement

With regard to open listings, once the property is sold by anyone, broker or owner, all listing agreements pertaining to the property are automatically terminated; the objective has been completed, there is no further need for the agency to exist. Similarly, with an exclusive agency listing, if the owner sells the property himself, the agency with the exclusive broker is terminated.

Abandonment   Agency can also be terminated by improper performance or abandonment by the agent. Thus, if a broker acts counter to his principal's best financial interests, the agency is terminated, no commission is payable, and the broker may be subject to a lawsuit for any damages suffered by the principal. If a broker takes a listing and then does nothing to promote it, the owner can assume that the broker abandoned it and has grounds for revocation.

Because an agency is a personal contract, it is automatically terminated by the death of either the principal or the agent. The same holds true if the principal or agent is judged legally incompetent by virtue of insanity or bankruptcy. Destruction of the listed property also terminates the agency because the object of the agency no longer exists.

DEPOSIT MONEY DISPOSITION   When an earnest money deposit accompanies an offer to buy, the normal procedure is to return it to the buyer if the offer is rejected. However, suppose that the offer is accepted and subsequently the buyer does not fulfill his obligations and forfeits the deposit to the seller as damages. If the broker is to share in any part of that money, there must be an agreement between the seller and the broker. Such an arrangement is usually made on the binder or sales contract. The most common arrangement is for the broker and owner to agree to split the deposit equally, but with the limitation that the broker's portion not exceed the amount of the commission he would have earned if the transaction had been completed. Not to have an agreement may leave the broker with nothing for his efforts and the owner with all the forfeited deposit.

BROKER'S RESPONSIBILITY TO THIRD PARTIES   A broker's responsibility is primarily to the principal who has employed him; state laws nonetheless make certain demands on the broker in relation to the third parties he deals with on behalf of his principal. Foremost among these is honest dealing. This includes the proper care of deposit money and offers, the responsibility for written or verbal statements made by the broker or his sales staff and any impression made by withholding information. Misrepresenting a property by omitting vital information is as wrong as giving false information. The result is that the broker loses his right to a commission, may lose his real estate license, and can be sued by any party to the transaction who suffered a financial loss because of the misrepresentation.

In guarding against misrepresentation, a licensee must be careful not to make statements about which he does not know the answer. When a prospect looks at a house listed for sale, he may ask if it is connected to the city sewer system. The agent does not know the answer, but sensing it is important to making a sale, says, "Yes." This is a fraud. If the prospect relies on this statement, purchases the house, and finds out that there is no sewer connection, the agent may find himself the center of litigation regarding sale cancellation, commission loss, damage lawsuit, and state license discipline. The answer should have been, "I don't know, but I will find out for you."

Suppose that the property owner had told the broker that the house was connected to the city sewer system, and the broker, having no reason to doubt the statement, accepted it in good faith and gave that information to prospective buyers. If this statement was not true, the owner would be at fault, owe the broker a commission, and be subject to legal action from the buyer for sale cancellation and money damages. When a broker must rely on information supplied by the owner, it is best to have it in writing. However, relying on the owner for information does not completely relieve the broker's responsibility to third parties. If an owner says his house is connected to the city sewer system and the broker knows that is impossible because there is no sewer line on that street, it is the broker's responsibility to correct the error.

One form of misrepresentation that is permitted by law is puffing. **Puffing** (or **puffery**) refers to nonfactual or extravagant statements that a reasonable person would recognize as such. Thus, a buyer would have no legal complaint against a broker who told him that a certain hillside lot had the most

PUFFING

beautiful view in the world, or that a listed property had the finest landscaping in the county. Besides, the buyer can see these things for himself and make up his own mind. However, if a broker in showing a rural property says it has "fantastic" well water, there had better be plenty of good water when the buyer moves in. The line between puffery and misrepresentation is a subjective one, but it can be easily defined by placing oneself in the position of the prospect about to pay a substantial amount of hard-earned money for a property.

PROPERTY
DISCLOSURE
STATEMENTS

The federal government through the Department of Housing and Urban Development (HUD), has enacted legislation to protect purchasers of property in new subdivisions from misrepresentation, fraud, and deceit. The HUD requirements, administered by the Office of Interstate Land Sales (OILS), apply primarily to subdivisions containing 50 or more vacant lots that are sold across state lines. The purpose of this law, which took effect in April 1969, is to require that developers give prospective purchasers more information regarding the property that they are being asked to buy. In passing this law, Congress recognized that all too often subdivision salesmen tell prospects untruths or withhold important information regarding the subdivisions that they are promoting. A color brochure might be handed to prospects picturing an artificial lake and boat marina within the subdivision, yet the developer has not obtained the necessary permits to build either and may never do so. Or, a developer, through his sales force, implies that the lots being offered for sale are ready for building when in fact there is no sewer system and the soil cannot handle septic tanks. Or prospects are not told that many roads in the subdivision will not be built for several years, and, when they are, lot owners will face a hefty paving assessment followed by annual maintenance fees, because the county has no intention of maintaining them as public roads.

Property Report

To give the prospective purchaser more information, OILS requires developers to file a property report that meets HUD specifications before any lots can be sold. A copy of this report must be given to each purchaser before a contract to purchase is signed. The report itself follows an easy-to-read question and answer format, with HUD asking key questions regarding the subdivision and the developer answering them. The following are typical questions.

What is the name and address of the developer? How far is it from the development to the nearest established city via paved and unpaved roads? Will the sales contract be recorded with the public recorder in the county where the land is located? If not, could the developer's creditors acquire title to the property free of any obligation to deliver a deed to the buyer, even though the buyer has made all his payments? What happens to a lot buyer's interest if he fails to make a payment on time as called for by his sales contract? Does the land present any special soil conditions that could cause problems in laying foundations? If so, what extra costs would the buyer incur?

Are schools, shopping, medical, and public transportation facilities available at or near the site of the development? How many homes and commercial-use buildings have already been built at the development site? Are all lots accessible by public automobile road and are they paved? If not, when will this occur and at what additional cost to the lot buyer? Are lots surveyed and staked so that the buyer can find his? Under what conditions will money paid by the buyer be returned to him if he is not satisfied with his purchase? Are there or will there be recreational facilities at the development? If so, who will pay to build and maintain them? What guarantee is there that these recreational facilities will actually be built? And when will they be built?

Is there a mandatory property owners' association with mandatory dues? What arrangements have been made for sewage and trash disposal and for water, gas, electricity, and telephone services to each lot? Are the cost of these in addition to the lot price? Is there an adequate water supply to service the lots once they are developed with buildings? What mortgage or other encumbrances are presently against the property that are senior to the buyer's land contract? What restrictive easements, covenants, reservations and building codes must the buyer observe if and when he builds on his lot? Who owns the oil and mineral rights and the surface right of entry to explore for them?

Government's Position

In enforcing disclosure requirements, neither HUD nor OILS takes a position as to whether a particular subdivision is a good investment or a bad one, and a disclaimer to this effect is printed at the top of the first page of every property report given a buyer. The primary purpose is to ensure that the developer and his sales agents disclose to third parties pertinent facts regarding the property before a sale is made.

A number of states have also enacted their own disclosure laws. Typically these apply to developers of house subdivisions, condominiums, cooperatives, and vacant lots, whereas the federal laws are primarily concerned with vacant land sales. Also, state disclosure laws deal with developments sold entirely within a state and in some cases with developments in other states sold to their residents, whereas HUD and OILS deal only with lots in one state sold to residents of another state.

FAIR HOUSING LAWS

There are two major Federal laws that prohibit discrimination in housing. The first is the Civil Rights Act of 1866. it states that, "All citizens of the United States shall have the same right in every State and Territory, as is enjoyed by the white citizens thereof to inherit, purchase, lease, sell, hold, and convey real and personal property." In 1968, the Supreme Court stated that the 1866 Act prohibits "all racial discrimination, private as well as public, in the sale of real property." The second is the Federal Fair Housing Law, officially known as Title VIII of the Civil Rights Act of 1968. This law makes it illegal to discriminate based on race, color, religion, sex, or national origin in connection with the sale or rental of housing. The 1968 Act also makes it illegal to discriminate in advertising the sale or rental of housing, in financing housing, or in providing brokerage services.

A real estate agent violates fair housing laws if he or she gives a minority buyer or seller less than favorable treatment. Specific examples include ignoring the customer or referring him to an agent of the same minority; offering property on less favorable terms; failing to use best efforts; failing or delaying submission of an offer; and inducing a seller to reject an offer because of race, color, religion, sex, or national origin.

Preventing a minority member from obtaining housing in a community of his choice is a violation of the law. Called **steering,** this includes efforts to exclude minority members from one community as well as efforts to attract them to minority or changing communities. Examples include showing only certain neighborhoods, slanting property descriptions, downgrading non-integrated neighborhoods to minority buyers and vice versa. **Blockbusting,** the practice of inducing panic selling because a minority member has recently purchased in the neighborhood, is also outlawed by the 1968 Act.

Steering, Blockbusting

Persons who feel discriminated against can file a complaint with the Department of Justice or the Department of Housing and Urban Development. Local and state agencies as well as civil rights organizations also stand ready to help.

VOCABULARY REVIEW

Match terms a–n with statements 1–14.

a. *Agent*	**h.** *Net listing*
b. *Commingling*	**i.** *Open listing*
c. *Dual agency*	**j.** *Principal*
d. *Exclusive agency*	**k.** *Procuring cause*
e. *Exclusive right to sell*	**l.** *Puffing*
f. *Middleman*	**m.** *Special agency*
g. *Multiple listing service*	**n.** *Third parties*

1. A person who authorizes another to act for him.
2. Listing giving a broker a nonexclusive right to obtain a purchaser.
3. Persons who are not parties to a contract but who may be affected by it.
4. An agency created for the performance of specific acts only.
5. A person who brings two or more parties together but does not assist in conducting negotiations.
6. Listing giving the broker the right to collect a commission if anyone sells the property during the listing period.
7. A listing wherein the owner reserves the right to sell the property himself, but agrees to list with no other broker during the listing period.

 8. Person empowered to act by and on behalf of the principal.
 9. A listing for which the commission is the difference between the sales price and a minimum price set by the seller.
10. An organization of real estate brokers that exists for the purpose of exchanging listing information.
11. One broker representing two or more parties in a transaction.
12. Mixing of clients' funds with an agent's personal funds.
13. Broker who is the primary cause of a real estate transaction.
14. Nonfactual or extravagant statements that a reasonable person would recognize as such.

QUESTIONS AND PROBLEMS

1. When we speak of an agency relationship, to what are we referring?
2. How does a universal agency differ from a general agency?
3. What does broker cooperation refer to? How is it achieved?
4. Why do brokers strongly prefer to take exclusive right to sell listings rather than exclusive agency or open listings?
5. What advantages and disadvantages does the open listing offer a property owner?
6. The laws of agency require that the agent be faithful and loyal to the principal. What does this mean to a real estate broker who has just taken a listing?
7. What does the phrase "ready, willing, and able buyer" mean in a real estate contract?
8. If a person holds a real estate license in your state, is he or she required to make a statement to that effect when acting as a principal?
9. How are listings terminated?
10. What is the purpose of HUD property disclosure statements?

ADDITIONAL READINGS

Gaines, Kenneth S. *How to Sell (and Buy) Your Home Without a Broker.* New York: Coward, McCann and Geoghegan, 1975, 160 pages. Covers the pricing, marketing, showing, negotiating, and closing the sale (or purchase) of a house or condominium as seen from the standpoint of an owner who wishes to undertake the task himself.

Kratovil, Robert. *Real Estate Law,* 6th ed. Englewood Cliffs, N.J.: Prentice-Hall, 1974, 479 pages. Chapter 10 deals with the legal aspects of listings, commissions, and broker's duties.

Powell, Richard R. *The Law of Property.* New York: Matthew Bender, 1975, 7 volumes. Volume 5, Chapter 70A, deals with federal regulation of interstate land sales and full disclosure requirements.

19

Licensing Laws and Professional Organizations

KEY TERMS

Ficticious name: a name other than one's own, such as a business operated under a name other than the owner's

Independent contractor: one who contracts to do work according to his own methods and is responsible to his employer only as to the results of that work

License revocation: to recall and make void a license

License suspension: to temporarily make a license ineffective

Principal broker: the broker in charge of a real estate office

Real Estate Commissioner: a person appointed by the governor to implement and carry out laws enacted by the legislature that pertain to real estate

Realtor: a term copyrighted by the National Association of Realtors for use by its members

Reciprocity: an arrangement whereby one state honors licenses issued by another state and vice versa

Recovery fund: a state-operated fund that can be tapped to pay for uncollectible judgements against real estate licensees

The first attempt in the United States to license persons acting as agents in real estate transactions was in the year 1917 in California. Opponents claimed that the new law was an unreasonable interference with the right of every citizen to engage in a useful and legitimate occupation and were successful in having the law declared unconstitutional by the courts on a technicality. Two years later, in 1919, the California legislature passed a second real estate licensing act; this time it was upheld by the Supreme Court. That same year, Michigan, Oregon, and Tennessee also passed real estate licensing acts. Today all 50 states and the District of Columbia require that persons who offer their services as real estate agents be licensed.

Although licensing laws do prevent complete freedom of entry into the profession, the public has a vested interest in seeing that salesmen and brokers have the qualifications of honesty, truthfulness, and good reputation. This was the intent of the first license laws. Some years later the additional requirements of license examinations and real estate education were added in the belief that a person offering his or her services as a real estate agent should meet special knowledge qualifications.

Experience to date clearly indicates that license laws have helped to upgrade technical competency and have increased public confidence in brokers and salesmen. Moreover, license laws are an important and powerful tool in reducing fraudulent real estate practices because a state can suspend or revoke a person's license to operate.

PERSONS REQUIRED TO BE LICENSED

A person who for compensation or the promise of compensation lists or offers to list, sells or offers to sell, buys or offers to buy, negotiates or offers to negotiate either directly or indirectly for the purpose of bringing about a sale, purchase or option to purchase, exchange, auction, lease, or rental of real estate, or any interest in real estate, is required to hold a valid real estate license. Some states also require persons offering their services as real estate appraisers, property managers, mortgage bankers, or rent collectors to hold real estate licenses.

Property owners dealing with their own property and licensed attorneys conducting a real estate transaction as an incidental part of their duties as an attorney for a client are exempt from holding a license. Also exempt are trustees and receivers in bankruptcy, legal guardians, administrators and executors handling a deceased's estate, officers and employees of a government agency dealing in real estate, and persons holding power of attorney from an owner. However, the law does not permit a person to use the exemptions as a means of conducting a brokerage business without the proper license. That is, an unlicensed person cannot take a listing in the guise of power of attorney and then act as a real estate broker.

The licensing procedure in use in nearly all states calls for two types of licenses: real estate broker and real estate salesman. In view of the present trend to remove the word "man" from occupational titles, we may see the word "salesman" replaced over the next few years by a new word, perhaps "salesperson." A **real estate broker** is a person licensed to act independently in conducting a real estate brokerage business. He brings those with real estate to be marketed together with those seeking real estate and negotiates a transaction. For his services he receives a fee, usually in the form of a commission based on the selling price or lease rent. The broker may represent the buyer or the seller, or, if he makes full disclosure, both at the same time. His role is more than that of a middleman who puts two interested parties in contact with each other, for the broker usually takes an active role in negotiating price and terms acceptable to both the buyer and seller. A broker can be an actual person or a business firm owned and operated by an actual broker. The laws of all states permit a real estate broker to hire others to work for him for the purpose of bringing about real estate transactions. These persons may be other licensed real estate brokers or they may be licensed real estate salesmen.

A **real estate salesman,** within the meaning of the license laws, is a person employed by a real estate broker to list and negotiate the sale, exchange, lease, or rental of real property for others for compensation, under the direction, guidance, and responsibility of the employing broker. Only an actual person can be licensed as a salesman (a business firm cannot be licensed as a salesman), and a salesman must be employed by a broker; he cannot operate independently. Thus, a salesman who takes a listing on a property does so in the name of his broker, and in some states the broker must sign along with the salesman for the listing to be valid. In the event of a legal dispute caused by a salesman, the dispute would be between the principal and the broker. Thus, some brokers take considerable care to oversee the documents that their salesmen prepare and sign. Other brokers do not, relying instead on the knowledge and sensibility of their salesmen, and accepting a certain amount of risk in the process.

BROKER–SALESMAN RELATIONSHIP

The salesman is a means by which a broker can expand his sales force. Presumably, the more salespeople a broker employs, the more listings and sales generated, and thus the more commissions earned by the broker. Against this, of course, the broker must pay enough out of these commissions to keep his sales force from leaving, provide sales facilities and personnel management, and take ultimate responsibility for any mistakes.

SALESMAN
COMPENSATION

Compensation for salesmen is usually a percentage of the commissions they earn for the broker. How much each receives is open to negotiation between the broker and each salesman working for him. For example, on a sale yielding a broker a 6% commission, the listing salesman may be entitled to 20%, the salesman finding the buyer 50%, and the broker 30%. Arrangements vary from broker to broker depending on how many services the broker provides, the emphasis on listing versus selling, and the sheer bargaining power of the broker and the salesperson. Thus, a broker who offers his sales staff office space, extensive secretarial help, a large advertising budget, and generous long-distance telephone privileges might take 40% to 50% for office overhead. A broker who wants to encourage listings might contract with his salesmen to take 30% for overhead and give 30% to the salesman who obtains the listing and 40% to the salesman who finds the buyer. Salespersons with proven sales records can usually reduce the portion of each commission dollar they earn that must go to the broker. This is because the broker feels that with an outstanding sales performer, a high volume of sales will offset a smaller house cut. Conversely, a new and untried salesperson, or one with a mediocre past sales record, may have to give up a larger portion of each dollar for the broker's overhead.

When one brokerage agency lists a property and another locates the buyer, the commission is split according to any agreement the two brokers wish to make. The most common arrangement is a fifty-fifty split. After splitting, each broker pays a portion of the money he receives to the salesperson involved in accordance with his commission agreements. If the sale is through a multiple listing service, the MLS fee is deducted before brokers and salesmen are paid.

A real estate salesperson is considered by the laws of agency to be an employee of the broker. At the same time however, the salesperson usually works strictly for commissions, sets his or her own working hours, and is given freedom in conducting sales activities. Consequently, labor and income tax laws have generally considered the salesperson to be an independent contractor rather than an employee of the broker. As a result, the broker has not been obligated to provide retirement benefits, or withhold income taxes, or pay social security taxes. The salesperson was responsible for these things. However, this situation is now changing. Recent government tax audits of brokers, particularly in large brokerage offices, have found that the broker exerts considerable control over when and how a salesperson works. This qualifies the salesperson as an employee and makes the broker responsible for withholding income and social security taxes from commissions and, in certain situations, for providing retirement benefits.

EMPLOYEE OR INDEPENDENT CONTRACTOR?

Of the two license levels, the salesman's license is regarded as the entry-level license and, as such, requires no previous real estate sales experience. By comparison, the broker's license, in nearly all states, requires 1 to 5 years of experience (2 or 3 years is most common) as a real estate salesman. Also, the salesman's license can usually be obtained at a younger age, as most states grant salesman licenses at age 18, whereas many states require the applicant to be 21 years old for a broker's license.

QUALIFICATIONS FOR LICENSING

Examination of the license applicant's knowledge of real estate law and practices, mathematics, valuation, finance, and the like, is now an accepted prerequisite for license granting in all states. Salesman exams average 2 to 4 hours in length, whereas broker exams range from 4 hours to as long as a day and a half. Salesman exams cover the basic aspects of state license law, contracts and agency, real property interests, sub-

Examination

division map reading, fair housing laws, real estate mathematics, and the ability to follow written instructions. Broker exams cover the same topics in more depth and test the applicant's ability to prepare listings, offer and acceptance contracts, leasing contracts, and closing statements, and test the applicant's knowledge of real estate finance and appraisal.

Education Requirements

In recent years education has also become an increasingly important part of license qualification requirements. More and more states are requiring that applicants take real estate education courses at community colleges, private real estate schools, or through adult education programs at high schools. (Chapter 1 gives current education requirements in effect in the 50 states.) Moreover, the reader should be fully aware that education requirements are increasing. Many states that started with a 30-hour broker education requirement several years ago have increased the requirement to 60 and 90 hours and more recently, in a few states to 180 and 270 hours. Several states, by the 1980s, plan to require broker applicants to hold a 4-year college degree with a specialization in real estate or an equivalent combination of courses and experience. Salesman education requirements are also increasing, although not as dramatically.

Also, as a rule, education requirements are structured so that the least rigorous requirements are for salesmen and the most rigorous are for brokers. For example, Arizona and New Jersey require 45 clock hours of real estate education for salesmen and an additional 90 hours for brokers. California and Rhode Island require special education only for the broker license. In addition, considerable thought is being given to the idea that salesmen and brokers should be required to take real estate education courses after they are licensed. Arizona, Iowa, Kentucky, Nebraska, Oregon, Texas, and Wisconsin require education for license renewal. Other states are either considering the matter or have developed a plan that will soon be implemented.

LICENSING THE BUSINESS FIRM

When a real estate broker wishes to establish a brokerage business of his own, the simplest method is a sole proprietorship under his own name, such as, John B. Jones, Real Estate

Broker. A few states still permit a broker to operate out of his residence. However, operating a business in a residential neighborhod can be bothersome to neighbors, and most states now require brokers to maintain a place of business in a location that is zoned for businesses.

When a person operates under a name other than his own, he must register that name by filing a **fictitious business name statement** with his county clerk and the state real estate licensing authority. This statement must also be published in a local newspaper. Thus, if John B. Jones wishes to call his brokerage business Great Lakes Realty, his business certificate would show "John B. Jones, doing business as Great Lakes Realty." (Sometimes "doing business as" is shortened to dba or d/b/a.)

Fictitious Name

A sole proprietorship, whether operated under the broker's name or a fictitious name, offers a broker advantages in the form of absolute control, flexibility, ease of organization, personal independence, ownership of all the profits and losses, and the freedom to expand by hiring all the salespeople and staff he can manage and afford. Against this the sole proprietor must recognize that he is the sole source of capital for the business and the only owner available to manage it.

Recognizing the need to accumulate capital and management expertise within a single brokerage operation, states also permit corporations and partnerships to be licensed. Since a corporation is an inanimate being (not an actual person), it cannot take a real estate examination. Therefore, laws require that the chief executive officer (usually the president) be a licensed real estate broker and be responsible for the management of the firm. Other officers and stockholders may include brokers and salesmen and nonlicensed persons. However, only those actually licensed can represent the corporation in activities requiring a real estate license. When a brokerage firm is formed as a partnership, the law requires each partner to be licensed as a real estate broker. The partnership must also file a fictitious business name statement showing the names of the partners and the name of the partnership.

If a broker expands by establishing branch offices that are geographically separate from the main or home office, each

Branch Offices

branch must have a branch office license and a licensed broker in charge. Referred to as an **associate broker** or a **principal broker,** this person can be a partner, a corporate owner who is a broker, or an employee who has a broker's license.

NONRESIDENT LICENSING

The general rule regarding license requirements is that a person must be licensed in the state within which he negotiates. Thus, if a broker or one of his salesmen sells an out-of-state property, but conducts the negotiations entirely within the borders of his own state, he does not need to be licensed to sell in the state where the land is actually located. State laws also permit the broker of one state to split a commission with the broker of another state provided each conducts negotiations only within the state where he is licensed. Therefore, if Broker B, licensed in State B, takes a listing at his office on a parcel of land located in State B, and Broker C in State C sells it to one of his clients, conducting the sale negotiations within State C, then Brokers B and C can split the commission. (Exceptions are Arkansas, Indiana, and Michigan; in these three states, license holders cannot split commissions with out-of-state brokers). If, however, Broker C comes to State B to negotiate a contract, then a license in State B is necessary. The standard practice has been to apply for a **nonresident license** and meet substantially the same exam and experience requirements as demanded of resident brokers. This is an expensive and time-consuming procedure.

License Reciprocity

In recent years, there has been considerable effort to design real estate licensing systems that permit a broker and his sales staff to conduct negotiations in other states without having to obtain nonresident licenses. The result is **license reciprocity** and it occurs when two states honor each other's licenses. In permitting reciprocity, state officials are primarily concerned with three matters: (1) the nonresident's knowledge of real estate law and practice as it applies to the state in which he wishes to operate, (2) the legal responsibility of the nonresident broker to local residents, and (3) the attitude of the broker's home state toward reciprocity. The knowledge aspect is solved by either designing a license examination that is equally acceptable to a given group of states that will reciprocate with each other, or by requiring the nonresident license holder to pass a local real estate exam. The exam may be the complete state exam or a short exam covering local law and practices.

With regard to broker responsibility, the standard procedure is to require the broker to file a **notice of consent** with the state government, usually with the secretary of state. This permits the secretary of state to receive legal summonses on behalf of the nonresident broker and provides a state resident an avenue by which he can sue a broker who is a resident of another state.

Finally, reciprocity arrangements are typically on a quid pro quo basis by individual states. If State T allows brokers of State L to work within its borders without taking an exam, then State L usually must allow brokers of State T to operate within its borders without taking an exam.

A major factor aiding reciprocity has been the emergence since 1970 of nationwide real estate license examination services by the Educational Testing Service of Princeton, New Jersey, and the California Department of Real Estate. Prior to the advent of these services, each state devised its own license exam, deciding the length, coverage, number, and difficulty of questions. This seemed reasonable as real estate laws and practices vary from state to state. Also, each state could control the difficulty of its testing standards. The result was that a person who passed the exam in his own state was not deemed qualified to practice in another state. There were two other problem areas: it was necessary for each state to devise its own sets of exam questions, and test writers had to be careful not to repeat questions so often that applicants would know the exact questions to expect on future exams.

EXAMINATION SERVICES

Sensing a need for a packaged examination that could be sold to real estate licensing authorities, Educational Testing Service (ETS) developed salesman and broker exam packages. Approximately three-quarters of the questions asked are applicable to all states and one-quarter are written for each state individually, based on that state's particular laws. By contracting with enough states, ETS reasoned that a large bank

Educational Testing Service

of questions applicable to all states could be developed and at the same time permit more careful preparation of the local questions. Moreover, the extensive experience of ETS in testing (e.g., ETS College Entrance Exams) meant better question writing and testing procedures. Today, ETS writes, schedules, administers, and grades real estate license exams in 23 states.*

Multi-State Exam   Differences in opinion about testing procedures and what an applicant should know on a license exam resulted in the California sponsored Multi-State Exam. California salesman and broker exams are separated into questions universal to all states and those questions specific to California. The universal questions are available to other states, where they are coupled with locally written questions pertaining to local law and practice. The resulting exams are scheduled, administered, and graded locally. An important consequence of this exchange is that participating states have instituted a limited reciprocity arrangement. Any salesman or broker who has passed the multistate portion since October 1973 may request credit for that portion of the exam when applying for a license in a participating state.†

REAL ESTATE   The legislature of each state has established a government
REGULATORY   agency for the purpose of regulating real estate licensing pro-
AGENCIES   cedures and real estate practices within its state. These regulatory agencies are variously known as real estate commissions, or departments or divisions of real estate, or they may be a part of the state's business and vocational licensing and regulation departments.

---

* States using ETS exams as of mid-1977 were Alaska, Hawaii, Indiana, Iowa, Kansas, Kentucky, Maine, Maryland, Massachusetts, Missouri, Montana, Nebraska, Nevada, New Hampshire, New Jersey, North Carolina, North Dakota, Pennsylvania, South Dakota, Vermont, Virginia, and Wyoming; also the District of Columbia and the Virgin Islands.

† Participating in the California Multi-State Examination program as of mid-1977 were Alabama, California, Colorado, Georgia, Guam, Idaho, Oregon, Utah, and Washington.

Although exact details vary from state to state, in the usual arrangement the legislature establishes a real estate department, a real estate commissioner, and a real estate commission. Let us look at the role of each in more detail.

The role of the legislature is to enact laws within constitutional limits for the purpose of promoting the safety, health, morals, order, and general welfare of the population. Laws so enacted must not be unreasonable or unnecessary and they must be applied evenhandedly. Acting under the right of police power, legislatures of all the states have deemed it in the public interest that persons offering their services as real estate brokers and salesmen have the qualifications of good reputation, honesty, truthfulness, and knowledge of the field. If an applicant meets the requirements, he must be issued a license.

Either the legislature or the governor appoints a **real estate commissioner** whose task is to implement and carry out the laws enacted by the legislature and the policies set forth by the commission. This includes screening and qualifying of applicants for licenses, investigating complaints against license holders and persons without licenses, and regulating subdivisions and real estate syndicates.

Real Estate Commissioner

To assist and advise the commissioner, there is a **real estate commission,** usually composed of four to eight persons active in real estate and appointed by the governor for 2- to 4-year terms. One or two additional members may be selected from the general public. Typically, commission members are volunteers selected to represent all geographical parts of the state. The full commission usually meets once a month. Its members provide input to the commissioner and other state officials on such matters as the needs of real estate licensees, state policies regarding real estate, and the welfare of the public in dealing with licensees. One of the most important tasks in recent years has been to draft plans for more extensive education and testing requirements for approval by state legislatures.

In addition to its advisory capacity, the commission makes

Real Estate Commission

decisions in accordance with the powers delegated to it by the legislature. Thus, the legislature enacts a law requiring a real estate examination for license applicants, the commission decides how many questions there will be, how long the exam will last, and what is considered a passing score. Similarly, many states permit an applicant to offer equivalent experience or education in meeting license requirements. The commission's task is to decide, on a case by case basis, the qualifications of each applicant claiming equivalent experience and education. It is also a duty of the commission to decide on license suspensions and revocations.

Real Estate Department   The day-to-day responsibility of real estate regulation rests with a **real estate department** or real estate division. Staffed by full-time civil service employees, the department answers correspondence, sends out application forms, arranges for examinations, collects fees, issues licenses, approves subdivision reports, and so forth. Manpower is also available for the investigation of alleged malpractices and for audits of broker trust fund accounts. Additionally, the department publishes a periodic newsletter or magazine to keep licensees informed about changes in real estate law and prints books or leaflets describing the state's license and subdivision laws. In short, it is the real estate department with which licensees have the most contact, but it is the commission, the commissioner, and the legislature that set license requirements and tell a licensee what he can and cannot do in real estate transactions.

LICENSING AND
EXAMINATION
PROCEDURES   The license applicant begins by filling out a license application form furnished by the real estate department. Applications may be secured either in person or by mail. When the application is completed, it is returned to the department along with a fee to cover application processing and the examination charge. On this application, the applicant is required to furnish his fingerprints and the names of character references. These are for the three-fold purpose of verifying the applicant's identiy, obtaining an indication of the applicant's honesty in business dealings in the past, and locating any criminal record the applicant may have that might dis-

qualify him from being licensed. If he is disqualified, the exam fee is returned.

Next, the department schedules a written examination for the applicant. Exams are held in various parts of the state so the applicant need not travel to the state capital. The same exam is given at each examining center on the same day and at the same time. The applicant is not allowed to bring any books or notes into the testing room. Exams are machine scored and the proper mark-sensing pencils are supplied. Depending on the state, exams may be offered as few as two times a year or as often as once a week. The most common arrangement is once every 3 months.

The applicant is notified of the results in approximately 4 to 6 weeks. If he passed, he now pays a fee for the license itself. Also, salesman applicants must name the broker they will be working for. This information is usually provided on a form signed by the employing broker. A broker applicant must give the address where he plans to operate his brokerage business. These forms are processed by the department and a license is mailed to the applicant. Upon receipt, the licensee can operate as a real estate salesman or broker, as the case may be.

If the applicant fails the written examination, the usual procedure is to allow him to continue taking it until he passes. The original application fee does not have to be paid each time; however, a fee is charged to retake the exam and the applicant must wait until the next testing date.

Once licensed, as long as a person remains active in real estate and meets any post-license education requirements, he may renew his license by paying the required renewal fee. No additional exam is required. If a license is not renewed before it expires, most states allow a grace period and charge a late renewal fee, but do not require reexamination. Once the grace period is passed, all license rights lapse and the individual must meet current application requirements and take another written exam. If a licensee wishes to be temporarily inactive from the business, but does not wish to let his license lapse, most states permit him to place his license on inactive status. When the licensee wishes to reactivate his license, he pays a fee to the department. Then his license is moved from inactive to active status, and he can start selling again.

LICENSE SUSPENSION AND REVOCATION

The most important control mechanism a state has over its real estate salesmen and brokers is that it can **suspend** (temporarily make ineffective) or **revoke** (recall and make void) a real estate license. Without one, the law will not permit a person to engage in real estate activities for the purpose of earning a commission or fee. Unless an agent has a valid license, a court of law will not uphold his claim for a commission from a client.

Reasons for license suspension and revocation include any violation of the state's real estate act, misrepresentation or false promises, undisclosed dual agency, commingling, and acting as an undisclosed principal. Licenses can also be revoked or suspended for false advertising, obtaining a license by fraud, negligence or incompetence, failure to supervise salesmen, conviction of a felony or certain types of misdemeanors, dishonest conduct in general, and, in many states, failure to have a fixed termination date on an exclusive listing.

When the real estate commissioner receives a complaint from someone who feels he was wronged by a licensee, an investigation is conducted by the real estate department staff. Statements are received from witnesses. Title company records, public records, and the licensee's bank records are checked as necessary. The commissioner may call an informal conference and invite all parties involved to attend. If it appears the complaint is serious enough and that a violation of the law has occurred, a formal hearing is scheduled. At this hearing, usually held in the presence of the full commission, the commissioner becomes the **complainant** and brings charges against the licensee. The person who originally brought the matter to the commissioner's attention is a **witness.** The licensee, called the **respondent,** may appear with or without legal counsel. Testimony is taken under oath and a written record is made of the proceedings. A hearing officer may be appointed by the state to hear the case and make a decision, which the commission may accept, reject, or modify. Or the commissioner may act as the hearing officer himself. If the decision is to suspend or revoke the respondent's license, the respondent has the right of appeal to the courts.

The fact that a salesman or broker can lose his or her license for a wrongdoing strongly encourages licensees to operate within the law. However, the threat and loss of a license do nothing to provide financial compensation for any losses suffered by a wronged party. This must be recovered from the licensee or his employer, either through a mutually agreed upon monetary settlement or a court judgment resulting from a civil lawsuit brought by the wronged party. But even with a court-ordered settlement in his favor, all too often court judgments turn out to be uncollectible because the defendant has no money.

Two solutions to the uncollectible judgment problem are in common use. The state may require that a person post a **bond** with the state before a salesman's or broker's license will be issued. In the event of an otherwise uncollectible court judgment against a licensee, the bond money is used to provide payment. Some states require bonds ranging from $1,000 to $10,000, with $2,000 to $5,000 being the most popular range. Licensees either can obtain these bonds from bonding companies for an annual fee, or they can themselves post the required amount of cash or securities with the state.*

The second method of protecting the public is through a state sponsored **recovery fund.** A portion of the money that each licensee pays for his real estate license is set aside in a fund which is made available for the payment of otherwise uncollectible judgments. The number of states that use such recovery funds is growing rapidly.†

The requirement for bonds and the establishment of re-

---

* Bonds are used in Alabama, Arizona, Arkansas, District of Columbia, Louisiana, Massachusetts, Montana, New Mexico, Rhode Island, Tennessee, Virginia, West Virginia, and Wyoming.

† Recovery funds are used in Alaska, Arizona, California, Colorado, Connecticut, Delaware, Florida, Georgia, Hawaii, Idaho, Illinois, Kansas, Kentucky, Minnesota, Nevada, New Jersey, North Dakota, Ohio, Oklahoma, South Dakota, Texas, Utah, and Virginia.

covery funds are not perfect solutions to the problem of uncollectible judgments because the wronged party must expend considerable effort to recover his loss, and it is quite possible that the maximum amount available per transaction or licensee will not fully compensate for the losses suffered. However, either system is better than none at all, which is still the case in some states.

EDUCATION AND RESEARCH

Along with the nationwide trend toward higher licensing standards and professionalization of the real estate brokerage industry, a number of states have embarked on real estate education and research programs. They are paid for out of license fees and serve three purposes. First is the development and staff support of a wide variety of real estate courses on a regular basis in as many geographical areas in a state as possible. Second, money is made available to educators and other qualified persons for the purpose of conducting research on real estate problems. Third, the real estate departments of some states make scholarships available to students wishing to pursue a college degree with a specialization in real estate.

PROFESSIONAL REAL ESTATE ASSOCIATIONS

Even before laws required real estate agents to have licenses, there were professional real estate organizations. Called real estate boards, they joined together agents within a city or county on a voluntary basis. The push to organize came from real estate people who saw the need for some sort of controlling organization that could supervise the activities of individual agents and elevate the profession's status in the public's mind. Next came the gradual grouping of local boards into state associations, and finally, in 1908, the National Association of Real Estate Boards (NAREB) was formed. In 1914, NAREB developed a model license law that became the basis for real estate license laws in many states.

Today the local boards are still the fundamental units of the National Association of Realtors (NAR; the name was changed from NAREB on January 1, 1974). These are the board to which licensees can voluntarily belong. Called boards of Realtors, real estate boards, and realty boards, they promote fair dealing among their members and with the public, and protect members from dishonest and irresponsible licensees. They also promote legislation that protects property rights, offer short seminars to keep members up to date with current laws and practices, and, in general, do whatever is necessary to build the dignity, stability, and professionalization of the industry. Local boards often operate the local multiple listing service, although in some communities it is a privately owned and operated business.

State associations are composed of the members of local boards plus salesmen and brokers who live in areas where no local board exists. The purposes of the state associations are to unite members statewide, to encourage legislation that benefits and protects the real estate industry and safeguards the public in their real estate transactions, and to promote economic growth and development in the state. Also, state associations hold conventions to educate members and foster friendships among them, offer group insurance plans, and sponsor work–pleasure travel trips.

The NAR is made up of local boards and state associations in the United States. The term "Realtor" is a copyrighted and registered term that belongs to NAR. Realtor is not synonymous with real estate agent. It is reserved for the exclusive use of members of the National Association of Realtors, who as part of their membership pledge themselves to abide by the Association's Code of Ethics. The term Realtor cannot be used by nonmembers and in some states the unauthorized use of the term is a violation of the real estate law. Prior to 1974, the use of the term Realtor was primarily reserved for principal brokers. Then in November of that year, by a national membership vote, the decision was made to create an additional membership class, the **Realtor-Associate,** for salespersons working for member Realtors.

Realtor

In the minds of many persons familiar with NAREB and later NAR, the single greatest contribution of the Association was the development of a strict code of ethics in the year 1913. Prior to that time, dealing with real estate agents was hazardous. Cutthroat competition prevailed, and the general spirit of the real estate business was "let the buyer beware." Into this vacuum, NAREB introduced a code of ethics that members agreed to abide by, and which it was hoped would generate public confidence and attract business to members.

Code of Ethics　　　The Code of Ethics has been revised several times since then and now contains 24 Articles that pertain to the Realtor's relation to his clients, to other real estate agents, and to the public as a whole. The full code is reproduced in Figure 19:1.

Although a complete review of each article is beyond the scope of this chapter, it can be seen in the Code that some articles parallel existing laws. For example, Article 10 speaks against racial discrimination and Article 12 speaks for full disclosure. However, the bulk of the Code addresses itself to the obligations of a Realtor that are beyond the written law. For example, in Article 2, the Realtor agrees to keep himself informed regarding laws and regulations, proposed legislation, and current market conditions so that he may be in a position to advise his clients properly. In Article 5, the Realtor agrees to willingly share with other Realtors the lessons of his own experience. In other words, to be recognized as a Realtor, one must not only comply with the letter of the law, but also observe the ethical standards by which the industry operates.

In some states, ethical standards such as those in the NAR Code of Ethics have been legislated into law. Called **canons**, their intent is to promote ethical practices by all brokers and salesmen, not just by those who join the National Association of Realtors.

In addition to its emphasis on real estate brokerage, the National Association of Realtors also contains a number of specialized professional groups within itself. These include the American Institute of Real Estate Appraisers, the Farm and Land Institute, the Institute of Real Estate Management, the Realtors National Marketing Institute, the Society of Industrial Realtors, the Real Estate Securities and Syndication Institute, the American Society of Real Estate Counselors, the American Chapter of the International Real Estate Federation, and the

Preamble . . .

Under all is the land. Upon its wise utilization and widely allocated ownership depend the survival and growth of free institutions and of our civilization. The REALTOR® should recognize that the interests of the nation and its citizens require the highest and best use of the land and the widest distribution of land ownership. They require the creation of adequate housing, the building of functioning cities, the development of productive industries and farms, and the preservation of a healthful environment.

Such interests impose obligations beyond those of ordinary commerce. They impose grave social responsibility and a patriotic duty to which the REALTOR® should dedicate himself, and for which he should be diligent in preparing himself. The REALTOR®, therefore, is zealous to maintain and improve the standards of his calling and shares with his fellow-REALTORS® a common responsibility for its integrity and honor. The term REALTOR® has come to connote competency, fairness, and high integrity resulting from adherence to a lofty ideal of moral conduct in business relations. No inducement of profit and no instruction from clients ever can justify departure from this ideal.

In the interpretation of his obligation, a REALTOR® can take no safer guide than that which has been handed down through the centuries, embodied in the Golden Rule, "Whatsoever ye would that men should do to you, do ye even so to them."

Accepting this standard as his own, every REALTOR® pledges himself to observe its spirit in all of his activities and to conduct his business in accordance with the tenets set forth below.

ARTICLE 1

The REALTOR® should keep himself informed on matters affecting real estate in his community, the state, and nation so that he may be able to contribute responsibly to public thinking on such matters.

ARTICLE 2

In justice to those who place their interests in his care, the REALTOR® should endeavor always to be informed regarding laws, proposed legislation, governmental regulations, public policies, and current market conditions in order to be in a position to advise his clients properly.

ARTICLE 3

It is the duty of the REALTOR® to protect the public against fraud, misrepresentation, and unethical practices in real estate transactions. He should endeavor to eliminate in his community any practices which could be damaging to the public or bring discredit to the real estate profession. The REALTOR® should assist the governmental agency charged with regulating the practices of brokers and salesmen in his state.

ARTICLE 4

The REALTOR® should seek no unfair advantage over other REALTORS® and should conduct his business so as to avoid controversies with other REALTORS®.

ARTICLE 5

In the best interests of society, of his associates, and his own business, the REALTOR® should willingly share with other REALTORS® the lessons of his experience and study for the benefit of the public, and should be loyal to the Board of REALTORS® of his community and active in its work.

ARTICLE 6

To prevent dissension and misunderstanding and to assure better service to the owner, the REALTOR® should urge the exclusive listing of property unless contrary to the best interest of the owner.

ARTICLE 7

In accepting employment as an agent, the REALTOR® pledges himself to protect and promote the interests of the client. This obligation of absolute fidelity to the client's interests is primary, but it does not relieve the REALTOR® of the obligation to treat fairly all parties to the transaction.

Figure 19:1

ARTICLE 8

The REALTOR® shall not accept compensation from more than one party, even if permitted by law, without the full knowledge of all parties to the transaction.

ARTICLE 9

The REALTOR® shall avoid exaggeration, misrepresentation, or concealment of pertinent facts. He has an affirmative obligation to discover adverse factors that a reasonably competent and diligent investigation would disclose.

ARTICLE 10

The REALTOR® shall not deny equal professional services to any person for reasons of race, creed, sex, or country of national origin. The REALTOR® shall not be a party to any plan or agreement to discriminate against a person or persons on the basis of race, creed, sex, or country of national origin.

ARTICLE 11

A REALTOR® is expected to provide a level of competent service in keeping with the Standards of Practice in those fields in which the REALTOR® customarily engages.

The REALTOR® shall not undertake to provide specialized professional services concerning a type of property or service that is outside his field of competence unless he engages the assistance of one who is competent on such types of property or service, or unless the facts are fully disclosed to the client. Any person engaged to provide such assistance shall be so identified to the client and his contribution to the assignment should be set forth.

The REALTOR® shall refer to the Standards of Practice of the National Association as to the degree of competence that a client has a right to expect the REALTOR® to possess, taking into consideration the complexity of the problem, the availability of expert assistance, and the opportunities for experience available to the REALTOR®.

ARTICLE 12

The REALTOR® shall not undertake to provide professional services concerning a property or its value where he has a present or contemplated interest unless such interest is specifically disclosed to all affected parties.

ARTICLE 13

The REALTOR® shall not acquire an interest in or buy for himself, any member of his immediate family, his firm or any member thereof, or any entity in which he has a substantial ownership interest, property listed with him, without making the true position known to the listing owner. In selling property owned by himself, or in which he has any interest, the REALTOR® shall reveal the facts of his ownership or interest to the purchaser.

ARTICLE 14

In the event of a controversy between REALTORS® associated with different firms, arising out of their relationship as REALTORS®, the REALTORS® shall submit the dispute to arbitration in accordance with the regulations of their board or boards rather than litigate the matter.

ARTICLE 15

If a REALTOR® is charged with unethical practice or is asked to present evidence in any disciplinary proceeding or investigation, he shall place all pertinent facts before the proper tribunal of the member board or affiliated institute, society, or council of which he is a member.

ARTICLE 16

When acting as agent, the REALTOR® shall not accept any commission, rebate, or profit on expenditures made for his principal-owner, without the principal's knowledge and consent.

Figure 19:1

ARTICLE 17

The REALTOR® shall not engage in activities that constitute the unauthorized practice of law and shall recommend that legal counsel be obtained when the interest of any party to the transaction requires it.

ARTICLE 18

The REALTOR® shall keep in a special account in an appropriate financial institution, separated from his own funds, monies coming into his possession in trust for other persons, such as escrows, trust funds, clients' monies, and other like items.

ARTICLE 19

The REALTOR® shall be careful at all times to present a true picture in his advertising and representations to the public. He shall neither advertise without disclosing his name nor permit any person associated with him to use individual names or telephone numbers, unless such person's connection with the REALTOR® is obvious in the advertisement.

ARTICLE 20

The REALTOR®, for the protection of all parties, shall see that financial obligations and commitments regarding real estate transactions are in writing, expressing the exact agreement of the parties. A copy of each agreement shall be furnished to each party upon his signing such agreement.

ARTICLE 21

The REALTOR® shall not engage in any practice or take any action inconsistent with the agency of another REALTOR®.

ARTICLE 22

In the sale of property which is exclusively listed with a REALTOR®, the REALTOR® shall utilize the services of other brokers upon mutually agreed upon terms when it is in the best interests of the client.

Negotiations concerning property which is listed exclusively shall be carried on with the listing broker, not with the owner, except with the consent of the listing broker.

ARTICLE 23

The REALTOR® shall not publicly disparage the business practice of a competitor nor volunteer an opinion of a competitor's transaction. If his opinion is sought and if the REALTOR® deems it appropriate to respond, such opinion shall be rendered with strict professional integrity and courtesy.

ARTICLE 24

The REALTOR® shall not directly or indirectly solicit the services or affiliation of an employee or independent contractor in the organization of another REALTOR® without prior notice to said REALTOR®

Where the word REALTOR® is used in this Code and Preamble, it shall be deemed to include REALTOR®-ASSOCIATE. Pronouns shall be considered to include REALTORS® and REALTOR®-ASSOCIATES of both genders.

The Code of Ethics was adopted in 1913. Amended at the Annual Convention in 1924, 1928, 1950, 1951, 1952, 1955, 1956, 1961, 1962, and 1974.

Women's Council of Realtors. Membership is open to Realtors interested in these specialties.

Realtist   The National Association of Real Estate Brokers, Inc. (NAREB) is a national trade association representing minority real estate professionals actively engaged in the industry. Its members have adopted the designation **Realtist** as their trade name and the organization extends through 14 regions across the country with more than 40 active local boards.

GRI Designation   To help encourage and recognize professionalism in the real estate industry, state Boards of Realtors sponsor education courses leading to the GRI designation. Course offerings typically include real estate law, finance, appraisal, investments, office management, and salesmanship. Upon completion of the prescribed curriculum, the designation, Graduate Realtor's Institute is awarded.

VOCABULARY REVIEW   *Match terms a–m with statements 1–13.*

a. *Broker*
b. *ETS*
c. *Fictitious name*
d. *Principal broker*
e. *Real estate commissioner*
f. *Real estate salesman*
g. *Realtor*

h. *Realty board*
i. *Recipcrocity*
j. *Recovery fund*
k. *Respondent*
l. *Revoke*
m. *Suspend*

1. A company based in Princeton, New Jersey, that writes, administers, and grades real estate exams for about 20 states.
2. A person who is licensed to bring about real estate transactions for a fee, but who must do so only in the employment of a real estate broker.
3. A copyrighted term owned by the National Association of Realtors for exclusive use by its members.
4. Broker in charge of an office.
5. An arrangement whereby states honor each other's licenses.
6. A business operated under any name other than the owner's name.
7. An agent who negotiates transactions for a fee.

8. A person appointed by the governor to implement and carry out those laws enacted by the state legislature that pertain to real estate.
9. To temporarily make ineffective.
10. To recall and make void.
11. A real estate licensee against whom a complaint has been filed with the real estate commission.
12. A local trade organization for real estate licensees and other persons allied with the real estate industry.
13. A state-operated fund that can be tapped to pay for uncollectible judgments against real estate licensees.

QUESTIONS AND PROBLEMS

1. What was the purpose of early real estate license laws?
2. When is a person required to hold a real estate license?
3. What factors does a broker consider when deciding what percentage of commissions should be paid to the salespersons in the office?
4. Does your state subscribe to the ETS or multi-state exam services or does it write all its own questions? How often are the broker and the salesman exams given?
5. What trends are apparent in your state with regard to real estate education requirements?
6. Regarding license reciprocity, in what other states can a person holding a real estate license from your state negotiate transactions for a commission?
7. What is the name of the person currently serving as real estate commissioner for your state? What are his (her) duties and responsibilities?
8. How is the real estate commission selected in your state? What are its duties and responsibilities?
9. Under what circumstances are real estate licenses suspended or revoked in your state?
10. What is the purpose of a bond or recovery fund? What does your state require?
11. What is the purpose of the National Association of Realtors?

ADDITIONAL READINGS

"Do You Need a BA to Sell Real Estate?" *Real Estate Today*, May/June 1975, pages 15ff. A round-table discussion by seven Realtors on the pros and cons of education requirements for real estate licenses.

Ellis, John T. *Guide to Real Estate Examinations.* Englewood Cliffs, N.J.: Prentice-Hall, 1974, 311 pages. A combination text and workbook designed for real estate salesmen and broker applicants. It provides nontechnical coverage of examination subjects and features several hundred examination-type questions.

Howe, Jonathan T. "Update: The Independent Contractor Issue," *Real Estate Today,* Oct. 1975, pages 40ff. Discusses whether the traditional independent contractor status is best for real estate salespeople, or whether it would be better to change to an employee–employer relationship.

Mortell, Arthur L. *Why Real Estate Salesmen Succeed and Why They Don't.* Los Angeles: Systematic Achievement Corporation, 1970, 224 pages. Discusses why some salesmen succeed for a year and others for a lifetime and what the successful salesmen have in common.

Semenow, Robert W. *Selected Cases in Real Estate.* Englewood Cliffs, N.J.: Prentice-Hall, 1973, 638 pages. Pages 464–503 contain a series of cases and court decisions regarding the granting and revocation of real estate licenses.

Weston, Joseph E. *Weston's Real Estate Mathematics.* Portland, Ore.: Wesley Publishing Company, 1972, 241 pages. Written to aid the applicant in passing the mathematics section of his state's real estate license examination.

20

Condominiums, Cooperatives, and Townhouses

Bylaws: rules that govern how an owners' association will be run

CC&Rs: covenants, conditions and restrictions by which a property owner agrees to abide

Common elements: real property that is owned jointly by condominium owners as a group

Condominium: individual ownership of separate portions of a building plus joint ownership of the common elements

Cooperative: land and building owned or leased by a corporation which in turn leases space to its shareholders

Enabling declaration, Master

deed: a document that converts a given parcel of land into a condominium subdivision

Limited common elements: common elements, the use of which is limited to certain owners; for example walls and ceilings between individual units

Proprietary lease: a lease issued by a cooperative corporation to its shareholders

Time-sharing: part ownership of a property coupled with a right to exclusive use of it for a specified number of days per year

Townhouses: individually owned row houses with joint ownership of common areas

The idea of combining community living with community ownership is not new. Two thousand years ago, the Roman Senate passed condominium laws that permitted Roman citizens to own individual dwelling units in multi-unit buildings. This form of ownership resulted because land was scarce and expensive in Rome. After the fall of the Roman Empire, condominium ownership was found in the walled cities of the Middle Ages. However, this was primarily a defensive measure as residing outside the walls was dangerous due to roving bands of raiders. With the stabilization of governments after the Middle Ages, the condominium concept became dormant until the early twentieth century, when in response to land scarcity in cities, the idea was revived in Western Europe. From there the concept spread to several Latin American countries and, in 1951, to Puerto Rico.

UNITED STATES   Puerto Rican laws and experience became the basis for the passage by the U.S. Congress in 1961 of Section 234 of the National Housing Act. This section provides a legal model for condominium ownership and makes available FHA mortgage loan insurance on condominium units. Currently, the District of Columbia, Guam, Puerto Rico, the Virgin Islands, and 49 states (Louisiana is the exception) permit the ownership of real estate on a condominium basis. By 1976, roughly one in four new residences being built in the United States was a condominium.

Condominium ownership is not the only legal framework available that combines community living with community ownership, although it is currently the best known. Prior to the enactment of condominium legislation, cooperative ownership of multifamily residential buildings was popular in the United States, particularly in the states of Florida, New York, and Hawaii. A more recent variation in community ownership is the individually owned row house combined with joint ownership of common areas; it is usually referred to as a townhouse.

Of the forces responsible for creating the need for condominiums, cooperatives and townhouses, the most important are land scarcity in desirable areas, continuing escalation in construction costs, disenchantment with the work and expense of maintaining a single-family house, and the desire to own rather than rent.

Land-use Efficiency   When constructing single-family houses on separate lots, a builder can usually average four to five houses per acre of land. In a growing number of cities, the sheer physical space necessary to continue building detached houses either does not exist or, if it does, it is a long distance from employment centers or is so expensive as to eliminate all but a small portion of the population from building there. As in ancient Roman times, the solution is to build more dwellings on the same parcel of land. Instead of four or five dwellings, build 25 or 100 on an acre of land. That way not only is the land more efficiently used, but the cost is divided among more owners. From the standpoint of construction costs, the builder does not have the miles of streets, sewers, or utility lines that would be necessary to reach every house in a subdivision. Furthermore, the facts that there are shared walls, that one dwelling unit's ceiling is often another's floor, and that one roof can cover many vertically stacked units can produce savings in construction materials and labor.

Amenities

For some householders, the lure of "carefree living," wherein such chores as lawn mowing, watering, weeding, snow shoveling, and building maintenance are provided, is the major attraction. For others, it is the security often associated with clustered dwellings or the extensive recreational and social facilities that are not economically possible on a single dwelling unit basis. It is commonplace to find swimming pools, recreation halls, tennis and volleyball courts, gymnasiums, and even social directors at condominium, cooperative, and town-house projects.

A large rental apartment project can also produce the same advantages of land and construction economy and amenities. Nevertheless, we cannot overlook the preference of most American households to own rather than rent their dwellings. This preference is typically based on a desire for a savings program, observation of inflation in real estate prices, and advantageous income tax laws that allow owners, but not renters, to deduct property taxes and mortgage interest.

To further explore the topic of owner-occupied community living, the remainder of this chapter is divided into two broad sections: (1) the legal and mechanical aspects, and (2) the human side of these forms of living.

DIVIDING THE LAND

Let us begin our discussion of the legal aspects of condominiums, cooperatives, and townhouses by illustrating the owner's estate in each and comparing each to the estate held by the owner of a house. Notice in Figure 20:1 that the ownership of house A extends from lot line B across to lot line C.

Figure 20:1

COMPARISON OF ESTATES
(Presume fee simple ownership in each case)

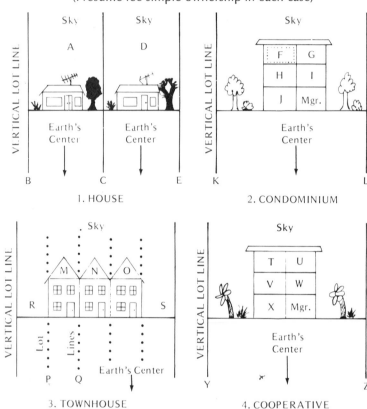

Except where limited by zoning or other legal restrictions, the owner of house A has full control over and full right to use the land between his lot lines from the center of the earth to the limits of the sky. Within the law, he can choose how to use his land, what to build on it or add to it, what color to paint his house and garage, how many people and animals will live there, what type of landscaping to have, from whom to purchase property insurance, and so on. The owner of house D has the same control over the land between lot lines C and E. The owner of A cannot dictate to his neighbor what color to paint his house, what kind of shrubs and trees to grow, or from whom to buy hazard insurance if he buys it at all. (Occasionally, one will find deed restrictions in housing subdivisions that give the owners a limited amount of control over each other's land uses in the subdivision.)

In a condominium, each dwelling unit owner owns as his *Common Elements* separate property the cubicle of air space that his unit occupies. This is the space lying between the interior surfaces of the unit sides and between the floor and the ceiling. The remainder of the building and the land are owned jointly by the owners as a group; these are the **common elements** or common areas. In Figure 20:1, the owner of dwelling unit F owns as his separate property the air space enclosed by the dotted lines. Except for the individual unit owners' air spaces, an **owners' association** composed of F, G, H, I, and J owns an undivided interest in everything between lot lines K and L. This includes the land and the shell of the building, plus such things as the manager's apartment, lobby, hallways, stairways, elevators, and recreation facilities. In some states the walls and ceilings between individual units are called **limited common elements.** The word "limited" means that their use is limited to the abutting units.

A third ownership arrangement combines features of both a house and a condominium. In Figure 20:1, each townhouse owner owns as his separate property the land that his dwelling unit occupies. For example, the owner of townhouse M owns the land between lot lines P and Q from the center of the earth skyward. Together, owners M, N, and O jointly own the land at R and S and any improvements thereon, such as recreation facilities or parking lots.

In a cooperative there is no separate property at all. Rather, the owners hold shares of stock in a cooperative corporation, which, in turn, owns the land and building and issues proprietary leases to the owners to use specific apartments. A **proprietary lease** differs from the usual landlord–tenant lease in that the "tenant" is also an owner of the building. In the cooperative in Figure 20:1, all the land and building lying between lot lines Y and Z are owned by a corporation that is owned by shareholders T, U, V, W, and X. Ownership of the corporation's shares carries the right to occupy apartment units in the building.

Having now briefly illustrated the estates created by the condominium, townhouse, and cooperative forms of real estate ownership, let us take a closer look at their organization, financing, and management.

CONDOMINIUM

A condominium is created when a person, usually a real estate developer, files an **enabling declaration** with his state government that converts a parcel of land held under a single deed into a number of individual condominium estates, plus an estate that includes the common elements. Included in the declaration is a description of the location of each individual unit with respect to the land, identification of the common elements to be shared, and the percentage interest each unit owner will have in the common elements. If the condominium is to be on leasehold land, the declaration converts the single leasehold interest into individual subleases. The right of a person to file an enabling declaration is outlined in each state's condominium laws. These laws are variously known as the **Horizontal Property Act,** Strata Titles Act, or Condominium Act, or by a similar name. Basically, they all follow the model FHA legislation, plus each state's own particular refinements.

Owners'
Association

In addition to filing the enabling declaration, also known as the **master deed,** plan of condominium ownership, or condominium subdivision, the developer must provide a legal framework by which the unit owners can govern themselves. Often, a nonprofit condominium **owners' association** of which each unit purchaser automatically becomes a member is incorporated. The association can also be organized as a trust or unincorporated association. However, in the event of a lawsuit against the association, these do not offer the members the legal protection normally provided by a corporation.

Bylaws

Bylaws must also be recorded with the master deed. They provide the rules by which the association's board of directors is elected from among the association members and set the standards by which the board must rule. They also set forth how association dues (maintenance fees) will be established and collected, how contracts will be let for maintenance, management, and repair work, and how personnel will be hired.

Finally, the developer must file a list of regulations by which anyone purchasing a unit in the condominium must abide. These are known as **covenants, conditions, and restrictions** (CC&Rs) and tell a unit owner such things as what color the exterior of his living room drapes must be and whether or not he can have children or pets living in his apartment. Additional regulations may be embodied in a set of **house rules.** Typically, these govern such things as when the swimming pool and other recreation facilities will be open for use and when quiet hours will be observed in the building. *CC&Rs*

Once the units in the building have been sold and the association turned over to the unit owners, the unit owners can change the rules. Generally, the bylaws require a three-fourths vote and the CC&Rs require a two-thirds vote from the association members for a change. House rules can be changed with a simple majority or, in some cases, by the board of directors without a vote of the association. Votes are weighted in accordance with the bylaws, and three variations are presently in use. The most straightforward is to give each unit owner one vote. In other associations, the weight of one's vote depends on the percentage of the building he owns. Thus, in a condominium composed of 1,000- and 1,500-square-foot apartments, the owners of the 1,500-square-foot units would have one and one-half times the vote of those with 1,000-square-foot units. In the third variation, the weighting is by the sales price of the unit. The argument for weighted voting is that owners of the larger and more expensive units are often required by the bylaws to bear a proportionately larger share of the cost of maintaining the building. *Voting Rules*

For condominium owners to enjoy maintenance-free living, the association must employ the services of a building manager. If the project contains only a few units, the association may elect to employ one of its members on a part-time basis to take care of the landscaping, hallways, trash, and the like and to keep records of his expenses. For major maintenance items such as painting, roof repairs, and pool refurbishing, independent contractors are hired. *CONDOMINIUM MANAGEMENT*

In larger projects, the association can either hire a full-time manager or a professional management firm. A management firm supplies a management package that combines an on-site resident manager plus off-site services, such as accounting for the building's expenses and handling the payroll. The management firm will also contract for gardening, trash hauling, and janitorial services. Each month the firm bills the association for the package of services rendered.

Whether hired directly by the association or by the management firm, the resident manager is usually responsible for enforcing the house rules, handling complaints or problems regarding maintenance, and supervising such matters as the handling of the mail and the use of the swimming pool and recreation areas. The extent of his duties and responsibilities is set by the owners' association. The association should also retain the right to fire the resident manager and the management firm if their services are not satisfactory.

MAINTENANCE FEES   The costs of maintaining the common elements in a condominium are allocated among the unit owners in accordance with percentages set forth in the enabling declaration. These **maintenance fees** or **association dues** are collected monthly. Failure to pay creates a lien against the delinquent owner's unit. The amount collected is based on the association's budget. This in turn is based on the association's estimate of the cost of month-to-month maintenance, insurance, legal counsel, and accounting services, plus reserves for expenses that do not occur monthly.

The importance of setting aside reserves each month is illustrated by the following example. Suppose it is estimated that the exterior of a 100-unit building will have to be painted every 5 years, and that the cost, allowing for inflation, will be $18,000. The association has two choices: the members can either wait until the paint job is needed and then divide the $18,000 cost among the 100 owners, or they can pay a small amount each month into a reserve fund so that in 5 years there will be $18,000 available. The first choice means a special assessment averaging $180 per owner at the time the job needs to be done. The second choice requires an average of $3 per month from each owner for 60 months. If the reserves are kept in an interest-bearing savings account, as they should be, less than $3 per month would need to be collected.

PROPERTY TAXES
AND INSURANCE

Since condominium law recognizes each condominium dwelling unit as a separate legal ownership, property taxes are assessed on each unit separately. Property taxes are based on the assessed value of the unit, which is based on its market value. As a rule, it is not necessary for the taxing authority to assess and tax the common elements separately. The reason is that the market value of each unit reflects not only the value of the unit itself, but also the value of the fractional ownership in the common elements that accompanies the unit.

The association is responsible for purchasing hazard and liability insurance covering the common elements. Each dwelling unit owner is responsible for purchasing hazard and liability insurance for the interior of his dwelling.

Thus, if a visitor slips on a banana peel in the lobby or a hallway of the building, the association is responsible. If the accident occurs in an individual's unit, the unit owner is responsible. In a high-rise condominium, if the roof breaks during a heavy rainstorm and floods several apartments below, the association is responsible. If an apartment owner's dishwasher overflows and soaks the apartments below him, he is responsible.

If the condominium unit is being rented, the owner will want to have landlord insurance, and the tenant, for his own protection, will want a tenant's hazard and liability policy.

CONDOMINIUM
FINANCING

Because each condominium unit can be separately owned, each can be separately financed. Thus, a condominium purchaser can choose whether or not to borrow against his unit. If he borrows, he can choose a large or small down payment and a long or short amortization period. Once in his unit, if he wants to repay early or refinance, that is his option too. When he sells, the buyer can elect to assume the loan, pay it off, or obtain new financing. In other words, while association bylaws, restrictions, and house rules may regulate how an owner may use his unit, in no way does the association control how a unit may be financed.

Since each unit is a separate ownership, if a lender needs to foreclose against a delinquent borrower in the building, the remaining unit owners are not involved. They are neither responsible for the delinquent borrower's mortgage debt, nor are they parties to the foreclosure.

Loan Terms

Loan terms offered condominium buyers are quite similar to those offered on houses. Typically, lenders will make conventional, uninsured loans for up to 80% of value. With private mortgage insurance, this can be raised to 90% or 95%. On FHA-approved buildings, the FHA will insure up to 97% of the first $25,000 of appraised value, 90% of the next $10,000, and 80% above that to a maximum loan guarantee of $45,000. Amortization periods typically run 25 to 30 years. Financing can also be in the form of an installment contract or a purchase money mortgage.

When a condominium is being sold by a developer to private buyers for the first time, the usual procedure is for the developer to find a lender who will advance the money the developer needs to build and offer to finance the unit purchasers. As purchasers sign their mortgage papers, the lender is credited on his loan. Although a buyer can still pay cash or obtain his own lender, having a loan package ready for the buyer is a valuable marketing tool.

Deposit Practices

If a project is not already completed and ready for occupancy when it is offered for sale, it is common for the developer to require a substantial deposit. The best practice is to place this in an escrow account payable to the developer upon completion. However, some developers use deposits to help pay the expenses of construction while the building is being built. Unfortunately, if such deposits are spent by a developer who goes bankrupt before the project is completed, the buyer receives neither a finished unit nor the return of his deposit. If the deposits are held in escrow, the buyers do not receive a unit but they do get their deposits back.

LEGISLATION AGAINST ABUSES

The legal documents involved in purchasing a house are few in comparison to those involved in purchasing a condominium. Because the master deed, bylaws, and restrictions

often total 100 or more pages of legal language, unit purchasers are discouraged from reading them. As a result, in
numerous cases developers have buried in these documents the
fact that they are retaining substantial rights and title in their
projects, even after all the units have been sold.

Two specific areas of abuse have been recreation and management. Some developers retain title to recreation areas and
then charge unit owners escalating monthly-use fees that are
far more than actual costs. The developer then keeps the
difference. If a unit owner protests by refusing to pay, the
developer can place a lien against the unit and ultimately have
it sold at foreclosure. In the second area of abuse, the fine
print appoints the developer as manager of the project for
25 years. When the unit owners find their management fees
out of proportion to the level of services received, the developer points out the clause appointing him manager and
reminds them that he cannot be fired.

In some instances, developers have used declaration fine
print to bury the fact that they are retaining the fee title to
the land and that the unit owners are lessees. Thus, not only
are unit owners required to pay a lease fee to the developer
each month, but they will never own the land beneath them.
There is nothing fundamentally wrong with having a condominium on leased land; it is the intentional burying of this
fact with the hope that it will not be detected before the sales
contracts are signed that creates trouble.

Legislation

Various state legislatures have reacted to these abuses and
enacted protective measures. A number of jurisdictions prohibit condominiums on leased land (Colorado, Delaware, Illinois, Kansas, Minnesota, Missouri, Montana, New Hampshire,
New York, Pennsylvania, West Virginia, Wyoming, and the
Virgin Islands). New York prohibits developers from retaining
the ownership of recreation facilities. Illinois, New York, Virginia, and others have pioneered legislation that requires important contract passages be printed in red ink or large type,
that contracts be written in ordinary English, and that the developer be more descriptive about the fees that will be assessed to owners once they buy. Arizona, California, Hawaii,
Oregon, Washington, and others require that a public sub-

division report, prepared by a state agency, be handed to buyers before they sign any sales contract. These reports must give numerous facts about a project in a readable format.

The FHA has also taken a firm stand on these issues. Recognizing that owner discontent can lead to mortgage foreclosure and subsequent FHA insurance losses, the FHA requires that deposit money go into an escrow account, that unit owners own in fee all the common elements, and that the developer does not retain the management contract. The FHA also imposes guidelines as to construction quality, building design, recreation facilities, and number of units on the site.

Note that laws to prevent developer abuses fall into two categories: the outright prohibition of something, such as building on leased land, and the attempt to make documents more readable. However, neither is the total answer. In Hawaii, although lease abuses are rare, leasehold condominium owners are automatically denied FHA insurance. In states that endeavor to make documents easier to read, the effort is to no avail when a buyer refuses to read them or obtain legal counsel.

PHYSICAL APPEARANCE OF A CONDOMINIUM

Before we turn our attention from condominiums, let us reemphasize that a condominium is first and foremost a legal concept. It tells how title to real property is owned. It does not, by itself, tell us what a condominium looks like. Physically, a condominium can take the shape of a two-story garden apartment building, a 20-story tower, row houses, clustered houses, or detached houses sharing a single parcel of land. You will hear them called low-rise and high-rise condominiums, townhomes, garden-rises, walled garden apartments, villas, and cluster housing.

Condominiums are not restricted to residential uses. In recent years, a number of developers across the nation have built office buildings and sold individual suites to doctors, dentists, and lawyers. The same idea has been applied to shopping centers and industrial space. A condominium does not have to be a new building. Starting in the late 1960s, many existing apartment houses were converted from rental status to condominium ownership with only a few physical changes to the building.

The townhouse combines features of a house and a condominium. As illustrated in Figure 20:1, the legal concept is that the owner enjoys the separate ownership of his dwelling and the land immediately beneath his dwelling, plus joint ownership of the common areas surrounding the dwelling units.

Since the townhouse owner owns his land and dwelling as separate property, presumably he may use and maintain it as he wishes. However, there may be mutual restrictions upon all separately owned lots and dwellings. The right to establish and enforce these restrictions is usually vested in an owners' association. The association can dictate what color an owner can paint his window shutters, how he can landscape the front of his lot, and how many children and pets can reside in his dwelling. Also, title to the common areas is vested in the association, and it governs how these areas shall be used by the residents.

Of all the forms of community living, the townhouse comes the closest to combining the advantages of a house and a condominium. Structurally, townhouses are built to look more like houses than apartments and generally contain more living area than apartment buildings. Because vertical stacking is limited to one owner, densities are usually limited to eight or ten units per acre. Even though this is twice the density of a house subdivision, by careful planning, a developer can give each owner the feeling of more spaciousness. One way is by taking advantage of uneven terrain. If a parcel contains some flat land, some hilly land, some land covered with trees, and a running stream, the dwellings can be clustered on the land best suited for building and thus preserve the stream, woods, and steep slopes in their natural state. A developer building detached houses would have to remove the grove of trees, fill in the stream, and terrace the slopes, and would still be able to provide homes for only half the number of families.

Such thoughtful planning, of course, is not limited to the townhouse form of ownership. Some of the attractive planned residential developments in the nation combine natural surroundings with townhouses and cluster houses, plus low- and high-rise condominium apartments. So skillfully has this been

TOWNHOUSE

done that residents are far more aware of the project's green vistas and lakes than they are of neighboring buildings.

COOPERATIVE APARTMENTS

Prior to the availability of condominium enabling legislation, owner-occupied community housing took the form of the cooperative housing corporation. Although the condominium is dominant today, there are still substantial numbers of cooperative apartments in New York City, Miami, Chicago, San Francisco, and Honolulu.

A **cooperative apartment** is organized by forming a nonprofit corporation. This is usually done by a developer who is planning to convert an existing rental building to cooperative ownership or build a new structure. Sometimes, the tenants in a rental building will organize a cooperative corporation to buy their building from the owner. To raise the funds necessary to pay for the building, the corporation borrows as much as it can by mortgaging the building. The balance is raised by selling shares of stock in the corporation.

The Cooperator

The shareholder, or **cooperator,** receives a proprietary lease from the corporation to occupy a certain apartment in the building. The more desirable apartments require the purchase of more shares than the less desirable ones.

In return for this lease, the cooperator does not pay rent; instead, he agrees to pay to the corporation his share of the cost of maintaining the building and his share of the monthly mortgage payments and annual property taxes. This sharing of expenses is a unique and crucial feature of this form of ownership. If one or more cooperators fail to pay their pro rata share, the remaining cooperators must make up the difference. Suppose that the monthly loan payment on a 10-unit cooperative building is $2,000 and it is shared equally by its 10 cooperators, each contributing $200 per month. If one shareholder fails to contribute his $200, only $1,800 is available for the required payment. If the lender is paid $1,800 rather than $2,000, the loan is delinquent and subject to foreclosure. The lender does not take the position that, since 9 of the 10 cooperators made their payments, nine tenths of the building is free from foreclosure threat. Therefore, it is the responsibility of the remaining nine to continue making the $2,000 monthly payments or lose the building. They can seek voluntary reimbursement by the tardy cooperator, or, if that does not work, terminate him as a shareholder.

In most cooperative leases written today, shareholder termination is the worst that can happen to a nonpaying cooperator, because under American corporation law a shareholder is not liable for the debts of the corporation. Thus, even if the cooperative corporation owes more than it owns and is in foreclosure or bankruptcy, the shareholders cannot be dunned for deficiency payments. The lender can look only to the value of the corporation's property for recovery of its loan. In view of this, lenders are especially cautious when making loans to cooperatives, and this has made it difficult for them to raise money. To counteract this situation, the FHA, under Section 213 of the National Housing Act, will insure lenders against losses on loans made to nonprofit housing cooperatives.

As the entire building serves as collateral for the loan, obtaining new financing on an individual apartment unit in the building is impossible. If there is to be new financing, it must be on the entire building. When the original mortgage loan is substantially reduced and/or apartment prices have risen, as evidenced by a rise in the value of shares, this can be a severe handicap if a cooperator wants to sell. To illustrate, suppose that a family buys into a cooperative for $5,000. Several years later the family wants to sell, and is offered $15,000 for its shares. Unlike the purchaser of a house or a condominium who can obtain most of the money he needs by mortgaging the dwelling he is buying, the cooperative purchaser cannot mortgage his unit. Consequently, if the buyer does not have $15,000 in cash, he must mortgage his other assets or seek an unsecured personal loan. With such a loan, the lending decision is based on the buyer's character, income, and assets in general, but no specific security is pledged as collateral. If a personal loan is not possible and the seller is willing to help the buyer with financing, the solution may be to sell on an installment contract.

Refinancing Methods

Board of Directors

How a cooperative will be run is set forth in its articles of incorporation, bylaws, covenants and restrictions, and house rules. The governing body is a board of directors elected by a vote of the cooperators and voting can either be based on shares held or on a one-vote-per-apartment basis. The board hires the services needed to maintain and operate the building and decides on how cooperative facilities will be used by shareholders. The annual budget and other matters of importance are submitted to all shareholders for a vote. Between shareholder meetings, normally scheduled annually, unhappy cooperators can approach board members and ask that a desired change be made. Or, at election time, they can vote for more sympathetic contenders for board membership or can run for board positions themselves.

Owner's Association

In two very significant areas, the authority of a cooperative owners' association and its board differs from that found in a condominium. First, as the interior of a cooperator's apartment is not his separate property, the association can control how he uses it. This right is based on the principle that the entire building is owned jointly by all cooperators for their mutual benefit. Thus, if a cooperator damages his apartment or is a constant nuisance, his lease can be terminated. As a rule, this requires at least a two-thirds vote of the shareholders and return of the cooperator's investment.

Second, in a cooperative, the owners' association has the right to accept or reject new shareholders and sublessees. (The latter occurs when a shareholder rents his apartment to another.) If there is much turnover in the building, the association will delegate this right to the board. Thus, whenever a shareholder wishes to sell or rent, the transaction is subject to approval by the board. Although this may seem discriminatory, particularly in view of the current trend toward non-discrimination, this feature has been upheld by the courts. The legal basis is that cooperators share not only mutual ownership in their building, but also a joint financial responsibility. However, the courts have also ruled that board approvals cannot be capricious or inconsistent.

From a social standpoint, the right to approve purchasers

and renters helps to foster and maintain the economic and social status of residents, which some persons find attractive. It is also a very useful feature when a person wants to own in a building that excludes children and/or pets.

Although owners of houses and condominium units have always enjoyed deductions for mortgage interest and property taxes on their federal income tax returns, such was not always the case with cooperatives. Originally, cooperators were excluded because it was the corporation, not the shareholder, that was liable for interest and taxes. Now, however, if 80% of a cooperative's income is derived from tenant–owner rentals, the individual cooperators may deduct their proportionate share of property taxes and loan interest. If the land or building is leased to the corporation and the fee owner pays the taxes, he is entitled to the deduction, not the cooperators.

Income Tax Treatment

Most cooperatives are organized as corporations. It is a practical way to take title, select and control management, administer the day-to-day affairs of the cooperative, and at the same time insulate the individual members from direct liability for the obligations of the corporation. It is also possible to form a cooperative as a general or limited partnership, or as a trust arrangement with the cooperators as trust beneficiaries, or as a tenancy in common. None of these has been widely used, primarily because partnerships and trusts do not provide the legal insulation of a corporation, and because the tenancy in common idea has been replaced by the condominium concept.

Other Cooperative Forms

Low-cost cooperatives can be found in a number of United States cities. Sponsored by the FHA or the city itself, these cooperatives are subsidized by public tax revenues and provide low- and moderate-income families with an opportunity for home ownership. Leases in these buildings are usually written for only 1 to 3 years and are not automatically renewable by the cooperator. This feature reflects the possibility that public funds may be cut back in the future. Also, when a cooperator sells, he is not permitted to retain any profits made upon resale. Rather, he is restricted to recovering only the money he has actually invested (i.e., his down payment, mortgage amortization, and improvements).

TIME-SHARING OWNERSHIP

Thus far, we have been concerned only with the three-dimensional utilization of real estate (i.e., the sharing of land and air space). Since 1970, a fourth dimension, time owner-ship, has received increasing attention in the United States. Used primarily in resort areas, the principle of time sharing ownership is that a person buys the right to the exclusive use of real estate for a specified length of time each year, such as a week or a month.

Two systems are in operation. One is the long-term lease wherein a promoter purchases a motel, hotel, or apartment building in a resort area; for each unit in the building, he sells 25 two-weeks-a-year leases for 30 years. (The remaining two weeks are generally reserved for maintenance work.) The sale of these leases pays for the building, and the lessee is charged only his share of the cost of managing, servicing, and main-taining the building. The lessee may be assigned to a specific unit to be used each year or allowed to use any unit in the building that is available when he wishes to visit. To obtain his 2 weeks each year, the lessee makes a reservation through the on-site manager, often on a first-come first-served basis. As 30 years at the same resort is a long time, the lease should permit the lessee the right to sell his lease to another person.

The second system is to establish a condominium and sell each unit to several owners in common ownership. With ownership, each owner obtains the right to use the unit for a certain period each year. For example, a unit might be sold to 12 buyers as tenants in common, each of whom obtains the right to the exclusive use of the unit for 2 weeks in the winter and 2 weeks in the summer. The ownership agreement should also state how user priorities are set, who is responsible for maintenance, what procedures must be followed if an owner wants to sell his interest, and what happens if one or more owners fail to pay their share of expenses and the mortgage.

THE HUMAN ASPECT

Although the condominium and townhouse concepts are still relatively young in the United States, considerable infor-mation has been collected on how residents have fared with these new life styles. Let us briefly review the highlights of their experiences.

The two most important reasons are the desire for owner- *Why They Buy*
ship and the fact that condominiums and townhouses usually
cost less than houses do. Other reasons include freedom from
maintenance, availability of recreation facilities, attractive
views and settings, close-in locations, security systems, and
new friends among other unit owners.

At one time, condominium living was considered strictly *Who Buys*
for the "newly wed or nearly dead," reflecting a philosophy
that this form of living was but a stepping-stone for young
couples on their way to house ownership and a refuge for older
persons no longer able to maintain their houses. It is now
apparent, however, that the predominant age group in condominiums is 30 to 39 years old, followed by those in their
twenties, forties, fifties, and sixties. Moreover, young buyers
are deciding to stay longer. A key reason for this is the increasing cost of single-family houses. In hot and dry climates,
where considerable effort is required to have attractive landscaping, persons who have houses are moving to condominiums and townhouses.

To date, condominium purchasers are primarily from the
white-collar professions, far outnumbering blue-collar and retired residents. However, in sharp contrast to this homogeneity
is the wide range of incomes often represented in the same
condominium building. Whereas single-family house prices are
usually consistent within a given neighborhood or suburb, in
a high-rise condominium it is not unusual to find $20,000 to
$40,000 units on the lower floors, larger $50,000 to $60,000
units on upper floors, and perhaps several $100,000 pent-
house units on the top floor.

People still have a desire for privacy even though they *Privacy*
may live in a multifamily building. The most common complaint is that neighbor's conversations, radios, children, appliances, and plumbing can be heard through the walls, and
that footsteps from the unit above can be heard through the
ceiling. Another complaint stems from windows that look onto

neighboring dwellings at close range and windows that permit outsiders to see in. Popular in townhouses is a small, but totally private, backyard or patio. Although a developer can increase privacy by building thicker walls and ceilings and planning lower densities, these items cost money. Consequently, owner dissatisfaction with community living is more prevalent among low-priced than high-priced units.

Children

More and more couples with children are turning to condominiums and townhouses because they cannot afford a single-family house. In a well-planned project, children can actually benefit by having more and closer recreation areas than would be found in a house subdivision. Also, because of higher densities, schools are often located closer to children's homes. Unfortunately, in poorly planned projects, children are forced to play in the streets and on residents' front lawns. Problems also arise when children and teenagers take over swimming and recreation facilities and exclude adults. As a result, buyers without children often go to great lengths to find adult-only projects.

Pets

Most residents do not mind a neighbor with a small, well-trained pet, but they are unhappy when large dogs are permitted to run loose on association property. Consequently, some projects flatly prohibit pets.

Owners versus Renters

Unless prohibited in the bylaws, an owner may rent his apartment. All too often, however, renters exhibit little interest in maintaining the visible portions of their units and flagrantly disregard association rules. This creates discontent with owner–occupants nearby and, if the problem is acute enough, will depress unit resale values. Owners of rental units can compound the problem by taking little interest in the owners' association. The renting of unsold, developer-owned units is another source of this problem. Prohibiting renting, however, can work a financial hardship on an owner who must move but is unable to sell his unit owing to poor market conditions.

Developers and Sales Agents

Shoddy construction practices are no less a problem in a community development than in a house subdivision. Common complaints include leaking basements, doors and cabinets not hung straight, thin carpets, cheap paint, noisy appliances, and faulty plumbing. Other bad experiences stem from developers who promise but do not deliver (the swimming pool is left out or the project is finished late), salespeople who promise things the developer never intended to deliver, builders who are either slow or unwilling to correct mistakes, and developers who purposely underestimate maintenance costs in order to promote sales. Another complaint is that the transition of the association from developer to owner control is often not smooth.

Developers who place green areas within sight of each unit, provide adequate parking and recreation facilities, and avoid monotonous looking buildings will receive praise from owners. Also popular are generous interior and exterior storage space, off-street recreational vehicle parking, larger kitchens, fewer stairs, and closer laundry facilities. Conversely, if it is obvious that the project architect has never lived in a condominium or townhouse and that the builder's sole concern is how many units he can legally squeeze onto a parcel of land, owner dissatisfaction is inevitable. Although it is tempting for a developer to view his project strictly from the standpoint of selling the units as quickly as possible, the owner views it as a long-run investment. *Layout and Planning*

Some people feel that association regulations are a straightjacket control on their lives. Others feel that regulations provide a pleasant, controlled environment. There is no question that some control must exist in any community living arrangement. The question is where to draw the line. One owner may consider rules against loud parties an abridgement of his separate unit ownership, whereas his neighbor considers the rule an absolute necessity. Similar differences occur regarding children, pets, and use of recreation facilities. Experience has shown that the best solution is for the developer to set the tone of a project before the first unit is sold. If the restrictions and covenants he files with the enabling declaration specifically prohibit loud parties, children, and pets, he will attract buyers who prefer this life style. Once in charge of the *Restrictions and Regulations* association, owners can perpetuate these policies, and subsequent resales will continue to attract this type of owner.

Enforcement Provisions

If restrictions, covenants, or house rules are broken, what right of enforcement does the association have? In a cooperative, the ultimate sanction is lease cancellation, but in a condominium or townhouse the association does not have that option. The only comparable power is the ability to place a lien against a unit if maintenance fees are not paid. In other areas, if friendly persuasion does not work, civil methods can be used. In the case of a trespasser on association property, the police can be called and the matter pursued as a standard trespass violation. If an association member or his invited guest is causing a nuisance, trespass laws do not apply, but nuisance laws can usually be enforced.

Courts of law do recognize torts (wrongdoings) for which damages can be collected. Plaintiffs are allowed to collect reasonable damages, exemplary damages, and, in certain circumstances, damages for mental suffering. Thus, if an owner allows his dog to foul the common areas in clear violation of association rules, a court of law could be called upon by the association to award damages to the association. Courts can also be called upon to order injunctions against noncomplying behavior. For example, suppose that an owner moves himself, his wife, three children, and two barking dogs into a one-bedroom condominium apartment in violation of association rules. If prohibitions against these acts are reasonable, clearly stated, available for inspection to all occupants, and uniformly enforced, a court will order that such behavior cease. Failure to comply can result in court-ordered fines and imprisonment. Unfortunately, a lawsuit can be quite slow, sometimes taking a year or more. It is also expensive and it may be difficult to convince the association to vote the money to pursue the issue, especially if the problem only affects a few of the residents.

If the violation in question is of city health and safety ordinances, another alternative is open to the association. Local public health departments have regulations regarding the use of community swimming pools and the power to enforce them. The same is true of local building and safety departments regarding structural alterations to the building.

Despite claims by salespeople that condominium and townhouse living is carefree, there must be some system of self-government. Attracting interested and capable people who have the time to serve can often be difficult. Yet without such persons, the entire project can suffer. Persons capable of being board members for a multimillion dollar project may not exist among the owners, or those willing to serve may have the enthusiasm but not the administrative talent. A solution used by many associations is to hire an expert in condominium affairs to sit at board and association meetings as an advisor. Sometimes such a person is provided by the management company as part of their package of services. Experience has shown that such a person is especially helpful when a project is new and the association has just been turned over to the owners by the developer.

Owners' Association

VOCABULARY REVIEW

Match terms a–l with statements 1–12.

a. *Bylaws*
b. *Common elements*
c. *Condominium*
d. *Cooperative*
e. *Cooperator*
f. *Enabling declaration*
g. *Horizontal property act*
h. *House rules*
i. *Limited common elements*
j. *Maintenance fees*
k. *Owners' association*
l. *Proprietary lease*

1. Individual ownership of separate portions of a building plus joint ownership of the common elements.
2. Land and building owned or leased by a corporation which in turn leases space to its shareholders.
3. Real property jointly owned by condominium owners as a group.
4. An organization composed of condominium unit owners in which membership is automatic upon purchase of a unit.
5. Walls and ceilings between two condominium units.
6. Type of lease issued by a cooperative corporation to its shareholders.
7. State legislation that permits the creation of condominiums.
8. A document that converts a given parcel of land into a vertical subdivision. Also called a master deed.
9. Rules that govern how the owners' association will be run.
10. Rules that govern the day-to-day use of condominium and cooperative facilities by owners and tenants.
11. A shareholder in a cooperative apartment.
12. Charges levied against unit owners to cover the costs of maintaining the common areas. Also called association dues.

QUESTIONS AND
PROBLEMS

1. What has caused the explosive growth in condominium construction since the late 1960s?
2. Who owns the land in a fee simple condominium project? Cooperative?
3. What is the key difference between a proprietary lease in a cooperative and a landlord–tenant lease?
4. What is the purpose of the enabling declaration in a condominium project?
5. To whom does the wall between two condominium units belong?
6. What are CC&Rs and how do they affect a condominium owner?
7. How are condominium owners' association dues set? What happens if they are not paid?
8. If the condominium owners' association carries hazard and liability insurance, why is it also advisable for each unit owner to purchase a hazard and liability policy?
9. Briefly explain the concept of time-sharing condominiums.
10. Why do condominium and cooperative owners prefer to live in projects that are primarily owner-occupied?

ADDITIONAL READINGS

Butcher, Lee. *The Condominium Book.* Princeton, N.J.: Dow Jones Books, 1975, 143 pages. A large format paperback that covers condominiums, planned unit developments, management, financing, legal pitfalls, and the human side of community living.

Clurman, David, and **Hegard, Edna.** *Condominiums and Cooperatives.* New York: John Wiley, 1970, 395 pages. Legal aspects, financing, and management of condominium and cooperative apartments; also low-income and FHA condominium and cooperative programs.

Rothenberg, Henry H. *What You Should Know About Condominiums.* Radnor, Pa.: Chilton, 1974, 151 pages. Advice on selecting a condominium to purchase and live in. Includes a checklist for buyers, sample association regulations, and a glossary. Also contains a section on Canadian condominiums.

Urban Land Institute. *The Homes Association Handbook,* Technical Bulletin 50. Washington, D.C.: The Urban Land Institute, n.d. Gives practical guidelines for organizing an owner's association, plus association leadership, finances, operation and the maintenance of common property.

21

Property Insurance

All-risks policy: all perils, except those excluded in writing, are covered

Assured: the insured party

Broad-form policy: a policy that covers a large number of named perils

Coinsurance: the division of risk between the insured and the insurer

Endorsement or Rider: an addendum to an insurance policy stating certain provisions that become a part of the policy

Insurable interest: a requirement that a person have an actual interest in a property in order to be paid in event of a loss.

Insurance premium: the amount of money one must pay for insurance coverage

Mutual insurer: an insurance cooperative owned by its policyholders

Public liability: the financial responsibility one has toward others as a result of his actions or failure to take action

Underwriter: one who insures others; the insurer

Real estate ownership exposes one to a multitude of risks, the consequences of which range from very good to very bad. These risks fall into two categories, speculative risks and pure risks. **Speculative risk** exists when the consequence can be positive or negative. Thus, the purchaser of a vacant lot hopes that it will increase in value, but at the same time he takes the risk that he may have to sell it at a loss. In contrast, **pure risk** results in only unfortunate consequences to both the individual and society as a whole. For example, a house burns down or an elevator malfunctions and personal injuries result. This chapter is concerned with pure risk.

Dealing with pure risks is called **risk management.** It involves discovering existing risks, estimating the probability and seriousness of potential losses, and then doing something about them. To illustrate, a prospective homebuyer can learn

RISK MANAGEMENT

from fire department statistics the probability and seriousness of the risk of damage to his home by fire. In deciding what to do, he has four choices. The first is to avoid the risk entirely. In this example, it would mean renting instead of buying. The second choice is prevention. The prospect buys the home and then takes measures to prevent, or at least reduce, the possibility of an unfortunate consequence. For example, he can lessen the risk of losing his home to a flood by not purchasing in a flood-prone area. He can reduce the chance of a furnace fire by having the furnace checked and repaired. Also, he can install smoke detectors so that if a fire does start it will be quickly noticed before it spreads. However, no matter how careful one is, prevention cannot remove all possible risks. A family pet may chew the insulation off an electrical cord, starting a fire, or a strong wind may blow the roof off.

Where avoidance and prevention are impossible or impractical, a decision must be made to either personally assume the risk that remains or transfer it to someone else. Personally assuming the risk (risk retention) makes sense where the potential loss is small or the risk is insignificant. Retention also results when a risk has not yet been identified, or when there is no known way of handling it, or when one takes the optimistic attitude that, although the risk exists, he will be lucky. In a few instances, retention may be the result of a carefully made decision to set aside money reserves every year to meet the loss when it does occur. In all cases, however, the outcome of assuming or retaining risk is the same: one waits for the loss to occur and then personally pays for it.

INSURANCE   The alternative to risk retention is the transfer of risk to others, and that is the function of insurance. The underlying principle of insurance is that a large number of individuals each make a small contribution to a pool that can then be used to reimburse losses suffered by members of the pool. Thus, insurance spreads the risk of loss among many persons so that each can exchange the small possibility of a major loss for a known cost of manageable proportions.

For insurance to work successfully, there are two key requirements. First, the probability and size of the losses expected must be predictable with a reasonable degree of accuracy. Second, there must be a large number of persons in the pool. To illustrate, suppose that fire-fighting statistics for the past 15 years show that, for every 1,000 houses of a given type of construction, there have been an average of four fires a year. One fire resulted in total (100%) destruction, one in 50% destruction, and two in 25% destruction. Suppose that owners of 1,000 dwellings of similar exposure to fire hazards want to form an insurance pool and that the average replacement cost of their homes, excluding land, is $40,000. With this information, we can anticipate that losses will amount to $80,000 during the coming year. To cover these anticipated losses, each homeowner contributes $80. In other words, for $80, each homeowner can rid himself for one year of the small possibility of a loss that might be as high as $40,000. The mere formation of a pool does not reduce the chance of a fire, but it does soften the financial blow to a pool member who suffers a loss.

Law of Large Numbers

The larger the number in the insurance pool, the more predictable the outcome. This is the **law of large numbers.** A good demonstration of this law, and one the reader can try, involves flipping a coin. In any ten consecutive tosses, it is relatively easy to get six or more heads or tails, even though we know the statistical average must be five of each. But now try to flip 60 or more of one kind out of 100 tosses. This is much more difficult. And, if you have the time, you will find that flipping 600 out of 1,000 is practically impossible. The larger the number of events in the sample, the more predictable the outcome, in this example, 50% heads and 50% tails. The same principle applies to insurance pools. Thus, with 1,000 houses in the pool and an average of four fires expected per year, in each individual year there will probably be from two to six fires, with more or less than that number rather unlikely. With 10,000 houses in the pool, 35 to 45 fires can be anticipated with reasonable certainty.

Even though having a large number in the pool makes loss estimates more predictable, some years insurance claims will exceed the amount of money collected. The solution is for each member of the pool to pay a little more than his proportionate share of expected losses so that a reserve fund can be established. Also, each member must pay something extra above the pure cost of protection to cover overhead expenses of the pool, such as office space, staff salaries, and commissions paid to insurance agents. The total annual cost of providing for expected losses plus a reserve fund and overhead expenses is the **insurance premium.**

STOCK VERSUS MUTUAL INSURERS

There are two predominant methods by which an insurance pool can be formed and operated: the stock company and the mutual. **Stock companies,** as the name implies, are corporations that issue shares of stock. This stock is sold to investors, who provide the operating capital, supply additional reserve funds, take the risks of losing their investment if the company does poorly, and receive the rewards if it does well.

In contrast, **mutuals** are cooperative organizations owned entirely by their policyholders. In effect, the policyholder also takes the role of the stockholder by providing operating capital and participating in its financial success or failure. In a mutual organization, the policyholder is both the insured and the insurer.

From the policyholder's standpoint, each approach has its advantages and disadvantages. With a stock company, the policyholder is quoted a fixed price for his insurance, and the stockholders take the risk that the premiums collected will be sufficient to cover company overhead and policyholder losses that follow. The insured is strictly a customer of the company. With a mutual, the premium is set a little higher than would be needed in a stock company. At the end of the policy year, any excess is returned to the policyholder as a **dividend.** However, if overhead and losses exceed premiums and reserves are exhausted, in some mutuals the policyholder can be asked to pay an assessment.

There is considerable argument as to whether a stock company or a mutual is better for the policyholder in terms of price, service, and coverage. However, the fact that both systems are very much in use today seems to indicate that the public considers them to be equally acceptable. Ultimately, the price a policyholder pays for his coverage will depend on the insurer's sales costs and other overhead, ability to select the people it insures, ability to reduce claims for losses, and the general quality of its management.

In Colonial America, fire insurance premiums paid for members' losses and also subsidized volunteer fire-fighting companies. Each member received a plaque, which he prominently displayed on his building to indicate that he was insured. Although the volunteer fire companies would answer all calls, they probably put more effort into saving houses displaying the plaque. Going back further, historians have reported that an even more interesting system existed 2,000 years ago. A Roman by the name of Crassus would bring his fire fighters to the scene of a fire and set a price for putting it out. If the owner refused, Crassus offered cash on the spot for the burning building and, if accepted, sent in his firemen to salvage as much as possible.

The concept of a fire insurance policy for which one pays a premium to an insurance company and, in turn, receives money if a loss is suffered witnessed its initial growth in the United States during the nation's first century. Unfortunately, early policies lacked uniformity from one insurer to the next, and some insurers took advantage of policyholders with policies designed to pay off as little as possible. This was accomplished by writing policies that could not be understood, even by learned men, and by including numerous exceptions to coverage in small, hard-to-read print. The phrase, "The large print giveth and the small print taketh away," is said to have its origins in early fire policies. In response to consumer complaints, the Massachusetts legislature, in 1873, and the New York legislature, in 1886, established standardized fire policy forms. If a company wanted to sell fire insurance in those states, it was required to use the state-mandated form. Since then, the New York fire form has been revised twice, in 1918 and 1943, and today nearly all states use it or a form very similar to it. The New York fire form serves as the foundation for nearly all property damage policies now written in the United States.

New York Fire Form　　The 165 lines of court-tested language in the New York fire form cover (1) loss by fire, (2) loss by lightning, and (3) losses sustained while removing property from an endangered premises; coverage can be on real property improvements, personal property, or both. Let us briefly discuss these three **perils** (also called hazards or risks).

To be covered for loss by fire, there must be flames. Smoke or heat damage or damage by explosion, no matter how severe, does not qualify unless preceded by flames. Also, the fire must be hostile as opposed to friendly. A hostile fire is a fire where it is not intended to be. A friendly fire is a fire burning in a place designed for it, such as a furnace, fireplace, gas stove, or water heater. However, if a friendly fire gets out of control, it is then classed as hostile and losses are covered. Insurers are required to pay whether the fire was purely accidental or the result of negligence by the insured or some other person. For example, suppose that you have a fire in the fireplace of your home and do not bother to close the fireplace screen. If, while you have left the room, the fire throws out a live ember onto a rug and starts a fire, you are covered even though you were negligent in not closing the screen. However, if the insured intentionally starts a hostile fire, the insurer is excused from paying for the damage.

Damage caused by lightning is covered whether or not an actual fire develops. However, man-made electrical discharges are not covered. For example, melted wires caused by an electrical short circuit are not covered unless the cause was lightning or a fire on the premises.

To encourage the removal of personal property from an endangered building, the New York form also covers certain types of loss or damage resulting from removal and storage elsewhere. Coverage is good for 5 days at a new location, after which a new policy must be obtained.

ENDORSEMENTS　　Although fire is the single most important cause of property damage in the United States, a property owner is also exposed to many other perils, including hail, tornado, earthquake, riot, windstorm, smoke damage, explosion, glass breakage, water-pipe leaks, vandalism, freezing, and building collapse. Coverage for each peril can be purchased with a separate policy or it can be added to the fire form as an **endorsement.** An endorsement, also called a **rider** or **attachment,** is an agreement by the insurer to extend coverage to losses by perils not included in the basic policy. Using endorsements, a policyholder can create a single policy that covers only the perils he is exposed to so he does not pay for coverage he does not need.

Thus far, we have been primarily concerned with insuring financial losses resulting from damage to the insured's property. However, the ownership of real property also entails **public liability,** which is the financial responsibility one has toward others as a result of one's actions or failure to take actions. For example, if you are trimming the limbs from a tall tree in your backyard and a limb falls on your neighbor's roof and damages it, you are liable to your neighbor for damages. Or, if you have a swimming pool in your backyard and a neighbor child drowns in it, the child's parents may be able to successfully sue you for money damages.

PUBLIC LIABILITY

Generally, you are liable when there exists a legal duty to exercise reasonable care and you fail to do so, thereby causing injury to an innocent party. Even though you did not intend for the limb to fall on your neighbor's roof or the child to drown in your pool, you are not excused from liability. You can be held accountable, in money, for the amount of damage caused. This amount, coupled with legal defense costs, may run to many thousands of dollars. Fortunately, for most people, the possibility of a large settlement is slim. For a small annual fee, one can obtain liability insurance and avoid the risk of having to pay a substantial liability claim. Note that liability is an artificial concept; if laws did not provide for the liability of one person to another, there would be no need for liability insurance.

For major commercial and industrial property owners and users, carefully identifying each risk exposure and then insuring for it is a logical and economic approach to purchasing insurance. But for the majority of homeowners, owners of small apartment and business properties, and their tenants, purchasing insurance piecemeal is a confusing process. As a result,

HOMEOWNER PACKAGE POLICIES

package policies designed for owners and tenants of specific kinds of properties have been developed.

Of these, the best known and most widely used is the **homeowner's package policy,** which contains the coverages deemed by insurance experts to be most useful to persons who own or rent the home in which they live. Not only does this approach avoid overlaps and lessen the opportunity for gaps in coverage, but the cost is less than purchasing separate individual policies with the same total coverage. Moreover, homeowner policies go beyond covering only damage and public liability directly connected with the insured property. They also include coverage for theft of the insured's real and personal property and public liability arising from the personal activities of the insured. Let us take a closer look.

Policy Formats

There are six standardized homeowner policy forms in use in the United States. Each contains two sections. **Section I** deals with property insurance and includes a standard fire policy with a wide variety of endorsements, plus a theft policy. Buildings and their contents and, to a certain extent, personal property when it is taken off the insured premises are covered. **Section II** deals with liability on the premises, plus personal liability. All six homeowner forms will be discussed here; however, Form HO-2 for owner–occupants of houses and Form HO-4, the form used by tenants, will receive the most attention.

Form HO-2

Form HO-2 covers damage and loss to buildings and contents caused by such perils as fire, lightning, hail, windstorm, explosion, riot, smoke, vandalism, theft, sonic boom, falling objects, weight of ice, snow, or sleet, building cracking or collapse, accidental plumbing leakage or overflow, freezing of pipes, artificial electrical discharge, and hot-water-system malfunction. Major exceptions are loss or damage caused by an enemy attack, insurrection, rebellion, revolution, civil war, or usurped power. As a group, these exceptions are sometimes referred to as a **war clause exemption.** Also excepted are the perils of earthquake, flood, landslide, mudflow, tidal waves, or underground seepage. If a property owner is exposed to these perils, he must buy additional insurance. With regard to theft, major exceptions to coverage are motorized vehicles, business property, and animals. These require separate policies or endorsements.

Section I

The dollar amount of coverage that one obtains in Section I is automatically related to the amount of insurance purchased on the dwelling. To illustrate, suppose that the dwelling is insured for $40,000. Under HO-2, the policyholder is automatically covered for 10% of that amount for damage to appurtenant structures. This gives the policyholder $4,000 in coverage for damages to structures located on the insured premises that are not attached to the dwelling (e.g., a detached garage, greenhouse, barn, garden-tool shed, or playhouse). Damage or theft of personal property on the insured premises is covered up to 50% of the dwelling insurance (i.e., $20,000 in this example). Damage or theft of personal property off premises is covered up to 10% of on-premises personal property coverage (i.e., $2,000). However, special limits per loss apply to money ($100), securities, passports, deeds, and related property ($500), jewelry and furs ($500, but only with respect to theft), and landscaping (5% of dwelling insurance with $250 maximum per plant or tree). Also, there is a $50 or $100 deductible clause designed to discourage policyholders from filing claims that would cost as much to process as would actually be paid out. Finally, in Section I, if damage to the premises requires the insured to live elsewhere while repairs are being made, HO-2 pays for additional living costs up to a limit equaling 20% of the dwelling insurance.

Section II

Section II of the policy includes liability insurance, medical payments coverage for injuries to others, and insurance for physical damage to the property of others. This section covers such incidents as a tree falling onto a neighbor's house, the family dog biting a visitor, a guest slipping on a freshly waxed kitchen floor, and the insured or the insured's child kicking a football through someone's window.

Section II coverage applies to the premises where the insured lives, not owned property where the insured is temporarily staying (such as on a vacation), plus vacant land and cemetery plots and vaults owned by the insured. Specifically excluded are farms owned or rented by the insured, and business or rental property owned or operated by the insured. However, the temporary rental of one's dwelling to another is covered. Liability for bodily injury or property damage resulting from the personal activities of the insured is covered, subject to certain exclusions such as liability resulting from the ownership, maintenance, or operation of aircraft, motor vehicles, recreational vehicles, or watercraft.* Also excluded is liability resulting from professional pursuits. For example, on a golf course, Form HO-2 covers the amateur who slices a golfball into another player or bystander and causes injuries. However, a homeowner's policy would not cover a professional golfer who suffered the same fate. Also excluded in Form HO-2 are liabilities covered by worker's compensation insurance (discussed later) and situations in which the insured intentionally inflicts injury or property damage.

Persons Insured

The persons insured in Section II are those named in the policy (the **named insured**), plus the insured's spouse, relatives of either spouse, and any person under the age of 21 years in the insured's custody, provided they reside with the named insured. The named insured is also covered for injury to third parties by his animals.

The minimum amount of insurance that can be purchased in Section II is $25,000 per occurrence for combined bodily and property liability, medical payments of $500 per person, and $25,000 total per occurrence. Higher limits can be purchased to give the policyholder more protection. The key aspect of medical payments coverage is that an injured third party can obtain them without having to first prove that the insured was at fault, as is necessary to receive compensation under liability coverage. Section II also covers up to $250 of property damage per occurrence, without first having to conclusively prove that the insured was at fault.

---

* There are several major exceptions to this in that homeowner policies cover liability arising from the personal use of golf carts on a golf course, the operation for pleasure of sailboats and motorboats under specified length and horsepower limits, and the operation of power mowers, snowblowers, and similar equipment on the insured premises.

With regard to Section II coverage, all six homeowner policy forms are like Form HO-2. The differences are in Section I coverage. **Form HO-4,** often referred to as a **tenant's policy,** provides the same coverages as HO-2 except that there is no coverage on building structures. The balance of the Section I limits depend on the base amount of personal property coverage the tenant elects. The off-premises amount is 10% of the base amount, and additional living expenses are 20%. If a tenant makes additions or alterations to the rental unit that he occupies, these are covered up to 10% of the base amount. Form HO-4 is also available to owner–occupants of buildings ineligible for homeowner insurance. This includes, for example, a person living in the loft of a warehouse that he owns and the shop owner who lives in a room at the back of his store.

HO-4 Tenant's Policy

Form HO-1 is a homeowner policy that covers fewer perils and has more restrictions than HO-2. These limitations deal with aircraft and vehicle damage to the insured property, smoke damage, glass breakage, and theft.

HO-1 and HO-3

Form HO-3 covers more perils to the building structure and is sometimes referred to as an **all-risks** policy. However, property damage by flood, earthquake, war, termites, rodents, wear and tear, marring and scratching, rust, mold, and contamination (nuclear, for example) are still excluded. The difference between an all-risks policy and a **named-peril** policy, such as HO-1 or HO-2, is that in a named-peril policy each peril must be named in the policy in order to be covered. In an all-risks policy, all perils except those excluded are covered. The term **broad-form** is used to describe policies that cover a large number of named perils. Form HO-2, for example, is a broad-form policy.

Form HO-5 is the most liberal of the six forms from the standpoint of the insured. It extends the all-risk coverage described in Form HO-3 to personal property and increases the amount of dollar coverage.

HO-5 and HO-6

Form HO-6 is designed for condominium and cooperative owners where the owners' association carries property damage and public liability insurance on the common elements. Form HO-6 covers the same perils as the tenant's form, but increases the additional living expense limit to 40% of the base amount and puts addition and alteration coverage on a replacement cost basis with a maximum recovery of $1,000. Endorsements can be added to increase these coverages, cover appurtenant structures on the premises that are solely owned by the insured, and pay for special assessments levied against the policyholder for uninsured property or liability losses of the association.

Homeowner Endorsements   Any of the six homeowner policies can be endorsed for additional coverage. For example, endorsements are available that will pay for losses due to credit card forgery, cover buildings on the insured premises that are rented to others, and provide Section II coverage to rentals owned by the insured but located off the insured premises. (Real estate investors who own rental houses can insure them by adding a Section II endorsement to their homeowner's policy and purchasing a separate policy covering property damage.) **Inflation guard** endorsements are also available that automatically increase property damage coverage by 1½%, 2% or 2½% per quarter, as selected by the insured. Off-premises coverage and jewelry coverage can be increased in both dollars and in terms of perils covered, and deductibles can be changed. Also, a few insurers will combine a homeowner's policy with automobile and life insurance to form a single package.

PACKAGE POLICIES
FOR BUSINESS   Package policies for owners of apartment buildings, stores, offices, and industrial buildings have become widely available since 1960. Like a homeowner policy, a business package policy provides the owner of a small or moderate-sized business property more coverage at a lower price, with fewer gaps in coverage, and is more convenient than purchasing a number of separate policies. These packages contain provisions for a standard fire policy with endorsements, plus public liability coverage on the premises, product liability, and medical payments coverage. Perils to the property can be limited to those named in the policy, or the insured can purchase all-risks coverage.

The insurance premium that one pays is based on anticipated losses, which in turn are based on loss history. The
insurer can obtain this information from its own past experience or from publicly maintained loss records. However,
most often it comes from **rating bureaus** which are actuarial
organizations that collect information on the property and
liability loss experience of many insurers. From this, bureaus
develop and publish insurance rates, or **bureau rates.** For
example, fire insurance rates are expressed per $100 of cover-
age per year. Thus, if the rate is $0.25, the cost of a $44,000
policy would be $110 per year. In some states, insurers are
required by law to charge bureau rates. In these states, the
legislative philosophy is that to charge more is to overcharge
the public, and to charge less may mean that the insurer will
not be able to cover loss claims. In other states, the bureau
rates are only advisory, and each insurer is free to set its own
rates.

In selecting a rate to charge policyholders, the problem is
not only to charge enough to cover losses, but also to set them
fairly among policyholders so that some are not overcharged
and others undercharged. Thus, the owner of a wood-frame
house, 10 miles from the nearest fire station, would be charged
a higher rate for fire insurance than the owner of a brick
house located 2 miles from the fire department. Similarly, a
house that borders vacant, brush-covered land is a higher
fire risk than one in town and hence is charged more. Even the
quality of the local fire department makes a difference in fire
rates.

Relatively few fires (or other natural perils, for that matter) result in total loss of the insured property. The rest cause
only partial damage. Since fire insurance is sold on a rate per
$100 of coverage, this means a building owner could cut his
fire insurance bill in half by insuring his building for only half
its worth, yet still be quite well protected. However, this is
unfair to the property owner who insures for full value with
the same company. Consequently, insurers may require policyholders to carry insurance equal to, or close to, the value of
the property being insured. The penalty for not doing so is
that the insured will not be able to recover his loss in full, even

though the loss is less than the face value of the policy. (**Face value** is the dollar amount of coverage given by a policy; this amount is usually printed on the face, i.e, first page of the policy. Also, some policies refer to the insurer as the **underwriter** and the insured as the **assured**.)

When a person underinsures his property, he is said to be a coinsurer with the insurance company, hence the term **coinsurance**. (This is actually a loose application of the term, as it is questionable whether a person who fails to buy enough insurance can rightly be called an insurer.) The most common arrangement among insurers is to require the policyholder to carry coverage of at least 80% of the value of the property that is subject to loss or damage. If he does, he will be compensated in full for the value of his loss, up to the amount of insurance carried. If the policy is for less than 80% of the property's value, the following coinsurance formula shows how much the policyholder will receive:

$$\frac{\text{Insurance carried}}{\text{Insurance required}} \times \text{Amount of loss} = \text{Recovery}$$

Coinsurance Example   To illustrate coinsurance, suppose that you own a small apartment building with a replacement cost of $100,000, not counting the value of the lot and the foundation. (The philosophy is that the lot, excavations, foundations, pipes, and wiring below ground level are not subject to damage and therefore are excluded from the calculation.) Suppose, further, that you purchase an $80,000 fire policy, and subsequently a fire destroys $20,000 of the building. Using the coinsurance formula, you recover $20,000 from the insurer as follows:

$$\frac{\$80,000}{\$100,000 \times 80\%} \times \$20,000 = \frac{\$80,000}{\$80,000} \times \$20,000 = \$20,000$$

If you had $100,000 in insurance, would you be able to recover $25,000? In other words,

$$\frac{\$100,000}{\$100,000 \times 80\%} \times \$20,000 = \frac{\$100,000}{\$80,000} \times \$20,000 = \$25,000 \ (?)$$

The answer is no, of course, because one cannot collect more than the amount of the loss just as one cannot collect more than the amount of insurance carried.

Continuing with the apartment building example, suppose that you buy $100,000 of fire insurance and continue to carry that amount, while inflation pushes the building's replacement cost to $125,000. Since $100,000 is still 80% of $125,000, you would be covered in full for a loss up to $100,000. Beyond that, the loss would come out of your pocket. Now suppose that the replacement cost of your building rises to $150,000, but you still carry a $100,000 policy. If a $20,000 fire occurs, your recovery would be calculated as follows:

$$\frac{\$100,000}{\$150,000 \times 80\%} \times \$20,000 = \frac{\$100,000}{\$120,000} \times \$20,000 = \$16,667$$

The remaining $3,333 is not recoverable.

Coinsurance clauses are almost universally found in property damage policies written for business operations. Home-owner policies do not, as a rule, carry them. However, they do have a coinsurance-like feature that one should be familiar with and which will be discussed next.

A special problem in recovering from damage to a building is that, although the building may not be new, any repairs are made new. For example, if a 20-year-old house burns to the ground, it is absurd to think we can put back a used house, even though a used house is exactly what the insured lost. Thus, the question is whether insurance should pay for the full cost of fixing the damage, in effect replace "new for old," or simply pay the actual cash value of the loss. **Actual cash value** is the new price minus accumulated depreciation and is, in effect, "old for old." Under "old for old," if the owner rebuilds, he pays the difference between actual cash value and the cost of the repairs. Since this can be quite costly the alternative is to purchase a policy that replaces "new for old."

For the owner of an apartment building, store, or other property operated on a business basis, obtaining "new for old" coverage is a matter of substituting the term "replacement cost" for "actual cash value" wherever it appears in the policy. Also, the policyholder must agree to carry coverage amounting to at least 80% of current replacement cost and to use the insurance proceeds to repair or replace the damaged property within a reasonable time.

NEW FOR OLD

Under a homeowner's policy, if the amount of insurance carried is 80% or more of the cost to replace the house today, the full cost of repair will be paid by the insurer, up to the face amount of the policy. If the face amount is less than 80% of replacement costs, the insured is entitled to the higher of (1) the actual cash value of the loss or (2) the amount calculated as follows:

$$\frac{\text{Insurance carried}}{\left(\begin{array}{c}\text{80\% of cost to}\\ \text{replace new today}\end{array}\right)} \times \left(\begin{array}{c}\text{Today's cost to replace}\\ \text{the damaged portion}\end{array}\right) = \text{Recovery}$$

To illustrate, consider a 12-year-old house that would cost $54,000 to construct new today, not counting the lot. Excavation work and the foundation account for $4,000, leaving a replacement cost for insurance purposes of $50,000. Suppose that there is a fire in a bedroom, and it will cost $7,000 to fix the damage. If the house is insured for at least $40,000, the insurer will pay the $7,000 in full. If the policy is for less than $40,000, the amount the isurer will pay is reduced. On a $35,000 policy, the insurer would pay $6,125 thus:

$$\frac{\$35,000}{80\% \times \$50,000} \times \$7,000 = \$6,125$$

The least the insurer will pay is the actual cash value of the damage. However, on an older building, this may not amount to much. Appraisal manuals, such as those discussed in Chapter 16, are used in determining construction costs and for estimating accumulated depreciation.

Two interesting conclusions may be drawn. First, although homeowner policies do not carry coinsurance clauses per se, they do encourage homeowners to carry at least 80% of replacement cost by promising "new for old" for those that do, and "old for old" for those that do not. Second, this is one of the extremely rare situations in which one can come out ahead on a disaster. For example, a 15-year-old roof that will need replacing in 5 years (due to normal wear and tear) is blown off in a windstorm. "New for old" gives the homeowner a new roof in place of his old roof.

FLOOD INSURANCE

Until 1968, an important gap in property damage policies had been the unavailability of flood insurance. Many insurers felt that only those persons in flood-prone areas would be interested and too large a number of them would be affected by the same catastrophe. Consequently, on numerous occasions, usually following a major flood somewhere in the country, Congress took up the idea of a government-sponsored flood insurance program. The outcome was legislation in 1968 that created the National Flood Insurance Program. This program is a joint effort of the nation's insurance industry and the federal government to offer property owners coverage for losses to real and personal property resulting from the inundation of normally dry areas because of (1) the overflow of inland or tidal waters, (2) the unusual and rapid accumulation or runoff of surface waters, (3) mudslides resulting from accumulations of water on or under the ground, and (4) erosion losses caused by abnormal water runoff.

To encourage persons with property in flood-prone areas to purchase flood insurance and at the same time discourage more new construction in flood areas, the program has taken a "carrot and stick" approach. For example, before flood insurance can be marketed in a community, community officials must demonstrate a need for flood insurance to the Federal Insurance Administration and must enact and enforce land-use and building permit controls to reduce the community's exposure to flood damage. (Without controls, the availability of inexpensive flood insurance might actually encourage construction in flood-prone areas.) To encourage people to buy flood insurance, the federal government subsidizes insurance rates, and to encourage private insurers, reinsures them against catastrophic losses. Also, federally regulated lenders are not permitted to finance in flood-prone areas without flood insurance, and one year after the availability of flood insurance in a community federal flood disaster assistance is no longer available. Flood insurance for all types of structures and their contents is available through private insurance agents.

A property damage or public liability policy can be canceled at anytime by the insured. Since the policy is billed in advance, the insured is entitled to a refund for unused coverage. This refund is computed at short rates, which are somewhat higher than a simple pro rata charge. For example, the holder

POLICY CANCELLATION

of a 1-year policy who cancels one-third of the way through the year is charged 44% of the 1-year price, not 33⅓%. Similarly, a person who wants to purchase a 4-month policy will be charged 44% of the 1-year rate. Short-rate tables also tell us that a policy for 1 week costs 9% of the annual rate; for 1 month, 19%, for 6 months, 61%, and for 11 months, 94%. The justification for short-rate pricing is that the cost of setting up a policy is the same whether it runs for a day, a month, or a year. Also, short rates discourage spur of the moment cancellations to switch to another insurer. Policies longer than one year can act both as a useful hedge against rising premiums and as a means of continuing coverage when insurers are reluctant to issue new policies.

The insurer also has the right to cancel a policy. However, unlike the policyholder, who can cancel on immediate notice, the New York fire form requires the insurer to give the policyholder 5-day notice. Also, the cost of the policy, and hence the refund of unused premium, must be calculated on a pro rata basis. For example, the insured would be charged one half the annual premium for 6 months of coverage.

Policy Suspension

Certain acts of the policyholder will suspend his coverage without the necessity of a written notice from the insurer. Suspension automatically occurs if the insured allows the hazard exposure to the insurer to increase beyond the risks normally associated with the type of property being insured, for example, converting a dwelling to a restaurant. Suspension also occurs if the insured building is left unoccupied for more than 60 days, because unoccupied buildings are more attractive to thieves, vandals, and arsonists. If the condition causing the suspension is corrected (returning the restaurant to a dwelling or reoccupying the building) before a loss occurs, the policy becomes effective again.

Willful concealment or misrepresentation by the insured of any material fact or circumstance concerning the policy, the property, or the insured, either before or after a loss, will make the policy void. Thus, if a person operates a business in the basement of his house and conceals this from the insurer for fear of being charged more for insurance, the money he pays for insurance could be wasted.

An injured party cannot collect twice for the same loss: once from the insurance company and once from the person causing the loss. For example, a neighbor child maliciously throws rocks at your home, breaking a number of windows. If the child's parents pay you for the damage, you cannot also collect from the insurer. If the child's parents do not pay you and your insurer must pay for the damage, your insurer acquires the right to collect from the child's parents. This is **subrogation.** Subrogation rights exist under common law without special mention in the insurance policy. Nonetheless, it is the practice to state them in the policy to remind the insured of their existence.

SUBROGATION

The inclusion of an apportionment clause, also known as a pro rata clause, in a property damage policy removes the possibility of financial gain to the policyholder who insures the same property with two or more insurers in hopes of collecting more than the actual loss. To illustrate, suppose that the owner of a building valued at $100,000 buys a $100,000 fire policy from insurer X and an $80,000 fire policy from insurer Y, and then suffers a $36,000 fire loss. Will he be able to collect $36,000 twice? No. Insurer X will pay $20,000 and insurer Y will pay $16,000. This is in proportion to the amount of coverage carried by each insurer.

APPORTIONMENT

When an insured property loss occurs, the usual procedure is for the policyholder to obtain an estimate of the repair costs and submit it to the insurer. The insurer then assigns an insurance adjuster to the case. His job is to verify the loss and to adjust, on an amicable basis, any differences between what the insured feels he should receive and what the insurer will pay. If an agreement cannot be reached, each party hires an independent appraiser to estimate the loss. The appraisers select an umpire, and the differences are submitted to him for a binding decision.

ARBITRATION

Coverage in the standard fire policy is for the financial interest of the named insured only. Thus, if two persons own a building on a 50–50 basis, and the building is insured for its full value, but only one owner is named on the policy,

NAMED ON POLICY

then only one half of the loss can be recovered. Although unfortunate for the owners, this happens because the named insured owns only a half-interest in the building. Therefore, it is of the utmost importance that all persons with a financial interest in an insured property be named as insureds in the policy. Also, when improved real property is secured by a mortgage or trust deed, the holder thereof will want a **loss payable endorsement** in the policy. This endorsement provides that the insurance proceeds check will be made out jointly to the insured and the holder of the mortgage or trust deed.

An insurance policy is a personal contract between the insurer and those named as insured. Consequently, when a building or other property is sold, the new owner cannot automatically assume the existing insurance policy from the seller. Only the insurer can make the assignment, although this is usually a routine matter.

WORKERS' COMPENSATION LAWS*

Under workers' compensation laws, if an employee suffers an accident or contracts a disease while on the job, he has a legal right to compensation from his employer. All states have these laws and they cover nearly all employee job classifications from office secretaries to assembly-line workers. If you own or operate income-producing property and hire people to help run it, they are covered. Workers' compensation coverage is not available to individual proprietors but is available for business partners. A broker may or may not be required to cover his salespeople, depending on whether or not his state regards them as employees for workers' compensation purposes.

Prior to the introduction of workers' compensation laws early in this century, an employee had to prove in court that his injury or disease was caused by his employer's negligence in order to obtain compensation. Today, proving negligence has been eliminated. This has vastly increased worker welfare, but at the same time has increased the employer's exposure to employee liability losses. To offset this liability exposure, em-

---

* "Workers' compensation" is the more modern term and has replaced the term "workmen's compensation."

ployers purchase workers' compensation insurance from private insurers or through state-operated funds; by doing so they substitute a relatively certain premium for an uncertain loss. The insurer handles the investigation and the paperwork of the claim and the payments resulting therefrom. For the employee, such a policy is assurance that he or she will be able to collect on an approved claim.

The cost of workers' compensation insurance is set by the amount of the employer's payroll and the claim history for the job classification of each employee. Thus rates for carpenters are considerably higher than for school teachers.

Benefits to employees include medical services for the injury or disease itself, weekly cash payments if temporary disability results, rehabilitation programs, weekly or lump-sum benefits for permanent disability, and death benefits. The weekly cash payments are tax free, are paid for temporary or permanent, partial or total disability, and can be as much as 60% to 100% of the worker's wage, depending on the state.

A long-standing concern of home buyers has been the possibility of finding structural or mechanical defects in a home after buying it. In new homes, the builder can usually be held responsible for repairs, and in some states he is required to give a 1-year warranty on his product. Additional protection is available from builders associated with the Home Owners Warranty Corporation (HOW). Under this program, the builder warrants against defects caused by faulty workmanship or materials for the first year and against defects in wiring, piping, ductwork and major structural defects in the second year. If the builder cannot or will not honor this warranty, the HOW program underwriter will do so. Then for 8 more years, the underwriter directly insures the home buyer against major structural defects.

In a growing number of cities, the purchaser of a used house can obtain a warranty for 12 to 18 months to cover most things that can go wrong. Available through real estate brokers, this coverage is sold through two plans. Under one plan, the insurer makes an inspection of the home and issues a policy covering all defects not identified by the inspection.

HOME BUYER'S INSURANCE

Under the second plan, there is no inspection. However, a participating broker must agree to insure all homes sold by him.

INSURABLE INTEREST   The policyholder must have an insurable interest to be reimbursed for losses. You cannot buy a fire insurance policy on a home belonging to a neighbor and then collect if the home burns down. Similarly, if you sell your home and keep the policy, you cannot collect if the new owner has a loss, as the sale terminated your insurable interest. An insurable interest is required because, without it, an insurance policy would be no more than a gambling contract, and gambling contracts are unenforceable at law. Nonetheless, isn't insuring one's property and liability still gambling? The answer is no: insurance is the exact opposite of gambling. In gambling, a risk is deliberately created. With insurance, a risk already exists, and an attempt is being made to neutralize it.

VOCABULARY REVIEW   *Match terms a–r with statements 1–18.*

a. *Actual cash value*	**j.** *Mutual insurer*
b. *Apportionment*	**k.** *Named insured*
c. *Arbitration*	**l.** *Perils*
d. *Dividends*	**m.** *Replacement cost*
e. *Face value*	**n.** *Stock company*
f. *Homeowner's policy*	**o.** *Subrogation clause*
g. *Inflation guard*	**p.** *Tenant's policy*
h. *Insurable interest*	**q.** *Underwriter*
i. *Loss payable endorsement*	**r.** *War clause*

1. An insurance firm owned by investors.
2. An insurance cooperative owned by its policyholders.
3. A policy endorsement that automatically increases the amount of insurance coverage periodically during the life of the policy.
4. Also called hazards or risks.
5. Words inserted in an insurance policy to limit the extent of coverage for damages caused by warfare, insurrection, etc.
6. Persons whose names appear in a policy as the insured.

7. A combined property and liability policy designed for persons who do not own the dwelling in which they live.

8. Paid to mutual policyholders when income exceeds losses.

9. Amount of insurance coverage; usually shown on the first page of the policy.

10. Current cost of replacing damaged property less depreciation; in effect, "old for old."

11. Cost of replacing damaged property at current prices; in effect, "new for old."

12. A clause found in insurance policies that allows the insurer to recover losses from the party causing damages.

13. A system to prevent a policyholder from insuring the same risk twice in order to collect more than the actual amount of the loss.

14. A method used to settle differences between what an insurer offers to pay on a loss and what the insured feels he should receive.

15. A policy endorsement directing that payments for losses suffered are to be paid jointly to the property owner and his mortgage holder.

16. Requires that a person have an actual interest in a property in order to receive insurance coverage.

17. A combined property and liability policy designed for residential owner–occupants.

18. One who insures others; the insurer.

QUESTIONS AND PROBLEMS

1. What is the difference between speculative risk and pure risk? With which one is the insurance industry concerned?

2. What is the law of large numbers? Why is it necessary in order for insurance pools to function successfully?

3. Do fire policies cover losses caused by negligence? Losses intentionally caused by the insured?

4. What role does an endorsement or rider play in an insurance policy?

5. What is the purpose of public liability insurance?

6. In a homeowner's policy, what type of loss does Section I deal with? Section II?

7. How do all-risk insurance policies differ from broad-form policies?

8. How are insurance premiums set?

9. What is the purpose of coinsurance?

10. What does the phrase "new for old" refer to when talking about insurance policies that cover property damage?

11. What is the purpose of workers' compensation laws? Workers' compensation insurance?

ADDITIONAL READINGS   **Chernik, Vladimir P.** *The Consumer's Guide to Insurance Buying.* Los Angeles: Sherbourne Press, 1970, 288 pages. A fast-reading book that deals with the purchase of insurance from the policyholder's viewpoint. Includes chapters on selecting an insurer and an insurance agent.

Kratovil, Robert. *Real Estate Law,* 6th ed. Englewood Cliffs, N.J.: Prentice-Hall, 1974, 479 pages. Chapter 15 deals with fire insurance.

Long, John D., and **Gregg, Davis W.** *Property and Liability Insurance Handbook.* Homewood, Ill.: Richard D. Irwin, Inc., 1965, 1,265 pages. A very informative series of 76 articles written on all aspects of property and liability insurance. Also contains sample policies.

Pfeffer, Irving, and **Klock, David R.** *Perspectives on Insurance.* Englewood Cliffs, N.J.: Prentice-Hall, 1974, 513 pages. Looks at insurance from historical, legal, psychological, economic, actuarial, managerial, and consumer's perspectives, as opposed to dividing the subject into traditional property, liability, health, and life categories.

Riegel, Robert T., Miller, Jerome S., and **Williams, C. Arthur, Jr.** *Insurance Principles and Practices,* 6th ed. Englewood Cliffs, N.J. Prentice-Hall, 1976, 619 pages. A very readable and up-to-date textbook that deals with risk management, property insurance, liability insurance, package policies, and government insurance programs.

22

Property Management

Landlord-tenant codes: special codes or acts passed by government that regulate the rights and responsibilities of landlords and tenants to each other

Option clause: one that gives the tenant the option of renewing his lease at a pre-set figure, but does not obligate him to do so

Participation clause: allows the landlord to pass along increases in property taxes, maintenance and utilities to the tenant during the life of the lease

Percentage lease: a lease wherein the amount of rent paid is related to the income the tenant receives from using the premises

Prelease: to obtain tenants before a building is ready for occupancy

Rent concession: discounts, free services and free gifts given to attract tenants

Rent control: government imposed limitations on the rents that a landlord can charge

Rent-up: the process of filling a new building with tenants

Unconscionable contract: a contract that no fair and honest person would make or accept

At one time in the United States, the majority of residential rental properties were small buildings managed by the owner, who showed vacant apartments, collected rents, and maintained and repaired the building. Many small, owner-occupied buildings still exist, but today the majority of new apartment buildings are large and complex, owned by absentee owners, and the emphasis is on maximizing rental income, property value, and tax benefits. The result is a growing need for property managers who are professionally qualified in a broad range of management skills. At the same time, owners of small properties are also recognizing the need to adopt management techniques used for larger properties.

PLANNING
MARKETING
STRATEGIES

To the casual observer it may appear that the marketing of a newly constructed rental building begins on the day ads are placed in newspapers and pennants are strung across the property. In reality, however, marketing begins with choosing a location suitable for the intended market, designing a structure that is both popular with tenants and easy to maintain, finding good tenants, and then keeping them. Let us consider these points in more detail.

Residential Property
Merchandising

The first step in successful property management is to have a property that will merchandise itself. In residential management, this means offering an apartment unit that is designed for living. As more and more families are priced out of the single-family-house market, the demand for rental apartments suitable for permanent residency increases. In the past, many apartment dwellers considered renting to be a stepping-stone to home ownership. Today renting is becoming a permanent way of life. As a result, the trend in apartment construction (and the remodeling of existing apartments) is toward such features and amenities as wall-to-wall carpeting, dishwashers, self-cleaning ovens, large closets, decorator-designed kitchens, sunken living rooms, extra bathrooms, more attractive landscaping, recreation centers, and enclosed parking facilities. Moreover, these features must be installed and visible to the prospective tenant before he rents. Unlike the house buyer who can install a dishwasher or plant a tree after he moves in, the prospective tenant must assume that what is there is what he gets; if it is not presently there, it never will be.

Commercial Property
Merchandising

In office and industrial property, the first step in merchandising is to have space suitable to the business needs of tenants. One way to do this is to design a building to suit a tenant's needs. However, if the tenant moves out, it may be very hard to find another business with exactly the same space needs. As a result, design emphasis today is on buildings with movable walls and partitions. Thus, if an owner of an empty 10,000-square-foot building is approached by a prospective tenant who needs 6,000 square feet, the owner can move partitions to section off 6,000 square feet and begin earning rent on that space, rather than having to wait until he can find a tenant who needs exactly 10,000 square feet. The remaining 4,000 square feet can be rented to any combination of tenants that add up to 4,000 square feet. If 5 years later the 6,000-square-foot tenant moves out and a tenant in another part of the building needs expansion space of 1,000 square feet, the walls can again be moved, and the remaining 5,000 square feet let to new tenants.

The astute property manager attempts to find as many tenants as possible before the building is actually completed. This is called **preleasing** and involves showing prospective tenants architectural drawings of the finished building and perhaps a model built especially for sales purposes. This is done for two important reasons: (1) a preleased building is more attractive to lenders, and (2) once a building is completed and approved for occupancy, each day that it remains vacant a day's rent is lost. Preleasing programs are especially effective with commercial and industrial properties, since business tenants often know their space needs in advance. Residential tenants, by comparison, are far more likely to enter the rental market only a few days ahead of when they need space. Consequently, for new apartment buildings, the bulk of management's advertising and renting campaign efforts are timed to coincide with the project's completion.

RENT-UP PHASE

For renting apartments, radio and television advertising usually costs more than it produces in tenants. The traditional search pattern for the prospective apartment tenant is to drive through the neighborhoods he or she is interested in and to read the newspaper classified advertisements for rentals in that area. Thus, advertising money is most effectively spent on classified newspaper advertisements, plus billboards, signs, and arrows placed on nearby roads and highways. Full-page ads are not necessary; quarter-page or smaller ads cost less and are usually sufficient to catch the interest of the person looking for an apartment to rent.

Advertising Methods

To motivate salespeople to fill newly built apartments as quickly as possible, a bonus system is often used. For example,

Bonus Systems

during the rent-up phase, cash bonuses of $25 can be paid for every tenant signed up who moves in within 3 days of completion, $15 within 1 week, and $5 within 1 month. This is in addition to the normal salary or commission that would be paid for each apartment rented. A larger bonus may be offered for renting the more expensive units in the project.

Once a project has passed the rent-up phase, the bonus system is redesigned so that the manager on the property has an incentive to keep the project full. For example, with apartment buildings, a popular arrangement is to pay the manager one-fifth of the rents collected above the 95% occupancy level. If rents are set at market level, under normal management, 95% occupancy is expected; if the manager is superior in his efforts and obtains a higher occupancy, he should be rewarded.

TENANT SELECTION

Programs to fill buildings should be accompanied by a sound tenant selection system. For apartment developers, tenant selection begins with building design. For example, a project may be designed for adults only, or single people, or families with children.

In taking this approach, the developer's objective is to increase the appeal of his project to certain tenants, who, in turn, will be attracted to the project because they will be living with people of the same life style. To illustrate, beginning in the 1960s, apartment complexes developed specifically for single persons became powerful magnets for singles preferring to rent in a project with other singles rather than with married persons or families with children.

However, predetermining tenant type does not automatically solve the problem of tenant quality. Decisions must be made on an individual basis as prospective tenants apply to rent space. An extensive application form, a seasoned manager, and a substantial security deposit are valuable screening tools for identifying tenants who have a high probability of being compatible with the other tenants in a project and of paying their rent on time. If it appears that a prospect, once moved in, will not pay his rent or will be obnoxious to the neighbors, the time to avoid the problem is before he moves in.

A lengthy application form acts to discourage prospects who themselves feel only marginally qualified or who prefer not to divulge the information requested. It also provides a basis for checking the tenant's references. This includes talking with his former landlords to ask why he left, checking with the local credit bureau to learn if he pays his bills on time, and, in some cities, checking with a landlord's reference bureau to find out if he left a previous apartment without paying his rent. The purpose of the interview is to determine if the prospect has the income to support the rental he wants and if he will be compatible with the other tenants. For example, if the project does not allow children or pets, the manager will want to be sure the prospect understands this. Finally, the security deposit (against which the manager can deduct for unpaid rent or damage to the building) also serves as a screening device. If, for example, a prospect wants to rent a $200 per month apartment but does not have the money for a $100 security deposit, it is doubtful that he will be able to pay $200 rent each month.

Application Process

In some communities, there are firms that specialize in referring prospective tenants to apartment managers. However, the usefulness of this source depends on the level of pre-screening provided. If the firm simply channels all its apartment inquiries directly to the apartment manager without any prescreening, the service loses its usefulness; the manager may be better off relying on less costly newspaper advertising to draw prospects.

At one time an owner had complete choice in the selection of his tenants, a situation that caused undue hardship among minority groups. However, state and federal civil rights laws now require an owner and his manager to disregard all matters of race, color, or creed in selecting tenants. Some states also do not permit owners to refuse welfare recipients, provided they can pay the rent.

Renting to families with children usually means higher maintenance costs, and these costs must be built into the rent. Yet, because of the expense of feeding and clothing children, families with children can least afford higher rents. As a result,

Family Projects

relatively few apartment projects in the United States have been specifically designed to accept children. In contrast, tenants without children can afford more rent and maintenance costs are lower. Consequently, there has been a proliferation of adult-only apartments projects in recent decades. Families with children often find that the only apartments available to them are those that cannot be kept filled with an "adults only" policy. Whether this will be an adequate and satisfactory source of apartments for the families of the tens of millions of children born after World War II remains to be seen.

Commercial Tenants   Tenant selection for commercial and industrial properties is similar in principle to residential rentals. The property manager will want to know about the prospect's financial strength, how the prospect intends to use the space, and whether the use is compatible with adjacent tenants. Because of their financial strength, major corporations and government agencies are considered to be excellent tenants.

RENTAL AGREEMENT   The purpose of a rental contract is to transfer to a tenant possession of and the right to use property for a stipulated period of time. In return, the tenant promises to pay rent and observe the conditions set forth in the contract. At the end of the rental period the tenant's right of possession and use terminates unless provision is made for extension or renewal. To be a valid, binding contract, the tenant and owner must be legally competent, and the rental agreement must describe the property, the rental period, the amount of the rent, and any special agreements. In residential rentals, special agreements typically cover such topics as house rules, how the apartment may be used (e.g., no children, no pets), provisions for contract cancellation, and the conditions under which the tenant's security deposit will be returned. In addition, the manager is usually given the right to enter the tenant's unit for maintenance purposes and to show the property if the tenant plans to move.

Flexibility   Of particular interest to both the tenant and the owner is the period of time each is committed to the other. A month-to-month rental is the most flexible arrangement. It allows the owner to recover possession of the property on one-month notice and the tenant to leave on one-month notice with no further obligation to the owner. In rental agreements for longer periods of time, each party gives up some flexibility to gain commitment from the other. Under a one-year lease, a tenant has the property committed to him for a year. This means that the tenant is committed to paying rent for a full year, even though he may want to move out before the year is over. Similarly, the owner has the tenant's commitment to pay rent for a year, but loses the flexibility of being able to regain possession of the property until the year is over.

Inflation is a major concern of tenants and landlords who agree to rentals of more than a year. On a month-to-month rental, the rental fee can be changed monthly if prices change that fast. Thus, an owner can quote a **fixed rental** fee, knowing that he can change it a month later if need be. On a yearly rental that opportunity arises only once a year, and on a 10-year lease, once every 10 years. Consequently, to be fair to both the owner and the tenant during periods of rising prices, the rental contract may call for step-up rents, participation clauses, percentage rents, or options. For example, suppose that you own an office building and have been asked by a prospective tenant for a 5-year lease. You are enthusiastic about the prospect as a tenant, but are concerned that property taxes, maintenance, and utility costs will rise to the point that the rental price charged today will soon be inadequate.

Inflation

One solution is a series of predetermined rent increases designed to offset inflation. Thus, the rental contract might call for monthly rents of 60¢ per square foot of floor space the first year, 63¢ the second year, 67¢ the third year, 71¢ the fourth year, and 75¢ the fifth. This is a **step-up rental.** It is simple and straightforward; however, the major weak point is that it may be difficult to accurately predict what inflation will be like several years from now. As a result, **participation clauses** are often written into rentals of more than 1-year duration. Under these clauses, the building owner passes along to the tenant any increases in such items as property taxes, utility charges, or janitorial fees.

Another system for setting rents is the **percentage basis** wherein the owner receives a percentage of the tenant's gross receipts as rent. For example, a farmer who leases land may give the landowner 20% of the value of the crop when it is sold. The monthly rent for a hardware store might be $600 plus 6% of gross sales above $10,000. A supermarket may pay $7,500 plus 1½% of gross above $50,000 per month. By setting rents this way, the tenant shares some of his business risk with the property owner. Also, there is a built-in inflation hedge to the extent that inflation causes the tenant's receipts to increase.

Option Clauses

Option clauses in long-term lease contracts can be used to give a tenant more flexibility. For example, suppose that you are starting a new business and are not certain how successful it will be. Therefore, in looking for space to rent, you want a lease that will allow you an "out" if the new venture does not succeed, but will permit you to stay if your venture is successful. The solution is a lease with options. Thus, you might arrange for a 1-year lease, plus an option to stay for 2 more years at a higher rent, and a second option for an additional 5 years at a still higher rent. If your venture is not successful, you are obligated for only 1 year. But if you are successful, you have the option of staying 2 more years, and if still successful, for 5 years after that.

Rent Concessions

When a building owner is trying to attract tenants in an otherwise soft rental market, he can either keep rents the same and increase the quality of services offered to tenants, or he can provide a monetary inducement. If he selects the latter, he has two choices: (1) reduce the monthly rent, or (2) offer a rent concession. With a **rent concession,** the property owner keeps the rents at the same level, but offers a premium to a prospective tenant to entice him to move in. Often this takes the form of giving a free month's rent to prospects who will sign a 1-year lease. Other concessions include offering the tenant a cash moving allowance or giving him a free weekend vacation at a nearby resort. The philosophy behind using concessions rather than outright rent reductions is that, when the rental market firms up, it is easier to quietly stop offering concessions than it is to raise rents.

Tenant retention begins with selecting tenants who can pay the rent and who will be compatible with existing tenants. Having once found good tenants, the property manager's most important task is to keep them as long as possible. Besides the rent lost while the apartment is empty, the costs of apartment clean-up and finding a new tenant are high.

Statistically, about one third of the units in a typical apartment project must be rerented each year. Certainly, many moves are due to job relocation or the need for larger or smaller quarters. But some moves occur because tenants find something they dislike about the way their apartments are managed. For example, if a building is poorly kept up or the manager gives the impression that he does not care about his tenants or the owner increases the rent with no apparent justification, people will move out. To retain tenants, the property owner and manager should think of them as permanent residents, even though turnover is expected. This begins with using a rental contract that an average tenant can read and understand. A complicated and legalistic contract may be seen by the tenant as the first step in a sparring match with management that will last as long as he resides there. The tenant also expects the property to be clean and properly maintained, and if repairs become necessary to his unit that they will be made promptly.

Communications

Good communications between management and tenants is also crucial to tenant retention. If the swimming pool is closed or the electricity shut off to the building with no announcement or no apparent reason, tenants become disgusted and add it to their private lists of reasons for ultimately leaving. As a minimum, tenants expect management to keep them informed through bulletin board announcements or notices placed under their doors. In many larger apartment projects, managers publish newsletters to keep tenants informed about how the project is being managed, and to provide an avenue by which tenants can communicate with each other. For example, one page can explain why rents must go up because of rising property taxes, maintenance, and utility costs, while another page announces the formation of a bowling league among project dwellers.

Leases   A very straightforward approach to improving tenant retention is to use leases. Once signed to a 1-year lease, a tenant is much less likely to leave after a few months if he has a minor complaint than he would be on a month-to-month agreement. Similarly, leases for longer than 1 year will reduce tenant turnover even more, although residential tenants are often wary about committing themselves that far into the future. A tenant can also be encouraged to stay by offering him a renewal lease at a slightly lower rate than that being offered to new tenants. Another technique is to offer long-time tenants free carpet shampooing, drape cleaning, and wall painting, all things normally done if the tenant leaves and the apartment must be rerented.

Recreation Facilities   Recreation centers may aid in tenant retention. However, to effectively do that, they must be useful. To a first-time renter, a flashy recreation center may be one of the reasons he chooses a particular apartment building. However, if after he moves in he finds the gym equipment inadequate, the swimming pool too small, and the billiard tables overcrowded, he soon thinks about another place to live.

COLLECTING RENTS   Ultimately, the success of a rental building depends on the ability of management to collect the rents due from tenants. In accomplishing this, it is generally agreed among property managers that a firm and consistent collection policy, handled in a businesslike manner, is the best approach. For commercial and industrial properties, the standard practice is for the property manager to mail a monthly rent statement to the tenant and for the tenant to mail his rent check to the manager. For residential properties, monthly rent statements can also be mailed to each tenant, but more often, the tenant is told in his rental contract when his rent is due each month, and he is expected to pay it on time. Rents can be collected door to door, but most managers prefer that rent checks be mailed or brought to their office when due.

When a tenant's rent is not received on time, the manager must decide what to do. Is the lateness simply a matter of delayed mail or temporary but honest forgetfulness, or is the delay an early sign of a much deeper problem, one that may cost the property owner lost rent and ultimately lead to eviction? The accepted procedure is to wait 5 days before sending the tenant a reminder. This avoids generating a negative feeling when the problem was only due to a minor delay, for it is a fact that the vast majority of tenants do pay their rent on time. However, if payment is not received by the tenth day after it was due, a second reminder goes out requesting that the tenant personally call on the manager. By meeting with the delinquent tenant, the manager may obtain an indication as to what the underlying problem is. If the tenant is suffering from a temporary financial setback, the manager can weigh the humanitarian side and the cost of rerenting the apartment against the possibility that payment will never be received.

Late Rents

When it is apparent that a delinquent tenant will never bring his rent up to date, it is time to ask the tenant to leave and to rerent the space. What happens if the tenant will neither leave nor pay his rent? Years ago, it was not uncommon for an owner to enter a tenant's unit, remove all his belongings, and lock them up. The key to the apartment door was changed and the apartment rerented; if the delinquent tenant wanted his belongings back, he had to pay the back rent. Today's laws provide more protection for the tenant, and he may sue his landlord for removing his belongings and locking him out. Moreover, under current laws, although a manager can get a court order telling the tenant to leave, and even call upon a sheriff to enforce it, a nonpaying tenant who is well versed in the law can remain for several rent-free weeks. This is possible because of the time required to go through the legal procedures of eviction. When the delinquent tenant finally leaves a month or two later, he may owe several hundred dollars in back rent. The legal cost of forcing payment

Eviction Problems

may be more than what is owed. The tenant knows this and hopes he will not be pursued.

MANAGER REMEDIES

More and more tenants are learning that if they are brash enough they can use the method just described to live rent-free and then move on. Others stop just short of the sheriff knocking on their door and leave on their own. Called **skipping out,** the delinquent tenant moves out without paying his back rent, hoping the manager or owner will not go to the trouble of pursuing the issue. Tenants are also learning to use the small claims courts as an inexpensive way to legally pursue all sorts of real and fancied complaints against management, and managers are learning that judges often favor the tenant in these cases. What can owners and managers do about this? The best defense is careful tenant selection, good service, and a businesslike policy on rent collection. In other words, the old idea of filling up a building as fast as possible and later weeding out the problem tenants is no longer practical. Beyond that, the presence of a full-time manager means tenants are likely to take better care of the premises and are less likely to leave without paying the rent.

Managers can also make more effective use of the law by using the small claims courts to obtain judgments for unpaid rent claims against delinquents, skips, and those who write bad checks for rent payments. Although a tenant may have left the area and it may not be worth the effort of locating him, the fact that a manager does take a firm stand serves as a deterrent to those planning the same tactics. For the nonpaying tenant, the judgment against him becomes a part of his credit record and a warning to the next manager he approaches for an apartment. Small claims cases that go against managers can often be appealed to a municipal court, where lawyers are permitted and more weight is given to contracts.

TENANT REMEDIES

If a property owner provides an honest service for a reasonable price, he is entitled to the rent. However, just as some tenants try to take advantage of their landlord, some landlords try to take advantage of their tenants. What remedies does the tenant have? Traditional legal thinking has viewed the rental agreement as a conveyance of real property for a specified period of time. Seen from this standpoint, if the property owner agreed in the contract to make repairs or provide certain services and failed to do so, the tenant could claim breach of contract. This allowed the tenant to abandon the premises or order the repairs made or the services performed, and deduct the cost from the rent. Alternatively, the tenant could pay the rent in full and sue the owner for the deficiencies, or pay a reduced rent reflecting the value of the premises without the needed repairs and services. Also, the owner could be held liable for injury suffered as a result of the contract breach.

If a repair or service was not promised in the contract, the owner was not obligated to provide it, and it became the tenant's responsibility. Thus, if the contract said nothing about keeping the roof in repair and it leaked after the tenant moved in, the tenant either lived with a leaky roof or fixed it at his own expense. This still applies to a large degree to commercial and industrial property rentals.

Residential Properties

However, with regard to residential properties, courts and legislatures are now taking the position that the owner is obligated to keep the property repaired and in habitable condition even though this is not specifically stated in the rental contract. Such laws may also give the tenant the right to move out if repairs are not made, or to make repairs and deduct them from the rent. In a few states, when building code violations occur, the tenant can sue for a refund of rent paid or can withhold rent by placing it in a neutral escrow, with instructions that it be paid to the property owner when repairs are made. This is an important change in legal thinking; rental agreements are now seen less as a strict conveyance of property and more as contracts that provide the service of shelter.

Another trend is for courts to refuse to enforce unfair (**unconscionable**) provisions in rental contracts. For example, a lease may state that it cannot be canceled for building violations. This is unenforceable. Similarly, rental contracts that are overly advantageous to the owner or that take advantage of the tenant's inability to understand law are also being looked upon with disfavor. In response, owners are beginning to write simplified contracts in plain English that clearly spell out the responsibilities of both the tenant and the property owner.

LANDLORD–TENANT CODES

In an attempt to equalize the rights of residential tenants and their landlords and to set forth these rights in readable language, a number of states have adopted landlord–tenant codes or acts. This trend is gaining strength, and the concept will be introduced as legislation in more and more states in the next few years.

Basically, a landlord–tenant code describes the responsibilities of the landlord to his tenant and the tenant to his landlord. While tenants often complain that the codes are pro landlord, and owners complain that they are pro tenant, the codes do fill important gaps. Among these are situations where the rental agreement is not in writing, where a landlord does not know how to write a complete rental contract, or where the landlord and the tenant do not fully understand what their rights and responsibilities are.

Landlord–tenant codes currently in use vary somewhat from state to state, but the following provisions are among those usually included:

1. The tenant is to receive a copy of each document signed, plus a pamphlet listing his rights and responsibilities under the code.
2. Security deposits cannot exceed 1 month's rent and must be returned to the tenant within 14 days after the tenant moves out, provided the tenant lives up to the agreement. If the landlord intends to withhold part or all of the security deposit, he must notify the tenant within 14 days after the tenant moves and state the reasons. If the security deposit is being withheld because of tenant-caused damages, the landlord must include estimates, invoices, or receipts showing the cost of repairs. If the tenant disagrees with the amount being withheld, the issue is to be settled in a small claims court. If the landlord knowingly cheats the tenant on the return of the security deposit, the court can award the tenant return of the deposit, plus damages and court costs. If the court finds that the tenant has no case, the court shall award the landlord damages and court costs at the expense of the tenant.

3. A landlord may not word a rental contract so that it exempts him from his duties and responsibilities under the landlord–tenant code or from other health, safety, building, or legal requirements pertaining to the premises. For example, a tenant cannot waive (sign away) his right to an accounting of his security deposit.

4. If the landlord fails to deliver possession of the apartment to the tenant on the date called for in the contract, the tenant is not liable for rent and may cancel the contract.

5. If, after the tenant moves in, the landlord fails to live up to the rental agreement or fails to maintain the premises in a fit condition, the tenant may terminate the rental agreement during the first week of occupancy and move out. If conditions on the premises later become a threat to the health and safety of the tenant, as verified by public health officials, he may terminate even though the first week has passed.

6. The tenant agrees to obey the house rules provided they are clearly stated, reasonable, and applied fairly to all tenants.

7. The landlord has the right to enter the tenant's apartment only for reasonable purposes and only upon 2-day notice, except in the event of a legitimate emergency.

8. The tenant agrees to keep his unit clean and safe, dispose of rubbish promptly, use electrical and plumbing fixtures properly, not damage the premises, and inform the landlord of defects in need of repair.

9. If, after being informed by the tenant, the landlord fails to make repairs within 30 days, the tenant has several options. If the repairs do not exceed $100 in cost and the tenant notifies the landlord of his intention to do so, the tenant may have the repairs made and either bill the landlord or deduct the cost from the next rent payment. Repair expenses up to the amount of 1 month's rent are permitted where a public health official documents an objectionable condition.

10. A landlord may not evict a tenant or increase his rent because he complains to a government health, safety, or building department about his unit or the premises.

11. If the landlord must take court action to recover unpaid rent from a tenant, the tenant is responsible for paying the landlord's legal costs plus the unpaid rent.

12. If the rental agreement is on a month-to-month basis, the tenant must give the landlord a minimum of 1-month notice of his intent to vacate.

13. If the tenant remains past his rental period without the landlord's consent and becomes a holdover tenant, he must pay double rent.
14. The landlord can go to court to evict a tenant and recover possession of his unit if the rental agreement has expired, or the tenant has not paid his rent after 5-day written notice. A court-ordered eviction can also be requested if the tenant has abandoned the unit, has broken his agreement with the landlord regarding the use of the premises, or has used it contrary to law. For example, a tenant who brings a pet into a no-pet building or a tenant who sets up a business in a residential apartment could be evicted.

TENANT UNIONS

In a large apartment project, one tenant acting alone usually has little bargaining power against his landlord. However, many tenants banded together into a tenant union have considerable bargaining power. For example, a small group of unhappy tenants can gather support among other tenants and ultimately present their demand in the form of paying their collective rents into a neutral escrow until the problem is resolved. Or, if rents go up, tenants may simply keep paying the old rate, all in unison. Even though an owner might have legal grounds for eviction based on nonpayment of rent, evicting all the tenants in a building is not only a major task, but would leave the whole building to be rented again.

Sometimes the urge to form a tenant union comes from outside the project. However, whether the impetus is from outside or inside, if the majority of the tenants in the project have received open communications from the management (particularly in regard to rent increases), courteous treatment, good service, fast repairs, and fair rent charges, the odds of success of an organized complaint group are small. If a tenant union does form, the problem that created it must be resolved with considerable diplomacy, for tempers usually run high in an organized confrontation.

RENT CONTROL

For the most part, until 1970, the concept of residential rent control was reserved for wartime use in the United States. During World War I, six states and several major cities and, in World War II, the federal government imposed limits on how much rent an owner could charge for the use of his real property. The purpose was twofold: (1) to discourage the construction of new housing so that the resources could be channeled to war needs, and (2) to set ceilings so that American households would not drive up prices by bidding against each other for available rental housing. With limits on rents, but no controls on the cost of construction materials and labor, the construction of new housing was slowed without the need for a direct government order to stop building.

Within a few years after World War I, and again after World War II, rent controls disappeared in nearly all parts of the country. The notable exception was New York City, where they have survived since the end of World War II and are still in use. In addition, a number of other cities have opted for rent control since 1970. They include Berkeley, California; Miami Beach, Florida; Fairbanks, Alaska; Washington, D.C.; Boston, Massachusetts; and several suburban communities around New York City. Rent controls were also in effect nationally between August 15, 1971, and January 11, 1973, as part of a federally imposed price control program.

The major attraction of rent control today is that since 1965 prices of nearly all goods and services have been climbing at a relatively rapid rate for Americans. Moreover, during parts of the 1970 decade, prices have risen faster than wages. Although it is true that since 1956 residential rents in the United States have not risen as rapidly as the general level of consumer prices, any relief from rent increases would nonetheless be welcomed by the 36% of American households that rent. Most tenants recognize that newly constructed properties must command higher rents to meet higher construction, land, and interest costs. However, in existing buildings they resent rent increases that have nothing to do with the original cost of the building or the cost of operating it. The argument of rent control supporters is that only increases in such things as property taxes, utilities, and maintenance should be passed on to tenants. The tenant's assumption in this argument is that rent alone is enough to attract dollars into housing investments. In reality, rents would have to be even higher if the investor could not also look forward to price appreciation of his property.

Experience to date, however, strongly suggests that rent control creates more problems than it solves. In New York City, for example, it is generally agreed that controlled rents have discouraged new residential construction and have taken existing dwelling units out of circulation. In fiscal year 1974–1975, there were an estimated 35,000 abandoned dwelling units, costing the city millions of dollars a year in lost property taxes. These abandonments were primarily due to rent control levels that did not rise fast enough to allow for increases in property taxes, maintenance, and utilities. As a result, property owners were actually better off abandoning their properties than operating them. In other parts of the city where rents are artificially low but the building continues to operate, black markets occur. For example, a tenant vacating a controlled apartment may demand a substantial cash payment from a tenant who wants to move in. Although this is illegal, the vacating tenant may attempt to circumvent the law by requiring the incoming tenant to purchase his furniture for several times its actual worth. This places the actual cost of the controlled apartment much closer to the value of the unit on the open market, and the advantage of low, controlled rents is lost to the incoming tenant.

In Washington, D.C., a side effect of rent control has been a surge of conversions of existing rental apartments to condominiums, as there are no controls, as yet, on prices of dwelling units offered for sale. Because this removed rental apartments from the market, laws were enacted to restrict conversions. This encouraged owners to demolish and build new condominiums; however, laws were then enacted to restrict demolition permits.

After Berkeley, California, adopted rent control by public vote in 1972, new rental apartment construction stopped because investors and lenders did not know if rent-controlled prices would allow them enough income to meet operating expenses, debt repayment, and a reasonable return on the investor's capital. The irony was that although no new construction was taking place, artificially low rents actually increased demand for apartments in Berkeley. (In 1976, the State Court of Appeals affirmed the finding of the Alameda County

Superior Court that the Berkeley rent control law was unconstitutional. Thus, the fate of rent control in that city remains to be seen.)

Experience with rent control in the United States has also shown that there is a significant cost to the public to operate the government offices that administer the controls and, to the extent that controls hold down rents, the rich tenant benefits as much as the poor. Finally, a new phenomenon is beginning to emerge: communities are beginning to realize that with rent control they can keep rents low on existing rentals and at the same time foster a no-growth policy, because the controls discourage new construction.

PROPERTY MANAGERS

Property management responsibilities can be divided into two categories: off-site and on-site. **Off-site management** consists of those duties that can be accomplished without actually having to be on the premises, for example, accounting for rents collected, handling payrolls, attending to legal matters, and paying bills. **On-site management** refers to such matters as showing vacant space to prospective tenants, maintaining the premises, supervising repairs, handling tenant complaints, and in general looking after the building and the welfare of the tenants.

Management Qualifications

Commercial and industrial property management positions tend to be filled by persons who have had prior property management experience and who have a good understanding of how business and industry make use of real estate. Residential properties are managed by persons with a wider variety of experience backgrounds. The most successful apartment managers seem to be those who have had previous experience in managing people and money and who are handy with tools. Those with prior military experience or experience as owners or managers of small businesses are eagerly sought after. Least successful as on-site property managers are those who see it as a quiet, peaceful retirement job, those who are unable to work with and understand people, those who cannot organize or make decisions, those without a few handyman skills, and those looking for strictly an 8-to-5, Monday-to-Friday job.

The last item is particularly critical as the manager who lives on the property is on call 24 hours a day, in addition to regular working hours that may stretch from early morning janitorial supervision to late night security checks of the premises.

Management-Unit Ratios

The rule of thumb in apartment management is that one on-site manager can handle 50 or 60 units by himself. Between 60 and 100 units, the manager needs an assistant to help with management chores and to make it possible to have someone on the property at all times. In projects over 100 units, an approach that is gaining popularity is to hire husband–wife teams, placing both on the payroll and adding assistants in proportion to project size. For example, a 150-unit apartment building would be managed by a husband–wife team and one assistant (usually a full-time custodian). A 200-unit building would have a husband–wife team plus two full-time assistants, and so on, adding an additional employee for each additional 50 to 60 apartment units. Larger projects also mean assistants can specialize. For example, in a 625-unit complex with a husband–wife team and nine assistants, two assistants might run the leasing office, two specialize in cleaning apartments when tenants leave, one act as a gardener, one as a repairman, one as a custodian, one as a rent collector and bookkeeper, and one as a recreational facilities director.

Training Programs

Finding experienced and capable property managers is not an easy task. There is little formal education in property management available in the United States. Instead, most managers learn their profession almost entirely by experience. An individual property owner can place an advertisement in the newspaper and attract a manager from another project, but most professional management firms have found it necessary to develop their own internal training programs. With such a program, a management firm can start a person with no previous property management experience as an assistant manager on a large project. If he or she learns the job and enjoys the work, there is a promotion to manager of a 50- or 60-unit building and an increase in salary. If this works well, the manager is moved to a larger complex, with an assistant and another increase in salary. Each step brings more responsibility and more pay. This system provides a steady stream of qualified managers for the management firm.

The dominant professional organization in the property management field is the Institute of Real Estate Management (IREM). Established in 1933, the institute is a division within the National Association of Realtors. Its primary purposes are to serve as an exchange medium for management ideas and to recognize specialists in the field. The exchange of ideas is accomplished through the IREM *Journal of Property Management*, IREM written reports and studies, and IREM-sponsored seminars. Professional recognition is by designation as a Certified Property Manager (CPM), a title awarded IREM members who meet experience, education, and ethical standards, and pass written examinations. The institute also has an Accredited Management Organization (AMO) program whereby property management firms that meet institute-established standards of management capability and integrity can receive the AMO designation.

Whereas the IREM is designed for managers of all types of property, the Building Owners and Managers Association International consists primarily of owners and managers of office buildings. The association provides educational programs, encourages professional development, sets ethical standards for members, and publishes its own magazine.

PROFESSIONAL MANAGEMENT ORGANIZATIONS

VOCABULARY REVIEW

Match terms a–m with statements 1–13.

a. *CPM*
b. *IREM*
c. *Off-site management*
d. *On-site management*
e. *Option clause*
f. *Participation clause*
g. *Percentage lease*

h. *Prelease*
i. *Rent concession*
j. *Rent control*
k. *Skipping out*
l. *Step-up rent*
m. *Unconscionable*

1. To obtain tenants before a building is actually ready for occupancy.

2. A lease that calls for specified rent increases at various points in time during the life of the lease.

3. A lease clause that allows the landlord to add to the tenant's rent any increases in property taxes, maintenance, and utilities during the life of the lease.

4. A lease clause that gives a tenant the opportunity of renewing his lease at a predetermined rental, but does not obligate him to do so.

5. A lease where the amount of rent paid is related to the income the lessee obtains from the use of the premises.

6. When a tenant who is behind in his rent moves out without paying.

7. Contract provisions considered by the courts to be grossly unfair.

8. Government-imposed limitations placed upon the rents that a landlord can charge.

9. Property management functions that can be performed away from the property such as bill paying and payroll accounting.

10. A professional property management organization sponsored by the National Association of Realtors.

11. A professional designation available to persons in the property management field.

12. Property management tasks that include showing vacant space to prospects, maintaining the premises, supervising repairs, etc.

13. Discounts, free services, and free gifts given in order to attract tenants.

QUESTIONS AND
PROBLEMS

1. Why should a property rental program begin before a building is even built?

2. Why are preleasing campaigns usually more successful with commercial and industrial properties than apartments?

3. If you were an apartment building manager interviewing prospective tenants, what questions would you ask?

4. Where will the high school students in your community find housing in the next few years?

5. From the standpoint of the tenant, what are the advantages and disadvantages of a lease versus a month-to-month rental?

6. Have rental-property owners in your community offered rent concessions at any time in the past 3 years? If so, describe the concessions offered.

7. What remedies does a property manager in your state have when a tenant does not pay his rent and/or refuses to move out?

8. Does your state have a landlord–tenant code? What are its major provisions? If no specific code or act currently exists in your state, where does one look for laws pertaining to landlords and tenants?
9. Is rent control currently in effect in your community? If so, what effects have these controls had on the sales of investment properties and on the construction of new rental buildings in your community?

ADDITIONAL READINGS

Downs, James C., Jr. *Principles of Real Estate Management*, 11th ed. Chicago: Institute of Real Estate Management, 1975, 488 pages. Considered by many to be *the* authoritative text in real property management, it covers a wide range of property management topics.

Glassman, Sidney. *A Guide to Residential Management*. Washington, D.C.: National Association of Homebuilders, 1971, 92 pages. Topics include renting procedures, rent collections, delinquent rent, security deposits, tenant–management relations, maintenance, personnel policy, and computer use, with an appendix of sample forms and documents used in property management.

Hanford, Lloyd D., Sr. *The Property Management Process*. Chicago: Institute of Real Estate Management, 1972, 86 pages. What a property owner can expect when he hires a professional property management firm and what the obligations of a professional manager are to the owner.

House and Home Press. *Managing Apartments for Profit*. New York: House and Home Press, 1972, 72 pages. A very readable collection of articles that have appeared in *House and Home* magazine and deal with apartment management. Includes such topics as building design, rent-up phase, advertising, maintenance, tenant standards, property managers, security systems, and condominium management.

Institute of Real Estate Management. *The Property Manager's Guide to Forms and Letters*. Chicago: Institute of Real Estate Management, 1971, 245 pages. Contains over 200 forms and documents used in real estate management in the United States. Included are sample leases, subleases, lease renewals, expiration and cancellation forms, delinquency and eviction notices, security deposit forms, tenant letters, rent increase notices, and house rules.

Institute of Real Estate Management. *The Resident Manager.* Chicago: Institute of Real Estate Management, 1973, 88 pages. A guidebook for on-site apartment and condominium managers. Topics include the manager's responsibilities, public relations, rental collection, record keeping, resident communications, and building maintenance and operation. Includes sample forms and documents.

23

Land-Use Control

Building codes: local and state laws that set minimum construction standards

Certificate of occupancy: a government issued document that states a structure meets local zoning and building code requirements and is ready for use

Environmental impact statement (EIS): a report that contains information regarding the effect of a proposed project on the environment

Land-use control: a broad term that describes any legal restriction that controls how a parcel of land may be used

Master plan: a comprehensive guide for the physical growth of a community

Nonconforming use: an improvement that is inconsistent with current zoning regulations

Restrictive covenants: clauses placed in deeds to control how future landowners may or may not use the property; also used in leases

Transferable development right (TDR): a legal means by which the right to develop a particular parcel of land can be transferred to another parcel

Variance: a permit granted to an individual property owner to vary slightly from strict compliance with zoning requirements

Zoning: public regulations that control the specific use of land in a given district

The concept of land planning and land-use control is by no means new. When man gave up his nomadic existence and settled into villages, he concentrated his tribal huts so as to provide maximum protection against marauders. Similarly, the walled cities of pre-Christian and medieval Europe and Asia were not accidents of history, but carefully thought out land-use designs dictated by the need for protection. Homes, shops, and government were concentrated in a small area around which a strong wall was built. Outside the wall, agriculture took place, but only within the area that a city resident could   *515* walk to in the morning, do his work, and then return to the city gates before nightfall.

PLANNING IN THE
COLONIAL PERIOD

In North America, the primary intent of early European arrivals was to establish permanent outposts to validate the territorial claims of England, France, Spain, and the Netherlands. From the beginning, there was considerable interest in planning and controlling land uses in the newly founded settlements so that they would not only be economically and socially successful, but also capable of absorbing additional settlers from Europe. The whole process of town planning was greatly aided by the fact that land ownership was in the name of the king or colony company sponsoring the settlement.

Many towns founded during the Colonial American period were local adaptions of land-use patterns found in English towns where the residents had lived before. Some of these original land-use patterns can still be seen in New England today. Other American communities were planned as the result of the inspiration of a single person who attempted to combine the best features of many European cities. Examples are Philadelphia (planned in 1682), Annapolis (planned in 1695), Williamsburg (planned in 1699), and Savannah (planned in 1733). When the newly emerged government of the United States selected Washington, D.C., as its new home, an artist and engineer named Pierre L'Enfant was selected to prepare the city plan, which he did in 1791.

PLANNING IN THE
NEW COUNTRY

Unfortunately, interest in city planning declined shortly after the new American government became established. The primary causes were the loss of land control by the king of England, the American emphasis on development of the country's rural lands rather than its towns and cities, and the adoption of the rectangular survey system. The result was a headlong rush by an army of land speculators to buy up the cheap lands to the west, survey them into townsites, and sell the freshly platted lots at a high markup to unsuspecting buyers. The "towns" thus created usually followed the rectangular street pattern characteristic of William Penn's plan for Philadelphia. However, this was not to provide the large number of open spaces that Penn used, but because a gridiron was easy to survey. Little thought was given to whether the newly platted townsites were economically useful or pleasant to live in. Simultaneously, in Philadelphia and Washington, D.C., the plans of Penn and L'Enfant were compromised as areas reserved for open spaces were used for buildings. But the country was too busy expanding its territory and enhancing its economic influence under the doctrine of Manifest Destiny to give thoughtful consideration to land-use planning and to provide adequately for such things as sanitation standards, water supplies, parks, and paved roads.

The number of cities in the United States with populations of 25,000 or greater increased from 12 in the year 1840 to 77 in the year 1880, and it became apparent that more than hastily prepared plat maps were needed to give cities economic and social vitality. The initial reaction was to give more attention to water supplies, sanitation, and paved roads. Then in the late 1800s, there came a period of intense interest in city beautification programs. A number of cities established planning commissions, but the emphasis was primarily on using public money to purchase downtown property and convert it to attractive parks and boulevards. Little was done about the formless urban sprawl that made beautification programs necessary. Moreover, beautification programs sidestepped the issue of whether the community had the power to control how land could be used without first having to purchase it.

Beginning in 1916, a number of cities and towns began to experiment with zoning ordinances that dictated to a landowner what he could and could not do with his land without providing him compensation for the rights taken away. This did not seem constitutional to many people, and the issue reached the Supreme Court of the United States. In 1926 the court ruled that zoning laws were constitutional, and thus communities gained a valuable land-use control tool. In theory, zoning laws were to be the teeth in comprehensive land-use plans designed to provide for the orderly and logical development of land in and around cities. In practice, however, popular acceptance of zoning laws came only after it was widely

TWENTIETH CENTURY PLANNING

touted that zoning would stabilize and protect real property values.

Today, over 98% of all U.S. cities with a population of 10,000 or more have zoning ordinances. It is generally agreed that these laws do a good job of protecting the character of existing neighborhoods. But there is considerable debate as to whether they have resulted in sensible land planning at the developing edges of a city. Moreover, zoning decisions were too often based solely on the physical aspects of land planning, that is, streets, transit systems, parks, and civic appearance. Not until the experience of the Great Depression of the 1930s was much thought given to the notion that land-use decisions should consider the overall economic and social vitality of a community, as well as its physical appearance.

The Post-World War II Period   After World War II, more attention was paid to the economic and social impact of land-use controls. Planning was becoming a profession, and by 1950 nearly 20 universities offered graduate degrees in city planning. The postwar period also brought a series of state and national housing acts, transportation acts, and urban development acts that required cities to have land-use plans. But the most impelling factor for thoughtful land planning resulted from the general economic prosperity that followed World War II and the growth of the U.S. population by 60% between 1940 and 1975.

During the past several years, the American public has become more concerned with land-use planning and control. This is evidenced at the federal government level by the passage in 1969 of a law requiring environmental impact statements. At the state level, the trend toward regional and statewide planning is shown by the growing number of states that control land use along their coastlines and by at least one state, Hawaii, where statewide land planning is currently practiced. At the local level, individual towns and cities are thinking in terms of controlling their growth by refusing to grant water or sewer hookups to new buildings and by limiting the number of building permits granted each year.

More than anytime since 1776, land is being regarded as a community resource, and individual landowners are expected to be more accommodating to the public as a whole. However, the passage of two centuries has not brought us to a land-use utopia. The individual property owner does not consider his property to be a community resource. Thus, any substantial progress in land planning and control in the future must also consider the right of the individual to develop his land.

With this brief background in mind, let us consider the specific topics of zoning, planning, subdivision controls, building codes, deed restrictions, environmental impact statements, new communities, and windfalls versus wipe-outs.

No other aspect of land-use control affects the American public to a greater degree than zoning. Since the first zoning law went into effect in 1916 in New York City, nearly every town and city in the United States, plus a large number of counties, has adopted zoning ordinances. (The original purpose for adopting zoning in New York City was to keep the expanding garment industry out of the fashionable Fifth Avenue business and residential areas.) These laws divide land into zones (districts) and within each zone regulate the purpose for which buildings may be constructed, the height and bulk of the buildings, the area of the lot that they may occupy, and the number of persons that they can accommodate. Through zoning, a community can protect existing land users from encroachment by undesirable uses, ensure that future land uses in the community will be compatible with each other, and control development so that each parcel of land will be adequately serviced by streets, sanitary and storm sewers, schools, parks, and utilities.

The authority to control land use is derived from the basic police power of each state to protect the public health, safety, morals, and general welfare of its citizens. Through an enabling act passed by the state legislature, the authority to control land use is also given to individual towns, cities, and counties. These local government units then pass zoning ordinances that establish the boundaries of the various land-use zones and determine the type of development that will be permitted in each of them. By going to his local government offices, a landowner can see on a map how his land is zoned. Once he knows the zoning for his land, he can consult the zoning ordinance to see how he will be allowed to use it.

ZONING CONCEPTS

Zoning Symbols   For convenience, zones are usually identified by code abbreviations such as R (residential), C (commercial), I or M (industrial–manufacturing), and A (agriculture). Within each general category there are subcategories, such as R-1 (single-family residence), R-2 (two-family residence), R-3 (low-density, garden-type apartments), R-4, high-density, high-rise apartments), and RPD (residential planned development). Similarly, there are usually three or four manufacturing zones ranging from light, smoke-free industry (I-1 or M-1) to heavy industry (I-4 or M-4). However, there is no uniformity in zoning classifications in the United States. One city may use R-4 to designate high-rise apartments, while another uses R-4 to designate single-family homes on 4,000-square-foot lots and the letter A to designate apartments.

Land-Use Restrictions   Besides telling a landowner the use to which he may put his land, the zoning ordinance imposes additional rules. For example, land zoned for low-density apartments may require 1,500 square feet of land per living unit, a minimum of 600 square feet of living space per unit for one bedroom, 800 square feet for two bedrooms, and 1,000 square feet for three bedrooms. The zoning ordinance may also contain a set-back requirement which states that a building must be placed at least 25 feet back from the street, 10 feet from the sides of the lot, and 15 feet from the rear lot line. The ordinance may also limit the building's height to 2½ stories and require that the lot be a minimum of 10,000 square feet in size. As can be seen, zoning encourages uniformity.

Enforcement of Zoning Laws   Zoning laws are enforced by virtue of the fact that in order to build upon his land a person must obtain a building permit from his city or county government. Before a permit is issued, the proposed structure must conform with government-imposed structural standards and comply with the zoning on the land. If a landowner builds without a permit, he can be forced to tear down his building.

When an existing structure does not conform with a new zoning law, it is grandfathered-in as a **nonconforming use.** Thus, the owner can continue to use the structure even though it does not conform to the new zoning. However, the owner is not permitted to enlarge or remodel the structure or to extend its life. When the structure is ultimately demolished, any new use of the land must be in accordance with the zoning law. If you are driving through a residential neighborhood and see an old store or service station that looks very much out of place, it is probably a nonconforming use that was allowed to stay because it was built before the current zoning on the property went into effect.

Once an area has been zoned for a specific land use, changes are made by **amending the zoning ordinance** or by obtaining a variance. The amendment approach is taken when a change in zoning is necessary. An amendment can be initiated by a property owner in the area to be rezoned or by local government. Either way, notice of the proposed change must be given to all property owners in and around the affected area, and a public hearing must be held so that property owners and the public at large may voice their opinions on the matter. By comparison, **variances** allow an individual landowner to deviate somewhat from zoning code requirements and do not involve a zoning change. For example, a variance might be granted to the owner of an odd-shaped lot to reduce the set-back requirements slightly so that he can fit a building on it. Variances usually are granted where strict compliance with the zoning ordinance or code would cause undue hardship. However, the variance must not change the basic character of the neighborhood, and it must be consistent with the general objectives of zoning as they apply to that neighborhood.

Zoning Changes

A zoning law can be changed or struck down if it can be proved in court that it is unclear, discriminatory, unreasonable, not for the protection of the public health, safety, and general welfare, or not applied to all property in a similar manner.

It must be recognized that zoning alone does not create land value. For example, zoning a hundred square miles of lonely desert or mountain land for stores and offices would not appreciably change its value. Value is created by the number of people who want to use a particular parcel of land for a

Property Values

specific purpose. To the extent that zoning channels that demand to certain parcels of land and away from others, zoning does have an important impact on property value.

PLANNING AHEAD
FOR LAND
DEVELOPMENT

When a community first adopts a zoning ordinance, the usual procedure is to recognize existing land uses by zoning according to what already exists. Thus, a neighborhood that is already developed with houses is zoned for houses. Undeveloped land may be zoned for agriculture or simply left unzoned. As the community expands, undeveloped land is zoned for urban uses in a pattern that typically follows the availability of new roads, the aggressiveness of developers, and the willingness of landowners to sell. All too often the result has been a hodgepodge of land-use districts, all conforming internally because of tightly enforced zoning, but with little or no relationship among them. This happens because they were created over a period of years without the aid of a land-use plan that took a comprehensive view of the entire growth pattern of the city. Since uncoordinated land use can have a negative impact on both the quality of life and economic vitality of a community, more attention is now being directed toward land-use master plans to guide the development of towns and cities.

Master Plans

To prepare a master plan (or general plan), a city or regional planning commission is usually created. The first step should be a physical and economic survey of the area to be planned. The physical survey involves mapping existing roads, utility lines, and developed and undeveloped land. The economic survey looks at the present and anticipated economic base of the region, its population, and its retail trade facilities. Together the two surveys provide the information upon which a master plan is built. The key is to view the region as a unified entity that provides its residents with jobs and housing, as well as social, recreational, and cultural opportunities. In doing so, the master plan uses existing patterns of transportation and land use and directs future growth so as to achieve balanced development. For example, if agriculture is important to the area's economy, special attention is given to retaining the best soils for farming. Similarly, if houses in an older residential area of town are being converted to rooming houses and apartments, that transition can be encouraged by planning apartment usage for the area. In doing this, the master plan guides those who must make day-to-day decisions regarding zoning changes and gives the individual property owner a long-range idea of what his property may be used for in the future.

To assure long-run continuity, a master plan should look at least 15 years into the future and preferably 25 years or more. It must also include provisions for flexibility in the event that the city or region does not develop as expected, such as when population grows faster or slower than anticipated. Most importantly, the plan must provide for a balance between the economic and social functions of the community. For example, to emphasize culture and recreation at the expense of adequate housing and the area's economic base will result in the slow decay of the community, because people must leave to find housing and jobs.

SUBDIVISION REGULATIONS

In addition to controlling the use of land through planning and zoning laws, government can also control the process by which raw land is subdivided into lots. As noted earlier in this chapter, there was a time when subdivisions could be platted and sold with little regard to the adequacy of streets, sewers, utilities, and grading. However, this picture has greatly changed as state and local governments now use their police power rights to enforce minimum subdivision standards.

Today, before a lot can be sold, a subdivider must comply with government regulations concerning street construction, curbs, sidewalks, street lighting, fire hydrants, storm and sanitary sewers, grading and compacting of soil, water and utility lines, minimum lot size, and so on. In addition, the subdivider may be required to either set aside land for schools and parks or provide money so that land for that purpose may be purchased nearby. Until he has complied with all state and local regulations, the subdivider cannot receive his subdivision approval. Without approval he cannot record his plat map, which in turn means he cannot sell his lots to the public. If he tries to sell his lots without approval, he can be stopped by a government court order and fined in some states. Moreover, permits to build will be refused to lot owners, and anyone who bought from the subdivider is entitled to a refund.

Subdivision laws are not subjective in their application. If a subdivider complies with the rules, approval must be granted. However, government approval does not necessarily mean the lot is a good investment. First, requirements for subdivision approval vary widely in the United States; some localities are very exacting, while others are quite lax. Second, subdivision approval deals with the physical aspects of the property and how buyers' money is handled, not with the economic worth of the land.

BUILDING CODES

Recognizing the need to protect public health and safety against slipshod construction practices, state and local governments have enacted building codes. These establish minimum acceptable material and construction standards for such things as structural load and stress, windows and ventilation, size and location of rooms, fire protection, exits, electrical installation, plumbing, heating, lighting, and so forth.

Before a building permit is granted, the design of a proposed structure must meet the building-code requirements. During construction, local building department inspectors visit the construction site to make certain that the codes are being observed. Finally, when the building is completed, a **certificate of occupancy** is issued to the building owner to show that the structure meets the code. Without this certificate, the building cannot be legally occupied.

Although the idea of using building codes to protect the public is widely accepted, it is also generally agreed that the codes are not as efficient as they could be. One major problem has been that codes vary from one community to the next, making it difficult for the construction industry to realize cost savings through product uniformity. Another has been that building codes have not always kept up with technology. As a result, in the past several years there has been a movement toward the establishment of statewide building codes and the use of performance rather than **specification codes.** When building-code laws first became popular, they specified the materials the builder must use (e.g., 2 x 4 wood studs every

16″ in the walls and cast iron pipe for waste lines). If a builder wanted to use aluminum wall studs or heavy plastic sewer pipe, he could not, even though they might do the job as well or even better. With **performance codes,** any material can be used as long as it properly performs the task set forth in the building code. This encourages the development and application of new materials that can make construction less expensive, but just as safe.

Private land control

DEED RESTRICTIONS

Although property owners tend to think of land-use controls as being strictly a product of government, it is possible to achieve land-use control through private means. In fact, Houston, Texas, with a population of more than 2 million persons, operates without zoning and relies almost entirely upon private land-use controls to achieve a similar effect.

Private land-use controls take the form of deed and lease restrictions. In the United States, it has long been recognized that the ownership of land includes the right to sell or lease it on whatever legally acceptable conditions the owner wishes, including the right to dictate to the buyer or lessee how he shall or shall not use it. For example, a developer can sell the lots in his subdivision subject to a restriction written into each deed that the land cannot be used for anything but a single-family residence containing at least 1,200 square feet of living area. The legal theory is that, if the buyer or lessee agrees to the restrictions, he is bound by them. If they are not obeyed, any lot owner in the subdivision can obtain a court order to enforce compliance. The only limit to the number of restrictions an owner may place on his property is economic. If there are too many, the landowner may find that no one wants his property.

Legal Limitations

Deed restrictions, also known as **restrictive covenants,** often carry time limits. Thus, a house developer may set a 35-year time limit on his deed restrictions, recognizing that when the houses become old they may be replaced with apartments or other structures. An alternative is to use renewals. For example, a deed might start out with a 25-year restriction followed by one or more 10-year renewals. When the time comes for renewal, if the majority of property owners affected by the restriction vote against renewal, the restriction is terminated. Restrictions can be removed at anytime by unanimous agreement of all those affected, and they can be terminated if the seller permits the controls to be breached and does not enforce them.

Deed restrictions can cover such matters as the purpose of the structures to be built, architectural requirements, setbacks, size of the structure, and aesthetics. They cannot be used to discriminate on the basis of sex, race, color, or creed; if they do, they are considered unenforceable by the courts. Courts can also strike down restrictions or covenants that are frivolous or not in keeping with the times. Some years ago, for example, avid believers in alcohol and tobacco temperance used deed restrictions that prohibited all future owners from smoking or drinking on the property.

View Lots   The fact that a city has zoning does not preclude the use of deed restrictions, nor are deed restrictions used strictly by professional subdividers. To illustrate, suppose that you own a house and an adjacent vacant lot, both of which have scenic views. You want to sell the vacant lot, but are concerned about the type of structure that the buyer may build on the lot and whether it might block the view from your home. If the lot is zoned for houses, you know that he must use it for that purpose. However, you are concerned about the exact placement of the house on the lot and the height of any trees the buyer may plant, because they could block your view. By using a deed restriction you can specify the size and location of any structures built on the lot and limit the height to which any trees may be permitted to grow.

Houston   In Houston, normal economic and social forces dictate what zoning would probably enforce. Thus, land that is in demand for stores and offices does not attract residential users because they cannot afford the price. Similarly, industrial users do not locate in residential areas because of the aggravation they would cause, and homebuilders do not build homes in industrial areas because of smoke and noise. Furthermore, when a landowner does impose deed restrictions on a buyer, it is with the intent of making the property more valuable and more salable to everyone involved. Of special interest is the fact that the city has the power to deny building permits where a proposed structure will violate a private deed restriction. The Houston method is not perfect, but it appears to be no less perfect than the use of zoning laws. In the meantime, without the government red tape of zoning, developers have become more efficient. This has been an important factor in making the cost of housing (and construction in general) less expensive in Houston than in most other cities in the United States.

NEW COMMUNITIES

To many people, the idea of starting a new community from scratch with homes, shopping, and industry all carefully planned in advance is the ultimate in land utilization. There are, in fact, about two dozen such communities in the United States. In each, many square miles of land were brought under one ownership in order to control development. A master plan was then drawn that allowed for the orderly growth of the new city over a period of 20 years or more.

The two best known new communities in the United States are Reston, Virginia, and Columbia, Maryland. Developed by private enterprise, both of these communities are beautiful to drive through and pleasant to live in. Other new communities include Jonathan, Minnesota; Irvine, California; Park Forest, Illinois; Forest Park, Ohio; Sharpstown, Texas; and Sun City, Florida. What is evident in all of these is the great care that has been taken to avoid the formless urban sprawl that surrounds most American cities.

If new communities are so pleasant to live in, why aren't there more of them? The main problem is the cost of holding the land. Before planning can begin, all the land that will eventually be in the new community must be purchased, even though large portions will not be developed until 10 or 20 years later. In the meantime, however, each year the developer must pay interest and property taxes on that land although it produces no income.

ENVIRONMENTAL IMPACT STATEMENTS

The purpose of an environmental impact statement (EIS) (also called an **environmental impact report**) is to gather into one document enough information about the effect of a proposed project on the human environment so that a neutral decision maker can judge the environmental benefits and costs of the project. For example, a city zoning commission that has been asked to approve a zone change can request an EIS that will show the expected impact of the change on such things as population density, automobile traffic, noise, air quality, water and sewage facilities, drainage, energy consumption, school enrollments, employment, public health and safety, recreation facilities, wildlife, and vegetation. The idea is that with this information at hand better decisions regarding land uses can be made. When problems can be anticipated in advance, it is easier to make modifications or explore alternatives.

The compelling force in the EIS movement was the passage of the National Environmental Policy Act of 1969. This act required that an environmental impact statement be prepared whenever the federal government proposed a project that would have an effect on the environment. Subsequently, the idea caught hold at the state level; by 1975, similar laws were established in 32 states and 14 were actively considering the issue. At the local government level, towns, cities, and counties have either broadly construed state EIS requirements to include them or simply added the requirement to their local zoning or planning ordinances. Also, several landmark court cases since 1969 have found in favor of requiring impact statements before land development could begin.

EIS Applications   Applied liberally, all proposed development and construction, ranging from a huge federally sponsored dam to a lot owner wishing to build a home for his family, would require the filing and approval of an EIS before necessary building permits could be issued. However, there are threshold levels so that an EIS is not required until a project reaches a certain size in terms of square feet, acres, or housing units, or requires a zoning change.

At the city and county level, where the EIS requirement has the greatest effect on private development, the EIS usually accompanies the development application that is submitted to the planning or zoning commission. Where applicable, copies are also sent to affected school districts, water and sanitation districts, and highway and flood control departments. The EIS is then made available for public inspection as part of the hearing process on the development application. This gives concerned civic groups and the public at large an opportunity to voice their opinions regarding the anticipated benefits and costs of the proposed development. If the proposed development is partially or wholly funded by state or federal funds, state or federal hearings are also held.

Although interpretation as to what should be included in an EIS varies from state to state, most state and local EIS laws are patterned after the 1969 federal law. This law requires a description of present conditions at the proposed development site, plus information on the following five points: (1) the probable impact of the proposed action on the physical, economic, and social environment of the area, (2) any unavoidable adverse environmental effects, (3) any alternatives to the proposed action, (4) the short-term versus long-term effect of the proposed action on the environment, and (5) a listing of any irreversible commitment of resources if the action is implemented. In addition, some states and localities require that the EIS describe how the applicant plans to lessen the negative features of the proposed action and forecast what effect approving the proposal will have on causing future growth. A few states also require an economic cost–benefit analysis, and the U.S. Department of Housing and Urban Development requests statements as to the effect of the environment on the proposed action, and, for large projects, a statement on the environment that will be created within the project.

Content of an EIS

For a government-initiated project, the EIS is prepared by a government agency, sometimes with the help of private consultants. In the case of a private development, it may be prepared by the developer, a local government agency for a fee, or by a private firm specializing in the preparation of impact statements. Experience has shown that none of these approaches is perfect. Developer-prepared statements tend to cast the proposed action in a favorable light, government

Preparation of an EIS

agencies tend to advocate their position, and with private consultants there is little as yet in the way of qualification standards for competency.

Side Effects of EIS Laws   Although the concept of examining the environmental impact of a proposed action is now considered an important part of good planning, EIS laws have not been without their adverse side effects. The most significant has been the cost. From the public at large, tax money must be collected to pay for the additional government employees who must be hired to accept and review impact statements. For the developer there is the cost of preparing the statement, a cost that can easily run from $5,000 to $10,000 for a modest-sized tract of homes; this must ultimately be passed on to the home buyer. There is also the cost of delays caused by the EIS requirement. For example, for each month of delay a developer incurs in constructing a $40,000 house, interest and inflation add $400 to the price the purchaser must pay. Before 1970, housing developers usually estimated 3 months between land purchase and the start of grading and construction. In 1976, it took from 9 to 18 months; the EIS requirement was a major contributor to the extra delay.

Another side effect has been that growth opponents have seized upon the EIS as a means of stopping growth rather than controlling it. There is also an effect on persons who already own developed land: their property becomes more valuable because similar vacant land being developed today must shoulder the costs of an EIS and the delays and restrictions it brings. Finally, an EIS provides only a one-project-at-a-time perspective to land-use planning. As such, it is the exact opposite of comprehensive planning.

WINDFALLS AND   Planning and zoning tend to provide windfall gains for the
WIPE-OUTS   owners of land that has been authorized for development, while landowners who are prohibited from developing their land suffer financial wipe-outs. This has been a major stumbling block to the orderly utilization of land in America. It is only natural that a landowner will want his land to be zoned for a use that will make it more valuable; however, not all land can be zoned for housing, stores, and offices. Some

land must be reserved for agriculture and open spaces. If local and state governments embark upon bold land planning programs, how will these financial inequities be resolved?

The past and current position of government and the courts is that, if land-use restrictions are for the health, safety, and general welfare of the community at large, then under the rules of police power the individual landowner is not compensated for any resulting loss in value. Only when there is an actual physical taking of land is the owner entitled to compensation under the rules of eminent domain. In today's environmentally conscious society, this often results in pitting the landowner who wants to develop his land against those who want to prevent development without compensation. For example, a government planning agency in one state stretched the limits of police power to deny an urban landowner a permit to build on his property and instead told him he should grow flowers for the public's enjoyment. Many decisions like this could ultimately undermine planning efforts. Yet, government planning agencies do not have the money to buy all the land that they would like to see remain undeveloped.

Transferable Development Rights

The solution may come from some radical new thinking about land and the rights to use it. Previously, the right to develop a parcel of land could not be separated from the land itself. Now planners are exploring the idea of separating the two so that development rights can be switched to land where greater density will not be objectionable. Figure 23:1 illustrates this concept. Parcel A lies in an area of high-quality farmland that planners feel should be retained for agriculture and not be paved over with streets and covered with buildings. Parcel B lies in an area deemed more suitable for urban uses and is an area where government will concentrate on constructing streets, schools, parks, waterlines, and other public facilities. To direct growth to this area, it is planned and zoned for urban uses. Meanwhile, areas designated for agriculture are forced to remain as farmland. Ordinarily, this would result in windfall gains for the owner of parcel B and a loss in land value for the owner of parcel A.

The new planning idea is to eliminate windfalls and wipeouts by creating **transferable development rights** (TDRs). The

Figure 23:1   **TRANSFERABLE DEVELOPMENT RIGHTS (TDRs)**

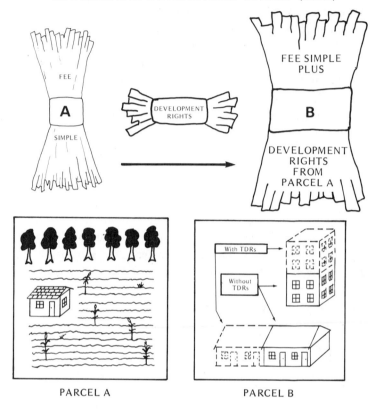

PARCEL A   PARCEL B

By purchasing development rights from Parcel A,
the owner of Parcel B is allowed to develop his land more intensely.

owner of parcel A would transfer his development rights to
parcel B. By purchasing these rights from owner A, owner B is
allowed to develop his land more intensely than he otherwise
could. This compensates owner A for the loss of his right to
develop his land. For the TDR concept to work, there must be
a comprehensive regional master plan with EIS approval.

TDRs could be traded on the open market like stocks and
bonds. Alternatively, a government agency could pay cash for
the value of rights lost. This would be financed by selling
those rights to owners in districts to be developed.

To date, Chicago and New York City have attempted a
limited use of TDRs for the purpose of protecting historical

buildings not owned by the government. Under this system, an owner who agrees not to tear down his building is given TDRs, which can be sold to other nearby landowners. New Jersey and Puerto Rico use TDRs to protect open spaces, as well as agricultural and environmentally sensitive lands. The TDR concept is also being considered or used in parts of Maryland, Virginia, Pennsylvania, California, Florida, and the District of Columbia.

To date, the reception by the courts has not always been favorable. However, it appears that much of the debate centers on the concept of separating the right to develop land from the land itself. The idea is new and has little legal precedence. But, for that matter, neither did zoning before 1916.

Match terms a–l with statements 1–12.

VOCABULARY REVIEW

a. *Certificate of occupancy*
b. *EIS or EIR*
c. *Land-use control*
d. *Master plan*
e. *Nonconforming use*
f. *Performance codes*
g. *Restrictive covenants*
h. *Specification codes*
i. *TDR*
j. *Windfall gain*
k. *Wipe-out*
l. *Zoning*

1. A broad term used to describe any legal restriction (such as zoning) that controls how a parcel of land may be used.
2. Public regulations that control the specific use to which land in a given district may be put.
3. An improvement that is inconsistent with current zoning regulations.
4. A comprehensive guide for a community's physical growth.
5. Building codes that require the use of certain types of materials and construction techniques.
6. Building codes that are written in terms of results rather than particular materials and construction techniques.
7. Clauses placed in deeds to control how future landowners may or may not use the property.
8. A document issued by a building department stating that a structure meets local zoning and building code requirements and is ready for use.
9. A report that contains information regarding the effect of a proposed project on the environment.
10. An increase in property value resulting from a publicly made decision; i.e., a zoning change from agricultural to residential use.

11. A decrease in property value resulting from a publicly made decision, such as a change in zoning from urban uses to open space.

12. A means by which the rights to develop a given parcel of land can be conveyed to another parcel of land.

QUESTIONS AND
PROBLEMS

1. For land-use control to be successful, why is it necessary to consider the rights of individual property owners as well as the public as a whole?

2. Explain how a city obtains its power to control land use through zoning.

3. What is the purpose of a variance? How does it differ from a zoning ordinance amendment?

4. In your community, what are the letter/number designations for the following: high-rise apartments, low-rise apartments, single-family houses, stores, duplexes, industrial sites?

5. What is the difference between master planning and zoning?

6. Why is financing such a major problem to developers of new towns?

7. What is the purpose of an environmental impact statement?

8. What are the pros and cons of requiring an EIS before a housing subdivision can be built?

9. How would the use of transferable development rights reduce windfalls and wipe-outs for land owners?

10. Does any city or county in your state currently use transferable development rights? What have been the results?

ADDITIONAL READINGS

American Society of Planning Officials. *Planning.* Published 11 times a year, this magazine focuses on current issues in urban planning, including zoning, planning, transportation, and city growth.

Burchell, Robert W., and **Listokin, David.** *The Environmental Impact Handbook.* New Brunswick, N.J.: Rutgers University, 1975, 239 pages. Emphasizes how to prepare an EIS and what to include in it. Also discusses the EIS review process.

Crawford, Clan, Jr. *Handbook of Zoning and Land Use Ordinances.* Englewood Cliffs, N.J.: Prentice-Hall, 1974, 207 pages. Written to help those who plan and write zoning ordinances.

Kratovil, Robert. *Real Estate Law.* Englewood Cliffs, N.J.: Prentice-Hall, 1974, 479 pages. Chapters 28 and 29 deal with building restrictions and zoning ordinances and contain numerous examples and legal references.

24

Investing in Real Estate

Blind pool: investment pool wherein the properties are purchased after the investors have invested their money

Cash flow: the number of dollars remaining each year after collecting rents and paying operating expenses and mortgage payments

Downside risk: the possibility that an investor will lose his money in an investment

Equity build-up: the increase of one's equity in a property due to mortgage balance reduction and price appreciation

Investment strategy: a plan that balances returns available with risks that must be taken in order to enhance the investor's overall welfare

Mortgage-equity: a method for valuing income producing property that takes into consideration the price and availability of loan money

Negative cash flow: a condition wherein the cash paid out exceeds the cash received

Prospectus: a disclosure statement that describes an investment opportunity

Tax shelter: the income tax savings that an investment can produce for its owner

The monetary returns that are possible from real estate ownership make it a very attractive investment. However, at the same time the real estate investor takes two risks: he may never obtain a return on his investment and he may never recover his investment. There are no simple answers as to what is a "sure-fire" real estate investment. Rather, success depends on intelligently made decisions. With that in mind, we shall consider investment benefits, property selection, investment timing, investment strategy, property pricing, and limited partnerships.

BENEFITS OF REAL
ESTATE INVESTING

The monetary benefits of investing in real estate come from cash flow, tax shelter, mortgage reduction, and appreciation. **Cash flow** refers to the number of dollars remaining each year after collecting rents and paying operating expenses and mortgage payments. If nothing is left over for the investor and he must dip into his pocketbook to keep the property going, it is called **negative cash flow.** **Tax shelter** refers to the income tax savings that an investor can realize. This is possible because depreciation is deductible as a cost of doing business when computing income taxes, although it is not an out-of-pocket expense. This usually means that part or all of the income from the property is not subject to taxation. In fact, sometimes it is possible to generate tax shelter in excess of that needed to shelter the income from the property itself. Income tax laws in effect at this writing permit the taxpayer to use these tax losses to offset gains in other investments, business profits, and salaries. **Mortgage reduction** occurs because the investor uses a portion of the property's rental income to reduce the balance owing on the mortgage, thus increasing his equity. **Appreciation** refers to the increase in property value that the owner hopes will occur while he owns it. Mortgage balance reduction and price appreciation together are referred to as **equity build-up.** This is shown in Figure 24:1.

Figure 24:1

CALCULATING EQUITY BUILD-UP

Equity at Time of Purchase		Equity 5 Years Later		Equity Buildup	
Purchase price	$200,000	Net sales price	$220,000	Ending equity	$100,000
Mortgage loan	−140,000	Less loan balance	−120,000	Less beginning equity	− 60,000
Down payment (equity)	$ 60,000	Equals equity	$100,000	Equals equity build-up	$ 40,000

PROPERTY SELECTION

The real estate market offers a wide selection of properties for investments, including vacant land, houses, condominiums, small, medium, and large apartment buildings, office buildings, stores, industrial property, and so forth. Selecting a suitable type of property is a matter of matching an investor's capital with his attitudes toward risk taking and the amount of time he is willing to spend on management. Let us begin by looking at the ownership of vacant land.

The major risk of owning vacant land as an investment is that one will have to wait too long for an increase in value. Vacant land produces no income, yet it consumes the investor's dollars in the form of interest, property taxes, insurance, and eventually selling costs. The rule of thumb is that the market value of vacant land must double every 5 years for the investor to break even. If this increase does not occur, the owner will find he has spent more on interest, insurance, property taxes, brokerage fees, and closing costs than he has made on the price increase.

Vacant Land

Income tax laws currently in effect improve land speculation benefits somewhat, since insurance, interest, and property taxes plus any other costs of holding the investment are tax deductible at ordinary rates in the year paid. Yet the increase in property value is taxed only after the property is sold, and then at capital gains rates that are about one half of ordinary rates. (Note that what is one person's tax deduction here is another's taxable gain. The person receiving the interest must count it as taxable income.)

The key to successful land speculating is in outguessing the general public. If the public feels that development of a vacant parcel to a higher use is 10 years in the future, the market price will reflect the discounted cost at current interest rates and property taxes for that waiting period. If the land speculator buys at these prices, and the higher use occurs in 5 years, there is a good chance his purchase will be profitable. However, the speculator will lose money if the public expects the higher use to occur in 5 years and it actually takes 10 years.

Finally, land speculators expose themselves to an extra risk that owners of improved property can usually avoid: when it comes time to sell, unless buildings will immediately be placed upon the land by the purchaser, very few lenders will loan the purchaser money to buy the land. This may force the seller to accept the purchase price in the form of a down payment plus periodic payments for the balance. If the interest rate on the balance is below prevailing mortgage rates, as often happens in land sales, the seller is effectively subsidizing the buyer. Furthermore, if the payments are made over several years, the seller takes the risk that the money he receives will buy less because of inflation.

Houses and Condominiums

Houses and condominiums are the smallest properties available in income-producing real estate and as such are within the financial reach of more prospective investors than apartment buildings, stores, or offices. Moreover, they can usually be purchased with lower down payments and interest rates, because lenders feel that loans on houses and condominiums are less prone to default than on larger buildings. With a small property, the investor can fall back upon his salary and other income to meet loan payments in the event rents fall short. With larger buildings, the lender knows he must rely more on the rental success of the property and less on the owner's other sources of income.

Houses and condominiums are usually overpriced in relation to the monthly rent they can generate. This is because their prices are influenced both by the value of the shelter they provide and the amenity value of home ownership. Thus, an investor must pay what prospective owner–occupants are willing to pay, yet when the property is rented, a tenant will pay only for the shelter value. However, when the investor sells, he will be able to sell at a higher price than would be justified by rents alone. What this means to the investor is that he can usually expect a negative cash flow while he owns the property. Consequently, there must be a substantial increase in property value to offset the monthly negative cash flow, as well as to give the investor a good return on his investment.

From time-to-time substantial appreciation has occurred. During parts of the 1970 decade, house prices rose very rapidly and produced excellent returns to those with single-family houses as investments. This rise can be traced to the relatively low number of new housing starts compared to the large number of children born between 1940 and 1960 reaching the age of household formation. In contrast, during the early 1960s, houses were poorer investments because sufficient new housing kept the prices of existing houses from rising rapidly. In many cities of the United States, condominiums were overbuilt in the early 1970s resulting in unsold new units. Consequently, investors in existing units could not get the appreciation needed to provide a decent return on investment. In areas where the supply and demand for condominiums have been closer, more appreciation has occurred.

Small Apartment Buildings

Because considerable appreciation must occur to make house and condominium investments profitable, many investors who start with these move to more income-oriented properties as their capital grows. This reduces investment risk because returns from rental income can be more reliably forecast than changes in prices. Particularly popular with investors who have modest amounts of investment capital are duplexes (two units), triplexes (three units), and four- and five-unit apartment buildings.

If it were necessary to hire professional management, such small buildings would be uneconomical to own. However, for most owners of two- to five-unit apartment buildings, management is on a do-it-yourself basis. Moreover, it is possible for the owner to live on the premises. This eliminates a cash outlay for management and allows the owner to reduce repair and maintenance expenses by handling them himself. Also, with the owner living on the property, tenants are encouraged to take better care of the premises and discouraged from moving out without paying their rent. Finally, the ownership of a residential rental property provides the owner with a wealth of experience and education in property management.

Medium-size Buildings

Apartment buildings containing 6 to 24 units also present good investment opportunities for those with sufficient down payment. However, in addition to analyzing the building, rents, and neighborhood, thought must be given to the matter of property management before a purchase is made. An apartment building of this size is not large enough for a full-time manager; therefore, the owner must either do the job or hire a part-time manager to live on the property. If the owner does the job, he should be willing to live on the property and devote a substantial amount of his time to management, maintenance, and upkeep activities. If a part-time manager is hired, the task is to find one who is knowledgeable and capable of maintaining property, showing vacant units, interviewing tenants, collecting rents on time, and handling landlord–tenant relations in accordance with local landlord–tenant laws. As the size of an apartment building increases, so does its efficiency. As a rule of thumb, when a building reaches 25 units, it will generate enough rent so that a full-time professional manager can be hired to live on the premises. With a live-in manager, the property owner need not reside on the property nor be involved in day-to-day management chores. This is very advantageous if the owner has another occupation where his time is better spent.

Larger Apartment Buildings   As the number of apartment units increases, the cost of management per unit drops. Beyond 60 units, assistant managers can be hired. This makes it possible to have a representative of the owner on the premises more hours of the day to look after the investment and keep the tenants happy. Size also means it is possible to add recreational facilities and other amenities that are not possible on a small scale. The cost of having a swimming pool in a 10-unit building might add so much to apartment rents that they would be priced out of the market. The same pool in a 50- or 100-unit building would make relatively little difference in rent. As buildings reach 200 or more units in size, it becomes economical to add such things as a children's pool, gymnasium, game room, lounge, and a social director.

Since larger apartment buildings cost less to manage per unit and compete very effectively in the market for tenants, they tend to produce larger cash flows per invested dollar. However, errors in location selection, building design, and management policy are magnified as the building grows in size. Also, many lenders, particularly small- and medium-sized banks and savings associations, are simply not large enough to lend on big projects. Finally, the number of investors who can single-handedly invest a down payment of $500,000 or more is limited. This has caused the widespread growth of the limited partnership as a means of making the economies of large-scale ownership available to investors with as little as $2,500 to invest.

Office buildings offer the prospective investor not only a higher rent per square foot of floor space than any of the investments discussed thus far, but also larger cash flows per dollar of property worth. This is because office buildings are costlier to build and operate than residential structures, and because they expose the owner to more risk.

Office Buildings

The higher construction and operating costs of an office building are due to the amenities and services office users demand. To be competitive today, an office building must offer air-conditioning to all tenants on a room-by-room basis thus adding to construction and operating costs. Office users also expect and pay for daily office housecleaning services, such as emptying waste baskets, cleaning ashtrays, dusting, and vacuuming. Apartment dwellers neither expect these services nor pay for them.

TENANT TURNOVER: Tenant turnover is more expensive in an office building than an apartment building because a change in office tenants usually requires more extensive remodeling. To offset this, building owners include the cost of remodeling in the tenant's rent. Another consideration is that it is not unusual for office space to remain vacant for long periods of time. Also, if a building is rented to a single tenant, a single vacancy means there is no income at all. To reduce tenant turnover, incentives such as lower rent may be offered if a tenant agrees to sign a longer lease, such as 5 years instead of 1 or 2 years. Care, however, must be taken on longer leases so that the owner does not become locked into a fixed monthly rent while operating costs escalate rapidly due to inflation.

LOCATION, TAXES: The risk in properly locating an office building is greater than with a residential property since office users are very particular about where they locate. If a residential building is not well located, the owner can usually drop rents a little and still fill the building. To do the same with an office building may require a much larger drop; then, even with the building full, it may not generate enough rent to pay the operating expenses and mortgage payments. Finally, the tax shelter benefits available from offices are not as attractive as comparably priced apartments for two reasons. First, federal and state governments encourage residential construction and ownership by allowing investors to take depreciation on residential buildings faster than on nonresidential. This difference is important. Even though tax laws do not permit an investor to take depreciation in excess of the fair market value of the improvements at the time of his purchase, the sooner in a property's life that depreciation is allowed, the more valuable it is to him. Second, compared to office buildings, residential properties tend to have a higher percentage of their value in depreciable improvements and less in nondepreciable land.

INVESTMENT TIMING

The potential risks and rewards available from owning improved real estate depend to a great extent on the point in the life of a property at which an investment is made. Should one invest while a project is still an idea? Or is it better to wait until it is finished and fully rented? That depends on the risks one can afford and the potential rewards.

Land Purchase

The riskiest point to invest in a project is when it is still an idea in someone's head. At this point, money is needed to purchase land; but beyond the cost of the land, there are many unknowns, including the geological suitability of the land to support buildings, the ability to obtain the needed zoning, the cost of construction, the availability of a loan, the rents the market will pay, how quickly the property will find tenants, the expenses of operating the property, and finally the return the investor will obtain. Even though the investor may have a feasibility study that predicts success for the project, such a report is still only an educated guess. Therefore, the anticipated returns to an investor entering a project at this point must be high to offset the risks he takes. As the project clears such hurdles as zoning approval, obtaining construction cost bids, and finding a lender, it becomes less risky. Therefore, a person who invests after these hurdles are cleared would expect somewhat less potential reward. The 1976 Tax Reform Act now requires that interest and property taxes incurred during the construction period be expensed over a period of several years, rather than the year of construction. Nonetheless, the investor is buying into the project at a relatively low price; if it is successful, he will enjoy a developer's profit upon which no income tax must be paid until the property is finally sold. Against this, he takes the risk that the project may stall along the way or that, once completed, it will lose money.

Another major milestone is reached when the project is completed and opens its doors for business. At this point, the finished cost of the building is known, and during the first 12 months of operations the property owners learn what rents the market will pay, what level of occupancy will be achieved and what actual operating expenses will be. As estimates are replaced with actual operating experience, the risk to the investor decreases. As a result, the investor entering at this stage receives a smaller dollar return on his investment, but is more certain of his return than if he had invested earlier. The tax benefits at this stage are very attractive, but not quite as rewarding as in the earlier stages.

Project Completion

A building is new only once, and after its first year it begins to face competition from newer buildings. However, in an inflationary economy that forces up the construction cost of newer buildings, existing buildings will be able to charge less rent. Furthermore, newer buildings may be forced to use less desirable sites. During this period of 10 years or so, occupancy rates are stable, operating expenses are well established, tax benefits are good, and the building is relatively free of major repairs or replacements.

First Decade

As a building approaches and then reaches its tenth birthday, the costs and risks it presents to a prospective investor change. He must ask whether the neighborhood is still expected to remain desirable to tenants and whether the building's location will increase in value enough to offset wear and tear and obsolescence. A careful inspection must be made of the structure to determine whether poor construction quality will soon result in costly repairs. Also, the buyer must be

Second Decade

prepared for normal replacements and expenses such as new appliances, water heaters, and a fresh coat of paint. As a result, an investor buying a 10-year-old building will seek a larger return than when the building was younger.

Third & Fourth Decade Building Life   Larger returns are particularly important as a building reaches its twentieth year and major expense items such as a new roof, replacement of plumbing fixtures, repair of parking areas, and remodeling become necessary. As a building approaches and passes its thirtieth year, investors must consider carefully the remaining economic life of the property and whether rents permit a return on investment as well as a return of investment. Also, maintenance costs climb as a building becomes older, and decisions will be necessary regarding whether or not major restoration and remodeling should be undertaken. If it is, the cost must be recovered during the balance of the building's life. The alternative is to add little or no money to the building, a decision the surrounding neighborhood may already be forcing upon the property owner. Older properties have been a strong magnet to real estate investors who hope to find attractive buys that can be fixed up for a profit. However, care must be taken not to overpay for this privilege in light of the foregoing discussion.

Building Recycling   More buildings are torn down than fall down, and this phase in a building's life also represents an investment opportunity. However, like the first stage in the development cycle, raw land, the risks are high. In effect, when the decision is made to purchase a structure with the intention of demolishing it, the investor is counting on the value of the land being worth more in another use. That use may be a government-sponsored renewal program, or the investor may be accumulating adjoining properties with the ultimate intention of creating plottage value by demolishing the structures and joining the lots. Because the risks of capital loss in this phase are high, the potenial returns should be too.

GLITAMAD   The acronym GLITAMAD, developed by Maury Seldin and Richard Swesnick, is a helpful way to remember the various phases in the life cycle of improved real estate investments.

"GLITAMAD"   Figure 24:2

G = Ground (the raw land stage)

L = Loan (long-term loan commitment)

I = Interim (short-term loan and construction)

Increasing risk,
Increasing returns

T = Tenancy (building filled with tenants)

A = Absorption (second through tenth year)

Least risk,
Least returns

M = Maturity (eleventh through thirtieth year)

A = Aging (more than 30 years)

Increasing risk,
Increasing returns

D = Demise (demolition, reuse of the land)

As the risk that an investor will suffer a loss increases, the expected returns must increase.

Source: Maury Seldin and Richard H. Swesnik, *Real Estate Investment Strategy*, copyright © 1970, John Wiley & Sons, Inc., New York, N.Y. By permission.

The objective in developing a personal investment strategy is to balance the returns available with the risks that must be taken so that the overall welfare of the investor is enhanced. To accomplish this, it is very helpful to look at lifetime income and consumption patterns.

In Figure 24:3 the broken line represents the income that a person can typically expect to receive at various ages during his or her life. It includes income from wages, pensions, and investments, and is the same income curve that was discussed in Chapter 15. The solid line represents a person's lifetime consumption pattern. Taken together, the two lines show that, during the first 20 to 25 years, consumption exceeds income. Then the situation reverses itself and income outpaces con-

*DEVELOPING
A PERSONAL
INVESTMENT
STRATEGY*

sumption. If one is planning an investment program, these are the years to carry it out.

Figure 24:3   **LIFETIME INCOME AND CONSUMPTION PATTERNS**

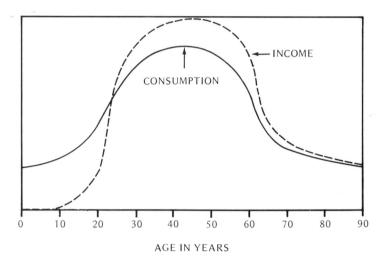

AGE IN YEARS

Risk Taking   The graph shows that an investment opportunity that offers a high risk of loss is better suited for a person under the age of 45. Then, even if the investment does turn sour, the investor still has a substantial amount of working life remaining to recover financially. An investor between 45 and 55 years of age should be somewhat more cautious in terms of risk taking, since there is less time to make a financial recovery if the need arises. Above the age of 55, high-risk investments are even less appropriate for the same reason. Therefore, as a person reaches 55, 60, and 65, there should be a program of moving toward relatively risk free investments, even though the returns will be smaller. Upon retirement, the investor can live off the investments he or she made when younger.

Debt Repayment   Mortgage debt commitments that require a portion of the investor's personal income should also be considered in light of one's position on the lifetime income and consumption curves. This is done to ascertain whether there will be sufficient income in the future to meet the loan payments. Not to consider the future may force a premature sale, perhaps in the midst of a very sluggish market at a distressed price. For the investor who has passed his income peak, financing with less debt and more equity means a higher probability that his properties will generate enough income to meet monthly loan payments. Also, with fewer dollars going to debt repayment, more can be kept by the investor for living expenses. By comparison, a relatively young investor may be handicapped by the lack of starting capital; however, he has the advantages of time and increasing income on his side.

Tax Planning

The income curve in Figure 24:3 provides us insight with regard to tax planning using tax shelter investments. During the peak income years, a person is in the highest tax brackets of life; a larger portion of each dollar of income is paid out as income taxes than later in life. Thus, a strategy to minimize taxes calls for sound investments that emphasize tax shelter during the peak income years. Later in life when income falls and the investor moves to successively lower tax brackets, there is less concern with finding investments that shelter income or selling properties in which there is a taxable gain. Developing a workable tax strategy requires thoughtful advance planning. If a person aged 40 purchases a real estate investment that offers excellent tax shelter for 5 years and then is to be resold at a profit, the income curve shows that, while his short-run tax picture will be improved, his tax problems 5 years hence will be made worse. To solve that problem, the investor must either trade for another property in the fifth year or, if he sells, be prepared to invest in another tax shelter investment large enough to shelter the taxable gain from the first.

The same points made here in connection with investments can also be applied to one's home. If a homeowner can purchase a home with a mortgage and then pay down the mortgage during those years in life when income substantially exceeds consumption, the home can be carried debt free into retirement to provide a place to live without mortgage payments. The home then becomes an investment in every sense of the word.

VALUING AN
INVESTMENT

The most crucial decision in any real estate investment is deciding how much to pay. Chapter 17 discussed the principle that the worth of something today depends on the rewards it will return to its owner in the future. Let us now apply this to a more difficult, but certainly very typical, valuation question. How much should an investor offer for a property that has a projected net operating income of $100,000 a year if he plans to purchase it with a 9½% interest, 20-year amortized loan for 70% of the purchase price? He plans to hold the property 10 years, during which time he expects it will increase 30% in value (after deducting for brokerage and closing costs), and he wants an 18% annual yield on each dollar he invests.

The best known method for solving this type of investment question involves using the Ellwood Tables, published in 1959 by L. W. Ellwood, MAI. However, for the person who does not use these tables regularly, the arithmetic involved can prove confusing. As a result, Irvin Johnson, in 1972, and the Financial Publishing Company, in 1974, published **mortgage-equity tables** that allow the user to look up a single number, called an **overall rate** (OAR), and divide it into the net operating income to find a value for the property.

The answer to the investment question just described is found by looking at the mortgage equity table for a 10-year holding period, 18% equity yield, and a 70% loan. Within this table we look for a 20-year mortgage carrying 9½% interest. Finally, within this group of numbers we look for appreciation of 30%. In Table 24:1 we find that the OAR for this investment is .111223. This number has all the investment conditions as described in our problem built into it. The .111223 is then divided into the net annual operating income. The result, $899,095, is the price the investor should pay.

$$\frac{\text{Income}}{\text{Rate}} = \text{Value}, \qquad \frac{\$100,000}{.111223} = \$899,095$$

This is not the only type of real estate investment question that these valuation tables will solve. For example, if a property is for sale at a specific price, one can determine the yield it will provide for the investor. In fact, one can determine any

MORTGAGE-EQUITY TABLE—OVERALL RATES
10-Year Holding Period / 18% Equity Yield Rate / 70% Loan Ratio

Loan Term	Appreciation, Depreciation	Loan Interest Rate		
		9%	9½%	10%
20 years	+40%	.103948	.106971	.110028
	+30%	.108200	**.111223**	.114379
	+20%	.112451	.115474	.118531
	+10%	.116703	.119725	.122782
	0%	.120954	.123977	.127034
	−10%	.125206	.128228	.131285
	−20%	.129457	.132480	.135537
	−30%	.133709	.136731	.139788
	−40%	.137960	.140983	.144040

Source: Irvin E. Johnson, *The Instant Mortgage-Equity Technique,* copyright 1972, by Lexington Books, D.C. Heath & Company, Lexington, Mass. By permission.

of the following if the other seven factors are known: holding period, equity yield rate, loan ratio, loan term, loan interest rate, appreciation, net operating income, price or value of property. In addition to these eight factors, the mortgage-equity tables published by the Financial Publishing Company incorporate increases in net operating income during the holding period, accelerated depreciation, and the investor's income tax bracket.*

LIMITED PARTNERSHIPS

As discussed earlier in this chapter, large investment properties have a number of economic advantages over small ones. Yet the vast majority of investors in the United States do not have the capital to buy a large project single-handedly. Moreover, many persons who would like to own real estate for its yield and tax benefits do not do so because they wish to avoid the work and responsibilities of property management. As a result, the United States has witnessed the widespread use of limited partnerships for real estate investment. This popular form of investment offers investors the following advantages:

1. Management of the property and financial affairs of the partnership.

---

* *Financial Capitalization Rate Tables,* Boston: Financial Publishing Company, © 1974, 776 pages.

2. Limited partner financial liability is limited to the amount invested.
3. The opportunity for a small investor to own a part of large projects and to diversify.
4. The same tax benefits as enjoyed by sole owners.

The organizers of a limited partnership are responsible for selecting properties, putting them into a financial package, and making it available to investors. As a rule, the organizers are the general partners and the investors are the limited partners. For their efforts in organizing the partnership, the general partners receive a cash fee from the limited partners or a promotional interest in the partnership or both.

Property Purchase Methods

Property is purchased by one of two methods. The organizers can either buy properties first and then seek limited partners, or they can find limited partners first and then buy properties. The first approach is a **specific property offering.** The second is a **blind pool.** The advantage of the specific property offering is that the prospective limited partner knows in advance precisely what properties he will own. However, this approach requires the organizers either to find a seller who is willing to wait for a partnership to be formed or to buy the property in their own names using their own capital. If they use their own capital, the organizers risk the chance of financial loss if limited partners cannot be found.

The advantage of the blind pool is that the organizers do not buy until money has been raised from the limited partners. This requires less capital from the organizers, and avoids the problem of holding property but not being able to find sufficient investors. Also, the organizers can negotiate better prices from sellers when they have cash in hand. However, if the organizers are poor judges of property, the investors may wind up owning property that they would not have otherwise purchased.

Property Management

Once property is purchased, the general partners are responsible for managing the property themselves or selecting a management firm to do the job. In addition, the general partners must maintain the accounting books and at least once a year remit to each investor his portion of the cash flow, an accounting of the partnership's performance for the year, and profit or loss data for income tax purposes. With regard to selling partnership property, the partnership agreement usually gives the limited partners the right to vote on when to sell, to whom to sell, and for how much. In practice, the general partners decide when to put the matter up to a vote, and the limited partners usually follow their advice.

The word "limited" in limited partnership refers to the limited financial liability of the limited partner. In a properly drawn agreement, limited partners cannot lose more than they have invested. By comparison, the general partners are legally liable for all the debts of the partnership, up to the full extent of their entire personal worth. Being a limited partner does not eliminate the possibility of being asked at a later date for more investment money if the properties in the partnership are not financially successful. When this happens, each limited partner must decide between adding more money in hopes the partnership will soon make a financial turnaround, or refusing to do so and being eliminated from the partnership. By way of comparison, an individual investor who buys real estate in his own name takes the risks of both the limited and general partner combined, since he is exposed to all the risks of ownership.

Financial Liability

Investment groups provide the means for an investor to diversify. For example, a limited partnership of 200 members each contributing $5,000 would raise $1,000,000. This could be used as a down payment on one property worth $4,000,000 or on four different properties at $1,000,000 each. If the $4,000,000 property is purchased, the entire success or failure of the partnership rides on that one property. With four $1,000,000 properties, the failure of one can be balanced by the success of the others. Even greater diversification can be achieved by purchasing properties in different rental price ranges, in different parts of the same city, and in different cities in the country. Regarding income tax benefits, a very important advantage of the limited partnership is that it allows

Investment Diversification

the investor to be taxed as though he was the sole owner of the property, because the partnership itself is not subject to taxation. All income and loss items, including any tax shelter generated by the property, are proportioned to each investor directly.

Service Fees

The prospective investor should carefully look at the price the organizers are charging for their services. Is it adequate, but not excessive? To expect good performance from capable people, they must be compensated adequately, but to overpay reduces the returns from the investment that properly belong to those who provide the capital. When is the compensation to be paid? If management fees are paid in advance, there is less incentive for the organizers to provide quality management for the limited partners after the partnership is formed. The preferred arrangement is to pay for management services as they are received, and for the limited partners to reserve the right to vote for new management. Similarly, it is preferable to base a substantial portion of the fee for organizing the partnership on the success of the investment. By giving the organizers a percentage of the partnership's profits instead of a fixed fee, the organizers have a direct stake in the partnership's success.

Pitfalls

Although the limited partnership form of real estate ownership offers investors many advantages, experience has shown that there are numerous pitfalls that can separate investors from their money. Most importantly, a limited partner should recognize that the success or failure of a limited partnership is dependent on the organizers. Do they have a good record in selecting, organizing, and managing real estate investments in the past? Are they respected in the community for prompt and honest dealings? Will local banks and building suppliers offer them credit? What is their rating with credit bureaus? Are they permanent residents of the community in which they operate? Do the county court records show lawsuits or other legal complaints against them?

With reference to the properties in the partnership, are the income projections reasonable and have adequate allowances been made for vacancies, maintenance, and management? Overoptimism, sloppy income and expense projections, and outright shading of the truth will ultimately be costly to the investor. Unless the investor has extreme confidence in the promoters, he will personally visit the properties in the partnership and verify the rent schedules, vacancy levels, operating expenses, and physical condition of the improvements. He will also want to make an estimate of the partnership's **downside risk** (i.e., the risk that he will lose his money).

The careful investor will consult with a lawyer to make certain that the partnership agreement does limit his liability and that the tax benefits will be as advertised. He will also want to know what to expect if the partnership suffers financial setbacks. Are the partnership's properties to be sold at a loss or at a foreclosure sale, or do the general partners stand ready to provide the needed money? Will the limited partners be asked to contribute? The prospective investor should also investigate to see if the properties are overpriced. Far too many partnerships organized to date have placed so much emphasis on tax shelter benefits that the entire matter of whether the investment was economically feasible has been overlooked. Even to a 50% bracket taxpayer, a dollar wasted before taxes is still 50¢ wasted after taxes.

Finally, to receive maximum benefits from his investment, the investor must be prepared to stay with the partnership until the properties are refinanced or sold. The resale market for limited partnership interests is almost nonexistent, and when a buyer is found, the price is usually below the proportional worth of the investor's interest in the partnership. Moreover, the partnership agreement may place restrictions on limited partners who want to sell their interests.

DISCLOSURE LAWS

Because investors are vulnerable to unsound investments and exploitation at the hands of limited partnership organizers, state and federal disclosure laws have been passed to protect them. Administered by the Securities & Exchange Commission at the federal level and by real estate regulatory departments and commissions at state levels, these laws require organizers and salesmen to disclose all pertinent facts surrounding their partnership offerings. Prospective investors must be told how much money the organizers wish to raise, what portion will go for promotional expenses and organizers' fees, what properties have been (or will be) purchased, from whom they were bought, and for how much. Also, prospective investors must be provided with a copy of the partnership agreement and given property income and expense records for past years. They must be told how long the partnership expects to hold its properties until selling, the partnership's policy on cash flow distribution, the right of limited partners to a voice in management, the names of those responsible for managing the partnership properties, and how profits (or losses) will be split when the properties are sold.

The Prospectus

The amount of disclosure detail required by state and federal laws varies with the number of properties and the partners' relationship. For a handful of friends forming a partnership among themselves, there would be little in the way of formal disclosure requirements. However, as the number of investors increases and the partnership is offered to investors across state lines, disclosure requirements increase dramatically. It is not unusual for a disclosure statement, called a **prospectus,** to be 50 to 100 pages long.

Blue-Sky Laws

The philosophy of disclosure laws is to make information available to prospective investors and let them make their own decisions. Thus, an investor is free to invest in an unsound investment as long as the facts are explained to him in advance. An alternative point of view is that many investors do not read nor understand disclosure statements; therefore, it is the duty of government to pass on the economic soundness of an investment before it can be offered to the public. The result has been the passage of **blue-sky laws** in several states. The first of these was passed by the Kansas legislature in 1911 to protect purchasers from buying into dubious investment schemes that sold them nothing more than a piece of the blue sky. Some states still retain these laws and apply them to limited partnerships and other securities offered within their borders.

Match terms a–j wtih statements 1–10.

a. *Blind pool*
b. *Cash flow*
c. *Downside risk*
d. *Equity build up*
e. *GLITAMAD*

f. *Mortgage-equity technique*
g. *Negative cash flow*
h. *Overall rate*
i. *Prospectus*
j. *Tax shelter*

1. Number of dollars remaining each year after collecting rents and paying operating expenses and mortgage payments. *b* *g*
2. Requires the investor to dip into his own pocket.
3. Income tax savings that an investment can produce for its owner. *j*
4. Results from mortgage balance reduction and price appreciation. *d*
5. An acronym that refers to the various phases in the life cycle of an improved property. *e*
6. A method for valuing an income-producing property that takes into consideration the price and availability of mortgage loans. *f*
7. A number that takes into consideration equity yield, loan terms, holding period, and appreciation. When divided into the net operating income of a property, it tells us the property's value. *h*
8. A limited partnership wherein properties are purchased after the limited partners have invested their money. *a*
9. The possibility that an investor will lose his money in an investment. *c*
10. A disclosure statement that describes an investment opportunity. *i*

1. What is a tax-sheltered real estate investment?
2. What monetary benefits do investors expect to receive by investing in real estate?
3. What is the major risk that a vacant land speculator takes?
4. What advantages and disadvantages do duplexes and triplexes offer to a prospective investor?
5. Is an investor better off investing in a project before it is built or after it is completed and occupied? Explain.
6. As a building grows older, why should an investor demand a higher return per dollar invested?
7. How does age affect one's investment goals and the amount of investment risk that one should take?

8. An investor is looking at a property that produces a net operating income of $22,000 per year. He expects the property to appreciate 40% in 10 years, plans to finance with a 20-year, 10% interest, 70% L/V loan, and wants 18% yield on his equity. How much should he offer (Table 24:1)?

9. Another investor looks at the property described in number 8, but he feels it will appreciate only 20% in value. How much would he offer to pay?

10. What advantages does the limited partnership form of ownership offer to real estate investors?

11. What can a prospective investor do to increase his chances of joining a limited partnership that will be successful?

12. What are the purposes of disclosure and blue-sky laws?

ADDITIONAL READINGS

Anderson, Gordon J. *How To Compete Successfully in Real Estate Investing.* Hicksville, N.Y.: Exposition Press, 1973, 191 pages. Emphasizes that no matter how lucky a person may be in his or her first real estate investment, long-run success depends on understanding the factors that affect real estate values.

Financial Publishing Company. *Financial Capitalization Rate Tables for Appraisers.* Boston: Financial Publishing Company, 1975, 776 pages. Mortgage-equity tables for computing property value. Includes factors for the effects of inflation, accelerated depreciation, and the investor's tax bracket.

Johnson, Irvin E. *The Instant Mortgage-Equity Technique.* Lexington, Mass.: Lexington Books, D.C. Heath, 1972, 375 pages. Contains over 150,000 precomputed rates for finding property value, equity yield, appreciation and depreciation, loan terms, net operating income, and holding period. Explanations and examples are included.

Mader, Chris. *The Dow Jones–Irwin Guide to Real Estate Investing.* Homewood, Ill.: Dow Jones–Irwin, Inc., 1975, 236 pages. A very readable book that discusses inflation, the real estate market, and the purchase of real estate as an investment. Includes investment analysis tables.

Messner, Stephen D., et al. *Marketing Investment Real Estate: Finance Taxation Techniques.* Chicago: Realtors National Marketing Institute, National Association of Realtors, 1975, 353 pages. Emphasis is on taxation, financing techniques, and inflation.

Seldin, Maury, and **Swesnik, Richard H.** *Real Estate Investment Strategy.* New York: John Wiley, 1970, 248 pages. A very readable and thoughtful book designed to aid the prospective real estate investor in choosing the type of property to invest in. Emphasizes risks versus returns.

provement having the same usefulness as the one being appraised, 356

Reproduction cost: the cost, at today's
prices, of constructing an exact replica of the subject improvements,
using the same or similar materials,
356

Rescind: to cancel or nullify, 139

Reserves for replacement: money set
aside for the replacement of items
that have a useful life greater than
one year, 373

RESPA (Real Estate Settlement Procedures Act): a federal law that
deals with procedures to be followed in a real estate closing, 297–
299

Restrictive covenants: clauses placed in
deeds to control the way future
owners may or may not use the
property; also used in leases, 525–
527

Return on investment, 368–76

Revenue stamps: a tax on deeds payable at the time of recording, 282–
283

Reversionary interest: the right to
future enjoyment of property presently possessed or occupied by another, 41, 45

Reversionary value: the expected worth
of a property at the end of the projected holding period, 381

Rider, 473; *see* **Endorsement**

Right of survivorship: the remaining
co-owners of a property automatically acquire a deceased co-owner's
interest, 61, 64–65

Riparian right: the right of a landowner whose land borders a river or
stream to use and enjoy that water,
13–14

Risk rate: the rate of return on investment necessary to attract capital, 369

Risk management: the process of discovering risks, estimating the probability and seriousness of loss and
taking action, 467–68

Risk taking, 546

Running the chain: the process of constructing a chain of title from the
public records, 111

Safe rate: the guaranteed return
available on U.S. government bonds,
368–69

Sale and leaseback, 263

Sale by advertisement, 196; *see* **Power
of sale**

Salesman, real estate, broker-salesman
relationship, 421–22; compensation,
422; defined, 421–22; independent
contractor issue, 423

Salesman license requirements, education, 2–6, 424; examination, 423–
424, 430–31; experience, 4–6, 423

Sandwich lease: the name given to a
lease held by a lessee who sublets
a portion of his rights to another
party, 49

Savings and loan associations, growth,
239; history, 237–38; interest ceilings, 240–41; regulation, 240

Savings certificate, 240–241

Scheduled gross (projected gross): the
estimated rent that a fully-occupied
property can be expected to produce
on an annual basis, 371–72

Second mortgage: one which ranks immediately behind the first mortgage
in priority, 191

Secondary mortgage market: the marketplace in which a lender can sell
a mortgage loan to another investor,
254–55

Section: an area of land one mile long
on each of its four sides; contains
640 acres, 22–24

Section 203b: a federal program that
provides FHA mortgage insurance
for single family residences, 220–23

Sector theory of land use, 329, 330

Secular event: a long-lasting and noncyclical economic event, 333–34

Seller's affidavit of title: a document
provided at the settlement meeting
by the seller which states that he has
done nothing to encumber title since
the title search was made, 289–90

Seller's market: one with few sellers
and many buyers, 321

Seller's points: loan discount points
paid by a seller so that a buyer can
obtain a loan, 231

Senior mortgage: the mortgage against

Surface right: the right to travel upon and use the surface of a parcel of land, 10, 54

Surplus money action: a claim for payment filed by a junior mortgage holder at a foreclosure sale, 192–93

Surrogate court, 93; *see* **Probate court**

Survey books, 24–25; *see* **Map books**

Syndicate: a combination of persons or firms united to pursue a financial enterprise too large for any of them to undertake individually, 71

Take-off: a construction cost estimate based on the cost of each material item and the labor necessary to install it, 356–57

Take-out loan: a permanent loan arranged to replace a construction loan, 219

Tandem plan: a subsidy program wherein the GNMA supports the price of residential mortgage loans, 254

Taxable gain, 279–81

Tax basis: the sum of the price paid for a property plus certain cost and expense adjustments; used in calculating income taxes, 277

Tax certificate: a document issued at a tax sale that entitles the purchaser to a deed at a later date if the property is not redeemed, 270–271

Tax deed: a document that conveys title to a property purchased at a tax sale, 270

Taxes, conveyance, 282–83; income, 276–82, 536, 547; property 267–76

Tax-free exchange: the trade of one real property for another without the need to pay income taxes on the gain at the time of the trade, 164–67

Tax lien: a charge or hold that the government has against property to insure the payment of taxes, 51, 270, 282

Tax-option (Sub-chapter S): laws that allow shareholders in closely held corporations to elect to be taxed just once on their profits, 72

Tax postponement, homes 278–79; installment sale, 280; trades, 164–67

Tax shelter: the income tax savings that an investment can produce for its owner, 536

Tenancy by the entirety: a form of joint ownership reserved for married persons; right of survivorship exists and neither spouse has a disposable interest during the lifetime of the other, 65–66

Tenancy in partnership: ownership by two or more persons as business partners, 68

Tenant, 49–50, 262–64; *see also* **Property management**

Tenant selection, 494–496

Tenants in common: shared ownership of a single property among two or more persons, interests need not be equal and no right of survivorship exists, 60–62

Tenant's insurance policy, 477

Tenant unions, 506

Termite inspection, 150, 159

Term loan: a loan requiring interest-only payments until the maturity date (due date) at which time the entire principal is due, 209–10

Testator: a person who makes a will, 93

Testimony clause: a declaration inserted in a document that reads, "In witness whereof the parties hereto set their hands and seals" (or a similar phrase), 86

Thin market: a market with few buyers and few sellers, 321–22

Third parties: persons who are not parties to a contract but who may be affected by it, 395, 412–15

Tight money: a situation wherein the demand for money exceeds the supply and loans are hard to get, 230

Time deposit: a savings deposit wherein the saver agrees not to withdraw his money for a specified period of time, 240–241

Time is of the essence: means the time limits of a contract must be faithfully observed, 163

Time-sharing: part ownership of a property coupled with a right to ex-